Gower Handbook
of Project
Management
4th edition

GOWER HANDBOOK OF PROJECT MANAGEMENT 4TH EDITION

Edited by
J. Rodney Turner

GOWER

First edition published 1987
Second edition published 1994
Third edition published 2000

This edition published by
Gower Publishing Limited
Wey Court East
Union Road
Farnham
Surrey GU9 7PT
England

Gower Publishing Company
Suite 420
101 Cherry Street
Burlington, VT 05401-4405
USA

British Library Cataloguing in Publication Data
Gower handbook of project management. – 4th ed.
   1. Project management
   I. Turner, J. Rodney (John Rodney), 1953- II. Handbook of
   project management
   658.4'04

   ISBN 978-0-566-08806-3

Library of Congress Cataloging-in-Publication Data
Gower handbook of project management / edited by J. Rodney Turner. – 4th ed.
     p. cm.
   Includes bibliographical references and index.
   ISBN 978-0-566-08806-3
   1. Project management–Handbook, manuals, etc. I. Turner, J. Rodney (John Rodney),
1953- II. Title: Handbook of project management.

   T56. 8. G69 2007
   658.4'04–dc22

                     2007014525

Typeset in Century Old Style by IML Typographers, Merseyside.

Printed and bound in Great Britain by
TJ International Ltd, Padstow, Cornwall.

Contents

Part III   Process

List of Figures

Notes on Contributors

THE EDITOR

Rodney Turner is Professor of Project Management at the Lille School of Management, and at the Kemmy Business School of the University of Limerick. He is also Adjunct Professor at the University of Technology, Sydney, Educatis University, Zurich, and Henley Management College. For the spring semester of 2007 he was a visiting scholar at George Washington University. Rodney Turner is the author or editor of ten books, including the third edition of this book, and is editor of *The International Journal of Project Management*. He has written articles for journals, conferences and magazines. He teaches project management world wide. From 1991 to 2004, Rodney was a member of Council of the UK's Association for Project Management (APM), serving as Treasurer and Chairman. He is now a Vice-President. From 1999 to 2002, he was President and then Chairman of the International Project Management Association, the global federation of national associations in project management, of which APM is the largest member. He also helped to establish the Benelux Region of the European Construction Institute as Operations Director. Rodney is a Member of the Institute of Directors, and a Fellow of the Institution of Mechanical Engineers and of the Association for Project Management.
Email: rodneyturner@europrojex.co.uk

THE AUTHORS

Erling S. Andersen is professor of Project Management and Information Systems at BI Norwegian School of Management, Oslo. He holds a Master in Economics from University of Oslo. Before joining BI NSM he was Associate Professor in Economics at University of Oslo, Dean of NKI College of Computer

Science and Professor of Information Science at University of Bergen. He has been a visiting professor to University of Tokyo, Japan and Nanyang Technological University, Singapore. He has published several books and articles on information technology, systems development, project management and management in general. His book *Goal Directed Project Management* is translated into several languages.

Colin Bentley has been a project manager since 1966 and has managed many projects, large and small, in several countries. He has been working with PRINCE2™, PRINCE and its predecessor, PROMPT II, since 1975. He was one of the team that brought PROMPT II to the marketplace, wrote the major part of the PRINCE2™ manual and is the principal author of the various revisions to the manual for the Office of Government Commerce. He has had over twenty books published, has lectured widely on PRINCE2™ and has acted as project management consultant to many high profile firms. He is the Chief Examiner in PRINCE2™ for the APM Group.

Chris Chapman is Emeritus Professor of Management Science in the School of Management at the University of Southampton. He holds a BASc in Industrial Engineering (Toronto), an MSc in Operational Research (Birmingham) and a PhD in Economics and Econometrics (Southampton). His teaching, research and consultancy have focussed on risk management for 30 years, with a wide view of the subject in terms of perspectives and contexts. He has designed processes adopted by organizations which include BP International, National Power, Gulf Canada, AEA Technology, IBM UK, UK Nirex, ESCW/Bombardier and NatWest Bank. He has provided reviews of corporate practices for organizations which include the Highways Agency, MoD, Ontario Hydro, Railtrack and BNFL Engineering. He has provided advice on process development for organizations which include Cerrejon Coal, Consorzio Venezia Nuova and Union Rail (North) Limited. He was the Founding Chair of the Project Risk Management Special Interest Group of the Association for Project Management, and he has been involved in the development of the PRAM and RAMP guides. He has published widely on risk management and related topics. He is a Past President of the Operational Research Society, and an Honorary Fellow of the Institute of Actuaries.

Zhen Chen is Senior Lecturer in the School of the Built Environment at Liverpool John Moore University; he is former Senior Research Fellow in the School of Construction Management and Engineering at the University of Reading, and Visiting Research Fellow to the School of the Built Environment at Oxford Brookes University. He received his BSc degree in building engineering from Qingdao Technological University in Tsingtao, his MSc degree in construction

engineering from Tongji University in Shanghai, and his PhD degree in construction management under Heng Li's supervision from the Hong Kong Polytechnic University. Since 1990, he has been working as an academic at many universities in Asia, Australasia and Europe; and has generated more than 200 research publications and reports covering a wide range of topics related to construction engineering and management. He also has worldwide professional experience in freelance consultancies to numerous projects. His previous books include *Intelligent Methods in Construction*, *Handbook of Buildings Construction*, and *Environmental Management in Construction*.
Email: z.chen@reading.ac.uk

Terry Cooke-Davies is the Executive Chairman of Human Systems International, a company which he founded and which exists to help organizations enhance their project delivery capability and demonstrate results. He has been a practitioner of both general and project management since the end of the 1960s and a consultant to blue-chip organizations for over twenty years. With a PhD in Project Management, a bachelor's degree in Theology, and qualifications in electrical engineering, management accounting and counselling, Terry has worked alongside senior leaders and managers in both the public and the private sectors, to ensure the delivery of business critical change programmes and enhance the quality of leadership. He is an Adjunct Professor at the University of Technology, Sydney, an Honorary Research Fellow at University College, London, and co-author with Paul C. Dinsmore of *The Right Projects Done Right*, published by Jossey-Bass in October 2005. In October 2006, the Association for Project Management awarded Terry its premier Award, the Sir Monty Finneston Award, for his outstanding contribution to the development of project management as a vehicle for effective change.

Lynn Crawford is Associate Professor and Director of the Project Management Research Group, University of Technology, Sydney, Professor of Project Management, ESC Lille, France and Director, Human Systems International Limited. She is involved in project management practice, education and research. Through Human Systems, she works with leading corporations developing organizational project management competence by sharing and developing knowledge and best practice through a global system of project management knowledge networks. She is currently involved in two PMI® funded research projects – *Exploring the Role of the Executive Sponsor*, and *The Value of Project Management*. Results of a completed study have been published by PMI® in a book titled *Project Categorization Systems: Aligning Capability with Strategy for Better Results*. Lynn has been leading the development of global standards for project management since the late 1990s.

Christian Dawson is a full-time lecturer in the Department of Computer Science at Loughborough University. He completed his PhD in 1994 in software development management. Since then he has become an active researcher in project management and is often involved in project management and risk management consultancy work.

Christopher Dobson is a PRINCE2™ practitioner and Member of the Association for Project Management. He has worked in the IT industry for 20 years. He spent 9 years with LloydsTSB Bank in various roles before joining IBM Global Services, where he was involved in outsource service delivery, management   training & development and technical project management. Whilst working for IBM he was a member of a team of project managers responsible for the outsourcing of the entire IT staff and technical infrastructure of the Bank of Scotland. He has been Head of IT for an International Charity, responsible for their global IT infrastructure, service delivery and project management, and a Director of Research for Project Management Belgium, where he researched project management software. This was followed by a white paper on project management software for the European Market. He is currently Project & Resources Manager for Cognisco, an online assessment company in the UK, managing projects for national and international blue chip companies.

Jack S. Duggal is the managing principal of Projectize Group LLC, Avon, Connecticut, USA specializing in next generation tools, training and consulting in project management and business process management. He works with leading companies worldwide in consulting and training engagements. An international speaker, consultant and coach, Jack is a leading practitioner who brings a unique blend of practical hands-on experience with innovative ideas and solutions to deal with the real-world challenges of complex environments. He has implemented PMO's for multiple Fortune companies, facilitated large-scale organizational change, designed and led comprehensive training programmes, personally managed multi-million dollar technology projects, and been an executive coach and mentor to different levels of management. Jack Duggal is also an adjunct professor at the University of Hartford in Connecticut, USA. He teaches graduate courses in the MBA and Executive programmes, teaching project management, managing technology and strategic information systems courses. Jack is a seminar leader in Project Management Institute's (PMI®) Seminars World programme and leads seminars on Next Generation PMO and Portfolio Management around the world. He frequently presents and publishes at industry conferences. Jack is a certified PMI® Project Management Professional (PMP). jduggal@projectize.com

Roland Gareis is Professor of Project Management at the Vienna University of Economics and Business Administration, and director of their MBA Programme 'Project and Process Management'. He is owner of ROLAND GAREIS CONSULTING, a consultancy specializing in project, programme, portfolio and strategic management, with offices in several countries. He is programme manager of the research programme *project orientation [international]*, project manager of the EU project: ABS International, and project owner of the annual international Austrian project management days. He is the author of *Happy Projects* (Manz 2005), which has been translated into four languages, and editor, with David Cleland, of *The Global Project Management Handbook*, (McGraw-Hill 2006). He graduated from the University of Economics and Business Administration, Vienna, and received his Habilitation at the University of Technology, Vienna, in the Department of Construction Industry. From 1979-1981 he was Professor of Construction Management at the Georgia Institute of Technology in Atlanta. He was Visiting Professor at the ETH Eidgenössische Technische Hochschule, Zurich (1982), at the Georgia State University, Atlanta (1987), and at the University of Quebec, Montreal (1991). For 1986-2003 he was President of PROJEKT MANAGEMENT AUSTRIA, the Austrian Project Management Association, and for 1998-2003 Director of Research of the International Project Management Association.

Alistair Godbold is a Senior Programme Manager with NATS. He has over 17 years of project and programme management experience in a variety of areas; from building and relocation projects through safety critical applications to IT enabled business transformation using discrete technology and ERP solutions. He is also helping to lead the further development of the project management capability and maturity of NATS using a mixture of process and capability based techniques. He has contributed to other Project Management books on Ethics and Professionalism, including the APM Body of knowledge 5th edition. Alistair has a BSc (Hons) and an MBA in Project Management, he is a member of the Institute of Engineering and Technology, the Association for Project Management and is a Chartered Engineer. Alistair is also active within the Major Projects Association.

Bob Graham is an independent management consultant and educator in project management organizational creativity and implementation of change. He is also a Senior Associate at Primavera Systems in Bala Cynwyd, Pennsylvania, and the Strategic Management Group in Philadelphia. At the Wharton School of the University of Pennsylvania, Dr Graham taught project management in the Executive Education Programme. His work stressed the importance of people in project management. He was also a Research Associate with the Management and

Behavioural Science Centre. Dr Graham holds a BS in systems analysis from Miami University, an MBA and Ph.D. in business administration from the University of Cincinnati and an MS in cultural anthropology from the University of Pennsylvania.

Martina Huemann is assistant professor in the Project Management Group of the University of Economics and Business Administration, Vienna and since 2003 a Research Fellow of the University of Technology, Sydney. In her research she concentrates on Human Resource Management in project-oriented companies, management auditing of projects and programmes and maturity of project oriented individuals and organizations. Martina has project management experience in organizational development, research, and marketing projects. She is a board member of Project Management Austria and board member of the IPMA research board. She is a trainer for assessors and lead assessor of the IPMA excellence award. Martina is also a network partner of ROLAND GAREIS CONSULTING. Email: martina.huemann@wu-wien.ac.at

Ashley Jamieson worked for many years as a business manager, senior programme manager and project manager with global aerospace and defence companies. Recently he has been working with Peter Morris on various research projects. At Manchester, he carried out research into design management in major construction projects, and was a visiting lecturer in project management. At UCL he completed the PMI® funded research project on how corporate strategy is translated into project strategy. He is also a contributor to the Wiley Guide to Managing Projects, and has co-authored a number of papers on project management. In 2004-5 he was Research Fellow on a project updating the APM BOK. He became an independent business management consultant and member of the BASG network in 2005. He has been Chairman of the Board of Directors of a charitable company for a number of years.

Anne Keegan is Associate Professor at the Amsterdam Business School, University of Amsterdam. She delivers courses in Human Resource Management at undergraduate, postgraduate and executive level. Her research interests include critical analyses of transformations in the HR function, managing employees in knowledge intensive and project based work, and leadership and change in project based organizations. Dr Keegan has published a number of articles in leading journals including the Journal of Management Studies, Journal of Applied Psychology, Long Range Planning, Management Learning and the Human Resource Management Journal. She studied management and business at Trinity College Dublin, and did her doctorate there on the topic of *Management Practices in Knowledge Intensive Firms*. Dr Keegan has previously worked at the

Rotterdam School of Management, Erasmus University, and has also worked as a consultant in the areas of Human Resource Management and Organizational Change to firms in the computer, food, export and voluntary sectors in Ireland and the Netherlands.

Heng Li is Professor in the Department of Building and Real Estate and the Director of Research Centre for Construction Innovation at Hong Kong Polytechnic University. He started his academic career from Tongji University in 1987. He then researched and lectured at the University of Sydney, James Cook University and Monash University before joining Hong Kong Polytechnic University. During this period, he has also worked with engineering design and construction firms and provided consultancy services to both private and government organizations in Australia, Hong Kong and China. He has conducted many funded research projects related to the innovative application and transfer of construction information technologies, and he has published 3 books, about 200 journal papers in major journals of his field and numerous conferences papers in proceedings. His previous books include *Machine Learning of Design Concepts*, *Implementing IT to obtain a competitive advantage in the 21st Century*, and *Environmental Management in Construction*. He is a review editor of the *International Journal of Automation in Construction* and holds editorship from other six leading Journals in his area. His research interests include intelligent decision support systems, product and process modelling, and knowledge management.
Email: bshengli@polyu.edu.hk

Dennis Lock, who began his career as an electronics engineer in a research laboratory, now specializes in project management. After a series of successful management posts in industries ranging from miniature hearing aids to giant machine tools and international mining, he spent ten more recent years as an external lecturer on the MSc and MBA programmes of two English universities. Now a full time freelance writer, Dennis has edited or written some 35 books, mostly for Gower, including the hugely successful *Project Management* (now in its ninth edition). Dennis is a Fellow of the Association for Project Management, Fellow of the Institute of Management Services and a Member of the Chartered Management Institute.

Bill McElroy is an Executive Director of the Nichols Group, a leading UK project and programme management consultancy. He has over 20 years programme and project management experience, including managing a wide spectrum of projects, from capital investment to organizational change, and strategic advice and support to senior executives responsible for the direction and management of large scale change across both public and private sectors, with particular focus on the transportation sector. Bill has twice won the Association for Project Management's (APM) 'Sir Monty Finniston Award' for 'an outstanding contribution to Project Management'. These awards in 1995 and 1997 recognized his work in the management of strategic change through projects, and the need for effective communication strategies to manage key stakeholders. Bill is a Visiting Lecturer on strategic programme management to MBA and MSc courses at the Tanaka Management School of Imperial College London, a technical referee for the International Journal for Project Management, and contributor to the APM's 'Year Book' (2003) and 'Body of Knowledge' (2005), and the 'Parliamentary Year Book and Diary' (2001). Email: bill.mcelroy@nichols.uk.com

Mary McKinlay worked in Aerospace and Defence for over 27 years starting as a Systems Engineer. She is now a practitioner, researcher and trainer of Project Management, works as an Adjunct Professor of Project Management at ESC Lille and is Managing Director of Mary McKinlay Projects Ltd. Whilst working in industry Mary participated in research programmes involving collaboration between industry and academics e.g. Alvey, SERC and ESPRIT. One of these projects was to generate a process model for Project Management. This underlined the need for Project Management improvement and influenced her later work. She was instrumental in the introduction of Lifecycle Management and has carried out external assessment of Project Management Plans for many major projects. She works as a Lead Assessor for the IPMA International Project Management Awards and also a Judge for the APM Annual Awards. Having been a Council Member for IPMA, she is now a Vice President. She has also been active in APM and was a contributor to the APM Body of Knowledge v5. Mary has written many articles and is a frequent speaker at Project Management Conferences. She is a Governor of the University of Greenwich and also a member of Institute of Directors.

Chris Mills is a senior consultant with the Nichols Group and has provided expertise and advice on managing programmes and projects for clients in the utilities and transportation sectors in the UK and overseas since 1989. He holds an honours degree in civil engineering from Imperial College, London, a MBA from Cranfield University and is a member of the Institution of Civil Engineers, the Chartered Institution of Water and Environmental Management and the Association for Project Management.
Email: chris.mills@nichols.uk.com

Peter Morris is Professor of Construction and Project Management at University College London, and Executive Director of INDECO, a management consultancy.

He was Chairman of the Association for Project Management from 1993-96 and is currently a Vice President. He was Deputy Chairman of IPMA from 1995-1997. He is a Fellow of the Institution of Civil Engineers, Chartered Institute of Building, and the Association for Project Management. His research has largely been on the competencies required to develop and deliver projects and programmes successfully. He is the principal proponent of 'the management of projects' perspective – see *The Wiley Guide to Managing Projects* (Wiley 2005); *Translating Corporate Strategy into Project Strategy* (PMI® 2004); *The Management of Projects* (Thomas Telford 1994) and *The Anatomy of Major Projects* (John Wiley & Sons 1987). He is the author of over 110 papers and was the recipient of the PMI® 2005 Distinguished Research Award. He was previously a main board director of Bovis Ltd., Executive Director of the Major Projects Association, a consultant with Arthur D Little, and Booz Allen & Hamilton, and an engineer with Sir Robert McAlpine.

Ralf Müller is Assistant Professor at Umeå University, School of Business in Sweden and visiting faculty member at TiasNIMBAS Business School in The Netherlands. He researches and lectures in project management, governance of project-based organizations, as well as in research design and methodology. His own research is on leadership and communication in projects, as well as on programme and portfolio management. Before doing a doctorate in project management and starting an academic career, he spent several decades managing project-based organizations, and consulting large enterprises and governments in project management and its governance. This included work in more than 40 countries in different roles, such as worldwide Director of Project Management in NCR Teradata, or as global 'flying doctor' for project recovery. Ralf is the author of three books and a number of articles in international management journals, as well as a frequent speaker at researcher and practitioner conferences. He is the co-founder of several PMI® chapters in Europe and co-developer of PMI® Standards for Organizational Project Management Maturity (OPM3), as well as for Programme and Portfolio Management. He can be reached at ralf.mueller@usbe.umu.se

Mark O'Callaghan is CEO of Reponsa, a company that markets a device to capture responses to advertisements He lectures at the University of Malta and is a freelance management consultant. He runs a number of management training programmes. He is a psychologist by profession and has managed health institutions in the United Kingdom as well as chaired academic programmes of Clinical Psychology and Hospital Management.

David Partington is a Senior Lecturer at Cranfield School of Management, where he is Director of Management Research Programmes. He is a chartered engineer whose career spans 35 years as a practitioner, consultant and lecturer in project and programme management. He has practical experience of managing many types of projects and project organizations in the UK, South America and the Middle East. He has an MSc in project management and a PhD in organizational behaviour. David has published widely in the fields of project and programme management, organizational change, and management research methods. He is co-author of the Proaction® project and programme management simulations. His current research interests include programme management and organizational learning.

Richard Pharro is MD of The APM Group. Richard conceived the idea of Accreditation and Certification associated with OGC's PRINCE2™[1] in 1995. Since then PRINCE2™ has become established throughout the world. APMG's partnership with OGC has expanded to include MSP™[2], M_o_R®[3] and ITIL® accreditation and qualifications. APMG is now a global business providing accreditation and certification services via an international network of Accredited Consultancy and Training Organizations. Richard has spearheaded APMG's expansion into wider fields of business accreditation. The organization's business partners include TSO (The Stationery Office Ltd), The Association of Proposal Management Professionals (APMP), The UK's Financial Services Skills Council (FssC), and the UK's Chartered Management Institute.

He is a chartered Civil Engineer who has worked on projects in the UK and the Middle East. His book, The Relationship Manager – The Next Generation of Project Management, was published by Gower in January, 2003. Richard is a non executive Director of the PRINCE2™ Best Practice User Group. In December 2006, he was awarded the Institute of Director's professional qualification C.Dir.

Jim Pearce is a senior consultant with the Royal Society for the Prevention of Accidents. Originally a chemical technologist, he is a safety practitioner of over 30 years experience. He is a Chartered Fellow of the Institute of Occupational Safety and Health with extensive experience in safety training up to and including teaching the National Examination Board in Occupational Safety and Health's National Diploma. For several years he was a training provider representative on NEBOSH's Executive Committee and a provider of examination questions. Currently he specializes in auditing health and safety management systems (HSMS) and providing support to organizations to aid the development of HSMS systems appropriate to their needs.

---

[1] PRINCE2™ is a registered Trade Mark of the office of Government Commerce.
[2] MSP™ is a Trade Mark of the Office of Government Commerce.
[3] 3 M–O–R® is a Registered Trade Mark of the office of Government Commerce in the United Kingdom and other countries.

David Rees was professionally trained in work study, organization and methods, and spent his formative career in the UK telecommunications industry. Leaving to take up a lecturing post, he spent eight years teaching communication and business studies before returning to the commercial world. After creating the Centre for International Communication as a training company, a partnership was created with a Belgian organization to provide cross-cultural language and culture programmes for European and American students. During the 1990s the business expanded and a new company, Cultural Fluency, was formed to focus specifically on helping organizations manage cross-cultural strategy, operations and teams. David works extensively in consultancy and development roles with many high profile, project-based organizations. He is a Fellow of the Chartered Institute of Personnel and Development, a Member of the Chartered Institute of Management and Visiting Fellow at Henley Management College.

Tony Reid is a business performance coach, mentor and project facilitator. He has an MA in Management Learning; is a Registered Practitioner of the Myers Briggs Psychometric Indicator; a Practitioner for Emotional Freedom Therapy; a Lead Assessor for Quality Assurance, and an Open Licensed Trainer and Assessor for the EFQM. He has been a Chairman with the Academy for Chief Executives; a coach and facilitator for Tomorrow's Company; has facilitated the initiation of major projects in the UK and Middle East; and tutored project management programmes for many major construction organizations. He has been the chair of the Project Organization and Team Working Special Interest Group for the APM for ten years. He is presently the lead facilitator with Lancaster Business Academy and exploring the establishment of a new Special Interest Group focused on Innovation for the APM. Tony is a Fellow of the Royal Society of Arts and Member of the Association for Project Management.

Lizz Robb is a partner in Yellowhouse.net, an Australian company based in Brisbane, Queensland, which has a focus on programme and project management training and consulting. Lizz specializes in the PRINCE2® and Managing Successful Programmes (MSP™) methodologies from the Office of Government Commerce, UK, as well as the Project Management Institute's Project Management Body of Knowledge (PMI® PMBoK®). Lizz gained a Masters In Project Management from the University of Technology, Sydney (UTS) and has continued to be with the programme. She has taught PRINCE2™ at UTS and ESC Lille in Paris. Lizz has worked across a range of industry sectors, from construction to international aid to pharmaceuticals and information systems, both in Australia and internationally. Lizz has a keen interest in the deployment of project and programme management methodologies. She has a commitment to enhancing both individual and corporate capability through programme and project management in complex organizations. Lizz is a member of the PMI®.

Stephen Simister is a member of the academic faculty and lead tutor in project management at Henley Management College and a visiting lecturer at Reading University. He has over 25 years experience of project management and has worked in most business environments. He is a chartered project management surveyor with the Royal Institution of Chartered Surveyors (RICS), a fellow of the Association of Project Management (APM) where he is also chair of the Contracts & Procurement (SIG) and a Certificated Value Manager with the Institute of Value Management (IVM).
Email: stephen.simister@henleymc.ac.uk

Michel Thiry has over 30 years' professional experience and is founder and Managing Partner of Valense Ltd. (www.valense.com), a PMIR Global Registered Education Provider that offers consultancy, education and research services to Project-Based Organizations. He is also the initiator of the Valense Network, an International multi-disciplinary network of professionals. He has worked worldwide in many cultural environments and provides his expertise to major organizations, in various fields and at different levels. Michel is a regular Keynote Speaker for major International events and Adjunct Professor with the Lille Graduate School of Management (France) and visiting professor at UTS in Sydney (Australia). He has written and lectured widely in International forums, both at the Academic and Practice levels. In addition to his book 'Value Management Practice', published in 1996, he has written a number of book chapters on Value, Program and Portfolio Management in prominent PM books. He is a regular writer and referee for the International Journal of Project Management and Contributing Editor PM Network, in which he authors the 'Executive Speak' Quarterly Column. He has particular expertise in the structures and integration principles of Project-Based Organizations (PBO), in particular, the link between strategy and projects, project selection methodologies and project governance systems.

Stephen Ward is Professor of Management at the School of Management, University of Southampton, UK, and Deputy Head of the School. He holds a BSc in Mathematics and Physics (Nottingham), an MSc in Management Science (Imperial College, London), and a PhD in developing effective models in the practice of operational research (Southampton). Before joining Southampton University, he worked in the OR group at Nat West Bank. For more than twenty five years his research and consulting activities have focused on risk and uncertainty management, usually in a project context. He has published widely, including two books co-authored with Chris Chapman: *Project Risk Management – processes, techniques and insights* (Wiley, second edition 2003), and *Managing Project Risk and Uncertainty – a constructively simple approach to decision making* (Wiley 2002). His latest book *Risk management: organization and context* was published by Witherby in early 2005. He is a member of the PMI®, a Fellow of the UK Institute of Risk Management, and a lead examiner for the Institute's Diploma. He is also a member of the British Standards Institute Committee on Risk Management.

Terry Williams has been Professor of Management Science at Southampton University since mid 2005. He worked in Operational Research for 9 years at Engineering Consultants YARD (now within BAE SYSTEMS), developing Project Risk Management, and acting as Risk Manager for major projects (mainly defence industry). He (re-)joined Strathclyde University in 1992 and became Professor of Operational Research (OR) and Head of Department. He continued research and consultancy modelling the behaviour of major projects, both post-project review and (thus informed) pre-project risk. He was one of a team which supported post-project claims, particularly Delay and Disruption, totalling over $1.5 billion in Europe and North America. Terry is a speaker and writer on modelling in project management; he has written around 60 articles in refereed OR and Project Management journals and a book on 'Modelling Complex Projects'. He is a member of a number of research networks worldwide, particularly the Project Management Institute (PMI®), where hc is one of the Research Members Advisory Group. He edits the Journal of the OR Society and sits on a number of other journal advisory boards. He is a PMP, PhD, Chartered Mathematician, and Fellow of the IMA and ORS. He was educated at Oxford and Birmingham Universities, UK.

OTHER BOOKS BY RODNEY TURNER PUBLISHED BY GOWER

The Gower Handbook of Project Management, 3rd edition, 2000, edited with Steve Simister, ISBN: 0-566-08138-5, (Hardback), ISBN: 0-566-08397-3, (CD-ROM).
People in Project Management, 2003, editor, ISBN: 0-566-08530-5.
Contracting for Project Management, 2003, editor, ISBN: 0-566-08529-1.
The Management of Large Projects and Programmes for Web Delivery, 2004, ISBN: 0-566-08567-4,

Preface

Welcome to the 4th edition of the *Gower Handbook of Project Management*. In this edition I have focused more on producing a handbook rather than an encyclopaedia, but the book is still intended a as reference book for practicing project managers. It should also remain a useful text for people studying for professional exams in project management and for people seeking certification around the world.

The 3rd edition was successful, being translated into two other languages, and resulting in two spin off books, People in Project Management (Gower 2003) and Contracting for Project Management (Gower 2003). The first of those was also translated into two other languages, and the second into one other.

Project Management is a rapidly expanding subject. In the early 1990s I tried to write three books covering the whole of project management as I saw it:

- *The Handbook of Project-based Management* (2nd edition, McGraw-Hill 1999) covering the core concepts of how you manage a project to convert vision to reality
- *The Commercial Project Manager* (McGraw-Hill 1995) covering the commercial issues of finance and contracting
- *The Project Manager as Change Agent* (McGraw-Hill 1996) describing people management issues

I think at the time they gave a fairly comprehensive view of the then status of project management. Also I profiled the 3rd edition of this book as an encyclopaedia, trying to cover the whole of project management in one book. I don't think that is possible anymore; perhaps it wasn't possible in the late 1990s. The 3rd edition had 44 chapters in seven parts: Projects, Context, Functions, Process, Commercial, Contractual and People. If, this, the 4th edition, were to cover all the previous material plus the new areas of project management, it would become unwieldy. I had to leave something out. That is a positive indication of the growth of our subject, so I am pleased that Project Management is such an expanding subject. I have left out parts of Context, Commercial and Contractual.

As I have merged the rest of Context with Projects, and changed the name of Functions to Performance, I have left out the three Cs and left in the four Ps. It was suggested I should also leave out People. After all it is covered by People in Project Management, and we might look forward to a second edition of that book. However, I think that projects don't exist, let alone happen, without people, so leaving out People would be like building a car without the engine. So it stays in. As far as the commercial parts of Context, Commercial and Contractual are concerned, I hope it might be possible to produce a *Handbook of Commercial Project Management.* It is now twelve years since The Commercial Project Manager was published and so it is due for an update.

As before, I don't necessarily share the views of all the authors. I think it is healthy that a book like this should have a wide range of perspectives. Again, there is nothing that I violently disagree with, and since I think Project Management is a social construct, I would not even say anything is 'wrong', just different perspectives of the same thing. A cylinder looks like a circle if you view it along one axis and a square if you view it from the side. So you can put a square peg in a round hole; it can look like a circle to some people and a square to others. None are wrong for expressing their views. Project Management is the same.

Each chapter has a list of references and further reading. Not all the references are cited in the text. Some are there as further reading. For me, in a book like this, references fulfil two purposes:

- they provide additional sources for people who want to explore the topic further
- they acknowledge the source of somebody else's material or ideas

Only books really satisfy the first purpose. Perhaps some magazines and readily available academic research journals also meet that need. PhD theses, papers in conference proceedings and arcane academic journals do not. So I have tried to avoid including those as references. They are only included if they satisfy the second purpose and there is not other text that does so.

In the 3rd edition I said I hoped the book would run to further editions, and asked people to e-mail me their suggestions for improvement. The hope remains there will be a demand for further editions, and I repeat the request – though nobody e-mailed me as a result of the 3rd edition. If Project Management continues to be an expanding subject, perhaps next time I will need to leave out the People section and devote a whole book to it.

Finally, I would like to thank Judy Morton for her help in editing the book.

Rodney Turner
East Horsley
rodneyturner@europrojex.co.,uk; www.europrojex.co.uk

1

A Handbook for Project Management Practitioners

Rodney Turner

Projects and project management are now widely recognized by organizations as being essential to achieving their strategic objectives. Achieving the strategic objectives often involves change, and that change needs managing in a different way from managing the routine work of the organization. The change can take several forms:

- it may be an engineering construct, a new building, new infrastructure or a new product or production machinery
- it may be an information system, involving new information and communication technology (ICT)
- or it may be a social construct, new processes, a new organizations structure, or new skills in the work force

In each case, the organization that wants the new asset creates a temporary organization, a project, to which resources are assigned to do the work to deliver that beneficial change. The change itself is some new facility or asset. We have just seen that the facility or asset may be an engineering construct, an ICT system, or a social construct. Once the project is finished, that asset will be operated to deliver benefit to the owning organization. During its life, the temporary organization needs managing to deliver the asset and achieve the benefit on completion. The asset and desired benefit (the objectives) must be defined, as must the process of achieving the objectives, and the work and delivery of the objectives must be monitored and controlled. The management of the project (the temporary organization) is the responsibility of project management practitioners.

This book is intended as a handbook for project management practitioners. The aim is to give an introduction to and overview of the essential knowledge required for managing projects. In Chapter 32, Lynn Crawford defines competence as the knowledge, skill and behaviours required to perform according to defined standards. Through this book I can introduce the reader to the knowledge and skills required to manage projects. Competence the individual will develop

1

through experience, and through the essential traits bought to the job. The project management professional societies throughout the world take several different approaches to defining the competence required to manage projects.

(a) Some focus on the knowledge and skills required. This is the approach taken by the Project Management Institute (PMI®, www.pmi.org), a global organization based in North America, through its body of knowledge and certification programme (PMI® 2004). This is an input based approach to competence.

(b) Some focus on what project managers have to be able to do to manage projects, what functions they have to perform. This is the approach taken by the Association for Project Management (APM, www.apm.org.uk), the UK's national association, through its body of knowledge and certification program (APM 2006), and by the International Project Management Association, (IPMA, www.ipma.ch), a global federation of 36 national associations of which APM is the largest, (IPMA 2006). This is a performance based approach to competence.

(c) Some focus on what project managers must deliver. This is the approach adopted in the UK by the Engineering Construction Industry Training Board (ECITB, www.ecitb.org.uk), in its National Occupational Standards for Project Management, and by the Australian Institute for Project Management (AIPM, www.aipm.com.au), in its National Competency Standards for Project Management (AIPM 2004).

Lynn Crawford (Chapter 32) says that competence is the ability to perform according to defined standards. Those standards can take different forms:

1. They may be global standards. The PMI® Guide to the Project Management Body of Knowledge, PMBoK®, (PMI® 2004) is often presented as a global standard. The International Standards Organization has produced a standard for Project Management, ISO 10,006, (ISO 2004). Lynn Crawford herself is leading a global working party to produce global standards for project management

2. They may be national standards. The PMI® Guide to the PMBoK® (PMI® 2004) is also an American national (ANSI) standard. In the UK, the ECITB has produced the National Occupation Standards for Project Management (ECITB 2003) and in Australia AIPM has produced the National Competency Framework for Project Management (AIPM 2004).

3. They may be standards produced by professional associations, such as the PMI® Guide to the PMBoK® (PMI® 2004), the APM Body of Knowledge (APM 2006) and the IPMA Competency Baseline, ICB (IPMA 1999).

4. They may be job descriptions produced by individual organizations for specific jobs within the organization.

As I say, in this book I can only give a guide to the knowledge and skills required by project management practitioners in their work, not to the performance required by project managers. Figure 1.1 shows the content of this book, and how it relates to three of the standards, the APM Body of Kowledge, the PMI® Guide to the PMBoK® and the IPMA ICB.

In the next section I give a brief description of the contents of each chapter, and in the following section a brief description of knowledge areas not covered in this book.

THE GOWER HANDBOOK OF PROJECT MANAGEMENT

The book consists of four parts

- the first describes projects and the context within which they take place, including projects and programmes
- the second part describes the functions that a project manager has to perform in execution of the project
- the third part describes the process that needs to be followed in managing the project
- the fourth part describes how to manage the people

PART I: PROJECTS

The first part of the book describes issues that relate to why projects exist, their nature and the nature of project management. We also consider why organizations undertake projects, how they contribute to the achievement of corporate strategy, and how they adopt strategies for undertaking projects, including the adoption of programme and portfolio management.

Chapter 2: Implementing strategy through programmes of projects: Organizations undertake projects and programmes to achieve beneficial change. They need to do something differently than the way it has been done in the past, and so they undertake projects and programmes to develop new facilities and assets and implement the new way of working, and those new facilities will give the organization benefit and help it achieve its development objectives.

Chapter 3: Managing portfolios of projects: Often an organization will be undertaking a portfolio of projects with unrelated objectives, but which need to draw on a common pool of resources (labour, money, information). To achieve the best results the organization should manage the portfolio in a coordinated way,

Gower Handbook of Project Management 4th edition, Chapter	APM BoK, 5th edition APM, 2006		PMI® Guide to the PMBoK®, 3rd edition PMI, 2004		IPMA ICB IPMA, 2006	
1. Introduction						
Projects						
2. Implementing strategy	1.5	Project sponsorship	2.3	Organizational influences	3.06	Business
3. Managing programmes	1.2	Programme management			3.02	Programme orientation
4. Managing portfolios	1.3	Portfolio management			3.03	Portfolio orientation
5. Projects and project management	1.1	Project management	1.2	What is a project	3.01	Project orientation
			1.3	What is project management		
6. Success and strategy	2.1	Project success and benefits management			1.01	Project management success
7. Processes and procedures	6.9	Methods and procedures	3	Project management processes	3.04	Project, programme and portfolio implementation
8. Systems	3.7	Information management and reporting			1.17	Information and documentation
9. The project office	1.6	Project office				
10. Maturity and benchmarking						
11. Audits	6.6	Project reviews				
12. Managing context	1.4	Project context	1.6	Project management context		
	6.10	Governance of projects	2.3	Organizational influences		
Performance						
13. Managing benefit	5.1	Business case	2.3	Organizational influences		
14. Managing requirements	4.1	Requirements management	4.1	Develop charter	1.03	Project requirements and objectives
15. Managing scope and configuration	3.1	Scope management	4	Project integration management	1.10	Scope and deliverables
	3.5	Change control	5	Project scope management	1.15	Changes
	4.7	Configuration management			2.08	Results orientation

16. Managing value	2.3 4.5	Value management Value engineering				
17. Managing quality	2.6	Project quality management	8	Project quality management	1.05	Quality
18. Managing project organization	6.7 6.8	Organization structure Organizational roles	9	Project human resource management	1.06	Project organization
19. Managing the schedule	3.2 4.3	Scheduling Estimating	6	Project time management	1.11	Time and phases
20. Managing cost	3.4 3.6 4.3	Budgeting and cost management Earned value management Estimating	7	Project cost management	1.13	Cost and finance
21. Managing resources	3.3	Resource management	6.3 9	Resource estimating Project human resource management	1.12	Resources
22. Managing risk	2.5 3.8	Project risk management Issue management	11	Project risk management	1.04	Risk and opportunity
23. Managing health and safety	2.7	Health, safety and environmental management			3.09	Health, safety, security and the environment
24. Managing the environment	2.7	Health, safety and environmental management			3.09	Health, safety, security and the environment
Process						
25. The project life-cycle	6.1	Project life-cycles	2.1 3	The project life-cycle Project management processes		
26. Project start	2.3	Project management plan	4.1	Develop project charter	1.19	Start-up
27. Proposal, feasibility, and design	4.2 6.2 6.3	Development Concept Definition	4.2	Develop initial project scope statement		
28. Project modelling	4.6	Modelling and testing			1.09	Project structures
29. Managing implementation, progress and performance	6.4 3.5	Implementation Change control	4	Project integration management	1.16	Control and reports

Figure 1.1 The structure of this book and its relationship to the project management of bodies of knowledge of leading professional institutions *continued*

	6.56 Handover and close-out	4.7 Close project	1.20 Close-out
30. Project close-out			
People			
31. Human resource management	7.6 Human resource management	9.1 Human resource planning	3.08 Personnel management
32. Developing people	7.7 Behavioural characteristics 7.8 Learning and development	1.5 Areas of expertise	
33. Enterprise pm capability			
34. Managing teams	7.2 Teamwork	9 Project human resource management	1.07 Teamwork
35. Leadership	7.3 Leadership		2.01 Leadership 2.02 Engagement and motivation
36. Managing stakeholders	2.2 Stakeholder management	2.2 Project stakeholders	1.02 Interested parties
37. Managing communication	7.1 Communication	10 Project communications management	1.18 Communication
38. Managing conflict	7.4 Conflict management 7.5 Negotiation		2.10 Consultation 2.11 Negotiation 2.12 Conflict and crisis
39. Managing culture			2.06 Openness 2.14 Values appreciation
40. Ethics	7.9 Professionalism and ethics		2.15 Ethics

Figure 1.1 *Concluded*

Competencies not included	APM BoK	PMI® Guide to the PMBoK®	IPMA ICB
Commercial			
Appraisal	5.3 Project financing and funding		
Finance	5.3 Project financing and funding		3.10 Finance
Taxation			
Insurance			
Contracts			
Contracts	5.4 Procurement	12 Project procurement management	1.14 Procurement and contract
Procurement	5.4 Procurement	12 Project procurement management	1.14 Procurement and contract
Legal	5.5 Legal awareness		3.11 Legal
General management areas			
Human resource management			2.03 Self-control 2.04 Assertiveness 2.05 Relaxation 2.09 Efficiency 2.13 Reliability
Operations	4.4 Technology management		3.05 Permanent organization
Finance			
Markets	5.2 Marketing and sales		
Information technology			1.08 Problem resolution
Finance and accounting			
Innovation and change			2.07 Creativity 3.07 Systems, products, technology
Governance			
Strategy			

Figure 1.2   Other areas of knowledge relevant to Project Management not covered in this book

prioritizing resources and coordinating interfaces between the projects. A portfolio of projects shares common inputs.

Chapter 4: Managing programmes of projects: Often an organization will undertake an extended programme of change, beyond the scope of a single project. They need to undertake several related projects to achieve their overall change objectives. To achieve the best results the organization should manage those projects as an integrated program. The projects in a program contribute to a common, shared objective, or outcome.

Chapter 5: Projects and their management: Projects are temporary organizations to which resources are assigned to do work to achieve beneficial change. Project management is the process which defines the objectives of the project (both the change and the benefit it should deliver), and the means of obtaining the objectives, and then monitors progress towards their successful delivery. From these simple definitions we can derive most of the competencies required to manage a project.

Chapter 6: Project success and strategy: To achieve a successful outcome for a programme, portfolio or project, the manager needs to develop a strategy for how he or she will manage it. First, the manager needs to identify how the stakeholders will judge successful achievement of the objective, and what key success factors will help to deliver those criteria. This will then form the basis of a strategy.

Chapter 7: Processes and procedures: As we have seen, international standards have been developed which give guidance about successful methods of delivering programme, portfolio and project objectives (based on standard success criteria and success factors). Organizations should maintain standard procedures and guidelines based on international standards and their previous experience, and develop individual project procedures manuals for the projects they undertake, and job descriptions for project management professionals.

Chapter 8: Software solutions for project, programme and portfolio management: As part of implementing procedures, and managing the successful delivery of projects, an organization needs a system for monitoring and reporting progress on projects to be able to take corrective action where necessary. The systems will be based on standard and individual project procedures. They may be computer or paper based.

Chapter 9: The project, programme or portfolio office: Many organizations have a project or programme office to administer the systems either for individual large projects, or all the projects in programmes or portfolios they are undertaking.

Chapter 10: Maturity models for company benchmarking in the project-oriented organization: The maturity of a project-oriented organization is a measure of its competence at undertaking its projects, a measure of its enterprise-wide project management capability. Competence can be measured at the individual, team, organizational or even societal level and maturity is a measure of competence at the last two of these. In order to judge its maturity and to improve its performance, an organization can benchmark its performance internally or against others.

Chapter 11: Conducting audits: Audits and health checks are undertaken for two reasons. The first is to ensure that a given project is progressing satisfactorily, in accordance with the systems and procedures, to deliver its objectives. The second is to learn from the success and failures of a completed project to improve the organization's standard procedures for future projects, to feed back into improving organizational maturity. Audits are conducted by external assessors and health checks by the project team.

Chapter 12: Managing the context: Projects and programmes take place in an external context, which creates the need for the project, influences people's perceptions of it, and can enhance or impede the successful delivery of the objectives. The analysis of these issues is sometimes called PESTLE analysis, (political, economic, social, technical, legal and environmental).

PART II: PERFORMANCE

The second part of the book looks at what the project manager must do and produce. The parent organization undertakes the project to achieve beneficial change. In order to achieve that it must deliver some outputs or requirements, and they must be delivered within constraints of time, cost and quality. The project involves risks which must be managed, and particular risks are threats to health and safety and potential impacts on the environment.

Chapter 13: Managing benefits: The parent organization undertakes the project to achieve development objectives, which satisfy some business need. It is expected that the project will deliver benefit, and without that benefit the project is not worth doing. Not only does the parent organization need to define what the expected benefit is; it needs to make sure that it is actually achieved once the project is completed.

Chapter 14: Requirements management: To achieve that benefit the project must deliver certain outcomes, or requirements. Those requirements must be defined, and that initiates the project planning process. The requirements must also be delivered and converted into the expected benefits.

Chapter 15: Managing scope – configuration and work methods: To achieve those requirements the project team needs to do work to deliver products. The products and their components need to be defined through a product breakdown structure, and the work to make and assemble those components identified through a work breakdown structure. Configuration management is a tool to control the identification and delivery of work and products.

Chapter 16: Managing value: The benefits only have any value to the parent organization if they can be produced at a cost that allows it to make a profit. Furthermore, the higher the benefit for a given cost, or the lower the cost for a given benefit, the better the project's value. Value management is a tool for optimizing the project's outcome.

Chapter 17: Managing quality: To perform effectively, the project's products must be delivered to certain standards. First, the product must perform to provide the functionality expected, and to solve the problem deliver the benefit and value expected of it. It must also meet other performance requirements or service levels, such as availability, reliability and maintainability, and have acceptable finish or polish.

Chapter 18: Managing project organization: In order to be able to do the work, it is necessary to determine what people are required, the roles and responsibilities they will fulfil, what skills they need, and the numbers required. These people need to be structured into the temporary organization that is the project, and the relationship of that temporary organization with the parent organization identified.

Chapter 19: Managing the schedule: Likewise, to provide benefit, the project's products must be obtained within a certain time to satisfy the need, and to cover both interest and capital payments on the finance. Hence, the timing of the work must be managed. Sometimes very tight time constraints must be met, but normally they are more flexible. Also on many projects, the work of different resources must be carefully coordinated, and that will also be achieved through the management of the timing of the work.

Chapter 20: Managing cost: To be of value, the functionality must not cost more than a certain amount. Clearly the more benefit it delivers, the more that can be spent on its delivery. The cost of the product, and the value it gives, must be estimated, and the cost controlled within those limits while the work is done.

Chapter 21: Managing resources: The actual resources required (money, materials and people), must be identified and estimated, and their assignment to the work managed.

Chapter 22: Managing risks: Projects, being unique, novel and transient, are inherently risky; more so than the routine work of organizations. This is what differentiates project management from the management of normal operations. Risk management is therefore an essential part of project management.

Chapter 23: Managing health and safety: In all working environments, the safety and health of people doing the work must be of paramount concern to managers, mainly for moral reasons. However, a safe working environment usually results in more cost effective outcomes. Since some managers do not seem to behave ethically towards their employees, this area is now also tightly controlled by law.

Chapter 24: Managing the environment: The impact of the project on the environment must also be carefully managed. Most people sweep managing the environment in with health and safety. However, my view is that they are fundamentally different issues with different processes adopted to manage them.

PART III: PROCESS

Because projects are transient, their delivery goes through a cycle of development, from germination of the idea, through initiation, design, and delivery, to commissioning, handover to the client, and close-out of the work. This cycle is known as the 'life-cycle'. Someone once suggested to me it should be called the 'life', since 'cycle' implied a return to the start. However, I think life-cycle is a good biological metaphor, as the project goes from germination through growth, maturity and eventual metamorphosis into a new and successful operation. As we progress through the life-cycle, the plans, and design of the product or objectives, are developed in increasing detail. We gain greater understanding of the objectives and how they will be delivered, and that feeds into increasing detail in the plans. Because we develop the lower level definition at successive stages of the life-cycle, the levels are essentially linked to the stages.

Chapter 25: The project life-cycle: There are many versions of the life-cycle, but they all essentially contain the steps of germination of the idea, proposal and initiation, design and appraisal, mobilization of the team, execution and control, integration of the team and their work, testing, commissioning and handover of the project's product and close-out of the work.

Chapter 26: Project start process: The difference between project start and start-up has been likened to the difference between starting the engine of a car and the complex sequence of activities required to start the diesel engine of a ship. A complex sequence of activities are required to start the project, to mobilize the team, to initiate the project definition process, to obtain agreement to the project objectives and plan to deliver them.

Chapter 27: Project proposal initiation: The problem the project is to solve (or opportunity it is to exploit), is identified. Several options are developed, functional designs produced, and respective costs and benefits estimated to the current level of accuracy. The best solution is chosen for further definition. A high level, strategic plan for the design and execution of the project is developed. The information generated so far is incorporated into a Project Definition Report or Project Brief. The chosen solution is developed further. A systems design is produced, and the costs and benefits estimated in more detail. The project is appraised and if found acceptable, it is sanctioned. The information generated at this stage is incorporated into a Project Manual or Project Initiation Document.

Chapter 28: Project modelling: Projects are complicated systems, and managers cannot generally analyse all the aspects of a project in their head. Modelling can be useful to help managers understand their projects, and so lies at the heart at project planning and development. It can be particularly useful on complex projects.

Chapter 29: Managing implementation: Work is undertaken to deliver the project's products. The first step is to produce detailed plans to control execution, as opposed to the systems level plans required for appraisal. As work progresses, it must be measured and controlled to ensure the project delivers the required performance. A key feature of project management, which sets it apart from normal operations, is the integrative function. Operations management emphasises discrete functions; project management integrated teams. This is in evidence throughout the life-cycle, but particularly at this stage. The work of the project members must be integrated, the work of the design, execution and commissioning teams must be integrated, the work of project team and client must be integrated.

Chapter 30: Project closure and aftermaths: The work of the project is brought to a timely and efficient conclusion. The product is tested and commissioned, and handed to the operations team, who must be trained in its use, and operational and logistical procedures must be put in place. The clients ensure they receive the benefit required to repay the project finance, and the contractor obtains sign off from the client and receives final payment. The project team is disbanded, and debriefed. The project performance is audited, and lessons learnt for future projects.

PART IV: PEOPLE

Project management may be viewed as a systems science or a social science. I believe it is more social science than systems science, but in most of what appears above you may have gained the impression that it is more systems science. This final part of the book redresses the balance and is primarily about the social science, managing the needs of all the people involved in the project. It was suggested I leave this out and make it a separate book. Gower published a spin-off book from the 3rd edition, *People in Project Management* (Turner 2003a), and so it was suggested I didn't need this part in the main handbook. However, I think projects don't exist without people, and so it was essential to include it. I could also see all the charges levelled at me that I don't care about the people if I didn't include it.

Chapter 31: Managing Human Resources in the project-based organization: Projects are unique, novel and transient, and hence standard Human Resource Management concepts do not apply to project-based firms. Every project requires a new structure, and every time a new project is created the human resource configuration of the parent organization changes. Thus, some of the core concepts of HRM need rethinking. There are three core concepts of HRM theory in particular which need novel approaches in a project organization. These are the selection of people to work for the organization, the management of their careers and their and the organization's learning and development. There are also three new processes required, the assignment of people to projects, their development on projects, and their dispersement after projects have been completed.

Chapter 32: Developing individual competence: To undertake its projects, an organization needs competent individuals. It needs to develop people competent in the technology of the project and people competent in the management of projects.

Chapter 33: Developing project management capability of organizations:
The organization also needs to be competent itself in the technology used and in the management of projects, and so needs to develop enterprise project management capability. The competence of the people is a component of this, but there are also other things the organization can do to develop its capability and to innovate in the processes it uses. These include the use of procedures, reviews and benchmarking, knowledge management, and the development of a project management community.

Chapter 34: Managing teams: Project teams are formed to undertake a unique and novel task, and are transient in their existence. The team needs to be formed and raised to peak performance. This is part of the mobilization process. Achieving peak team performance is critical to project success. The team needs to be composed of a balanced set of individuals with complimentary strengths and weaknesses. The team also needs to be properly disbanded at the end of the project so that its members can look forward to their future work, and they need to be properly debriefed so that the organization can learn from their experiences.

Chapter 35: Leadership: Volumes have been written on the elusive quality of leadership, and volumes devoted to the question of whether leaders are born or made. My view is that the majority of people are born with inherent leadership skills, and they can learn to develop these. Understanding the skills and styles of good leadership can improve the performance of a project manager in leading the team and motivating the individuals in the team to great things. One of the most important skills of a good leader is to be able to communicate the vision for the project, and the process of achieving that vision.

Chapter 36: Managing stakeholders: The wider project team encompasses people beyond those actually doing the work of the project. There are many people whose lives are affected by the project and its outcomes, and most of these have a view on the project. Some people view it positively, some negatively. Some can influence the outcome, some cannot. Where they view the project negatively, and can influence the outcome, they will work to undermine the project and that can lead to conflict. The project manager needs to communicate the vision, communicate the process, to win everybody over to the sense of the project. He or she also needs to negotiate everybody's involvement in the project, making them aware of how it can lead to positive outcomes for them, and what contribution is expected from them.

Chapter 37: Managing communication: Communication between the project manager and the client, between the client and the project manager and between both and the other stakeholders is essential for maintaining cohesion of the project team. The client in particular wants to be comfortable about project progress and to trust the project manager. The right type of communication from the project manager is essential to maintain that comfort and trust. But in order for the client to be able to trust the project manager, the latter must know what the client wants and needs, and so communication in the opposite direction must also take place. Communication with all the stakeholders is essential for keeping them committed and resolving conflict.

Chapter 38: Managing conflict: Conflict often arises on projects, either because people have differences of opinion about the expected project outcomes, or because some people misunderstand or fear the expected outcomes, or because there are personality clashes. Unresolved conflict can be damaging to the project's performance and so must be managed. People who fear or misunderstand the expected project outcomes may be persuaded to accept them if they are properly explained.

Chapter 39: Managing culture: The team is composed of many individuals, with different backgrounds. International teams are now common, and the project manager and team members need to be aware of cultural differences. However, there is a view that the cultural differences between different professions can be greater than those between nations. Hence even people working within a single country need to be aware of differences that can arise from professional, religious, class, educational, gender, age and other backgrounds.

Chapter 40: Ethics: Several times I have said people should behave morally, especially with regard to health, safety and the environment. So often the law has to intervene. Experience shows that even though many people think the moral road is the more expensive road, it often leads to greater rewards, and on earth, not just in heaven. The ethical approach usually leads to the greater good for everyone, and people respect that and respond in like fashion.

OTHER PROJECT MANAGEMENT KNOWLEDGE AREAS

In compiling the book, choices had to be made about what was to be included. I said above that it was suggested I leave out the part dealing with people, but I decided people are so essential to project management I would include it. However, I did decide to leave out the commercial and contractual parts. (I have included the four Ps, projects, performance, process and people, but left out the two Cs, commercial and contractual.) People might say both those issues are just as important as the people issues. Projects cannot happen without finance and contracts. That is true, but I thought they were of less general interest. Also I thought I would be less exposed to criticism if I left them out. Both were included in the 3rd edition, and the contractual issues have been included in a spin-off book, *Contracting for Project Management* (Turner 2003b). For completeness of this overview of the project management body of knowledge, I include brief descriptions of these areas.

COMMERCIAL

There are several commercial and financial issues relating to the way the project is financed.

Project appraisal: The value for the project must be appraised, by comparing projected cash inflows (revenues and savings) to expected cash outflows (costs) using investment appraisal techniques.

Finance: Finance must be raised from any of a number of sources. The simplest is to obtain money from the parent organization. Alternatively, money can be obtained from other equity shareholders, or as loans from banks. There are also a number of specialist sources of finance. The costs and benefits of different sources of finance must be compared, and a financial package produced for the project.

Taxation: Even rich people have to pay their taxes. It is important to understand the tax laws of the country. What counts as capital expenditure and what as revenue? What tax exemptions and grants are available? How can capital exemptions be worked to the best advantage? How can expenditure be phased to obtain the best tax advantage?

Insurance: The sponsor's investment needs to be protected against unexpected loss. Some risks are insurable, such as fire, civil strife, transport losses. Severe weather can be insured, but not inclement weather. Projects may be insured with insurance companies. However, there are also ways of insuring the projects, such as setting aside a contingency in the budget, or buying currency futures. That is related to risk management.

CONTRACTUAL

On anything but the smallest projects, the sponsor will not have the necessary resources in-house to undertake the project. Hence, it is almost always necessary to buy in external goods and services. On a project there is an essential difference between the procurement of a service, such as works or labour, which is used over an extended period of time, and the procurement of goods and materials, which are delivered at an instant in time. The term 'procurement' tends to be used for the latter and 'project contract management' for the former, even though both involve procurement and contracts.

Project contract management: The client must develop a contract strategy, deciding the best form of contract from several available to appropriately motivate the contractor and govern the relationship between them. They must choose an appropriate contractor to do the work and govern the relationship with the contractor. Contractors must bid for work and administer the relationship with the client. Both the client and contractor need ways of managing variations, to minimize claims arising, and to try to prevent claims becoming disputes.

Procurement: The word 'procurement' strictly applies to the purchasing of all goods and services, but in projects it does tend to be limited to the procurement of goods and materials. Similar processes apply as applied to the selection of contractors as described above, but at a more detailed level.

Contract law: In most countries the law of contract involves concepts of offer, acceptance, consideration, functions, validity, mistakes, terms and conditions, termination and remedies.

GENERAL MANAGEMENT KNOWLEDGE AREAS

Most versions of the project management body of knowledge also deal with some of the general management skills required by project managers. Some of these are directly related to knowledge topics above, those knowledge topics just being their interpretation in the unique, novel and transient context of projects or project-based organizations.

Human Resource Management: There are many elements of human resource management, terms and conditions of employment, industrial relations, career development, work and organizational design, organizational learning, leadership, team development, individual empowerment and motivation.

Marketing and customers: Marketing is the process by which an organization identifies its customers, and the products they want to buy, and tries to influence their buying habits. There are ways of identifying the marketing mix (the four P's: product, price, promotion and place of sale), and the product portfolio, and making improvements to both. Marketing is significant to projects in two ways.

17

The project-based firm, selling bespoke products and services, needs to identify its customers and the products and services they want to buy, like anyone else. In routine organizations, the marketing process will lead to the identification of new products, technologies or organizational structures needed to service the market, and the implementation of those changes will be undertaken through projects (or at least it ought to be).

Operations: Above we have identified the processes required to manage projects. Organizations also need to define the processes required to manage their routine operations.

Information Technology: I talked above about identifying the information management needs of projects. Organizations need to identify the information needs of all their business processes across all areas of management and all functions.

Finance and accounting: Organizations must manage the cash. Firms in the private sector need to generate cash to operate and to grow, and they need to make profits to provide returns to shareholders. Organizations in the public and voluntary sectors need to ensure that they do not over-spend their budgets, and ensure that they get value for money. That will not happen by accident; it must be planned and controlled.

Innovation, technology and change: Technology may be viewed as part of operations and innovation part of marketing. I have included this separately, because I see operations as being about defining the business processes. The knowledge of the technology that adds value for the organization is a key part of its competitive advantage, and so that knowledge, that technology, should be managed carefully, and separately from routine operations. Innovation and change are essential to maintain competitive advantage. Innovation usually refers to improvements in the products and technology of the organizations, and change to improvements in the process and effectiveness of the organization.

Governance: Absolutely nothing happens in an organization without governance. In a narrow sense governance (in the private sector) is the legally defined roles of directors and the company secretary. In a wider sense governance is the process by which the organization defines its objectives, and the means of obtaining those objectives and the means of monitoring performance. It is strategic planning and implementation through projects, and it is leadership (communicating the vision, communicating the process).

Strategy: At the end we are back where we started. Projects are undertaken to help organizations deliver their strategic plans. The strategic planning process is essential for the survival of organizations, and it is the strategic planning process that generates projects. There is not one without the other, and there is no organization without either.

REFERENCES AND FURTHER READING

APM, 2006, *APM Body of Knowledge,* 5th edition, High Wycombe, UK: Association for Project Management.

AIPM, 2004, *National Competency Standards for Project Management*, Hawthorn, VA, AU: Innovation and Business Skills Australia.

ECITB, 2003, *National Occupational Standards for Project Management,* Kings Langley, Herts, UK: Engineering Construction Industry Training Board.

IPMA, 2006, *ICB: IPMA Competence Baseline,* Zurich. CH: International Project Management Association.

ISO, 2004, *ISO 10,006: Quality Management – Guidelines to Quality in Project Management,* 2nd edition, Geneva, CH: International Standards Organization.

PMI®, 2004, *The Guide to the Project Management Body of Knowledge,* 3rd edition, Newtown Square, PA: Project Management Institute.

Turner, J.R., (ed) 2003a, *People in Project Management,* Aldershot, UK: Gower.

Turner, J.R., (ed) 2003b, *Contracting for Project Management,* Aldershot, UK: Gower.

Part I
Projects

INTRODUCTION TO PART I

In Part I, we consider the raison d'etre of Project Management, as a tool to help organizations achieve their corporate strategy. We also consider the strategy of undertaking a project or programme of projects, how an organization approaches the need to deliver a project successfully.

CHAPTER 2: IMPLEMENTING STRATEGY THROUGH PROGRAMMES OF PROJECTS

In Chapter 2, Peter Morris and Ashley Jamieson set the scene. Based on research they undertook for the Project Management Institute (PMI®), they describe how organizations link the projects, programmes and portfolios they are doing to corporate strategy. They outline the way corporate strategy is developed and implemented via the management of portfolios, programmes, and projects. Through an analysis of four case studies, they show that to align projects with corporate strategy, organizations need to adopt appropriate business models and hierarchies of plans through portfolios of projects and programmes. Firms need to adopt appropriate project strategies, supported by project management processes and procedures, with roles, responsibilities and accountabilities assigned. They also need to develop people with appropriate competencies to accept those roles, responsibilities and accountabilities.

CHAPTER 3: MANAGING PORTFOLIOS OF PROJECTS

Most projects do not take place on their own, but as part of a larger grouping. A portfolio of projects is a group of projects that share a common resource pool; a programme is a group of projects that jointly contribute to a higher order objective. As Peter Morris and Ashley Jamieson describe in Chapter 2, most projects are part of an organization's investment portfolio, sharing the funds that the organization makes available for investment and development. A more limited portfolio shares other resources like project staff and materials. In Chapter 3, Michel Thiry describes project portfolio management. He focuses on two aspects of the management of portfolios: the selection and prioritization of projects, based on contribution to organizational benefits and achievability; and the allocation and prioritizing of resources between those projects that have been chosen so that they can deliver the expected benefits. He suggest there are four key activities to accomplish this: analysing the portfolio of existing and potential projects; selecting the projects to be implemented as part of this portfolio; allocating resources to those projects that have been selected; and collecting and storing project data for performance measurement and portfolio reorientation.

CHAPTER 4: MANAGING PROGRAMMES OF PROJECTS

Often the change or strategic development required by an organization cannot be achieved by one project alone. It is necessary to do several, sometimes unrelated, things to achieve the desired change. The collection of projects contributing to that change is a programme. Michel Thiry describes Programme Management in Chapter 4. Many organizations that have adopted a project management approach have had to deal with the inconsistency between the flexibility and dynamism of the project approach and the desire of firms' financial and strategic stakeholders to exercise control at corporate level. In this chapter, Michel Thiry shows how programme management can help resolve this inconsistency by enabling the implementation and control of business strategies while allowing for the dynamism and flexibility inherent to the project approach. He describes a programme management life-cycle, and also considers how other tools, considered later in this book, can contribute to the effective management of programmes. This chapter just gives an overview of Programme Management as a context for Projects. Anyone wishing to study the subject further should read the *Gower Handbook of Programme Management*, a sister compendium to this book.

CHAPTER 5: PROJECTS AND THEIR MANAGEMENT

Chapter 5, described projects and their management. This is of course the core topic of this book, but the four previous chapters should have set projects in the context of the parent organization and the programmes or portfolios of which they are a part. In this chapter I (Rodney Turner) describe the three dimensions of project management and give an overview of projects and management, by describing a theory of project management. I start with three simple premises, and show that much of what we understand as project management follows naturally from those three premises. I show that if we assume those premises to be correct then we need many of the tools and techniques described in this book to manage our projects.

CHAPTER 6: PROJECT SUCCESS AND STRATEGY

In Chapter 2, Ashley Jamieson and Peter Morris describe how to link projects, programmes and portfolios to the strategy of the parent organization. But we also need a strategy for the temporary organization that is the project. That requires us to define the objectives of the project, both the asset the project is required to deliver, and the business objectives we will use that asset to achieve; how we will judge the successful achievement of those objectives (success criteria), and success factors that will influence their achievement. In this chapter I describe how to formulate a project strategy by identifying the success criteria and success factors.

CHAPTER 7: PROCESSES AND PROCEDURES

In Chapter 7, Richard Pharro and Colin Bentley consider the use of project processes and procedures. In Chapter 5, I showed that the transience of projects implies that their management is more process-based than functionally-based, and that the life-cycle represents that process. Several standard procedures have been developed to represent that process, including BS6079, PRINCE2™ and ISO 10,006. Many organizations develop their own standard procedures, and these can be tailored to an individual procedures manual for each project.

CHAPTER 8: SOFTWARE SOLUTIONS FOR PROJECT, PROGRAMME AND PORTFOLIO MANAGEMENT

In Chapter 8, Chris Dobson describes the information systems available for programme planning and portfolio management. The current breed of software tools vary in their complexity and functionality. With the development of faster and more powerful computers, we are at the point where virtually anything is possible and an organization needs to think strategically before investing in a tool. Chris Dobson categorizes software tools, examines for their functionality and suggests applicability to the project environment discussed. He gives a description of the information systems and their use, and provides a practical overview of how they support and facilitate the project, programme, and portfolio management process. The aim is to help an organization searching for a software tool to find one suitable for their needs.

CHAPTER 9: THE PROJECT, PROGRAMME OR PORTFOLIO OFFICE

Jack Duggal describes the project management office (PMO) in Chapter 9. PMOs have been a growing trend in recent years, and more and more companies are establishing them. In this chapter Jack illustrates the reasons and need for a

PMO. He presents a PMO Framework that focuses on both the strategic and tactical aspects of a PMO. He outlines the PMO continuum and presents the range of PMO functions. He also addresses various aspects of a PMO – the different types and levels of PMOs; the role and purpose of a PMO; the PMO focus areas and functions; PMO implementation lifecycle; organizational structures; risks and challenges; demonstrating and measuring PMO value; and PMO success criteria.

CHAPTER 10: MATURITY MODELS FOR THE PROJECT-ORIENTED COMPANY

In Chapter 10, Roland Gareis and Martina Huemann describe benchmarking and maturity models for project management. After introducing the strategic, structural, and cultural characteristics of the project-oriented company, they categorize maturity models, and then they present general maturity models and project management-related maturity models. A family of *mature* models is introduced. For selected models of this 'family' the underlying management approach, the dimensions of the model, the process of application, and the results of the analysis and the benchmarking are described.

CHAPTER 11: CONDUCTING AUDITS

In Chapter 11, Martina Huemann describes the use of Project Management Audits to control the quality of project management processes, and to increase the chance of project success. She aims to introduce the auditing of projects as a learning instrument to add value to the project as well as to the project-oriented company. Project management auditing can be perceived as an instrument for improving the management processes of a project, and thus it may contribute to a project's success. To perceive project management auditing as a learning opportunity calls for a reinvention of this quality assurance instrument. This is reflected in the auditing process and in the methods applied as well as in the attitude of the auditor and the cultural aspects of the audit. This chapter advocates routine auditing on a regular basis and promotes a co-operative auditing style to add value to the project or programme.

CHAPTER 12: MANAGING THE CONTEXT

What was a whole part in the 3rd edition is reduced to one chapter. Mark O'Callaghan describes the management of the project's context in Chapter 12. He uses PESTLE analysis, to look at the Political, Economic, Social, Technical, Legal and Environmental impacts on a project, and how they can be managed.

2 Implementing Strategy through Programmes of Projects

Ashley Jamieson and Peter Morris

A project is a temporary organization to which resources are assigned to deliver benefit for the parent organization. To ensure the investments it makes in its projects are wisely spent, an organization will want to ensure it undertakes appropriate projects to deliver desirable outcomes and benefits that contributes to its overall goals and objectives. Thus it will want to ensure the projects it undertakes are wisely chosen and are aligned to its corporate strategy.

Corporate strategy is the means by which an organization thinks through and articulates how its corporate goals and objectives will be achieved. This strategy is typically operationalized at a strategic business unit [SBU] level, and strategic initiatives are then clustered into portfolios of programmes and projects for implementation. Much of traditional management writing tends only to cover the strategic management processes that formulate and implement strategy at the corporate level. But there is a dearth of writing about how corporate strategy gets translated into implementation at the programme or project level. Yet in practice the two sets of activities are well connected; projects and programmes are important ways for strategy to be implemented in the enterprise and we ought to understand much better how this occurs.

Strategic management is often an ambiguous and complex process, fundamental and organization-wide, and generally has long-term implications. While the typical corporate planning process is generally ordered and analytical, strategy management is a dynamic process. Mintzberg and Quinn (1996) distinguished 'deliberate' strategy from 'emergent' strategy. Emergent strategy is that which becomes evident as it, and events, emerge with time. This emergence suggests a more incremental approach to strategy formulation and implementation, where results are regularly appraised against benefits and changes are made and managed against the evolving picture of performance.

This chapter outlines the way corporate strategy is developed and implemented via the management of portfolios, programmes, and projects. Through an analysis of four case studies, we show that to align projects with corporate strategy, organizations need to adopt appropriate business models and hierarchies of plans through portfolios of projects and programmes. They need to adopt appropriate project strategies, supported by project management processes and procedures, with roles, responsibilities and accountabilities assigned. They also need to develop people with appropriate competencies to accept those roles, responsibilities and accountabilities.

INTERACTION BETWEEN PROJECTS, PROGRAMMES AND CORPORATE STRATEGY

The interaction between projects, or programmes, and the enterprise's strategy also may be either 'deliberate', as formal vehicles for strategy implementation, as in capital expenditure projects for example, or 'emergent', in that as they are implemented they create new conditions which in turn influence and shape the intended strategy. Consequently projects and programmes often have a two-way relationship with the corporate environment in which they evolve. And though there may be formal strategy planning processes and practices, strategy may not be realized in as rigid or formal a manner as many planners assume. Nevertheless, a formal strategy process does bring clarity and discipline.

ROLE OF PROJECT MANAGEMENT IN FORMULATING AND IMPLEMENTING STRATEGY

Recent research has revealed that the role of project management in implementing such strategy is often not clear. For example some senior managers believe project managers should not be involved in strategy formulation (Crawford 2005). Others see project management as strongly execution oriented and as such it is not perceived as strategically important by senior managers. More significantly perhaps, some propose that project managers should be involved in strategy formulation but are not competent to carry out implementation effectively since they will not have been exposed to the factors that initiate change in projects. And moreover there is a growing view, at least in the UK, that business and organizational change projects are really managed best by programme management, as defined say by the Office of Government Commerce (OGC 2003), rather than by project management.

BUSINESS MANAGEMENT AND PROJECT MANAGEMENT

It is important that organizations understand properly their business management model and the position of project, or programme, management within it; and hence for project management to see how they sit alongside, and are perceived by, the business management functions. Research shows, for example, that one of

28

the reasons new product innovation projects often fail is because they lack wider organizational support. While project management practitioners may think their function is central to the success of a company, it may have little meaning within the enterprise unless it is clearly established and embedded within the enterprise's structure and business management models and processes.

The involvement of some discipline explicitly concerned with the management of projects in strategy implementation is essential in order for senior management to have some control over expenditure and intended action. Conversely senior management involvement is required if project management is to be successful in strategy implementation. Good governance practice in fact now explicitly requires, among several things, formal alignment between business, portfolio, programme and project plans and transparent reporting of status and risks to the Board (APM 2004).

Not all strategy implementation is just downwards from the corporate level through portfolios to programmes and projects. Just as in strategic planning there is upward flow from SBUs, so in implementation there is management information and action bearing up from programmes and projects onto portfolio, business unit and corporate strategy.

A HIERARCHY FOR IMPLEMENTING STRATEGY

Hierarchy is usually important in any discussion of implementing strategy. A hierarchy of objectives and strategies can generally be formed as a result of using a strategy planning process; this can be a highly effective means of structuring and managing strategy, and communicating it to the organization. One such model is Archibald's hierarchy of objectives, strategies and projects (Archibald 2003). This model proposes that objectives and strategies are developed at the policy, strategic, operational and project levels and cascaded down, thereby ensuring alignment and continuity of strategy. Another model is the Stanford Research Institute's 'System of Plans' (Mintzberg et al 1998).

Levels of strategy have been defined as corporate, business and operational, where the operational level strategies tend to focus on programmes and projects. Recent research indicates that the linkage often starts, or can start, even higher. Others have defined the levels slightly differently (Turner 1999). Figure 2.1 shows how organizations position business strategy, portfolios, programmes and projects to achieve their development objectives.

PRACTICES AND TECHNIQUES FOR MANAGING STRATEGY

A number of practices are used for managing the strategic-portfolio-project linkage in multiple project environments and a number of techniques have been

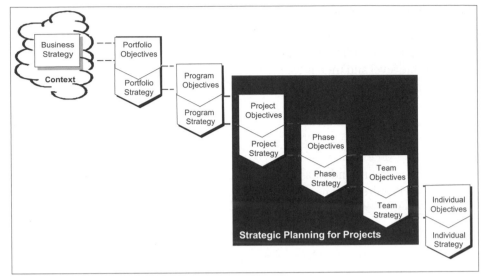

Figure 2.1 Linking corporate and project strategy

proposed to move corporate strategy into portfolios, programmes (and projects). These include scenario planning, force-field analysis, stakeholder analysis, and 'attractiveness/implementation difficulty' analysis.

PORTFOLIOS, PROGRAMMES, AND PROJECTS

PORTFOLIO MANAGEMENT

The majority of projects take place as part of a portfolio of several projects or programmes (see also Chapters 3 and 4). Project portfolio management has been described as the art and science of applying a set of knowledge, skills, tools, and techniques to a collection of projects or programmes to meet or exceed the needs and expectations of an organization's investment strategy, and a project portfolio as a set of projects that are managed in a coordinated way to deliver benefits which would not be possible if the projects were managed independently. A slightly different but widely accepted view is that a project portfolio is a collection of projects to be managed concurrently under a single management umbrella where each project may be related to or independent of the others. It has been suggested that portfolio management is pre-eminently about selecting, or prioritising, the best projects or programmes to proceed with. Project portfolio management, then, is predominantly about 'choosing the right project', in contrast to project management which is about 'doing the project right'.

Portfolio frameworks, processes and practices

Archer and Ghasemzadeh (1999, 2004) have provided a general framework for project portfolio selection which demonstrates the need for strategy to be set at the corporate level and then filtered down to the project level (see also Chapter 3). They emphasize the importance of aligning resource demand with resource availability to achieve a set of strategic goals. Considerable research into key aspects of portfolio management has been undertaken in recent years, some of which is listed in Figure 2.2.

A key criterion for successfully applying risk evaluation in portfolio selection is that risk assessment and quantification be uniformly applied across all projects and teams, a requirement now mandated by good governance (APM 2004).

PROGRAMMES

Programme management is a powerful way of coordinating projects that have a shared business aim and is perceived by some as the most suitable methodology for ensuring the successful implementation of strategies, since it is subtler and more able to respond to emerging data. Both portfolio management and programme management focus on prioritising resources and optimising the business benefit. Programme management is more involved in day-to-day implementation management than portfolio management which is more periodic and is strongly analytical. Implementing strategy through programme management involves continuous updating and adjustment.

Most commentators define programme management as involving the management of a collection of interrelated projects, often clustered to achieve a shared strategic benefit (outcome). Several perspectives exist on the optimal ways to configure programmes to achieve strategic objectives and to deal with change. Some emphasize the technology base, as in platform projects. Others, particularly those coming from Information Technology, emphasize the importance of business benefit. And a few have proposed more generic portfolio and programme typologies.

Programmes are often ongoing or long-term and are subjected to both uncertainty and ambiguity. Programmes and programme management are frequently used in large organizations to implement strategic initiatives. The UK Office of Government Commerce (OGC) for example considers the alignment between strategy and projects to be one of the main benefits of programme management (OGC 2003), though this seems rather dated in the light of the more recent guidance on good governance (APM 2004): they require a decision management paradigm which takes into account the appropriate strategic perspective. Programmes often have to strive for the achievement of a number of conflicting aims whereas projects aim to achieve single predetermined results

Topic	Source
A general framework for project portfolio selection. A project portfolio management process which provides a means of consistently and objectively evaluating projects. And thereby making the most effective strategic use of the resources.	Archer and Ghasemzadeh (1999) Knutson (2001)
Strong portfolio selection and management practice in new product development. Using formal portfolio management methods to manage portfolio strategy within the context of the enterprise business strategy.	Archer and Ghasemzadeh (2004) Cooper, et al (2001). Cooper, et al (1999).
Examples of portfolio management practice employed by a diversity of major companies. Examples of portfolios of different project types and an outline of the major types of methodologies used in portfolio selection.	Cooper et al (1998) Artto and Dietrich (2004)
A strategic portfolio classification framework based on the need to select projects due to their strategic impact and to form a policy for project selection.	Shenar and Dvir (2004)
Strong impact of risk and outsourcing on portfolio selection and management.	Archer and Ghasemzadeh (2004)

Figure 2.2 Portfolio management sources

within set time and cost constraints. Many commentators position projects as appropriate more for implementing 'deliberate' (planned) strategies while seeing programmes for both deliberate and 'emergent' (unplanned) strategies, although in the case studies described below we found this to be so for the aerospace case but not for the drug development or construction cases.

PROJECTS

Turner (1999) advocates the development of a comprehensive definition of a project at the start of the project, in which business plans are aligned with project plans containing key elements of project strategy. The development of business cases and strategic briefs is generally considered to be an integral part of the project definition process. Gardiner (2005) provides several authoritative case studies on project strategy and Morris and Hough (1987) summarize the elements of a project strategy based on an analysis of many projects.

Work by the authors in integrating what the PMBOK® (PMI 2004) and the APM BOK (APM 2006) have to say about the way strategy shapes project definition shows the large number of factors involved in creating project strategy at the front end (Morris and Jamieson 2004). This highlights the need for an effective way to manage project strategy creation, covering not only the front end of a project but the entire life-cycle. Many organizations have in fact developed structured approaches for creating and managing project (and programme) strategy that covers the entire project life-cycle and are integrated with the business strategy development processes.

COMPETENCIES, ROLES, RESPONSIBILITIES AND ACCOUNTABILITIES FOR MOVING STRATEGY

Corporate strategy is not translated into project strategy by process alone. Moving strategy through such processes and practices as we have just reviewed requires an extensive range of personal competencies and a clear definition of roles, responsibilities and accountabilities. Several definitions of competence (and capability) have been offered. For example competency is the knowledge, skills and qualities of effective managers, with the ability to perform effectively in a specific work situation.

The UK Institution of Civil Engineers' competency framework (ICE 2000) comprises twelve key management roles and approximately 140 associated competencies. Elements of strategy management are covered in both the corporate and business management roles and project management is shown as having responsibility for project strategy. Examples of core competences related to project strategy are provided in the case studies in Morris and Jamieson (2004) and outlined below. We shall also see evidence in the case studies that project leadership is increasingly being recognized as a key competence in shaping and implementing project strategy (see the drug development and transportation case studies).

FOUR CASE STUDIES OF MOVING FROM CORPORATE TO PROJECT STRATEGY

We studied four companies to find evidence and insight into the way corporate strategy is created and moved into programmes and projects. The companies were:

- a global aerospace company
- a division of a global pharmaceutical company
- a group within a global financial services company
- an international transportation facility owner and operator – for our purposes, a leading construction client and owner

AEROSPACE COMPANY

The company is a Tier 2 supplier. All of its business activities are assigned to a programme and each programme has a client. There is a hierarchical cascade of objectives from the corporate level, through SBUs, to programmes and projects. Orders are progressed through a stage-gated development process. Eleven key project management topics are reviewed at each gate, one of which is project strategy. Project strategy is managed, in considerable detail, by project teams throughout all the stages and all the associated phases of the project management process, as illustrated schematically by Figure 2.3. The company also has a specific process for managing a rapid response to changes impacting strategy. The importance the company attaches to project strategy, and its effective management, is clearly demonstrated by the mandatory use of a highly integrated, structured approach to translate corporate and business strategies into project strategy, and then to manage the project strategy through the entire project management process and project life-cycle.

GLOBAL FINANCIAL SERVICES COMPANY

The company has a highly structured process for developing and approving its corporate plan but the role of project management in its implementation is not explicit. The programme and project processes are self-standing and begin with reference to the business unit's vision, mission, strategies and objectives. Once the project is authorized, work begins on defining the business case. This defines, inter alia:

- the programme operational vision
- the relationship with the business strategy plan
- programme/project organization structure
- risk and resource plans
- delivery plan
- project briefs

Upon approval of the business case, the project is prepared for execution using a 'Mobilize Programme' process which takes the results of the previous planning processes and incorporates them into the project management plan. 'Project strategy' as a term and activity is not mentioned in the project management process from this point onward. However, the way in which the project is to be managed is covered in detail in the following sections of the project management plan:

- project objectives
- project schedule

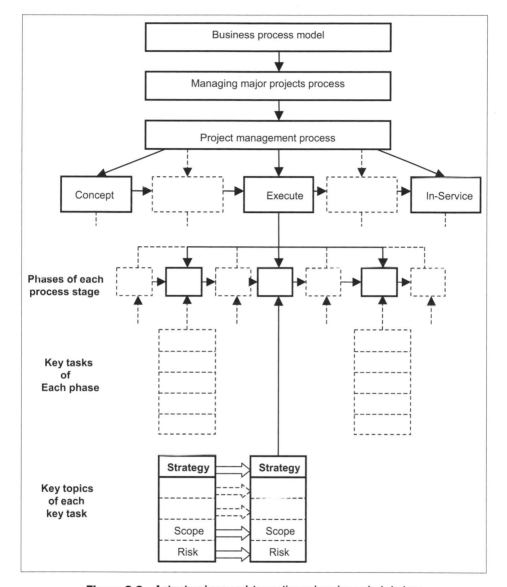

Figure 2.3 A structured approach to creating and moving project strategy

- project budget
- resource plan
- risk management plan
- a complete set of project briefs.

The strategy for the project is managed and maintained through the operational vision within the business case, and is in force until the close of the project. The lack of a single coherent project strategy document, clearly related to the business case, can lead to loss of business rationale in some cases. It is recognized that there could be a tighter linkage between business strategy and project implementation.

GLOBAL DRUG DEVELOPMENT COMPANY

Drug development involves the progression of chemical entities discovered in the laboratory through a highly structured series of tests. Several dozen chemical entities may be being progressed through the pipeline at any one time. The management of this activity involves a complex matrix of functional 'lines', projects and programmes.

The attrition rate is enormously high, certainly in the earlier stages of the pipeline. However large pharma companies typically have many more entities in hand than they have resources available to work on them. Hence there is an on-going dialogue between senior management on portfolio prioritization and resource allocation.

A portfolio in the drug development industry is a group of actual or potential chemical entity projects that are being or could be undertaken. Portfolios are very important: they essentially form 'the hand' from which the future of the company is being played. They are frequently rebalanced, at which point portfolio strategy is revised and the next phase of implementation shaped. This may require modifications for project or programme strategy and this may in turn influence portfolio strategy.

The term 'programmes' is less well embedded. Programmes are seen as constituting a technical platform, a particular chemical entity which may have different indications, delivery mechanisms or dosages. These essentially constitute different development projects which will be being moved, within the portfolio, along the development funnel at different rates.

Projects have two meanings:

1. the major project of developing chemical entities from discovery to regulatory approval and into the marketplace
2. the activity of getting the entity to the next milestone review point in its development

The company uses a very structured project management process to manage projects. The process is geared to each of the phases of the life-cycle and linked to a series of project management methodologies, which identify the actions to be taken by the project team at any point in the project or phase of the development life-cycle. Project strategy is identified as one of the topics that needs to be implemented by the project team, during each of the phases of the life-cycle, using a standard procedure.

Because of the high rate of attrition, spending too much time detailing long-term project strategy is not seen to be useful. However, it is still considered essential to develop and maintain a flexible strategy for the success of the project. Thus project strategy is aligned with the portfolio strategy and is revised as the project progresses.

Most pharmaceutical project management organizations distinguish between a Project Leader (or Director) role and the Project Manager. Typically, the former has a strong feeling for the science of the development; the latter is more concerned with the operational management of the project. The project leader/director typically assumes a much more prominent role in shaping project strategy, though this is not always the case.

TRANSPORTATION (CONSTRUCTION) COMPANY

The company is one of the largest and most efficient airport operators in the world. It applies the 'OGSM' methodology to define its Objectives, Goals, Strategies, and Measures in a sequential manner cascading these down through business units to programmes and projects. Figure 2.4 shows that the strategic business units, capital investment plans (CIPs), business governance, project

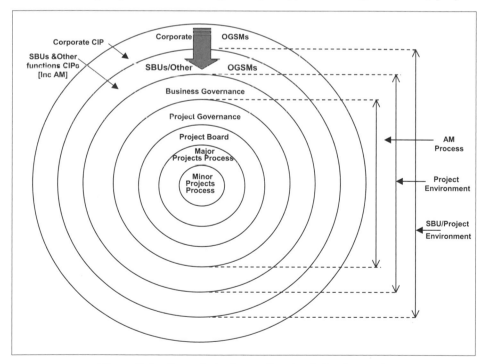

Figure 2.4   Corporate, business unit, and project environments

37

governance and major and minor projects are all set within the 'environment' of the corporate OGSMs, and that each level determines that of the next in descending order.

The company does not use the term 'portfolio' but does use a process for measuring the strategic contribution, uncertainty/complexity, and value-for-money of its capital investments at the SBU levels and for evaluating, selecting and prioritising its programmes and projects. Programme management is seen as the management of a group of projects with similar aims.

Projects are managed via a stage gate process with a project board responsible to project governance for the day-to-day running of the project. The project is split into two stages: development and project delivery. The former is managed by a development manager, the latter by a project leader (not 'project manager' – the term is deliberately avoided by the company as seeming too bureaucratic and not sufficiently emphasizing the required level of leadership).

The gated review process ensures that projects are aligned to business strategy (and corporate strategy) as they are set up, authorized and executed. A project management process is used to develop the project definition and key project management plans, a summary of which is considered to encapsulate project strategy. However, 'project strategy' as a term and practice is not used in the company. The performance of the project team is not measured against the objectives of the project, expressed in terms of project strategy, but only in terms of business strategy.

CROSS-COMPARISON OF CASE STUDY FINDINGS

The following general findings can be drawn from the case studies.

BUSINESS MODELS

The aerospace company had a very powerful business process model in which programme management (and project strategy) played a prominent part. The pharmaceutical company had a process model which was dominated by the drug development process; this is not the same as a business model *per se* but is common to all drug development, being driven by regulatory requirements; and was clearly the major business process. Project and portfolio management (and programme management to a lesser extent) are important aspects of this process. The financial services company had a high-level business process but this was less visible than the aerospace and transportation business models. The international transportation company/construction owner also had a strong business process model, though project management as a formal discipline had a less visible role.

CASCADING CORPORATE STRATEGIES INTO PROJECTS

All the companies created corporate objectives, goals and strategies using typical strategic management processes. These objectives, goals and strategies were cascaded to the SBUs or equivalent organizational entities, which in turn, and in conjunction with corporate strategy planners, developed their own objectives, goals and strategies. The SBUs subsequently developed objectives, goals and strategies with and for their respective programme and project teams, again in some instances using fully interconnecting business and project management processes.

HIERARCHY OF PLANS

The business case was the key element of the corporate and project management interface in all the companies. In all four cases the programme and/or project teams developed project strategies that aligned with the SBU and corporate strategy using project strategy or similar processes. The outputs of the processes containing the objectives, goals, and strategies included strategy plans, business plans, deployment plans and project plans, the hierarchy of which, in most cases, was similar to Archibald's hierarchy of objectives, strategies and projects, as reflected in the aerospace case, Figure 2.3. The pharmaceutical development company reviewed and rebalanced its portfolios frequently. This required new proposals for project or programme strategy.

PORTFOLIO MANAGEMENT

The importance of project portfolio management was recognized by all the companies. Within the companies, portfolio management was used primarily to select and prioritize programmes and projects, not to manage programmes or projects. Corporate and business units assembled a strategic portfolio of programmes and projects, or measured the strategic contribution of a programme or project, using a number of strategic and project management processes, tools and techniques. Company management boards or committees of senior managers adopted or rejected projects based on this information. The pharmaceutical company had a dedicated project portfolio management practice that played a very important part in project development.

PROGRAMME MANAGEMENT

Programme management was practiced by all the companies primarily in the sense of managing a group of high value projects sharing a common aim and/or of delivering regular benefits over a protracted period of time. In the aerospace company programme management was positioned as the management of a number of interrelated projects but critically also covering operations and maintenance. This is crucial in this company since much of the product margin is in operations and logistics support rather than initial capital sales. In the financial services company there was much more emphasis in programme management on managing multiple, interrelated projects for business benefit. In the pharmaceutical case the emphasis was on 'asset' management, in the sense that the programme represented a basic chemical entity (a technology platform) which can be promoted as a brand. Programme management in the transportation case was used to manage multiple, interrelated projects.

PROJECT STRATEGY

The business case was the key element of the corporate and project management interface in all the companies. An outline project strategy was developed early in all the projects and was aligned with corporate and business strategies. Subsequently, business strategy, in most of the companies, was turned into a comprehensive project strategy following project management processes and incorporating many of the usual project management practices.

The aerospace company formally reviewed project strategy as a project management topic alongside other prescribed aspects of project management at each 'stage gate' review. The drug company reviewed project strategy at major gate reviews. Two of the companies used a very structured approach to create and manage project strategy. The aerospace company had institutionalised a project strategy management practice that was equivalent to, for example, risk management or technical management. The pharmaceutical company had identified specific project strategy-related issues for each phase and stage of the project development life-cycle. Both companies above assigned roles and responsibilities for managing the execution of these processes. The other two companies used a less structured approach. Though they developed management plans for their projects, they tended not to summarize the plans nor to develop a single project strategy statement from them. The companies above also tended not to use the term 'project strategy' in their project management processes. The aerospace and pharmaceutical companies managed project strategy for effectively the entire project life-cycle and not just at the front end of a project. The other two companies managed the project strategy as part of managing the business case for the project. It is important to note that good governance practice now clearly requires that projects and programmes have an approved implementation plan which is aligned with the overall business strategy – and that this should be reviewed at pre-defined authorization points (APM 2004). Many companies now do this on a routine basis.

PROCESSES AND PROCEDURES

The processes that were most consistently used within the companies were those in which the structure and content were described at a practical level, such as flowcharts with inputs and outputs for key processes; and those which identified who were accountable and responsible for carrying out the process activities. Conversely, where procedures were described in too much detail, staff tended not to use them. The best examples of the deployment of the business models and associated processes were those that were fully documented and incorporated within the company's Quality Management System, and were web-based, and available online throughout the organization. Where this approach was not used, companies nevertheless linked the activities of their SBUs and projects to ensure alignment of strategy.

Strategy was consciously and systematically 'value managed' in the pharmaceutical company. The transportation company had a strong 'value-for-money' orientation but did not use value management as a special practice. All companies integrated other key project development practices into their strategy development processes, such as risk management, technical and commercial management, and safety management. Programme management and project management activities were carried out in all cases using the same set of common processes, variously called integrated programme management, programme management, or even project management. The development of programme strategy and its alignment with corporate and business strategy was, as a consequence, achieved in a similar way to that for projects.

ROLES, RESPONSIBILITIES AND ACCOUNTABILITIES

In the pharmaceutical and transportation companies, project strategy was developed and maintained by governance and project leadership teams through business related processes and not exclusively through project management processes. In the pharmaceutical case it was driven by the characteristics of the regulated development process and governance review of the 'emerging' portfolio and individual project data. Project managers focused on scheduling, follow-up and 'control' activities in support of the project leaders' strategy-shaping activities. In the transportation company, strategy was developed using the OGSM method cascaded down through SBUs in classical 'deliberate' manner. In the financial services company, a family of project management job descriptions was used to identify the jobholder's roles, responsibilities and accountabilities for specific project management process activities and outputs which provided an unusually high degree of integration between the process and the individual or team. In the aerospace company, the roles, responsibilities and accountabilities were incorporated in the business and programme/project management processes, while the competences of the project management staff were linked to generic project management processes and key practices. The companies also employed a number of other methods to identify and specify the skills, knowledge, behaviours and experience required to develop and manage project strategy. These included competencies for senior project management staff, such as managing vision and strategy; and project management functional competencies covering knowledge and experience of strategy related areas like scope management.

COMPETENCIES AND FRAMEWORKS

In general, within all the companies, project management resources and capabilities figured highly in creating, deploying and maintaining enterprise, portfolio, programme and project strategies. All the companies specified the roles, responsibilities and accountabilities of those involved in the business management and project management processes, some using comprehensive sets of tables and matrices, for example RACI tables (Responsible, Accountable, Coordination/Consultation, Information), that were linked directly to the processes. These covered in detail all the phases and stages of the project management process and project life-cycle, including those for creating and maintaining project strategy or for implementing enterprise strategy within the context of the project business case. The RACI tables identified 'who' does 'what' and 'when' at any point along the process.

OVERALL FINDINGS AND CONCLUSIONS

We can draw several conclusions from these results.

MOVING FROM CORPORATE TO PROJECT STRATEGY

Project and programme management is widely used as a means of implementing corporate and business strategy and is a key business process. Normatively, we should expect strategies to be aligned and moved from the corporate level through portfolios, programmes and projects in a systematic and hierarchical manner that provides cohesion, visibility and an effective means of communication. Not all is 'deliberate' however: there is emergence and iteration. Project strategy is managed dynamically.

BUSINESS MANAGEMENT AND STRATEGY

Enterprise-wide business models are seen to play an important part in effecting this transformation. Business models are used widely by organizations and the business units within many of these organizations apply them collectively. The models may differ in size and complexity but most appear to incorporate project/programme management processes as key business management processes. Processes having a high interconnectivity between corporate, business and project levels are an important means of translating corporate goals, objectives and strategy into programmes and projects; and of ensuring that continuity of strategy is achieved in a systematic and structured way. Hierarchies of objectives and strategies allow organizations to cascade strategy in a systematic way.

Project and programme strategy is not always managed as a formal process. Often it is developed and maintained by project or programme leadership teams and governance through business case processes and not exclusively through project management processes.

PORTFOLIO MANAGEMENT AND PROGRAMME MANAGEMENT

Some form of portfolio management is implemented by many organizations but in a recent survey carried out by the authors, respondents perceived it to be about managing projects around a common theme rather than maintaining a balanced portfolio or selecting the right project (contrary to the literature). In contrast, three of the case study companies implemented portfolio management mainly as a process for selecting and prioritising 'the right projects'.

Programmes are important vehicles for implementing corporate strategy and for implementing change. Most companies considered that programme management emphasizes the management of benefits (as well as the ideas of product, brand or platform management). There is broad agreement that programme management includes the management of a portfolio or group of projects using integrated project teams, managing resources in an integrated manner, together with the management of benefits and of aggregated risk. Some organizations use a single fully integrated project management process for managing both programmes and projects.

PROJECT MANAGEMENT AND PROJECT STRATEGY

Project strategy management is widely recognized as an important project management practice that systematically relates project definition and development to corporate goals and strategies. Project management approaches are now being used by organizations at all stages of the project life-cycle with project strategy development, review and optimization occurring at specific points. A combination of programme or project plans and other management plans is most commonly used to manage programmes and projects, parts of which describe how the project is to be undertaken – in other words, its strategy. These parts may not be summarized in a single project strategy document. Value Management is quite widely used in optimising the strategy, often in combination with Risk Management.

PROJECT MANAGEMENT COMPETENCIES

Project resources and capabilities are key factors in creating, deploying and maintaining programme and project strategies. The project management roles, responsibilities and accountabilities required for this are generally well defined. Competency is seen by some to be role-specific and covers the knowledge, skills, and behaviours needed to perform the role. Organizations use competency frameworks to define the competency requirements for all the key jobs within the organization or all the jobs in a job family. A recent survey by the authors showed that a high percentage of organizations define the personal project management competencies required to develop project strategy. Furthermore, several organizations stressed the leadership qualities that they expected of their executives in shaping and delivering strategy, at both the project level and the corporate level.

It can be concluded therefore that though project strategy management is an under-explored and insufficiently described subject in the business and project literature, it is in fact a relatively well-trodden area, deserving of more recognition, formal study and discussion.

REFERENCES AND FURTHER READING

Archer, N.P. and Ghasemzadeh, F., 1999, 'An integrated framework for project portfolio selection', *International Journal of Project Management*, 17(4), 207–216.

Archer, N.P. and Ghasemzadeh, F., 2004, 'Project Portfolio Selection and Management' in: *The Wiley Guide to Managing Projects*. Morris, P.W.G. and Pinto, J.K., (eds). New York: John Wiley & Sons Inc.

Archibald, R., 2003, *Managing High-Technology Programmes and Projects*. 3rd edn., New York: John Wiley & Sons Inc.

Artto, K.A. and Dietrich, P.H., 2004, 'Strategic Business Management through Multiple Projects' in: *The Wiley Guide to Managing Projects*. Morris, P.W.G. and Pinto, J.K., (eds). New York: John Wiley & Sons Inc.

APM, 2004, *Directing Change: A guide to governance of project management*, High Wycombe, UK: Association for Project Management.

APM, 2006, *APM Body of Knowledge,* 5th edition, High Wycombe, UK: Association for Project Management.

Cooper, R.G., Edgett, S.J. and Klienschmidt, E.J., 1998, *Portfolio management for new products*. Reading, MA: Perseus Books.

Cooper, R.G., Edgett, S.J. and Klienschmidt, E.J., 1999, 'New product portfolio management: Practices and performance', *Journal of Product Innovation Management,* 16, 333–351.

Cooper, R.G., Edgett, S.J. and Klienschmidt, E.J., 2001, *Portfolio Management for New Products*, Cambridge, MA: Perseus Publishing.

Crawford, L.H., 2005, 'Senior management perceptions of project management competence', *International Journal of Project Management*, Vol. 223(1) pp.7–16.

Gardiner, P.D., 2005, *Project Management: A strategic planning approach*. London: Palgrave.

ICE, 2000, *Management development in the construction industry – Guidelines for the construction professional,* London: The Institution of Civil Engineers.

Knutson, J., 2001, *Succeeding in Project-driven Organizations: People, Processes and Politics,* New York: John Wiley & Sons, Inc.

Mintzberg, H., Ahlstrand, B., and Lampel, J., 1998, *Strategy Safari: A complete guide through the wilds of strategic management.* London: Pearson Education.

Mintzberg, H., & Quinn, J.B., 1996, *The Strategy Process: Concepts, Contexts and Cases.* 3rd edn. New Jersey: Prentice-Hall.

Morris, P.W.G. and Hough, G.H., 1987, *The Anatomy of Major Projects.* Chichester: John Wiley & Sons.

Morris, P.W.G. and Jamieson, H.A., 2004, *Translating Corporate Strategy into Project Strategy: Achieving corporate strategy through project management.* Newtown Square, PA: Project Management Institute.

OGC, 2003, *Managing Successful Programmes.* London: The Stationery Office.

PMI, 2004, *The Guide to the Project Management Body of Knowledge,* 3rd edition. Newtown Square, PA: Project Management Institute.

Shenar, A.J., and Dvir, D., 2004, 'How Projects Differ, And What to Do About It', in: *The Wiley Guide to Managing Projects.* Morris, P.W.G. and Pinto, J.K., (eds). New York: John Wiley & Sons Inc.

Turner, J.R., 1999, *The Handbook of Project-based Management,* 2nd edition., Maidenhead: McGraw-Hill.

3 Managing Portfolios of Projects

Michel Thiry

Organizations that adopt projects as a means to achieving change and delivering results often find it difficult to prioritize projects and to make best use of their resources. Portfolio management is a management approach that aims to align project efforts with the corporate strategy and optimise the efficient use of resources throughout the organization. This chapter focuses on two aspects of the management of portfolios:

- the selection and prioritization of projects, based on contribution to organizational benefits and achievability
- the allocation and prioritizing of resources between those projects that have been chosen so that they can deliver the expected benefits

The chapter identifies four key activities to accomplish this:

1. Analysing the portfolio of existing and potential projects
2. Selecting the projects to be implemented as part of this portfolio
3. Allocating resources to those projects that have been selected
4. Collecting and storing project data for performance measurement and portfolio reorientation

WHAT IS PROJECT PORTFOLIO MANAGEMENT?

The concept of portfolio is used in many domains; finance, strategy and marketing, education and politics. To be able to understand the project portfolio management concept, it is essential to understand these different approaches, especially finance and strategy.

In *finance*, a portfolio is a collection of investments held by an institution or a private individual. Portfolio theories generally promote a risk-limiting strategy through diversification of investments. By owning varied assets, individuals or organizations aim to reduce the concentration of certain types of risk. The main objective of portfolio management is to maintain and increase monetary value of the overall portfolio of assets. Portfolio management is the process by which potential assets are analysed and included in the portfolio with regard to the objectives and risk strategy of the portfolio owner. Asset selection involves a comparison of performance estimates, typically expected return, and a measure of the risk associated with this return for different combinations of assets.

In *strategic management and marketing*, a portfolio is a collection of products, services, or brands that are offered by a company. In building up a product portfolio a company can use various analytical techniques including a combined market share/market growth rate developed by the Boston Consulting Group (BCG Analysis) (Johnson & Scholes 2003), contribution margin analysis, which measures the effect of a change in the portfolio on its other elements in financial or resourcing terms, and Quality Function Deployment (QFD), which analyses customer, organizational and technology-development needs. Typically portfolio optimization is based on the use of analytical-rational tools where good portfolio balance is achieved by combining maximum profit with minimal risk.

Authors in the fields of marketing and strategic management have identified several issues with currently used portfolio models and techniques (Nagar & Rajan 2005):

1. Often the *selection criteria used are generic*: capabilities that should always be present and are usually linked to the business or organization but do not guarantee that the strategy will be successful, just more likely to be successful. These generic factors do not adequately assess competitive advantage in specific situations.
2. Rational *decision models are usually static and linear* and are not appropriate to assess turbulent environments and rapid change. The data they use are often based on the analysis of slowly evolving markets and environments, but cannot easily predict radical change.
3. Because these models are typically cross-sectional, they consider a stable situation, which *does not take into account the influence emergent strategies* can have on existing market characteristics.
4. These, usually financial, *simplified models limit the range of factors* that need to be taken into account to evaluate success and may miss important influences.
5. Portfolio models are generally market-driven and *deny goal-directed or mission-driven strategies*. Organizations must first define their objectives and only then develop strategies. Markets are analysed independently of the mission of the organization.

Project portfolio management as currently practiced is a derivate of financial and strategic portfolio management, and so the same issues are also true of project portfolio management.

As the need to prioritize resources across the organization becomes more and more urgent, project portfolio management has essentially become a selection process to choose which projects the organization should undertake and to allocate limited resources to those projects that thereby constitute the organization's investment portfolio. In order to achieve this, managers tend to use simple tools such as NPV (net present value), IRR (internal rate of return), ROI (return on investment), or other pre-set financial measures, and then make decisions based upon intuitively perceived outcome and political clout. To create sustainable results it is necessary to link the expenditure of resources to specific corporate strategy criteria, not solely generic project selection criteria, applicable to most projects.

Many writers in strategic management have also identified the lack of horizontal interrelationships as a key problem in portfolio decision-making, as little attention is given to business unit interdependencies. Unfortunately, the same can be said of project portfolio management, which often relies on computer tools that collect and collate financial and quantitative performance data from individual projects without taking into account organizational interdependencies.

Portfolio management is a management approach for project-based organizations; its objective is to guarantee efficient use of resources in support of the corporate strategy. As such, its role is to prioritize resources across potential and existing programmes and projects in a consistent and stable way. A consistent prioritization model based on the satisfaction of corporate needs and the wise use of resources must be developed for each organization. It should take into account more than financial feasibility and consider a system's perspective of organizational effectiveness and competitive advantage, as well as programme and project achievability. Additionally the process has to be implemented in a way that enables ongoing assessment and realignment of resources and projects; a flexible, dynamic decision model.

Recently a few strategic authors have argued that organizations focus too much on facilitating the optimal utilization of existing productive resources and sharing of residual wealth, but do not take into account processes by which resources are increased or transformed. Value creation is an essential element of good project portfolio management, privileging not only programmes and projects that limit risks, but also those that maximize opportunities. Good portfolio management is meant to deal with fairly stable environments, so, in anything but a stable environment, can only be effective if combined with programme management (Chapter 4), which is designed to deal with more turbulent environments and emergent strategies.

In summary, taking into account most current definitions, Project Portfolio Management could be defined as:

The process of analysing and allocating organizational resources to programmes and projects across the organization on an ongoing basis to achieve corporate objectives and maximize value for the stakeholders.

PROGRAMME AND PORTFOLIO: KEY DIFFERENCES

Figure 3.1 shows the major difference between programmes and portfolios. One of the key differences between programmes and portfolios concerns the approach to change and the control and evaluation process. Whereas portfolios rely on a relatively stable long-term corporate strategy, with clear preset performance indicators, programmes are linked to dynamic business strategies that are highly responsive to their immediate environment. Business strategies, by nature, are rather emergent, whereas corporate strategies are mostly deliberate. Because of the higher level of abstraction of corporate strategies, this is not necessarily a paradox; typically, corporate strategies should ensure the stability of the organizational purpose, whereas business strategies enable it to adapt to its changing environment. At portfolio level, because of the degree of abstraction, parameters can be set that consider the environment as stable; at programme level the approach is largely responsive and at project level, because of the bounded scope and set parameters, the environment is stabilised. In the case of programme management, change is seen as inevitable, if not necessary; in the case of portfolio management, change is generally perceived as incremental, therefore relatively negligible. Only in the case of major change deficit would it radically modify corporate goals. The change deficit represents the difference between the rate of change of an organization and its environment (competitors, market, and so on).

In terms of control, researchers have distinguished 'summative' evaluation from 'formative' evaluation; the former consists of a retrospective assessment against a preset standard; the latter consists of a prospective improvement process against objectives. Corporate strategy, and therefore portfolio management, is most often based on preset performance indicators that reflect long-term corporate goals, assuming a relatively stable context. Business strategy and programme management, on the other hand, are largely responsive, taking into account emergence and complexity. In these fluid situations, each stakeholder will construct different evaluation criteria, and evaluation measures will therefore need to be negotiated; parameters and boundaries are determined through an interactive negotiated process.

MANAGING TACTICAL BENEFITS AND EFFICIENCY

Management of a project portfolio usually includes four major activities:

Area	Programmes	Portfolios
Scope	Broad scope with flexible boundaries to meet medium-term expected business benefits	Organizational scope adapted to corporate goals
Change	Change is first seen as an opportunity	Monitor environmental changes that affect the corporate strategy
Success maximum	Measured in financial terms, value creation and benefits delivery	Measured in terms of overall portfolio performance: results, minimal resources
Leadership	Facilitating style, management of powerful stakeholders, conflict resolution. Intuitive decision-making	Administrative style focused on adding value from allocation of resources. Rational decision-making
Role	Pacing and interfacing of projects; business benefits delivery	Resource management; deliver value to corporate stakeholders
Responsibility	Strategic decision implementation, develop opportunistic emergent strategies	Align portfolio with corporate strategy, adjust portfolio to changes in organizational environment
Main Tasks	Coordinate project resources and key deliverables; market programmes and build business case on a regular basis; develop and maintain project managers' team spirit and contribution to programme	Allocate resources to portfolio components; reassess portfolio on an ongoing basis; collect and use program and project data to make decisions
Control	Appraise project deliverables and resource usage prospectively against expected benefits; report to business stakeholders	Measure aggregate value of portfolio retrospectively against preset corporate performance indicators; report to corporate stakeholders

Figure 3.1   A comparison of programmes and portfolios

1. *analysing* the portfolio of existing and potential projects
2. *deciding* on which projects to include in the portfolio to implement
3. *allocating resources* to those projects that have been selected

4. *collecting and storing project data* for performance measurement and future assessment

ANALYSIS

Portfolio analysis is the first step of the selection process, in an organizational context. Analysis is ongoing as projects are reviewed and analysed on a continuous basis and information is collected to inform decision-makers on the realignment of the portfolio.

Typically organizations evaluate projects on cost or schedule data; less often on quality or scope criteria. This type of evaluation is valid, but gives only a partial view of the project performance. Projects are usually undertaken to create value for the business; therefore organizations need to spend the necessary time and resources at strategic level to set meaningful critical success factors (CSF) and key performance indicators (KPI) which will be used to assess the portfolio on a regular basis. CSFs should be based on expected organizational performance. There are basically two types of CSFs:

1. **Generic CSFs:** capabilities that should always be present and are usually linked to the business or organization, such as effective communication, top management support or user involvement. They are generally imposed from above and can be used as a framework for portfolio management; if absent they may jeopardize the success of the portfolio, but their presence does not necessarily guarantee success.
2. **Specific CSFs:** actions required to achieve a specific strategy in its determined context or circumstances, such as build hospital, improve IT system performance or develop new financial product. These are in direct correlation to the portfolio's success. Specific CSFs are related to stakeholders' needs and expectations, and should be expressed in measurable terms.

While generic CSFs are often too general to provide meaningful project guidance, they should be used as a framework for the portfolio. On the other hand, specific CSFs are at the core of stakeholder's satisfaction and are the ones portfolio managers should focus on when analysing programmes and projects within the portfolio. Many organizational performance models have been described in the management literature. Some of the currently most popular include: the *Business Excellence Model*; *Balanced Scorecard*; and *Six Sigma*.

Business Excellence Model

Also called the EFQM Model (http://www.efqm.org/), this was developed by the European Foundation for Quality Management in 1992. In recent years, many organizations in Europe and elsewhere have adopted it as their organizational effectiveness template. It is based on the principle that organizations are composed of 'enablers'; things you need to improve, and 'results'; the things you need to measure. Its basic assumption is that there is a cause-effect relationship between enablers and results. Excellence is divided into nine criteria, Figure 3.2.

Enablers	Results
1. Leadership	6. Customer Results
2. Policy and Strategy	7. People Results
3. People	8. Society Results
4. Partnerships and Resources	9. Key Performance Results
5. Processes	

Figure 3.2 Excellence criteria in the EFQM Business Excellence Model

Balanced Scorecard

This was developed by Kaplan and Norton as a measurement tool in the early 1990s (http://www.12manage.com/methods_balancedscorecard.html). In 2000, they modified its approach to be used as a strategy formulation method. As for the Business Excellence Model and Six Sigma, it considers a wide range of organizational criteria. The concept of strategy maps, derived from the balanced scorecard, has recently gained a strong following in major organizations. The balanced scorecard and strategy maps are based on four main perspectives of the business, and suggest we develop metrics, collect data and analyze it relative to each of these perspectives:

- The *Learning and Growth Perspective* or Organizational Development Perspective, which focuses on the creation of capabilities in employees and systems
- The *Business Process Perspective* or Internal Business Perspective, which focuses on the enhancement of internal processes
- The *Customer Perspective* or Stakeholder Perspective, which focuses on stakeholder and customer satisfaction
- The *Financial Perspective*, which focuses on economic factors of success

Six Sigma

The fundamental objective of the *Six Sigma* methodology is the implementation of a measurement-based strategy that focuses on process improvement and variation reduction (http://www.12manage.com/methods_six_sigma.html). Six Sigma focuses on three elements: the customer, the process and the employee. Six Sigma revolves around a few key concepts:

- *Quality:* Attributes most important to the customer
- *Defect:* Failing to deliver what the customer wants
- *Capability:* What your process can deliver
- *Variation:* What the customer sees and feels
- *Stability:* Ensuring consistent, predictable processes to improve what the customer sees and feels
- *Design:* Designing to meet customer needs and process capability

The *MESA* methodology described below, in the section Portfolio Selection Matrix, is the method preferred by the author; in addition to considering a wide ranging view of organizational performance, it is based on a value concept. Whereas the models described above usually cover only the formulation aspect of the strategy, the method promoted further embraces the concept of *strategy formation*, which includes the formulation of a deliberate strategy and its reformulation with regards to realized strategy or achievability factors.

It requires the establishment of stakeholder-based needs and expectations, which are translated into very specific expected benefits; and then takes into account aspects of supply and demand which are essential to successful implementation. All these methods focus on the establishment of CSFs and KPIs representative of the organization's values and mission. Whatever the method used, these CSFs or KPIs should be clearly linked to the organization's corporate strategy, its goals and objectives.

DECISION AND IMPLEMENTATION

Only the key organizational stakeholders can decide what benefits the organization should expect from its programmes and projects. It is therefore useful to establish a portfolio steering committee or council composed of the key stakeholders to make decisions and approve project selection. When deciding which projects to undertake, an organization can choose to treat all projects at the same level and only use a scoring matrix to select projects. Alternatively, projects can be divided into categories, and the organization can decide in advance to allocate a determined percentage of their annual resources to each type of project and the selection process would then occur within each category. For instance, in product development categories might be:

- *derivative projects*: extension of existing or past projects
- *platform projects*: new developments in known markets
- *breakthrough projects*: breaking new ground or penetrating new markets
- *research and development*: visionary innovative new undertakings

The best use of scoring matrices is to create a list of prioritized programmes and projects, based on their contribution to the corporate strategic goals. The right mix and pace of endeavours will be selected from this list, according to available resources and synergy between programmes and projects. This list enables decision-makers to decide on a portfolio to fund immediately and programmes or projects that will be held in reserve if resources become available or if circumstances change. Once this portfolio is publicised, senior management will commit themselves to funding the portfolio and to its expected results. The portfolio mangers will allocate funds, resources and skills to the programmes and projects as they are needed. During implementation, it is important to plan for regular programme appraisals and project reviews that will enable the portfolio manager to reallocate resources if needed.

RESOURCE ALLOCATION

One objective of portfolio management is the sharing and allocation of resources (human, financial, physical and others) to programmes and projects across the organization. Following analysis of the current portfolio and available resources, the portfolio management team examines the programme and project proposals and their resource requirements. If the resources required are lower or equal to the resources available, a number of new programmes can go ahead, up to the available resources. If there are fewer resources available than required (see Figure 3.5), then choices must be made using the programme and project prioritization (see Portfolio Selection Matrix Section) which will help decide which programmes or projects to disengage from and which should be accelerated. Resource allocation is divided into two distinct processes: Resource availability assessment and Resource assignment / Procurement.

Resource availability assessment

This requires the comparison of supply and demand. Demand concerns the resources required by all the programmes and projects currently part of the portfolio as well as any proposals that have been approved for implementation: this workload must be prioritized and paced. Supply, on the other hand, concerns the available resources, not only in terms of number, but also in terms of capacity, competence, and capabilities. This concerns human resources, for which it is self evident, as well as financial resources. For example it could concern the capacity to manage a large number of assets, or the competence of its financial advisors, or the capability of the firm to obtain external funding. In any case, the supply must always be greater or equal to the demand. On the other hand if there is a great surplus of available resources over the resources required, then it is not an optimal use of resources and the organization should review its selection processes to enable more programmes and projects to be ready to implement.

Resource assignment and Procurement

This consists, with the input of programme managers and managers of significant projects, of defining the key resources required and available for each action (programme or project). The key here is to make sure the best people are assigned to the most significant programmes and projects, and that, where there are gaps, they are identified and the organization procures the necessary skills and competences externally if not available internally. Finally, this process is iterative and should be continually updated and programmes and projects reprioritized if necessary.

Balancing the supply and demand of programme and project team members is a constant challenge. To address this issue, more and more organizations are seeking an enterprise level system to manage programme and project resources. Any solution considered should be able to answer the following questions:

- What percentage of resources is currently invested in high priority initiatives?
- What resources can the organization free to undertake new projects?
- Considering resource constraints, what mix of projects is best?
- Where are the specific skills located within the organization?
- Can we have at any point in time a good image of the portfolio?
- What is the impact of current programmes and projects on any new programme or project?

Resource allocation cannot be effective without first having a sound selection and prioritization process, which will allow the right choices to be made.

PROGRAMME AND PROJECT DATA COLLECTION

Again here, as for analysis, organizations usually collect basic quantitative data from projects; financial and schedule data are often the only elements collected. Since the popularisation of earned value, the collection of earned value data has also become more common. Sadly, the validity of the data is often not questioned and the data collected are not used in the right way. Remembering that programmes and projects are undertaken to create value to the portfolio, the data collected should be linked to the creation of value and as such, should be both qualitative and quantitative.

Managers often make the mistake of thinking that only quantitative data are measurable; in fact both quantitative and qualitative data can be measured numerically. Quantitative data can be added up, whereas qualitative measures could be described as a function, which is independent from a sum. For example 'customer satisfaction' is a qualitative measure, which can be measured, using the number of complaints, the number of references, the number of repeat contracts, etc. On the other hand 'annual revenue', 'number of customers' or 'numbers of contracts' are quantitative measures, which give us a different kind of information on the organization.

There are a **few rules** that need to be applied to the collection of portfolio data:

- Data should correspond to measures that are meaningful to the strategic intention and expectations
- Measures should be based on needs analysis, taking into account strategic justification
- Organizations must recognize the difficulty of identifying cause-effect relationships in complex situations and acknowledge the validity of qualitative measures
- Management support and resources should be secured to allow effective evaluation of results
- For the overall portfolio, results should be set and measured at organizational level
- For programmes, results should be set and measured at benefits level
- For projects, results should be set and measured at deliverable level
- Measures of interfacing activities should also be identified and collected

Setting data to be collected is in fact linked to the definition of KPI. Each KPI should be linked to a CSF and should provide data that can be used to improve performance and effectiveness. KPIs should be:

- *Measurable*: In either quantitative or qualitative terms
- *Feasible*: In terms of finances, equipment, skills and time
- *Relevant and accurate*: Reflect what is to be measured in an accurate way
- *Sensitive*: Capable of identifying changes over time
- *Timely*: Inform in time for effective decision-making

There are three steps in setting effective KPI measures:

1. The first step is to identify one or more criteria of measure
2. The second step is to decide what is an acceptable level of performance
3. The third step is to define a level of flexibility (minimum/maximum acceptable level)

For example, if we take the critical success factor: *'Involve customers in decisions'*, the measures could be as shown in Figure 3.3.

When identifying data to be collected, the portfolio management team must also clarify the means by which this should be done and make sure that data collection is achievable, both in terms of resources and in terms of capabilities (expertise and technology). The data register shown in Figure 3.4 identifies the CSFs and KPIs, the measures and measuring method. It also allows tracking of collected data to be used for ongoing control and realignment.

KPI	No. of decisions	Customer buy-in	Customer participation
Criterion	Decisions made with customer present	Proposals endorsed by customer	Proposals initiated by customer
Level	80%	50%	20%
Flexibility	- 10%	- 5%	- 2%

Figure 3.3 Examples of key performancce indicator measures

PRIORITIZING PROJECTS AND PROGRAMMES: CORPORATE STRATEGY AND RESOURCES

The prioritization of programmes and projects could be separated into two elements: their contribution to the organization's expected benefits; and the resources they require to achieve these benefits. This benefits/resources ratio is defined as 'value'. Corporate strategies define the organization's expected benefits, and are at the core of an organization's vision; they are medium or long-term forecasts of the organization's future position. As such they should be fairly stable and not influenced much by context changes, unless these are of great magnitude. However, because of this, they are also fairly abstract, high-level and not very agile and need to be combined with clear, responsive business strategies. Their implementation is usually a top-down process and is concerned with the high level direction of the corporation. Corporate strategies typically identify corporate goals which are mostly expressed qualitatively; business strategies, on the other hand, translate the corporate goals into more quantifiable business benefits that are the basis for programmes and projects. Typically, large organizations engage in both corporate and business level strategy, where business strategies are formulated at business unit level and coordinated at corporate level; small organizations, on the other hand, usually have business

CSFs	Criterion (KPI)	Level	Flexibility	Measuring Method	Actual Results	Difference in %
Choose best suppliers	Competence	Selection criteria 70%	-5%	Weighted matrix	Pending	
	Price	≥ Estimate	+5%	Tender	Pending	
	Past Perform.	2 successful past project	1	Historical data	List of 5	-
Communicate regularly	Agreed report. syst.	100% conformance	-10%	# reports / # events	18/20	-10%
	Frequency	weekly	3/ month	# reports / # weeks	12/14	-14%
	Significance	5% CPI, 10% SPI deviation	none	Comparison EV/Report	100%	-
Involve customers in decisions	No. of decisions	80% decis. w/ customer	-10%	Record	85%	+5%
	Customer Buy-in	50% prop. endorsed	-5%	Record	40%	-10%
	Customer participation	20% prop./ customers	-2%	Record	22%	+2%

Figure 3.4   **Example of data register**

level strategies as they are more affected by the environment. Whereas business strategies typically relate to changing an unsatisfactory situation, corporate strategies are concerned with continuity, which could also mean the progression of a change process. One of the key measures of success of strategies is the match between strategic intent and results. The whole process of portfolio management is based on the capacity to clearly link means and ends, so that the projects chosen will achieve the expected strategic outcomes.

Value is often associated with economic factors; the author recommends a wider view of value, based on the concepts developed in the field of value management (BSI 2000; Thiry 1997). Figure 3.5 illustrates these concepts. The concept of value is based on the assumption that the better stakeholders' needs (strategic intent) are satisfied (results), and the less resources are used to achieve this satisfaction, the higher the value. Figure 3.5 takes this concept a step further by introducing the notion of realized value. Whereas typically, value is measured as the difference between expected benefits and the resources required to achieve them, a planned value, value will be realized only if the resources available are equal to or greater than the required resources and if the benefits offered are greater than or equal to the expected benefits. In business, the expected benefits are translated in agreed critical success factors and the offered benefits in the options offered to the stakeholders; the ratio between available resources (supply) and required resources (demand) constitutes the achievability factor.

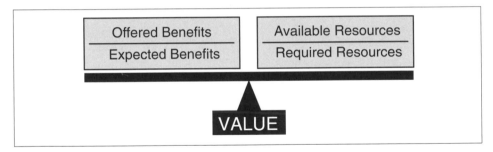

Figure 3.5   Benefits and resources: a value perspective

Programmes and projects that are part of an overall corporate strategy, managed through a portfolio approach, must be given clear sets of **tangible success factors**, linked to the corporate objectives and based on a wide range of criteria, these could include both: *Economical Factors* like: ROI, IRR, NPV, EVA® (economic value added), etc. and *Non-Economical Factors* like: business impact (short & long term expected results); level of opportunity (strategic to operational); customer significance, credibility and user satisfaction. Their **achievability** must be assessed on (Thiry 2003):

- *financial factors:* capital cost, cash flow, life-cycle costs
- *parameters & constraints*: schedule, budget, type of contract
- *human resources:* expertise, spread, external *versus* internal
- *people factors*: availability, customer perception

- *complexity*: innovativeness, clarity of scope, interdependencies, and stakeholders

Large-scale studies have demonstrated that 30 percent of projects are cancelled before the end (Standish 1996; KPMG 1997). These studies and others have sorely exposed the failure of organizations to use the right selection criteria for programmes and projects, as well as the lack of integration between expected strategic outcomes and the outputs generated by projects. It is a blatant case of the mismatch between means and ends. Interestingly, though, managers are usually judged, and rewarded or punished, on short-term results, while a project's actual benefits can only be measured effectively in the medium or long term. Cooke-Davies (2002) has clearly linked project benefits to operations and stated that the successful delivery of project outputs cannot be sufficient to measure success. Benefits are a key element of programme and project success and therefore of their significance and priority; benefits delivery goes beyond simple financial and generic measures.

SELECTION MODELS

There are basically two types of selection models: numeric and non-numeric. Most organizations surveyed by researchers use more than one model to select programmes and projects, especially in areas of higher uncertainty like new product development and research.

Non-numeric models

For research and new product development, where the relationship between means and ends cannot accurately be estimated, non-numeric techniques like *market studies* can be used. These would include prototyping and preference mapping. Project choice will be based on functional rather than technical outputs. *Comparative approaches* like advantages-disadvantages, comparative benefit models, Q-Sort and others classify projects according to relative merit. They consider a wide range of qualitative, quantitative and judgement criteria and are basically used on a limited set of projects as a comparison technique. These models, although intuitive, should not be dismissed as they are goal-oriented and reflect the organization's preoccupations. One issue though is that they can be used only once to compare a limited set of projects and have to be redeveloped each time, therefore limiting the comparability of projects in the long-term.

Numeric models

Most numeric models are *financial* and are based on profitability; for example, Internal Rate of Return (IIR), Return on Investment (ROI), Net Present Value

(NPV) or even Breakeven Point or Payback Period (see Turner 1995). The models are usually fairly simple and most managers understand how they work, although many do not really understand their limitations. Because the use of *economical factors* depends so much on accuracy of estimates, they can be used effectively only in circumstances or industries where reasonable accuracy can be expected and therefore historical data is expected to reasonably match future undertakings, like in construction for example. But even in fairly stable environments, concentrating solely on short-term financial evaluation techniques by focusing only on the projects' returns will marginalize some of the real measures of benefits. Many of these models are biased towards one type of project and the use of one or the other model could lead to different portfolio solutions. All the financial models depend on an estimation of cash flows, but it is not clear, in the context of project evaluation, how cash flow can be defined and linked to the project. The most popular models are usually the simplest, but they lack all the depth required to select a portfolio and, because different models yield different results, they basically end up being a justification for an intuitive or political decision.

Project management authors generally agree that *scoring models* are probably the most effective in that they combine advantages of both the non-numerical models by focusing on what is important and the quantitative objectivity expected from financial models. Although certain firms still use non-weighted criteria, it is generally accepted that weighted criteria are the most effective. Two rules should guide the use of these models: the number of criteria used should be reasonable – usually 5 to 8, 12 being a maximum – and each criterion should be clearly differentiated from the others. Another advantage of these models is that they can be used to verify project proposal improvement by scoring a project in a first round and rescoring it again after a value and risk management process.

PORTFOLIO SELECTION MATRIX

The author has developed and used a scoring model called MESA© (Model for Evaluation of Strategic Alternatives) (Thiry 2003) based on a ratio between the satisfaction of needs (benefits) and use of resources (investment), which is the definition of value found in Value Management Standards. The technique used is based on the classification principle used in risk management for prioritizing risks. Whereas risks are assessed against their probability of occurrence and their impact on project objectives, potential programmes and projects will be assessed on their contribution to stated benefits, or impact on the organization, and their achievability – the equivalent of probability of occurrence.

A portfolio selection matrix needs to classify programmes and projects, based on their ability to deliver benefits to stakeholders and the effort required to achieve those benefits; a **value ratio**. In value management, needs are usually expressed as expected benefits; once they are agreed between all the key stakeholders, they become the Critical Success Factors (CSF), which are a qualitative representation of needs and expectations. Resources required to achieve the expected benefits should be assessed, not in absolute terms, but in terms of their availability; a demand/supply ratio. In addition to strict resource availability, achievability takes into account a number of other factors that are detailed below; they include: financial factors, parameters/constraints, human resources and people factors, and complexity.

Contribution to Benefits

Establishing the CSFs is a key element of the portfolio selection process as they measure the contribution to the overall benefits. A few points are important in establishing CSFs:

- The CSFs have to be **organization-specific** and reflect the needs (expected benefits) of the key stakeholders;
- They must be derived from the needs **established by the stakeholders**;
- They must cover the **whole range of needs**, not be focused on only a few (weighting will prioritize them);
- They should **not be too numerous** but be detailed enough to enable establishment of measures.

These CSFs are the basis for the evaluation of the contribution of options to the overall benefits. Their weighting translates the key stakeholders' perception of their relative importance. The technique uses the following five steps:

1. **Stakeholder analysis:**
   Task: Identification and classification of stakeholders
   Output: List of stakeholders classified by influence (impact on programme) categories
2. **Function analysis:**
   Task: Identification of stakeholders' needs and expectations; classification by importance; agreement on CSFs and weighting of these (combined weight of all CSFs must be 100)
   Output: Benefits breakdown structure and list of weighted CSFs
3. **Options Scoring (First cut):**
   Task: score each option on a scale of 1 to 10 against each weighted CSF
   Output: List of scored options (maximum points 1000)
4. **Options Improvement:**
   Task: Perform Value Management (VM) and Risk Management (RM) on selected options
   Output: List of recommended options

5. Options Scoring (Final cut)

Task: Score recommended options against weighted CSFs
Output: Final list of options prioritized

Once the needs have been identified and classified and the CSFs agreed and weighted, a first scoring is performed to enable the team to eliminate a number of options that are not in line with the portfolio's objectives (see Figure 3.6). Following this scoring, the team performs risk and value management on all the remaining options and includes the improvements/risk responses to the revised options, which will then be reassessed against the weighted CSFs. This provides a final list of prioritized options that will be assessed for achievability.

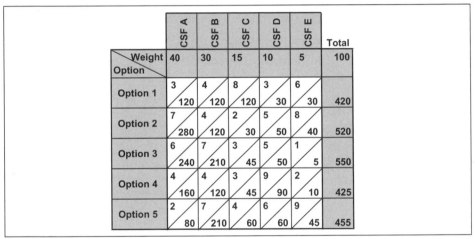

Option	CSF A	CSF B	CSF C	CSF D	CSF E	Total
Weight	40	30	15	10	5	100
Option 1	3 / 120	4 / 120	8 / 120	3 / 30	6 / 30	420
Option 2	7 / 280	4 / 120	2 / 30	5 / 50	8 / 40	520
Option 3	6 / 240	7 / 210	3 / 45	5 / 50	1 / 5	550
Option 4	4 / 160	4 / 120	3 / 45	9 / 90	2 / 10	425
Option 5	2 / 80	7 / 210	4 / 60	6 / 60	9 / 45	455

Figure 3.6   Weighted scoring matrix – contribution to benefits

Achievability Assessment

Again, based on value management concepts, achievability is defined as an organization's capability to undertake a set of programmes and projects, taking into account current or future workload. This concept is closely linked to the supply/demand ratio, and therefore in line with current developments in project and general management. Based on research and practice, the author presents a series of possible factors for measuring achievability; one must be careful though not to take them for granted and become too dependent on any classification system for fear of losing flexibility and understanding of its elements, as any classification system must be meaningful for its users.

Demand and supply are the key elements of achievability; the resources available must be equal to or higher than the resources required, for a set of projects to be achieved successfully (see Figure 3.7). If supply is greater than or equal to demand, achievability can vary from very high to medium; if supply is less

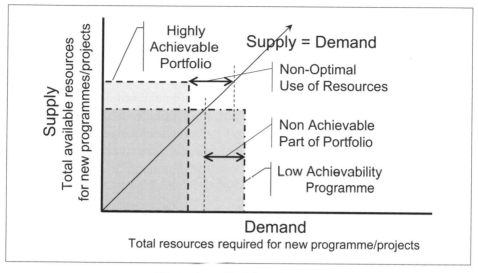

Figure 3.7 **Portfolio achievability**

than demand, achievability varies from low to very low. The factors used and their description must be relevant to each organization: such as total budget (supply) versus estimated cost of project (demand), expertise of organization (supply) versus innovativeness of project (demand), and so on.

Based on project and organizational effectiveness research, the matrix uses 4 major areas:

1. **Financial Factors**: the traditional measure of feasibility
2. **Parameters and Constraints**: the criteria related to pace, uncertainty and size.
3. **Human Resources and People Factors**: all the factors related to communication, competence and familiarity.
4. **Complexity**: the difficulty of *'doing the right thing'* and delivering actual benefits, also related to familiarity

These factors are detailed for each organization, prior to evaluation and used in a grid. Measurable descriptors are defined to indicate levels of achievability and are set as a *non-linear cardinal scale*. They are all described further below:

Financial Factors: These factors are all related to the difficulty of achieving projects with regard to the overall availability of funds. They include: total estimated capital cost; impact on company cash flow; source of funding; delay in expected return/benefits and life-cycle-cost, if the organization is committed to the operation of the deliverable.

Parameters and Constraints: This set of factors includes all the criteria imposed by the client, the organization's structure or the project itself; they are: number of members in team; level of familiarity with contract type; geographical spread of work; and as acceptability of schedule and budget.

Human Resources and People Factors: The quality of human resources is crucial to the achievability of a project within a programme; the factors listed here have all to do with the capability of resources to deliver the product. They are: spread of resources; familiarity with resources; other critical work being undertaken by the organization at the same time; customer perception of resources allocated; and staff expertise.

Complexity: The last point concerns the degree of difficulty of achieving the project, based on its complexity. Complexity factors include: familiarity with type of work/innovativeness; interdependency of deliverables; number of stakeholders; stakeholders spread; clarity of objectives, benefits and CSFs; clarity of scope statement. The technique uses the three steps:

1. **Identification of achievability criteria:**
   Task: Agree list of criteria that define achievability for the organization and descriptors from very low to very high achievability
   Output: Achievability assessment grid (maximum achievability score must be 10)
2. **Weighting of achievability criteria:**
   Task: Agree proportional value of each criterion with regard to the organization's capabilities and structures
   Output: Weighted criteria (total weight must equal 100).
3. **Scoring of options:**
   Task: Identify right descriptor for each option against each criterion and calculate final achievability score (maximum score must be equal to 1000)
   Output: List of scored options.

As shown in Figure 3.8, the achievability criteria are detailed and weighted for each organization, prior to evaluation. Measurable descriptors are defined to indicate levels of achievability and are set in a *non-linear cardinal scale*. The example shows five weighting descriptors and a scale of 0.625–1.25–2.5–5.0–10.0.

Combined Benefits/Achievability Scoring

Once project options have been scored against benefits contribution and achievability the programme manager or portfolio/resource manager will calculate the combined benefits/achievability score in order to be able to decide

Impact Criteria \ Specific Factors	10	5	2.5	1.25	0.625	Weighting*	Score** Project A	Score** Project B	Score** Project C
Financial Factors									
Total estimated capital cost	<5% of all projects	5-10%	10-15%	15-20%	>20% of all projects	7	70	17.5	35
Impact on company cash flow	<5%	5-10%	10-15%	15-20%	>20%	7	70	17.5	8.75
Funding	100% internal availability	25% external	50% external	75% external	100% external	4	40	40	40
Expected Return/Benefits	Short term (<3 months)	3-12 months	Medium term (1-2 yrs)	2-5 years	Long term (>5 years)	5	12.5	3.125	25
Life-Cycle-Cost (optional)						0	0	0	0
Parameters & Constraints									
No. members in team	01-Feb	03-May	6 – 10	Nov 60	>50	4	20	10	2
Type of contracts	Standard contracts	<-->	Some customized	<-->	All customized	3	7.5	3.75	7.5
Spread of work	Single location	2 – 3 sites	+3 sites	Base team + virtual	Fully virtual team	6	30	15	15
Schedule	Acceptable timeframe	<-->	Tight timeframe	<-->	Inadequate timeframe	5	25	12.5	50
Budget	Acceptable budget	<-->	Tight budget	<-->	Inadequate budget	3	30	7.5	7.5
Human Resources / People Factors									
Spread of resources	Team (same division)	Internal (2 areas)	Team + outsourced	All outsourced	Internal + outsourced	5	25	12.5	12.5
Familiarity with resources	All known	<-->	Some new	<-->	All unknown	3	15	3.75	15
Other critical work	None	little	Few but significant	Major	Major and significant	6	30	60	15
Customer perception	Above expectations	<-->	As expected	<-->	Below expectations	2	5	20	1.25
Staff expertise	Good skills/ experience	<-->	Half with neces expert	<-->	Expert staff not avail.	7	70	7.25	35
Complexity									
Type of work / Innovativeness	Known technique	variation from known	Some new developmt	Sig. new development	Breakthrough	7	17.5	8.75	8.75
Interdependency of deliverables	negligible	minor	significant	major	essential	6	30	3.75	7.5
No. of stakeholders	one or two	Few at project level	Multiple at project lvl	Multiple prjt / prog	Multiple internal & ext	5	25	3.125	3.125
Stakeholders spread	Similar business area	<-->	Multiple bus areas	<-->	Large spread ax enviro	6	30	3.75	3.75
Objectives, benefits & CSF's	Very clear	Unclear	unspecified	undefined	Unknown	6	15	7.5	30
Scope statement	Very well defined	Minor clarify. req.	Some elmts undefind	Major elmts undefined	undefined	3	7.5	1.5	15

* Considering programme / business level

** Impact x Weighting

Total Score 100 | **575** | **273.25** | **337.62**

Figure 3.8   Example of Achievability Assessment Matrix

which options to implement, or create a priority list for the allocation of financial and human resources. The matrix (Figure 3.9) is designed much in the same way as an inverted risk assessment matrix. Because contribution to benefits is considered more important than the achievability (e.g. an option having a high contribution to benefits and a medium achievability will be favoured over a highly achievable option with medium contribution to benefits), the scoring factors of benefits grow exponentially whereas the scoring factors of achievability grow linearly.

All options that get a combined score over 0.15 are implemented if the budget allows; all options that get a score between 0.05 and 0.15 are implemented if they are synergetic to a high priority option or if they have a high marketing value; otherwise they are re-examined to see if they can be further improved to make the

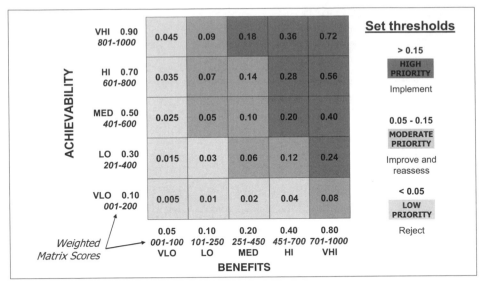

Figure 3.9 Combined Benefits and Achievability Matrix

upper tier of the programme. All options that score below 0.05 are rejected because they either do not contribute to benefits enough or are too difficult to implement.

SUMMARY

MESA© is a *decision-making model* that provides guidance for prioritization or reprioritization of projects that are part of a programme or portfolio. It is based on both the project's contribution to the programme's success and its achievability within the current workload and available resources. If the methodology described in this chapter is thoroughly followed, it generates consistent decision-making, based on stakeholder needs and expectations, and on the organizations' capabilities. When finalizing the selection process, decision-makers should always take a wide view of organizational issues that includes the whole programme, interdependencies between actions, interface with other programmes and the organizational context, including competitiveness specifically, factors like; project synergy, marketing value, acceptability, etc.

The MESA© tool reflects the strategic objectives of each organization *at the time of the decision*. Critical success factors must be directly linked to expected **benefits** that reflect the stakeholders' needs and expectations for that programme/portfolio/strategy. The author has defined a series of possible factors for measuring **achievability**; each programme/organization must define its own achievability factors, based on the understanding of its own context. The MESA©

has to be *'meaningful'* to its stakeholders. It is also crucial to involve senior management in the process; this will reduce the probability of high-level decisions overturning investment recommendations. If the process is shared and agreed with the key stakeholders beforehand, the MESA© offers a sound, objective and robust framework that prevents undue political or power-based influence and stabilizes the programme or portfolio prioritization and change process.

CONCLUSION

Although in most portfolios, projects and programmes can be independent from each other, they should all contribute to the organization's corporate objectives. Therefore the critical success factors used to assess and prioritize them must correspond to specific corporate needs of the organization. Corporate strategies are relatively stable and provide a long-term vision to the organization; the mission and goals of the organization should drive the portfolio approach and its analysis. An organization should not fear to weed out programmes or projects that do not fit within its corporate perspective and it must provide portfolio managers with a set of stable criteria with which to assess strategic decisions. At the same time, decision models have to be dynamic and flexible enough to provide for continuous realignment of the portfolio with regard to changes in the environment. Many organizations do not reassess portfolio decisions on an ongoing basis and this often leads to white elephants or poor investments. Portfolio analysis must be open to emergent inputs and provide for the possibility of regular realignment, and analysis should not be solely based on financial factors, but take into account a range of organizational factors linked to the organization's effectiveness in its environment.

REFERENCES AND FURTHER READING

BSI, 2000, *PD 6663: Guidelines to BS EN 12973: Value Management – Practical guidance to its use and intent,* Chiswick: British Standards Institution.

Cooke-Davies, T., 2002, 'The 'real' success factors on projects', *International Journal of Project Management,* 20(3), 185–190.

Johnson, G. and Scholes, K., 2003, *Exploring Corporate Strategy*, Hemel Hempstead, UK: FT Prentice Hall.

KPMG, 1997, 'What went wrong? Unsuccessful information technology projects', <http://audit.kpmg.ca/vl/surveys/it_wrong.htm>

Meredith, J.R. and Mantel, S.J., 2005, *Project Management A Managerial Approach*, 6th edition, New York, NY: Wiley.

Nagar, V. and Rajan, M.V., 2005, Measuring Customer Relationships: The Case of the Retail Banking Industry. *Management Science.* 51 (6): 904–919.

Reiss, G., Anthony, M., Chapman, J., Leigh, G., Pyne, A., and Rayner, P., 2006, *The Gower Handbook of Programmeme Management,* Aldershot, UK: Gower.

Standish Group International, 1996, *A Standish group research on failure of IT projects,* Yarmouth, MA: The Standish Group.

Thiry, M., 1997, *Value Management Practice,* Sylva NC: Project Management Institute.

Thiry, M., 2003, 'Select and prioritize projects with the MESA© (Matrix for the Evaluation of Strategic Alternatives)', in *Proceedings of the PMI Global Congress North America 2003, Baltimore, September,* Newton Square, PA: Project Management Institute.

Turner, J.R, (ed.), 1995, *The Commercial Project Manager*, London: McGraw-Hill.

4 Managing Programmes of Projects

Michel Thiry

We saw in Chapter 3 that organizations aim to implement business strategies that generate benefits for the business and their customers. However, if projects are managed independently this objective is seldom achieved. Programme management offers the means to manage groups of projects with a common business purpose in an integrated and effective way. In recent years, project-based organizations (PBOs) have received increased consideration as an organizational form, but many organizations that have adopted a project management approach have had to deal with the inconsistency between the flexibility and dynamism of the project approach and the desire of firms' financial and strategic stakeholders to exercise control at corporate level. In this chapter, we show how programme management can help resolve this inconsistency by enabling the implementation and control of business strategies while allowing for the dynamism and flexibility inherent in the project approach.

WHAT IS PROGRAMME MANAGEMENT (PGM)?

In project management practice and the associated literature, programme management (PgM) is defined in many ways. Etymologically, the word programme derives from the Greek *prographein,* meaning: to write before. It has evolved in Latin and French to mean a 'notice or list of a series of events'. One of the definitions of the Merriam Webster Collegiate Dictionary 2000 is: 'a plan or system under which action may be taken toward a goal'. The concept of programme used in the project management community probably originates from a number of sources. Today, typical uses of the word programme are quite varied. A search on the Internet (www.google.co.uk) using the word 'programme' yielded the following:

- UN and Governmental Programmes (United Nations Development Programme and National Toxicology Programme)

- computer programmes (Windows XP and Adobe Acrobat Programmes)
- Space Exploration Programmes (Mars Exploration Programme)
- Non Governmental Non Profit Programmes (Fullbright Programme, International Baccalaureate Programme)
- television programmes (BBC Programme)
- large publicly funded undertakings (Chesapeake Bay Programme, Endangered Species Programme).

This search shows the diversity of the uses of the word by the public, but, except for the computer programme, seems to point towards defining a programme as:

> a larger undertaking consisting of multiple actions of smaller scale.

Some authors also draw a difference between governmental and non-profit organizations and commercial or for-profit organizations:

> Non-profits usually refer to programmes as ongoing, major services to clients, for example, a Transportation Programme, Housing Programme, etc. For-profits often use the term for very large business efforts that have limited duration and a defined set of deliverables. Non-profits and for-profits might refer to programmes as a one-time or ongoing set of activities internal to the organization, for example, a Total Quality Management Programme, Workplace Safety Programme, the Space Programme, etc. (McNamara 1999)

PgM has emerged as a discipline distinct from project management (PjM) as practitioners and managers have started applying PjM concepts at a more strategic level or to the management of multiple interrelated projects to produce strategic benefits. But mainstream project management literature still holds the view that PgM is just an extension of PjM where the same 'principles of project management apply at every level of the hierarchy' (Wideman 2004, p.52). The Project Management Institute (PMI®), in their Organizational Project Management Maturity Model, OPM3®, (PMI® 2003), and their new Programme and Portfolio Management Standard (PMI® 2006a, 2006b), makes an attempt to distinguish PgM and PjM but states that the 'process groups' are the same; it weakly adds that 'The challenge, however, is more complex' (PMI® 2003, p.25). Interestingly, though, it recognizes the programme life-cycle is different and separates it in phases, either four (Programme Definition; Mobilisation; Delivery; Operation and Benefits Realization) or five (Pre-Programme Set Up; Programme Set Up; Establish Programme Management & Technical Infrastructure; Deliver Incremental Benefits; Close the Programme). Although it is difficult to understand the use of a different rhetoric for phases, it clarifies the distinction between project and programme management.

One of the key issues with current programme management mainstream literature is that it maintains a clear boundary between the project and the business domains. For example, in its publication, *Managing Successful*

Programmes, the UK government's Office of Government Commerce (OGC 2003), suggests that responsibility for the realization of benefits will fall to the business managers in the relevant areas. They go on to suggest that the achievement of benefits should be assessed independently from the process of delivery (the programme). The PMI® Draft Programme Management Standard seems to be the only exception as it clearly includes in the role of the programme manager the 'transition of the programme into ongoing operations and benefit sustainment' (PMI® 2006b, section 1.7.1).

In Japan, the *Guidebook for Project and Programme Management for Enterprise Innovation* (P2M) defines third generation project management as a 'philosophy of project management [which] lies in deciphering complex issues, developing or interpreting missions for breakthroughs, and paving roads to optimal solutions through programmes, which in turn consist of organically interrelated projects.' (PMCC 2002, p.7). To them, programme management is the key to 'value creation'.

In summary, taking into account most current definitions, Programme Management could be labelled as:

> The governance and harmonized management of a number of projects and other actions to achieve stated business benefits and create value for the stakeholders.

PROJECTS AND PROGRAMMES: KEY DIFFERENCES

A survey of recent project and programme literature identified four main areas of distinction between projects and programmes, Figure 4.1. Each of these areas constitutes a continuum between projects and programmes. It is the combination of all these areas that differentiates a 'pure' programme from a 'pure' project. In real life the boundary is more blurred and many instances like small dedicated programmes or large complex projects exist on a continuum between the 'pure' forms suggested by Figure 4.1. A fifth area of difference that has been identified in a number of recent research papers is the *organizational aspects* – roles and responsibilities and organizational structures. However, this aspect is outside the scope of this chapter. One can also distinguish projects from programmes in more specific aspects of management, as illustrated in Figure 4.2.

Area of Comparison	Project	Programmes
Multiplicity	Single deliverable	Multiple deliverables
Predictability	Well-defined	Complex
Alignment	Tactical, operational	Strategic
Focus	Product	Market

Figure 4.1   Four main differences between projects and programmes

Area	Project	Programmes
Scope	Set, limited scope with clearly defined deliverables	Broad scope with flexible boundaries to meet medium-term expected business benefits
Change	Change to be avoided; baseline is key	Change is first seen as an opportunity
Success	Measured through respect of cost, time, quality preset parameters: the PM triangle	Measured in financial terms, value creation and benefits delivery
Leadership	Transactional leadership, authority-based directive style, management of subalterns, conflict resolution. Rational decision-making	Transformational leadership, facilitating style, management of powerful stakeholders, conflict resolution. Intuitive decision-making
Role	Task and parameters management; product (project output) delivery	Pacing and interfacing of projects; business benefits (outcome) delivery
Responsibility	Project output delivery to parameters; reporting, performance-based focus	Strategic decision implementation, develop opportunistic emergent strategies
Main Tasks	Negotiate scope, define WBS, minimise adverse risks, manage delivery of the product of the project. Maintain project team stamina and motivation, monitor and control external team	Coordinate project resources and key deliverables; market programme and build business case on a regular basis; develop and maintain project managers' team spirit and contribution to programme
Control	Monitor and control tasks and project parameters retrospectively against the baseline; report to project sponsor	Appraise project deliverables and resource usage prospectively against expected benefits; report to business stakeholders

Figure 4.2   A detailed comparison of projects and programmes

In a recent paper (Thiry 2004a), I also distinguished the knowledge areas of project management as defined by the PMBOK® Guide (PMI® 2004) with those of programme management, Figure 4.3. These are further detailed in the section entitled 'Developing the right approaches and methodologies' below. This distinction was made on the basis that the management of single projects is much more restrictive in scope than that of multiple interdependent projects.

Based on current literature and common practice, the key distinction between projects and programmes could be identified as the extent of their mutual scope. However, as stated in the Japanese P2M: 'in this age of rapid and discontinuous social changes, perceptive approaches to complicated events, speed and uncertain factors have become significant challenges for programme management rather than a scale issue' (PMCC 2002, p.30). It is also the experience of the author, shared by other writers, that 'predictability' is an intrinsic element of the distinction between projects and programmes. Projects have a certain degree of

Project Management	Programme Management
Integration Management	Strategic Decision Management
Scope Management	Stakeholder Value Management
Time Management	Pace Management
Cost Management	Resource Management
Quality Management	Benefits Management
Human Resources Management	Stakeholder Relationship Management
Communications Management	Communication/Marketing Management
Risk Management	Uncertainty Management
Procurement Management	Partnership Management

Figure 4.3 **A comparison of the knowledge areas of projects and programme management**

predictability, which corresponds to stable environments or environments stabilised by limited resources, time and costs, whereas programmes often evolve in turbulent environments because of their business scope, multiple stakeholders and changing circumstances where the interaction of multiple 'agents' breeds ambiguity. Projects have to deal with what has been called the 'known-unknowns', which correspond to uncertainty or risk management, whereas programmes often have to deal with 'unknown-unknowns', which require ambiguity management and uncertainty management.

LINKING BUSINESS STRATEGY WITH PROJECTS THROUGH PROGRAMMES

The first question one must resolve when dealing with portfolios and programmes of projects is: What is the organizational purpose? Classic theories of organizational purpose, and governance, describe a tension between shareholder and stakeholder approaches, with the former being the dominant approach and the latter being the challenging approach, probably closer to Project-Based Organizations. Recently concepts of value creation have emerged, claiming that the two classic theories are only concerned with allocating resources whereas value creation is the real competitiveness issue. Value creation involves the use of intangible assets; what some authors have referred to as: 'human and organizational capital', the non-transferable assets. So the question really is: 'does your organization create programme and portfolio structures to manage existing resources or to innovate and create value?'

Organizations develop corporate strategies as deliberate medium or long-term forecasts of the future. However, they are always subjected to either external or internal pressures that force them to change to adapt or compete. In order to deal with these pressures, organizations respond with business strategies. Business strategy can be seen from two perspectives: an environment-responsive strategy, based on competitive advantage or a capability-based strategy, focused on available resources. The principle of the business strategy that is managers are constantly looking for the best ways to balance strengths and weaknesses of the organization with opportunities and threats in the environment. The business strategy, because of its dynamic nature, is continually updated and charts the course of a firm's activities in individual industries or domains; it is often an adaptive, bottom-up process. There are two ways to develop business strategies:

1. each unit competes with each other for the same resources, which, alas, is the case in most organizations because of a dominant top-down approach to strategy
2. interdependence and integration are created between units, which would be the case in an organization that privileges a more horizontal and collaborative approach

Business units, because they are closest to the action, will best be able to deal with turbulent environments by developing emergent strategies, strategies that evolve in directions that could not be predicted (see Figure 4.4). In organizations that

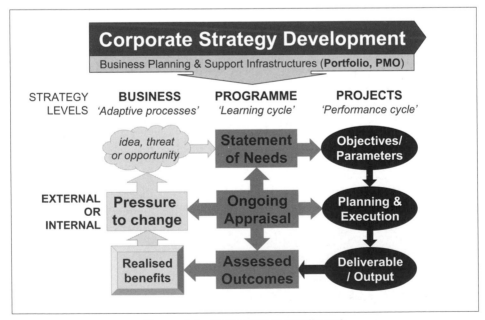

Figure 4.4   The business strategy life-cycle

adopt a project-based management approach, the advantage of an integrated programme/project management approach *versus* a single project management approach can easily be seen.

Sadly, in many organizations, managers are happy to deliver project outputs without assessing the outcomes: results and realized benefits. Projects, within a strategic framework, modify the condition of the firm in its environment because through them, resources and competencies are mobilized to create competitive advantage and other sources of value. If managers consider only planned strategies and do not assess outcomes and realized benefits, they are losing opportunities to use emergent strategies to create value for the organization. When the link between strategy and projects is strong, the project outputs will produce outcomes that will contribute to the expected business benefits and this, in turn, will ease the pressure.

The situation described in Figure 4.4 is ideal though seldom achieved in practice, often due to political or power pressures. Most of the time, strategies are deliberate long term plans that do not take into account emergent situations and cannot adapt quickly to external and internal pressures. Projects, on the other hand, often concentrate on product delivery and project or programme managers are not accountable for the delivery of benefits to the organization.

As shown in Figure 4.4, programmes are at the heart of a business strategy meant to deliver business results. Programme management is a cyclic learning-performance strategy management process. It combines performance (project-based) and learning (value-based) loops, which include decision making and decision implementation. Programme management requires thorough stakeholder analysis and management as well as the coordinated management of interdependent actions (projects and related work outside of the scope of the individual projects) to achieve business benefits. It is based on the setting of clear critical success factors (CSF) shared by the key stakeholders and leading to effective business results that can be measured. Once expected outcomes have been clearly defined, project management becomes a performance process intended to deliver those outcomes with the highest possible efficiency (best scope-quality versus lowest cost-time).

MANAGING BENEFITS DELIVERY AND PROJECT INTERFACES

There are two characteristics that make programme management the most suitable methodology to ensure successful implementation of strategies:

● It is a cyclic learning-performance process, which enables regular assessment of outcomes, ongoing appraisal and evaluation of emergent opportunities, and pacing of the process

● Its emphasis on the 'interdependencies' of projects, which ensures strategic alignment and delivery of outcomes rather than outputs.

To implement business strategies whilst supporting the corporate strategy and to take advantage of the two preceding characteristics, programme management processes must be distinct from those generally recommended for projects. Programmes are more complex and unpredictable than projects and require management of numerous interdependencies between stakeholders, projects and benefits; whereas project deliverables and parameters should be clearly defined from the start; programmes are not constrained by parameters and deliverables – outputs – but rather by the creation of value for the stakeholders –outcomes that can be satisfied through many different outputs – and are therefore more open to realignment and adjustment as the programme develops.

THE PROGRAMME MANAGEMENT LIFE-CYCLE

The programme life-cycle must be iterative, rather than linear; include periods of stability, where benefits can impact the organization and therefore be measured; and have a systems perspective. The programme management life-cycle shown in Figure 4.5 is iterative in nature and reflects the extended and evolving nature of strategic decisions. It is composed of five phases (Thiry 2004b):

1. *Formulation:* where the purpose is defined and stakeholders, along with their needs and expectations, are identified. It is also in this phase that programme benefits are determined and defined through critical success factors (CSFs) and key performance indicators (KPIs). Unlike project initiation, it is a

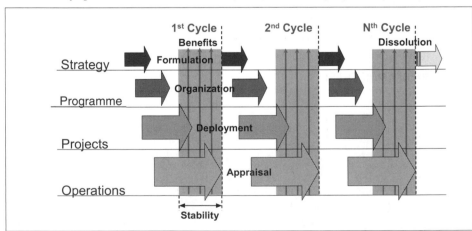

Figure 4.5 The programme management life-cycle

complex process, where ambiguity is high. It is the initial learning cycle of programmes where sensemaking, ideation, and evaluation of alternatives take place and which ends with the decision to undertake the programme. It is iterated regularly during the programme and confirms or redefines the direction of the programme and the actions required to support it. The main objectives of this phase are to understand stakeholders' needs and expectations, identify opportunities, and select the best course of action for the programme.

2. *Organization* is the process of selecting and prioritizing projects and actions required to deliver benefits and setting up the programme team and structures. It includes installation of procedures and structures to enable project interdependencies and interrelationships to be managed, as well as pacing the programme and ensuring ongoing benefits delivery.

3. *Deployment* involves the actual initiation of projects and other actions; management of interdependencies and resources; project sponsor type control, including scope verification and closeout; and benefits delivery. It is made up of review, pacing, and approval of project outputs and change/configuration control, including realignment and reprioritizing of resources and projects.

4. *Appraisal* essentially concerns the programme-level assessment of benefits. It is a process that requires constant re-evaluation of the programme's circumstances and CSFs and typically corresponds to a period of stability, enabling benefits to be measured with regard to their impact on the organization.

5. *Dissolution* happens when the rationale for the programme no longer exists. Uncompleted work, projects, and resources are reallocated to other programmes, which are reformulated as needed; a post-programme feedback is carried out; and knowledge is recycled. It is a phasing-down process, much more extensive than project closing.

THE FORMULATION PHASE

The formulation phase aims to identify internal or external pressures to change and to determine the best way to address them to add value for the stakeholders. In programmes, it is crucial to take a value perspective to formulation, seeking the best balance between the satisfaction of expected benefits and the resource investment required to achieve them.

Formulation starts with the identification of the expected benefits and the assessment of their achievability; this is best achieved through a *sensemaking* process. Sensemaking is the process by which needs and expectations of the stakeholders are identified, translated into expected benefits and prioritized. The

79

key elements of the sensemaking process are to allow the necessary time for all the stakeholders to understand all the issues involved and to agree on a shared definition of expected benefits. These benefits are then prioritized to become the critical success factors (CSF) of the programme. This is a key element in the structuring of the programme organization: expected benefits must be agreed and CSFs identified and prioritized before any action can be initiated.

Once these have been agreed, an *ideation* process – the generation of as many alternatives as possible to help decision-making – should be initiated to creatively seek alternative courses of action. The use of creativity and lateral thinking are crucial in this part of the process. The *elaboration* process, which follows ideation, seeks to develop alternatives or combine them in order to identify the most promising ones; once developed these alternatives are typically called 'options'. In programmes of projects each option is a potential project to be assessed. Often decision-makers will also have to take into account values other than economic, and in this case they will have to make *trade-offs*, which are judgments about how much they are willing to sacrifice on one element of the value equation to receive more of another. To help the decision-making process programme managers can use a number of decision support techniques; the author's experience is that a value-based system is most appropriate as it takes into account both the contribution to benefits and the achievability of each option and enables prioritization and mapping of the options (see Chapter 4 – Portfolio Selection Matrix). At this stage, options must include value improvements and risk responses.

Deciding the best course (or courses) of action is the last step of this phase; a decision will be made, based on the strategic purpose of the programme, its critical success factors and key performance indicators, as well as on its expected benefits. It is also the stage where 'fit' with the strategy is confirmed; priorities are set between different programmes within the organization and 'business cases' are compiled. The decision will seek to secure approval and support for the programme and allocation of funding and authority to undertake it.

Especially in programmes, decisions must be founded on the basis of alternatives, available information, and expressed value *at the time of the decision*. As these may evolve during the course of the whole programme, they must be reassessed regularly; this is the main purpose of the appraisal stage.

THE ORGANIZATION PHASE

Once funds are allocated to a programme, or to the first 'cycle' of a programme, and the authority of the programme manager is secured, the programme's organization phase can begin. In programmes, the organization phase essentially consists of *strategic level planning* for the programme; the *strategic plan*, which could be considered the business case for the programme; and of the *selection of actions* (projects and other actions), which will compose it.

Strategic Plan

The strategic plan of the programme should be viewed as a business case and as such should not only outline the tasks and projects to be implemented, but also identify the benefits to be expected. The first step is to create and plan the organization that will be put in place to implement the programme; this consists essentially of the allocation of roles and responsibilities and the control of interactions between the projects within the programme as well as the communication systems to be put in place. The programme manager should ensure that a responsible party is appointed to manage each critical success factor of the programme. If a *function breakdown structure* (FBS) has been developed as a means of identifying and prioritizing the needs and expectations, the programme organization should be based on it. The FBS should be to the programme what the WBS is to the projects.

The programme organization structure should also identify the *communication* channels for the programme; how information should be filtered and sorted to suit different organizational levels and how access to systems should be allowed or restricted.

The efficient management of *resources* across the organization is a key component of programme management; but this process must also foster the effective use of resources in each project. Programme resource planning essentially consists of matching demand – required resources – with supply – available resources. It is a value-based concept (see Chapter 3, Managing Portfolios of Projects, and the section entitled 'Prioritizing projects and programmes'). Demand consists of the prioritization of the workload required to implement the programme, whereas supply consists of the evaluation of the capacity, capability and availability of resources to match the demand. Matching demand and supply allows for use of the best resources for the most significant assignments, it provides enhanced flexibility through regular reprioritization and re-evaluation, as well as proactive, rather that reactive resource allocation. The concepts developed in the *Critical Chain*, (Goldratt 1997) like the holistic view, sequential tasking, the focus on a *'drum'* resource and the use of buffers, can also be applied effectively to programme organization.

Another major issue of the strategic plan is the *pacing* of the programme. Periods of stability, during which benefits are allowed to impact the organization, should be spread significantly throughout the programme to pace it (Figure 4.6). Their distribution depends on benefits sought and the significance of those benefits for the business. The key concept behind the duration of cycles and the

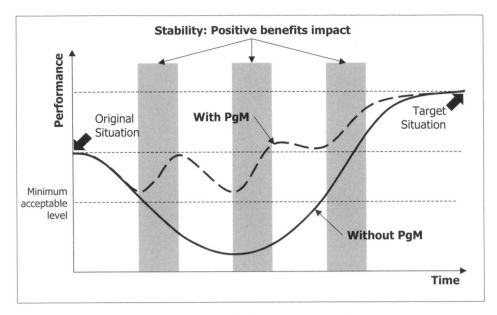

Figure 4.6   The planning of programme cycles

interval between periods of stability is based on a minimum acceptable level of performance, which cannot be crossed (Figure 4.6). Financial issues such as cash flow, funding, human resource issues like the organization's culture (such as risk seeking or risk averse) resistance to or acceptance of change determine this minimum. Programme planning must focus on early benefits, positive cash flow and maintenance of the motivation of stakeholders. The programme appraisal process is also built around the programme 'cycles' (see Figure 4.5).

Major project changes and benefits appraisal, both of which involve the programme manager in their sponsor role, are usually planned around the gateways of projects; these must be significantly spread to correspond both to major project deliverables and to expected benefits delivery for the programme. They are not related to the programme cycles, but rather to project milestones; on the other hand, to be valid, the project milestones must be linked to expected programme benefits.

The last element of the programme's strategic plan is the *change management system*. In programmes, the change process must be value-based. This signifies that, because the programme's critical success factors and objectives are very likely to be modified as it progresses, opportunities and threats are to be evaluated on a regular basis, as well as the capacity and capability of the programme organization to respond to them. This system has to be clearly established from the beginning.

Selection of actions

The selection of actions consists of identifying and prioritising projects and operational actions required to support them; and of developing the project *initiation* documents, if possible, in collaboration with the project managers. During this phase as well as during appraisal, the programme manager acts as the sponsor of projects.

The selection of actions takes into account the *'interdependability'* of projects, in terms of effects on each other, and in terms of their combined contribution to the benefits sought by the organization. The programme team must undertake a thorough analysis of the interactions or interfaces between the project and other actions that are part of the programme. The decision to implement must not be made solely on the individual value of each project, but also on its capability to contribute to the programme as a whole, and to align with the strategy.

The *prioritization* of actions in the overall programme must ensure that synergies between projects are taken into account, that there are no overlapping or conflicting actions and that benefit delivery is optimized. The criteria against which projects will be prioritized should include the critical success factors of the programme, but also take into account elements discussed in the pacing. Financial factors include payback period, cash flow, cost-benefit and risk elements; the objective being to make early gains to 'fund' the rest of the programme and motivate stakeholders, especially investors, to support the programme on an ongoing basis.

Concerning human resources issues, the programme team must take into account the responsiveness to change of the organization in which the programme is implemented; the demonstration of benefits for the users; the assessment of expectations of those affected by the change; and the measures put in place to support smooth transition from the original situation to the target situation. Interdependability issues should also be part of the prioritization of projects. Finally, the prioritization plan should be flexible enough to allow regular re-prioritization as the programme progresses and priorities or objectives change; if the initial plan has been well documented, this should pose no problem. The last point requires the identification of *constraints and assumptions* and their documentation. It is crucial that the constraints and other factors on which the assumptions have been based are well identified, because they will evolve and change as the programme progresses and will need to be reassessed regularly. This should be an integral part of the risk management process of the programme.

THE DEPLOYMENT PHASE

In the case of programmes, the implementation phase includes the actual initiation of actions, as well as the continuous reassessment of project benefits and priorities. Once actions are initiated, the programme manager needs to manage and prioritize resources and exercise formative evaluation of deliverables. The deployment process essentially consists of the *execution of actions* and of their *monitoring and control*.

Execution of actions

During this phase of the programme, the main task of the programme manager is to act as the sponsor of projects and allocate or reallocate funds and other resources according to priorities. In developing and approving project management plans, the programme manager will authorize or confirm the allocation of resources to undertake the detailed planning of projects and the 'working' of this plan.

The programme managers' role also requires the continuous assessment and management of the programme environment; particularly stakeholders' needs and expectations. They must also manage the communications to and from project managers and especially act as a buffer to control senior management's direct influence on the projects. It is not reasonable to expect project managers and project teams to, at the same time, focus on delivering specific project objectives within a performance paradigm; and develop effective responses to emergent change; the latter activity which requires a learning paradigm, is clearly the responsibility of the programme team. The identification of emergent (unplanned) inputs on the programme, which could trigger the need for changes, also needs to be monitored and managed in an orderly way. This is where the use of risk and value management techniques becomes essential.

This role requires the programme manager to concentrate on project inter-dependencies, rather than on project activities; even in terms of the project product, the programme level intervention should only consist of assessing benefits of major project deliverables and output-input relationships between projects; not solving the technical or operational level problems. Programme management requires that the projects review/approval process be put in place to regularly assess benefits and deliverables of projects at the major milestones; these correspond to the 'gateways' of the project management process.

Monitoring and Control

In programmes, control is not only a simple deductive (comparison to set parameters) and 'summative' (assessment perspective) type of control, based on performance criteria, but rather a continuous re-evaluation or 're-formulation' of the programme, with regard to the achievement of organizational benefits; an inductive (based on emergent inputs) and 'formative' (improvement perspective) type of control. Programme level control of projects concentrates on the impact of deliverables on the overall programme benefits and strategic alignment; the need to adjust the programme to respond to results that do not correspond to the business case, rather than a simple assessment of cost and schedule; or even earned value. All these measures become valid only as a means to make the necessary adjustments to achieve overall benefits. A mistake often found in the management of programmes is to link the programme with the delivery of project deliverables; the responsibility of the programme manager should extend beyond the simple delivery of projects to the delivery of business benefits, which often can be measured only after the projects are finished and their '*products*' have been '*operationalised*' in the organization or delivered to the market.

One of the roles of the programme manager is to assess the need for project plan review or readjustment; to propose or implement changes in projects and assess their impact on the critical success factors. The programme manager will consider project deliverables against key performance indicators and analyse project outputs, like schedule, budget or earned value results, with a view to the reallocation or reprioritization of resources and contingencies amongst projects, as well as deciding whether to continue, realign or stop the individual projects. Because of this, a sound aggregated information management system should be put in place both at project level and at programme level. The programme level information management will address both the information between project and programme level stakeholders, especially the reporting system, but also all the information circulating between projects that need to be managed at programme level.

THE APPRAISAL PHASE

The periods of stability which mark the end of each cycle, are the ideal time to appraise the programme. These are the periods when the organization, whether the programme is internal or undertaken externally, must evaluate the need to carry on with the programme, review its purpose, or stop it. The programme team should ask itself several questions such as:

- Have the expected benefits for this cycle been achieved?
- Have the programme or business circumstances changed?
- Have stakeholders' needs or expectations changed?
- Does the rationale for the programme still exist?
- If not, should the programme be reviewed; should it be stopped?

The *appraisal process* itself requires the programme team to loop back to the formulation and strategic plan of the programme, in order to reassess the validity of the original needs with regard to external or internal developments since the programme was started, including positive or negative impact on the business of outcomes from previous cycles. Any changes in the critical success factors must be identified and examined to understand how they could modify the expected benefits of the programme.

Following that exercise, the actual benefits of the cycle are evaluated against the expected benefits and a gap analysis is performed. If gaps are identified, the team needs to define how the programme plan should be modified to take them into account; alternatives are examined and options evaluated; finally a decision is made on how to modify the plan for the next cycle; this is again a learning loop where value and risks must be assessed. If everything has gone as planned and nothing has changed in the expected benefits, then the decision is made to carry on according to the original plan.

When assessing the delivery of benefits from a programme management point of view, the team must have a broad perspective and look at two different levels:

At the *organizational level*, the team needs to produce feedback on the effective delivery of expected benefits and satisfaction of critical success factors. Specifically it must assess the continuous and effective management of:

- changing corporate or client objectives
- shared and/or limited resources
- interface between function and project managers
- clear definition of roles and responsibilities and mutual support to achieve corporate goals
- project review and approval process
- project managers' focus on key business issues

At the *project level*, the programme team needs to review relevance of projects that are spanning over a number of cycles and the aggregated benefits of all the projects that are part of the cycle. In particular, to:

- Assess overall performance of projects against business benefits, including emergent factors
- Identify new threats and opportunities and implement changes, if required
- Re-plan work and relative priorities, at business level, for the next phases or projects
- Loop back to project definitions and readjust, if required (learning loop)
- Ensure information is recycled into a feedback loop, for the next phase or future programmes

In summary, this *learning/improvement process* needs to outline and feedback: the programme team's success in achieving expected benefits; *response to emergent change* in business environment, including changing needs and to bottom-up initiatives; the *overall performance against CSFs*, including identification of threats and opportunities; the *management of resources* in general and of line and project manager's complementary roles, in particular; and finally, *knowledge management*. It is on these elements that the justification for continuation will be demonstrated.

THE DISSOLUTION PHASE

A programme may extend over a period many months, (IT supported change programmes, Business Process Reengineering, etc.) or many years (drug development, transportation infrastructure refurbishment, etc.). Some programmes – typically portfolio or incremental – (account management, continuous improvement, etc.) are even ongoing. Even in the ongoing programmes, the appraisal process must be carried out on a regular basis and every time the programme team must ask itself: 'Should the programme be stopped?'

A programme should be stopped if the rationale for its existence is no longer defensible: when the initial benefits have been achieved; when the cost of the programme is greater than the benefits it is bringing to the organization; but also, when the environment or context have changed and the benefits that the programme was seeking to achieve are no longer required, or when the implementation of the first cycle(s) has demonstrated that the programme's ultimate purpose cannot be achieved. The first two are typical examples of performance-based decisions; the latter two, of learning- or value-based decisions.

Like for projects, the closing, or dissolution, of the programme is not an easy task; when a decision to stop a programme is made, people and funds will be reallocated to other ventures and therefore there is likely to be resistance from the team to 'let go'. For this reason, some organizations even choose to involve a team external to the programme in the closing phase, to make it more efficient. There will always be some uncompleted work that needs to be either completed within a reasonable period of time, or re-allocated to other programmes, which are then re-formulated as required. All the documentation must be updated and filed and a post programme review conducted; these are then fed back into the organization through a learning/innovation loop such as the one recommended in the EFQM® Business Excellence Model. Once this has been achieved, the programme dissolution team is disbanded and re-assigned.

DEVELOPING THE RIGHT APPROACHES AND METHODOLOGIES

The life-cycle process alone is not sufficient to run successful programmes. Sustainable programme management also requires a cultural change from a project approach to a management approach. The following section identifies the key elements required to successfully address this challenge.

87

STRATEGIC DECISION MANAGEMENT

Programme size and time span make for a more complex environment. Continually changing circumstances require a combination of both *deliberate* and *emergent* strategies; strategies are planned and, as they unfold through the programme and projects, new strategies emerge that modify the planned strategy; a process called *enactment*. PgM also takes a *formative* approach to change; whereas projects require a *transactional* leadership approach, the emergent nature of PgM requires more of a *transformational* leadership approach. Programme management should be linked to a strategic decision management process aimed at achieving strategic and or tactical benefits through a series of learning and performance loops. The learning loops focus on a value-based decision process, including change management, whereas the performance loops focus on the delivery of results. *Strategic Decision Management* is the programme management equivalent of the *Integration Management* knowledge area in project management; it should be a cyclic, benefits-oriented process capable of dealing with emergent inputs and continually evolving circumstances.

STAKEHOLDERS' VALUE MANAGEMENT

The PgM process should combine value management and project management, where value management is used to reduce ambiguity to identify and agree stakeholders' needs and expectations and translate them into measurable critical success factors (CSF) that constitute the scope of the programme. Value management is then used as a learning framework to address emergent changes and ongoing stakeholders needs management.

OGC (2003) suggests that some stakeholders will be a key group for assessing the realization of the programme's benefits and that it is important to recognize their specific interest areas in order to ensure that their expectations can be managed effectively. The process they advocate in the stakeholder management chapter, though, is basic and concerns only their identification and the establishment of communication channels to manage their expectations.

In a PgM framework, the role of initiator or sponsor of a project is clearly that of the programme manager. PgM cannot therefore be content with simply defining and controlling what is and is not included, but must take an evolving, systemic view of the customers and other stakeholders' needs and expectations. Each project, which form the programme, is prioritized on the basis of its value (contribution to benefits (CSFs) *versus* achievability); this is what determines the scope of the programme.

It can be safely argued that the equivalent of the *Scope Management* knowledge area in projects would be *Stakeholders' Value Management* in programmes: the management of the stakeholders' needs and expectations is expressed in measurable terms (CSFs) and prioritized, and the sum of them constitutes the programme's purpose.

PACE MANAGEMENT

Programme managers take a strategic view and give their attention to major deliverables and interfaces between projects. As part of the programme plan, the OGC (2003) identifies: a *dependency network* showing the optimum sequencing of the projects and their dependencies on each other and a *schedule of all the benefits* to be delivered by the projects and when they will be achieved. In the case of programmes, beginning and, particularly end, are usually 'fuzzy'. Because of the evolving and complex context of programmes, programme managers need continually re-evaluate project priorities and benefits delivery. Programme time management focuses on resource availability and benefits delivery, not on activity dependencies or duration. Pacing includes prioritization of actions based on interdependencies and benefits delivery. It must focus on early benefits, positive cash flow and maintenance of the motivation of stakeholders.

Rather than using the project's *Time Management* concept, it would be more appropriate to talk about *Pace Management* for programmes, since it concerns the management of relative project priorities in accordance with emergent inputs and 'optimal' benefits delivery – not shortest delivery time. It is a deterministic and formative approach whereas time management is a probabilistic and summative approach.

RESOURCE MANAGEMENT

The programme manager is involved in setting project budgets and is usually asked to justify, or 're-justify' the budgets on a regular basis. Additionally, a programme's budget includes elements of support activities and investment in supporting structures, which go beyond a simple delivery process.

Programme managers build long-term relationships and partnerships with their stakeholders, who can be either providers or customers, sometimes both. The management of funding and cash flow is directly related to these 'partnerships', which also involve an aspect of stakeholder relationship management, when securing human resources for the programme and negotiating commitments.

Programme budgeting is prospective, as opposed to cost management that is retrospective. It includes reliance on a much wider range of resources that cost alone can cover. It would be more appropriate, instead of *Cost Management*, to talk about *Resource Management* to describe this. It involves the long-term management of all the resources necessary to successfully carry out the programme and is closely linked to pacing management.

BENEFITS MANAGEMENT

Benefits are the key success factors of a programme, as quality is one of the key success factors of a project. Benefits are tightly linked to the stakeholders' needs and expectations as quality is to scope in projects. OGC (2003) suggests that benefits management provides the programme with a target and a means of monitoring achievement against that target on a regular basis. They suggest that care should be taken not to shift the focus of benefits management to the delivery of new capability. Benefits emerge from strategic intent, but cannot be evaluated until project deliverables are operated and marketed; it is therefore essential that PgM covers the whole benefits life-cycle if it is to be effective.

More and more, organizations agree that it is the responsibility of the programme manager to deliver benefits to the business, but this requires authority over the resources necessary to do so. The OGC puts the responsibility for benefits delivery in the hands of the business managers. This position is in line with the operational responsibility usually devoted to Business Managers, but runs the risk of taking away all accountability from the programme manager for the delivery of benefits and may be desirable only when it is not possible to delegate such authority to the programme manager. In such case the programme manager should be involved in the benefits delivery if only in a learning and advisory role.

What is known in projects as *Quality Management* becomes *Benefits Management* in programmes: the management of benefits over time so that the ultimate impact of project deliverables corresponds to expected benefits.

STAKEHOLDER MANAGEMENT

The PMI®'s PMBOK® Guide, 2004 considers stakeholder management a major challenge for project managers. Stakeholder management and the resolution of differences to identify expected benefits is one of the key roles of the programme manager. Stakeholder management is a two-way relation that involves the contribution of the stakeholders to the programme and, in certain cases, the forming of partnerships, the equivalent of team development in projects, but on a much larger scale and with much less formal power. While leadership involves formal power on projects – 'the project management team [can] use disciplinary action to maintain order' (PMI® 2004, p.163) – leadership in programmes requires more of a facilitating or negotiating approach, since many of the stakeholders have more formal power than the programme manager. Human resources in programmes encompass much more than the programme team, where relationships are based on trust rather than formal power, therefore requiring skills and competences much broader than simple human resource management.

Whereas in projects one can talk about *Resource Management*, in programme management we rather talk about *Stakeholder Management*: the management of all the stakeholders of a programme to maximize their contribution to the ultimate delivery of benefits.

COMMUNICATIONS AND MARKETING MANAGEMENT

OGC (2003) defines the communication strategy as how information about the programme will be disseminated to stakeholders, people directly involved in the programme, the rest of the organization, and any other external organizations. This view is consistent with the PMBOK® Guide (PMI® 2004) view for projects, but personal experience and research have demonstrated that well marketed programmes are much more successful than those which solely rely on communication management, as described above. Unlike in project management, information and data management is just one aspect of PgM communications. Programme management practice has seen the emergence of a new and crucial aspect of communications in programmes: *marketing*. Marketing is more than just advertising; good marketing encompasses strategic integration and not only follows strategy but drives it through learning and knowledge management.

Programme *Communication and Marketing Management* could be summarized as: developing an interactive communication system aimed at gaining stakeholders' support in terms of the strategy and delivery of the programme benefits.

UNCERTAINTY MANAGEMENT

The management of risks in programmes is not very different than in projects, except that a greater emphasis should be put on opportunities, because of the formative nature of programmes. The focus of programme risks is of a higher and more systemic level than that of projects. Differences also include the emergence of three distinct levels of risks: programme risks, project risks and 'aggregated' risks – project level risks that affect more than one project and are better managed at programme level. Programme risks definitely encompass both threats and opportunities, and take into account ambiguity and a scope outside of the simple known unknown of projects. Chapman & Ward (2000) suggest the term 'uncertainty management', which is also in line with the concepts of emergent strategy. It would be appropriate to use the term *Uncertainty Management* for programmes: 'an iterative, learning approach' covering both threats and opportunities, where 'uncertainties are allowed for at organizational level' and that covers uncertainty related to ambiguity (Chapman & Ward 2002, p.416).

PARTNERSHIP AND VALUE CHAIN MANAGEMENT

In programmes, long-term relationships are built, which are not contractual, but based on mutual needs. Often, the programme manager has to deal with stakeholders who have enormous power and clout. Therefore the standard procurement relationship is not appropriate any more.

In terms of programmes it would be more appropriate to talk about partnership management or Value Chain management, which Pinto and Rouhainen (2001) have very well described in their book: 'Building Customer-Based Organizations' (pp.127–142). Value chain management involves much more than managing relationships required to procure goods and services; it is an organizational level process.

The recommendation is to use the term *partnership management* rather than *procurement management* to describe the programme knowledge area required to acquire resources and support for the programme from parties within or outside the performing organization. Relationships could be subjected to contractual agreement or not.

CONCLUSION

Programmes are an essential aspect of Project-Based Organizations as they provide the link between the strategic decisions and their implementation. PBOs that only use project and multi-project or portfolio management are avoiding the key issue of decision implementation, which requires constant realignment, and denying the interdependencies that exist between projects which are part of the same strategic decision. Programme management helps manage business strategies from their inception to the delivery of their expected benefits; it has the necessary flexibility to adjust to contextual changes and still maintain its strategic focus. It is meant to deal with multiple stakeholders and emergent change.

Programme management is a strategic decision management process.

REFERENCES AND FURTHER READING

Chapman, C.B. and Ward, S., 2002, 'Project risk management: the required transformations to become project uncertainty management', in Slevin, D.P., Pinto, J.K. and Rouhiainen, P., and Cleland, D.I. (eds.), *The Frontiers of Project Management Research,* Newton Square, PA: Project Management Institute, 405–418.

Goldratt, E., 1997, *The Critical Chain,* Great Barrington, MA: North River Press.

McNamara, C., 1999, 'Programme planning and management', extracted from: <http://www.mapnp.org/library/prog_mng/prog_mng.htm> on 15–06–2005

OGC, 2003, *Managing Successful Programmes,* London: The Stationery Office.

Pinto, J.K., and Rouhiainen, P., 2001, Building Customer-Based Project Organizations, New York, NY: Wiley.

PMCC, 2002, *A Guidebook of Project and Programme Management for Enterprise Innovation (P2M)-Summary Translation*, revised edition, Tokyo: Project Management Professionals Certification Center, Japan.

PMI®, 2003, *Organizational Project Management Maturity Model (OPM3): Knowledge Foundation*, Newton Square, PA: Project Management Institute.

PMI®, 2004, *Guide to the PMBOK®,* 3rd edition, Newton Square, PA: Project Management Institute.

PMI®, 2006a, *The standard for portfolio management,* Newtown Square, PA: Project Management Institute.

PMI®, 2006b, *The standard for programme management,* Newtown Square, PA: Project Management Institute.

Reiss, G., Anthony, M., Chapman, J., Leigh, G., Pyne, A., and Rayner, P., 2006, *The Gower Handbook of Programmeme Management,* Aldershot, UK: Gower.

Thiry, M., 2004a, 'Towards a programme management body of knowledge', in *Proceedings of the PMI® Global Congress, Europe 2004, Prague, April,* Newton Square, PA: Project Management Institute.

Thiry, M., 2004b, 'FOrDAD: a programme management life-cycle process', *International Journal of Project Management*, 22(3); 245–252.

Wideman, R.M., 2004, *A Management Framework for Project, Programme and Portfolio Integration*, Victoria, BC: Trafford.

5 Projects and their Management

Rodney Turner

To achieve the new business objectives identified through its strategic planning process (Chapter 2), an organization will undertake projects or programmes of projects (Chapter 4). The projects and programmes may be grouped into portfolios so the organization can choose which projects and programmes the organization will or will not do to optimize value, and to share resources between those projects it does decide to do (Chapter 3). Projects themselves are temporary endeavours to bring about beneficial change. Project management is the process by which that change is successfully delivered (whatever 'successfully' means, Chapter 6), and the benefit achieved. But what does this mean? What is the nature of projects and project management? What are the elements of project management essential for their successful delivery? To answer these questions we need a theory of project management.

At the time of writing I was a member of two research networks taking a fresh look at project management.

1. One, called 'Rethinking Project Management', was sponsored by the Engineering and Physical Sciences Research Council (EPSRC), and led by the University of Manchester (Maylor, 2006).
2. The other was investigating the value of Project Management, and was sponsored by the Project Management Institute of North America (PMI®). It was led by Athabasca University in Canada.

In both networks, the view was expressed that Project Management lacks a comprehensive theory, and what theory does exist is dominated by the systems perspective (Cleland and King 1983). A problem with the early theories is they are based on a large number of assumptions, some involving advanced concepts, so the theory is only as good as the assumptions and the definition of the concepts. For instance, Cleland and King assume:

● the project organization is a temporary matrix coordinated by the project team

- projects move through a life-cycle
- the project management process is inherently one of planning and control
- the project organization delivers against objectives of time, cost and functionality set outside the project
- tools such as work break-down structure and critical path analysis are useful

The resultant theory is only as sound as the definition of the word 'matrix', and the assumptions of project life-cycle, project management life-cycle, the importance of time, cost and functionality and the usefulness of break-down and critical path analysis as tools. The theory draws upon a considerable amount of empirical evidence in its assumptions and so is only as sound as that empirical evidence.

In this chapter, I outline a theory of project management based on a small number of simple, natural premises, and try to find what elements of project management are inherently implied by them. Starting with just three premises, one defining the project, one project governance, and the third what we mean by the value of the project, I try to show that the project life-cycle, the project management life-cycle, all nine body of knowledge areas in the PMI® Guide to the Project Management Body of Knowledge, PMBoK®, (PMI® 2004), and some additional project management functions, are an inherent part of Project Management. Further:

- some tools, such as product, work, organization and cost break downs can be shown to be an inherent part of Project Management
- some tools such as Earned Value Analysis (EVA) and investment appraisal can be derived from theories in other disciplines
- some tools must have certain features; for instance Configuration Management to manage scope must involve the planning and control of both product and work break-down
- the justification for the use of other tools such as Critical Path Analysis (CPA) is empirically based, and so the justification remains only as good as the empirical evidence

In this chapter I introduce two other premises:

1. one to define what we mean by the project-based or project oriented organization, including programme and portfolio management
2. one to suggest that the project is managed on behalf of the stakeholders

THE PROJECT

The first premise defines the project:

Premise 1: A project is a temporary organization to which resources are assigned to do work to bring about beneficial change.

Ralf Müller and I (2003) have shown that this premise encompasses most of the traditional definitions of a project. Particularly, all organizations can be viewed as systems. So this does not preclude the systems perspective. That is another view which can be useful, but it is not the primary focus.

A TEMPORARY ORGANIZATION

Whenever people gather together to do something they form an organization. So a project is an organization; that is axiomatic. All we are saying is: it is temporary. People have challenged the definition of a project as a temporary organization:

1. Some projects are not so temporary. In the extreme, some projects have lasted hundreds of years. The most extreme I have heard about is the Rhine to Danube Canal which was 1200 years (sic) from first works to final completion.
2. Other people say that all organizations are temporary; none last for ever. The oldest organization I know about is the Roman Catholic Church which is 2000 years old. That is temporary on some time scales.

The response to both these objections is that with projects the intention is they should be temporary. The project is created to bring about change, and when that change is achieved, the project is disbanded, whereas with other organizations the intention is they should be permanent (though the likelihood is their existence will be transient). The difference in intention (a social construct) produces a different approach to the management of a temporary versus permanent organization.

Ralf Müller and I (2003) also differentiate between a temporary task given to the routine organization and a project. A temporary task can be unique, novel and transient, but it is undertaken by the routine organization, by people who don't change their job function to do the task. For instance when I take my car to be serviced, the service is unique, novel and transient, but it is performed by the garage as part of their routine work, so it is temporary task, not a project. For a project, we create a temporary organization, and give people new functions for its execution.

Defining a project as a temporary organization sets Project Management firmly as part of Organizational and Management Theory and suggests we can draw on ideas from there to enlighten our understanding of projects. It also leads to our first conclusion.

Conclusion 1: Project Organization Management, or Integration Management, (Chapter 18) is an inherent component of Project Management.

There are other views of a project:

A nexus of contracts

It has been suggested that a project is a nexus of contracts. But every organization can be viewed as a nexus of contracts (Jensen 2000). So a project is just a temporary nexus of contracts. Some contracts will be informal, the word 'treaties' is sometimes preferred. But some will be formal legal contracts and so Project Contract Management and Procurement is an inherent component of Project Management.

Conclusion 2: Project Contract Management and Procurement (Turner 2003) is an inherent component of Project Management.

An information processing system

Winch (2005) suggests that a project is a system for processing information. However, that view is encompassed by Premise 1. Information is a resource, which is assigned to (and managed by) the temporary organization. That means Information Management is an inherent component of Project Management.

Conclusion 3: Information Management (Chapter 8), including Communication Management (Chapter 37) is an inherent component of Project Management.

So far we have shown that three of the nine of PMI®'s body of knowledge areas, Integration Management, Contract Management, and Communication Management, are an inherent part of project management.

THE BENEFICIAL CHANGE

A project produces a change. It delivers an output, a new facility or asset. The asset may be an engineering construct, it may be an information system, it may be a social construct or it may be entirely abstract. The asset is desired to produce a beneficial outcome, some return, to satisfy some purpose, to solve a problem or exploit an opportunity. In order to produce the desired beneficial outcome, the asset must function in certain ways. Thus the management of the delivery of those functions is an inherent part of project management. Also the achievement of the benefit must be managed.

Conclusion 4: Benefits Management (Chapter 13), Requirements Management (Chapter 14) and Quality Management (Chapter 17) are inherent parts of Project Management.

The project consumes resources, which costs money. We define the owner as the person who provides the money to buy the asset and receives benefit from its operation. (Throughout this chapter, whenever I say 'person' I may mean a natural person, a human being, or a legal person, or an organization). The owner pays the money to a contractor who does the work; effectively the owner buys the asset off the contractor. The owner may delegate operation of the asset to operators or users. The owner may gain the benefit from the operation of the asset directly. Or the asset may produce some product or service, and the owner gains the benefit by selling that product or service to third parties. So we have defined four inherent roles:

Role 1: The owner, who buys the project's output, the new asset, and receives the benefit from its operation or outcomes.

Role 2: The contractor, who receives money from the owner to do the work to deliver the asset or output.

Role 3: The users or operators, who operate the project's outputs on behalf of the owner to produce the outcome, product or service desired.

Role 4: The consumers, who are the people who buy a product or service produced by the operation of the asset.

THE WORK

In order to deliver the desired outcome or asset, Premise 1 suggests it is necessary to do work. Premise 1 thus implies a break-down structure, Figure 5.1, and to define a project, each level of this break-down must be defined.

Conclusion 5: Break-down Structure (Chapter 15) is an inherent component of projects.

Conclusion 6: To define a project we need to define

- the expected outcome, benefit or purpose
- the output, facility or asset that will enable us to achieve that
- the work required to deliver the output

Projects are fractal. The asset will consist of components, each requiring work to deliver them. Each component and each element of work to deliver a component will have the features of a project in that it will be temporary organization requiring resources to deliver beneficial change, namely the ability to do other

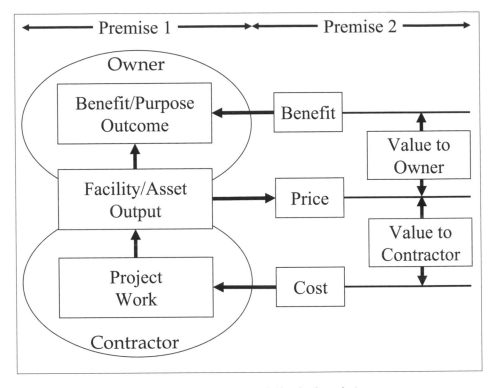

Figure 5.1 Three essential levels of a project

work and achieve the overall asset. Further the components will have sub-components, and so on.

Conclusion 5A: Product and Work Break-down Structures are inherent components of projects.

The work of the project needs to be managed. Thus Scope Management is inherent. In order to manage the work we need to define the output and its components at all levels of breakdown, and the work at all levels of breakdown. Thus the tools used for managing scope will include product and work breakdown. But we need further tools to help us define and manage those. Configuration Management is a tool with appropriate features, which has been shown from empirical evidence to perform that task (Turner 1999).

Conclusion 7: Scope Management is an inherent component of Project Management, and Configuration Management (Chapter 15) is a tool with the appropriate features which has proved useful for managing scope.

THE RESOURCES

Premise 1 says that resources are required to do the work. Indeed Premise 1 says the project is an organization so people are involved by definition.

Conclusion 8: Human Resource Management (Chapter 31) is an inherent part of Project Management.

Resources can include materials, plant and equipment and financial resources (money). These resources need to be managed. In order to plan the resources required it is necessary to define them at each level of work and product breakdown. Thus organization break-down is an inherent tool for managing resources. At any level of break-down, it will be useful to define which resources will perform which duties at a given level of breakdown, either to do work or deliver components of the asset. A Responsibility Chart is a tool with appropriate features, which has been shown from empirical evidence to perform that task (Turner 1999).

Conclusion 9: Resource Management (Chapter 19) is an inherent part of Project Organization Management.

Conclusion 10: Organization break-down is an inherent tool for managing resources, and Responsibility Charts are a tool with the appropriate features which have proved useful for managing resources and project organization.

A key resource is money. Those discussed above are direct costs. But there are also transaction costs associated with the creation of the temporary organization, and to manage the contracts and treaties. There are also economic costs such as inflation and taxation. Thus cost break-down is inherent. Further, 500 years of theory from Cost and Management Accounting says that in managing cost it is necessary to monitor the volume of work done and the cost per unit of work. I have shown that when applied to Project Management this results in Earned Value Analysis (Turner 1999). Thus another management discipline (Accounting, Finance and Economics) suggests that EVA is the appropriate tool for managing cost.

Corollary 11: Cost Management (Chapter 20) and Financial Management (Turner 2005) are inherent components of project management, and Earned Value Analysis (Chapter 20) is an appropriate tool for managing costs on projects.

Conclusion 12: Cost break-down (Chapter 20) is an inherent tool for managing costs.

UNIQUE, NOVEL AND TRANSIENT

It has been said, (Turner 1999, 2004), that projects are unique, novel and transient.

● every project is different from every other project
● the work of the project is novel
● the project has a transient existence

The third statement is part of Premise 1. The first is a tautology. Every organization is unique, no two are the same, whether projects or routine organizations. But with a project we expect the work to be non-routine; that is the work of the project will be unlike anything we have done before. Some projects are more or less routine than others. A popular categorization of projects defines four types of project (Turner 2004; Crawford et al 2005):

● repeaters: virtually routine batch processing
● runners: quite similar to previous projects
● strangers: essentially different from previous projects but with some common elements
● aliens: unlike anything we have done before

If the work of the project is non-routine, there is some uncertainty about whether the work will deliver the desired output, and whether the output will operate properly to deliver the desired outcome. This suggests that this uncertainty or risk needs to be managed.

Conclusion 13: Risk Management (Chapter 22) is an inherent component of Project Management.

From Premise 1, I have shown that eight of the nine of PMI®'s body of knowledge areas are an inherent part of project management, in the order we first encountered them:

● Integration Management
● Contract Management
● Communication Management
● Quality Management
● Scope Management
● Human Resource Management
● Cost Management
● Risk Management

We have also seen that many of the popular tools, such as product, work and organization breakdown and Earned Value Management are also inherent.

THE VALUE OF THE PROJECT

The second premise defines what we mean by the value of the project:

Premise 2: The change delivered by the project will be of value if the benefit justifies the cost.

There are two major parties making a judgement of the value of the project, the owner and contractor. The owner pays the contractor a price to buy the asset (change or output), and the contractor spends some of that price, the cost, to do the work, Figure 1. The asset will be of value to the owner if the benefit received from the operation of the asset justifies the price paid for it. The project will be of value to the contractor if the price is greater than the cost. The benefit and the price may include intangibles; they need not be purely financial. For the rest of this discussion I focus on the value to the owner.

Thus before the project starts the owner will want to be convinced the project is worthwhile and conduct investment appraisal to provide assureance of that. The theory of Accounting, Finance and Economics suggests many investment appraisal techniques, such as discounted cash flow or options pricing. Different ones are appropriate in different circumstances.

Conclusion 14: Investment Appraisal (Turner 1995) is an inherent component of the Financial Management of projects.

The owner will also want to optimize the value of the project; that is to obtain the best benefit possible for a given cost, and so may want to undertake Value Management to optimize the ratio of benefit to cost.

Conclusion 15: Value Management (Chapter 16) is an inherent component of Project Management.

Completing the project within a certain timescale will also optimize the value. There are several reasons for that, including:

- The theory of Accounting, Finance and Economics tells us there is time value of money. The earlier the benefit is obtained the higher its value.
- Sometimes the benefit can only be obtained in a limited time window. The earlier the project is completed in that time window the greater will be the benefit.
- Sometimes the benefit can only be obtained on a certain day. This is especially true for sporting or cultural events, or scientific conferences. The project must be completed by that day or the benefit is lost completely.
- Some costs are time dependent. Many indirect costs are proportional to time; the longer the project takes, the greater they will be. Some direct costs are

inversely proportional to time; the shorter the project is, the more they are. Thus there is a time that optimizes the cost of the project and another that optimizes the ratio of benefit to cost.

The project is a temporary organization, and so to manage the time it is necessary to define and control the start and finish dates, and communicate those to the people involved in the project. But the project is fractal, and so it will also be necessary to plan and control the start and finish dates of work elements and to communicate them to the people involved in those work elements. Empirical evidence suggests that bar charts (Gantt charts) are a useful tool for planning, communicating and monitoring the schedule. Mathematical theory suggests that Critical Path Analysis can be used to plan and control the schedule, but it is just a suggestion.

Conclusion 16: Time Management (Chapter 21) is an inherent component of Project Management, and bar charts are a tool with the appropriate features which has proved useful for managing the timescale of a project.

Time management is the ninth of the PMI® body of knowledge areas, and so we have now seen that all nine are inherent. However, we have also seen that other body of knowledge areas such as benefits management and requirements management are also inherent. Further, we have seen that every chapter in Part 2 describes an inherent feature of project management. (Every chapter, that is, except Chapters 23 and 24, Safety, Health and the Environment, but they are needed for moral reasons.) We now turn our attention to the management process.

PROJECT GOVERNANCE AND MANAGEMENT

For a definition of Project Governance I turn to the OECD definition of governance (Clarke 2004):

Premise 3: Project governance provides the structure which helps define:

- the objectives of the project
- the means of attaining those objectives
- the means of monitoring performance

Premise 1 implied it is necessary to define the objectives and the means of obtaining them. What Premise 3 adds is that governance provides the structure to do that and also to define the means of monitoring performance. Premises 1 and 3 together define Project Management.

Conclusion 17: Project Management is the means by which the work of the resources assigned to the temporary organization is managed and controlled to deliver the beneficial change.

PROJECT LIFE-CYCLE

Premise 3 suggests there is a project life-cycle. On its own, it suggests that there are three inherent steps to the project-life-cycle:

- definition: when the objectives are defined
- design: when the means of obtaining those objectives are defined
- execution: when the work is done and performance monitored

Combining Premises 1, 2, and 3 identifies five inherent steps in the project life-cycle:

- concept: when possibility of beneficial change is first identified, and the outcome (desired benefit) and possible outputs (project deliverables) to achieve that outcome are identified
- feasibility: when possible means of obtaining the outputs are identified, their feasibility and comparative values assessed, and one chosen for further development
- design: when definition of the desired outputs and outcomes is refined, the means of achieving them defined and the value to the owner proven
- execution: when the work to deliver the output is undertaken and performance monitored
- close-out: when the output is commissioned and handed to the owner or users for them to operate to produce the desired outcome

Some people suggest that not all projects have a life-cycle, and quote Extreme Programmeming. I disagree. The life-cycle may take place in strict series, but sometimes it will overlap as in fast-track, sometimes stages will run in parallel, sometimes stages will be repeated, and sometimes (as in Extreme Programmeming), they will be cyclic. The project-life-cycle, however, is inherent.

Conclusion 18: The project-life-cycle (Part 3) is an inherent part of project management.

Premise 3 also identifies four additional project roles, Figure 5.2. For the second I use a term suggested by Anne Keegan and I (2001).

Role 5: The sponsor is the person who defines the objectives of the project, the desired outcome (benefit) and defined output (deliverable, facility or asset).

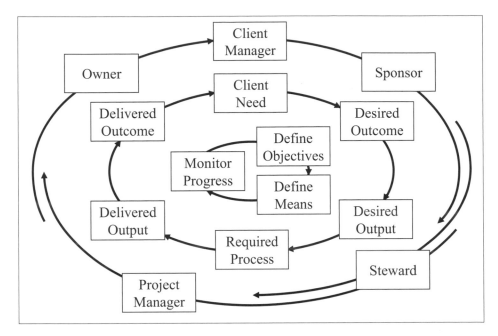

Figure 5.2 Four governance roles on projects

Role 6: The steward is the person who defines the means of achieving the objectives.

Role 7: The project manager is the person who monitors performance of the project to ensure the appropriate output is delivered.

Role 8: The project owner is the person who monitors performance of the output to ensure the desired outcome is achieved.

The project manager may also be the steward, and the project sponsor may also be the broker, but not necessarily so.

PROJECT MANAGEMENT LIFE-CYCLE

Premises 1 and 3 also suggest that there is a management life-cycle, with four inherent steps:

- planning: the work of the temporary organization is planned
- organizing: the resources required to undertake the work are identified
- implementing: the work is assigned to the resources
- controlling: performance is monitored, and corrective action taken to ensure the desired output (change) is obtained and that it is capable of delivering the desired outcome (benefit)

106

Conclusion 19: The Management Life-cycle is an inherent part of Project Management.

It is sometimes said that there are eleven body of knowledge areas in PMI®'s PMBoK®. We have now encountered the other two elements, the project life-cycle and the management processes. These are the focus of Part 3 of this book.

QUALITY MANAGEMENT

Conclusion 4 suggested that Quality Management is an inherent component of Project Management. Premises 1 and 3 now suggest what the elements of Quality Management are. From Premises 1 and 3 we can conclude we need to manage both the quality of the objectives delivered by the project, the asset, and the means of achieving the objectives, the management process. Premise 3 also tells us that in Quality Management we need to define the means of meeting our quality objectives, Quality Assurance, and the means of monitoring achievement of our quality objectives, Quality Control. Thus we can deduce the necessity of four of the five elements of my five element model for managing quality (Turner 1999), and see that quality management comprises four components:

Conclusion 20: Quality management includes:

1. quality assurance of the project's outputs
2. quality control of the project's outputs
3. quality assurance of the management process
4. quality control of the management process

THE PROJECT-BASED OR PROJECT-ORIENTED ORGANIZATION

Premise 4 defines the project-based organization, and programme and portfolio management:

Premise 4A: The project-based organization is one in which the majority of work is organized as projects.

Premise 4B: A programme of projects is a group of projects contributing to a common outcome, which cannot be achieved by any of the projects on its own.

Premise 4C: A portfolio of projects is a group of projects sharing common resources.

The literature suggests a difference between a project-based organization and a project-oriented one. Anne Keegan and I (2001) suggest project-based organizations are such perforce. The products or services they supply are bespoke, and so they necessarily undertake projects to deliver them. Gareis and Huemann (Chapter 10) suggest project-oriented organizations are such by choice. They choose to use temporary organizations to do their work. Premise 4A covers both. Many of the above premises and conclusions can be repeated for the governance of the project-based organization and its programmes and portfolios.

THE STAKEHOLDERS

There are two parts to the OECD definition of governance (Clarke 2004). I used only one part in Premise 3. The other leads to our final premise:

Premise 5: The project is governed on behalf of all the stakeholders, including the owner and contractor.

The governance literature suggests that there are two paradigms for the governance of the corporation:

- one suggests that it should be governed for the benefit of the shareholders only, and that the board of director's sole objective is to maximize shareholder value
- the second suggests that the corporation should be governed on behalf of a wider set of stakeholders, including the staff, customers and local community as well as the shareholders, and that all their needs should be balanced against each other

There is evidence that those boards of directors which look after the wider set of stakeholders, actually maximize shareholder value *en passant*, whereas those who focus just on the interests of shareholders do not achieve such good results.

The same two views can be taken for projects:

- the project manager's sole responsibility might be to maximize the value of the project for the owner
- or his or her responsibility might be to a wider set of stakeholders to maximize the value for all of them

Unfortunately projects are coupled systems. Making a change in one area can have an impact in another. So you do not optimize the whole project by optimizing each bit of it. You have to optimize a project as a whole, and that almost certainly means balancing the interests of stakeholders across the project. For instance, Figure 1 shows that if you try to increase the profit to the owner, by reducing the price, you reduce the profit to the contractor, and if you take that too far it is of no value to the contractor to do the work, and the project does not happen. On the other hand, if you try to increase the profit to the contractor by increasing the price, you reduce the value to the owner, and if you take that too far it is of no value to the owner to do the work and so the project does not happen. What is best for the project is to achieve a balance between the owner's and the contractor's interests.

Conclusion 21: A project should be optimized for all parties, not just one, the owner, and so the project should be undertaken as a partnership between all the parties involved, but particularly the owner and contractor.

Ralf Müller and I (2004) have shown that forming a partnership between the client and the project manager, where they work cooperatively and rationally towards mutually beneficial outcomes is a *necessary* condition for project success. Unfortunately it does not always happen.

CONCLUSION

From just three premises I have shown that all of Parts 2 and 3 of this book are inherent components of projects and project management, and I have shown that the nature of some of the tools is also inherent. I have also shown that Human Resource Management (Part 3) is also inherent. They do not need to be assumed as Cleland and King (1983) did. I have shown that the use of some common tools and techniques are inherent, and some can be derived from other management disciplines. With others I have shown the tools and techniques must have certain features, which existing tools do have, but it can only be shown empirically that the existing tools do actually meet the need.

The theory presented here does not preclude existing theories, such as the systems approach (Cleland and King 1983), the process approach (Turner 1999), and the project as an information processing system (Winch 2005). But they can be overlaid on this theory to provide additional insights. They do not need to be the primary focus of the theory, nor should they be. The theory presented here sets Project Management firmly as part of Organizational and Management Theory, enabling the discipline to draw on insights from other management disciplines.

REFERENCES AND FURTHER READING

Crawford, L.H., Hobbs, J.B. and Turner, J.R., 2005, *Project Categorization Systems: aligning capability with strategy for better results,* Newtown Square, PA: Project Management Institute.

Clarke, T., (ed.), 2004, *Theories of Corporate Governance: the philosophical foundations of corporate governance,* London: Routledge.

Cleland, D.I. and King, W.R., 1983, *Systems Analysis and Project Management,* 3rd edition, New York: McGraw-Hill.

Jensen, M.C., 2000, *The Theory of the Firm: governance, residual claims, and organizational forms,* Harvard University Press, Cambridge, MA.

Maylor, H., (ed.), 2006, 'Rethinking project Management', special issue of *The International Journal of Project Management,* 24(8), (653–637).

PMI®, 2004, *A Guide to the Project Management Body of Knowledge,* 3rd edition, Newtown Square, PA: Project Management Institute.

Turner, J.R., 1999, *The Handbook of Project Based Management,* 2nd edition, London: McGraw-Hill.

Turner, J.R., (ed), 2003, *Contracting for Project Management,* Aldershot: Gower.

Turner, J.R., 2004, *The Management of Large Projects and Programmes for Web Delivery,* Aldershot: Gower.

Turner, J.R., 2004, 'The financing of projects', in *The Handbook of Managing Projects,* ed P.W.G. Morris and J.K. Pinto, New York: Wiley.

Turner, J.R. and Keegan, A.E., 2001, 'Mechanisms of governance in the project-based organization: the role of the broker and steward', *European Management Journal,* 19(3), 254–267.

Turner, J.R. and Müller, R., 2003, 'On the nature of the project as a temporary organization', *International Journal of Project Management,* 21(1), 1–8.

Turner, J.R. and Müller, R., 2004, 'Communication and cooperation on projects between the project owner as principal and the project manager as agent', *The European Management Journal,* 22(3), 327–336.

Winch, G.M., 2005, 'Rethinking project management: project organizations as information processing systems?', in Slevin, D.P., Cleland, D.I. and Pinto, J.K., (eds.), *Frontiers of Project Management Research, volume 2,* Newtown Square, PA: Project Management Institute.

Project Success and Strategy

6

Rodney Turner

I said as part of the introduction to the last chapter, that project management is the process by which projects are successfully delivered, whatever 'successfully' means. In this chapter I am going to look at the issue of project success. There are two components of project success, project success criteria and project success factors:

- project success factors are those elements of the project and its management which can be influenced to increase the chance of a successful outcome – they are the independent variables through which we try to influence the achievement of project success
- project success criteria are the measures (both quantitative and qualitative) against which a project is judged to be successful – they are the dependent variables by which we judge whether or not we achieved a successful outcome

John Wateridge (1995) suggested that when addressing a project, our thought processes should follow a three step process:

Step 1: First we should think about how we are going to judge our project to be successful
Step 2: Then we should think about what success factors will help us achieve those desired outcomes
Step 3: Then we can think about what tools and techniques can be used to help us to implement those success factors

Unfortunately, many people's thinking follows the reverse process. They start assembling tools and techniques to manage the project, then they start thinking about how they can use those to influence the outcome, and sometime towards the end of the project they start considering how they might judge it to be successful. John Wateridge also identified a necessary condition for project success. That was to:

agree the success criteria with all the stakeholders before you start, (and repeatedly at configuration review points throughout the project)

You need to think about how you will judge project success before you start, and get the agreement of all the stakeholders. Everybody working on the project must have a common vision of what you are trying to achieve, so they are all working towards the same end objective, and all following the same road to get there. Even small differences of opinion can lead to sizeable divergences later. Just having a different idea about the relative importance of time, cost and functionality can lead to different people taking different decisions in response to project issues, generating to quite large differences at the end.

In this chapter, I will follow the three steps outlined above. I will start by considering how we judge project success, then I will consider what factors will help us achieve the desired outcomes, and finally I will explain how to formulate a project strategy and choose appropriate tools to help achieve a successful outcome.

PROJECT SUCCESS CRITERIA

Beauty is in the eye of the beholder, and so it is with project success. Much has been written over the last thirty years about how we judge project success, but the reality is that different people judge the same project to be successful or not in different ways, and indeed some people can judge a certain project to be successful while others judge the same project to be unsuccessful. Senior management may judge a change project to be a success, while some middle managers who have a reduced sphere of influence may think that they did not achieve their personal aims. Staff members whose jobs have been enriched may be happy, while others who have been made redundant unhappy, while yet others who took early retirement happy. The important thing, as I said above, is to try to obtain an overall consensus about what the aims of the project are and how success will be judged.

John Wateridge (1995) sent out a questionnaire to people involved in IT projects. He asked them their role in the project, were they a sponsor, user, designer or project manager. He then asked them to think of two projects they had been involved with, one a success and the other a failure, and asked them to say how they judged the result. On almost all successful projects all four groups of people said it had been a success because it had provided value to the sponsor, whereas on unsuccessful projects they all had different views. The sponsors said it had been unsuccessful because it didn't provide them with value, the users because it didn't provide them with the functionality they wanted, the designers because it was a poor design, and the project managers because it was late and overspent. What a surprise! When everybody is aiming towards the same outcome, value for the sponsor, the project is a success. But when they are all ploughing their own furrow and concentrating on what is important to them the project is a failure (at least to some of them). What is sad about the unsuccessful project is that what people are focusing on is important, but there seems to be a way that you can focus on what is important to you, to the detriment of the project, or you can focus on what is important to you, but balance that against the needs of the rest of the project. Projects are coupled systems. To achieve the best outcome for the project, you need to do what is best for the project overall, and not isolated parts of the project. That means you need to balance the functionality against the feasibility of the design, and both against cost and time to deliver what is best value for the sponsor.

Figure 6.1 shows a list of possible success criteria for a project, the stakeholders who are interested in each criterion, and the timescales over which they are judged. We see in fact that meeting the performance targets, the dreaded golden triangle of time, cost and quality that has dominated project management thinking for so long, is just one of many. Unfortunately, it, together with the satisfaction of the project team and satisfaction of suppliers, is judged at the end of the project, and so may dominate the appreciation of stakeholders at the time. The other criteria are not judged for months or even years later. However, that can lead to a situation where the project team are ecstatic at the end of the project, but appreciation of the project can change over the months and years that follow as it becomes apparent that the asset delivered does not function and is not delivering the desired benefits.

The list in Figure 6.1 can be criticised because it focuses on people directly involved in the project or the asset it produces. There are other stakeholders, bystanders and on-lookers, who have a view of what is happening. Their appreciation can be judged during the project or over the months or years that follow.

The message behind Figure 6.1 is that the success of the project is in the eye of the beholder, and it is necessary to balance the needs of all the stakeholders to achieve the best overall outcome for the project. Value for the sponsor is the key criterion, but in order to deliver that, the asset must function and be delivered at or near the desired cost, time and other performance targets. The project is a coupled system, and the best overall balance of the success criteria must be sought rather than just focusing on one of them.

Some project managers have heard me say this and said that in their annual appraisal they are judged on how many of their projects were finished on cost and time. They are not judged on how many of their projects delivered value to the sponsor. So they ask me what should they focus on: completing their projects to cost and time, or providing value to the sponsor? I say they should focus on

Success criteria	Interested stakeholder	Period over which judged
Satisfies providers of finance	Providers of finance	Project end plus years
Achieves purpose	Governance council	Project end plus years
Satisfies sponsor and owner	Governance council	Project end plus years
Satisfies consumers	Consumers	Project end plus months
Satisfies users	Users	Project end plus months
Functions as intended	Users	Project end plus months
Meets performance targets	All	Project end
Satisfies project team	Project team	Project end
Satisfies suppliers	Suppliers	Project end

Figure 6.1　Project success criteria, interested stakeholders and time horizon

changing the appraisal system because it is not consistent with good project management. But then of course you cannot judge a project manager in his or her annual appraisal on benefits to the owner obtained years down the track. The solution is to judge the project manager on the first year's revenue generated by the new asset. That can be measured at the time of an annual appraisal.

WEIGHTINGS OF AND PERFORMANCE AGAINST THE SUCCESS CRITERIA

Ralf Müller and I, in work we have done for PMI® (2006), were able to judge the relative weightings different project managers gave to the different success criteria, and how well they performed against the criteria. We were able to judge project managers depending on:

- the type of project
- whether they worked in the public or private sector
- their nationality
- their age
- their gender
- whether or not they were certified
- their level of education
- their job title

We found very few differences in either the weightings given to success criteria or their performance against the criteria. There was absolutely no difference by gender in either rating or performance. The few differences we found were as follows:

114

(a) The weightings that project managers gave to the success criteria varied by age. Across the board, project managers in their-mid twenties rated all the success criteria less highly than managers in their mid-thirties. The ratings fell again for managers in their mid-forties and rose for managers in their mid-50s. There seems to be an element of pessimism for managers in their twenties, but as they become experienced they become more optimistic. Then cynicism sets in during their forties, but they then become totally self-confident in their fifties.

(b) Managers from Western countries rated all the success criteria lower on average than managers from Asian countries.

(c) Managers from Asian countries rated the satisfaction of other stakeholders significantly higher than in Western countries, perhaps indicating the importance of relationships in those countries.

(d) Managers from the private sector rated repeat business with the client more highly than managers from the public sector, perhaps understandably.

(e) There was no difference in the performance of project managers by level of educational qualification, which would suggest that project management is not an intellectual skill. There was no difference between certified and non-certified project managers on low performing projects. But on high performing projects, certified project managers performed significantly better than non-certified project managers. This would indicate that certification does not make a bad project manager any better; there are flaws in his or her competence that certification cannot correct. But certification does help competent project managers; it makes them more competent.

KEY PERFORMANCE INDICATORS

It is worthwhile on a project to identify key performance indicators, KPIs. These are measures of the success criteria that can be tracked throughout the project to see that the project is on course for a successful completion. You don't want to wait until the end of the project and find it has not met its targets. You would like forewarning so you can take corrective action.

The KPIs you use will depend on the important success criteria for your project. On a recent major project, an oil company tracked the following KPIs:

1. capital cost
2. schedule
3. accidents involving its staff
4. accidents involving contractor staff
5. variations to plan
6. predicted first year production

7. satisfaction among other stakeholders including:
   ● government agencies
   ● contractors
   ● partners

A tool that is used to monitor KPIs is the project dashboard, Figure 6.2. In this figure, quantitative KPIs are tracked by the bars. The arrow under the line represents the target for the KPI, and the cross indicates the current predicted out-turn value. It is common to colour the bars green for on or ahead of plan, yellow for slightly behind plan, but controllable, and red for crisis. The traffic lights are used for qualitative criteria such as stakeholder satisfaction. Green indicates satisfied, yellow slightly unsatisfied and red very unsatisfied.

A problem with the dashboard as indicated is it shows performance today. It does not show how it is changing with time. The milestone tracker chart, Chapter 19, and earned value chart, chapter 20, can do that for time and cost respectively. Similar tools can be developed for other quantitative KPIs.

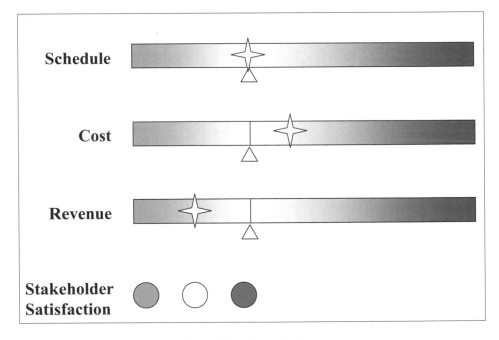

Figure 6.2 Project dashboard

PROJECT SUCCESS FACTORS

Over the last 40 years there has been a changing understanding of what contributes to project success. Kam Jugdev and Ralf Müller (2005) described how our understanding of project success has changed in that time. They identified four periods during which our view of what contributes to success has successively widened:

1. In the 1960s to 1970s, project success focused on the implementation stage, measuring time, cost and functionality improvements.
2. In the 1980s and 1990s, the quality of the planning and hand-over was identified as important. Lists of Critical Success Factors (CSF), which also took into account organizational and stakeholder perspectives, became popular.
3. More recently, new CSF frameworks have been developed on the basis that success is stakeholder dependent and involves interaction between project supplier and recipient. Additional dimensions taken into account during this period have been: the project's product and its utilization; staff growth and development; the customer; benefits to the delivery organization; senior management; and the environment.
4. For the future, Jugdev and Müller anticipate a continuation in the broadening of the definition of success, especially taking into account factors from the conceptual stages of the project life-cycle and the close-down of the project's product, together with an increasing understanding of the importance of the project sponsor's view of success.

1960s and 1970s

In the 1960s and 1970s, project management focused very much on the application of CPA (critical path analysis) and PERT (the programme evaluation and review technique) as the tools to be used, mainly in the management of time and resource usage. Therefore the focus was on the use of tools, rather than on the identification of critical success factors. Also, somewhat to the detriment of project management, people forgot about tools such as work breakdown and earned value analysis invented by the US military in the early 1950s but discarded as people focused on CPA and PERT.

1980s

In the 1980s there was an explosion of research. First, people rediscovered some of the discarded tools, but there was also a recognition that the management of time and resources and the focus on time, cost and quality was not the whole answer. People began to research critical success factors on projects. Andersen et al (2003), in the first Norwegian edition of their book published in 1984, were the first to identify a list of success factors (or in their case failure factors) on a project. Based on Kristoffer Grude's work as managing director of a software house they

117

identified pitfalls at four stages of a project. Their opposite of pitfalls are expressed as success factors in Figure 6.3. Next Peter Morris (1988) identified a list of success and failure factors, again at four stages of a project. His list is in Figure 6.4. Pinto and Slevin (1988) produced the most widely quoted list. Their list is still the most commonly used. Many other lists were produced, but there is not space to reproduce them all here.

Project stage	Success factors
Foundation	Align the project with the business Gain commitment of involved managers Create a shared vision
Planning	Use multiple levels Use simple friendly tools Encourage creativity Estimate realistically
Implementation	Negotiate resource availability Agree cooperation Define management responsibility Gain commitment of resource providers Define channels of communication Project manager as manager not chief technologist

Control	Integrate plans and progress reports
	Formalize the review process through
	  ▪ defined intervals
	  ▪ defined criteria
	  ▪ controlled attendance
	Use sources of authority

Figure 6.3 Project success factors after Andersen *et al* (2003)

1990s to now

During the early 1990s, the focus switched to success criteria, Wateridge (1995). It was Wateridge who suggested that you should first identify how we would judge our project to be successful, and then from that focus on appropriate success factors, and then choose the right tools to facilitate the use of those factors.

However, it was felt that even though the lists of success factors suggested above had led to improved project performance, they were not the whole answer. Project success rates had improved considerably during the 1980s, but many were

Stage	Success factors	Barriers
Formation	Personal ambition Top management support Team motivation Clear objectives Technological advantage	Unmotivated team Poor leadership Technical limitations Money
Build-up	Team motivation Personal motivation Top management support Technological expertise	Unmotivated team Conflict in objectives Poor leadership Poor top management support Technical problems
Execution	Team motivation Personal motivation Client support Top management support	Unmotivated team Poor top management support Deficient procedures
Close-out	Personal motivation Team motivation Top management support Financial support	Poor control Poor financial support Ill-defined objectives Poor leadership

Figure 6.4   Project success factors after Morris (1988)

still failing. So in the late 1980s there was renewed interest in identifying further success factors. This does not mean the work of the 1980s was wrong. It was just not enough. The most significant contribution was made by Terry Cooke-Davies (2001). He picked up on an idea that had been around for a while, namely that there is a difference between the success of the project, and the success of the project management. In my book (1999), I give examples of projects that were well managed, but still did not meet their business objectives, and projects that were badly managed but in spite of that were still deemed successful. Terry Cooke-Davies suggested that successful project management would help achieve the performance measures of project success, particularly time and cost, but the project would only be successful if it achieved its business objectives, the upper items in Figure 6.1. He identified factors which help achieve the performance measures of project success, and factors which help achieve business success, Figure 6.6. Notice that he talks about having an effective benefits delivery programme, which he writes about in Chapter 13, that you need effective programme and portfolio management, (Chapters 1, 2 and 3), and that you need to develop enterprise-wide project management capability, (Chapter 33).

Success factor	Description
1. Project mission	Clearly defined goals and direction
2. Top management support	Resources, authority and power for implementation
3. Schedule and plans	Detailed specification of implementation process
4. Client consultation	Communication with and consultation of all stakeholders
5. Personnel	Recruitment, selection and training of competent personnel
6. Technical tasks	Ability of the required technology and expertise
7. Client acceptance	Selling of the final product to the end users
8. Monitoring and feed back	Timely and comprehensive control
9. Communication	Provision of timely data to key players
10. Trouble-shooting	Ability to handle unexpected problems

Figure 6.5　Project success factors after Pinto and Slevin (1988)

THE CONTRIBUTION OF THE PROJECT MANAGER

Ralf Müller and I (2006) identified that the above lists almost studiously ignore the project manager. Andersen et al say that the project manager should be a good manager, not the chief technologist, and Peter Morris does mention poor leadership as a failure factor at one stage of the project. The other two lists do not mention the project manager at all. There appear to be two beliefs in the project management community:

1. The first is that the project manager's competence makes no contribution to project success. As long as he or she uses the right tools and techniques the project will be successful.
2. The second is that as long as a given project manager has learnt to apply those tools and techniques well, he or she can apply them to any type of project, regardless of technology, discipline or domain.

At first sight these two beliefs appear different, but in fact they are two sides of the same coin. The first says the project manager makes no contribution to project success; all that is important is to use the right tools and techniques. The second says that having learnt the tools and techniques, the project manager can apply them to any project; that their own technical knowledge and emotional intelligence makes no contribution. Both these beliefs undervalue the project manager. They suggest that anybody, even the proverbial chimpanzee, can manage any project well, as long as they apply the right tools and techniques. The tools manage the project, not the person. It is also in stark contrast to the general management literature where it has been shown over the last seventy years that the manager's competence makes a direct contribution to the success of the organization they manage, and different competency profiles are required in different circumstances. We should expect it to be the same in the temporary organization that is a project.

Project management success factors contributing to time completion:
F1 Adequacy of company-wide education on risk management
F2 Maturity of organization's processes for assigning ownership of risk
F3 Adequacy with which a visible risk register is maintained
F4 Adequacy of an up-to-date risk management plan
F5 Adequacy of documentation of organizational responsibilities on the project
F6 Project or stage duration as far below three years as possible, preferably below one year

Project management success factors contributing to budget completion:
F7 Changes to scope only made through a mature scope change control process
F8 Integrity of the performance measurement base-line

Additional project success factors contributing to successful benefits realization:
F9 Existence of an effective benefits delivery and management process that involves the mutual cooperation of project management and line management functions
F10 Portfolio and programme management practices that allow the enterprise to resource fully a suite of projects that are thoughtfully and dynamically matched to the corporate strategy and business objectives
F11 A site of project, programme and portfolio management metrics that provide 'direct line of sight' feedback on current project performance and anticipated future success, so that project, programme, portfolio and corporate decisions can be aligned
F12 An effective means of learning from experience on projects that combines explicit knowledge with tacit knowledge in a way that encourages people to learn and to embed that learning into continuous improvement of project management processes and practices.

Figure 6.6   **Project success factors after Cooke-Davis (2001)**

The project manager has not been totally ignored. Various authors have attempted to match the project manager's leadership against the schools of leadership described by David Partington in Chapter 35. From work with my students at Henley Management College, I identified seven traits of effective project managers (Turner 1999). Davidson Framc (2003) developed the idea of four leadership styles of project managers, and showed how different styles are appropriate at different stages of the project life-cycle. Anne Keegan and Deanne den Hartog tried to show that a transformational management style is appropriate for project managers. However, although they found a preference for the transformational style, their results were not statistically significant. Ralf Müller and I (2006) felt that if they had limited themselves to complex projects they would have found that transformational leadership was best, because, in fact, transformational leadership is appropriate on complex projects, but transactional leadership is best on simpler projects, and there transformational leadership does not work. Liz Lee-Kelley and Loon Leong (2003) showed that what is important is the project manager's perception of success, and that is based on self-confidence that comes with experience. Finally Lynn Crawford (2005) and Dainty et al (2005) explored the competence of project managers in different circumstances.

School	Authors	Idea
Trait school	Turner (1999)	Seven traits of effective project leaders
Behaviour school	Frame (2003), Turner (1999)	Four leadership behaviours: Laissez-faire, democratic, autocratic, bureaucratic
Contingency school	Frame (2003), Turner (1999)	Different behaviours at different stages of the life-cycle
Charismatic school	Keegan and den Hartog (2004)	No preference on projects for transformational or transactional leadership
Emotional intelligence school	Lee-Kelley and Leong (2003)	Perception of success depends on the manager's emotional intelligence and experience.
Competence school	Crawford (2005)	Different competence profiles for different projects
	Dainty et al (2005)	Twelve behavioural competencies associated with construction project management

Figure 6.7 Project leadership and the schools of leadership

Ralf Müller and I (2006) adopted a leadership competency model developed at Henley Management College (Dulewicz and Higgs 2003) with fifteen leadership competencies grouped into three competency areas. We showed that the project manager's leadership style is a success factor on projects. We showed that project managers should score highly on emotional competencies, and that they should be conscientious and good at motivating and communicating. We also found differences by types of projects. On almost all project types project managers should score highly on emotional competencies. But, as I said above, managers of simple projects should have a transactional leadership style whereas the managers of complex projects should have a transformational style. Further, managers of engineering projects should be conscientious and good at motivating; the managers of information systems projects should be self-aware and good at communicating; the managers of organizational change projects should be good at communicating and motivating. So the project manager's leadership style is a success factor on projects, and different styles are appropriate for different types of projects.

Because people, including the project manager, are important on projects, the last part of this book is devoted to the management of people.

A STRATEGY FOR PROJECT IMPLEMENTATION

Chapter 2 looks at how to link project strategy to corporate strategy, and how to move from corporate strategy to project strategy. What I have said here should be consistent with what Peter Morris and Ashley Jamieson say in that chapter. I have suggested that you should start by identifying the success criteria for your project and from that choose the success factors that will help you achieve the identified criteria. From there you can develop the strategy for implementing your project. The success factors for your project should be driven by corporate strategy, and thus the project strategy should be linked to corporate strategy. To determine your project strategy, you can use one of the models for the project management body of knowledge, Figure 1.1. Based on the work of Peter Morris (Morris and Hough 1987; Morris 1997) I developed the seven force model of project management as a guide to developing a project implementation strategy.

Group	Competency
Intellectual (IQ)	1. critical analysis and judgement
	2. vision and imagination
	3. strategic perspective
Managerial (MQ)	4. engaging communication
	5. managing resources
	6. empowering
	7. developing
	8. achieving
Emotional (EQ)	9. self-awareness
	10. emotional resilience
	11. motivation
	12. sensitivity
	13. influence
	14. intuitiveness
	15. conscientiousness

Figure 6.8   Fifteen leadership competencies after Dulewicz and Higgs (2003)

SEVEN FORCES MODEL OF PROJECT MANAGEMENT

This model shows seven forces acting on a project, and you need policies for managing all seven forces. The forces are:

Two forces external to the parent organization:

I   The drivers arising from the sponsorship of the organization's financiers, the benefit they expect, and the urgency that creates

123

II The resistance arising from political, economic, social, technical, legal and environmental influences in the project's context

Two forces internal to the parent organization, but external to the project:

III The drivers arising from the definition of the project required to deliver the returns to the financiers
IV The resistance arising from the attitudes of people within the organization

Three drivers from within the project:

V The people working on the project, their knowledge and skills, needs for careers, team working, leadership and industrial relations
VI The management systems to be used to manage functionality, configuration, work, organization, quality, cost, time, risk and safety, and the life-cycle to be followed
VII The organization of the project, the roles and responsibilities of the people working on the project, the numbers required, and the need to procure additional skills from outside the parent organization where they don't exist internally.

THE SEVEN FORCES AND THE BODY OF KNOWLEDGE

There is a simple relationship between seven forces and the areas of the body of knowledge as outlined in Chapter 1. The seven forces model does not change the Body of Knowledge, it is just another way of mapping it.

1. Forces I and II make up the context of the project (Part I of this book), and the need to finance the project. We need policies for managing all the influences from the project's context. These are the returns expected by the project's and parent organization's sponsors, promoters or financiers, and the influences arising from the project's environment, including stakeholders in the community.
2. Forces III and VI make up the systems for implementation of the project. We need policies for how we will manage functionality, configuration, project organization, quality, cost, time, risk, and safety (Part II of this book), and the life-cycle (Part III of this book). Force III addresses policies on how the project will be defined to meet the needs of the parent organization. This includes objectives, functionality and configuration. Figure 5.2 also shows that Force III includes policies on the technology to be used in the development of the project's product.

124

3. Forces IV and V represent the people on the project and in the parent organization (Part IV of this book). We need policies for leadership and team building, industrial relations and stakeholder management. We also need policies for ethical behaviour.

4. Finally, Force VII represents the resourcing of the project and the need to procure goods and service externally. (Procurement is not covered in this book).

REFERENCES AND FURTHER READING

Andersen, E.S., Grude, K.V., and Haug, T., 2003, *Goal Directed Project Management*, 3rd ed, London: Kogan Page.

Cooke-Davies, T., 2001, 'The "real" project success factors', *International Journal of Project Management,* 20(3), 185–190.

Crawford, L.H., 2005, 'Senior management perceptions of project management competence', *International Journal of Project Management,* 23(1), 7–16.

Dainty, A.R.J., Cjeng, M. and Moore, D.R., 2005, 'Competency-based model for predicting construction project managers' performance', *Journal of Management in Engineering, 2005* (January), 2–9.

Dulewicz, V. and Higgs, M. J., 2003, 'Design of a new instrument to assess Leadership dimensions and styles', *Henley Working Paper Series* HWP 0311, Henley-on-Thames, UK: Henley Management College.

Frame, J.D., 2003, *Managing Projects in Organizations,* 3rd ed, San Francisco, CA: Jossey Bass.

Judgev, K. & Müller, R. 2005, 'A Retrospective Look at Our Elvolving Understanding of Project Success'. *Project Management Journal,* 36(4), 19–31.

Keegan, A.E. and Den Hartog, D.N., 2004, 'Transformational leadership in a project-based environment: a comparative study of the leadership styles of project managers and line managers', *International Journal of Project Management,* 22(8), 609–618.

Lee-Kelley, L., and Leong, K.L., 2003, 'Turner's five functions of project-based management and situational leadership in IT services projects', *International Journal of Project Management,* 21(8), 583–591.

Morris, P.W.G., 1988, 'Managing project interfaces', in Cleland, D.I. and King, W.R., (eds.), *Project Management Handbook,* 2nd edition, New York, NY: Van Nostrand Reinhold.

Morris, P.W.G., 1997, *The Management of Projects,* 2nd edition, London, UK: Thomas Telford.

Morris, P.W.G. and Hough, G., 1987, *The Anatomy of Major Projects: a study of the reality of project management,* Chichester: Wiley.

Pinto, J.K. and Slevin, D.P., 1988, 'Critical success factors in effective project implementation', in Cleland, D.I. and King, W.R., (eds.), *Project Management Handbook,* 2nd edition, New York, NY: Van Nostrand Reinhold.

Turner, J.R., 1999, *The Handbook of Project-based Management: improving the processes for achieving strategic objectives,* 2nd edition, London, UK: McGraw-Hill.

Turner, J.R. and Müller, R., 2006, *Choosing Appropriate Project Managers: Matching their Leadership Style to the Type of Project,* Newtown Square, PA: Project Management Institute.

Wateridge, J. H., 1995, 'IT projects: a basis for success', *International Journal of Project Management,* 13(3).

7 Processes and Procedures

Richard Pharro and Colin Bentley

Is it a process, is it a methodology, is it a method, is it a framework, or is it a standard? Whatever it is called, its purpose is to aid management of the process to successfully deliver a project. Projects are always undertaken within an enterprise culture. An enterprise can be either for or not for profit. Projects require the complete involvement of a project team, a consistent vocabulary, appropriate tools, a framework within which they are managed, a process by, and a standard to which they are delivered. The culture and focus of the project team and the critical success factors will vary significantly but all projects need to be managed in a way that engenders confidence in the project sponsors. During the delivery process, the project sponsors require interim milestones or checkpoints to be met and that the final product, rather than the original idea, be right for their needs, thereby giving them maximum opportunity to obtain the business benefits from the project.

The rationale for a project stems from the corporate objectives and its part in the programme or portfolio to deliver them (Chapter 2, 3 and 4). Rodney Turner and Bob Cochrane (1992) in their now famous Goals and Methods Matrix, Figure 7.1, introduced four different types of project depending on how well defined are the goals of the project and the methods of delivering them. Projects are classified in terms of clarity of *what* is required and *how* to do it. A good process should be capable of dealing with all four types of projects, with:

1. Clear requirements: clear delivery process (solution)
2. Clear requirements: unclear delivery process
3. Unclear requirements: clear delivery process
4. Unclear requirements: unclear delivery process

In this chapter we consider standard methods of project management; that is, standard processes and procedures. We start by considering what we understand by a method (framework, methodology, standard), and then describe the three commonly used in Europe BS6079, PRINCE2™1 and ISO 10,006.

<hr>

1 PRINCE™ is a Registered Trade Mark of the Office of Government Commerce.

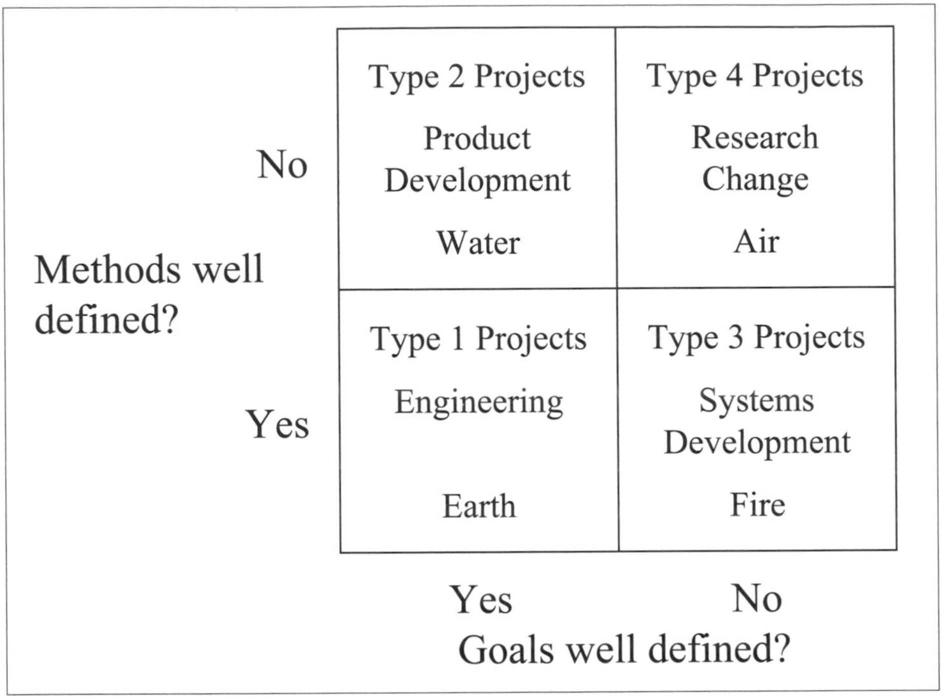

No	Type 2 Projects Product Development Water	Type 4 Projects Research Change Air
Methods well defined? **Yes**	Type 1 Projects Engineering Earth	Type 3 Projects Systems Development Fire
	Yes	No

Goals well defined?

Figure 7.1 Goals and methods matrix

METHOD

A *method*, or *methodology*, is a structured approach for delivering a project. It should be derived from a defined project process, and be capable of accommodating all four types of project. Its purpose is to provide clarity in the following areas:

1. The project's objectives
2. Roles and responsibilities of the key project participants
3. A series of check points at which progress and relevance can be reviewed and checked
4. A set of procedures for the day to day management of the project team
5. Control metrics for work within stages to provide early warnings of potential problems

The project's deliverables are developed as part of the corporate management or strategic planning process (Chapters 2 and 15) used to establish the business case for the project. There are various techniques available by which the project's objectives are established which will vary depending on the type of project.

Developing the business case is usually omitted from the project management method but is an essential part of the *process* of project management. This is not a semantic differentiation but is important in understanding the benefits of both a process and a method. The method is therefore a part of the process.

WHAT IS THE PROJECT MANAGEMENT PROCESS?

The *process* must include all stages of the project management life-cycle to define how inputs are to be converted into desired customer outputs, Chapter 25. Within this life-cycle two stages are usually outside the responsibility of the project team, Figure 7.2, namely:

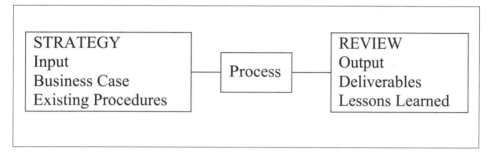

Figure 7.2   The project management process, from inputs to outputs

1. *Strategic Planning:* Developing the business case
2. *Review:* Ensuring the lessons learned are used to update the organization's corporate and project management procedures

Once approved by the sponsoring organization, the business case or rationale for the project will define in high level terms the reason for the project and what outcome is sought. This will determine the type of project. For example, if the business case identifies a requirement for a new production line to increase capacity by 30%, both the requirements and solution should be capable of being developed in detail by the project team. If the business case identifies an opportunity to launch an entirely new product the project team would want to undertake a series of feasibility studies before selecting a single option for detailed development. In this case both the 'what and the how' for providing maximum benefit are unclear. Regardless of the type of project, the project management *method* must be capable of delivering the project to achieve the objectives defined in the business case.

WHAT IS A METHOD?

The method is a set of management processes each with clearly defined resources and activities, which transform inputs into the outputs defined in the business case. This encompasses all the traditional project management activities essential to planning, doing, managing, reviewing and controlling the work required to deliver the project. Many methods are available; most are either proprietary or based on specific planning techniques, but there are only three which are clearly in the public domain and are non proprietary namely:

1. BS 6079 A guide to Project Management
2. PRINCE2™ Managing successful projects
3. ISO 10006 Quality Management – guidelines to quality in project management

They vary in approach and depth of content due to the different objectives of the sponsoring organizations and the background and make up of the authoring panels. The benefit of this is that one of these 'standard' processes should be suitable for your project. None should be used blindly and probably none is the perfect solution, but any of them should help you establish an environment in which to increase the chance of project success.

This chapter covers the content of these three processes in depth and does not attempt to compare or recommend, as to do this in isolation would be meaningless.

BS 6079: A GUIDE TO PROJECT MANAGEMENT

The guide identifies ten stages in a project

1. *Concept, basic ideas:* consideration of technical feasibility, commercial acceptability and a balance between costs and benefits (Chapters 2, 3, 13, 14, 15, 27 and 28)
2. *Feasibility:* identify those ideas worth developing further and find a senior manager to champion the project. Collect information from throughout the organization and appoint the project manager (Chapters 14, 15, 18, 27 and 28)
3. *Evaluation:* planning and full evaluation of all activities, (Chapter 15, 16, 19, 20 and 21)
4. *Applications:* defining the desired output in financial terms (Chapter 13, 14, 15 and 16)
5. *Authorization:* obtained at the appropriate level within the organization (Chapter 2)
6. *Implementation including design:* performance of the work of the project (Chapter 29)

7. *Control/accountability, periodic reviews and updates:* ensuring the project is completed in accordance with its success criteria (Chapters 5 and 26)
8. *Completion and handover:* the project team are disbanded and dispersed to other projects, (Chapters 30 and 31)
9. *Operation:* running of the facility or asset to deliver the expected benefit, and pay for the cost of doing the project, and for the cost of decommissioning
10. *Close down and cessation of operations:* shut down of the facility
11. *Termination and disposal of residual assets:* clear-up

Senior management are responsible for establishing the objectives and constraints of the project. They must also ensure proper operational procedures and controls are in place and subsequently used, and they must delegate the appropriate level of authority to the project manager to ensure the delivery of the project.

THE PROJECT MANAGEMENT PROCESS IN BS 6079

The project management process in BS 6079 is divided into two parts:

1. project planning
2. project control

Project planning is the development of a workable project plan that describes tasks in terms of who does what, when, at what cost and to what specification. This needs to be at a level of detail the project manager considers necessary and sufficient for effective and efficient project control. The second part of the process is to use the plan to control and co-ordinate the progress of the project. A basic project plan should contain:

1. Introduction and summary
2. Commitment acceptance
3. Project Work Breakdown Structure
4. Schedule
5. Statement of Work

The suggested process within BS 6079 is shown in Figure 7.3.

PROJECT PLANNING

The following are the steps of project planning

1. **Authorization**: for the whole project or up to specified milestones, at which point further authorization will depend on satisfactory progress.
2. **Establish the project team**: includes setting limits of authority for the Project Manager, developing incentive mechanisms, and setting up a communications framework for the project team.

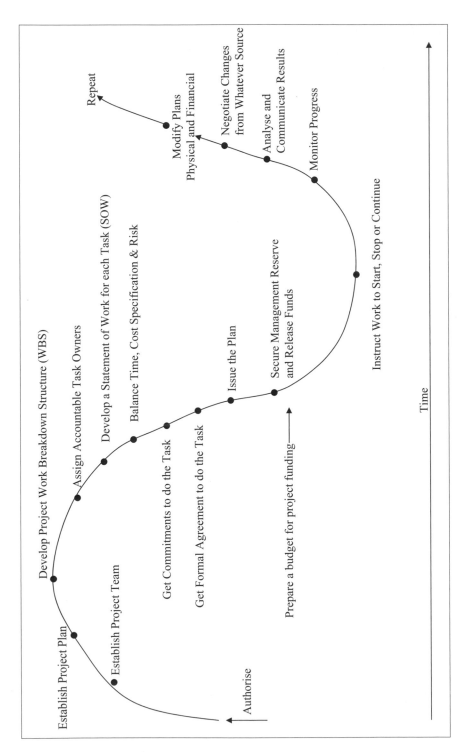

Figure 7.3   The BS 6079 project management process flow

3. **Development of Project Work Breakdown Structure (WBS)**: this is the most useful form of project breakdown, but it could be broken down by activity or cost elements.

4. **Assign a single accountable task owner to project tasks**: essential for the successful delivery of the task, but at the same time it is important to avoid having too many task owners, as this could lead to an unmanageable number of tasks and owners.

5. **Develop a Statement of Work (SOW) for project tasks**: This provides the requirements for each task and should contain:
   - A task reference code
   - A summary description of the requirement
   - The name of the person accountable for the completion of the task
   - A list of key deliverables
   - Timescales for the deliverables
   - A schedule of task dependencies and subsidiary tasks
   - A schedule of costs by cost element
   - An assessment of risks associated with the task
   - Performance measurement and task completion criteria
   - A description of the work content of the task
   - Reporting requirements
   - The names of the task owners (if known)

6. **Balance time, cost, integrity of specification and risk**: achieves the optimum solution for carrying out the project.

7. **Obtain commitments to do project tasks**: task owners should formally agree the appropriate tasks, and that the work can be completed as defined in the plan.

8. **Finalize the agreement**: the Project Manager is content that the plan satisfies requirements against agreements.

PROJECT CONTROL

Once the plan has been issued, the following guidelines should be used to manage changes to the plan:

- The Project Manager should be responsible for the control of the project plan and should authorize any changes. BS 6079 clearly assumes that the project manager has authority for approving changes and revisions to the plan.
- Issue of a revised, agreed project plan should automatically cancel all previous issues.
- Each issue of the project plan should have a unique reference number.
- The reasons for the changes should be fully documented and cross-referenced.

- Work should not be released from a draft project management plan.
- No item of work should be included in more than one project plan.
- The plan does not need to be reissued if the change is minor provided all the plan holders are notified of the change.
- The project manager should confirm that the revised plan does not jeopardize any contractual obligations.

The following are the suggested elements of project control:

Manage the project budget

Funds should be released to the task owners in accordance with the project budget, whilst retaining a management reserve to cover unexpected problems or small changes. The task owner is responsible for ensuring that the costs incurred in performing the work are allocated the correct code in the project WBS.

Instruct work to begin, continue or stop

The project manager controls the project by releasing or stopping work according to the plan, and is responsible for the formal termination of the project following formal acceptance of the final project deliverables by the sponsor.

Monitor progress

Progress is monitored through regular reports from the task owners to the project manager. The following are considered essential elements of the progress reports:

- actual costs reported against planned costs and variances
- time and cost at completion for each task
- earned value

Manage the project

The project manager is responsible for coordinating the reports submitted by the task owners and keeping them and the sponsor informed of any potential difficulties.

Assess risks

The risk of success or failure should be assessed continuously by means of cost and time estimates of the interdependent network of tasks that make up the project.

Manage risks

The Project Manager identifies those tasks where an alternative course of action is needed to mitigate the risk, and selects the best risk avoidance tactics.

Motivate task owners

The Project Manager is responsible for motivating the task owners through good communication and performance incentives.

Negotiate

Project managers succeed or fail depending on their ability to negotiate effectively pre- and post-contract. They should particularly convince the task owners of their role as stakeholders in the project.

Summary of BS 6079

BS 6079 assumes a full product life-cycle from its inception through to decommissioning of the completed project at the end of its useful life. It is most suitable for large engineering projects, and once the project is underway expects the project manager to have full control with only limited recourse to the sponsor or owner. It is not prescriptive regarding project management techniques but does recommend that a product breakdown structure is used and highlights the benefits of using earned value for measuring progress.

PRINCE2™

PRINCE2™ (**P**rojects **in** **C**ontrolled **E**nvironments) is a method covering the organization, management and control of projects (OGC 2005). PRINCE was first developed in 1989 as a UK Government standard for IT project management. PRINCE2™, first published in 1982, was a substantially enhanced version developed for a wider range of projects, and so is a generic approach for the management of all types of project. PRINCE2™ is far more detailed than BS 6079 and provides greater detail on what should be done within the process.

THE PROJECT MANAGEMENT PROCESS IN PRINCE2™

The process model in PRINCE2™ is shown in Figure 7.4. PRINCE2™ uses the following eight processes to manage the project.

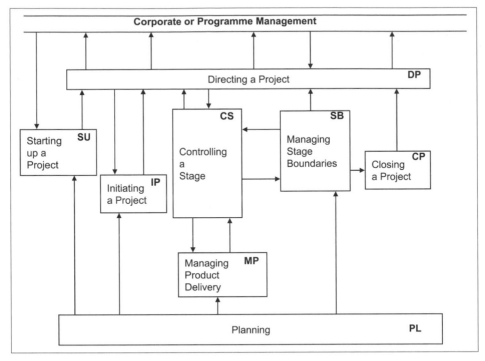

Figure 7.4 The PRINCE2 process model
© Crown Copyright 2007 – Reproduced under licence from OGC

Directing a Project (DP)

Directing a Project runs from the start-up of the project until its closure. This process is the responsibility of the Project Board that represents the business, user and supplier interests in the project. The high level representation of these three parties ensures that timely decisions can be made by informed people representing all the interests associated with the project. Some people get concerned with the supplier's involvement but providing appropriate commercial safeguards are agreed PRINCE2™ does encourage a partnership approach in delivering projects. The Project Board manages by exception and through pre-agreed decision points and its key responsibilities are:

1. Establishing the project management team and ensuring that there is sufficient reason to initiate a project (*Authorising Initiation*)
2. Starting the project off on the right foot (*Authorising a Project*)
3. Committing resources for the next stage (*Authorising a Stage or Exception Plan*)
4. Monitoring progress, providing advice and guidance, reacting to exception situations (*Giving Ad Hoc Direction*)

5. Confirming the project outcome and bringing the project to a controlled close (*Confirming Project Closure*)

This process does not cover the day-to-day activities of the Project Manager.

Starting Up a Project (SU)

This is the first process in PRINCE2™. This pre-project process is driven by the Project Mandate, which should define in high level terms the reason for the project and the required outcome. The amount of detail and clarity of the defined outcome depends on the type of project. It often takes far more time and effort than originally envisaged by the Project Sponsor to complete this process, which involves developing and agreeing the following project management documents (these are called products In PRINCE2™ terminology):

- a Risk Log
- the Project Approach (in general terms how a solution will be provided)
- the Project Brief
- designing and as far as possible appointing the project management team
- the initiation Stage Plan

Initiating a Project (IP)

This process develops the Project Plan in detail and records it in the Project Initiation Document which forms the baseline for the project. The objective of the Projecct Initiation Document are to:

- document and confirm that an acceptable Business Case exists for the project and that there is sufficient justification to proceed
- enable and encourage the Project Board to take ownership of the project
- ensure a firm and accepted foundation to the project prior to commencement of the work by establishing a stable management basis on which to proceed
- agree to the commitment of resources for the first specialist stage of the project
- provide the baseline for the decision-making processes required during the project's life
- ensure that the investment of time and effort required by the project is made wisely, taking account of the risks to the project

Managing Stage Boundaries (SB)

This process provides the Project Board with key decision points to enable it to decide whether to:

1. Continue with the project as planned, or
2. Make minor or major changes dictated by factors external to the project, or

3. Revise the expected outcome of the project in line with a changed business case, or
4. Terminate the project as its deliverables are no longer viable or the risks are considered too great.

For projects in the **fire** or **air** categories (Figure 7.1) the stage boundary is the point at which the Project Board agrees the details for the next stage. The benefits of this process are:

- assuring the Project Board that all deliverables planned in the current stage plan have been completed as defined
- providing the information needed for the Project Board to assess the continuing viability of the project
- providing the Project Board with information needed to approve completion of the current stage and authorize the start of the next stage, together with its delegated tolerance level
- recording any measurements or lessons that can help later stages of this project and/or other projects

The products of this process are:

- the status of the current stage plan showing performance against the original stage plan
- the next stage plan, for which approval is sought
- a revised project plan
- the updated risk log
- a revised business case
- an updated lessons learned report
- changes to the structure or staffing of the project management team
- an end stage report prepared by the project manager detailing the stage achievements

Controlling a Stage (CS)

This process describes monitoring and control activities of the project manager involved in ensuring a stage stays on course and reacts to unexpected events. The process forms the core of the project manager's work on the project. Throughout a stage there will be a cycle of:

1. authorizing work to be done
2. gathering progress information about that work
3. reviewing the stage and project situation
4. reporting
5. taking any necessary corrective action

6. risk management
7. change control

Products produced during this stage, on a cyclical basis are:

- new work packages
- highlight reports
- the quality log updated with planned dates for product quality checks
- project issues (suggestions, change requests, reports of items outside of specification)
- an updated risk log
- a regularly updated stage plan

There may also be the need for:

- an exception report/exception plan (notification when the project is expected to exceed its agreed tolerances)

Managing Product Delivery (MP)

The objective of this process is to ensure that whatever products are defined in Work Packages are delivered by:

1. negotiating details of work packages with the project manager
2. making certain that work on products contained in the work packages is effectively authorized and agreed
3. ensuring work conforms to the requirements of interfaces identified in the work package
4. ensuring that the work is done
5. assessing work progress and forecasts regularly
6. ensuring that completed products meet quality criteria
7. obtaining approval for the completed products

Products created or updated during this process are:

- team plans
- quality log updates, giving the project manager a view of quality work being done
- new project issues
- risk log updates
- checkpoint reports, regular progress reports from a team to a project manager

Closing a Project (CP)

The purpose of this process is to execute a controlled close to the project. The process covers the project manager's work to wrap up the project either at its end or at premature close. Most of the work is to prepare input to the Project Board to obtain its confirmation that the project may close; and the outcome of the project is handed over to the customer. The objectives of closing a project are, therefore, to:

1. check the extent to which objectives set out in project initiation document have been met
2. check to what extent all expected products are handed over and accepted by the customer
3. confirm the customer's acceptance of the deliverables
4. confirm that maintenance and operation arrangements are in place (where appropriate)
5. make any recommendations for follow-on actions (follow-on action recommendations)
6. capture lessons resulting from the project and complete the lessons learned report
7. prepare an end project report
8. archive the project files
9. produce a post project review plan
10. notify the host organization of the intention to disband the project organization and resources (end project notification)

Planning (PL)

Planning is a repeatable process, and plays an important role in other processes. It is covered in detail in Part III. PRINCE2™ uses a product-based approach which involves:

1. establishing what products are needed
2. determining the sequence in which each product should be produced
3. defining the form and content of each product

In addition, the process produces:

- the activities necessary for the creation and delivery of the project's products
- a product checklist, which is a table of the products to be produced by the work planned
- the risk log updated with any risk situation changes brought about by the plan

PRINCE2™ COMPONENTS

The above processes drive the project management activities and use eight components to produce the management documents, Figure 7.5.

Figure 7.5 The PRINCE2 components

© Crown Copyright 2007 – Reproduced under licence from OGC

Organizational Structure

The PRINCE2™ project management structure is based on a customer/supplier environment. The structure assumes that there will be a *customer* who will specify the desired outcome, make use of the outcome and probably pay for the project, and a (prime) *supplier* who will provide the resources and skills to create that outcome. The customer and supplier may be part of the same corporate body or may be independent of one another. In order to be flexible and meet the needs of different environments and different project sizes, PRINCE2™ defines roles which might be allocated, shared, divided or combined according to the project's needs. Associated with this is the concept that responsibilities for a role can be moved to another role or delegated, but should not be dropped. Some of the PRINCE2™ roles cannot be shared or delegated if they are to be undertaken effectively. The project manager role cannot be shared, nor can the project manager or project board roles be delegated. Corporate cultures differ, but PRINCE2™ can be used no matter what corporate organization structure exists. PRINCE2™ separates the management of the project from the work required to develop the products, and concentrates on the former. A fundamental principle is that the project organization structure has four layers responsible for:

- direction of the project
- day-to-day management of the project
- team management
- the work to create the products, that is the team members

The first three are known as the PRINCE2™ project management team.

Planning

When asked to describe a plan, many people think only of some sort of bar chart showing timescales. A PRINCE2™ plan is more comprehensive. It should contain the following elements (making maximum use of charts, tables and diagrams for clarity):

- the products to be produced
- the activities needed to create those deliverables
- the activities needed to validate the quality of deliverables
- the resources and time needed for all activities (including quality control)
- the dependencies between activities
- external dependencies for the delivery of information, products or services
- when activities will occur
- the requirements for people with specific skills
- the points at which progress will be monitored and controlled

PRINCE2™ proposes two basic levels of planning, the project plan and the stage plan, to reflect the needs of the different levels of management involved in the project. A stage plan may be broken down into a number of team plans (where, for example, a number of teams may be contributing to the work). Where a stage or project plan is forecast to exceed its tolerances, an exception plan is put forward which will replace a stage plan or lead to a revised project plan. The principal idea behind the levels is that the lower the level, the shorter the plan's timeframe and the more detail it contains. The project chooses the levels and, therefore, the number of plans it needs according to its size and extent of risk exposure.

Controls

There are various levels of control in the project. Most controls in PRINCE2™ are event-driven, including all the decision-making ones. There are some time-driven controls such as regular progress feedback. At the project level there is overall control by the Project Board, which receives information from the project manager (and any assurance roles appointed) and has control over whether the project continues, stops or changes direction or scope. PRINCE2™ applies the concept of 'management by exception' where the Project Board is concerned. Once a stage plan has been approved the Project Board is kept informed by reports during the stage. The project manager informs the Project Board immediately if any exception situation is forecast. The major controls for the Project Board are:

1. Project initiation:
   ● Should the project be undertaken?
2. End stage assessment:
   ● Has the stage been successful?
   ● Is the project still on course?
   ● Is the business case still viable? Are the risks still under control?
   ● Should the next stage be undertaken?
3. Highlight reports:
   ● Regular progress reports during a stage
4. Exception reports
   ● Early warning of any forecast deviation beyond tolerance levels
5. Ad Hoc Advice
   ● The project board members jointly consider what action to take in response to a forecast deviation or the Project Manager's request for advice
6. Project closure
   ● Has the project delivered everything expected?
   ● Are any follow-on actions necessary?
   ● What lessons have been learned?
   ● When and how can we measure achievement of the benefits expected in the business case?

Work Package Authorization is a control which the project manager uses to allocate work to individuals or teams. It includes controls on quality, time and cost and identifies reporting and hand-over requirements. The individuals or teams monitor progress through the work package and report back to the project manager via checkpoints or other identified means (such as risk 'triggers'). There is a controlled close to ensure that the project does not drift on for ever, but does not finish until the project manager can satisfy the Project Board that the objectives specified in the Project Initiation Document have been achieved.

In some methods the word 'phase' is used as an equivalent to the PRINCE2™ stage. Most of what in PRINCE2™ terms will be stages will be divisions of 'implementation' in the product life-cycle. Product life-cycle phases are not the same as PRINCE2™ stages. Stages are partitions of the project with decision points. A stage is a collection of activities and products whose delivery is managed as a unit. As such it is a sub-set of the project, and in PRINCE2™ terms it is the element of work which the Project Manager is managing on behalf of the Project Board at any one time.

The use of stages in a PRINCE2™ project is mandatory; the number of stages is flexible and depends on the needs of the project. A small project may need only two stages: an initiation stage with the remainder of the project as the second stage. The initiation stage may last only a matter of hours, but is essential to ensure that there is a firm basis for the project, understood by all parties. Most projects need to be broken down into more manageable stages to enable the correct level of planning and control to be exercised. PRINCE2™ uses stages to deal with management decision points. The decisions form the basis of the end stage assessments carried out in authorizing a stage or exception plan. The benefits of these end stage assessments are:

● providing a 'fire break' for the project by encouraging the project board to assess the project viability at regular intervals
● ensuring that key decisions are made prior to the detailed work needed to implement them
● clarifying previously unknown or ill-defined parts of the project's direction or products
● clarifying what the impact will be of an identified external influence such as the corporate budget round or the finalization of legislation

Uncertainty can often mean that it is only possible to plan in detail the activities and products of a limited amount of the work of the project. The rest of the project's work can only be planned in broad outline. The adoption of stages handles this situation by having two different but related levels of plan, that is a detailed Stage Plan and an outline Project Plan.

MANAGEMENT VS TECHNICAL STAGES

Technical stages cover elements such as design, build and implementation and are a separate concept from the management stages used in PRINCE2™. Technical stages are typified by the use of a particular set of specialist skills. Management stages equate to commitment of resources and authority to spend. Often the two types of stage will coincide, for instance, where a management decision is based on the output from a technical stage. However, on other occasions the stages will not coincide. There might be more than one technical stage within a management stage. For example, the Project Board might decide to combine all the technical stages which investigate a need and produce a specification into one management stage. One plan would be approved to cover all the work, with Project Board commitment before the work started and a review at the end. In a project which is (technically) innovative, a technical stage might be divided into more than one management stage.

The PRINCE2™ approach is to concentrate the management of the project through the management stages since these will form the basis of planning and control processes. This ensures the customer's management rather than letting the technical teams drive the project. Where the desired management stages do not coincide with the technical stages, technical work can be broken down so that its activities can be divided over two or more management stages. This can be problematic where the management stage ends part way through one or more large elements of specialist work, since it can be difficult to establish whether the specialist work is under control. Product based planning is invaluable here since by using it the project manager can identify the detailed products involved in any element of specialist work, and identify all the products which are due to be produced within the confines of any given management stage. This can then be used to assess completion or otherwise of the stage.

The process of defining stages is fundamentally a process of balancing how far ahead in the project it is sensible to plan and where the key decision points need to be on the project. This makes it flexible enough to cater for any type of project.

Risk

Risk is a major factor to be considered during the management of a project. Project management must control and contain risks if a project is to stand a chance of being successful. The management of risk is covered in chapter 22.

Quality

Within projects, quality is a question of identifying what it is about the project's products or services that makes them fit for their purpose of satisfying stated needs (Chapters 14 and 17). Projects should not rely on implied needs. These lead to uncertainty and, as such, are of little use. The product description may need to be updated if a change to the product is agreed. A product description should not be changed, once approved, without passing through change control. The Quality Review is the primary technique in making quality work for PRINCE2™. A Quality Review is a partnership of all those with a vested interest in the product to ensure its completeness and adherence to standards by a review procedure. It is a team review of a product with the emphasis on checking the product for errors (as opposed to, say, improved design). The deliverable, in the context of a Quality Review, is any product which has been evaluated against mostly subjective criteria involving elements of judgement or opinion. This will typically be a document, such as a plan, a report or a drawing, but could be other products such as models, mock-ups or prototypes. The objectives of a Quality Review are to:

- assess the conformity of a product against set criteria
- provide a platform for product improvement
- involve all those who have a vested interest in the product

- spread ownership of the product
- obtain commitment from all vested interests in the product
- provide a mechanism for management control

Quality reviews must be properly planned with input from the assurance function by:

- identifying the products which will be subject to quality review
- planning the timescale for each quality review
- identifying the reviewers and adding them to resource plans

Quality management is dealt with in more detail in Chapter 17 and requirements management in Chapter 14.

Configuration management

No organization can be fully efficient or effective unless it manages its assets, particularly if the assets are vital to the running of the organization's business. The project's assets likewise have to be managed. The assets of the project are the products that it develops. Within the context of project management the purpose of configuration management is to identify, track and protect the project's products. Configuration management is part of the quality control of a project. Without it, managers have little or no control over the products being produced, what their status is, where they are, whether they can be changed, what the latest version is. If more than one version of a product has been created, then configuration management is required. Configuration management for documentation products (both management and specialist) is of equal importance to configuration management for deliverables. Configuration Management is dealt with in detail in Chapter 15.

Change

Changes can potentially ruin any project unless they are carefully controlled. Change is, however, highly likely. In PRINCE2™ all potential changes are dealt with as project issues. One consideration at project initiation should be who can authorize changes to what the project is to produce. In a project where few changes are envisaged, it may be reasonable to leave this authority in the hands of the Project Board. But projects may be in a dynamic environment where there are likely to be many requests to change the initial agreed scope of the project:

- Is the Project Board prepared to make the time available to review all change requests?
- Does it wish to consider only the top priority changes and delegate decisions on minor changes to another body?

- How will changes be funded?
- Will the Project Board go back to corporate or programme management to vary funding, timetable or scope each time a change is desired?

In some projects the Project Board may choose to delegate consideration of changes to a group, called a *'change authority'*. A budget to pay for changes is normally given to this change authority. This arrangement can avoid a number of Project Board assessments in projects where the frequency of project issues is forecast to be high. The Project Board needs to decide before the project moves out of Initiation where the authority for making changes lies, and these responsibilities must be written into the appropriate job definitions. Change is dealt with as part of configuration management in Chapter 15.

SUMMARY OF PRINCE2™

PRINCE2™ assumes a developed business exists prior to initiating the project and explicitly recognizes the role of the project's owner and users in the decision making process. It also differentiates between management, technical and life-cycle stages, which makes it easier to link into a business management system. It requires the development of a product based plan but is non-prescriptive regarding the management tools and techniques used on the project.

ISO 10006: GUIDELINES FOR QUALITY MANAGEMENT IN PROJECTS

ISO 10006: Guidelines for Quality Management in Projects recognizes that successful projects demand appropriate quality of both the project processes and the project product. Detailed consideration of the quality of the project product is outside the scope of the guide, which focuses on the quality of the project management process. The guide does not identify specific techniques or develop much detail on how these areas should be managed and controlled. Ten processes are identified.

Strategic

These processes organize and manage realization of other processes, with focus on satisfying the stakeholder's requirements through a combination of processes and products to meet the project's objectives. The processes set the direction for the project and manage realization of the other project processes (see Chapters 2, 6, 13, 14 and 36).

Resource Related Process

These processes aim to plan and control resources. They help to identify what is required, for how long, and where they fit within the project schedule. There are two main sub-processes:

- **Resource Planning**: identifying, estimating, scheduling and allocating all resources (see Chapters 18 and 21)
- **Resource Control**: Comparing actual usage against resource plans and taking action if needed (see Chapters 21)

Personnel Related

The quality and success of a project depends on the participating personnel. These processes aim to create an environment in which people can contribute effectively and efficiently to the project, through organizational structures, staff allocation and team development.

- **Organizational Structure**: Defining a project organizational structure tailored to suit the project needs, including identifying roles in the project, and defining authority and responsibility (Chapter 18)
- **Staff Allocation**: Selecting and assigning sufficient personnel with appropriate competence to suit the project needs (Chapter 31 and 32)
- **Team Development**: Developing individual and team skills and ability to enhance project performance (Chapter 34)

Interdependency Related

These processes recognize that an action in one area of the project will usually affect other areas. It covers the following areas:

- **Project initiation and project management plan development**: evaluating customer and other stakeholder requirements, preparing a project plan and initiating other processes (see chapters 15 and 27).
- **Interaction Management**: Managing interactions between the project processes (Part 3)
- **Change Management**: Anticipating change and managing it across all processes (see Chapter 15 and 29)
- **Process and Project Closure**: Closing processes and obtaining feedback (Chapter 30)

Scope Related

The processes include a broad description of the project's product, its characteristics and how they are to be measured or assessed, together with its breakdown into manageable activities and the control of those activities. This includes the following:

- **Development**: Defining in broad outline what the project product will do (see Chapters 13, 14 and 15)
- **Scope development and control**: Documenting the product's characteristics in measurable terms, and controlling them (see Chapters 15, 16 and 17)
- **Definition of activities**: Identifying and documenting activities and the steps required to achieve the project objectives (see Chapters 15 and 21)
- **Control of activities**: Controlling the actual work carried out in accordance with the project management plan (see Chapter 19)

Time Related

These processes aim to determine dependencies and the duration of activities, and to ensure timely completion of the project. The processes are (see Chapter 19):

- **Activity Dependencies Planning**: Identifying interrelationships and the logical interactions and dependencies among project activities
- **Estimation of Duration**: Estimating the duration of activities in connection with specific conditions and the required resources
- **Schedule Development**: Interrelating the project time objectives, activity dependencies and their durations as the framework for developing general and detailed schedules
- **Schedule Control**: Controlling the realization of the project activities, to confirm the proposed schedule or to take adequate actions for recovering from delays

Cost Related

These processes aim to forecast and manage the project costs to ensure completion within budget by appropriate estimating, budgeting and cost control (see Chapter 20):

- **Cost Estimation**: Developing cost estimates for the project
- **Budgeting**: Using results from the estimates and schedules to produce the project budget
- **Cost Control**: Controlling costs and deviations from the budget

Communication Related

These processes aim to facilitate the exchange of information necessary for the project, covering its generation, collection, dissemination, storage and its ultimate disposition (see Chapters 36, 37 and 38):

149

- **Communication Planning**: Planning the information and communication systems of the project
- **Information Management**: Making necessary information available to project organization members and other stakeholders
- **Communication Control**: Controlling communication in accordance with the planned communication system

Risk Related

Risks deal with uncertainties throughout the project and may affect the project processes or the project product. These processes aim to minimize the impact of potential negative events and take full advantage of any opportunities for improvement. Processes should exist to identify, assess and treat the risk; and control all risks (see Chapter 22):

- **Risk Identification**: Determining risks in the project
- **Risk Assessment**: Evaluating the probability of occurrence of risk events and the impact of risk events on the project
- **Risk Treatment**: Developing solutions for responding to risks
- **Risk Control**: Implementing and updating the risk plans

Purchasing Related

These processes deal with obtaining products for the project. They include definition of requirement, contractor analysis, tendering procedures and contract control.

- **Purchasing Planning and Control**: Identifying and controlling what is to be purchased and when
- **Documentation of Requirements**: Compiling commercial conditions and technical requirements
- **Supplier Evaluation**: Evaluating, determining and keeping a record of which supplier should be used
- **Subcontracting**: Issuing invitations to tender, tender evaluation, negotiation, preparation and placing of the subcontract
- **Contract Control:** Ensuring that subcontractor's performance meets contractual requirements

There was not space to include chapters on purchasing and contract management in this edition of the book.

SUMMARY OF ISO 10006

The guide is explicit on what should be considered in ensuring that the project management process covers the appropriate issues. It is not comparable to either

BS 6079 or PRINCE2™ but provides an excellent checklist. It does not differentiate between simple and complex projects but anyone using the guide would be left in no doubt regarding what should be considered to achieve the required quality of the process. The guide focuses on the standard of management of the project and does not cover the 'doing' of the activities necessary to complete the project.

CONCLUSION

Probably the biggest difficulty facing the authors of any process is drafting a document suitable for a wide variety of users. None of these processes can be used in isolation and assure a project's success. They all need to be applied by someone who understands what is required and can tailor the processes to their particular project – in short a project manager!

As can be seen from each model the project process is initiated by a defined business need. Without this mandate the project manager cannot establish personal terms of reference and the rest of the project plan. The strategic planning and decision-making tools used to identify what should be undertaken rightly lie in the corporate, rather than the project toolkit. Consequently there can be no project without this stage and no project can deliver any business benefit if this stage is done badly. Without a clear recognition of need, no project management process can economically deliver a project of benefit to the business.

On completion the lessons learned from the project need to be incorporated into the corporate and project procedures if they are to be of any real benefit. For this simple, but often-overlooked reason, the process must be flexible and adaptable. Without this continuous improvement and development of the processes they soon fall into disrepute and shortly thereafter are ignored.

To obtain maximum benefit projects must be seen as making a significant contribution to the introduction of new ways of working or new products to the organization. A project-aware organization should establish a corporate framework (BS 6079) as one way of including the corporate needs. Within this framework the projects should be managed in a structured and controlled way to ensure timely and accurate delivery of the project deliverables and clear reporting procedures to senior corporate management. PRINCE2™ provides a method suitable for any project type and tailorable to suit the scale and importance of the project and skill level of the project manager.

ISO 10006 provides a comprehensive checklist to ensure all elements of the project are managed in a way that is compatible with the corporate quality management systems and at the appropriate level of detail for the specific project.

Project management processes have a reputation of being straightjackets rather than flexible management guidelines. It is not the method that is at fault but the way they are used by the project management team.

Good luck with your process.

REFERENCES AND FURTHER READING

BS6079, *A Guide to Project Management,* London: British Standards Institute.

ISO, 2004, *ISO 10,006: Quality Management – Guidelines to Quality in Project Management.* 2nd edition, Geneva, CH: International Standards Organization.

OGC, 2005, *Managing Successful Projects with PRINCE2™,* 4th edition, London: The Stationery Office.

PMI®, 2004, *The Guide to the Project Management Body of Knowledge,* 3rd edition, Newtown Square, PA: Project Management Institute.

Turner, J.R. and Cochrane, R.A., 1992, 'The goals-and-methods matrix: coping with projects with ill defined goals and/or methods of achieving them', *International Journal of Project Management,* 11(2), 93–102.

Software Solutions for Project, Programme and Portfolio Management

8

Christopher Dobson

This chapter describes the information systems available for programme planning and portfolio management. The current breed of software tools vary in complexity and functionality. With the development of faster and more powerful computers, we are at the point where virtually anything is possible and an organization needs to think strategically before investing in a project management tool. Not long ago technology was unable to perform all the tasks business required of it. This is no longer the case. It is true to say that some suppliers will not sell a solution to a company that does not have a structured methodology and governance in place to enable the tool to function effectively.

In this chapter, software tools are categorized, examined for their functionality and a suggested applicability to the project environment discussed. A description of the information systems and their use will be provided, and a practical overview of how they support and facilitate the project, programme, and portfolio management process will be discussed. This may help an organization searching for a software tool to find one suitable for their needs.

PROJECT PLANNING AND CONTROL TOOLS

There is a wide range of project planning and control tools available commercially. Most are called project *management* tools, but I suggest that this term is inappropriate. There is a great deal more to project management than is offered in a software package. They are mainly planning and control tools. There are a large number of software tools available, and to help understand the different types, and how they may apply to project management, I think it is worthwhile categorising the applications. Therefore, I propose five categories:

1. Standalone
2. Companion

3. Modular
4. Hosted
5. Methodology.

STANDALONE TOOLS

Standalone tools are the most basic of the project management software tools. These are available for purchase online, or off the shelf from vendors, who sell a range of software applications. Designed for companies who manage projects independently, standalone systems provide the basic toolkit to manage projects. What these tools lack is the collaboration and the complex resource management functionality of their bigger cousins. To make it more confusing, it is now possible to use a hosted tool as a standalone product. This means that you can hire a fully formed system that is accessed via your web browser, which will give you increased functionality and the ability to add more project managers seamlessly. However, for clarity I will talk about this in more detail in the relevant section.

Standalone tools can be used for programme management, but I would advise against it unless the company has tight version controls. The project manager creates a project plan in isolation. Whilst this is not a problem for a single project manager working on several projects, it can become an issue if there are multiple project managers working on sub-projects or as part of a programme. The only way to predict multi-project resource demands and logical conflicts is to merge the project plans, creating a master project plan. Any changes to the plan have to be communicated to the specific managers to enable them to update their own project plan. As you can imagine, the margin for error is great and for a large programme, configuration management is key.

These tools are dominated by Microsoft operating systems, and are predominantly based on the following basic processes:

- create a critical path model of the project
- analysis of the plan
- financial planning
- production of bar charts and other scheduling reports
- creation of management reports
- add resources to the tasks and produce resource histograms
- add costs to the tasks and produce cost forecasts
- set a baseline and monitor actual progress against that baseline

Standalone systems tend to use their own internal database, which is not accessible by the user. To exchange data between the system and other software applications the user must use one of the following:

1. *OLE2 (Object Linking and Embedding version 2) and DDE (Dynamic Data Exchange):*
   When mastered these allow data transfer between software packages that support the appropriate protocols.
2. *File Export:*
   Most systems offer a file export command that copies the data into a file format such as XML or HTML that can be accessed by another software package or transferred into a database.
3. *Cut and Paste:*
   Most Windows systems support the concept of cutting data out of one software package for pasting into another.
4. *ODBC:*
   This is a version of the File Export method. Some systems support Open Database Connectivity, which is a standard language for reading and writing files. Selecting the ODBC option normally saves the file in a common format.

Figure 8.1 shows a sample of standalone tools currently available. Costs vary from free to £600 per package.

Name	Supplier
Project Standard Edition	Microsoft Corporation
Open Workbench	NIKU\Computer Associates
Sure Trak	Primavera Systems
Milestones Professional	Kidasa Software

Figure 8.1   A selection of standalone tools currently available

COMPANION TOOLS

As mentioned in the previous section, standalone tools lack the functionality of larger software solutions. Companion tools however are designed to add a specific set of functions to an existing project management tool. It is not surprising to note that most companion tools are designed to interface with popular project management tools such as Microsoft Project and other Microsoft Office applications such as Excel, Word, and PowerPoint.

Companion tools are not project management tools in their own right. Although some companion tools can be used in isolation, such as mind mapping tools, they cannot function as a classic project management tool without the host. For example, Mind Manager requires mind maps to be uploaded to Microsoft Project. It is therefore prudent to check that the companion tool you want is compatible with the project management tool you have. One of the issues with companion tools is that an upgrade of your project management software may mean that your companion tool ceases to function. The benefit of such a tool is that you can enhance the functionality of existing applications without dramatically changing the tool you are using, therefore not incurring a large implementation or training cost.

The companion software is designed to interact seamlessly with the host application. This solution allows you to decide how many copies of the tool you require. For example, a company may have Microsoft Project running on five PCs, when only one is required to perform risk management. Therefore, only one PC requires a companion tool added to Microsoft Project. This enables comprehensive risk management processes such as Monte Carlo simulations, 'what if' analysis and management reports to be run on project plans performed by the project manager.

Companion tools have been developed to service a specific competency such as risk management. Other tools exist to compliment the methodology a company may use. For example, a companion tool can assist PRINCE2™ project planning by providing the project manager with a form to complete before the project plan is created. The tool installs interactive help facilities to guide the less experienced project manager through the process, thus ensuring that the project plan is accurate. Some tools also extend the functionality of the host, to allow project, programme, and project office management.

There are three types of companion tool.

1. The first is an add-in tool. Once loaded into the host, a menu bar is created, and from this menu bar, all the new functions can be run on either existing or new projects. The companion tool will work independently of the host and does not disable any of the functions of the host tool. Any templates or files relating to the companion tool will be stored in a separate directory. This will not affect the location of your project files.
2. The second type has the companion tool as part of another application such as Microsoft Excel. Files are imported from the host tool, analysed and enhanced before being uploaded back to the project management tool.
3. The third type of companion tool can also be used as a non-project standalone product, such as Mind Manager. This type of tool can plan a project; however, it requires a project management tool such as Microsoft Project to turn the files into classic project plans.

Figure 8.2 shows a sample of companion tools currently available. The price for companion tools varies considerably, between £99 and £1380 per copy, depending on the complexity of the product. Twelve months maintenance, including helpdesk support and discount for multiple purchases, is offered by most companies.

Name	Supplier	Function
Project Risk	PertMaster	Risk Analysis
@risk	Palisade	Risk Analysis and Reporting
P2MSP	P2MSP	PRINCE2® and PMI Processes and Forms
Mind Manager	Mindjet	Mind mapping and conversion to task lists
Project Kickstart	Technology Associates	Project Start up
Precision Tree	Palisades	Decision Analysis

Figure 8.2   A selection of companion tools currently available

MODULAR TOOLS

Modular software tools function as a multi-user project and programme management planning system. The fundamental change in recent years is that these tools have the ability to perform project portfolio management. A modular system is usually based on a database structure. The database will normally be a proprietary tool such as SQL or Oracle, accessed via a modular user interface. This means that once you have purchased the basic system you can chose which modules best fit your company's requirements immediately, but you can also plan the implementation of future modules in line with your strategic plans. While this looks like a tool for only large organizations, medium sized companies are now finding themselves requiring more than the classic project management toolset. Modular systems are capable of providing almost any function, for example:

● resource management
● programme and portfolio management
● governance
● management reports
● collaboration of teams
● stakeholder management
● managing portfolios
● access for third parties
● interface with financial systems
● interface with HR systems
● timesheet reporting
● access via mobile computing
● document management

Modular systems are expensive and usually require professional consultancy at the implementation stage. The tool chosen can have a wide-ranging effect on how the company works. It can assimilate all existing project processes, procedures, and governance, linking to HR, finance and other key systems in the organization. Although not all modular systems are this complex, the bigger solutions require the company to have well-established project governance and methodology in place. Implementation of a fully integrated modular system takes time and once in place it will require a partnership with the company that has provided the software to maintain upgrades and maintenance. A significant commitment from the company at all levels is required if modular systems are to be effective and realize the predicted cost benefits. It is not surprising that some software companies will only sell to an organization which they believe has the maturity to complete an implementation successfully.

Utilization of web interfaces and mobile technologies help to make this type of tool very powerful. Individual team members are presented with only the information they require to do their role, and it is presented in an easy to understand format, allowing members to update timesheets and documents whilst away from the office. This tool is aimed at full time planners who run major projects.

Figure 8.3 shows a sample of modular tools currently available. The cost of such a system is dependent on the number of user licences and services required. I have recently priced a system for a small company consisting of 30 users requiring a portfolio management system with web access and timesheet functionality for £21,000. Creation of the database and user training is included in the price. The cost of hardware is not included and should always be costed separately based on the system requirements.

Name	Supplier
Artemis	Artemis International Solutions Corporation
Asta TeamPlan	Asta Development Plc
Openplan	Deltek
Planview	PlanView Inc
Primavera	Primavera Inc
Clarity	Computer Associates (formerly NIKU)
Hydra	Program Management Group

Figure 8.3   A selection of modular tools currently available

HOSTED TOOLS

If you cannot justify the expenditure in money, time, and equipment that a modular system requires, there is now a 21st century alternative and that is the hosted tool. Hosted tools will allow you to manage either a single project or multiple projects from different locations with remote teams. Quite simply, a hosted tool is web-based and all you require is a web browser and an Internet connection. Data resides, or is 'hosted' on a database on your supplier's server and can be accessed by anyone who has Internet access and the appropriate security clearance.

The advantage of such a system is that you receive some of the functionality of a modular system but at a fraction of the cost. Most web-based applications include the ability to manage a portfolio of projects, matrix manage resources and have a repository for all project documentation. This can be secured to enable staff with only the appropriate authorization to access documents. Using such a facility allows a project manager to decide who can view and edit documents and who has 'read only' access. Version tracking ensures that all documents are time and date stamped showing the latest version and who amended it. When an authorized change has taken place all members of the project team can be informed via email. The disadvantage of a hosting system is that it does not belong to you, and the data from completed projects need to be archived to your own systems, unless you wish to pay an ever-increasing charge for disk space. Companies with sensitive projects may wish to keep them in-house and not use a remote server that is based in another company.

Many companies find it extremely useful using a hosted system, as suppliers, project teams and stakeholders can use the same system but with restrictions in place to prevent them from accessing sensitive information. If suppliers log onto the system they will only see the information pertaining to their part of the project; all other information is hidden. This facility allows real time updating of work packages that can be validated by the project manager prior to the updates being applied. The flexibility of hosted tools means that they can be used by one project manager with one project for a month, or they can be used for a portfolio of projects using 100 project managers and an unlimited resource. However, the cost increases with the number of people accessing the system and the amount of space required.

Most hosting companies charge on a per user basis that includes a fixed amount of storage space (space on the server). Extra storage is usually charged on a per megabyte basis. You do not have to worry about disaster recovery or server capacity as this is managed by the supplier as part of the service. Suppliers usually have a selection of support agreements, which are agreed upon when the accounts are set up.

Figure 8.4 shows a sample of hosted tools currently available. As the price is based on number of users and space required it is difficult to give an average price. Most companies provide discounts for multiple users and have flexible pricing structures. The price includes fixed allocated storage. Extra storage is usually charged on a per megabyte basis.

Name	Supplier
Projistics	Nagarro Inc
PAT (Project Assistant Toolkit)	Ninthwave
ProjectPlace	Project Place
eRealize.net	Pan Atlantic Software Inc

Figure 8.4   A selection of hosted tools currently available

METHODOLOGY TOOLS

With the growth of structured project management, the use of recognized methodologies by practitioners and companies is now well established, with PRINCE2™ and the PMBOK® being two of the most popular. Both methods are best practice guides with templates and guidelines to assist the project manager. However, every project is unique and it is the experience and understanding of individual project managers that allows them to apply methods to their particular project. Currently there is an army of project managers sitting their accreditation exams but it cannot be assumed that all project managers have been through a 'standard' project management course. Many untrained project managers are assigned to the job and are learning through trial and error.

A well-rounded project management environment includes some formal training, which complements the on-the-job training. Project management methodology tools provide a defined structure for project managers to work in. It will not do their jobs for them, but will allow them to plan the project in a structured way. Methodology is all about standardising the process in order to concentrate on the deliverables and the product. Methodology tools may or may not include software applications. A methodology tool provides project templates, training for the project manager, or even an 'end to end' project process, ensuring that all project staff adhere to procedures.

Many of the tools discussed so far in this chapter have some form of support for methodologies, indeed some of the modular tools can be adapted to not only follow a given method, but also provide a job description for each role. This can be particularly useful in a situation where staff are promoted to a role before formal training can be given, ensuring that consistency is maintained.

Figure 8.5 shows a sample of methodology tools currently available. I am unable to give an average price for methodology tools as they vary in complexity and implementation requirements, which affects the costs.

160

Name	Supplier
TenStep Project Management Process	Tenstep
Launch Pad Professional	SPOCE Project Management yd
P2MSP	Structured Project Management Solutions Ltd
P2-Toolbox	Fortes Solutions

Figure 8.5   A selection of methodology tools currently available

IN CONCLUSION

There are clear differences between programme, portfolio, and project planning. In the past project management software tools have been unable to provide the senior programme manager with the ability to oversee the status of a portfolio of projects at a glance. This is no longer the case with the emergence of new software solutions, which allow programme and portfolio managers to oversee projects no matter where in the world those projects are being run. Modular tools in particular are designed with the senior manager in mind. They allow accurate forward planning, the running of impact analysis and risk assessment in a real-time environment, with the ability to apply changes in real time.

Without the current emergence of fully rounded project software applications that allow full collaboration across departments and companies, effective portfolio management would have not been possible, as the portfolio manager would not be able to manage the changes in real time that are needed.

9 The Project, Programme or Portfolio Office

Jack S Duggal

The use of the Project or Programme Management Office (PMO) continues to be a growing trend among major companies worldwide according to recent surveys by the Project Management Institute (PMI®) and other private and academic organizations, (CIO Magazine 2003). While the concept of the PMO has been around for a number of years, only recently has it evolved as a popular organizational role. PMOs can be found in different areas within an organization at the departmental level, or the enterprise or corporate level. A wide variety of organizations have implemented PMOs, including: Citigroup, Honda, HP, IBM Global Services, Prudential, SAP and Government and Non-profit organizations.

The use of PMOs is growing in the information technology (IT) industry, primarily in the United States and Canada, but increasingly in Europe. A joint survey by PMI® and CIO magazine (2003) confirmed that 67% of IT organizations have a PMO or are thinking about establishing one. IT organizations worldwide have had a high project failure rate, and IT executives are more open to improving their project performance and institutionalizing the discipline of project management and best practices in the form of a PMO. Some of the IT PMOs that have been successful over time are moving outside IT and becoming role models for enterprise or corporate PMOs.

Senior managers and executives are gradually recognizing the value of project management and the strategic aspects of PMOs. There are examples of organizations which are mandated by the board to establish a PMO. This is also fuelled by a worldwide focus on compliance, regulatory and ethical considerations that emphasizes formal processes and disciplined management. Particularly regulations like the US Sarbanes Oxley law have spawned PMOs to provide data for compliance and also made PMOs more prominent. As more and more companies in different industries establish PMOs, differing expectations surround the role of the PMO, its purpose, functions and responsibilities. The success rate of PMOs has also been mixed. In the PMI®/CIO survey mentioned above only 50% or less of PMOs were perceived as successful. There is an air of misunderstanding and confusion surrounding the role, purpose, fit and functions of a PMO. *A Guide to the Project Management Body of Knowledge (PMBOK® Guide)* (PMI® 2004) states, 'There is no consensus on what PMOs must entail. They can operate on a continuum from providing project management support functions in the form of training, software, standardized policies and procedures, and templates to actual direct management and results of the projects.' This chapter outlines the PMO continuum and presents the range of PMO functions. It also addresses various aspects of a PMO – the different types and levels of PMOs; the need for a PMO; the role and purpose of a PMO; PMO framework that outlines the focus areas and functions; PMO implementation life-cycle; organizational structures; risks and challenges; demonstrating and measuring PMO value; and PMO success criteria.

TYPES OF PMO

WHAT'S IN A NAME?

In the process of implementing a PMO, it is imperative to establish a common ground, clarify terminology and align definitions which are often a cause for confusion. The 'P' in the PMO can stand for project, programme or portfolio or be used interchangeably, or mean all three of them, depending upon the focus of the PMO. PMO names range from project support office (PSO), project management support office (PMSO), enterprise programme management (EPM), enterprise programme management office (EPMO), corporate project office (CPO), PM centre of excellence (CoE), etc. Often the name of a PMO reflects its focus; a project support office (PSO) is typically a support oriented PMO, versus an enterprise project management office (EPMO), which is more strategic in nature.

PROJECT OR PROGRAMME OFFICE VERSUS ORGANIZATIONAL PMO

There are essentially two types of PMO:

1. a PMO for a particular project or programme
2. an organizational PMO

The former is often referred to as a Project Office or Project Support Office, and deals with the day-to-day project or programme issues, similar to the military concept of a 'war room,' which is a central point for all project/programme related information. The organizational PMO focuses on improving overall project, programme or portfolio management practices within the organization. It may also support a portfolio of multiple projects or programmes depending on its mandate.

The *PMBOK® Guide* (PMI® 2004) defines a PMO as:

> An organizational body or entity assigned various responsibilities related to the centralized and coordinated management of those projects under its domain. The responsibilities of the PMO can range from providing project management support functions to actually being responsible for the direct management of a project.

PMOS AT DIFFERENT LEVELS

Besides the project, programme or portfolio level the PMO can be organized at different levels – a departmental PMO for a particular department like human resources or information technology; or by geography, as a regional PMO; or at the business unit level; or a corporate or enterprise PMO. Large organizations may have multiple PMOs at different levels. The key for success with multiple PMOs in an organization is that they are aligned and they talk to each other and share best practices.

FUNCTIONS AND PURPOSE OF THE PMO

WHY HAVE A PMO? THE NEED FOR A PMO

Whether there is a need for a PMO at the organizational level depends on the response to key questions:

- Do we know how many projects are going on? Do we have an up to date status of the projects?
- Do we have too many projects and too few completed?
- Is constant fire fighting the norm?
- Is there burn-out among our best performers?
- Do we have the organizational capacity to take on more projects?
- Are 'flavour of the month' initiatives becoming a steady diet?
- Is too much focus on next-generation products forcing daily operations out of control?
- Can the pace and delivery be sustained realistically over a period of time?

Some organizations respond that they already have a high project success rate and question if they really need a PMO. However, questions that need to be considered are whether indeed they are well-organized, or is there a cost of successful project delivery, or is successful delivery a result of heroics? Certain individuals work long and hard and are good at putting out fires, and at the end of the day they deliver. This fosters a culture of heroism which results in increased fire-fighting. Over time fire-fighting symptoms proliferate – not enough time to solve all the problems; solutions are incomplete; problems recur and cascade; urgency supersedes importance; many problems become crises; performance drops; projects are delayed; there are cost-overruns; significant risks remain unmitigated. There is also a cost in terms of people, quality and other factors.

The following were actual observations from various organizations for reasons given for implementing a PMO:

> *'Inconsistencies in managing and reporting on projects…'*
> *'People waste a lot of time in finding out how to get things done… often find that they are reinventing the wheel…'*
> *'Documented processes are only on paper and are often not followed…processes are not understood, they do not have the inputs, outputs or clarity on roles and responsibilities to follow-through, thus slowing down execution…'*
> *'Too much bureaucracy which creates a lot of bottlenecks and slows down delivery…'*
> *'No mechanisms in place to improve or simplify business process…'*
> *'Projects move through the life-cycle without any structured governance or checkpoints…as a result sometimes cost-overruns, schedule delays, or critical risks do not surface at the appropriate level in a timely manner…'*
> *'Few opportunities to share information, ideas best practices and lessons learned… which leads to a lot of duplication and re-invention of the wheel…'*

The PMO provides an organized way of addressing these common causes of pain and bottlenecks in organizations. The PMO can enable information at multiple levels and provide answers to questions such as:

- How many projects and initiatives are currently going on?
- What is their value?
- Are our projects and initiatives aligned with the business needs?
- Are we meeting our commitments?
- What will be the impact if we miss our next milestone?
- Are we at risk of not achieving our fiscal year strategic initiatives?
- Can we take on this project?
- How long will it take?
- What will it cost? Is there an opportunity to finish early?
- Does the business unit know this?
- What is the most important project and priority in the organization that we should be focusing on?

THE ROLE OF THE PMO

Over the last few years the role of the PMO has evolved from a tactical to a more strategic focus. This has also caused misaligned expectations of the role of the PMO. Executives tend to expect a strategic focus, whereas traditionally the implementers of PMOs have maintained a tactical view of the PMO. Many PMO implementations fail because the purpose is not clear and the focus is fuzzy leading to different expectations among key PMO customers and stakeholders. The first step is to clarify and agree on the purpose of the PMO. In the author's experience in helping organizations establish PMOs in different industries around the world, the primary purpose of a PMO as illustrated in Figure 9.1 is threefold:

1. To increase capability to execute and deliver successful projects (tactical)
2. To Provide strategic decision support – business alignment and benefits realization (strategic)
3. To provide a governance structure

The PMO is the facilitating and enabling engine that helps realize business objectives, by translating strategies into portfolios of projects and programmes, and increases the capacity to deliver successful project performance (cost, schedule, quality). On the other hand in a more strategic role, the PMO can help in providing vital information for better decision-making regarding the projects/programmes in the portfolio – their strategic fit; business alignment; capacity to execute, etc. Increasingly PMOs get implemented to provide a sound governance structure that focuses on achieving compliance, performance management and linking the tactical with the strategic. These three aspects are further developed into PMO areas of focus see PMO Framework below.

This view also aligns with the role of the PMO in the context of the Organizational Project Management Maturity Model (OPM3) espoused by the Project Management Institute (PMI®), (PMI® 2003). OPM3 is the systematic management of projects, programmes, and portfolios in alignment with the achievement of strategic goals. The PMO achieves its objectives by focusing on the integration of people, process and tools (PPT) – the three main gears of effective execution (Figure 9.1). The PMO needs to identify the gaps and collaborate with its customers and stakeholders to provide the appropriate level of leadership, support, coaching, mentoring training, monitoring and information in each of the people, process and tools aspects.

One of the common myths about a PMO is that a major role of the PMO is to focus on tools, by implementing a project, programme or portfolio management system. The tool aspect of the PPT triad, though crucial, is not the answer. There are a number of examples that prove that companies that emphasize the tools alone often fail in achieving PMO objectives. Tools applied without a roadmap do not result in significant payoff. The emphases on people and processes are more important aspects in PMO implementations. The people aspect focuses on human resources, providing the appropriate resources with required capacity, knowledge, skills, training, mentoring and empowerment to deliver successful programmes.

Out of the three PPT elements, process is considered the glue that unifies the people and tools (Chapter 25). Process is a set of practices performed to achieve a

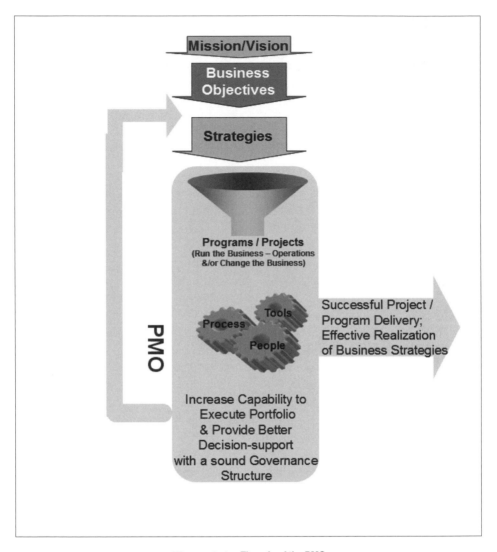

Figure 9.1 The role of the PMO

given purpose; it may include tools, methods; materials, and/or people. Processes provide a constructive high leverage focus; working harder may not necessarily be the answer, working smarter through process provides the leverage for focused, speedy delivery. Also tools and technology supported by the context of the appropriate process roadmap will provide the most benefit. One of the early functions of the PMO should be to inventory, outline, define and standardize core processes and support them with the right resources and tools to foster and create efficient and effective programme/project delivery.

ESTABLISHING A PMO

PMO FRAMEWORK: AREAS OF FOCUS AND PMO FUNCTIONS

To better communicate and apply the various aspects of a PMO, it is important to have an overall framework. Figure 9.2 outlines a PMO Framework to organize and align PMO areas of focus and PMO functions. This framework has been developed and applied in the planning and implementation of a number of PMOs in different organizations.

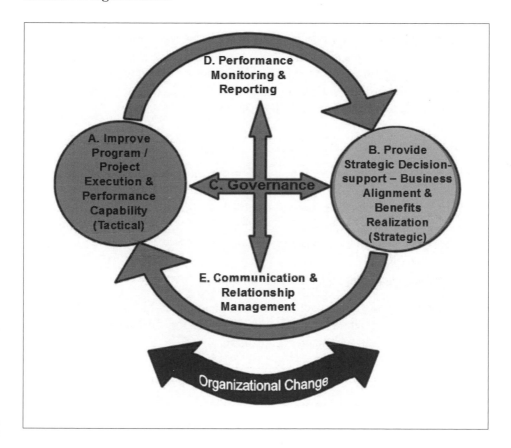

Figure 9.2 Framework for PMO: areas of focus

A: Improving programme/project execution and performance

Traditionally PMOs have focused on tactical aspects of projects, providing standardized processes, methodologies, tools, templates and training. In other words improving the capacity to deliver and focusing on doing the projects 'right.'

169

B: Providing decision-support – business alignment and benefits realization

Recently, there is an increased focus on strategic aspects of portfolio management, inventorying, selecting, evaluating and prioritizing projects. In other words, balancing the portfolio of projects and programmes to realize business strategies, by providing decision-support to focus on selecting and doing the 'right' projects.

As mentioned above this dichotomy between the tactical and strategic aspects causes misaligned expectations in the focus of the PMO. It should be emphasized that both aspects are important, and are two sides of the same coin; one cannot be effectively implemented without the other. To deliver successful projects (A), the right decision-support, priority, alignment and strategic view is necessary (B), and vice versa. Often there is emphasis on one aspect without attention to the other which creates gaps in effective PMO implementation. To bridge these gaps and link the strategic with the tactical, an integrated PMO Framework which includes three additional focus areas of the PMO is necessary.

C: Governance of the portfolio

A governance structure is required to link the strategic with the tactical, and to facilitate and escalate key project and programme decisions. This includes setting standards and processes, as well as establishing governance mechanisms like stage-gates to ensure the project/programme is still critical to the organization and to adjust or re-align the project as necessary.

D: Performance monitoring, information and reporting

The PMO also provides consolidated information that helps in tracking and monitoring project health and progress, to the right individuals up and down the organization, as well as across the organization.

E: A platform for communications and relationship management

This helps to relieve bottlenecks and resolve communications and interface issues across organizational silos and various stakeholders – customers, partners, contractors, vendors and internal resources.

A balanced approach to implementation is recommended that effectively integrates all of the above PMO framework focus areas. Which area is emphasized initially, and the priority of functions the PMO will assume, depend upon the current needs of the organizations.

PMO MODELS

Which area is emphasized also determines the dominant model of the PMO. For example, heavy emphasis on governance promotes a 'control tower' model where decisions and practices are controlled from the top-down. If the primary purpose is information and reporting, the PMO is like an 'information bureau' which monitors progress and reports passively on activity. A support oriented PMO providing training, coaching, mentoring and tools and templates is more of a 'consulting and supporting' PMO model. Focus on communications and relationship management is more of a 'community' based collaborative PMO model.

PMO FUNCTIONS

Each of the focus areas of the PMO has a number of possible functions. Figure 9.3 lists typical PMO functions. This is a comprehensive menu of possible functions and it is not suggested that a PMO adopt all these functions at once. The PMO functions should be selected and prioritized based on the specific needs of the organization at any given time.

A: Execution and Project Performance

Developing and maintaining PM process, standards and methods
- select, develop, maintain and deploy consistent methodology
- inventory, assess, develop and set PM processes
- align standards with existing procedures
- document compliance and update methodology

Planning and administration (assistance)
- scheduling
- estimation
- time and expense tracking
- project workbook maintenance
- report production and distribution
- project management software

Resource management and staffing
- project manager skill evaluation
- project manager candidate personnel identification
- project team member candidate personnel identification
- resource levelling across projects
- providing input on project managers' performance evaluation
- appropriate changes in policies and procedures

Figure 9.3 Functions of the PMO *continued*

Professional development
- project management skills assessment
- project management training
- design and development of training courses both for internal and external customers
- basics; advanced; soft skills
- PM certification
- PM career path
- rewards and recognition
- enhance experienced PM's skills through coaching

Professional development: consulting and mentoring
- confidential advice on sensitive issues and problems
- project start-up assistance
- providing quick response, expert guidance to support real-time project management needs
- group sharing sessions for project managers
- project recovery
- promoting and demonstrating use of preferred or best practices in project management
- endorsing professional development standards and opportunities
- working to maximize return on investments in project management tools and training
- standardizing a project management culture throughout the organizations

B: Decision-Support and Portfolio Management

Portfolio management
- develop and set portfolio management process
- project selection
- project inventory
- project evaluation
- project prioritization
- portfolio balancing and optimization
- portfolio risk assessment
- portfolio review
- oversight
- integrated reporting

Capacity planning
- assess organizational readiness and capacity to initiate new projects; identify inter-project dependencies
- identify potential resource overloads or log jams that pose risk to critical projects
- assist management in assessing performance throughout the life-cycle of the project
- support efforts to scope out appropriate resource levels and types to facilitate reliable project planning and schedule estimating

C: Governance

Establishing policies and procedures for:
- project and programme reporting

- project and programme review gates
- portfolio management
- project selection
- risk assessment
- change management
- resource management
- issue management
- escalation
- interface management
- time and expense
- utilization and billing
- oversight
- regulatory compliance (e.g. performance data requirements for Sarbanes-Oxley)

Setting standards for:
- methodology
- documentation
- estimation
- reporting
- regulatory compliance
- communications
- PM training and qualifications

D: Performance Monitoring and Reporting

Project monitoring - review and analysis
- report and track project status
- conduct ongoing project health checks
- assess progress in achieving business objectives through the projects underway
- identify and respond to weak or troubled project performance
- introduce project phase reviews
- implement post project (close out) reviews
- corrective actions

Knowledge management
Develop a KM taxonomy and appropriate tool to collect, organize and disseminate:
- records of prior project performance
- record of prior project plans
- issues and problem lists of previous projects
- historical project archives database
- description of techniques and templates
- lessons learned; best practices
- institutionalize a framework for PM communities of practice

---

E: Communication and Relationship Management

Communication and relationships
- identify and resolve bottlenecks and organizational interfaces
- market and communicate PMO products and services

- partner with customers to understand business / project needs
- manage customer demand for PMO services
- cultivate and manage PMO relationships with various stakeholders
- clarify, articulate and propagate business objectives
- aligning and mapping strategies
- filling and managing organizational gaps across business units and silos
- provide leadership for PM communities of practice

Figure 9.3 *Concluded*

PMO CONTINUUM

According to the *PMBOK® Guide* (PMI® 2004), PMOs can operate on a 'continuum'. Figure 9.4 charts the typical evolution of a PMO in stages, from fire-fighting and heroics to a fully integrated centre of excellence. It is based on a standard process model of standardization, measurement, control and improvement. The stages are:

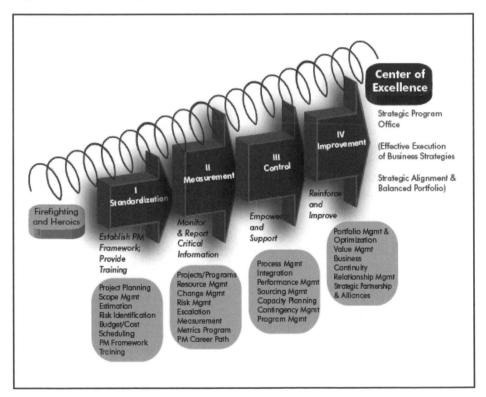

Figure 9.4 PMO continuum

1. Initially without standardization there is *fire fighting and heroics*: delivery structures are often disorganized, success is accidental, often based on single individuals, some processes exist, but project and programme management levels are inconsistent, producing unpredictable results.
2. The journey on the continuum starts with Stage I, *standardization*: this focuses on establishing common standards and practices by establishing a project and process management framework and providing training in these standards. The emphasis is on improving project planning; scope management; estimation; risk identification; budgeting and costing; scheduling.
3. Once the standards are established, Stage II focuses on *measurement*: monitoring and reporting critical information. Relevant project related metrics and KPIs are defined, collected and measured. At this coordinated measurement and multiple project reporting stage, results are more in line with plans, programmes are understood, PM is perceived as a career, resources are managed across projects, change and risks are managed, escalation processes are in place and supported by a measurement and metrics programme.
4. The next Stage, III, deals with *control*: controlling and fine-tuning the processes and providing the empowerment and support to continue what works and discontinue what does not work. Programmes and processes are managed, they are integrated into a portfolio, sourcing is well planned and integrated, partner relationship management and internal and external communication channels are well honed and contingencies are managed.
5. Stage IV highlights *improvement*: where practices are reinforced and improved and creativity and innovation are fostered. The PMO in this stage evolves towards mature portfolio management practices where the portfolio is consistently and continuously managed, investments and resources are optimized, value (financial and other) management processes are integrated, business continuity is ensured; relationship and interface management across vendor and partner PMOs and alliances is maintained.
6. The *centre of excellence* is the vision of a highly evolved and integrated model of a world-class PMO that is a key enabler and facilitator in executing business strategies and delivering consistent and repeatable results that are aligned to a balanced portfolio of projects and programmes.

It should be noted that the PMO continuum is a model that can be applied in different ways; it primarily provides a way to articulate and communicate the evolution of the PMO through various stages, areas that need to be focused, and expected timeframe to progress through the continuum. The evolution of the PMO continuum may not follow the neat evolution from Stages I to IV as some elements from different stages may be addressed at different times and may not necessarily follow a linear path along the continuum. The emphasis at each stage may also differ based on the organization's needs. The boxes below the stages in the PMO continuum can be used to define and tailor the activities at each stage that address the organization's current challenges as a part of PMO planning.

As the organization evolves through the stages of the PMO continuum it increases the overall PM maturity of the organization. It should be noted that these stages are consistent with generic process models which are the basis of different project management maturity levels, espoused in various PM maturity models. Initially it is easier to utilize a continuum approach, a practical way for communicating and setting the right expectations for the PMO. Once the PMO is established a PM maturity assessment like the PMI®'s Organizational Project Management Maturity Model (OPM3) can be conducted.

Timeline

As for the timeline of evolving through the various stages; there is no set benchmark. It varies depending on many factors like the organizational readiness, size, scope, culture, politics, etc. The timeline for implementing a PMO can range anywhere from 3 to 6 months for initial implementations, to 18 to 36 months for full-fledged PMO implementations. However that does not mean that the PMO cannot start to address key challenges, and deliver results in 30 to 60 days by focusing on quick-wins. Specific implementation plans at 60, 120 and 180 day should be outlined during PMO implementation planning.

PMO IMPLEMENTATION LIFE-CYCLE

Implementing a PMO is a project and should be treated like a project. Figure 9.5 depicts a PMO implementation life-cycle, listing typical activities and deliverables for each project management process. The key in the initiation stage is to develop a business case for the PMO that includes details about activities listed under this phase. Throughout the life-cycle it is imperative to focus on marketing and communication to address any concerns and issues among potential PMO customers and stakeholders. It should also be noted that this life-cycle is an iterative process and some activities will have to be repeated at different stages to sustain a PMO.

PMO IN THE ORGANIZATIONAL STRUCTURE

The structure, function, and use of any PMO within an organization varies based upon the application areas involved and the portfolios, programmes, or projects being addressed. There is no generally recognized single construct of a PMO

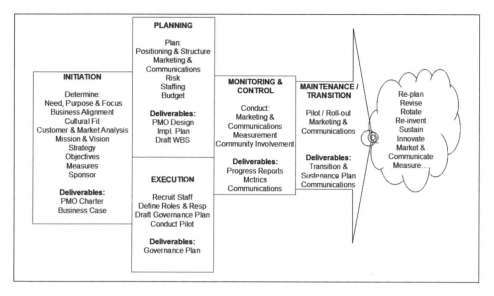

Figure 9.5   PMO Implementation Lifecycle

within the context of project management. The structure depends on the type of organization – functional, matrix or projectized; a PMO can exist in any of the organizational structures. The organizational structure may also determine the PMO model – supporting, monitoring/controlling, consultative or community based PMO. The influence, reach and authority of the PMO also depends on the PMO model and its reporting structure. Generally speaking, supporting or consultative PMOs have more of an advisory influence, limited to the recommendation of policies and procedures, compared to a monitoring and controlling PMO which may have more formal authority.

The trend is that successful PMOs that show results progress to higher levels of reporting within the organization and gain responsibility and authority. More and more PMOs are reporting at the executive level. Also project management maturity and the stage along the PMO continuum determines the reporting level and responsibility of the PMO. PMOs in Stage III and IV typically report at higher levels within the organization.

The size of the PMO can range from a one person PMO to a team of project management subject matter experts and consultants. Project managers may or may not report hard-lined into the PMO. Typically in functional and matrix organizations the project mangers report into their functional managers and are supported by the PMO in a dotted-line reporting structure. In projectized and strong-matrix organizations the project managers are more aligned to the PMO. Overall the PMO model and structure has to be enabling and facilitating and not constricting, and based on the organizational context and needs.

177

THE SUCCESSFUL PMO

WHY PMOS FAIL? RISKS AND CHALLENGES

There is a high failure rate of implementing PMOs. As mentioned above only 50% of PMOs were perceived as successful in a survey conducted jointly by PMI® and CIO magazine (2003). Many organizations start up a PMO and a year or two years later they are shut down—staff are let go or reassigned because the organization saw no value in having the PMO and looked at them as being additional overhead. There are a number of reasons why PMOs are not sustained. Figure 9.6 lists the top ten reasons why PMOs fail, based on a worldwide survey of organizations involved in implementing PMOs over five years, from 2000–2005, conducted by the Projectize Group, USA.

Top ten reasons why PMOs fail
Unclear purpose
No buy-in
Perception of more red tape, bureaucracy and overheads
Quick-fix to deep-rooted problems
PM policing
Too academic and far from reality – professionalism and quality for its own sake
Veneer of participation and hidden agendas
Politics and power struggles
High expectations and fuzzy focus
Hard to prove value

Figure 9.6   Top Ten Reasons Why PMOs Fail

DEMONSTRATING AND MEASURING PMO VALUE

One of the biggest challenges for the PMO is demonstrating value. The 'O' in the PMO is often referred to as the project management 'overhead.' PMO value is hidden, buried in improvements and intangibles that are hard to quantify. PMO value means different things to different stakeholders depending upon their perspective. Value creation cannot be an afterthought or taken for granted, it must be planned for from the beginning and outlined in the PMO business case.

To start with it is important to know where to look for value and what to look for. Ask the key stakeholders and the customers of the PMO what is important to them and what areas of the PMO can help them. The metrics should cover both tangible and intangible value. Examples of tangible value include increasing revenue, reducing cost, increasing productivity, reducing errors, etc. Intangible value includes increased customer satisfaction, increased morale, improved quality, enhanced effectiveness, etc.

Each deliverable or service of the PMO should have a payoff that should be quantified and linked to the stakeholder/s, showing a logical cause-and-effect relationship. The payoff and related metrics will have a greater degree of acceptability if developed collaboratively with the stakeholders. The measurement criteria and metrics for each PMO can be customized depending on the focus, functions and mandate of the PMO. Figure 9.7 provides a sample list of metrics organized according to the PMO Framework categories; other relevant metrics in each category can be identified and added as a part of the PMO measurement criteria.

A: Execution and Project Performance

- Increased project success rate (on-time, within budget, and to specification)
- Accuracy of estimates (cost, schedule, resources)
- Percentage of projects managed with detailed budget data
- Cost of projects running over budget
- Increase in customer satisfaction

B: Decision-Support and Portfolio Management

- Current inventory of all programs and projects
- Percentage of projects meeting alignment goals
- Number of reduction in redundant projects due to prioritization process
- Improved resource utilization

C: Governance

- Cost reductions from process
- Percentage of projects following standard process
- Faster resolution and reduction of issues

D: Performance Monitoring and Reporting

- Improvement in timeliness, accuracy, and quality of reports
- Increased sharing and reuse of best practices and lessons learned
- Reduced dependence on individual resources

E: Communication and Relationship Management

- Number of project management artefacts created
- Percentage growth of project management knowledge repository
- Number of cross-entity communications and knowledge sharing events
- Number of cross-entity interfaces developed/streamlined
- Number of new productive relationships developed with vendors, contractors, and partners

---

Figure 9.7   Sample PMO measurement criteria

SUCCESS CRITERIA

Establishing a PMO requires significant organizational change. It is a complex undertaking with political, cultural and organizational challenges. Organizational readiness for a PMO needs to be assessed and understood to mitigate the risks associated with PMO implementations. Without the appropriate sponsorship and buy-in, the expected change may not take root. PMO efforts may be further impeded due to hidden agendas and cultural issues. Figure 9.8 lists PMO success factors vital for a successful PMO.

PMO Success Factors

Link every PMO initiative to organization's business objectives
Deliver value now. Focus on quick wins with tangible results
Work on short-term initiatives and long-term solutions
Focus on high value/high impact projects
Communicate, 'What's in it for them' (WIIFT), the stakeholders of the PMO
Simplify and improve processes. The PMO should be the department of simplicity!
Measure, evaluate and reward compliance
Measure and quantify PMO value

Figure 9.8 PMO Success Factors

It is imperative to understand the business context for the PMO and be able to clearly articulate the role and purpose of the PMO. PMOs need to adapt to business environment and capabilities, and alleviate any fears and misconceptions of control and bureaucracy early on. Also it is important to demonstrate PMO value and deliver quick results by identifying current challenges that can be addressed quickly by the PMO.

REFERENCES AND FURTHER READING

Business Improvement Architects, 2005, 'The Impact of Implementing a Project Management Office – Report on the Results of Online Global Survey'.

CIO Magazine, 2003, 'Office Discipline: Why You Need a Project Management Office', *CIO Magazine*, July 1, <http://www.cio.com/archive/070103/office.html>

Duggal, J.S., 2001., Building the Next Generation Project Management Office. *Proceedings of the PMI® Conference, Nashville, TN.*

Hobbs, B. and Aubry, M., 2005, 'A Realistic Portrait of PMOs', *Proceedings of the North America PMI® Congress, Toronto, Canada.*

Projectize Group, LLC, USA, 2000–2005. Project/Programme Management Office Survey.

PMI®, 2003, *Organizational Project Management Maturity Model (OPM3)*, Newtown Square, PA: Project Management Institute.

PMI®, 2004, *The Guide to the Project Management Body of Knowledge,* 3rd edition, Newtown Square, PA: Project Management Institute.

10 Maturity Models for the Project-Oriented Company

Roland Gareis and Martina Huemann

The assurance of quality of personnel and of processes is a major concern of project-oriented companies. In order to analyze and to further develop the individual and the organizational competences maturity models have become popular. Maturities can be analyzed for individuals as well as for different social systems, such as teams, temporary and permanent organizations, and even societies. A family of maturity models is introduced. The advantages of a family of maturity models for different social systems are a common underlying management approach and the possibility to relate the models to each other. (Being able to measure the project management maturity of the organization is an important precursor to developing enterprise wide project management capability, described further by Lynn Crawford and Rodney Turner in Chapter 33.)

After introducing the strategic, structural, and cultural characteristics of the project-oriented company, maturity models are categorized and general maturity models and project management-related maturity models are presented. Then the family of *mature* models is introduced. For selected models of this 'family' the underlying management approach, the dimensions of the model, the process of application, and the results of the analysis and the benchmarking are described.

STRATEGY, STRUCTURE AND CULTURE OF THE PROJECT-ORIENTED COMPANY

Projects are applied in companies of all industrial branches as well as in non-profit companies to perform relatively unique processes of medium to large scope. Any company (or part of a company, such as a division or a profit centre), which applies projects and programmes can be perceived as being project-oriented. A project-oriented company has some or all of the following characteristics:

- Management by projects is considered as an explicit organizational strategy
- Projects and programmes are applied as temporary organizations
- Networks of projects, chains of projects and project portfolios are management objects of consideration
- Project management, programme management and project portfolio management are explicit processes
- Know-how, assurance and assignment of people to projects is organized by expert pools
- Project management quality is assured by a PM Office
- Strategic alignment of the project portfolio is performed by a Project Portfolio Group
- A 'New Management Paradigm' is applied
- Self-perception as being project-oriented

According to the 'organizational fit model' the project-oriented company can be described by its strategy, structure, and culture, Figure 10.1. These have to fit to provide good quality services, and to be cost and time efficient. The organizational strategy of the project-oriented company is 'Management by Projects' (Gareis 2005a). It has permanent and temporary organization structures, and a culture which is based on a 'New Management Paradigm'.

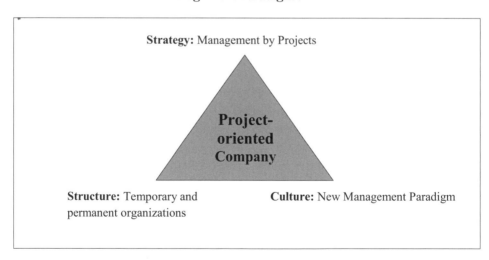

Figure 10.1 Strategy, structure, and culture of the project-oriented company

STRATEGY: MANAGEMENT BY PROJECTS

Project-oriented companies consider projects not only as ways of performing processes, but as a strategic option for the organizational design of the company. 'Management by Projects', is the organizational strategy of companies dealing with an increasingly complex business environment. By applying 'Management by Projects' the following objectives are pursued:

- organizational differentiation and decentralization of management responsibility
- quality assurance by project team work and holistic project definitions
- goal orientation
- personnel development in projects
- organizational learning in and by projects

For the implementation of 'Management by Projects', symbolic management measures, showing the importance of projects, are required. Such measures include:

- showing in the organization chart of the company not only the permanent organization structures, but also temporary organizations (see Figure 10.2)
- including project-related functions in job descriptions of all managers
- including a statement on the strategic importance of project management in the company mission statement
- promoting project management by appropriate marketing measures

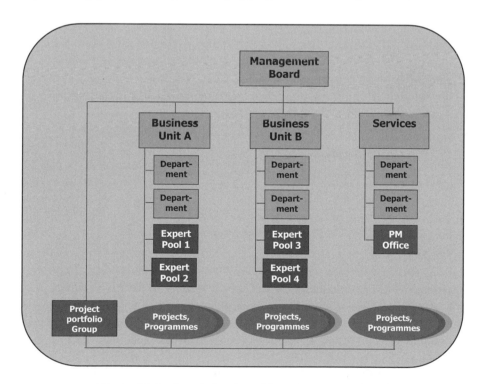

Figure 10.2 Organization chart of the project-oriented company

185

STRUCTURE: TEMPORARY AND PERMANENT ORGANIZATIONS

For the performance of processes of different strategic importance, or of different scope and duration and cost, different organizations are appropriate. Departments of the 'line organization' such as 'Procurement' or 'Production' are responsible for routine processes. However, for the performance of relatively unique processes of medium or large scope, and of short to medium duration, projects are the appropriate organizations. Projects can be defined for the performance of 'contracts' for external clients as well as for product developments, marketing campaigns, investments in the company infrastructure or for re-engineering processes for internal clients. A programme is a temporary organization for the performance of a process of large scope. A programme consists of several closely coupled projects and work packages. It is limited in time and is medium or long term in duration. Typical programmes are the development of a 'product family' (and not only of a single product), the implementation of a comprehensive IT-solution for an international concern, and the reorganization of a group of companies in a holding structure. Projects and programmes further differentiate companies. In addition to the permanent organizations of companies, such as divisions, profit centres and departments, temporary organizations are considered.

The greater the diversity of projects a company holds in its project portfolio, the more differentiated it becomes and the greater its management complexity will be. In order to support the performance of projects as well as to ensure the compliance of the objectives of the projects with the overall company strategies, specific integrative structures, such as a Strategic Centre, Expert Pools, a PM Office, and a Project Portfolio Group are required.

Experts from various Expert Pools of the project-oriented company perform the processes in projects and programmes. (The Expert Pool can be known by a number of names such as Resource Pool and Centre of Excellence.) It is the objective of Expert Pools to provide sufficient, appropriately qualified experts. The tasks to be fulfilled in the Expert Pools are personnel management, process management and knowledge management. Project-related tasks and their qualitative control are not performed in the Expert Pool but rather in the projects. In accordance with the model of the 'empowered' project organization, the project team members are responsible for the method of the performance – within the defined guidelines and standards – and for the quality of the performance of the work packages. Depending on the business operations of a project-oriented company several types of Expert Pools can be differentiated. In an engineering construction company, for example, there are various technical Expert Pools (Mechanical Engineering, Electrical Engineering, etc.), an Expert Pool 'Procurement', an Expert Pool 'Installation', etc.

The Project Portfolio Group is a permanent communication structure of medium-sized and large project-oriented companies. The Project Portfolio Group should be responsible for the assignment of a project or a programme and for project portfolio coordination. Only organizations with at least 200 to 300 employees which perform at least 15 to 20 projects simultaneously, achieve a complexity which makes a separate communication structure for the project portfolio management meaningful. In smaller companies, these tasks can be performed by the management in the course of management meetings.

The PM Office is to support the Project Portfolio Group in its preparation, performance and follow-up of coordination meetings. In particular, the PM Office can develop the project portfolio reports. PM Offices therefore not only perform services regarding the project and programme management, but also regarding the project portfolio management (see Chapter 9).

With the increasing importance of projects and programmes in organizations, there arises a need for standardizing the practices in projects and programmes and to ensure the quality of the project and programme management. The objective of a PM Office is to ensure a professional project, programme and project portfolio management in the project-oriented company.

CULTURE: NEW MANAGEMENT PARADIGM

The project-oriented company is characterized by an explicit project management culture; that is by a set of project management-related values, norms, and rules. For the project and the programme management processes, specific procedures exist, creating a common understanding for their performance of these processes, the roles involved, and the management methods to be applied.

Traditional management approaches, based on a mechanistic management paradigm such as that of Taylorism, emphasize detailed planning methods, focus on the assignment of clearly defined work packages for individuals, rely on contractual agreements with clients and suppliers, and use the hierarchy as a central integration instrument. 'New' management concepts, such as Lean Management, Total Quality Management, the Learning Organization, and Business Process Re-Engineering, introduce new approaches. Among the common features of these 'new' management approaches are:

- the use of the organization to create competitive advantage
- the empowerment of employees
- process-orientation and teamwork in flat organizations
- continuous and discontinuous organizational change
- customer-orientation
- networking with clients and suppliers

187

The application of a 'New Management Paradigm' supports efficiency in the performance of projects. Of course, projects can be performed within a traditional management culture. But this often results in costly, time consuming and, for the project team members, frustrating experiences. The real benefits, the added values of project management can only be achieved if some concepts of the 'New Management Paradigm' are applied.

MATURITY MODELS

In the Collins Dictionary the adjective 'mature' is defined as

- fully-developed or grown-up
- of plans or theories it can mean that they are fully considered, perfected
- of insurance policies or bills it can mean due or payable
- of fruit, wine or cheese it can mean ripe or fully aged

In an economic context maturity can be defined as 'fully developed processes', which implies that capabilities to carry out these processes must be grown over time. It connotes understanding or perception of why success occurs and ways to correct or prevent common problems (Cooke-Davies 2005, p 212). Based on the quality management movement over the last years different maturity models have been developed. A maturity model can be defined as a *'structured collection of elements that describe characteristics of effective processes'* (SEI 2005, p 12). The first model relating to the measurement of the quality of the software development process, the SEI Capability Maturity Model, was developed by the Software Engineering Institute (SEI) of Carnegie-Mellon University (Humphrey 1989; Paulk et al 1991). It uses 5 steps to describe and to measure the competence to perform a specific process. The scale used was initial, repeatable, defined, managed and optimized, Figure 10.3.

Due to the success of this maturity model and the growing number of users, the model was further developed. In 2002 the Capability Maturity Model Integration (CMMI) version 1.1 was published. In comparison to its predecessor model it integrated four disciplines (Systems Engineering, Software Engineering, Integrated Product and Process Development and Supplier Sourcing) and offered two representations (staged, continuous) which allowed an organization to pursue different improvement paths (SEI 2005). In 2006 the model CMMI for Development version 1.2 was published. The purpose of this further developed CMMI is *'to help organizations improve their development and maintenance processes for both products and services.'* (SEI 2006). For 2007 CMMI for Services and CMMI for Acquisition are planned.

Maturity Level	Description of the Level
5 = optimized	Continuous improvement of the process Continuous collection of data to identify Analysis of defects for prevention
4 = managed	Process is quantitatively measured Minimum of metrics for quality and productivity exist Collection of process experiences
3 = defined	Process defined and institutionalized Process groups defined
2 = repeatable	Process depends on individuals Minimum of process controlling/guidance exists Highly risky in case of new challenges
1 = initial	Ad-hoc process, not formalized No adequate guidance No consistency in product delivery

Figure 10.3   Maturity levels of the SEI Capability Maturity Model

PROJECT MANAGEMENT RELATED MATURITY MODELS

Project management-related maturity models can refer to different objects of consideration. For instance they can refer to different social systems or to different processes. Regarding the social system, considered maturity models usually refer to project-oriented organizations, such as a company or a division of a company. But the maturity can be analyzed also for a project manager, for a project, and even for a nation. In more general terms one can differentiate in maturity models for:

● individuals (project owner, project manager, project team member)
● teams (project owner team, project team)
● temporary organizations (programme, project)
● permanent organizations (company, division, profit centre)
● societies (nations, regions)

Regarding the processes considered maturity models usually refer to the project management process. Only OPM3 (PMI® 2003), considers programme and the project portfolio management processes in addition to project management processes.

Maturity models can further be differentiated in generic and company-specific models. An example of a company-specific model for the programme

189

management process is that of EDS, an international IT company (Figure 10.4). Most of the project management-related maturity models such as the Berkley Project Management Process Maturity Model (Ibbs et al 2005) or the PM Solution`s Project Management Maturity Model (Pennypacker and Grant 2003) are based on the PMI®'s Guide to the Project Management Body of Knowledge (PMI® 2004) and on maturity levels like the CMM®I, (SEI 2005, 2006). Others like Harold Kerzner's Project Management Maturity Model (PMMM) (Kerzner 2001), PRINCE2™ Maturity Model (P2MM) (OGC 2007), or PM Delta of the German Project Management Association (Schelle et al 2005, 499) are based on other project management approaches.

The most known and comprehensive generic maturity model to analyse the maturity of permanent organizations that has been developed in the last years is PMI®`s OPM3. OPM3 which stands for 'Organizational Project Management Maturity Model' was developed with a widespread participation of professionals and was published in 2003 by PMI®. Organizational project management is defined as the application of knowledge, skills, tools and techniques to achieve the strategic objectives of an organization through projects. Organizational project management comprises project, programme and portfolio management (PMI® 2003). OPM3 consists of three interlocking elements: knowledge, assessment and improvement. In addition to the terminology of the PMI®`s PMBOK® Guide it uses new terms: Best Practices, Capability, Outcome, Key Performance Indicators (KPIs). OPM3 also includes the incorporation of all three project management domains and a process improvement construct. In comparison to other maturity models it does not use maturity levels.

THE FAMILY OF '*MATURE*' MODELS

Maturity models for different social systems should relate to each other. Therefore the PROJEKTMANAGEMENT GROUP of the Vienna University of Economics and Business Administration and ROLAND GAREIS CONSULTING developed a family of '*mature*' models. This family comprises of the following maturity models:

- personnel *mature*
- team *mature*
- project *mature*
- programme *mature*
- project-oriented company *mature*
- project-oriented society *mature*

In contrast to excellence models, like the IPMA project excellence model (Chapter 17), maturity models are normative and need to be based on particular

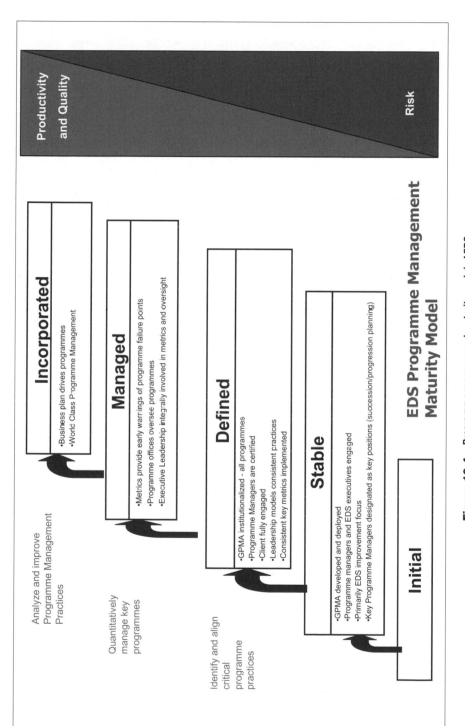

Figure 10.4 Programme management maturity model of EDS

191

management approaches. The family of the '*mature*' models is based on *ROLAND GAREIS Project and Programme Management*® and *ROLAND GAREIS Management of the Project-oriented Company*® and *ROLAND GAREIS Management in the Project-oriented Society*® (Gareis 2005a). For each maturity model there exists:

- a description of the underlying management approach,
- a questionnaire to be applied for the analysis,
- standards for the analysis report and for benchmarking reports, and
- descriptions of the analysis and the benchmarking process.

The results of an analysis with any *mature* model can be shown in a spider web presentation, which is multidimensional. The different maturities in different dimensions are visualized, the overall maturity is presented by the area resulting from the connection of the maturity points at the spider web axes. The results of a social system of a 'lower level' can be used as input for the analysis of the maturity of a social system at a 'higher level'. For instance the results of the analysis of a project belonging to a programme, can be used for the analysis of the maturity of this programme. Examples of the application of the models 'personnel *mature*', 'team *mature*', and 'project-oriented company *mature*' are described below.

APPLICATION OF PERSONNEL MATURE

Underlying management approach

In project-oriented companies, project owners, project managers, and project team members require competences to fulfil functions in the project management process. To be able to perform the role of a project owner adequately, they need project management competences, to communicate efficiently with the project manager and the project team. The functions to be performed by project owners, project managers, and project team members are described in role descriptions. As an example the role of the project manager is described in Figure 10.5. The project management maturity of a person can be defined as the competence and self-understanding (attitude) to fulfill a particular role in a process. Besides the project management knowledge and experience and a certain self-understanding, a project manager needs product, company, and industry knowledge. In international projects, cultural awareness and language knowledge are also prerequisites.

Dimensions of the model

The model 'personnel *mature*' can be applied for the analysis of the maturity of a project owner, a project manager, or a project team member. The overall maturity

Role Description: Project Manager
Objectives
Contribution to realization of the project objectives and to the optimization of the business case
Leading the project team and the project contributors
Representation of the project towards relevant environments
Organizational position
Member of the project team
Reports to the project owner team
Tasks
In the project start process
Know-how transfer from the pre-project phase into the project
Development of adequate project plans
Design of an adequate project organization
Performance of risk management
Design of project-context-relations
In the project controlling process
Determination of the project status
Redefinition of project objectives
Development of project progress reports
In the resolution of a project discontinuity
Analysis of the situation and definition of ad-hoc measures
Development of project scenarios
Definition of strategies and further measures
Communication of the project discontinuity to relevant project environments
In the project close-down process
Coordination of the final contents work
Transfer of know-how into the base organization
Dissolution of project-environment relations

Figure 10.5   Role description of a project manager

of a person is based on the maturities in the dimensions project start, project coordination, project controlling, management of a project discontinuity, project close-down, designing the project management process and social competence and self-understanding (see Figure 10.6). The analysis regarding the dimensions of the maturity model is based on the questionnaire 'personnel *mature*'. As an example one question relating to the project start process, asking for the knowledge and the experience of the project manager to design project-context relations is shown in Figure 10.7.

Project personnel require not only knowledge and experience to apply project management methods, but also to creatively design the project management process. The dimension 'designing the project management process' of the maturity model considers

● the application of appropriate project management methods
● the selection and the design of appropriate project communication structures

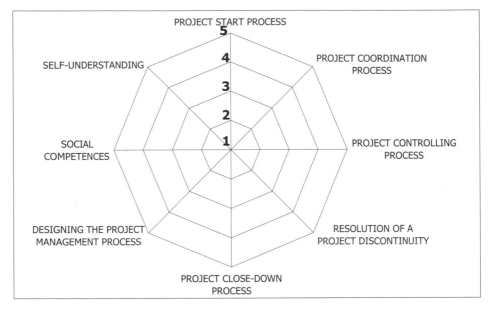

Figure 10.6   Spider web of the model 'personnel mature'

● the selection of an appropriate ICT infrastructure for the project

The social competence is an own dimension because of its importance. It considers competences regarding methods for presentation and facilitation, team development methods, conflict management, feedback and reflection, negotiating, and management of emotions. The dimension 'self-understanding' has different criteria for project owners, project managers and project team members. For project managers it considers the professional application of project management methods, the acceptance of an holistic project responsibility, the assurance of the project progress, etc.

Process of analyzing and benchmarking

It has to be decided for which project role the maturity model is to be applied; project owner, project manager, or project team member. The analysis is based on

Project start: Design of project–context relations		
1=none, 2=low, 3=average, 4=much, 5=very much	Knowledge	Experience
Project environment analysis		
Analysis: Pre- and post project phase		
Analysis: Relations to other projects		
Analysis: Relations to the company strategy		
Project marketing		
Business case analysis		

Figure 10.7   A question of the questionnaire of 'personnel mature'

a self-analysis questionnaire which comprises questions regarding the dimensions of 'personnel *mature*'. Also questions regarding the project management education attended and the project management experience gained in concrete projects are included. An external analysis is performed by an assessor. The assessor applies 1–2 hours interview with the person and analyses the project management documents of projects in which the person is involved. In the interview the results of the self-analysis are reflected and interpreted. In a benchmarking the maturities of different persons can be compared with each other. The results of the analysis (and the benchmarking) are documented in a maturity report. This becomes the basis for appropriate management measures.

Results of the analysis

The results of the analysis are shown in spider web presentations of the maturity model. Figure 10.8 shows the results regarding the project management

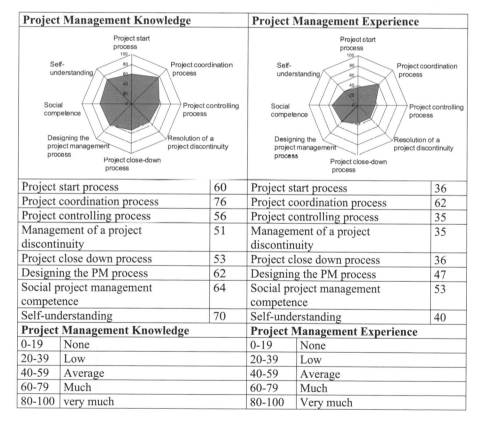

Project Management Knowledge		Project Management Experience	
Project start process	60	Project start process	36
Project coordination process	76	Project coordination process	62
Project controlling process	56	Project controlling process	35
Management of a project discontinuity	51	Management of a project discontinuity	35
Project close down process	53	Project close down process	36
Designing the PM process	62	Designing the PM process	47
Social project management competence	64	Social project management competence	53
Self-understanding	70	Self-understanding	40
Project Management Knowledge		**Project Management Experience**	
0-19	None	0-19	None
20-39	Low	20-39	Low
40-59	Average	40-59	Average
60-79	Much	60-79	Much
80-100	very much	80-100	Very much

Figure 10.8 Project management knowledge and experience of a project manager

195

knowledge and experience of a project manager. The blue areas visualize the overall competence and experience. The area for the project management knowledge is homogenous. The project manager has a high knowledge in the application of methods for the project start, the project coordination process, the designing the project management process, and also has a high social competence. There is average knowledge for project controlling, management of a discontinuity and project close-down. In comparison with the project management knowledge the project manager has less experience in most of the dimensions. The maturity of a project manager can be compared with the minimum knowledge and experience required to be certified as a project manager by IPMA-International Project Management Association.

Results of benchmarking

If several project managers are analyzed a comparison of their 'maturities' can be done.

The results of the benchmarking of one of the dimensions of the model, the self-understanding, of 12 project managers of an Austrian company are shown in Figure 10.9. This figure shows that the project managers have a relatively strong self-understanding to fulfil the role of a project manager. But there is space for improvement in the professional application of the project management methods.

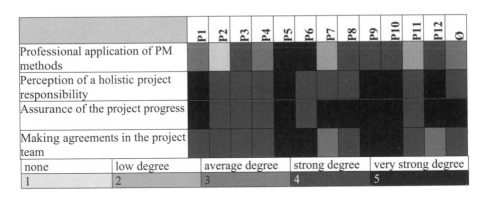

Figure 10.9 Benchmarking of the self-understanding of project managers

APPLICATION OF TEAM MATURE

Underlying management approach

In project-oriented companies project owner teams as well as project teams might be subject to a maturity analysis. In addition to the project management competences needed by the members of a project owner team or a project team, a team requires a specific team competence to perform its functions. The functions to be performed can be described in role descriptions. As an example the role of the project team is described in Figure 10.10.

Role Description: Project Team
Objectives
▪ Develop a common 'Big Project Picture'
▪ Ensure synergies in the project performance
▪ Ensure commitment
▪ Solve conflicts
▪ Organize learning in the project
Organizational position
▪ Part of the project organization
▪ Assigned by the project owner team
Tasks
In the project start process
▪ Exchange information between the project team members
▪ Jointly decide on the design of the project organization and about project planning
▪ Jointly decide on the design of the project context relationships
▪ Agree on project rules
In the project controlling process
▪ Jointly determine the project status
▪ Jointly agree on adaptions of project objectives, schedule, costs, etc
▪ Jointly agree on adaptions of the project organization and the project context relationships
In the resolution of a project discontinuity
▪ Jointly suggest the definition of a project discontinuity
▪ Jointly design the process for resolving the project discontinuity
▪ Jointly develop immediate measures
In the project close-down process
▪ Jointly design the project close-down process
▪ Jointly transfer know-how into the permanent organizations
▪ etc.

Figure 10.10   Role description of the project team

Dimensions of the model

The model 'team *mature*' can be applied for the analysis of the 'maturity' of a project owner team or a project team. The overall maturity of a team is based on the maturities in the dimensions, Figure 10.11:

- Competences of the team members
- Design of the project management process
- Development of the 'Big Project Picture'
- Assurance of synergies
- Commitment
- Conflict solution
- Learning and innovation

197

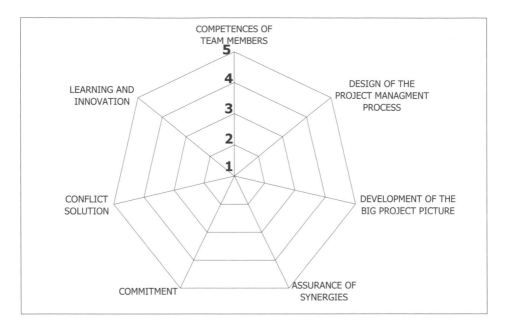

Figure 10.11   Spider web of the model 'team *mature*'

The analysis of the maturity of a team is based on the questionnaire 'team *mature*'. As an example a question relating to the joint development of the 'Big Project Picture' is shown in Figure 10.12. The dimensions of the model 'team *mature*' are briefly described:

Competences of team members: relates to the individual project management competences of the team members. These competences can either be analyzed roughly or can be subject to a detailed analysis applying 'personnel *mature*'. The possibility of integrating the results of the analysis of the individual competencies shows the relationships between the '*mature*' models.

Development of the Big Project Picture: reflects that a team needs the competence to consider all project dimensions, which means the project scope, its

Development of the 'Big Project Picture'		
1=none, 2=low, 3=average, 4=much, 5=very much	Knowledge	Experience
Consideration of all project dimensions		
Consideration of relationships between the project plans		
Application of project plans as communication instruments		
Application of a context orientation		

Figure 10.12   A question of the questionnaire 'team *mature*'

time, and costs, as well as its income, risk, organization, and culture. The consideration of relationships between the project plans, for example between the work break-down structure and the project environment analysis, contributes to the quality of project management. The project plans have to be understood as communication instruments.

Design the project management process: considers that the team jointly defines the required project communication structures, the adequate project management methods, the consulting support, and the adequate ICT infrastructure.

Assurance of synergies: considers that a team has the potential to create synergies and added value by team work. Open communication and sharing of information is the basis of real team work.

Commitment: considers that teams need to create commitment. Agreements made in the team need to be kept, responsibility has to be taken.

Conflict solution: reflects that teams need to have the competence to solve conflicts. For that methods like feedback and reflection are required.

Learning and innovation: reflects that teams need to organize learning and innovation in the project. Project controlling can be perceived as a process of organizational learning in a project.

Process of the analysis and benchmarking

The analysis is based on a questionnaire which comprises questions regarding the dimensions of 'team *mature*'. Results of the analysis of the single team members with 'personnel *mature*' can be integrated. The analysis can be performed as a self-analysis of the team and as an external analysis by an assessor. The important part of the self-analysis by the team is the communication process of the team members and the finding of consensus regarding the answering of the questions. The additional external analysis consists of a discussion of the results of the self-analysis with the team and of an observation of a team meeting. The dimensions of the maturity model serve as observation criteria. In a benchmarking the maturities of different teams can be compared. The results of the analysis (and the benchmarking) are documented in a maturity report. This becomes the basis for appropriate management interventions.

199

APPLICATION OF PROJECT-ORIENTED COMPANY MATURE

Underlying management approach

The strategy 'Management by Projects', the temporary and permanent organizations, and the 'New management paradigm' of the project-oriented company have been described above. Here selected, specific processes of the project-oriented company, namely project management, programme management, and project portfolio management, are described briefly.

Project management

The perception of projects influences the project management approach, to be applied. *ROLAND GAREIS Project and Programme Management®* represents a systemic approach to project management. Projects are perceived as temporary organizations and social systems. Therefore the objects of consideration in the project management process are not only the scope of work, the project schedule, and the project costs but also the project objectives, the project income, the project organization, the project culture, as well as project context dimensions, such as the relationships to the relevant environments, to other projects, and to the company strategies, and business case.

Project management is considered as a process of the project-oriented company, which includes the sub-processes project start, continuous project coordination, project controlling, resolution of a project discontinuity, and project close-down. The project management process starts with the formal project assignment and ends with the approval of the project results by the project owner. The objectives of the project management process are to:

- perform successfully the project according to the project objectives
- contribute to the optimization of the business case of the investment, initialized by the project
- manage the project complexity and project dynamics
- adjust the project boundaries continuously
- manage the project-context relationships

Programme management

Programme management has to be performed in addition to the management of the single projects of a programme. The programme management process has the same structure as the project management process. It includes the sub-processes of starting, coordinating, controlling, closing-down a programme, and possibly resolving a programme discontinuity. Also, programme management methods are similar to the project management methods. For instance there is a programme work breakdown structure, a programme bar chart, a programme environment analysis, and so forth.

In order to allow for autonomous projects while ensuring the benefits of organizational learning, economies of scale, and networking synergies in a programme, a specific programme organization has to be designed. Typical programme roles are Programme Owner, Programme Manager, Programme Office and Programme Team. The Programme Owner assigns the programme to the Programme Manager, who is responsible for the programme management. He or she is supported by the programme team members and the Programme Office. Typical programme communication structures are programme owner meetings and programme team meetings. The function of the programme organization is to integrate the different projects of a programme, in order to fulfil overall programme objectives and strategies. The advantages of designing a programme organization instead of defining a large 'project' with several sub-projects are:

- a less hierarchical organization
- a clear terminology: a programme manager and several project managers instead of one project manager and additional 'project managers' of the sub-projects
- empowerment of the projects (of the programme) by allowing for specific project cultures, specific relationships to social environments, and specific project organizations
- differentiation between programme ownership and ownerships of the different projects.

Project portfolio management

The objectives of the project portfolio management are to:

- assign the right projects and programmes,
- optimize the results of the project portfolio
- define project priorities
- coordinate internal and external resources
- organize learning of and between projects.

The basis for the management of the project portfolio is a project portfolio database, which typically includes data about the project types, relations of projects to other projects, the project organizations, relevant project environments, and project ratios. The project portfolio database is not a project information system but contains aggregated project data only. It might be integrated in a project information system. The project portfolio database allows the development of project portfolio reports. Typical project portfolio reports are the project portfolio bar chart, the project portfolio profit-risk graph, and the project portfolio progress chart. An integrative project portfolio reporting tool is the project portfolio score card. It shows how the actual project portfolio contributes to the implementation of the company strategies, reports on the structure of the project portfolio, and on the project portfolio status overall. Visualizing the project portfolio reports contributes to their acceptance as a communication instrument for management and top management.

A set of closely coupled projects can be viewed as a network of projects. Examples of the criteria which might relate projects in a network are a common technology applied, a common client, a common partner or supplier, or a common geographic region. The construction of a network of projects occurs at a point in time, in order to resolve a common problem or use a common opportunity. Therefore a network of projects is not an organization with a common objective and a manager, such as a programme, but it is an ad-hoc communication structure. The objective of networking between projects is to identify synergies and potential conflicts between projects and to define strategies and measures to resolve the conflicts and to use the synergies. The networking between projects might result in a redefinition of the objectives of one or more projects of the network, in an assignment of common resources to two or more projects, or in re-negotiations of contracts with the clients, partners or suppliers.

Dimensions of the model

The maturity model 'project-oriented company *mature*' includes the following dimensions:

- project management
- programme management
- assurance of the management quality of a project or a programme,
- assignment of a project or a programme,
- project portfolio coordination and networking between projects
- organizational design
- personnel management
- process management

In the questionnaire of 'project-oriented company *mature*' each dimension is dealt with by a set of questions. The number of questions for each dimension is shown in Figure 10.13. In total the questionnaire consists of 74 questions. An example of questions relating to the project start process is shown in Figure 10.14.

As well as questions relating to the maturity dimensions, the questionnaire also includes questions about the size of the company, its line of business, its types and

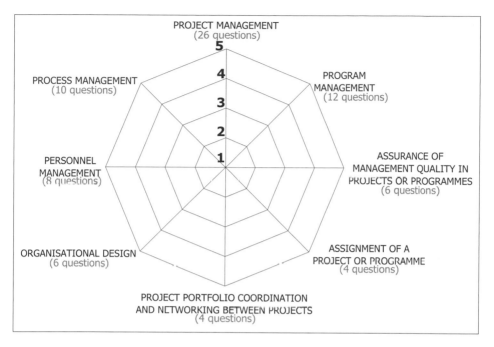

Figure 10.13   Spider web of the model 'project-oriented company *mature*'

number of projects and programmes, etc. This information is required to later interpret the data resulting from the analysis appropriately.

Process of the analysis and of benchmarking

A self-analysis is performed by a team of five to ten project management experts from the project-oriented company being analyzed. Senior project managers,

In the project start process the following methods are used for project planning	External projects	Internal projects
Project objectives plan		
Work break-down structure		
Work package specifications		
Project milestone plan		
Project bar chart		
CPM schedule		

1=always, 2=often, 3=sometimes, 4=seldom, 5=never

Figure 10.14   A question of the questionnaire of 'project-oriented company *mature*'

203

programme managers, members of the Project Portfolio Group, the PM Office manager, and project owners participate in the analysis. The questionnaire is filled out in a moderated workshop. The benefits of this process include the discussions between the experts, the agreements they reach about the applied practices, and the common construction of a reality as a project-oriented company.

In any external analysis documents, such as project management templates, project and programme management guidelines, project management documents of ongoing projects, project portfolio reports, a project management career path, etc., are analyzed. The assessor interviews some of the project management experts, in order to better understand the documents. Based on the results of the external analysis possibly the results of the self-analysis have to be challenged.

Through benchmarking the maturity of the company being assessed can be compared to other project-oriented companies. The results of the analysis (and the benchmarking) are included in a maturity report. This is a basis for the planning measures for the further development as a project-oriented company.

Results of the analysis and of benchmarking

From January 2004 to July 2005 a research project *'project orientation [austria]'* was performed by the PROJEKTMANAGEMENT GROUP of the Vienna University of Economics and Business Administration, (Gareis and Gruber 2005, 2006). The objectives of this project were to:

- analyze and benchmark the maturities of about 60 Austrian project-oriented companies
- analyze and benchmark the maturities of about 5 project-oriented industries
- analyze the maturity of Austria as a project-oriented nation
- develope strategies and measures for the further development of the maturities of the project-oriented companies and of Austria as a project-oriented nation
- present and publish the research results at conferences and in journals

The results of 60 Austrian companies analyzed are shown against the spider web model of 'project-oriented company *mature*' in Figure 10.15. The 60 project-oriented companies have an average maturity of 2.93, which is measured by the '*mature* ratio'. A *mature* ratio is calculated as a weighted average of the maturities of the different dimensions. As 'project management' is considered the most important dimension, this dimension has the weight of 20%. The dimensions 'assignment of a project or a programme' and 'organizational design' are weighted with 15%, the rest with 10%. The single questions in each dimension are equally weighted. If for example a question block consists of five questions each question will be weighted with 20%.

mature ratio of the project-oriented company	2.92
Project management	3.55
Programme management	1.87
Assurance of the management quality of a project or programme	2.04
Assignment of a project or programme	3.28
Project portfolio coordination, networking between projects	2.74
Organizational design	3.22
Personnel management	2.75
Process management	2.88

Figure 10.15 Average maturities of 60 project-oriented companies of Austria

The highest maturities are obtained in the dimensions 'project management', 'assignment of a project or a programme' and 'organizational design'. The lowest maturities are obtained the dimensions 'assurance of the management quality of a project or a programme' and 'programme management'. The maturity area is relatively homogeneous with the exception of the drop in 'programme management' and the 'assurance of the management quality of a project or a programme'. Some benchmarking results are shown in the Figures 10.16 and 10.17. The average maturity of the 60 project-oriented companies and the best and the worst are compared.

In addition the results of the 60 Austrian project-oriented companies have been compared by sizes of companies (small, medium and large) as well as by industries. It turned out that large project-oriented companies had a higher mature ratio than small and medium ones. Large companies carry out programmes and do consulting and auditing, to assure the management quality of projects and programmes. Large companies also have more possibilities regarding the organizational design, such as establishing a PM Office or a Project Portfolio Group, and take extensive measures regarding the development of the project personnel.

From the six industries considered (ICT, research, engineering, consulting, building construction, and public sector), the ICT industry had the highest, the public sector the lowest *mature* ratio. The fact that the ICT industry has the highest mature ratio was confirmed by Turner and Müller (2006).

	Worst POC	Best POC	Ø 60 POCs
A 1. Project start process	3,87	1,42	2,39
A 1.1. Methods used for project planning I (e.g. project objectives plan, project milestone plan, ...)	3,50	1,00	2,07
A 1.2. Methods used for project planning II (e.g. project resource plan, project cost plan, ...)	4,50	1,33	2,24
A 1.3. Methods used for the project context relationship (e.g. project environment analysis, business case analysis, ...)	4,00	1,33	2,77
A 1.4. Methods used for designing the project organization (e.g. project organization chart, responsibility chart, ...)	4,86	1,14	2,37
A 1.5. Consideration of representatives of 'external companies' as project team members ("integration")	3,20	2,60	2,22
A 1.6. Methods used for developing a project culture (e.g. project name, project logo, slogans, ...)	4,00	1,50	2,67
A 1.7. Methods used for project marketing (e.g. project homepage, project presentations, project newsletters, ...)	3,00	1,00	2,41

Always	1	Often	2	Sometimes	3	Seldom	4	Never	5

Figure 10.16   Maturity in the performance of the project start process

SUMMARY

The assurance of the quality of personnel, of teams and of processes is a major concern of project-oriented companies. The high number of different projects performed simultaneously, the high complexity of the organization, the dynamics in the project portfolio, and the relative autonomy of projects and programmes require specific integrative measures. Maturity models are important instruments to assure quality in project-oriented companies. Three models of the 'family *mature*' have been introduced, to show maturities can be analyzed for different social systems in the project-oriented company and that the models relate to each other.

	Worst POC	Best POC	Ø 60 POCs
Part G: Personnel management in the project-oriented company	7%	86%	47%
G 1. 'Project manager' considered as a profession	5,00	1,00	3,26
G 2. Professional recruiting of·project and program managers	5,00	2,00	3,61
G 3. Leading of project and program management personnel	4,67	1,00	2,52
G 4. Project-related incentive systems	3,50	3,25	3,48
G 5. Development of project and program management personnel	4,83	1,00	3,24

continually optimized	1	very relevant	2	limited relevance	3	existing informally	4	not existing	5

G 6. Project management competencies of the project and program management personnel	4,67	1,25	2,58
G 7. Project management competencies of managers	5,00	1,75	2,45

very high	1	High	2	Average	3	low	4	very low	5

Figure 10.17   Maturity in personnel management

REFERENCES AND FURTHER READINGS

Cleland, D.I. and Gareis, R., (eds), 2006, *Global Project Management Handbook*, 2nd edition, New York: McGraw Hill.

Cooke-Davies, T., 2005, 'Measurement of Organizational Maturity: Questions for Future Research', in *Innovations: Project Management Research 2004*, Newtown Square, PA: Project Management Institute.

Gareis, R., 2005a, *Happy Projects!*, Vienna: Manz Verlag.

Gareis, R., 2005b, 'Management of the project-oriented company', in Morris, P.W.G. and Pinto, J.K., (eds.), *The Wiley Guide to managing projects*, New York: Wiley.

Gareis, R., and Gruber, C., 2005, *Final Research Report: Analysis of Austria as a Project-Oriented Nation*, Vienna, August 2005.

Gareis, R., and Gruber, C., 2006, 'Project Management in Austria: Analysis of the maturity of Austria as a project-oriented nation'; in Cleland, D.I. and

Gareis, R., *Global Project Management Handbook*, 2nd edition, New York: McGraw Hill.

Humphrey, W., 1989, *Managing the Software Process*, Reading, MA: Addison-Wesley.

Ibbs, C.W., Reginato, J.M. and Kwak, Y.H., 2005, 'Developing project management capability: Benchmarking, maturity, modelling, gap analyses, and ROI studies', in Pinto, J.K. and Morris, P.W.G (eds.), *The Wiley Guide to managing projects*, New York: Wiley.

Kerzner, H., 2001, *Strategic Planning for Project Management Using a Project Management Maturity Model*, New York: Wiley.

OGC, 2007, *Improving Project Performance using PRINCE2™ Maturity Model*, London: Stationery Office.

Paulk, M.C., Curtis, B., and Chrissis, M.B., 1991, *Capability Maturity Models for Software*, Pittsburg: Carnegie Mellon University.

Pennypacker, J.S. and Grant, K.P., 2003, 'Project management maturity: An industry benchmark', *Project Management Journal*, 34 (1), 4–11.

PMI®, 2003, *Organizational Project Management Maturity Model*, Newtown Square, PA: Project Management Institute.

PMI®, 2004, *A Guide to the Project Management Body of Knowledge*, 3rd edition, Newtown Square, PA: Project Management Institute.

Schelle, H., Ottmann R., and Pfeiffer, A., 2005, *Projektmanager*, Frankfurt: GPM Deutsche Gesellschaft für Projektmanagement.

Senge, P., 1994, *The Fifth Discipline Fieldbook: Strategies and Tools For Building a Learning Organization*, London: Nicholas Brierly Publishing.

Software Engineering Institute, 2005, *Capability Maturity Model® Integration, (CMMI®) Overview*, Pittsburg: Carnegie Mellon University.

Software Engineering Institute, 2006, *CMMI® for Development, Version 1.2*, Pittsburg: Carnegie Mellon University.

Turner, J.R. and Müller, R., 2006, *Choosing Appropriate Project Managers: Matching their Leadership Style to the Type of Project*, Newtown Square, PA: Project Management Institute.

11 Conducting Audits

Martina Huemann

In many project-oriented organizations, different quality management methods are applied. These include excellence models, maturity models, benchmarking, certification, accreditation, evaluation, coaching, reviewing and auditing. Auditing is a quality assurance instrument which can add value to the project and the project-oriented organization which applies it.

Auditing is often connected with ISO certification or financial auditing. When project managers are asked about their experience with auditing, most report that it has been a rather stressful, sometimes even a hostile event. In many cases auditing is perceived as a formal box-ticking exercise, to ensure all documents and project plans exist. Project managers do not perceive any added value in this process.

As an alternative, this chapter aims to introduce the management auditing of projects as a learning instrument to add value to the project as well as to the project-oriented company. Project management auditing can be perceived as an instrument for improving the management processes of a project, and thus it may contribute to a project's success. To perceive project management auditing as a learning opportunity calls for a reinvention of this quality assurance instrument. This is reflected in the auditing process and in the methods applied as well as in the attitude of the auditor and the cultural aspects of the audit. This chapter advocates routine auditing on a regular basis and promotes a co-operative auditing style to add value to the project or programme.

PROJECT AUDITING

ISO 19011:2002 defines auditing as a 'systematic, independent and documented process for obtaining audit evidence and evaluating it objectively to determine the extent to which the audit criteria are fulfilled'. The audit criteria are a set of policies, procedures, or requirements set externally to the item being audited. Reasons for audits include certification, internal audits or contract compliance.

Auditing is also a method of quality assurance and quality improvement in the context of projects and programmes. A project audit is a systematic and independent investigation to check if the project is performing correctly with respect to product, project and or project management standards. Different terms are used such as project health checks, quick scans or most commonly reviews. Generally, these are considered to be less formal than audits. In many organizations the term audit tends to be used in the context of certification or financial auditing. In the context of projects or programmes the term review is often used instead.

We differentiate between controlling, reviews and audits. Project controlling, which aims to determine the progress and the status of a project, is done by the project manager and the project team. A specific form of review is the peer review. Peer reviews for projects and programmes are done by peer professionals such as programme managers or senior project managers to give feedback and advice to the project or the programme. However, an audit is always conducted by a party external to the project. Thus the auditor provides a perspective external to the project.

Either processes or results of processes can be audited. Depending on the objectives and the scope of the audit, different types of auditing or reviewing exist:

- Audits that consider specific project deliverables like for example design reviews or contract reviews
- Audits that consider (technical) project processes, often in combination with project deliverables, commonly referred to as project audit or project review
- Audits that solely consider the project management process and its results, referred to as management audits of projects or programmes or simply project management audits

Project audits to check the (technical) project processes and project deliverables are commonly applied in construction, engineering, and product development projects and programmes. They are applied at the end of project phases. The gate model for an integrated solution delivery of an international engineering company shows for instance the phases: concept, design, development, implementation, and benefits delivery. Reviews are carried out to evaluate the deliverables produced during the phases. These reviews are audits of the solution under development, which include the following

- *Concept phase review:* To assess the completeness of the design concepts, including consideration of alternative designs.
- *Design phase review:* To assess the completeness of design phase work, which includes process design and system requirements, logical design, operations plan, and test plan.
- *Detailed design review*: To do a complete technical assessment of the detail design before beginning extensive coding or purchasing of software.

210

- *Pilot readiness review*: To assess whether the solution is ready to pilot.
- *Implementation readiness review*: To assess the readiness to implement the solution to its planned full extent.
- *Implementation reviews:* To assess the implementation on each site that implements the new solution. It includes validation of implementation measurements, system performance, site adjustments, planning adjustments, implementation logistics, budget, and schedule.

These reviews are linked to stage-gates, which are go/no-go decision points. Only successful reviews allow a project to schedule a gate meeting. These quality assurance activities are an inherent part of the technical content processes and are visualized in the work breakdown structure, the bar chart, and the cost plan of such a project.

In project audits beside the contents processes also the project management process may be assessed. In many companies that carry out their projects according to project phase models no differentiation between contents processes and project management process is made. Generally, the processes need to be checked rather early in the project to ensure the quality of the project deliverables, as only sound processes lead to good products and solutions.

PROJECT MANAGEMENT AUDITING

Management auditing of a project or programme is an independent investigation to check if the management processes (project management or programme management) are performed according to the specified standards of the project-oriented company. To turn project management auditing into a learning instrument we add a competence perspective. In a project management audit the management competences of the project are assessed. These are the organizational, team, and individual competences to perform the project management process. Thus, the project or programme management process and its results are reviewed. Results of the project start process are, for instance, that adequate project plans exist, a project team has been established, the project roles are clear and communicated. Further in this chapter we will concentrate on management auditing of projects.

WE ONLY CAN SEE WHAT WE ARE LOOKING FOR

The management audit criteria depend on the project management approach used as a basis for the auditing. In project-oriented organizations, project management process description and guidelines can serve as a baseline. The possible learning is limited by the audit criteria applied, as we can only see what we are looking for through the filters we use. If our pair of glasses are traditional project management then the audit criteria are limited to the traditional project management objects of consideration like scope, schedule, and costs. Additional project management objects of consideration such as the project organization, the project culture, and the project context only become project management audit criteria, if a project management approach is used that considers these criteria, such as PRINCE2™ (OGC 2005). If projects are seen as temporary organizations and project management is considered as a business process consisting of the sub processes project start, project controlling, project coordination, management of project discontinuities, and project close down, the design of the project management process becomes an audit criterion. Only then will the auditor look to see if the project start process was designed adequately, for instance:

- if there has been a project start work shop and/or a project kick off presentation
- if the appropriate persons have been included in the project start

The auditing forms shown later in this chapter as examples are based on *ROLAND GAREIS Project and Programme Management*®, which is a systemic-constructivist project management approach that for instance values project organization, context, culture, process-orientation and considers project management as a business process (Gareis 2005).

The project management approach that serves as a base in a project management audit of a project has to be agreed beforehand. In most cases the audit will be based on the project management guidelines used in the company that is conducting the project. In other cases consultants from a consulting company may be invited to do the audit, explicitly for the purpose of using a different project management approach as auditing criteria. This can increase the added value of the audit for the project as well as for the project-oriented company.

AUDITS ON A REGULAR BASE

Project management auditing can be done randomly, regularly, or because of a specific reason. Routine project management audits on a regular base are rare. They are still very often carried out only if the client asks for it or if somebody in the line organization has a bad feeling about the project and suspects a project crisis. Then the method is used for problem identification and controlling purposes.

In some project-oriented companies the auditing is done on a regular basis. As the project is a temporary organization (Turner and Müller 2003; Gareis 2005), it needs to build up the project management competencies of its organization and its team. To add most value to the project the ideal point in time to do a project management audit is early in the project – for instance, after the project or programme start has been accomplished. This provides feedback and gives the project the chance to further develop its management competence. Further audits later in the project are possible to give further feedback but also to verify if the recommendations agreed on in earlier audits were taken care of by the project.

STRUCTURED AND TRANSPARENT PROCESS

An audit needs a structured and transparent approach (Corbin et al 2001). Before the audit, an audit assignment is necessary to initialise the auditing, appoint the audit owner (which in most cases will be the project owner), appoint the auditors, and provide first information about the auditing to the project. The result of the assignment is a project audit assignment that clearly points out the objectives, reason, scope, timing and the auditing methods used in the audit. A structured and transparent process supports the acceptance of the results.

An example of a project management audit assignment is shown in Figure 11.1. Depending on the complexity of the project or programme and the objectives of

Auditing Assignment	
Project: customer project: Implementation of an ERP system	Start date of auditing: 23. February
Reason for auditing: routine after project start	End date of auditing: 05. March
Auditing objectives : Analysis of the project management quality after the project has been started Analysis of the organizational, team and individual project management competences in the project Results are basis for an agreement between project owner and project team for further development of project management competences in the project	Non-objectives: Auditing the contents processes Interviews with all relevant environments
Auditing Methods : Documentation analysis Interviews with representatives of the project and selected relevant environments Self-Assessment of PM competences Observation of a project team meeting	Auditing Budget: Auditor: 7 days Representatives of the project: 6 days
Initiator Auditing: PM-Office	Project Manager: M. Haier
Auditing-Owner: R Turner (project owner)	Auditor: M Huemann

Figure 11.1 Auditing assignment for project 'Implementation ERP System'

the audit, one or more (normally not more than three) auditors are assigned. A project management audit process established in a project-oriented organization in accordance with the ISO 19011 (ISO 2002) should include the steps:

1. conducting a situational analysis
2. planning the auditing
3. preparing the auditing
4. performing the analysis
5. generating the audit report
6. performing the audit presentation
7. terminating the auditing

The objectives of the situational analysis are to clarify the reason for and expectations towards the auditing. The auditors formulate first hypotheses about the situation the project is in and the quality of its project management process. In the planning step of the auditing the auditors plan the macro design of the process and the meetings they will have with the audit owner and the project organization, the analysis methods they will apply (like documentation analysis, interviews, observations, etc) and the presentation methods that will be used. The result of this step is the audit plan as shown in Figure 11.2. The audit plan has to be agreed by the audit owner as well as by the project manager representing the project to be audited.

AUDIT METHODS

In a project management audit, a multi method approach is used. Methods used to gather information include:

● documentation analysis
● single and group interviews
● observation of project team meetings
● site visit

These methods are used for the analysis of the project management competence of the project. Which of these methods are applied depends on the specific case and on the audit assignment. Following the recommendation of the ISO 19011 (ISO 2002) an audit should at a minimum include documentation analysis and interviews. Further to these methods I have good experience of also applying self-assessment methods of the project management competences. The quality of the results of the audit depends very much on the scope of the methods and the professional application of these.

Auditing Plan for Project "Implementation ERP System"			
Working Format	**Participants**	**Date**	**Venue**
Meeting: Start of the auditing	Audit owner Auditor	23.02 Duration: 1 hour	Room: 2.22
Meeting: Clarification of the auditing	Project manager Auditor	25.02 Duration: 1,5-2 hours	Room: 2.22
Self-Assessment: PM competences of the project manager	Project manager	27.02 Duration: 1 hour	
Self-Assessment: Team PM competence	Project team	27.02 Duration: 3 hours	Room: 2.22
Group interview with the project manager and project team	Project manager Team members Auditor	01.03 Duration: 2 hours	Room: 1.12
Interview with the project owner	Project owner Auditor	01.03 Duration: 1 hour	Room: 1.12
Group interview with client representatives	Client "project manager" Further client representatives Auditor	01.03. Duration: 1,5 hours	At client's site
Observation: Project team meeting	Project team Project manager Auditor	02.03 Duration: about 1,5 hours	Room: 1.22
Presentation: Audit results	Audit owner Project manager Project team Client representatives Auditor	03.03. Duration: 2 hours	Room: 1.10
Meeting: Termination of Audit	Auditor Audit owner	05.03 Duration: 1 hour	Room: 2.22

Figure 11.2   Auditing plan for project 'Implementation ERP System'

215

Documentation analysis

In a documentation analysis the organizational project management competence of a project can be observed. Documents to be considered are project management documents such as the project work break-down structure, project bar chart, project environmental analysis, project organization chart, project progress reports and minutes of project meetings. Figure 11.3 shows some questions from a questionnaire used in an audit. This questionnaire supports the analysis. To add value to the project team the auditor does not stop with ticking boxes whether a certain project management document is there or not, but the auditor also analyses the quality of the project management plan and provides feedback.

Project planning methods in the project start	Document	Quality
Project objectives plan	2	2
Plan of objects of consideration	1	-
Project work break down structure	2	2
Work package specifications (for selected WP)	2	3
Gantt chart	2	3
Project finance plan (Demand?)	n.d.	-
Project cost plan	2	4
Project risk analysis	2	3

Document: n.d.= no demand, 0=no document, 1= Information available, 2=document available
Quality: 1=not adequate, 2=low quality, 3=average quality, 4=good quality 5=very good quality

Figure 11.3   Auditing questionnaire

Criteria for assessing the quality of the project management plans include completeness, structure and visualization; also the consistency between the single project management documents. The quality criteria very much depend on the project management approach used as a basis for the audit. In the case of a process-oriented project management approach, for instance, the auditor will always look for a process-oriented work break-down structure.

Interview

Interviews are conducted to obtain more detailed information based on questions that arose from the documentation analysis. The interviews are conducted with the project manager, the project owner, and representatives of the project team. In the case of a programme, interviews with the programme owner, the project managers, and project owners of the different projects are required. To get a holistic perception on the project it is often essential to conduct further interviews with representatives of relevant stakeholders such as the client and suppliers.

Self-assessment

To apply self-assessments of the project management competence of players such as the project manager, the project owner, a project team member or of the project team adds value to the auditing. Self-assessments provide the individuals and the project team with the possibility reflecting their current status of project management competences. The project management competence of the project team has temporary character. It needs to be established in the project start and needs to be developed during the project. The competence to act as a project team can be described as the knowledge and the experience of the project team to develop commitment, to create a common 'Big Project Picture', to use synergies in the project team, to solve conflicts, to commonly learn and to commonly design the project management process (Gareis and Huemann 2003). To apply self-assessments adds greatly to the learning perspective of the audit.

Observation

In the observation stage, the auditors collect further information about the project management competence in the observation criteria. Project owner meetings, project team meetings, project sub team meetings can be observed. For instance, by observing a project team meeting, the auditors gain insight into the project management competence of the project team.

Presentation

For presenting the project management audit findings, reports, presentations and even workshops can be applied. Figure 11.4 shows the structure of a project management auditing report. For making an audit a learning experience a presentation of the results is necessary. The results should at least be presented to the project manager, the project team and the project owner (who is the audit owner). That leads to better understanding and more acceptance of the results and provides the opportunity for the project to become a learning organization.

Structure: Project Management Auditing-Report

---

1. Executive summary
2. Situation analysis, context and description of the auditing process of Project XY
3. Brief description of the Project XY
4. Analysis of the project management of Project XY
5. Analysis of the project start
6. Analysis of the project coordination
7. Analysis of the project controlling
8. Analysis of the project close-down
9. Recommendations for the further development of project management of Project XY
10. Recommendations for the further development of project management in the company
11. Enclosures

Figure 11.4 Structure of an auditing report

CLEAR ROLES IN THE AUDITING SYSTEM

The auditing system is a temporary communication system in which the audit owner, the auditor(s), representatives of the project and representatives of relevant environments cooperate. One can differentiate between the initiator of the audit and the audit owner. Initiators of the audit can be for example the project office, a representative of a profit centre or the client.

Audit owner

In any case the audit owner should be the project owner, whose interest is to assure the project management quality of the project, provide a learning chance for the project team and to ensure that the audit can be performed. The audit owner is responsible for the assignment of the audit, agreements about scope, and timing of the audit with representatives of the project and the auditor. Further the audit owner has to ensure the (project) resources for the audit.

Auditors

Often the audit is performed by two to three auditors. Then one of the auditors takes over the role of the lead auditor. The auditors analyse the project management quality of the project and give recommendations regarding the further development of the project management of the project. The auditor needs not only profound project management competences but also auditing competences like designing the auditing process or performing an interview professionally. Thus attitude, social competence and emotional intelligence are important.

Those being audited

The role of the representative of the project is taken over by the project manager of the project that is audited. The objective of this role is to contribute information for the audit and to invest resources. Tasks of the project manager in an audit are for example to contribute to clarify the situation in the project, give feedback to the audit plan, to agree on scope and methods of the audit, provide documents for the documentation analysis, be a interview partner.

RULES, VALUES AND COMMUNICATION

The rules for the audit have to be agreed in the auditing system. The communication policy should be agreed between the auditor and project manager at the beginning of the audit. To provide a learning opportunity to the project, the audit needs to be performed in a cooperative style. That also means that the representatives of the project that is audited should be kept informed by the auditor. Circumstances that should lead to a cancellation of the audit and the consequences of a cancellation should also be agreed on at the start. The quality of the audit depends on the willingness of the project to cooperate and the time and resources available.

One major challenge to ensure is that the results of the audit are not perceived as a personal feedback to the single project manager who then will be blamed for mismanagement. This means also that there is the need for a certain culture of openness in the project-oriented organization.

FOLLOW-UP OF THE AUDIT

Often the results of the audit are not implemented by the project. A formal follow-up is necessary. An audit follow-up agreement signed by the project manager and the project owner ensures the implementation. After the auditor has provided his feedback and recommendations in the audit presentation and documented them formally in the audit report, he or she steps out. The audit is formally determined in a last meeting with the audit owner.

Which of the actions recommended in the audit report need to be implemented in the project is agreed between project owner and the project manager or project team. Thus also the follow-up of the audit is the task of the project owner and not the auditor.

AUDITING FOR THE GOVERNANCE OF PROJECTS

So far we have discussed the practices and process of management auditing of projects and programmes. In this section we consider the need and benefits. Finally we point out the role of the PM office.

NEED AND BENEFITS

The need for management auditing of projects derives from the empowerment of the project and programmes, which in an ideal project-oriented organization act autonomously with a minimum of intervention by the line organization. To assure quality and the application of agreed standards management, auditing is necessary.

In 2002, about 7% of the annual turnover of a global ICT consultancy company was spent on quality. About half of it was spent for management audits of projects and programmes. The company has a long tradition of applying the method of management auditing of projects and programmes and does it on a routine basis. Before they implemented management auditing of projects, they had a lot of troubles with their projects and clients. Nowadays management auditing of projects and programmes is part of their company governance system and supports the governance of projects and programmes.

The benefits of audits of projects are twofold. On the one hand they provide a learning opportunity to the single project to improve its project management competence. On the other hand, by evaluating the results of several management audits, patterns can be found. For instance, if a lot of the projects have a low-quality cost plan or do not apply a proper project controlling, these issues are general subjects for improvement in the parent organization. The results of the audits can further lead to an improvement of the business processes project management or programme management.

RESPONSIBILITY

Empowerment of projects and programmes is one of the key values of the project-oriented company. To govern the projects and to ensure quality of the project management and programme management processes, the PM office provides project management guidelines and procedures, standard project plans for repetitive projects, project management infrastructure, management consulting services and management auditing for projects and programmes. Thus the PM office is responsible for the development of guidelines and procedures of the management auditing of projects. A standardized auditing process ensures the comparability of the auditing results between projects.

Auditors may be recruited externally to the company (such as consulting companies), or internally. Auditing can be considered as job enlargement for senior project managers. The auditors are often organized in a (virtual) pool linked to the PM office. Further the PM office is responsible for the training of the auditors. Professional auditors need to be experienced project managers, but also need to know the auditing process and methods.

SUMMARY

The chapter draws a distinction between a project audit and the project management audit of a project, and shows what a systematic auditing process might look like. It has described auditing methods such as documentation analysis, interviews and observations. The roles in the auditing system are described and the need for a clear communication policy is stressed. Finally the responsibility of the PM office for the provision of auditing guidelines and forms is discussed and the benefits reflected. The benefits of management auditing of projects and programmes are to provide a learning opportunity to the project or programme as well as to the project-oriented organization as such. The evaluation of the results of several project management audits may serve as basis for the further development of project management in the project-oriented organization.

The chapter advocates that we should perceive management auditing of projects and programmes as a learning instrument. But there are some challenges to make auditing a learning instrument that adds value to the project, programme and the project-oriented organization. The recommendations as shown in this chapter can be summarized as follows:

- *A modern project management approach:* This has to be the basis for the auditing.
- *Auditing should be done on a regular basis:* For instance every project with a certain complexity should be audited after the start, and perhaps at significant project stage-gates.
- *A certain formalism is required:* Auditing process description and forms like auditing assignment, auditing follow-up agreement, support the standardisation and transparency of the audit.
- *Clear expectations and communication agreements:* the objectives, scope, and consequences of the audit have to be clear. It is not the project manager who is audited but the project. This has to be communicated! A communication policy has to be agreed.
- *Assessing the quality of the project methods and techniques:* It is not good enough to tick boxes whether a certain project management document exists or not,

but it is necessary to go one step further and assess the quality of project management and provide feedback.

- *Audit methods:* Interviews with the client and suppliers are very challenging but add a different and very important perspective to the audit. Also assess the individual and team project management competences in the project. Self-assessments are good instruments for learning. A presentation of the audit results adds to the understanding and supports the acceptance of the results.
- *Clear role and responsibility of the auditor:* The auditor provides his or her feedback to the project and recommends actions. Which of these actions need to be implemented in the project is agreed between project owner and the project manager or project team. The follow up of the audit is the task of the project owner and not the auditor.
- *Responsibility for the auditing:* The PM office can provide auditing as a service to the projects and programmes.
- *Professional auditors:* The auditors need to be experienced project managers, but also need to know the auditing process and methods. Auditing training is required.

REFERENCES

Corbin, D., Cox, R., Hamerly, R. and Knight, K., 2001, 'Project management of project reviews', *PM Network*, March.

Gareis, R., 2005, *Happy Projects!*, Vienna: Manz.

Gareis, R., and Huemann, M., 2003, 'Project management competences in the project-oriented company', in Turner, J.R., (ed), *People in Project Management*, Aldershot: Gower.

ISO, 2002, *ISO 19,011: Guidelines for Quality and/or Environmental Management Systems Auditing,* Geneva: International Standards Organization.

OGC, 2005, *Managing Successful Projects with PRINCE 2*, 4th edition, London: The Stationery Office.

Turner, J.R. and Müller, R., 2003, 'On the nature of the project as a temporary organization', *International Journal of Project Management*, 21(1).

12 Managing the Context

Mark O'Callaghan

It was suggested in Chapters 1 and 5 that projects are unique, novel and transient and are therefore inherently risky. The aim of project management is to manage this uncertainty. However, projects are borne out of and interact with an external environment which is not static. Merely concentrating on the internal workings of a project ignores the influences that shape its conception, design, operation and ultimately its success. The larger the scope of the project and the greater the timeline, the more interaction it is likely to have with its external environment. Analysing the external environment can be difficult given its vastness and complexity. A further complication is the difficulty of recognising what factors might directly influence the project amongst a host of rapid changes in the environment.

These external factors can have an influence on a range of aspects of a project including its customers or users, the industry or marketplace including competitors, the technology it uses, the staff building or running the project as well as on other key stakeholders such as the sponsor as well as on the organization itself. Failure to consider external factors can lead to project overrun of time and budget; it may even lead to complete project failure. However, sometimes a project may appear to be fatally flawed in terms of project management, but due to external factors its ultimate outcome may be a resounding success. A project supplying an alternative energy supply (to oil) may have dramatically gone over time and budget, but because of equally dramatic increases in oil costs may still eventually be judged a success. Analysis of the external environment links in with project risk management.

PESTLE (Political, Economic, Social, Technical, Legal and Environmental) Analysis along with other tools (such as Porter's Industry Analysis) is used for scanning the present and especially future external environment when engaging in strategic planning or change management. These tools identify the external factors that impact on the various aspects of an organization. They provide the external Opportunities and Threats, which together with the internal analysis of

223

the organization (Strengths and Weaknesses) give rise to the SWOT Analysis. Originally, the external analysis was confined to four factors: political, economic, social and technical (PEST), but subsequently two more categories have appeared, **L** for legal (and regulatory) and **E** for environment (PESTLE). These last two will be dealt with more briefly in this chapter as they are covered more extensively in the other chapters in this handbook. It does not really matter which label a disputed possible factor falls under (such as is a factor political or economic), as long as it is identified.

It is essential that those conducting a PESTLE Analysis have a sound knowledge of the industry. However, they should avoid just concentrating on issues that have always been crucial in the industry at the expenses of other factors or of 'group think'. They need to be aware of the wider environment and how it might interact with the project. Further, anyone conducting a PESTLE Analysis for a project should continuously update it to take into account the ever changing nature of the environment in which it is located. As every parent knows (possibly with apprehension), certain trends can be easily discerned over the television in programmes and especially advertisements. So it is with PESTLE Analysis; certain trends can be seen from viewing what happens in other countries.

DEFINITIONS AND IMPLICATIONS

We consider each of the elements of PESTLE Analysis in turn.

POLITICAL

The **P** in **PESTLE** stands for political factors, both current and future. These range from global and supra-national (such as the European Union) through to national, regional and local. The more public and controversial the project (especially if it is in the media spotlight), the more likely it is to be influenced by political factors, especially if the project duration spans possible changes in government. This provides a greater uncertainty over the project. In the health care field, for example, closing even part of a hospital can be considered a political 'hot potato'. Across Western Europe, decisions to close departments or even whole hospitals either due to rationalization efforts or as a result of a move to Care in the Community have led to vigorous protests. Even building a hospital can prove politically sensitive. For example, the large project of constructing a new hospital in Malta has passed through three national elections with two changes in government which has led to a number of complete reconsiderations of its purpose and scope, as the Foundation for Medical Sciences (2006) presented in its history of the project.

- The idea for a new hospital, to meet the needs of the people of the Maltese islands, was already being discussed in the early 1990s. The idea was to build a centre of excellence to complement the 50 year old St. Luke's General Acute Hospital which was to undergo an extensive programme of refurbishment. The 480 bed, state of the art specialized hospital was to operate in the fields of Diabetology, Cardiology and degenerative diseases and other chronic illnesses prevalent in Malta and other Mediterranean countries. The new hospital was also to have a strong research and teaching aspect.

- The initial and conceptual preparations for the new hospital started in the early 1990s. The first agreements between the Maltese Government and the Fondazione Centro S Romanello Del Monte Tabor were entered into in December 1990. Eventually, the design work was started in 1993 by Ortesa Spa and the construction in 1995 by Skanska Malta J.V.

- Due to a change in Government in 1996 the feasibility of the whole project was reconsidered. Eventually it was decided to expand the project into an acute general hospital with a capacity ranging from 825 to 1,000 beds. The new intention was to replace St. Luke's Hospital.

- Alluded to, but not specifically mentioned in the last bullet, was the possibility of the Labour government completely scrapping the whole project in 1996. The consideration of the financial penalties for doing so forced it to rethink the scheme and eventually propose a hospital twice the size of the original plan.

- A snap election in 1998 brought about another change in government. The new hospital project was re-evaluated and re-dimensioned to a 650 bed hospital with a possible extension to 825 beds. The new hospital was to cater for Malta's acute medical needs into the next century whilst incorporating secondary and tertiary services including all major specialties. All the clinical functions were to have a strong research and teaching component.

- The new hospital with 825 beds in 40 wards should open in 2007, seventeen years after the initial planning phase. Naturally such a project has attracted massive increases in costs, timeline as well as personnel involved.

The political instability of a country and poor relations with its neighbours will increase the uncertainty over a project. Countries undergoing civil unrest while possibly providing higher returns make projects uncertain, increasing costs and risks. Building refineries or oil pipelines in politically unstable areas such as in parts of the Middle East or the Balkans can be tricky. Countries which join a large supra-national organization (such as the European Union) will be influenced by it, possibly enjoying greater long-term stability at the expense of short term problems in adjusting to the new regimes imposed by it. Countries that have a general consensus amongst political parties are less likely to cause serious problems for projects during changes of government than those that move from a wholesale embrace of free market reform to a centrally controlled, interventionist and de-privatised economy. It must be noted that whilst a particular party that has a negative view of a project may not be in power, its influence may be felt should the project experience difficulties and therefore provide political ammunition to embarrass the party or authority in control. Finally, in the political arena we must not forget that other key stakeholders (such as Trades Unions and Non Governmental Organizations) in a project might exert considerable influence.

The questions that those planning the project must ask in this regard therefore are:

- How stable is the political scene likely to be over the lifespan of the project and beyond?
- How do the national (and local) parties view the project?
- Do you know what are the policies and priorities of the various parties as they might affect the project?
- What are the chances of national (and local) elections occurring during the project?
- What are the chances of a change in administration and how would this affect the project?
- Even should an administration not change, what is the chance that their policies might change over the lifetime of the project?

The project team as well as forecasting and accounting for such influences will also want to try to manage them. There will be a greater requirement for more effective consultation with all the stakeholders at the outset of the project. A proactive public relations and communication strategy, for example, will continuously promote the benefits of a politically sensitive project. It will also respond appropriately when problems are encountered throughout the project's life-cycle. Managers will need to be given the appropriate training in all these areas.

ECONOMIC

The **E** in **PESTLE** stands for economic factors. Once again these range from global and supra-national through to national, regional and local. In addition to the macro economic influences there are micro-economic considerations that affect a project. The large degree of control over their economies that countries enjoyed in the past has now gone. On a global level there is an ever escalating effect of globalization and a greater move towards free trade coupled with an increasing inter-dependency on interest rates. These combine with the constraints on a country imposed upon members by trade blocs such as the European Union, especially within the Eurozone. Massive and sudden economic shocks are felt world-wide and within days if not hours. Dramatic changes in economic conditions can make project process and outcome difficult to predict and manage. Any sudden interruption in oil supplies leads to massive fluctuations in energy and oil price which can not only affect the costs of a project but also its eventual outcome. For example, on a large scale, any decision to build an electricity power plant will be dramatically influenced by massive fluctuations in energy costs. On a small scale the decision to install central heating will also be affected by energy costs. All these influences cascade from the national to local level. Any individual project is likely to be affected by a host of economic factors and few industries escape their influences.

For example, the decision of a farmer in North County Cork in Ireland to build a sugar beet storage facility is affected by a cascade of influences on the sugar beet industry. The World Trade talks have resulted in agreement to reduce the subsidy to sugar beet farmers in the European Union so as to make a fairer playing field for other farmers. The European Union therefore no longer allows such subsidies. The Irish government follows suit leaving farmers with less money for their produce as well as the likelihood that there will be less demand for beet, thereby reducing the amount of beet they will produce as well as the money they will have for the construction project. The local sugar beet factory will also be in jeopardy and is therefore likely to close with a major loss of jobs in the region, adversely affecting the local economy and once again influencing the farmer's decision to proceed with his project.

Economic cycles and inflation rates can have an effect not just on the cost of a project (capital borrowed as well as prices of labour and materials) but also on its outcome (revenues versus operational costs), dramatically affecting its economic viability. On a national level changes in Gross Domestic Product and the disposable income of the people as a result of recession can seriously jeopardise projects such as leisure parks. Availability and price of capital would be affected by stock market instability, changes in interest rates and any ensuing currency fluctuations. Government economic policies including taxation rates may also have a bearing on the economic viability of a project.

In addition, on a micro level the wider economic circumstances of the organization(s) responsible for the project (whether project management or eventual operational management) also affect the project. An organization suffering severe financial difficulties is more likely to have problems managing a project.

The questions that those planning the project must ask in this regard therefore are:

- What is the current general economic environment like?
- How stable are economic conditions likely to be over the life of the project and beyond?

- If there are likely to be changes how will they affect the project in terms of capital funds available as well as project costs?
- Will there be any change to the reserves needed for the project?
- How will such changes affect future operational costs as well as revenues (or public funds if a public or voluntary organization)?
- How will such changes affect eventual users or consumers?

The project team will want to forecast such influences and try to manage them. Some economic risks can be insurable (the cost being shared or passed on to the sponsor). Other proactive strategies can include borrowing capital from a number of sources, buying foreign currency to reduce exchange risks or forward buying fuel at a fixed price to avoid fluctuating costs.

SOCIAL

The **S** in **PESTLE** stands for social factors. These can include widespread demographic and cultural changes. In the past these changes have been slow, but with globalization, economic growth has transformed some countries. For example, in a relatively few years Ireland has transformed from one of the poorest countries in Europe to one of the richest. Through what they have seen and read in the media the Irish have raised expectations with concomitant changes in culture and values. Ireland has gone from a country with a strong religious identity with little social mobility (except towards wholesale emigration of its youth) to one in which consumerism and materialism play a strong role in a more hedonistic lifestyle. The dramatic interplay of social factors can be seen in terms of the shopping experience. Developers of shopping malls in Ireland are well aware of these higher expectations of life as well as the greater economic power of the consumer. These goods are bought as a result of increasing wages or on credit against the expectation of increased equity in the family home. This is coupled with a lifestyle that regards shopping as no longer a drudgery of the housewife, but rather a leisure activity to be enjoyed by all the family even on a Sunday morning when in the past they might have all been at church.

Social factors will largely affect the long-term use of the project's product and in particular its economic viability. Differing demographic patterns, greater social mobility and changes in family and lifestyle can have a dramatic effect. In many countries, there has been an increase in the number of elderly people as a result of higher life expectancies. Their children have moved outside the family area for work purposes. There is also the increasing tendency for women to obtain paid employment rather than look after their parents as in the past. Thus there are no local family members to look after elderly parents. This has had a significant impact on health and social services with a greater requirement for residential and day places than in the past. On the other end of the age spectrum the declining birth rate has lead to fewer maternity beds and fewer schools being required. Similarly, changes in values and culture as well as a shift in life and leisure have also led to a greater degree of consumerism as well as increased desire for leisure. The increase in mobility as well as the influx of people of other countries with different traditions has led to a broadening of even local communities. Higher levels of education and increased power of consumers or users of services have led to higher expectations of projects. The questions that those planning the project must ask in this regard therefore are:

- Is the project based on a particular social model and could this change?
- What is the current and future demographic composition of the area in which the project is located or from which it draws its users?
- Is social mobility and lifestyle changing and, if so, how will this affect the project?
- Could these change the type of user of the project or the way it is used?
- Does the project meet the expectations of its community?
- Do these social changes affect the viability of the project?

The project team may well be able to forecast and account for such influences, but may have difficulty in trying to manage them. They may have to build flexibility into the project such that it develops in pace with the social changes in the environment.

TECHNOLOGY

The **T** in **PESTLE** stands for technological factors. These can include major technological advances affecting whole industries down to minor innovations which make life easier for consumers. The effect of technology can be considerable and alter social patterns. The Internet has had a dramatic effect on society and is changing patterns of work, with more people being able to work from home or on the move. However, this pales beside the speed of change of the introduction of mobile phones, which has revolutionised the telecommunications industry as well as having marked effects on the behaviour of individuals. In a relatively short time in many industrial countries the majority of the population has a mobile phone. This has led to the users, especially the young, being more mobile than previously. Appointments amongst youngsters can now be made and altered almost instantaneously. The rationalization of devices such as phones, cameras, audio devices and personal hand-held computers has started to have dramatic effects on the entertainment industry with the possibility of downloading and playing audio and video on the move. Other technological advances can include changes in computerization (both hardware and software), industrial processes, transportation, as well as in the type and use of materials. In project management technological advances can assist the project management process as well as its outcome, although one must be aware that in certain circumstances they can make the project obsolete.

Whilst in many industries technological innovation can lead to a simplification of processes and often a reduction of cost, in some industries it can appear to be a two-edged sword. For example, in the health care field the benefits of technological innovation such as micro and keyhole surgery can dramatically reduce operation time and complications, that patients can be operated and discharged on the same day, thereby reducing the requirement for hospital beds. On the other hand technological advances can increase the expense of a healthcare system. This is because patients who might otherwise have died can be kept alive longer and at possibly greater expense. In addition new surgical operations or medicines for complaints that previously were untreatable may dramatically increase the demand for the new procedures. The questions that those planning the project must ask in this regard therefore are:

● Is the project based on a particular technological model and could this change?
● How could any emerging technology affect the project process or outcome?
● Could technological changes affect the type of user of the project or the way it is used?

Once again, the project team may well be able to forecast and account for such influences, but may have difficulty in trying to manage them. They may have to build flexibility into the project such that it develops in pace with the technological changes in the environment. However, the major problem in adopting new technologies is the risk they it will not deliver their promise. Some projects (such as in health care) will be more risk averse than others. In technological projects, especially, the larger and more complex the project, with perceived longer-term benefits, the greater the risk of failure. The project management world is particularly littered with large-scale information technology projects that either do not work properly or do so at much greater expense or at considerable delay. Those managing such schemes must at the outset develop and agree a proper risk management strategy with the stakeholders (including sponsors as well as users) and continuously monitor the risks associated with the project.

LEGAL

The **L** in **PESTLE** stands for legal or regulatory factors. These can include wholesale introduction of new laws or regulations or modifications to existing ones. Such changes can derive from global or supranational entities. Countries within the European Union, for example, have witnessed dramatic changes in the employment field as a result of EU directives aimed at protecting the workforce and promoting equality and avoiding discrimination. National and local laws and regulations must now reflect such changes.

Working practices in projects that include a large building component have been transformed by new health and safety legislation that governs all aspects of construction including the issue of work equipment, manual handling, personal protective equipment, safety signs, noise etc. These have reduced short and long term risk to the project workers (both manual and administrative). They have generally resulted in a visible increase in project costs, although there is a possible reduction in invisible risk-related costs (e.g. compensation due to injury).

In the healthcare field the EU working time directive (93/104/EC) has had a dramatic impact on the hours of junior doctors. Many healthcare systems relied on such staff to work long hours often with very short breaks to provide adequate medical cover. Similarly, in many hospitals nursing shifts have also had to change to reflect the new working practices. The questions that those planning the project must ask in this regard therefore are:

- Are there new laws/regulations or amendments to existing ones that affect the project process or its continued operation?
- How could these affect the project process or outcome?
- Could these affect the way the project is eventually used?

The project team must evaluate, prevent and reduce workplace risks.

ENVIRONMENTAL

The final **E** in **PESTLE** stands for environmental factors. Once again these range from global and supranational influences through to national, regional and local. For example, the concern on global warming has resulted in global agreements on emissions of greenhouse gasses. These, coupled with concerns over waste management, have cascaded through national and local government to affect all aspects of life and especially in projects that involve construction both during the building phase as well as afterwards in the operational running of the new facility. Even before the plans are drawn up most of these projects require an environmental impact assessment. The construction of the building can incorporate many 'environmentally friendly' features such as measures to conserve energy. Another environmental effect of a project is on the community that surrounds it. Job creation (as a result of building a facility) or destruction (following closure) can dramatically transform a neighbourhood. For example, a large industrial complex will rely on workers being available. It in turn will spawn a number of industries which will give rise to further jobs. Such effects can more clearly be seen when a project involves closure of a particular facility. The knock on effects on the local economy can sometimes be quite widespread and dramatic.

The questions that those planning the project must ask in this regard therefore are:

- What existing environmental policies are there which might affect the project?
- Are there any best practices in the field that could be used to assist the project?
- Are there new environmental concerns that might arise that could affect the project process or its continued operation?
- How could these affect the project process or outcome?
- Could these affect the way the project is eventually used?
- How does the project affect its community and how can this be managed?

Once again, the project team must evaluate the environmental impact a project might have at the planning stage, but also continuously monitor and remedy any adverse problems that arise.

STEPS IN CARRYING OUT A PESTLE ANALYSIS

First brainstorm the possible Political, Economic, Social, Technological, Legal and Environmental factors that might change over the life of the project and beyond, using the questions that those planning the project must ask. Discuss how each of these might affect the project and list their implications (see for example Figure 12.1).

Type

Categorize factors as positive or negative. Positive factors can be sifted out at this stage and used to help in the design of the project. Our concern is with those factors having a negative impact.

Time span

Next decide at what stage these factors might impact on the project.

- Start of project (planning and design), S
- Execution and closure, M
- Aftermath affecting its operation and/or outcome, L
- Impact intermittent over time, I

Impact

Decide on what impact each might have on the project (see Figure 12.2):

Impact = Likelihood × Consequences

INITIAL PESTLE ANALYSIS

Project:	South Regis Day Care Centre
Project Champion:	John Locke
Project Manager:	David Hume

External Factors		**Implication for project**	**Time Span**	**Type (+ or -)**	**Impact**	
					Likelihood	**Consequences**
Political	Election of opposition party to local government that opposes centre	Project in jeopardy	S	-	M	H
Economic	Local government finances in deficit as a result of recession	Not enough money for full project	I	-	H	M
Social	Large projected increase in frail elderly people	Increases imperative for project	M	+	H	M
Technological	Increase in minor surgery away from hospital	More health work can be done at Day Care Centre	M	+	H	H
Legal	Part of site owned by third party reluctant to sell	Delay in starting construction	S	-	M	M
Environmental	Project site in sensitive conservation area	Problems obtaining planning permission	S	-	M	M

Figure 12.1 Initial PESTLE Analysis (one example from each factor)

233

		LIKELIHOOD		
		High	Medium	Low
CONSEQUENCES	High	Abandon	Seriously Question	Manage
	Medium	Seriously Question	Manage	Control
	Low	Manage	Control	Monitor

Figure 12.2 **Impact Assessment on a Project**

Likelihood of it happening:

3 = will or very likely to happen
2 = likely to happen
1 = unlikely to happen
0 = almost certainly will not happen

Consequences:

3 = critical – factors that would seriously harm the project such as to halt it, or so compromise its benefits that the project would not be worth doing
2 = very important – factors that threaten the carrying out of the project but it could still continue, or seriously compromise its benefits
1 = important – factors that would impact the project adding to cost, complexity or time, or dilute the project's benefits
0 – insignificant – factors that would affect the project very minimally and could be easily managed

PRIORITISING

Combining the Likelihood and Consequences scores gives an impact score which can be used to prioritize those factors that must feed into the design stage of the project and figure in Risk Analysis. Even if one listed only six items for each of the six PESTLE factors, this yields thirty six items. Using the Pareto Principle (the 20/80 rule), reduce and rank the above to those six or seven that figure highest on the combined impact score (Figure 12.2). Clearly those that score the highest (9) should call the whole project into question (Figure 12.3).

PLANNING

These factors can be used in the concept and design phase of a project. The results of the PESTLE analysis can be used to feed into scenario planning in which alternative futures are envisaged and their impact on the project explored. Sometimes, this is simplified into a 'worst case' and 'best case' scenario. For example, a project may involve building an electricity power plant fuelled by oil to provide electricity to the local population. Under the political factors one notes that an election is imminent with the strong chance that the existing government in favour of the project will fall and be replaced by one favouring 'alternative' energy sources. Under economic factors the price of oil is likely to rise dramatically following the strong possibility of war in the Middle East. Under social factors, the area where the plant is to be sited is being steadily depopulated due to migration of the population to areas where work is more readily available. Under technological factors, studies have indicated that alternative sources of energy (e.g. wind farms or wave energy) might be more cost effect in this region or that the existing plant that supplies electricity to this area might be made more efficient. On the environmental front the plant might be planned for a site of outstanding conservational importance. Finally, legal disputes might delay the project for many years. All the above factors could seriously question the wisdom of proceeding with the project.

On a narrower focus the results of the PESTLE analysis can be used to draw up contingency plans for the project and should feed into risk analysis and management. For example, have an agreement to buy oil at a fixed price to hedge against cost fluctuations.

Monitoring

Given the changing nature of the external environment, it is important to update regularly the PESTLE analysis and feed the results into the Risk Management strategy.

PESTLE ANALYSIS SHEET

Project: South Regis Day Care Centre
Project Champion: John Locke
Project Manager: David Hume

Rank	Time Span	External Factor	Implication for project	L'hd HML	Cons HML	Strategy
1	S	Election of opposition party to local government that opposes Day Care Centre	Project in jeopardy	M	H	Discuss benefits with party, involve medics and Social Services to lobby politicians
2	S	Local government finances in deficit as a result of recession	Not enough money for full project	H	M	Discuss finances with Health Authority and Private Finance Initiative
3=	S	Part of site owned by third party reluctant to sell	Delay in starting construction	M	M	Negotiate or if needed obtain compulsory purchase order or reconfigure plan
3=	S	Project site in sensitive area with opposition from environmental groups	Planning permission delayed and changes in plans required	M	M	Discuss with lobby groups and local planning authority
5=	L	Possible reorganization of social services	May make the running of the project difficult	M	L	Discuss possible implications of reorganization with Social Services
5=	M	Proposed changes in transport links in the community	Users will have problems accessing facility	M	L	Discuss with local transport authority, use Social Services or voluntary transport

Author: MOC   **Date:** 10 February 2006   **Issue:** A

Figure 12.3   PESTLE Analysis Sheet

CONCLUSION

Factors in the external environment (Political, Economic, Social, Technological, Legal or Environmental) can influence a project's process and outcomes, sometimes to a significant degree. Project planners and managers need to conduct a continuous PESTLE Analysis of the external environment asking how the various factors can impact on the project and what might be done to manage them.

REFERENCES AND FURTHER READING

Foundation for Medical Sciences, 2006, *History,* Retrieved February 10, 2006, from <http://www.fms.com.mt/mdhproject/history.asp>

Grant, RM, 2004, *Contemporary Strategy Analysis: Concepts, Techniques, Applications*, Oxford: Blackwell Publishing.

Part II
Performance

INTRODUCTION TO PART II

In the 3rd edition I called this part Functions, following the lead I had set in my book, *The Handbook of Project-based Management* (2nd edition, McGraw-Hill, 1999). Here I have called it Performance mainly for the alliterative effect. However, it is now common to talk about the so called golden triangle as time, cost and performance, or else to describe it as time, cost and functionality, and the three together as performance. On the Masters in Project, Program and Strategic Management at ESC Lille we have a subject on Project Performance Management. Thus it is now common to talk about the achievement of a project's objectives, and its time, cost and quality targets generically as the management of project performance. Thus the name of this part.

The first five chapters describe a chain through which we define and manage what the project will deliver. We start with the benefits we ultimately want to achieve and then define the requirements of the project to help us achieve those benefits. Then we need to manage the scope of work of the project, and the value of the project which is the ratio of the benefit to the cost of the work. Finally we need to manage the finish or quality of the new asset delivered. There are then a number of other components of performance, or constraints on its achievement. We have to create an organization to undertake the work of the project. The other two major components of performance are time and cost, and the manpower or resources we need to use are a component of cost. The project is subject to uncertainty, and so we need to manage that risk. Two key constraints are the health and safety of our workers and the impact on the environment. They can sometimes be viewed as additional components of both quality and risk.

CHAPTER 13: MANAGING BENEFITS

In Chapter 13, Terry Cooke-Davies describes benefits management. First he explores the topic of benefits management from each of the two points of view: the business perspective on the one hand, and the project management perspective on the other. He then describes the pivotal role of the 'executive sponsor', before finally examining the processes and practices that constitute 'benefits management' and suggests the ten most critical keys to success.

CHAPTER 14: MANAGING REQUIREMENTS

Mary McKinley describes Requirements Management in Chapter 14. First she reminds us why it is important, and then describes the Requirements Management Process (RMP). She explains Requirements Management throughout the project life-cycle and introduces a requirements management toolset.

CHAPTER 15: MANAGING SCOPE – CONFIGURATION AND WORK METHODS

Configuration Management is a technique for managing the functionality of the asset produced by the project, and the work methods to deliver it. The facility is broken into components, and the functionality of each component defined. This decomposition is known as *product break-down*. The way the components make up the facility is known as the *configuration*. Through the processes of configuration management, the project team manage the break-down, the functionality of each component, and their configuration into the facility to provide the overall functionality. This process is linked to value management since the control of the cost of each component and the overall cost of the facility will be part of the value management process. Each component should provide value commensurate with the overall value required from the facility. The techniques of configuration management can also be used to manage the work methods, that is the method of making each component, and the method of building them into the facility, and this is also described. Goal Directed Project Management is a structured technique for managing both the product breakdown and work methods in a way consistent with configuration management. The technique is introduced. Finally, a link is made between the work methods identified by configuration management and the management of resources and progress described later.

CHAPTER 16: MANAGING VALUE

All projects are undertaken to deliver value for the sponsor which in turn should add value to an organization. Understanding, defining and managing this value is critical to the success of a project. In Chapter 16, Stephen Simister describes the process of *Value Management*. Value management (and the related topic of *value engineering*) is a structured technique for understanding, defining and managing

242

value. One definition of value is the ratio between functionality and the cost of delivering that functionality. The link with configuration management is to ensure that the functionality of the various components of a project is managed in a co-ordinated manner. The broader concept of value is explored in considering how projects contribute to shareholder value.

CHAPTER 17: MANAGING QUALITY

Not only is it necessary to define the functionality of the facility, but also the quality of finish. This covers many attributes or service levels required. In this chapter, I consider the quality of projects. A five element model for delivering quality is described. I consider whether quality is free on projects, and introduce several techniques for solving quality problems.

CHAPTER 18: MANAGING PROJECT ORGANIZATION

Having identified what it is the project will deliver and how it will be done, we must define who will be involved in the project, their responsibilities and how they will be managed. In Chapter 17, Erling Andersen describes how to create a project organization. He identifies that there are two levels to project organization; how the project will be integrated into the parent organization, and how the project team will be structured and managed. He describes the issues involved. He then describes the use of responsibility charts to define people's involvement in the project.

CHAPTER 19: MANAGING THE SCHEDULE

In Chapter 19, Dennis Lock describes how to calculate the schedule of the project. He describes the use of calendars and then three techniques for determining and representing the schedule: bar charts; activity-on-arrow networks; and precedence networks. He then discusses several issues for optimizing the schedule.

CHAPTER 20: MANAGING COST

In Chapter 20, Dennis Lock describes how to manage the cost of the project. He starts by giving some definitions, and describing principles of project cost management. He then describes methods of estimating costs and the development of cost budgets. In the rest of the chapter he describes methods of monitoring costs. He describes simple methods, using graphs and milestones, and ends with the earned value technique which can be used to monitor both cost and time on a project.

CHAPTER 21: MANAGING RESOURCES

One of the issues for optimizing the schedule at the end of Chapter 19 is the use of resources, and the need to balance their inputs. Dennis Lock describes those issues fully in Chapter 21. He describes principles of resource scheduling and the role of critical path networks in resource scheduling, and the resolution of conflicts. He describes the use of computers in resource scheduling, how the outputs are used to manage the work of the project, including the resource input. He ends with some additional issues, such as the use of calendars, multi-project scheduling and scheduling resources in small departments.

CHAPTER 22: MANAGING RISK

In Chapter 22, Chris Chapman and Stephen Ward describe how to manage the risk inherent in the work of projects, and the uncertainty in all estimates. They describe a nine step risk management process (RMP) developed for the UK's Association for Project Management Special Interest Group on Risk Management, and published as the *Guide to Project Risk Analysis and Management (PRAM)*.

CHAPTER 23: MANAGING HEALTH AND SAFETY

In Chapter 23, Jim Pearce discusses a specific risk issue, health and safety. He gives an introduction to occupational health and safety and describes benefits from its management. He then describes the identification and management of risks to safety. He describes the role of occupational health and safety on projects and suggests how to develop a safety policy.

CHAPTER 24: MANAGING THE ENVIRONMENT

In Chapter 24, Zhen Chen, Heng Li and Rodney Turner describe environmental management. They present qualitative and quantitative approaches to environmental management. They describe how an organization can develop an environmental strategy, and basic principals of environmental management. They then describe methods for pollution prevention, control and reduction, including some quantitative approaches. These quantitative methods are further integrated under a knowledge-driven managerial frame based on a standard EMS process and other processes normally adopted in projects management. It is expected that this knowledge-driven approach can be used to effectively support conducting quantitative environmental management throughout the lifecycle of projects.

244

13 Managing Benefits

Terry Cooke-Davies

Anything but a careful and comprehensive reading of the project management literature prior to 2000 would be unlikely to turn up a reference to 'Benefits Management'. Rodney Turner as early as the first edition of his book (1993) recognizes that projects are undertaken to deliver business benefit, that achievement of the business benefit is the highest level of the project control cycle, and that should be one of the main concerns of project close-out. But he is almost a lone voice in the wilderness. This is surprising, since every project represents an investment by a sponsoring organization, and the investment is made to obtain benefit. A project is a unique piece of work designed to deliver beneficial change (Chapter 5), so managing benefits underpins project success (Cooke-Davies 2001a). When anticipated benefits are delivered, customers are satisfied, sponsors get their return on investment, and the project team can see that their job has been well done. When anticipated benefits are not delivered, the would-be beneficiaries are frustrated, and the project can be counted as a failure. That is why successful project management is all about managing benefit.

With its origins in engineering and construction, however, project management convention during much of the 20th century made a sharp distinction between the 'client', who was paying for the project and the 'contractor', whose job it was to deliver the desired products and services collectively referred to as the project's 'deliverables'. This sharp delineation of responsibilities was generally given expression in the contract. Whether or not the client was subsequently obtaining value from its investment was not the responsibility of the contractors and so lay outside the scope of project management. Further, with engineering projects such as buildings, dams, power stations, chemical plants, when the new asset was switched on it almost began to deliver the desired benefit perforce. No additional effort was required. So the omission of benefits management from the literature is perhaps understandable.

The last two decades of the 20th century saw more and more organizations applying project management techniques to more and more situations where a contract was not forthcoming (such as IT developed internally, or new product development or even business change). Consequently this division of responsibilities between client and contractor became less clear, and there was no external legal sanction to force clarity on the respective roles. In addition, the link between the new capabilities delivered by the new asset, and how they will be exploited to deliver the desired benefit is less clear. Under these circumstances, it could be argued that the growth of interest in benefits management was inevitable.

In this chapter, we will explore the topic of benefits management, first of all from each of the two points of view: the business perspective on the one hand, and the project management perspective on the other. The pivotal role of the 'executive sponsor' will then be described, before finally examining the processes and practices that constitute 'benefits management' and suggesting the ten most critical keys to success.

THE BUSINESS PERSPECTIVE

Businesses approve expenditure on projects for many and varied reasons, but underlying each one is the expectation that the investment will yield a positive benefit to the organization. For example an organization may undertake:

- Business Process Reengineering (BPR) projects to improve competitiveness
- corporate restructuring or merger/acquisition projects to enhance shareholder value
- projects to deliver innovative products or services to clients in order to make a profit
- projects to support or to improve operations (such as marketing projects, plant shutdowns, or production engineering projects) so as to improve bottom-line performance
- research projects and (in the case of some industries such as Pharmaceuticals) development projects to maximize return on R&D spend, leading directly to the creation of new streams of operating revenue
- development projects to improve time to market, and enhance competitive position, product sales or product margins
- IT/IS projects to deliver improved financial benefits (either directly or indirectly), and/or reduced wastage from aborted projects
- projects to design, procure and construct new capital assets so as to enhance time to market parameters, return on investment, reduced operating costs or some combination of all three

Each of these types of project (and many others not included in the list) contributes towards the creation of additional corporate value. But each

246

contributes in a different way. It is the role of the business case to articulate how the project will create additional value to the enterprise. The business case provides the justification for committing resources to the project, and answers the question, 'Why are we doing it?' A sound business case underpins a project charter and is a prerequisite for both project scope planning and benefits management. Since every project represents, in a sense, a new undertaking, it is laden with risks, including the risk that it might not justify the investment that the business intends making in it. From the business perspective, therefore, benefits management is a process for minimising corporate risk.

Implicit in the concept of 'a sound business case' is the consequence that if at any point during the project life-cycle it appears that the anticipated benefits no longer justify the future investment required, then the sponsoring business should take all necessary steps to minimize the financial and other risks to the business, including cancelling all further work on the project if necessary. Thus from the business perspective, managing benefit from a project is a key function of corporate governance and becomes, effectively, the point at which corporate governance and project governance converge.

Much of the recent literature on benefits management is to be found in relationship to programme management (Office of Government Commerce 2003; Project Management Institute 2006), but it is a mistake to restrict the topic simply to programmes. Benefit management is applicable to all projects, and following the lead of the UK's Office of Government Commerce (OGC 2005) and Association for Project Management (APM 2006) it is to be expected that all project management standards will sooner or later recognize the essential place that it occupies in the management of any project.

THE PROJECT MANAGEMENT PERSPECTIVE

From the point of view of project management, however, managing benefits is not an activity or group of activities that stands alone; it introduces additional activities into every process stage of project management.

- During initiation, the business case needs to be prepared in such a way that the end-benefits and intermediate benefits are clearly spelled out prior to project approval.
- During project planning, the project plan needs to take account of benefits delivery, and lock the beneficiary departments or business units into a benefits delivery plan.
- During project monitoring and control, periodic business reviews need to be conducted with a view to assessing the impact that any changes to the project

might have on delivery of benefits and thus on the integrity of the business case.

- During project execution, stakeholder management needs to ensure that any approved changes to the project are reflected in corresponding changes to the benefits delivery plan.
- During project closeout, the full impact of the benefits delivery plan needs to be reflected in the operations budgets and plans of the beneficiary departments.

In practice, these additional activities require a closer co-operation between the project team and the final owners and users of the product or service to be produced by the project.

THE PIVOTAL ROLE OF THE EXECUTIVE SPONSOR

For perfectly sound operational reasons, many organizations are structured so that the part responsible for planning, managing and delivering projects is distinct from the part charged with the responsibility for operating the products, services or capabilities delivered by those projects (see Figure 13.1). It has been argued that the executive sponsor provides a pivotal link between the part of the organization (the business enterprize) seeking beneficial change, and the temporary organization (the project) established to create the product or service designed to provide the benefits (Dinsmore and Cooke-Davies 2005). It is not the

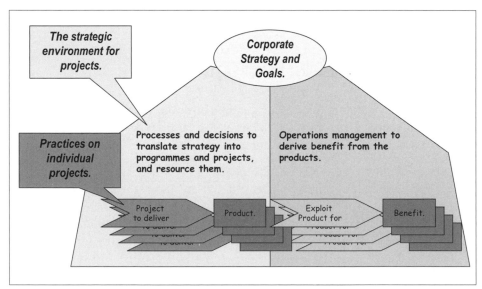

Figure 13.1   Organizational barriers to benefits management

purpose of this chapter to explore the role of the executive sponsor in either corporate or project governance. But the management of benefit calls for an overarching responsibility that extends from the initial discussions leading up to approval of the project right through to the time when the sponsoring organization can demonstrate to its stakeholders that the desired benefit has been achieved. This role is normally taken on by senior executives since only experienced top managers are likely to have credibility and knowledge of the permanent organization to interact effectively with other senior executives on the impact of the project on strategic and operational issues. Indeed, two aspects of the sponsor's role are essential preconditions to benefits management: the sponsor as

- Owner of the business case
- Harvester of benefits

THE SPONSOR 'OWNS' THE BUSINESS CASE

Another way of thinking about the business case is that it represents the essential deal between the sponsoring organization and the project team – 'We'll give you the agreed resources, if you give us the product or service specified, so we can get the business benefits,' (Turner 1999). As such, where no external contract exists, it stands as a kind of surrogate internal contract. But once the project is underway, there are likely to be changes both in the business environment and in the project team's own detailed understanding of what technical progress is and isn't possible. As these changes occur, there is a constant need to make sure that the deal or business case still looks attractive to the sponsoring organization. Just as 'single point responsibility' within a project rests upon the shoulders of the project manager, so it is helpful if 'single point responsibility' for the business case rests on the shoulders of the sponsor, whose job it is to provide oversight to the project so it achieves the benefits for which it was designed.

THE SPONSOR IS RESPONSIBLE FOR ENSURING THAT BENEFITS ARE HARVESTED

The project team is charged with delivering the specified product or service, but someone else in the organization is usually responsible for reaping the operational benefits for the organization. Thus the role of the sponsor extends beyond reviewing project progress; it includes reviewing the readiness of the operating departments to receive the product or service, and to operate it so that the benefits assumed in the business case are harvested. In classical project management, of course, this role is assumed by a representative of the organization that is procuring the project, referred to elsewhere in this book as the 'owner'. But the task is the same, whether the person responsible is referred to as sponsor or as owner.

And it is no simple task. The skills associated with the management of change may be required. Operations departments are often uninterested in becoming involved in projects until the products or services are nearing handover. That is understandable since the job of a line or unit manager is to manage functional activities, which usually generates sufficient workload without having to dedicate time to worry about future improvements. In the folklore of project management there is a saying that 'clients are people who don't know what they want until it is delivered – and then they know that it wasn't THAT!' The saying contains at least a kernel of truth, and embodies a particular barrier to harvesting benefits. So the sponsor does well to spot the 'wavering-expectations' syndrome early on, and articulate efforts to ensure that the project delivered will indeed generate results for the client and for the parent organization. This mismatch in expectations does not always lie with the client or receiving department. Some project teams pay little attention to stakeholder management, and prefer not to raise difficult issues and risks in a timely manner. In these situations, the sponsor's role, as one who knows the organization well, is to ensure the project team has the right stakeholder management practices in place (Chapter 36), including those stakeholders who will have to operate the product or service.

(Editor's note: In Chapter 5, Rodney Turner differentiates between the role of the sponsor and the role of the owner. The role of the sponsor is pre-project, defining the desired benefit, writing the business case, and monitoring the project during the design phase to ensure the asset as designed will provide new capabilities that can deliver the desired business benefit. The role of the owner is post project, monitoring delivery of the asset to ensure the desired new capabilities are obtained, and then using those capabilities to harvest the business benefits. The sponsor and owner are usually the same person, but not always. Prince2™ (OGC 2005), for instance, defines the Project Executive and Senior User, respectively. Here the two roles are being combined in one.)

PROCESSES AND PRACTICES

WHAT PROCESSES ARE INVOLVED?

Benefits management itself consists of a number of interlinked but discrete processes:

- As a part of the project strategy, identifying a benefits management strategy, proposing how the benefits are to be delivered, who is to be accountable for them, how they are to be assessed, and what the implications of this are for the project structure and governance

- Clarifying the outcomes that the product or service to be delivered by the project is intended to accomplish, and from these identifying what the benefits (and also any dis-benefits) are likely to be
- Mapping the linkages and dependencies between benefits
- Quantifying the benefits in practical terms that allow the areas of the organization that are responsible for realizing them to understand how their ongoing operations will need to change in order for the benefits to be realized
- Relating the specific benefits to the project deliverables that will enable them to be realized, and planning how the benefits will be realized and measured in the areas responsible for realizing them. Relating costs to specific benefits, and allocating responsibilities for realising each of the benefits
- Monitoring implications for benefits of changes to the project and business environment
- Measuring the realization of benefits

As has been noted above, these processes need to be integrated as appropriate into the relevant project management areas.

HOW WELL IS BENEFITS MANAGEMENT PRACTICED?

Unfortunately, such evidence as there is suggests good practice in benefits management is as rare as the literature on the subject was during the twentieth century. I have shown elsewhere that only 7% of all projects deliver 100% or more of the benefits expected of them, while more than two thirds deliver less than 75% of the expected benefits. And these figures apply only to those 75% of projects that are able to make an estimate – the remaining quarter are unable to assess the extent to which any benefits were delivered (Cooke-Davies 2005).

The same paper reports that although many project sponsors are broadly satisfied that 'the project has been approved on the basis of a well-founded business case linking the benefits of the project to explicit organizational goals (whether financial or not)', they are much less satisfied that 'the benefits realization process for each project assigns clear and unambiguous responsibility for the realization of business benefits', and even less so that 'there is a means of measuring and reporting on the extent to which benefits have been realized at any point in time', (Figure 13.2). The scale in Figure 13.2 represents a four point Likert scale ranging from Completely Untrue (1) to Completely True (4), and is based on the responses of 117 project sponsors, or managers of project management offices in USA and UK. This is disappointing, since the same piece of research indicates that assigning unambiguous responsibility for realizing business benefits is instrumental in delivering significantly improved project outcomes as measured

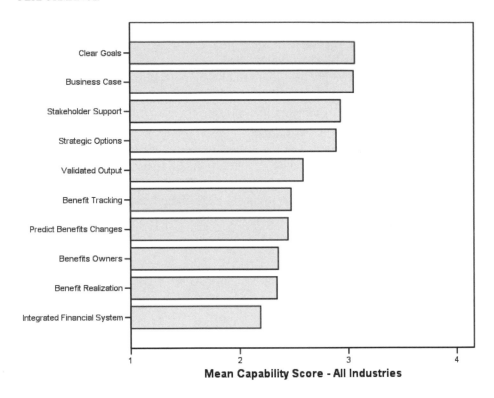

Figure 13.2 Reported sponsor capabilities

by project efficiency – an amalgam of the traditional measures of project performance: time, cost, quality, scope and safety (Figure 13.3).

Leading management consultants confirm the bleakness of the picture. One report states that nearly half of all senior executives are unable to track benefits realized against the original project targets or plans, while nearly 60% fail to link the benefits owner's success (or failure) in achieving the benefit target to performance evaluation and compensation (Deloitte 2005). Another report (KPMG 2005) includes among its 'big' messages that:

● The most popular definition of success today is meeting promised project benefits – in other words, keeping commitments
● in only 23 % of cases is delivery of project benefits tied to individual executive performance plans and rewards
● inadequate benefits management processes prevent the articulation of programme and project success and this creates a largely unquantifiable degree of benefits leakage
● only 2 % of organizations claimed they achieved targeted benefits all the time in the past 12 months

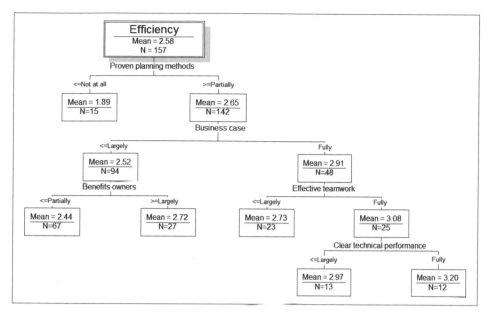

Figure 13.3 Significant influences on project results

It would appear that even if the message is getting through that benefits management is an important area of project management practice, the practice is still more talked about than implemented.

WHAT ARE THE KEYS TO SUCCESSFUL PRACTICE?

So what are the keys to implementing a successful management practice? A review of the practices of leading organizations suggests that there are three underpinning principles for an effective benefits management system, which break down into 'ten commandments' for effective benefits management, grouped into three challenge areas:

1. Create governance structures that involve both the project team and the functional line organization and that focus on business benefit.
2. Ensure that all decisions taken about the project at the governance level are driven by the business case.
3. Redesign all project management processes and practices so that benefits management is an integral part of them.

These are spelt out in a little more detail. (The practices described in this section are those identified by groups of practitioners whose organizations were members of a network that shared information about their practices and results as part of an ongoing knowledge exchange about project management. The practices

253

were first described in an article in *Project Manager Today*, November/December 2001, pp22 to 26.)

STRUCTURE TO HARVEST BENEFITS

The first challenge is to create a structure that encourages the harvesting of benefits by the organization. While the role of the project sponsor is crucial to achieving this goal, the sponsor is not the only person involved. The whole organization has a vested interest in the effective governance of the overall project portfolio. The word governance has been bandied about in project management circles in recent years. The term is used here to describe a layer of project control exercised by or on behalf of the people who are paying for the project. It sits at a higher level in the organization than that of detailed project control. It can involve the project sponsor, a higher-level programme director or an advisory board or steering group, which may involve representatives from joint venture partners, client and financing organizations. In some cases the project manager and core team members may be partially involved in the governance structure. Three areas of good practice (the first three 'commandments') illustrate how this first principle transitions from theory to implementation:

Commandment 1:

- Nurture a culture of cooperation between the line and the project organization, which has at its heart a clear accountability for the delivery of benefits and return on investment.
- Business change is delivered through a portfolio of projects (Chapters 2 and 3), managed by a project management community, and governed by some organizational body responsible for maximizing the success of both individual projects and the entire portfolio of projects. Taken as a whole, the sum of the projects represents the organization's efforts to implement its strategy for achieving its long-term goals.
- The realities illustrated in Figure 13.1 need to be reflected in governance structures for each project or programme in the portfolio, with the appointment of a suitably qualified and competent project manager, but also of a suitably qualified and competent executive sponsor. The performance of the executive concerned in his or her role as executive sponsor should be evaluated as an integral part of the appraisal and development process.

Commandment 2

- Define clearly the responsibilities of the project sponsor, project manager, end-users and other stakeholders so that the roles are coherent with the goal of garnering the benefits for which the project was funded.

254

- The structural adjustments recommended in the first best practice don't need to be implemented through a massive reorganization. It is appropriate to begin dealing with the issue through specifying clear roles and responsibilities for all project stakeholders in order to ensure that benefits planning, delivery and realization are clearly in the hands of those people best able to contribute to achieving ultimate benefits for the organization.
- One solution is to create a liaison for 'outcomes management' in each area of the company that will ultimately gain benefits from the product or service delivered by the project. This person, whose responsibilities will outlive the project, can work alongside the project team to ensure that decisions taken from within the project are likely to enhance benefits to the organization.
- The role of the project manager needs to be clearly defined with regards to benefits management. Some organizations in the financial services industry hold project managers accountable for the delivery of benefits, thereby expanding considerably the scope of traditional project management.

Commandment 3

- Identify all stakeholders who will need to be involved in the project in order for it to contribute the anticipated benefits to the business, incorporate their roles into the benefits delivery plan, and involve them in appropriate ways throughout the life of the project.
- This third good practice area ensures that the scope of the project includes all activities necessary to ensure the management of the project stakeholders.
- A subsequent step is to fix clear responsibilities for the delivery of benefits once project deliverables are produced, and to have these stakeholders work together with the project team to develop a benefits delivery plan, which can serve as the basis for future decisions about operational budgets and practices.

BASE DECISION-MAKING ON THE BUSINESS CASE

The second challenge to be overcome is to base all decisions in the sphere of project or programme governance on the business case for the project. Business cases are not simply documents to be used for gaining access to the necessary resources; they are the project's raison d'être. Using them to drive all decisions calls for a further three areas of good practice ('Commandments' 4 to 6):

Commandment 4

- Before approving the project, ensure that in the business case project plans show how deliverables will be produced, that benefits management plans show how benefits will be realized from utilising the deliverables, and that the benefits realized are a necessary contribution to corporate strategy (see Figure 13.4).

Commandment 5

- Ensure that the business case from each project is presented in a comparable form, so that the totality of an organization's project activity can be assessed against its overall corporate strategy. If practice Commandment 4 is concerned with ensuring that every project is necessary to the corporate strategy, then Commandment 5 is concerned with ensuring that the totality of project-based activity is sufficient to deliver the corporate strategy.
- Regular reviews should be conducted of the entire project portfolio, so as to assure the alignment of project activity with corporate strategy.

Commandment 6

- Review the integrity of the business case in the light of both project performance and the changing business environment at each 'stage gate' review point during the life of the project. Implicit in this process is the real possibility that a 'no go' decision will be taken if the business case, when reviewed, no longer justifies future investment of resources in the project.

MODIFY OR DEVELOP PROJECT MANAGEMENT PROCESSES, TO PUT BENEFITS MANAGEMENT AT THEIR HEART

The third challenge is to incorporate the processes described above into the organization's project management processes, and that leads to the final four specific areas of good practice ('Commandments' 7 to 10).

Commandment 7

- Incorporate benefits planning into the project planning process such that all appropriate stakeholders are committed to a benefits delivery plan. Planning for the delivery of benefits must be built into the planning process right from the start if delivery is to be successfully executed and monitored. In effect, the scope of the project has to extend to the creation of a benefits delivery plan that will show not only what benefits will be realized and when, but who will be responsible in the operational part of the organization for ensuring that they are delivered.
- Ensure that each project team develops an appropriate suite of metrics to assess the probable benefits that their project will or does contribute to the business, in such a way that they can be compared at any time during the

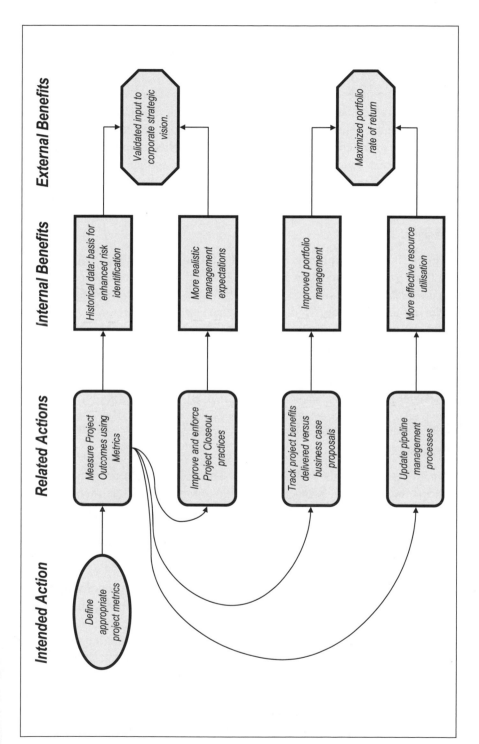

Figure 13.4 Examples of a benefits map

257

project life-cycle with the benefits that were anticipated in the business case, and with the benefits required by the business in the light of current trading performance.

- The second good practice principle is easier to say than to do. It is relatively easy to show when benefits will become available, if the benefits are explicitly linked to specific deliverables (see Commandment 4). It is less easy to develop 'early warning' systems of indicators (such as traffic lights or dashboard dials) that can predict the total value of the project as compared with the initial business case. This is where the rigorous use of some financial measure such as Net Present Value (NPV) can be of great assistance.

Commandment 9

- Integrate risk management principles into the benefits management process. The third good practice area is to take the benefits that can be released by specific deliverables, and then tie these into risk analyses associated with the timing of the deliverables in the project plan. Two separate reviews can prove useful in this context. Firstly, the size of the benefit compared with the time that it is forecast to become available during the project's life can encourage bringing benefits forward so as to improve the cost/benefit profile of the project. Secondly, the size of a benefit compared to the risks inherent in its associated deliverables can lead to a revised project strategy, using the principles of *Value Management* (Chapter 16).

Commandment 10

- Communicate both the benefits plan and current project status to all participants, in both the project and the line organization. Thus we come to the final good practice area, which is perhaps the most obvious, and yet one of the least commonly practiced. Companies that excel at benefits management major on the need to keep all parts of the organization continually informed of the current status of the benefits plan, as it is affected by current project status.

None of these ten 'commandments' is simple to implement – as is born out by the lamentable state of practice identified earlier in this chapter. From the point of view of senior management seeking to implement corporate strategy, however, or from the point of view of the project management profession seeking to raise the rate of 'success' of projects, there can be few more important areas of focus.

REFERENCES AND FURTHER READING

APM, 2006, *APM Body of Knowledge,* 5th edition, High Wycombe, UK: Association for Project Management.

Cooke-Davies, T., 2001a, 'The 'real' project success factors', *International Journal of Project Management,* 20(3), 185–190.

Cooke-Davies, T. J., 2001b, *Managing Benefits; the Key to Project Success,* London: Larchdrift Projects Limited.

Cooke-Davies, T. J., 2005, 'The Executive Sponsor – The Hinge Upon Which Organizational Maturity Turns?' in *Proceedings of the PMI® Global Congress Europe, Edinburgh, May 2005,* Newtown Square, PA: Project Management Institute.

Deloitte, 2005, *Adopting the Value Habit (and Unleashing More Value for Your Stakeholders),* New York: Deloitte Consulting.

Dinsmore, P.C and Cooke-Davies, T. J., 2005, *The Right Projects Done Right,* San Francisco: Jossey-Bass.

KPMG, 2005, *Global Programme Management Survey – a UK Perspective,* London: KPMG.

OGC, 2003, *Managing Successful Programmes,* London: The Stationery Office.

OGC, 2005, *Managing Successful Projects with PRINCE2®,* 4th edition, London: The Stationery Office.

PMI®, 2006, *The Standard for Programme Management,* Newtown Square, PA: The Project Management Institute.

Thorp, J., 1998, *The Information Paradox: Realizing the Business Benefits of Information Technology,* New York: McGraw-Hill.

Turner, J.R., 1993, *The Handbook of Project-based Management: improving the processes for achieving strategic objectives,* London, UK: McGraw-Hill.

Turner, J.R., 1999, *The Handbook of Project-based Management: improving the processes for achieving strategic objectives,* 2nd edition, London, UK: McGraw-Hill.

14 Managing Requirements

Mary McKinlay

This is the second in a series of chapters in which we define the scope of the project; that is we define what the project team have to do. In Chapter 5, Rodney Turner said a project is a temporary organization to which resources are assigned to do work to deliver beneficial change. In the previous chapter, Terry Cooke-Davies described how we define and manage the desired benefit. In this chapter we begin to define the desired change that will enable us to realize that benefit. Terry Cooke-Davies introduced the idea of a benefits map, to show how we will use the change we introduce, the new asset, to achieve the desired benefit. Figure 14.1 shows a stylized version of that, where the project delivers the new asset which in turn gives us new capabilities, which we can use, through a series of intermediate steps, to solve problems or exploit opportunities, to achieve some goal that will enable us to realize value, that is achieve the desired benefit.

The process of defining the required new asset, the new capabilities, and the components of the project required to deliver them, is known as Requirements

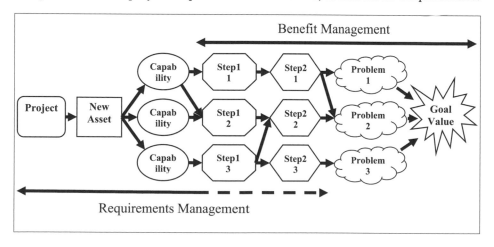

Figure 14.1   **Linking the required change to the desired benefit**

Management. The name reflects historically where project management has come from. Traditionally, the client approached the contractor with some idea of the asset they wanted or needed, their requirements, and asked the contractor to deliver that (Rodney Turner and Martina Huemann discuss wants and needs in Chapter 17). The client's requirement is actually the end benefit, but the label Requirements Management remains attached to the definition and delivery of the change that will enable us to deliver that benefit, and the label Benefits Management to the definition and delivery of the desired benefit.

In their body of knowledge, (APM 2006), the UK's Association for Project Management defines Requirements Management as follows:

Requirements Management is the process of capturing, analysing and testing the documented statement of stakeholder and user wants and needs. Requirements are a statement of the need that a project has to satisfy, and should be comprehensive, clear, well-structured, traceable and testable.

Figure 14.2 illustrates that the process is a bit more amorphous than implied by Figure 14.1.

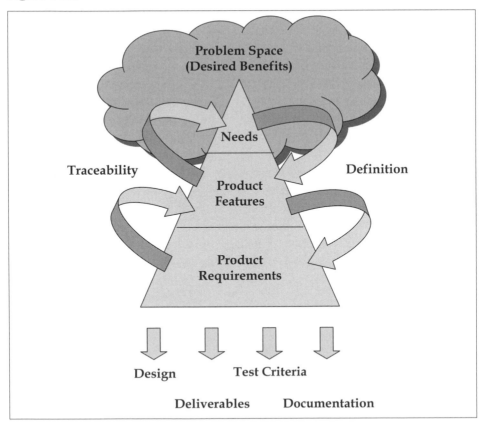

Figure 14.2 Requirements management

The Requirements Management process is described in this chapter. First we remind ourselves why it is important. Then we describe the Requirements Management Process (RMP), consider Requirements Management throughout the project life-cycle and introduce a requirements management toolset.

THE REQUIREMENTS MANAGEMENT PROBLEM

Why should requirements management be important to a project? Some comments from Project Managers may illuminate here:

- 'Ad hoc Requirements Management is the main cause for delayed milestone payments and project failure'
- 'Without a clear requirements baseline, contractual changes are missed and cannot be charged back'
- 'Missed out, misinterpreted or unclear requirements end up in rework, eroding the project margin'
- 'Without Requirements Management how does the project manager know what has to be accomplished by the project?'
- 'How does the client understand what will be the final result?'
- 'Properly managed requirements are the key to successful acceptance and closure of a project'

The 'requirements problem' can be stated very simply: What are we delivering? The answer has to be threefold:

1. What they specify
2. What they want
3. What they need

This leads to a further question: 'Who are they?', and the identification of stakeholders and resolution of possible conflict of their objectives (Chapters 36 and 38). Managing requirements is not just trying to improve the material definition or quality of the product, but trying to ensure:

- early resolution
- easy acceptance
- less conflict
- greater customer satisfaction
- getting paid for what was agreed!

Requirements management was at one time thought to be very simple. The customer would supply a requirements document – sometimes, albeit rarely, this would be a detailed specification – and the project team would deliver an implementation of this. Experience and data taken from past projects have shown the requirements are the 'Achilles heel' of many projects. Lack of understanding of requirements, incomplete requirements, changing requirements, unrealistic and unclear requirements are all common causes of perceived project failure. So why should this be so? The communication of requirements is a process that will involve at least two parties and, like all communications processes (Chapter 37), is prone to weakness.

It has to be asked 'What are requirements?' and in the answer to this question there is a wide range of ideas depending on who has answered it! Requirements may be expressed as functionalities, wishes, needs, requests, success factors, assumptions and not just the 'Quality/Scope, Cost and Time' elements that are often regarded as the so-called 'Golden Triangle' baseline for Project Managers. In addition to the range of requirements there is an added issue of how these are interpreted. This involves the project team in cultural and linguistic differences as well as different viewpoints and priorities of the various stakeholders. Requirements Management is very closely allied with Stakeholder Management, Communication Management, Conflict Management, Success Factors, Success Criteria, Scope Management, Change Control, Quality Management, and Implementation Management (Chapters 36, 37, 38, 6, 15, 17, and 29).

The project manager must have a clear understanding of the purpose of the project in order to be able to fully define the objectives and hence the success criteria. The starting point for this definition has to be the requirements which in turn should be comprehensive, understandable, unambiguous and, from the point of view of acceptance of the project deliverables, testable and traceable. The project manager must communicate this information to the project team and also to the stakeholders. In addition to the formal requirements, the project manager needs a full understanding of the business context of the project, the 'big picture'. This will enable identification of stakeholders and their influence on the project. Taken all together, the project manager will be able to create a comprehensive project mission statement that can be used throughout the life-cycle. It is apparent from the foregoing that a well run project should have a process to ensure that all these elements are considered, recorded and resolved.

WHAT ARE REQUIREMENTS?

Requirements are the characteristics of a project that a customer or other stakeholder desires to have present in the project deliverables. Figure 14.2 illustrates that we start with some vision of the desired future benefit, and that we need to convert this into a statement of need, and thence into a definition of the desired features of the new asset and thence into a statement of the requirements of that product. This will include a specification of the desired deliverables of the project, how they should be designed, and of the supporting documentation. The requirements statement should also indicate how the characteristics will be demonstrated and tested as part of the acceptance process. A project needs to have a requirements statement that expresses these in unambiguous terms and in such a way as to make sure that all parties involved with the project have the same understanding of what will be produced. We can identify different types of requirement.

1. **User requirements**: usually these will reflect the user's needs and may well concentrate on how they will view the deliverables from the perspective of attributes and outputs.
2. **Functional requirements**: express the specific functions of the deliverables and may frequently depend on systemic operation. A list of functional requirements will encompass the things that the deliverables must do and which must be delivered as part of the project.
3. **Derived requirements**: will become apparent as the definition of the requirements statement becomes clearer. These are requirements for the system that are not explicitly stated but are needed in order to fulfil the higher level needs.
4. **System, or technical requirements:** appear as a more detailed explanation of the physical and functional attributes of the project deliverables.

In essence, as the requirements for the project are explored, they will be decomposed to lower levels until the overall system can be viewed as a series of interconnected and practical elements to deliver the project as specified.

ADVANTAGES OF MANAGING REQUIREMENTS

In the process of managing requirements, links are created between higher and lower requirement levels. Figure 14.2 illustrates that the definition of requirements at a lower level should be driven by those at a higher level, and there should be an audit trail where the definition can be clearly traced through the various levels. This allows easy assessment of the impact of changes. Proper evaluation of the requirements helps to eliminate 'gold-plated' solutions; that is where more work is put into the job than is really necessary (see also Value Management, Chapter 16). The process provides more visibility of planning activities and deliverables through linkages with acceptance and validation and verification. The added control enables timely closure of contracts and milestone payments. The goals of the managing requirements can be summarised as:

● to clarify and interpret requirements
● to provide a clear, early and mutual understanding of what will be delivered and how compliance will be demonstrated

265

- to develop a process that will work with the customers so that they will be less inclined to challenge the project outputs

THE REQUIREMENTS MANAGEMENT PROCESS (RMP)

The RMP can be described as a process of developing requirements through an iterative, cooperative series of activities under the following headings:

1. **Capture:** where the requirements are collected, clarified, structured and documented
2. **Analysis:** to evaluate completeness, realism, effects, benefits and interfaces and present the resulting observations in a variety of representation formats
3. **Control:** to establish a baseline against which changes can be assessed.
4. **Testing:** documentation of how the project's deliverables will achieve the requirements and how this can be proved for acceptance by the stakeholders; that is checking the accuracy of the understanding gained throughout the project life-cycle

RMP is iterative because, although it would be desirable for requirements to be fixed at the outset of a project, requirements do change. These changes arise for a variety of reasons, including:

- The customers may change their minds; their needs may increase or decrease
- Technological change may be required as a result of obsolescence or other non-availability of components of the project system
- External factors may impact the project, such as legislation on health and safety, environmental factors or stakeholder intervention
- Improvements in process, understanding or technology

It is worth noting at this point that although the principles of Requirements Management apply to all projects, the implementation of the process will differ between simple and complex system projects. In the case of the latter, there are very sophisticated toolsets that will facilitate whereas for simple projects a spreadsheet database may suffice.

REQUIREMENTS DEVELOPMENT THROUGH THE PROJECT LIFE-CYCLE

Figure 14.3 demonstrates the processes needed during a typical project life-cycle. The requirements management process usually starts at the Bid or Proposal stage of a project. The Request for Proposal (RFP) received from a prospective customer will contain some information about the requirements. This information

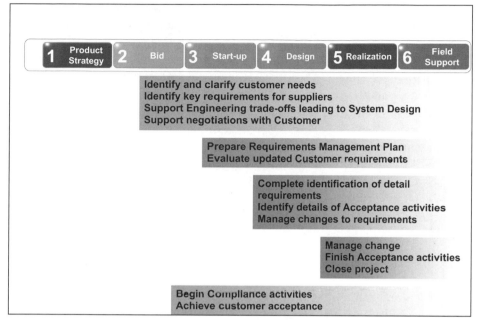

Figure 14.3   Requirements management through the life-cycle of a project

must be analysed and the separate requirements identified. Often at this stage it is useful to prepare a Requirements Matrix where each requirement is listed and cross related with whether or not, at this stage of the project, a technical solution is available or will need further work. This will often be a case of comparing the items listed in the RFP with an existing product or technical solution. Conventionally requirements are written in the form 'X shall be provided.' They can be statements of fact, such as 'Y will occur.' Or the process can become a mechanical one of listing all the 'wills' and 'shalls'. The result of this initial exercise is an indicator of the work that will be required during the project and how much additional development is needed beyond an existing solution. Another term conventionally used in requirements documentation is 'should' and this refers to goals of the project.

In addition to the exploration of the documentation provided by the customer, this is the time when the first assessment of the stakeholders should be made and, where possible, their strategic goals for the project identified (Chapter 36). These must be related to the objectives, as far as presently known, of the project. Whilst appreciating that, at the proposal stage, resources may be limited, this exercise is a valuable investment in future project success. At this time it is also essential to clarify the project objective statements, identify conflicts and contradictions and verify the real issues to be solved.

It may also become apparent that further definition will be required and agreement with the team and the customer on how this should proceed must be reached. The experience of the team is valuable in this process because it may become necessary to make estimates for the proposal without a detailed statement of requirements. The project team should put as much effort as possible into holding workshops with stakeholders, the customer and other interested parties, such as end users, to establish a factual baseline (Chapter 16). This is another area where 'Learning from experience' plays a vital part and the organizations that are successful here will benefit.

Figure 14.4 demonstrates the thinking processes to be implemented at this early stage of the project. At this stage, it is possible that there will be a very large list of requirements and it is necessary to decide which of these should figure in the requirements statement for the project. This is the analysis phase of the process and it is up to the project manager together with the technical manager, or system architect (as appropriate for the type of project) to decide on the criteria for inclusion. Some important issues at this stage will be:

1. **Verification:** can this requirement be verified once delivered?
2. **Achievability:** can the requirement be achieved within the constraints of budget, resources, time and available techniques?

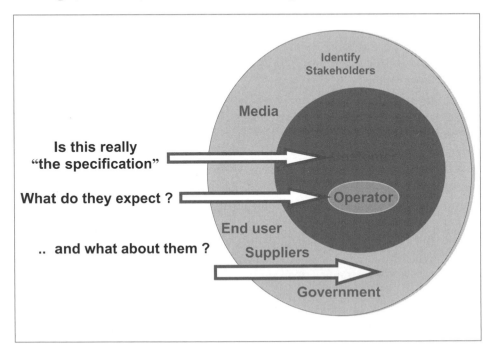

Figure 14.4   Initial elicitation process

3. **Criticality:** is this requirement one that is critical to the satisfaction of the customer?
4. **Priority:** how much do the customer and the other stakeholders value this requirement?
5. **Feasibility:** is this a practical proposition from the standpoint of technicality and financial resources?

The next phase of this process is to return to the customers and check that the requirements statement that has been generated is in line with their needs and desires. At this stage it is frequently found that assumptions have been made on both sides and these must be identified and their status clarified. Assumptions can be a costly area for projects and need to be documented and explained as early as possible. The results of the above activities must be documented fully and the documentation should be configured. The statement of requirements that has been derived will act as a baseline until the requirements have been developed as described below.

It is worth noting at this stage that the use of language is of importance here. The phrasing of requirements is of great significance. Each should be simple and unambiguous. Definition of terms must be rigorous and values or tolerances allocated for outputs. Remember that achievement of the requirement has to be verified. Some terms to be avoided in the requirements statement are:

- User friendly
- Rapid
- Adequate
- Maximize
- Minimize
- World Class
- Sufficient
- Efficient
- Effective
- Simple

There are a host of other terms like this but they can be checked by asking the question 'What does this mean, and how can we test it?' Projects have foundered on disagreements as to what constitutes 'User friendliness'.

REQUIREMENTS SPECIFICATION

The work needed to move from the Statement of Requirements to Requirements Specifications is a progressive one. Some complex systems will decompose into several requirements specifications depending on the number of components. Deriving a specification is the way to compile and harmonize the knowledge to form an agreed definition of the need. The deliverable outputs of the project will be compared to this specification and acceptance tests will be based upon this.

The next phase is to allocate the requirements: which means that we must roll down the definition to create discrete packages of work which will, when taken together, define the complete system. From a technical point of view, the project has to decide how a requirement will be fulfilled technically and how the work will be carried out; for example will a particular requirement be satisfied by a software or a hardware solution? In large complex systems this process may be the responsibility of the Systems Engineering Function in the project.

During the 1990s Systems Engineers worked hard to understand this process and the result has become known as the 'V Diagram', Figure 14.5. This is the mirror image of Figure 14.2, showing that as we create more detail we get greater resolution. Starting from the top left of the 'V' it is possible to follow the requirements process through project. Moving down the left hand side, the requirements are systematically provided with technical solutions; it is a process of breaking down into a hierarchy of requirements. The work that is done in this design activity may be helped by modelling, simulation or other means. What is important is to view the traceability of the process and the relationships between the developing elements of the system design and the requirements that they satisfy. It can be seen that once again, documentation is paramount. In this respect some of the software tools that have been developed to assist with Requirements Management can provide great support. Working up the right-hand side of the 'V' we see a process of synthesis ending with the final output product. The cross-links between the left and right hand sides of the diagram are important in providing evidence for acceptance. For complex systems it is often impossible to test for all functionality at final acceptance. Using this process, collected data from intermediate testing, modelling and simulation and design proving exercises can be documented and used as part of a progressive acceptance. The process of deriving specifications and allocating requirements leads to the following:

1. Generating a family of requirements with their links and hierarchy
2. Recording and coordinating the issues that have arisen during the process such as those given in the following list:
    ● Assumptions
    ● Gaps
    ● Clarifications
    ● Conflicts
    ● Risks and opportunities
3. Defining 'satisfaction arguments'
4. Organizing the 'whats' and the 'hows'.

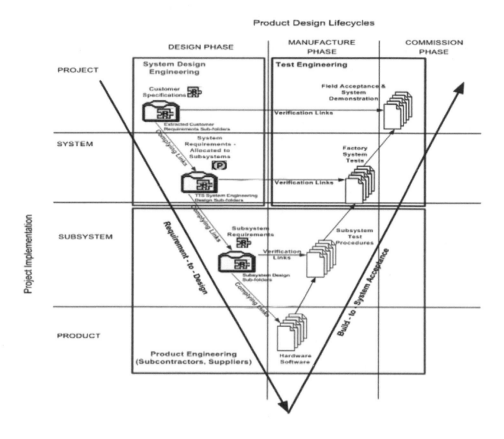

Figure 14.5 The 'V' Diagram, showing requirements management through the life-cycle

Traceabilty is established during this process and demonstrates that:

- The requirements have been understood
- The design has been done to meet the requirements
- Subsystems are specified that meet the requirements
- The final product has been programmed or built according to the design
- The final deliverables have met the requirements

TOOLSETS FOR REQUIREMENT MANAGEMENT

As mentioned earlier, the RMP may be relatively simple or very complex depending on the objects of the project. In all cases it is necessary to track requirements, their development and technical resolution and how they will be tested and validated for final acceptance and closure of the project. Toolsets can

271

therefore range from the use of a spreadsheet to some of the sophisticated Systems Engineering Requirements suites available on the market. There are several of these and the choice of the most suitable one depends on the project environment and resource availability. These tools are capable of analysing the initial documentation and mechanising the process of listing out all the requirements by identifying all the 'wills and shalls'. The data can be used and the progress of each element can be tracked. The toolsets often have design tools and modelling tools built into them and so can create complete documentation for the project. This is outlined in Figure 14.6. Although this might sound like magic, using the tools is a skilled job and requires training and understanding.

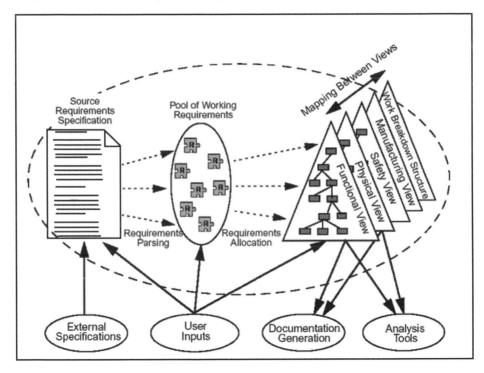

Figure 14.6   Using requirements management toolset in a complex system

CONCLUSIONS

Requirements Management is a necessary process for projects. There are still projects that do not use the techniques to make sure that success is more likely. It is still common to find projects that have not got a fully documented set of requirements, and one has to wonder how they know when the project has been completed.

REFERENCES AND FURTHER READING

APM, 2006, *APM Body of Knowledge,* 5th edition, High Wycombe, UK: Association for Project Management.

Hall, G., 'Requirements management', in Stevens, M., (ed), Project Management Pathways, High Wycombe, UK: Association for Project Management.

Robertson, S. and Robertson, J., 2004, *Requirements-led Project Management; Discovering David's Slingshot*, Boston, MA: Addison-Wesley.

Managing Scope – Configuration and Work Methods

15

Rodney Turner

In this chapter I describe the management of the scope of the project. Although scope is a simple word, it is very difficult to get agreement on precisely what is meant by 'managing the scope of the project'. The authors of the early editions of the IPMA Baseline of Competence (Caupin et al 1999), had difficulty finding a German word to translate the English word 'scope'. In my book, (Turner 1999, p93), I defined managing scope as the process of:

> ensuring enough, but only enough, work is undertaken to deliver the project's purpose successfully

There are three elements to this statement. We want to ensure:

- a sufficient amount of work is done
- unnecessary work is not done
- we achieve the stated purpose of the project

However, I now think that this definition is a bit narrow; it only focuses on the work of the project. In Figure 5.1, reproduced as Figure 15.1, I introduced three essential levels of a project, the work to be done, the asset to be delivered by that work, and the business benefit desired from the operation of the asset. These are the three essential components of Premise 1 in Chapter 5. Over a sequence of five chapters we are looking at how to manage the definition and delivery of these three components of the project:

1. In Chapter 13, Terry Cooke-Davies describes Benefits Management, how to define and manage the business benefits required from the project.
2. In Chapter 14, Mary McKinley describes Requirements Management, how to define and manage the requirements of the asset, and the work required to deliver the asset, so that the asset will perform to deliver the desired business benefit.
3. In this chapter I will discuss Scope Management, but I am mainly going to focus on the use of configuration management to identify and manage the

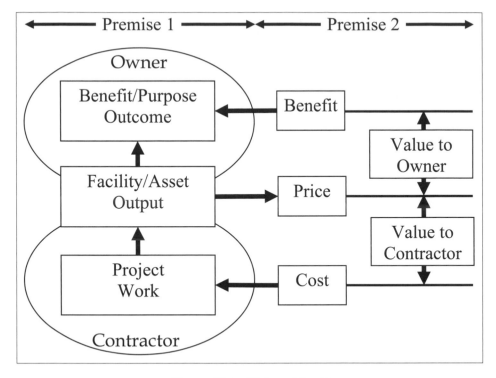

Figure 15.1   Work-asset-benefit

delivery of the components of the asset of desired functionality, and identify and manage the work required to make and assemble the components.

4. In Chapter 16, Steve Simister describes Value Management, and how it is used to balance the functionality of the asset and the benefit it will produce against the cost of doing the work, to obtain best value for money from the project (Premise 2 in Chapter 5).

5. In Chapter 17, Martina Huemann and I describe Quality Management, and how to ensure that the asset and work that delivers it are of the required standards and specification so that the asset delivered performs as required.

Thus Scope Management is part of an essential chain from identifying and managing the delivery of the desired business benefit through doing the optimum amount of work to the desired standard. But Scope Management itself is more than just managing the work. Yes, managing the scope of work is an important part of it, ensuring that enough, but not too much work is done to achieve our objectives. But so too is managing the scope of the asset:

● identifying its required functionality, based on outputs from Requirements Management

- identifying the components that make up the asset, and the desired functionality of each of them so that they perform as required
- identifying how the components should be assembled into the asset

This comes first. Having identified the components of the asset, then and only then can you identify the work required to make each component and to assemble them into the overall asset. In Chapter 5 I identified two break-down structures, the Product Break-down Structure, PBS, and the Work Break-down Structure, WBS. Often people only talk about the WBS. However, I believe that the PBS is essential, and it comes first. First you must identify the components of the asset, their desired functionality and how they fit together. Then and only then can you identify the work that has to be done to make and assemble them. The levels of the WBS and PBS will necessarily map on to each other one-to-one.

In Chapter 5, I also introduced a third break-down structure, the Organization Break-down Structure, OBS, defining organizational units and resources available to do the work. In Chapter 18, Erling Andersen describes the use of responsibility charts to identify which organizational units are responsible for making and assembling which components of the asset, and for doing which work. The levels of the OBS map one-to-one onto the levels of the PBS and WBS. (In Chapter 5 I also introduced a fourth break-down-structure, the Cost Break-down Structure, CBS, but it is decoupled from the other three.)

The inherent tool for managing scope is Configuration Management. Through its two dimensions, essentially the PBS and WBS, Configuration Management identifies the components of the asset, and their associated functionality, and the work required to make and assemble the components. In the next section I will describe how to use the outputs from Benefits Management and Requirements Management to do the initial Project Definition. Then I will introduce Configuration Management, describe how to control changes, and the changing role of configuration management throughout the life-cycle. I also describe Goal Directed Project Management, a project management methodology that supports the concepts of Configuration Management.

PROJECT DEFINITION

Project definition is the first step of scope management, where we draw on the outputs of Benefits Management and Requirements Management to define precisely what the project is about. Through project definition we need to link the business objectives we want to achieve from the project to the definition of the asset the operation of which we think will enable us to deliver those objectives. This requires us to identify three things:

- the Purpose of the Project
- the Deliverables of the Project (the asset)
- the Scope of the Project

PURPOSE

First we must identify the purpose of the project, its ultimate business objective. This may be a problem we want to solve. We may have identified that we are not processing data as well as we might, or we may have a shortage of office space, or a step in our production process is less efficient than it might be. Or it might be in the form of an opportunity we want to exploit. For instance, we may have identified that there is currently a gap in the market which we think we are able to supply. Of course there are some people who say they don't have problems, they only have opportunities for improvement. Thus every problem is an opportunity to improve; every opportunity is a problem of how we are going to exploit it.

If we can identify the problem or opportunity, then that will help us define the potential benefit of doing the project. Processing data better will help us take better decisions; increasing office space may enable us to expand our business; repairing the step in our production process will reduce costs; and exploiting the market with a new product will generate new sales and revenue. All of these are worth money to us, and hopefully from defining the problem we can identify the benefit and potential revenues.

Using an example from my own experience, let us consider a small company with an annual turnover of £12 million. In the annual audit one year the firm's accountant's point out that working capital amounts to £3 million, three months' turnover. Working capital is primarily made up of raw materials awaiting manufacture, work in progress on the production line and finished goods awaiting sale. The accountants say in their business working capital should only equal about one month's turnover, that is about £1 million. The problem is they have too much working capital. What is it costing them? Well, they have to borrow £2 million from their bank to finance that working capital, so at 9% interest it is costing £180,000 per year. But this company also had a product with only a very short shelf-life, about six months. Half the shelf-life is being used up in the production process. Reducing the amount of working capital will increase the useful life of the product making it more competitive. Thus we are able to identify the problem, and the benefit of being able to solve it.

SCOPE

I think that next we often have to think about possible ways of solving the problem. There may be several possible solutions to the problem. Each of those solutions will have a certain cost associated with it, and produce different amounts of benefit. From the possible solutions we want to choose the solution that gives us the highest value, that is the highest ratio of benefit to cost. We do not want to choose the lowest cost solution; that is doing nothing, zero cost. Nor do we want to choose the highest benefit option; that might involve inordinate cost for only small additional benefit. We want the highest value solution. Steve Simister describes Value Management in the next chapter.

Having identified the preferred solution, we are able to draw up the initial definition of the scope of the project. We can define what is included in the project, and what we think are not parts of the project, what is excluded. There are several reasons why work might be excluded: we may want to share or delegate work to other projects, or to avoid the nice-to-haves.

Included

We identify the initial scope of the project through a high level definition of the sorts of things we have to do to implement the preferred solution.

Nice-to-haves

Once we decide to do a project, lots of additional requirements start to ooze out of the woodwork as people try to achieve their own, covert objectives. These are nice-to-haves. Often they add a lot of extra cost for little additional benefit. Doing them reduces the value of the project to us. They must be avoided, and the best way of doing that is by stating explicitly that they are not to be included.

Shared and delegated work

Sometimes several projects may share a common component. It is inefficient for all projects to develop it. One solution is for one project to develop and the others to share it. Another solution is to create an additional project to undertake the work on behalf of all the projects. Other times it may be more effective to delegate work to a functional department. In these circumstances it often doesn't matter what you decide, just as long as you decide something and clearly communicate the decision to everybody involved.

In the case above of the small company with too much working capital, there are several possible solutions.

- The problem may be one of discipline and we think a training programme will solve it
- We may decide to adopt just-in-time working reducing the amount of raw materials and work in progress required

- Or we may adopt a computer system to plan the production process against known demands for our product

In this case we decide the computer system provides the best solution. Therefore what is included in the project is hardware, software, documentation and training of personnel. In avoiding nice-to-haves, we need to be clear about what software modules are necessary and which provide little value for us, and to minimize the amount of bespoke tailoring required to meet unnecessary requirements imposed by users. This may be part of a larger change programme, and so we may delegate recruitment to the personnel department.

DELIVERABLES

Having identified the preferred solution, we can then identify the asset required to deliver it. This is a statement of the end products of the project. We need to define the products and the functionality required in both quantitative and qualitative terms. We may also specify quality requirements. We also need to state the acceptance criteria at which the operators will accept responsibility for the new system.

For example in the production planning computer system above, the end deliverables are operating hardware, operating software, usable documentation and trained staff able to operate the system to deliver benefit. I also believe that the very last deliverable should be a check to show that the working capital is beginning to fall. The system should be put on load and begin to show benefit before the project team handover to the operations team. But the project team cannot be responsible for getting the working capital all the way down to £1 million. That is the responsibility of the operations team. So you should set a target of getting the working capital down to say £2.5 million by a certain time after the system is first put on load. If you achieve that target (plus/minus), the project team hands over to the operations team. If you don't, one of two things has happened. Either there is a mistake in the system, in which case the project team should diagnose the mistake and put it right before handing over. Or the system is not being used properly, in which case you may still handover to the operations team and give them the responsibility for the performance of the system.

BENEFITS MAPS

Terry Cooke-Davies introduced benefits maps as part of Benefits Management. A benefits map represents two parts of the project definition. Figure 15.2 shows a stylized benefits map. The right-hand side shows the goal of the project, the problem to be solved and the end benefit desired. The left hand side shows the new asset, its components, and the capabilities it will give the organization which

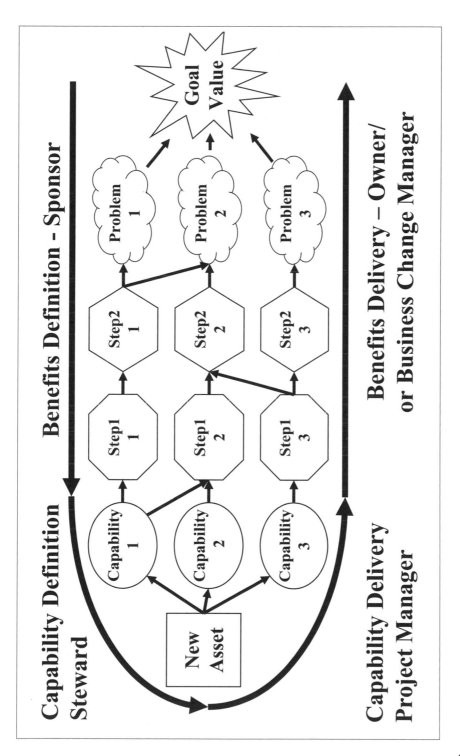

Figure 15.2 Project definition and the benefits map

will enable it to solve the problem. The steps in between show how the new capabilities can be used to solve the problem.

In the example above, the goal on the right hand side is to reduce working capital from £3 million to £1 million, and the benefit of doing that is reduced interest payments and extended useful life of the product. The new capabilities on the left hand side are operating hardware and software, documentation and competent people which will enable us to better plan and manage the production process.

Figure 15.2 also shows three governance roles in addition to the project manager, introduced in Chapter 5:

1. The project sponsor: a manager from the operations department responsible for identifying the problem, and showing how the new asset can be used to solve it, perhaps using the benefits map in that process. The UK Government, in its Prince 2 process (OGC 2005), calls this role the Project Executive.

2. The steward: a manager from the technical department, who will work with the sponsor to define the asset and show how it will be used to solve the problem. The steward will also lead the initial project definition, identifying the process required to deliver the asset, and the resources required to undertake the process. He or she will also be responsible for sourcing the required resources. On larger projects the steward will be the project manager. However on smaller projects, especially projects which are part of a larger programme, much of this will be done before the project manager is appointed. The UK Government in its Prince 2 process calls this role the Senior Supplier. In Managing Successful Programs (OGC 2003), the role is taken by the programme manager.

3. The owner or business change manager: a manager from the operations department responsible for ensuring that the new asset, and the new capabilities it delivers, are used to solve the problem and achieve the benefit. The project manager's responsibility ends with the delivery of the new capabilities, once it has been shown they are working (see above). It is the owner's responsibility to ensure they are used to achieve the full benefit. In the example above that is to get the working capital down to £1 million. The UK government in its Prince 2 process calls this role the Senior User, and in Managing Successful Programs it is the Business Change Manager.

PROJECT DEFINITION REPORT

The project definition should be captured in some way. It is the first step in the project plan, and so should be recorded. I suggest the use of a Project Definition Report (Turner 1999, Turner 2004). Figure 15.3 shows a possible contents page

---

EuroProjex

Project Definition Report

Project:	
Project Champion:	
Project Manager:	

CONTENTS

1. Project Context	Background
2. Project Mandate	Purpose/Scope/Objectives
	Work Areas
3. Project Strategy	Key Performance Indicators
	Mission Statement
4. Work Definition	Milestone Plan
	Work Package Definition
	Work Package Scope Statements
5. Organization	Departments Involved
	Project Roles
	Responsibility Chart
	Stakeholder Register
6. Project Plans	Activity Plans
	Network and Bar Chart

Figure 15.3   Contents page of a project definition report *continued*

283

	Quality Plan	
	Risk Register	
7. Project Control	Planning and Control System	
8. Project Appraisal	Cost Estimate	
	Revenue Estimate	
	Project Appraisal	
Author: JRT	**Date:** 21 Jan 2004	**Issue:** A

Figure 15.3 *Concluded*

for a project definition report, and Figures 15.4 and 15.5 show the first two pages, a statement of background, and the purpose, scope and project deliverables for an Intranet project (from Turner 2004). Prince 2 (OGC 2005) has a two stage project definition process, and calls the report at each stage the Project Brief and Project Initiation Document respectively. Figure 15.6 shows the contents for the Project Brief. They are very similar to my Project Definition Report. PMI® in its PMBoK® (2004) suggests the use of a Project Charter. Figure 15.7 shows the contents of the Project Charter.

CONFIGURATION MANAGEMENT

Configuration management is a tool for defining and managing the delivery of the new asset, and the work required to be done to deliver the asset. Figure 15.8 illustrates the concept. When we start the project we may be uncertain about:

- the exact component breakdown of the eventual facility
- the exact specification of the components and the overall facility
- how the individual components will be made and built into the overall facility

This is illustrated in Figure 15.8, by showing that we cannot precisely specify the goals or methods of delivering them. All we can say is that they lie within certain bounds. We agree those bounds as well as we are able with all the stakeholders, and freeze the definition in a baseline. We work to that baseline for a period of time, and refine our understanding of the goals and work methods. At predetermined review points, we agree the refined definition with the

284

TFS
Project Definition Report

Project:	Intranet Phase 1
Project Champion:	Martin Pacific
Project Manager:	Frances Seeker

Background

TFS is investigating the way it can use web-enabled technology to improve its operations and its contact with its customers and its employees. It is expected that in the medium term it will develop:

- a home page to market its products and services to potential customers
- an extranet, to provide internet and home banking services to customers
- an intranet

The intranet will be the first step in the process. Reasons for this are:

- TFS can gain experiences with web-enabling technologies testing them out on employees, before customers, so that the company has gained experience by the time it goes live externally
- all employees will automatically be logged on to the TFS home page at the start of every day, so as services for customers are introduced, employees will be familiar with the system, and automatically be on-line to support the new services.

The system will also automate several personnel processes, and enable information about the company benefits programme to be readily available on line. The system will support:

1. Processing of documents for personnel, including
   - expense claims
   - holiday requests
   - sickness reports
2. On line availability of personnel information, such as
   - procedures to be followed to submit the above
   - information about the company car scheme
   - statement of the company's personnel policy and psychological contract with its employees
3. Daily news reports on each person's desk top, including
   - news about the company
   - news from the financial services sector
   - briefings from the managing director

The benefits are that the company wants to

- communicate better with its employees, and hopefully improve the psychological contract
- speed up the processing of personnel documents, and reduce the administrative burden
- reduce administrative, printing and storage costs by making information available on line rather than in paper form

Author:	JRT	**Date:**	21 July 2003	**Issue:**	A

Figure 15.4 Statement of background for an Intranet project

285

TFS **Project Definition Report**	
Project: **Project Champion:** **Project Manager:**	Intranet Phase 1 Martin Pacific Frances Seeker
Purpose **Why?**	The purpose of Phase 1 of the Intranet will be to: ▪ communicate better with employees to improve psychological contract ▪ speed processing of personnel documents and reduce administration ▪ reduce personnel administration costs There is also the additional purpose of gaining experience of web-based technology for further development of the Intranet and for introduction of the Internet home page and extranet.
Outputs **What?**	The project will deliver an Intranet comprising: ▪ internal home page to automatically appear on employees' screens when they log on at the start of the day, containing news for employees, and linking to other pages containing further current information ▪ document processing pages for essential personnel information such as holiday requests, expense claims, sickness reports, and others as agreed; these pages will include information on when to complete these forms, how to complete and process them ▪ personnel information pages containing essential information relating to terms and conditions of employment, and information about company personnel schemes The project will also a deliver a report describing experience for Phase 1 to be used in the implementation of Phase 2 and the implementation of the Internet home page and the Extranet. The project will be complete when the system has gone live, and the report on experience for Phase 1 has been accepted by the managing director as a basis for proceeding to Phase 2.
Scope **How?**	**Discovery:** The overall content of the system will be planned and new procedures written. An audit will be conducted to produce an inventory of current hardware. **Design:** The site will be designed and developed. The new procedures piloted. New hardware requirements will be identified and orders placed. **Delivery:** The new procedures will optimized, and the site assembled and approved. **Deployment:** The new hardware will be installed and the data entered or migrated. The system will go live. **Exclusions:** Phase 1 will not include the management information and production pages.
Author: JRT **Date:** 21 July 2007 **Issue:** A	

Figure 15.5   Project definition for an Intranet project *continued*

286

<table>
<tr><td colspan="2" align="center">TFS
Project Definition Report</td></tr>
<tr><td>Project:
Project Champion:
Project Manager:</td><td>Intranet Phase 1
Martin Pacific
Frances Seeker</td></tr>
<tr><td>Areas of Work</td><td>There will be four areas of work:

M: Management approval
D: Design and development
P: Procedures and systems
H: Hardware and data</td></tr>
<tr><td colspan="2">Author: JRT   Date: 21 July 2007 Issue: A</td></tr>
</table>

Figure 15.5 *Concluded*

Project Brief

Background

Project definition
- project objectives
- project scope and exclusions
- outline deliverables/desired outcomes
- constraints
- interfaces

Outline business case
- how project supports business strategy
- reasons why project is needed (problem to be solved)

Project tolerances

Customer's quality expectations

Acceptance criteria

Known risks

Figure 15.6 Contents of the Project Brief for Prince 2, OGC (2005)

287

Requirements to satisfy customer and other stakeholders
Business needs
Project purpose and justification
Assigned project manager and authority level
Summary milestones
Stakeholder influences
Functional organization and their participation
Organizational environment and external assumptions
Organizational environment and external constraints
Business case justification
Budget

Figure 15.7 Contents of the Project Charter in the PMI® PMBoK® (2004)

stakeholders, and then freeze the revised definition as a new baseline. We continue this process until we deliver a fully agreed product at the end of the project. If at some point we cannot get agreement, then either the previous specification was wrong, or the refinements since the last agreement were wrong. In the former case we will need to change the specification; in the latter case we may need to repeat the last step in the process. Neither of these options will cost very much if the lack of agreement is identified early in the process. This can be achieved by holding the reviews reasonably frequently, especially in the design

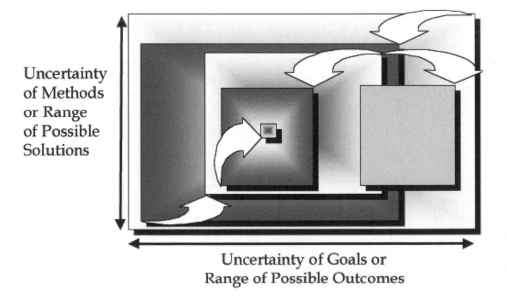

Uncertainty
of Methods
or Range
of Possible
Solutions

Uncertainty of Goals or
Range of Possible Outcomes

Figure 15.8 Configuration management

stages of the project. Both recovery mechanisms can be expensive if the lack of agreement emerges later in the life-cycle (leading to the stories mentioned above).

There are four steps in the configuration management process, Figure 15.9. The first column contains terms commonly used in the configuration management jargon; the second column tries to express steps using concepts developed elsewhere in this book.

CONFIGURATION IDENTIFICATION

Figure 15.10 represents the configuration identification of this book. There are four parts, each part consisting of several chapters, and each chapter several parts. At whatever level of breakdown, I can write a specification of the components, and work methods for how they will be delivered. On the one hand you might say that in this particular case the definition of the work methods is easy – write text. However, I might say that here the identification of the author is

Step	Action
1. Configuration identification	Develop a product breakdown of the facility to the current level of definition, (perhaps as part of the value management process) Identify the specification of the components in the breakdown, and of the overall facility
2. Configuration reviews	Meet with all the project stakeholders to agree the current definition
3. Configuration control	If agreement is achieved • repeat steps 1, 2 and 3, developing the breakdown and specification further, until the facility is fully defined If agreement is not achieved • either, cycle back to the configuration as agreed at a previous review, and repeat steps 1, 2 and 3, redoing the last steps of break-down and specification, until agreement is achieved • or, change the specification last obtained by a process of change control to match what people think it should now be
4. Status accounting	Memory of the current configurations, and all previous ones, must be maintained, so that if agreement is not reached at some point, the team can cycle back to a previous configuration, and restart from there. Also memory of the configuration of all prototypes must be maintained.

Figure 15.9   The four steps of configuration management

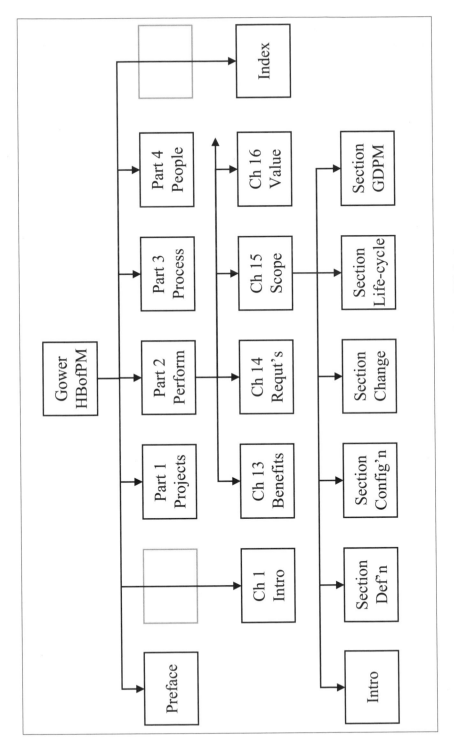

Figure 15.10 Configuration identification of this book

the work method, and I cannot do that until the specification of each chapter is determined. The definition of sections and sub-sections within each chapter could be said to be further levels of component breakdown, but in reality, also helps to define the method of writing each chapter. At the time of writing, I still do not know precisely how many chapters there will be in each part. I therefore have an initial specification of each part (from the body of Knowledge in Chapter 1, which is written), but that needs further refinement. I also still need to identify some of the authors, and agree with them the precise specification of the chapter they are to write, and the section and sub-section break-down.

CONFIGURATION REVIEWS

At predetermined points, the team will meet with the project stakeholders to agree the current definition of the configuration. The stakeholders may include:

- the sponsor, representing the project's financiers
- the owner, and others representing the users or operators
- representatives of the consumers, perhaps the marketing department
- trade union or staff council representatives
- representatives of the local community

These reviews are automatically built into the PRINCE 2 process (OGC 2005) as end of stage reviews, and they are required by ISO 10,006.

CONFIGURATION CONTROL

If agreement about the current configuration is obtained, then its further definition and refinement can continue. If agreement is not obtained, one of two problems has occurred:

1. An early definition was wrong, and needs to be changed, If an earlier definition was wrong, it can be put right through change control.
2. The work to come from the last definition to this has been wrong. If the work to reach the present position was wrong, then you must return to where the configuration was agreed, and redo the work from that point. Hopefully, it was the last definition that was right, and so it will only be necessary to cycle back to there. Sometimes, the problem can be at an earlier definition. The further refinement can help identify earlier weaknesses, and so the problem may have occurred earlier in the project.

If both of these types of problem are discovered at the design stage, their correction can be fairly simple. At the design stage, a change may cost nothing and cause no delay. Repeating the work will cost additional design effort and build in a delay. But you have to ask yourself, what is more important, the functionality which will generate revenue and provide the value, cost, or time, or some other parameter? Unfortunately, the answer to this question is not always clear cut, which is why the success criteria need to be agreed before you start (Chapter 6). If the problems are discovered during implementation, then their correction can cause considerable rework, with resulting additional costs and delay.

As an example of the problem that can occur, I might have specified Times Roman as the font for this book. If an influential stakeholder says they want Bookman, then I look at the previous specification and it says a printer's font was required. Both Times Roman and Bookman are printer's fonts, and so the wrong interpretation was put on the previous specification. Before the book is printed it costs nothing to redo the work and specify Bookman. Alternatively the stakeholder may say they want Courier. Courier is a typeface, and so the previous specification which said printer's font was wrong. Now we must change that to read typeface and specify Courier. Again it costs nothing to make the change before the book is printed.

STATUS ACCOUNTING

If a problem is found, then it will be necessary to refer back to the previous specifications. It is unfortunately a classic syndrome that as people refine the specification they lose the memory of what the previous specification was. When a problem is then discovered, it is impossible to cycle back. At each review, the current status of the specification must be filed. Also, if prototypes are being developed, the precise specification of each prototype must be recorded through all its stages of development.

With the status accounting of this book, I have a version of the contents where this is Chapter B3, the third chapter in the second part, and another where it is Chapter 15. The former lets me make changes to earlier parts and not interrupt the definition of this chapter. I also keep the author's draft of each chapter, so I can check back against the changes I make in my edit.

CHANGE CONTROL

Changes are an essential part of configuration management. The whole point is to refine our understanding of the design of the asset produced by the project, and the method of delivering it. Hence you must have a subsidiary process for change control. I am not a great believer in bureaucracy, but one bit I do believe in is a change control form. If everybody proposing a change is asked to fill in a change control form, many will evaporate. The change will not be worth the time to fill in the form. Figure 15.11 is a suggested change control form.

Key stakeholders: The first row has space for the name of the project and key stakeholders. You may add more. Every stakeholder must sign off every issue of the change control form.

EuroProjex		
Project **Sponsor** **Champion** **Manager** **Marketing**		**Signature**
Change no **Issue** **Date** **Proposer**		
Description of **Change**		
Impact		
Benefit		
Cost ➢ direct ➢ indirect ➢ rework		
Appraisal ➢ NPV ➢ IRR ➢ payback		

Figure 15.11 Example of a change control form

Status accounting information: The next row contains the status accounting information for the change control form.

Description of change: A description of the change follows. The nature of the change and it effects must be explained. Why the change is beneficial must also be explained.

Impact: The full impact of the change must be described. It should be explained what new work is required, and what rework and scrapping of previous work is required. There may be other indirect impacts, on quality, or the ability to do work elsewhere.

Benefit: A monetary value should be put on the value of the change.

Cost of the change: Likewise a monetary value must be put on the cost. This should include the cost of the direct work, indirect work and rework necessary.

Appraisal: The change should be appraised using standard techniques (Chapter 27 and 28 for changes of far reaching impact). Changes will usually be required to meet higher hurdles than the project itself. The reasons for this are:

- many changes are nice-to-have, and so should be subjected to greater rigour – changes to avoid show-stoppers will have infinite IRR and therefore have no problem being accepted
- the benefits are usually over-egged, and the costs understated

CONFIGURATION MANAGEMENT THROUGH THE LIFE-CYCLE

The cost of making changes increases throughout the life-cycle. Many industries have a rule of thumb, that the ratio of the cost required to make a change from feasibility to design to execution to close-out is:

$$1 : n : n^2 : n^3$$

For shipbuilding these ratios are said to be 1:3:9:27, and for information systems 1:10:100:1000. The impact and rework is greater in the later stages of the project, and delays are more expensive. Once execution is underway, and money is being spent in earnest, delays increase the financing costs of a project. Hence it is preferable if the specification is agreed by the end of feasibility, and essential it should be agreed by the end of design. Thus the emphasis of configuration management changes at the transition from design to execution. During feasibility and design, the emphasis is on agreeing the specification. And longer may be spent ensuring it is right. During execution and close-out, the emphasis of configuration management is on checking the specification of the product as it is delivered. As each chapter of this book is written by the author, I check it against what I intended for that chapter, as each part is produced, I check that, and at the end I check the overall book. The configuration identification becomes the test procedure for the facility as it is produced.

GOAL DIRECTED PROJECT MANAGEMENT

Goal Directed Project Management (Andersen et al 2003) is a technique which supports the configuration management process. It consists of two simple documents:

1. The Milestone Plan, which shows:
   - the intermediate delivery of components of the facility
   - the intermediate delivery of assemblages of the components
   - the final delivery of the full assembly of the facility
   - intermediate review points at which the definition of future milestones is agreed
   - completion of life-cycle stages at which one team accepts the intermediate design or products handed over from the team working on the previous stage
2. The Responsibility Chart, used at two levels to show:
   - at the milestone level, the overall work methods to deliver the milestones overall, by showing departments and functions involved and their roles and responsibilities
   - milestone by milestone, the work methods to deliver each milestone, by showing the activities required, the people involved and their roles and responsibilities

Figure 15.12 shows the overall application of the approach and the use of the forms. It is assumed that the overall project definition, as described above, has been done, and so the definition of the asset is known. Figures 15.13, 15.14 and 15.15 show the use of the forms for the Intranet project defined in Figure 15.5. You will see that early milestones are designed to gain agreement to the design of the systems and procedures, and the later milestones are designed to confirm delivery of the agreed systems and procedures, and to commission them. Erling Andersen describes the use of symbols in the responsibility chart to describe roles and responsibilities (and hence work methods) in Chapter 18.

Managing	Products and functionality	Organization and work methods
Management level Contract between the project team and the organization	Milestone plan ▪ what the project will deliver ▪ when the project will deliver ▪ gaining agreement to it	Project responsibility chart ▪ who will support the project ▪ what support will the give ▪ what will they do
Detail level Contract between the project team members		Activity responsibility chart ▪ activities to deliver each milestone ▪ who will do it and when

Figure 15.12 The use of the forms in Goal Directed Project Management

TriMagi   MILESTONE PLAN

Project:	Intranet Phase 1
Project Champion:	Martin Pacific
Project Manager:	Frances Seeker

Date	P	M	D	H	Milestone Name	Short Name	End Date
18 Aug		M0			When the managing director and personnel manager approve that the project is ready to start	Ready to start	18 Aug
26 Aug		M1			When the overall content and style of the web space has been agreed	Overall content and style agreed	26 Aug
28 Aug				H1	When the current inventory of hardware and data has been identified and logged	Hardware and data inventory	28 Aug
02 Sep		M2			When the content of the home and news pages has been agreed	Home and news pages agreed	02 Sep
02 Sep		M3			When the content of the document processing pages has been agreed	Document processing pages agreed	02 Sep
02 Sep		M4			When the content of the Personnel information pages has been agreed	Personnel information pages agreed	02 Sep
03 Sep	P1				When exisiting procedures have been reviewed and revised procedures writtenhen the software development toos have been	Procedures rewritten	03 Sep
09 Sep		M5			When the overall content has been agreed ready for design	Ready to design	09 Sep
15 Sep				H2	When the hardware requirements have been defined	Hardware defined	15 Sep
15 Sep	P2				When new jobs required by the revised procedures have been designed	New jobs designed	15 Sep
22 Sep				H3	When the hardware has been designed	Hardware designed	22 Sep
25 Sep			D1		When the home and news pages have been designed and developed	Home and news pages developed	25 Sep
25 Sep			D2		When the document processing pages havse been designed and developed	Document processing pages developed	25 Sep
25 Sep			D3		When the Personnel information pages have been designed and developed	Personnel information pages developed	25 Sep
29 Sep	P3				When the new procedures have been piloted and adjustments approved	New procedures piloted	29 Sep
07 Oct			D4		When the site has been assembled	Site assembled	07 Oct
14 Oct	P4				When the procedures have been optimized and adjustments made to the web site	Procedures optimized	14 Oct
17 Oct			D5		When the site has been signed off and is ready to be deployed	Site signed off	17 Oct
17 Oct	P5				When the user trial is complete and the operation of the procedures and sites tested and approved	Ready to deploy	17 Oct
11 Nov				H4	When the new hardware has been installed	Hardware installed	11 Nov
11 Nov				H5	When the data for personnel information has been entered or migrated	Data entered and migrated	11 Nov
12 Nov	P6				When the site goes live	Site goes live	12 Nov
14 Nov		M6			When the success of Phase 1 has been reviewed, a report produced and Phase 2 can begin	Ready to proceed to Phase 2	14 Nov

© 2003 Goal Directed Project Management Systems Ltd

Figure 15.13 Milestone plan for the Intranet project

TriMagi — PROJECT RESPONSIBILITY CHART / PROJECT SCHEDULE

Project: Intranet Phase 1
Project Champion: Martin Pacific
Project Manager: Frances Seeker

Period: 30-Jun-02 Target end: (blank)

Legend

- X = eXecutes the work
- D = takes Decisions solely/ultimately
- d = takes decisions jointly
- P = manages Progress
- T = on the job Training
- I = must be Informed
- C = must be Consulted
- A = may Advise

Responsibility matrix

No	Milestone Name	Managing Director	Board	Personnel Manager	Personnel Department	Marketing Manager	Marketing Department	IS Manager	IS Department	Users	Contractors	Project Manager	Project Team	Consultant	Procurement
M0	Ready to start	D	d	I	I							d	X	X	
M1	Overall content and style agreed	D	d	C	C	d	C	I	X	C		X	X	T	
H1	Hardware and data inventory			D	C	d	C	P	X				X	T	
M2	Home and news pages agreed	D	D	D	C	d	C	d	X	X		X	X	T	
M3	Document processing pages agreed	D	D	D	C	d	C	d	X	X		X	X	T	
M4	Personnel information pages agreed	D	D	D	C	d	C	d	X	X		X	X	T	
P1	Procedures rewritten	P		P	X			P	X			d			
M5	Ready to design	D	d	d		d		d				d			
H2	Hardware defined							P	X			d			
P2	New jobs designed	P		P	X			P	X			d			
H3	Hardware designed			d				PD	X				A	Xd	Xd
D1	Home and news pages developed			d	C	d	C	Pd	X	C	X		A	Xd	Xd
D2	Document processing pages develope			d	C	d	C	Pd	X	C	X		A	Xd	Xd
D3	Personnel information pages develop			d	C	d	C	Pd	X	C	X		A	Xd	Xd
P3	New procedures piloted			I	C					C					
D4	Site assembled							PD	X		X	X			
P4	Procedures optimized	P		P	X							X			
D5	Site signed off	I	I	I		I		D	X		d	X			
P5	Ready to deploy	D	d	d	X	d		d	X	X	d	X			
H4	Hardware installed				Pd			Pd	X	X					
H5	Data entered and migrated	C		C	Pd			Pd	X						
P6	Site goes live	I	I	I		I		D	X		d	X			
M6	Ready to proceed to Phase 2	D	d	d	X	d		d	X		d	X			

Schedule (Week ending / Duration / End Date)

Week ending columns: 22-Aug (1), 29-Aug (2), 05-Sep (3), 12-Sep (4), 19-Sep (5), 26-Sep (6), 03-Oct (7), 10-Oct (8), 17-Oct (9), 24-Oct (10), 31-Oct (11), 07-Nov (12), 14-Nov (13), 21-Nov (14), 28-Nov (15)

No	Milestone Name	Duration (d)	End Date
M0	Ready to start		18 Aug
M1	Overall content and style agreed	7	26 Aug
H1	Hardware and data inventory	9	28 Aug
M2	Home and news pages agreed	5	02 Sep
M3	Document processing pages agreed	5	02 Sep
M4	Personnel information pages agreed	5	02 Sep
P1	Procedures rewritten	6	03 Sep
M5	Ready to design	5	09 Sep
H2	Hardware defined	12	15 Sep
P2	New jobs designed	8	15 Sep
H3	Hardware designed	5	22 Sep
D1	Home and news pages developed	12	25 Sep
D2	Document processing pages develope	12	25 Sep
D3	Personnel information pages develop	12	25 Sep
P3	New procedures piloted	10	29 Sep
D4	Site assembled	8	07 Oct
P4	Procedures optimized	5	14 Oct
D5	Site signed off	3	17 Oct
P5	Ready to deploy	3	17 Oct
H4	Hardware installed	17	11 Nov
H5	Data entered and migrated	17	11 Nov
P6	Site goes live	1	12 Nov
M6	Ready to proceed to Phase 2	2	14 Nov

Figure 15.14 Responsibility chart for the Intranet project

© 2003 Goal Directed Project Management Systems Ltd

297

TriMagi ACTIVITY PLAN

ACTIVITY SCHEDULE

Project:	Intranet Phase 1
Milestone:	D3: Personnel information pages designed
Manager:	Ian Simmons

	eXecutes the work
X	eXecutes the work
D	takes **Decisions** solely/ultimately
d	takes decisions jointly
P	manages Progress
T	on the job Training
I	must be **Informed**
C	must be **Consulted**
A	may Advise

Period:		Day:		Target end:	25-Sep-03

No	Activity Name	Ian Simons	Ian Deptford	Procurement	Contractors	Personnel	Marketing	Selected users	Duration (d)	End Date
D31	Specify page based on agreed cont	P	X						7	11-Sep-03
D32	Appoint contractors	Xd		Xd					2	11-Sep-03
D33	Manage contractors	P							10	25-Sep-03
D34	Design and develop pages	P			X				7	22-Sep-03
D35	Obtain approval - personnel	PX	X		X	C			5	23-Sep-03
D36	Obtain approval - marekting	PX	X		X		C		2	24-Sep-03
D37	Obtain approval - selected users	PX	X		X			C	2	24-Sep-03
D38	Make necessary changes	PD	X		X		d	d	3	25-Sep-03

Day columns: 03-Sep, 10-Sep, 11-Sep, 12-Sep, 15-Sep, 16-Sep, 17-Sep, 18-Sep, 19-Sep, 22-Sep, 23-Sep, 24-Sep, 25-Sep (1–15)

Figure 15.15 Activity plan for the Intranet project

DEVELOPING THE MILESTONE PLAN AND RESPONSIBILITY CHART

Since the objective is to gain the agreement of the wider project team to the intermediate products and the method of their delivery, it is essential that the milestone plan and responsibility charts are developed in group working sessions. It is suggested that the milestone plan and project responsibility chart are developed in a project start-up workshop (Chapter 26), to which appropriate managers are invited. The ideal number of people is around eight, and they may include:

- the project champion, (a senior user arguing the project's case)
- the project manager
- work area managers
- managers of groups or sections providing resources
- a planner from the project support office
- somebody who has worked on a similar project in the past
- a facilitator of the group dynamic

To create a milestone plan, starting from the project definition report, a four step process is suggested:

1. Brainstorm potential milestones
2. Rationalize the list down to 12 to 24,:
   - rejecting milestones as not relevant
   - combining milestones
   - incorporating milestones as activities of others
3. Group the milestones into 3 or 4 areas of work
   - Andersen et al describe these as result paths
   - a white board or flip chart is useful for this
4. Sort the milestones into sequence and draw their logical dependency
   - this gives both a milestone plan and a precedence network for the project (Chapter 19)

A similar process is used to develop the responsibility chart at the project or activity level. The chart at the project level will be developed by the same team as did the milestone plan, but a different team may develop the chart at the activity level. Then it will be the actual people working on the milestone. The suggested process is as follows:

1. Using a flip chart, whiteboard, overhead projector or PC with a beamer, draw a grid
2. Enter the names of products or components in the rows
   - milestones at the milestone level
   - activities at the activity level

299

3. Enter the names of the resources involved in the columns
   - companies, functions, departments, groups at the milestone level
   - named individuals involved in the milestone at the activity level
4. Enter the roles and responsibilities of the resources in the body of the matrix
   - using the symbols suggested by Erling Andersen in Chapter 18

The body of the responsibility chart defines the work methods at that level, as opposed to the names of the rows which defines the components of the facility. The charts over several levels define a *work breakdown structure* for the project, as opposed to the *product breakdown structure* defined by the configuration of the facility into components.

MANAGING SCOPE OF WORK

Over this chapter, we have defined the scope of the project very much by the functionality of the product or facility it will deliver and the decomposition or configuration of that facility into components. This is a recommended principle of project management, that you should define the plan (at least at the higher levels) in terms of the products the project will produce, rather than the work to deliver them. That gives a much more stable and robust plan, as the definition of the products (at least the components if not their precise specification) is more stable than the work required to deliver them. However, in the process of defining the configuration of the facility, we have also defined the work methods required to deliver it.

The actual management of that work is not covered in this chapter. It is more natural to discuss that later, especially when discussing the management of the resources to do the work (Chapter 20), or the implementation and control of progress (Chapter 29).

REFERENCES AND FURTHER READING

Andersen, E.S., Grude, K.V., and Haug, T., 2003, *Goal Directed Project Management*, 3rd ed, London: Kogan Page.

Caupin, G., Knöpfel, H., Morris, P.W.G., Motzel, E., and Pannebäcker, O., (eds), 1999, *ICB: IPMA Competence Baseline,* Zurich, CH: International Project Management Association.

ISO, 2004, *ISO 10,006: Quality Management – Guidelines to Quality in Project Management.* 2nd edition, Geneva, CH: International Standards Organization.

OGC, 2003, *Managing Successful Programmes,* London: The Stationery Office.

OGC, 2005, *Managing Successful Projects with PRINCE 2,* 4th edition, London: The Stationery Office.

PMI®, 2004, *The Guide to the Project Management Body of Knowledge,* 3rd edition, Newtown Square, PA: Project Management Institute.

Turner, J.R., 1999, *The Handbook of Project Based Management,* 2nd edition, London: McGraw-Hill.

Turner, J.R., 2004, *Managing Web Projects: The Management Large Projects and Programmes for Web-space Delivery,* Aldershot: Gower.

16 Managing Value

Stephen Simister

The value a project contributes to an organization must be clearly defined from the outset if it is to be managed. The pressure for changes to be made during implementation can invariably be traced back to a poor understanding of value at a project's inception. Client organizations are by their very nature multi-faceted. Determining the exact value criteria for a project from such organizations requires a clear framework within which decisions can be made. Structuring this framework at the outset of the project will ensure that not only is value adequately defined, but also that it can be managed during the project life-cycle.

Clients should go through a series of stages in determining the project definition, producing the following documents at successive steps:

- Client's business case: The financial raison d'être for the project
- Project specific statement of need: An outline document setting out what is required to fulfil the business case
- Strategic project brief: An outline document stating how the project will fulfil the statement of need
- Project definition: A document setting out the exact details of the project, its scope

The framework produced by this procedure enables both the functionality and value of the project to be expressly defined and monitored.

In this chapter, I consider the concept of value, and how it is produced by the functionality of the facility delivered by the project. I define value as the relationship between function and cost, and introduce the concept of value management. I then describe a five step process used in each value management workshop for defining the functionality of a project and managing its associated value.

UNDERSTANDING VALUE

The term value is used rather loosely and often the context of its use can change its meaning. Primarily we are interested in value as it relates to a project. It is useful however to examine value at an organizational level as ultimately projects have to contribute at this level. In this context the link with programme and portfolio management is very important.

SHAREHOLDER VALUE

Major investors have become more activist about company performance. Once it was rare for top executives to be punished for failing to deliver returns; now it is common. A measure often used to measure performance is shareholder value. Shareholder value had no clear definition but was generally taken as a measure of whether a company had created (or destroyed) wealth for its shareholders. In recent years a more reliable measure has been sought and two methods have been developed; market value added (MVA) and economic value added (EVA).

(a) As a system of analysis MVA aims to strip out most of the anomalies created by accounting standards to paint a truer picture of shareholder value. The basic calculation is to take the amount of money entrusted to management, measured by adding up money raised through shares issued, borrowing and retained earnings. That gives a measure of how much outsiders have given to the company in the years since it was founded. It then takes the current value of the company's shares and debt, as a measure of how much money the investors could take out of the business. The difference is the MVA, which measures how the executives running a company have fared with the capital under their control since the company was established. If the MVA is positive that means value is being created for investors, if negative that means investors' money has been destroyed.

(b) EVA takes the after tax operating profit for a company and compares it with its cost of capital. Cost of capital is an economic concept that includes far more than just the interest paid to the bank and the dividend to shareholders. For each company the cost of capital varies, sometimes quite widely. Some industries are naturally more risky than others; investors will accept lower returns from a big established food group than from a young software company because it is more likely the big food group will generate stable returns while it is quite likely the software company will stumble. The EVA figure represents the difference between the profit a company makes and the cost of its capital. The idea is that it is not good enough for a company just to make a profit from its business. It also has to make enough to cover the cost of its capital. If it is not covering the cost of its capital, plus a reasonable margin, then the logical conclusion is that it would have been better if the investor's money had been placed elsewhere, or if a new management team were brought in to make better use of the capital.

If a company is consistently generating EVA every year, over time its MVA should start to rise. Conversely if its EVA is negative, in time its MVA will start to fall. MVA is a great guide to where a company has come from, but EVA is a better guide to where it is going. Of course shareholder value relates to those people who effectively own the company. What of the value of those who use a company's products or services – customer value.

CUSTOMER VALUE

There is considerable debate within the business world on whether companies should deliver value for their shareholders or customers. There is no simple answer, but new techniques such as *'lean production'* are designed to produce unique value for the customer. Project duration and cost are considered in 'project-as-production system' terms, making concern for total cost and duration more important than the cost or duration of any activity. Co-ordination is accomplished in general by the central schedule while the details of work-flow are managed throughout the organization by people who are aware of and support project goals (as opposed to activity or local) performance. Value to the customer and throughput, the movement of information or materials to completion, are the primary objectives. Improvements result from reducing waste, the difference between the current situation and perfection (defined as meeting the customer's unique requirements in zero time with nothing in stores). Lean thinking focuses attention on how value is generated rather than how any one activity is managed. Whereas traditional project management views a project as the combination of activities, lean thinking views the entire project in production system terms, that is as if the project were one large operation.

PROJECT VALUE

Organizations add value to their business through a series of processes. Increasingly such processes are undertaken within the context of a project. It is the cumulative effect of projects that decides on the success or failure of a company in delivering value to both its customers and shareholders. An aspect of project value is how this is used at a portfolio level to ensure the right projects are brought forward through the portfolio. When looking across the portfolio to determine the prioritisation of projects a key consideration is the value they add to the organization. This reinforces the importance of ensuring that the value a project contributes to an organization is clearly defined and articulated.

In order to create and sustain competitive advantage in the form of effective differentiation and/or cost savings, organizations need the help of their suppliers. The supply chain has recently received considerable attention in the business press. It is raised here because projects bring together a range of suppliers. Increasingly, these suppliers can only add value to a project if there is co-operation between them. This has driven the trend towards projects being undertaken in a spirit of partnership rather than in an adversarial manner.

VALUE MANAGEMENT

Value management is primarily concerned with ensuring that that the clients' needs are clearly defined and that a true scope of work is produced for the project such that the value a project will provide is defined. Value management has developed from value engineering which has been utilized for over 60 years.

Value engineering originated in the United States during the Second World War. Lawrence Miles of General Electric is credited with inventing value engineering as a way of identifying alternative materials to replace those that were in short supply because of the war. Miles developed a technique which could focus on what something did, that is the function, rather than what it was. By focussing on the function of components Miles found alternative solutions which were often cheaper than the original method. Value engineering was identified as a method of reducing procurement costs by the US Navy in 1954. Since then practically all US Federal procurement requires the use of value engineering as a way of demonstrating value in the procurement process. In value engineering value is defined as below, while Figure 16.1 shows a number of connotations available for increasing value:

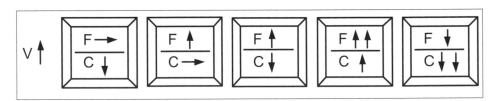

Figure 16.1   How value is increased

$$\text{Value} \quad = \quad \frac{\text{Function (what does it do?)}}{\text{Cost (How much does it cost?)}}$$

Value engineering is useful in situations where the functionality of a product can be clearly defined, typically during the design phase. It has its limitations and another technique has been developed to overcome these limitations – value management. Within many European industries there is growing view that value engineering is a special case of value management. Value management uses similar tools to value engineering but it is the scope of the technique that makes it so different.

Value management should commence during the early stages of a project as shown in Figure 16.2. Value engineering is one of the techniques that can be applied in the value management process during the later stages of a project.

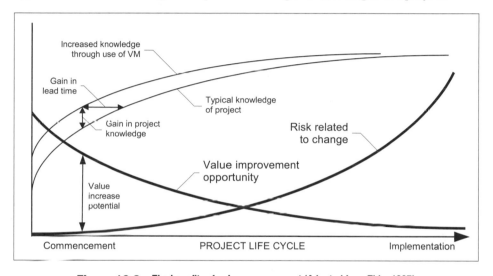

Figure 16.2 The benefits of value management (Adapted from Thiry 1997)

To utilize value management to its full effect it needs to be undertaken at the concept or briefing stage of the project. At this stage the technique is used to define the project's requirements. By this it is meant that the criteria that will guide the project throughout its entire life are established. During a project many changes can take place and a high level set of principles need to be maintained so any changes can be tested against these principles and their suitability judged. Without such principles it is all too possible for a project not to meet all the expectations of the client. By having a benchmark against which to judge changes the project team can ensure that the project will meet the client's requirements. Value management has been demonstrated to produce such benchmarks.

The benefits of using value management were highlighted in the 2004 report of the Auditor General for Scotland in the investigation of time and cost delays experienced in the construction of the Scottish parliament (Holyrood Palace):

Whatever construction method is chosen, sufficient time should be available for the planning stage, before construction starts. Good planning will involve (a) getting the construction sequence right to avoid delays and extra costs, (b) assessing and managing project risks and (c) using value management to assess the contribution of each part of the construction process to remove waste and inefficiency. There must always be sufficient time for procurement to allow the client's requirements to be adequately defined so that it may obtain fixed and firm prices for the work in a competition.

THE VALUE MANAGEMENT PROCESS

Most of the books and articles on value management may leave you with the impression that it is applied once in a project's life. This is not the case. Value management is a process which should be used throughout a project. What happens is that various tools and techniques are available which are applied at different stages to meet the particular requirements of that stage. In this section we are focussing on how the project requirements can be defined. This is the first stage at which value management should be used. Value management at this stage is concerned with producing the client's statement of need as shown below.

The value management process maps directly onto the project management process. Value management is undertaken as a series of workshops which can be considered as intervention points at strategic points in the life of a project, Figure 16.3. The number and exact timing of intervention points will depend upon the project, and workshops can be combined where required. Typical deliverables from the workshops are as follows:

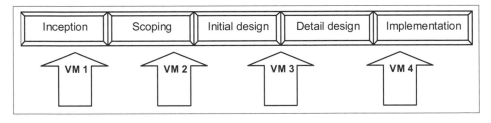

Figure 16.3   Value management workshops during the project life-cycle

- VM1: One of the prime purposes of a workshop at this stage is to present in clear and objective terms the mission of the project and its strategic fit with the corporate aims of the client organization.
- VM2: The aim of this workshop is to convert the output from VM1 into a project scope document which defines and specifies the performance of the elements of the project.

308

- VM3: Once the scope is defined the project team can begin to test various design options against agreed criteria and determine the most appropriate solution.
- VM4: This workshop can act as a catch-all refining the final stages of concurrently designed elements or dealing with changes in project requirements.

The VM3 and VM4 workshops are often referred to as value engineering exercises. A typical value management workshop consists of a five step process referred to as a job plan. The generic outputs of each of the steps for the early stages of a project are given in Figure 16.4. In utilising value management for the early stages of a project the main technique being used is that of facilitated decision making within a workshop environment. The five step process is used to structure the agenda for each workshop and depending on the stage of the project and required outputs, various tools and techniques may be used in each of the steps.

Job plan steps – Value management output	
Information	An information gathering process which focuses attention on the client's business drivers for the project. Particular importance is given to the use of facilitated workshops.
Speculation	Creative thinking techniques are used to generate alternative ways to provide the business drivers identified in step 1.
Evaluation	The solutions generated are evaluated in terms of their feasibility and cost. Ideas are combined and consolidated to produce a list of, say, five or six ideas which are worthy of further consideration.
Development	The surviving ideas are developed in detail, ensuring that all of the interfaces with the client's business are fully accounted for.
Recommendation / Implementation	The most suitable solution is identified and a formal recommendation made to the client for implementation.

Figure 16.4 Generic outputs for value management workshop

STEP 1 – INFORMATION

Think about the early stages of a project. The client is aware that there is a problem but does not know the exact nature of that problem. This obviously makes trying to define the project requirements very difficult. To define the project's requirements you need to have a clear understanding of the problem you are trying to solve. The client may know that more office accommodation is needed. So should you provide a building for 200 people or 300? Should you use this opportunity to re-engineer some of the business processes and relocate staff to other areas, or consolidate organizational functions in existing office accommodation? There are a multitude of questions the client needs to ask, explore, and then brief the project team accordingly. Value management is used to allow the client a forum for providing the answers to some of the questions that need asking.

At the early stages of the project the information is typically not held in documents but is held in the minds of people. The complex issues which gave rise to the need for a project are often locked up in the minds of the people who are running various functional departments within a company. To get the true picture of the problem this information needs to be extracted and documented in such a fashion as to be available to the project team.

The most appropriate method to get to the core information is to use a facilitated workshop. The facilitated workshop brings together all the key stakeholders from within the client organization and the project team and at this stage in the project life-cycle would be a VM1 type (see Figure 16.3). The workshop will typically last for two days and is used as a forum for obtaining the core information that will form the client's statement of need. Typically the facilitator is not a member of the project team. This person is an expert in the value management process and focuses on managing the process of the workshop and not its content. This facilitator will provide a structure around which the stakeholders can discuss the key elements of the problem which the potential project is aimed at solving. To commence the workshop the facilitator will ask each of the stakeholders in turn to outline their objectives, constraints and risks for the project. This information is listed onto flip charts by the facilitator under these three headings.

This basic information is then used as a starting point for facilitated discussion. This initial workshop will often be the first time that the key stakeholders have all met at the same time to discuss the project. The workshop provides the time needed to discuss the project properly. It is often the case that senior executives are not prepared to take time out of their busy schedule to discuss a project which could be vital to the future well being of their company. They will however be forced to make time later on should the project go wrong. Once there has been discussion on the objectives, constraints and risks of the project, the next phase is to organize this information into a graphical representation called a value tree.

The value tree is a way of organizing the information in such a manner as to allow people to visualize which are the most important elements of the project. Another key feature of the value tree is the ability to show the scope of the project. Often there are elements of a project upon which the client cannot decide until some initial design and costs work has been undertaken. By making explicit the areas which the client would like to include but are currently considered outside the scope of the project, the design team have a clearer remit upon which to work. A value tree for a new health centre is shown in Figure 16.5. This value tree demonstrates that whilst the internal layout of the health centre is important, its actual physical location in the community is of paramount importance. While this is ultimately a decision for the client to make, it reinforces to the design team that the facility they are designing has to be used by people with whom they will not have any contact. All information is second hand in being provided by the doctors who will work out of the health centre. One of the features of value management is the highlighting of such issues. It may be appropriate in this instance for some of the patients who use the health centre to be interviewed to find out what they would like to see in the building.

During later stages of the project where a VM2 or VM3 workshop is held a variant of the value tree is used called Function Analysis and Systems Technique (FAST). The concept in FAST diagrams is similar to that of value trees but more emphasis is given to defining functions. Following on from this information step, the next step is to generate ideas as to how some of the elements identified in the value tree can be provided.

STEP 2 – SPECULATION

During this step the team focuses on generating ideas as to how to provide the key elements identified in the previous step. For instance, are 5 consulting rooms adequate or should 4 be provided and provision made to provide a fifth at a later date? The principal feature of the speculation step is to stimulate creativity. The four golden rules are:

- suspend judgement – no criticism or evaluation; that comes during the next step
- freewheel – the odder the ideas the better
- quantity – the more ideas the better
- cross-fertilise – combine and improve on the ideas of others

The main technique used in the speculation workshop is brainstorming, where the team generates ideas, which are written onto flip charts. Creative thinking is essential to this step if the situation where the same old ideas are used to solve design problems is to be avoided. A constrained, conservative environment is detrimental to innovation, as shown in Figure 16.6. It is therefore necessary to ensure that the opposite environment prevails. Once the ideas for providing the key elements have been generated the next step is to evaluate them.

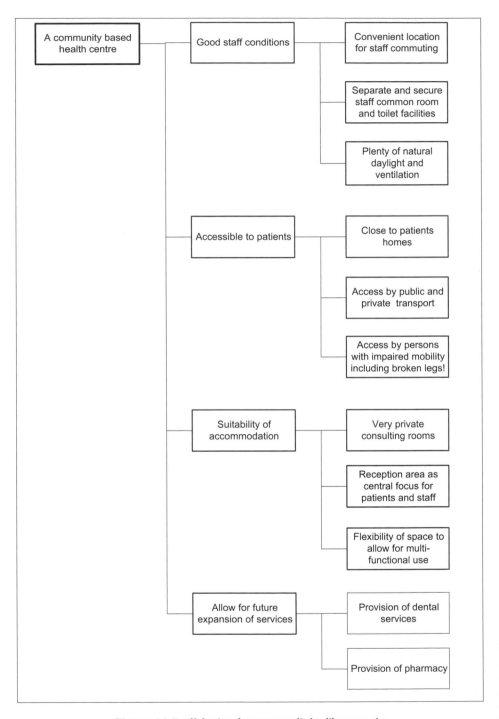

Figure 16.5 Value tree for a community health care centre

1895	*Heavier than air flying machines are impossible.*	Lord Kelvin, President, Royal Society, UK
1899	*Everything that can be invented has been invented.*	Charles Duell, Director US Patent Office
1923	*There is no likelihood man can ever tap the power of the atom.*	Robert Millikan, Nobel prize winner in Physics
1975	*There will not be a woman prime minister in my lifetime*	Margaret Thatcher

Figure 16.6   The need for creative thinking

STEP 3 – EVALUATION

In the evaluation step, ideas are sifted to identify those that might be worth investigating further. It takes time and money to develop ideas and therefore only the most promising can be chosen. During the speculation step it is normally very easy to generate as many as 200 ideas; these must now be pruned down to about 20 that will be developed further. Justification is the keyword of the evaluation step. The exercise should focus on justifying why an idea should be developed and, if no justification can be found, then it can be rejected. This process ensures that ideas are not simply dismissed because they will not work: the dismissal must be justified by a rational explanation of *why* they will not work.

STEP 4 – DEVELOPMENT

During this step the ideas that survived the evaluation step are developed further. Sufficient development work needs to be done to refine potential solutions to the point where they can either be rejected or taken further still and perhaps be incorporated into the client's brief. The amount of time and effort expended on any one proposal is only sufficient to allow the client to decide what that brief will contain.

STEP 5 – RECOMMENDATIONS/IMPLEMENTATION

This is the final level of the five step job plan. The findings of the value management exercise are written up into a formal report for presentation to the client. The purpose of the report is to provide an accurate record of the exercise for future reference. The report will often form the basis of the client's statement of need and therefore its accuracy is paramount. This report can be used in later VM studies to ensure consistency of decisions and act as an audit trail.

The five step job plan allows the client to define the project in such a manner as to ensure that there is little room left for ambiguity during the later phases of the project. It is the structure of the five step process that ensures all decisions are made in a consensus manner and against agreed, common criteria.

It has only been possible to provide a brief overview of the value management process. Suggestions for further reading have been made below.

SUMMARY

If project teams are to deliver successful projects they need to know what the client means by 'successful'. Success is invariably measured in terms of 'does the project meet the needs of client and does the client believe that value for money has been received?'

The value of a project can only be managed effectively on the client's behalf if the value itself is adequately defined in the first place. Clients are increasingly seeking guidance from their project teams concerning how projects can enhance their businesses processes. Project teams need to respond to this challenge positively and take on board new responsibilities and techniques to deal with this situation.

REFERENCES AND FURTHER READING

Auditor General for Scotland, 2004, *Management of the Holyrood Building Project*, Edinburgh: Audit Scotland.

Connaughton, J. and Green, S., 1996, *Value Management in Construction: A client's guide*, London: CIRIA.

Dallas, M., 2006, *Value & Risk Management: a guide to best practices*, Oxford: Blackwell Publishing.

Goodpasture, J.C., 2001, *Managing Projects for Value,* Sylva, NC: Project Management Institute.

Kelly, J., Morledge, R., Wilkinson, S., Male, S., and Drummond, G., 2002, *Value Management of Construction Projects,* Oxford: Blackwell Publishers.

Kaufman, J.J., 1998, *Value Management: creating competitive advantage*, Crisp Learning.

Male, S., Kelly, J., Fernie, S., Gronqvist, M. and Bowles, G., 1998, *The Value Management Benchmark: A good practice framework for clients and practitioners*, London: Thomas Telford.

Thiry, M., 1997, *Value Management Practice*, Sylva, NC: Project Management Institute.

17 Managing Quality

Rodney Turner and Martina Huemann

People have traditionally said the three measures of the success of projects are that they should be completed to time, to cost and to quality. However, when asked what they mean by quality, they are uncertain, and when asked how they manage it, they are even more uncertain. When you say to these people that the asset delivered by the project needs to perform in order to generate revenue, and hence pay for the project, they say performance and functionality are included in quality. In Chapter 15, Rodney Turner described the use of configuration management to deliver that functionality, and in Chapter 16, Stephen Simister described how to design functionality and value into the facility. This could reduce the definition of quality to a very narrow view, the 'finish' of the facility. In this chapter we take a somewhat wider view of quality, and describe its management. We consider what is meant by quality in the context of a project, describe a five element model for managing quality, and consider whether quality on projects is free. We also describe some tools for diagnosing quality problems, including the project excellence model.

QUALITY IN THE CONTEXT OF PROJECTS

There are several possible definitions of what is meant by good quality in the context of projects, and that they are the end product, the asset delivered:

1. meets customer requirements
2. meets the specification
3. solves the problem
4. is fit for purpose
5. satisfies or delights the customer

The customers will have an idea of the problem they are trying to solve, and will formulate a solution. That will become their requirements. They will enunciate their requirements, and a designer will try to capture them in a specification. When the project is delivered, it should be delivered in accordance with the specification. If there have been no mistakes in the preceding steps, the facility delivered will solve the problem; that is it will be fit for purpose, and it will delight the customer. Are these definitions the same thing? Well hopefully yes, but of course the phrase 'If there have been no mistakes in the preceding steps,' says it all. The chance is small that each step is performed correctly, that is it is unlikely that:

- the customers will solve their problem exactly
- they will perfectly convert their mental map into words
- the person writing the specification will hear exactly what they said and
- that person will convert his or her thoughts exactly into words

Thus the chance the facility exactly solves the problem and satisfies the customers, let alone delights them, is vanishingly small. The standard definition of quality is taken at the end of the chain, namely the asset delivered should be fit for purpose; it should solve the problem required of it, and (hopefully) thereby satisfy the customer. This requires acceptance that the specification may be imperfect, and therefore require some refinement. This gives us a dilemma. Traditional project managers think that the specification is sacrosanct, and therefore must not be changed. However, if it is imperfect, then the asset may not solve the problem. On the other hand, if the specification is changed constantly, the project will never finish. Thus it must be changed, but changed sparingly, at configuration review points, using the techniques of configuration management described in Chapter 15. You have the whole project to make sure the asset is going to perform as expected, and the whole project to massage the customers' expectations so that what they get at the end delights them.

The specification will define the finish expected. It will cover issues like:

- the required functionality of the facility and its components
- design standards it is required to meet
- the time and cost it should be delivered at
- various 'abilities', such as availability, reliability, maintainability, adaptability

THREE ADDITIONAL QUESTIONS

There are three additional questions we can consider:

Who is the customer?

The definitions of quality above said we should meet the customer's requirements, and satisfy or delight the customer. But who is the customer?

316

- **The owner or sponsor:** the person who is going to pay for the asset, and who is going to own it and receive the benefit from its operation?
- **The users:** the people who will operate the asset on behalf of the owner to make the product it produces?
- **The consumers:** the people who will consume the product produced by the asset, and therefore provide the revenue stream that gives the owner their benefit?
- **The media:** representing the community at large?

Whose requirements do we meet; whom do we need to satisfy? The answer is they are all customers and they all need to be satisfied. The owner has got to want to pay for it. The users can make failure a self-fulfilling prophecy. If they say it won't work, it won't work. And the consumers have got to want to buy the end product to provide the revenue stream. When discussing project success in Chapter 6, Rodney Turner said you had to attempt to satisfy the needs of all the stakeholders, and their needs have to be balanced. The ultimate objective is to provide value for the sponsor or owner, but you have to make an end product the consumers want to buy, and you have to make something the users are willing to operate (while not pandering to their every whim).

You have the whole project to massage the expectations of the three customer groups, so that what they get at the end is what they are expecting, and so that the three (or four) customers have a similar expectation of what will be delivered.

Do you give the customers what they want or what they need?

Through history there was a development of thinking on this question:

1. In the 1970s, arrogant engineers said their customers were stupid. They didn't know what you needed and you had to ignore what they said they wanted. The engineer was omniscient and would give the stupid customer what they (the engineers) knew the customer needed. The result was that the customers rejected the asset because it wasn't what they were expecting.
2. In the Total Quality Management days of the 1980s the customer was king. Whatever trivial whim they have, give it to them. The result might be that the asset did not work. The customer would complain it did not work, and the engineer would say, 'That is what you asked for, the customer is king, I gave you what you asked for.' But the customer would say, 'But you are the expert, you should have advised me it wasn't going to work.'

So the answer is, by the end of the project what the customer wants and what the customer needs must be the same thing. The customer's vision of what is needed may not be perfect, and so it may need to be adjusted. But the engineer's picture of what the customer needs may not be perfect either, so that may need to be adjusted.

317

You have the whole project to massage the customers' expectations so what they get at the end is what they want and what they need, it will be fit for purpose and operate to solve the problem it is meant to solve. Using configuration management you also have the whole project to make sure the engineer's design is going to deliver the appropriate product. (Are you getting the picture about the need to use configuration management to massage all the customer's expectations?)

Do you deliver good quality or high quality?

To answer this question, we ask, 'Is a Rolls-Royce a good quality motor car?' Usually people answer, 'Yes!' But then we ask, if your need is a small, economical motorcar that is easy to manoeuvre in traffic and easy to park, is a Rolls-Royce a good quality motor car? The answer is no. For almost any specification you draw up for a motor car, a Rolls-Royce doesn't satisfy it. You must deliver a product that will satisfy its purpose, provide value for the owner, and is value for money. Steve Simister described value management in the last chapter. This means that, in spite of what some people say, you should not always aim to delight the customers. If delighting them will cost 1% more than satisfying them, aim to delight them. If delighting them will cost twice as much, aim to satisfy, and spend the project massaging their expectations.

A FIVE ELEMENT MODEL FOR QUALITY

THE FIVE ELEMENTS

Figure 17.1 shows a five element model for delivering good quality. The components are:

- the quality of what: the product or the management processes
- quality assurance and quality control
- the attitudes

Quality of the product

It is the product that meets the criteria of the previous section. It is the product that provides the functionality, solves the problem and generates revenue. It is the quality of the product that is the ultimate arbiter of the quality of the project.

Quality of the management process

However, there is no doubt, that following well defined, previously proven successful ways of delivering the project increases the chance of delivering a

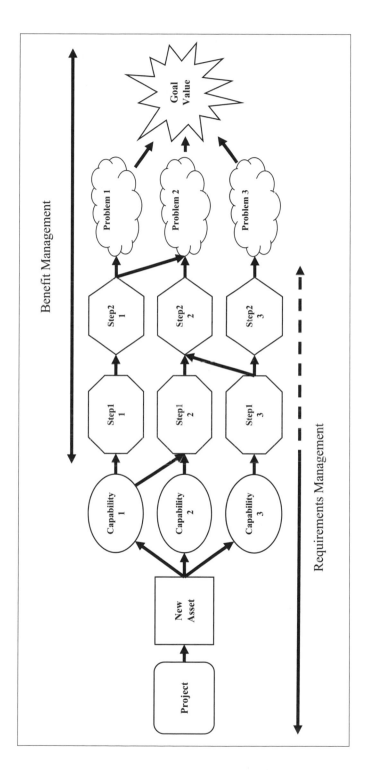

Figure 17.1 Five element model for project quality

successful solution. Part of the quality assurance of the product is following standard procedures for its delivery. However, the procedures must not be rigid rules, slavishly followed as more important than the quality of the product. Richard Pharro and Colin Bentley deal with this issue in Chapter 7. What is important is that for this project, you design a process or procedure that converts inputs into desired customer outputs that meet the needs of the particular customer requirement. That means taking the firm's standard procedures, which are flexible guidelines to best practice, and tailoring them to the needs of this project. Then at the end of the project, you should audit the process, to determine how you did, and change the firm's standard procedures to encompass new learning. ISO 10,0006 in its introduction discusses this issue. It says that both the quality of the product and the quality of the management process are important.

Quality assurance

Quality assurance is about taking steps to ensure that the product is delivered, and the management process is 'right first time'. The best result, in terms of time, cost and quality, will be obtained if the product is delivered correctly at the first attempt.

Quality control

However, human beings are fallible, and a last line of defence needs to be built in to check the product as it is delivered, and the management process as it is implemented. This is necessary to ensure that the product the project produces is 'right every time' with 'zero defects'.

Now there is a major difference between projects and routine production in the balance between quality assurance and quality control. In production, millions of products are produced. The production can be sampled, every one hundredth item destructively tested, and using the techniques of statistical process control, it can be determined when the production is going off specification. With a project, you cannot destructively test every one hundredth product. You only produce one. Wrong once means wrong every time. Destructively testing the one is 100% of the production. This pushes the emphasis much more back on to quality assurance, making sure the one that is made is right first time, and not relying on quality control. It also pushes the emphasis of quality control onto ensuring that the product and process are correct at the early stages, onto making sure the early components produced are right. If you get it right from the start, you find that a momentum of quality builds up.

Attitudes

Having the right attitude towards achieving success is an important element of achieving that success. Having all the stakeholders believe in the project from the start is an important contributor to project success. That was demonstrated in Chapter 6. And these attitudes are not solely the responsibility of senior management, middle management or junior management. It is the responsibility of all management, working together and doing their part for project success.

Some people develop the attitude that it is acceptable if we get it right 99.9% of the time. Human beings are fallible, that is an acceptable target. But if you adopt that attitude, 99.9% becomes an acceptable target, it becomes acceptable to fail 0.1% of the time. At Heathrow Airport, 99.9% correct is one crash a day – we would not accept that. You should aim for 100% correct. The quality technique Six Sigma aims for no more failures than one in 3 million products. (At Heathrow Airport a failure is not just a total loss of an aircraft, but would also include a puncture on landing, or an aborted take-off, say. So Six Sigma would be one incident every 10 years, which we don't think they achieve.)

THE FOUR QUADRANTS OF QUALITY ON PROJECTS

Figure 17.2 shows the four quadrants of quality, from combining the first four of the elements.

Quality assurance of the product

I cannot stress enough that the more you use previous experience, use standards, use qualified personnel, the more you increase the chance of success. The more you start with a blank sheet of paper, the more you increase the chance of failure. You also need to build in checks and balances. A well defined specification, reviews and change control (the configuration management process), all help to gain agreement and focus on quality.

Quality control of the product

There is a standard three-step control process. As you do work to produce results, you:

1. monitor what you are achieving
2. compare that to your plan, and
3. take action to recover progress

For quality this means you should have a plan for the quality of each component in the product breakdown, a plan for the quality of how those are configured into the facility, and a plan for the facility. As you deliver each component, you

321

Quality of	The Product	The Management Process
Quality assurance	<ul><li>Previous experience</li><li>Standards</li><li>Qualified resources</li><li>Well defined specification</li><li>Design reviews</li><li>Change control</li></ul>	<ul><li>Previous experience</li><li>Standards</li><li>Qualified managers</li><li>Well defined process</li><li>Health checks</li><li>Stable processes</li></ul>
Quality control	<ol><li>Monitor</li><li>Compare</li><li>Correct</li></ol><ul><li>Each component</li><li>Their configuration</li><li>The facility</li></ul>	<ol><li>Monitor</li><li>Compare</li><li>Correct</li></ol><ul><li>Processes</li><li>Reports</li><li>Results</li></ul>

Figure 17.2 Four quadrants of project quality

check its quality; as you configure the components, you check their quality; and you check the quality of the overall facility. You do not wait until you deliver the facility and then check it. That is wrong the only time. You build up a momentum of quality from the first component to carry you through. That is good attitude.

Quality assurance of the management process

The standards are now company standard processes, perhaps based on Prince 2 or ISO 10,006 (Chapter 7), tailored to the needs of this project and the facility it produces. The procedures also need to be configured as an integrated approved whole.

Quality control of the management process

The three step control process can also be applied to the management process. You can check that they are being applied well, that is the project is being well managed and is likely to deliver a successful outcome. There are three types of review:

1. **Control checks:** At every project control point constitutes a check on the project. Not only are you checking the performance of the project, (time, cost, functionality, and quality), you are also checking progress of the project, and you can make automatic checks that the controls are being well applied.
2. **Health checks:** The project team can also do periodic checks on the operation of the project management process and controls. These are called health checks. It is a useful habit to develop to be able to stand back from the coal face every now and again and think about what is going on. There is a

saying that it is difficult to think about draining the swamp when the alligators have chased you up a tree. Sometimes we become so focused on the project that we forget to think about its management. When something goes wrong, we feel that if we had spent just five minutes thinking about it we would have avoided the mistake, but we did not set aside five minutes. More formal health checks can be conducted at major project milestones, especially at stage transition. When one stage of the project comes to an end, you can conduct a formal check on the project, revisiting the business plan and project assumptions, and also checking the operation of the management processes before progressing to the next stage.

3. **Audits:** Health checks are checks conducted by the project team. Audits are formal checks conducted by a team from outside the project team. The audit may be conducted by other project managers from within the parent organizations, or by external consultants. Audits are formal checks, conducted using structured processes. They may be conducted at several different points on projects:

   - At major project milestones, or stage transition. The UK Government has a process of Stage Gate Reviews, where formal audits are conducted on all projects over a certain size as they progress from one stage to the next. (You can find information about them at <http://www.ogc.gov.uk/what_is_ogc_gateway_review.asp.>)
   - On a major, critical project, you may choose to conduct an audit at an early stage, to check that it has been set up correctly and is likely to deliver a successful outcome
   - On a project that is failing, an audit can be conducted at any time to see how it can be recovered, or after it has finished to determine why, as part of organizational learning and knowledge management.

Emotions can run high in audits, as the project team thinks you are checking up on them. However, you have to try to overcome this. You profile the audit as the audit team helping the project team to achieve a successful outcome for their project, not being there to check up on them. You can even do this when the audit team are helping to recover a failing project, though it is difficult to do in a post mortem of a failed project.

Martina Huemann describes the conducting of audits in Chapter 11.

IS QUALITY FREE?

It is suggested that improved quality is cheaper in the medium term than poor quality (Crosby 1979). Crosby's argument is as follows. There are three components of the cost of poor quality:

1. the cost of the quality assurance procedures
2. the cost of the control procedures
3. the cost of dealing with failures: scrap, rework, repairs under guarantee

To reduce the total cost, you must first increase the cost of the assurance procedures. So initially the cost of quality rises, and there will be no impact on the other two. However, with time the number of failures will begin to fall, and hence their cost. Later, you can reduce the amount of control effort, as your confidence of getting it right increases. Later still you can start to reduce the amount of your assurance effort. With time, the total cost of quality will drop below what it was before you started, and will eventually pay back the increased cost of assurance made initially. If you are a project based organization, undertaking many projects over a period of time, you will find that with time the cost of your projects reduces – the quality improvement is free. The problem is the whole cycle can take five years. The improvement takes longer than the first project on which it was implemented. The quality improvement is not free on the first project, just eventually for the organization as a whole.

If you are a contractor doing bespoke work for other organizations, the question arises: who pays for the initial effort, you or your clients? It was to overcome this problem that a contract arrangement called partnering is suggested (Scott 2001; ECI 2003), whereby clients and contractors work together over one or more projects to achieve improvements in project quality, thereby reducing costs.

Although quality is not free on the first project, the quality of the facility that results on the first project can reduce its life-cycle cost, that is the reduced maintenance costs outweighs the increased capital cost. Hence even though the project costs more, it can be worthwhile to put the increased effort into the increased quality of the project.

DIAGNOSTIC TOOLS FOR SOLVING QUALITY PROBLEMS

There are many tools to help diagnose quality problems:

Pareto analysis

Pareto analysis, named after an Italian economist, assumes that 80% of occurrences, here quality problems, result from 20% of causes, and 20% of occurrences result from 80% of causes, the so called 80:20 rule. Thus rather than trying to solve the vast majority of causes that cause just a few of our problems, (the 'insignificant many'), the suggestion is that you should identify and solve those 'vital few' causes which cause the majority of problems. As you eliminate the vital few causes, you can concentrate on the next most significant, but with decreasing impact. This is akin to a learning curve – where gaining greater and greater improvement requires proportionally greater and greater effort. This last sentence is a bit pessimistic, but the concept of concentrating your effort on those few causes which lead to the majority of problems is very powerful to produce quick, cost effective returns.

Cause and effect diagrams

Cause and effect diagrams attempt to trace back problems, as perceived through the symptoms or effects we see, to their root causes. They are sometimes called fish bone diagrams, because of their shape, or Ishikawa diagrams, after the man who first promoted their application to the solution of quality problems. They are constructed by repeatedly asking the question 'why?' or 'what?' A certain effect is perceived, so we ask, 'why does it happen?' or 'what causes it?' Once we have identified the main causes, we repeat the questions to find underlying sub-causes and so on, until we have identified the root causes of the effect we perceive. Obviously, when coupled with Pareto analysis, we will try to identify the vital few causes of the majority of our problems.

Structured problem solving

Having identified the vital-many causes of our problems, we will wish to eliminate them. A structured problem solving technique can help. Turner (1999) suggests a ten step process of three phases to aid problem solving and decision making and taking:

1. Decision making
   - identify the problem
   - gather relevant data
   - identify the causes
   - generate possible solutions
   - evaluate the solutions
2. Decision taking
   - choose one of the solutions for implementation
3. Implementation
   - plan implementation
   - communicate the plans
   - implement
   - monitor the results

Benchmarking

By the end of the 1970s companies like Xerox in the USA were suffering competition from Japan. They had to find out what their competitors were doing.

Benchmarking is a tool adopted to compare the performance and practices of one company with other companies. It is derived from the work of Robert Camp (1989). The aim is to understand the reason for the differences in performance by examining the process in detail. Benchmarking is a tool for improving performance by learning from best practices and understanding the processes by which they are achieved. Application of benchmarking involves following basic steps:

1. Firstly, understand in detail your own processes.
2. Next, analyze the processes of others.
3. Then, compare your own performance with that of others analyzed. Comparison can be done within your own organization or with other organizations from the same industry or different industries.
4. Finally, implement steps necessary to close the performance gap.

A number of benchmarking models and processes have been developed and are applied for a wide range of subject areas. In the context of project-oriented companies maturity models are often used as a basis for the benchmarking exercise (see PMI® 2003).

Accreditation

An accreditation is an external evaluation based on defined and public known standards. Accreditation was originally established to support customer protection. Consumers can be protected by certification, inspection and testing of products and by manufacturing under certified quality systems. Consumers need confidence in the certification, inspection and testing work carried out on their behalf, but which they cannot check for themselves. The certifiers of systems and products as well as testing and calibration laboratories need to demonstrate their competence. They do this by being accredited by a nationally recognized accreditation body. Accreditation delivers confidence in certificates and reports by implementing widely accepted criteria set by for instance the European Committee for Standardization (CEN) or international (ISO) standardization bodies. The standards address issues such as impartiality, competence and reliability; leading to confidence in the comparability of certificates and reports across national borders <http://www.european-accreditation.org/>.

Accreditation is a commonly used quality management method for instance in the health care sector, in which a lot of projects and programmes are carried out. There the accreditation was established to protect staff members and patients from faulty organizational processes. To participate in an accreditation programme is voluntary. The applying organization does a standardized self-assessment. The results of the self-assessment are the basis for a site visit, where the surveyor uses documentation analysis, observations and interviews for information gathering. Results of the site visit are summarized in a report. The applicant gives feedback to the report. This feedback discussion can be organized in the form of a workshop. Then the final result of the accreditation which can be numerical or a descriptive like 'substantial compliance, partial compliance, minimal compliance or non compliance' is provided. Accreditations have to be renewed every couple of years.

In the project management context accreditation is done by PMI® for project management education and training programmes. The degree and non-degree programmes are accredited for their content and progress compliance with the standards set by the Global Accreditation Centre for Project Management.

Excellence models

Excellence models are non-normative models which provide the framework to assess an organization in how far the organization is excellent in the application of practices. All excellence models differentiate between enabler criteria and result criteria as a basis for the assessment. The most important excellence models have been developed in the frame of regional quality programmes, which award organizations for outstanding quality improvement. We mention here:

- Deming Prize
- Malcom Baldrige National Quality Award
- European Quality Award
- IPMA Excellence Award

Deming Prize: The Union of Japanese Scientists and Engineers (JUSE) created a prize to commemorate Deming's contribution to quality management and to promote the development of quality management in Japan. The prize was established in 1950 and annual awards are still given each year. <http://www.deming.org/demingprize/>.

Malcom Baldrige National Quality Award: The Baldrige Award is given by the President of the United States to businesses and to education and health care organizations that apply and are judged to be outstanding in seven areas: leadership, strategic planning, customer and market focus, information and analysis, human resource focus, process management, and business results. Congress established the award programme in 1987 to recognize U.S. organizations for their achievements in quality <http://www.quality.nist.gov>.

European Quality Award: The European Foundation for Quality Management (EFQM) was founded in 1988 with the endorsement of the European

327

Commission. It is the European framework for quality improvement along the lines of the Malcolm Baldrige Model in the USA and the Deming Prize in Japan. The European Model for Business Excellence – now called the EFQM Excellence Model – was introduced in 1991 as the framework for organizational self-assessment and as the basis for judging entrants to the European Quality Award, which was awarded for the first time in 1992 <http://www.efqm.org/>.

International Project Management Association Project Excellence Award: An excellence model in the context of projects is the IPMA project excellence model, which is based on the European Model for Business Excellence, and has been developed by the International Project Management Association <http://www.ipm.ch>. The model is further described in the next section.

Coaching and Consulting

Coaching and consulting might not be considered as part of quality management at the first sight. But management consulting of projects and programmes as well as management consulting of project and programme managers are definitely quality management methods to assure the management quality. These methods are applied in advanced project-oriented companies. While in management coaching the client is an individual, for example the project manager or programme manager, the object of consideration in consulting is the project or programme. Coaching is often considered as a method to further develop personnel. If a new project management approach has been implemented in a company coaching is provided to project managers to support the implementation. That assures the quality of the management process. A typical situation for management consulting is a programme start up. The situation is generally rather complex but very important for the success of the programme as in the start process the quality for the programme management of the programme is set. Another typical situation for management consulting is project or programme crisis. Then the consultant helps to manage the discontinuity. Consulting activities can also support the programme to implement the corrective and preventive actions, which have been agreed on after a management audit of the programme. Large project-oriented companies provide these services through their project office and have internal project coaches and management consultants for projects and programmes.

IPMA PROJECT EXCELLENCE MODEL

The project excellence model was originally developed by the German Project Management Association (GPM <http://www.gpm-ipma.de> for the International project Management Association <http://IPMA, www.ipma.ch>. The project excellence model is applicable to any project type. The model, Figure 17.3, assesses nine criteria divided into two sections: Project Management and Project Results. The Project Management section evaluates how far the enabler processes are excellent, while the Project Results section evaluates the degree of excellence of the project results.

The criteria for the assessment of project management include the following:

- *Project objectives*: How the project formulates, develops, checks, and realizes its objectives.
- *Leadership*: How the behaviour of all leaders within the project inspires, supports, and promotes project excellence.
- *People*: How project team members are involved and how their potential is seen and utilized.
- *Resources*: How existing resources are used effectively and efficiently.
- Processes: How important project processes (content and management processes) are identified, checked, and changed, if necessary.

The criteria for the assessment of project results include the following:

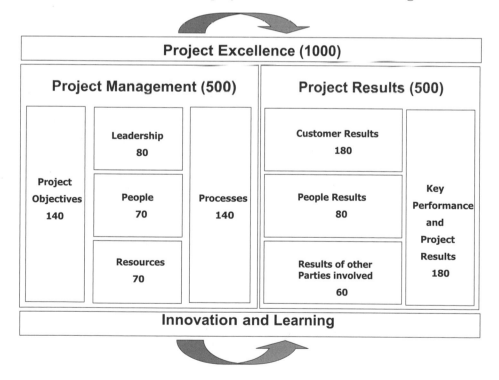

Figure 17.3 The Project Excellence Model

329

- *Customer result*: What the project achieves regarding customer expectations and satisfaction.
- *People results*: What the project achieves concerning expectations and satisfaction of the employees involved.
- *Results of other parties involved*: What the project achieves concerning expectations and satisfaction of other stakeholders involved.
- *Key performance and project results*: What the project achieves regarding the expected project results.

All criteria are further expanded. For example the criteria for project objectives of the section project management are shown in Figure 17.4. The model describes points of departure to assess the particular criterion. For example the points of departure for one sub criterion are shown in Figure 17.5. For the assessment of the criteria, assessment tables are applied. Figure 17.6 shows the assessment table for the project management section of the model. A similar table is used for evaluating how far the project results are excellent.

Criteria: Project Objectives (140 points)
How the project formulates, develops, checks, and realizes its objectives

---

1.1. Application and demands of parties involved are identified.
1.2. Project objectives are developed, as well as how competitive interests are integrated.
1.3. Project objectives are imparted, realized, checked, and adapted.

Figure 17.4   Criteria for assessing project objectives

The project excellence model may be applied in project health checks and evaluations and is quite commonly applied in companies for internal use as a self-assessment and possibility for reflection by the project team. Based on the self-assessment results, steps for further improvement are taken. In some bigger companies the evaluation results are used for internal project benchmarking exercises.

The project excellence model is a holistic project quality management model, as it provides a clear link between the quality of processes and the quality of results. It is applicable to any types of projects. A further strength is that the model is based on the European Model for Business Excellence, thus it especially asks for the consideration of different project stakeholder demands and issues like sustainability.

Nevertheless, there are limitations to the model as it is non normative. It is loosely based on the IPMA's Competency Baseline (IPMA 2006), but no particular Project Management approach is asked for or provided as a basis. Thus, no specific project management method has to be applied by the project. For

Sub Criterion: 1.1

It has to prove how the expectations and demands of parties involved are identified

Points of departure could be:

1. How the project:
   - guarantees to systematically identify all parties involved (eg interviews)
   - gathers, analyses, compresses and systematically uses necessary and sufficient information
   - uses the following sources to gather information:
     - initiator, users, sponsors and suppliers of the project
     - members of the project team
     - associations and other external organizations
     - internal achievement indicators
     - benchmarking-studies (internal/external)
     - achievements of competitors and 'best in class' projects/comparisons with other projects
     - studies and information about specific social, legal and environmental aspects
     - economic and demographic indicators
     - new technologies
2. How is/was the defined procedure for identifying stakeholders, ie to find out about groups that are potentially interested or concerned with the project?
3. Which stakeholders were determined?
4. How is/was the procedure for finding out about interests, requests, needs and fears of these stakeholders?
5. What is/was the result of this analysis - which needs etc. were determined?
6. Has it been observed if the stakeholders' interests have changed during the project?
7. Which changes have been noticed?

Figure 17.5   Points of departure for one subcriterion

Sound Process	Systems and Preventions	Checking	Sophistication and Improvement of Business Effectiveness	Integration into the Normal Project Work and Planning	Model for Other Projects	Evaluation
Clear and extensive proof	Clear and extensive proof	Frequently and regularly checked	Clear and extensive proof	Perfectly integrated	Could be an example	100%
Clear proof	Clear proof	Frequently checked	Clear proof	Very well integrated	—	75%
Proof	Proof	Occasionally checked	Proof	Well integrated	—	50%
Some proof	Some proof	Rarely checked	Some proof	Partly integrated	—	25%
No proof						0%

Figure 17.6   Assessment table for Project Management

instance, whether or not the stakeholder analysis is used may not matter as long as the project can prove that some kind of structured method is used to analyze their stakeholders. But for the project management section, it would be possible to go one step further and include the choice of a project management approach as the basis for the assessment. This kind of criticism is, however, inherent in excellence models, because they are non normative.

REFERENCES AND FURTHER READING

Camp, R.C., 1989, *Benchmarking: The Search for the Industry Best Practices that lead to Superior Performance,* Milwaukee, WI: ASQC Quality Press.

Corbin, D., Cox, R., Hamerly, R. and Knight, K., 2001, 'Project Management of Project Reviews', in *PM Network* March.

Crosby, P.B., 1979, *Quality is Free,* McGraw-Hill, New York.

European Construction Institute, 2003, *Long-term partnering: achieving continuous improvement and value,* Loughborough, UK: European Construction Institute.

IPMA, 2006, *ICB: IPMA Competency Baseline*, 3rd edition, Zurich: International project Management Association.

ISO, 2002, *ISO 19,011: Guidelines for Quality and/or Environmental Management Systems Auditing,* Geneva: International Standards Organization.

ISO, 2004, *ISO 10,006: Quality Management – Guidelines to Quality in Project Management.* 2nd edition, Geneva, CH: International Standards Organization.

OGC, 2005, *Managing Successful Projects with PRINCE 2,* 4th edition, London: The Stationery Office.

PMI®, 2003, *Organizational Project Management Maturity Model (OPM3): Knowledge Foundation*, Newton Square, PA: Project Management Institute.

PMI®, 2004, *The Guide to the Project Management Body of Knowledge,* 3rd edition, Newtown Square, PA: Project Management Institute.

Scott, R., (ed), 2001, *Partnering in Europe: incentive based alliancing for projects,* London: Thomas Telford.

Turner, J.R., 1999, *The Handbook of Project-Based Management*, London: McGraw-Hill.

18 Managing Project Organization

Erling S Andersen

As a temporary organization, a project at the outset has no resources. To achieve its objectives, a project needs competent and motivated people working tightly together in an organized manner. The project itself must create an organization of people well suited to meet its challenges. This means building an organizational structure, establishing the formal relationships of the organization, and clarifying the responsibilities of the individuals and organizational units involved. There are two basic topics to be approached when deciding the organization structure of the project:

- the external structure: the relationship between the project and its parent organization (base organization)
- the internal structure: the relationships between the project manager and the project participants and between all the project participants themselves

There is no one right way to organize a project. The choice depends on many factors, including the nature of the task and the length and size of the project. In this chapter I present the different options. First I describe different approaches to the external structure, before discussing which one to choose in a given situation. I then describe the internal structure.

EXTERNAL ORGANIZATIONAL STRUCTURES

There are three different external organizational structures, Figure 18.1:

- the 'fully incorporated' project organization
- the 'split authority' project organization
- the 'full authority' project organization

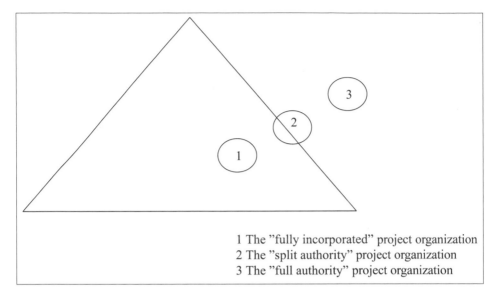

1 The "fully incorporated" project organization
2 The "split authority" project organization
3 The "full authority" project organization

Figure 18.1   Three different external organization structures

The fully incorporated organization

The fully incorporated project is established as part of an existing department or division in the parent organization. The project organization does not affect the basic structure of the parent organization. A line manager from the actual department heads the project. The project participants are mostly recruited from that organizational unit, even if others might be involved. This structure is of interest when the scope of the project is restricted to this one department. The task of the project could have been solved as part of the regular work of the parent organization, but organizing the task as a project may give it extra attention and effort. The problem of using this structure arises from the fact that the task of a project is seldom restricted to one part of the organization, meaning that the project is not considering all the factors important to the whole organization. That is what we call sub-optimization. There is also a danger the project is so intertwined with daily work it does not get the desired attention.

The split authority project

A split authority project is where the project members are partly or 'fractionally' allocated to the project. They are recruited from different parts of the parent organization. The project participants remain in their regular position in the parent organization during the project period. Project work and duties in the parent organization have to be done simultaneously, and the project members have to divide their time between the two. They will have two bosses at the same time, both the project manager and the line manager. The project manager will be in a position of split authority, sharing the authority with the line manager. The split authority project organization is an example of a matrix organization. We discuss the pros and cons of such an organizational structure below.

The full authority project

A full authority project is organized completely outside the parent organization. The project participants are 100% allocated to project work. The project manager is able exercise full authority over the project participants. This kind of organizational structure is also called the pure project organization. We discuss it in more detail later. In practise mixed forms of organizational structure may appear. In some projects we might have some participants who are working part time for the project and others being fully allocated to the project. This might be called a hybrid organizational structure.

THE SPLIT AUTHORITY AS A MATRIX ORGANIZATION

A matrix organization is an organizational structure well known from the general organizational theory. It means a combination of

- functional departments which provide a stable base for specialized activities and a permanent location for members of staff
- units that integrate various activities of the different functional departments

A certain company might be organized as a matrix consisting of functional departments on one hand and territories (geographical division) or products on the other. If projects are the units in the matrix, we have a split authority project organization. We know from organizational theory that the development of an effective matrix organization takes time, and a willingness to learn new roles and behaviour. The most important advantages of applying a matrix organization to project work are:

- every project has reasonable access to the entire reservoir of competence within the company; it makes specialized functional assistance available to all projects
- the project participants know at all times the problems and potentials of the parent organization; they maintain a close contact to the parent organization during the project
- better use of the resources of the company; it makes possible the maximum use of a limited pool of functional specialists

- there is little anxiety among the project participants about what happens when the project is completed; they all have their 'home' in the parent organization

The main advantage of a matrix organization is the access for all projects, large and small, to all the human resources of the company. The project could consider the company as a resource pool, from which it can draw the best available experts. Since the project may need the actual expertise for a rather short time, it might be easier to arrange this in-house than by engaging external consultants. Besides that, the in-house people are much more familiar with the actual situation of the company, which means that their input to the project work is more relevant. Sometimes the project may find it necessary to go outside the company to find competent and qualified personnel, but only after it has evaluated the availability of the internal resources. The matrix organization has its disadvantages:

- there is ambiguity of authority; a project participant has two bosses
- the project participant experiences a conflict between the demands for time and work from the parent organization and the project; the individual is confronted with a work load that is much greater than the time available

When people are asked to join a project and at the same time keep their position in the parent organization, they are usually promised some reduced workload in their permanent job. Practice shows that it is difficult to live up to this promise to its full extent. There are good reasons for that. It is difficult to find other people, who on short notice and for a short while, can do the job in a way that really lessens the burden of the permanent holder of the job. The problem, which arises from this, is that the project participant gets a very heavy workload. In the beginning of the project the person works hard to master the demands from both jobs. In the longer run the motivation for project work dwindles.

TASK CULTURE VS ROLE CULTURE

In a matrix organization people work for the project and parent organization at the same time. It is of importance to understand these two organizations represent different organizational cultures. The line organization is based on a role culture, while the project should be stamped as a task culture (Graham 1989; Handy, 1993). Working in these different cultures requires different attitudes and behaviour. It might be difficult for a person to move between the two jobs and adapt to the different cultures. However, the success of the project depends on the ability of the project manager to create a task culture, which is quite different from the role culture. The role (or bureaucracy) culture of the parent organization is characterized by:

- the organization is created to handle routine jobs and repetitive tasks
- each person is doing his or her job as described by procedures or job descriptions; they should not get involved in tasks which are outside their domain
- the influence and power of a person is determined by his or her position in the hierarchy or by the job title
- all tasks should be treated according to prescribed rules; logic and rationality is the general principle of management

On the other hand, the task culture of the project should have the following features:

- the organization is created to handle a unique task
- the task requires innovative behaviour and cooperation between functional specialists
- knowledge and expertise constitute power and influence on the results of the project
- the general principle of the management is to get the job done

Many project participants, who are used to the role culture, have problems in adjusting to the demands of the task culture of the project. They believe that they are appointed to the project because of their position in the parent organization and act accordingly. They do not fully grasp that the main reason for their participation in the project is that they possess certain knowledge and experience of value to the project. They also have problems in adjusting to the creative and innovative atmosphere of the project. The good project manager strives to create a task oriented culture within the project.

THE FULL AUTHORITY PROJECT ORGANIZATION (PURE PROJECT ORGANIZATION)

This kind of project is organized as a unit separate from the parent organization. It is a self-contained unit with its own staff, who work full time for the project. The most important advantages of this organizational structure are:

- the project manager has full line authority over the project and its human resources; all members of the project work force are directly responsible to the project manager
- the principle of unity of command exists; each subordinate has one, and only one, boss
- the project participants have the project as their sole commitment; they could devote all their attention to project work

The most pressing disadvantages are:

- it might be difficult to get access to certain kind of experts
- there might be a tendency to keep certain experts on the project without being able to utilize them all the time
- the project participants worry about what would happen to them when the project finishes
- the project may take on a life of its own, without having the modifying influence of the people from the parent organization

The pure project organization opens up for assembling a project team fully devoted to work on the tasks of the project. The most severe problem is access to and use of specialized experts. This is a lesser problem in a large project. In a small project it might be very difficult to attract the really good people and keep them occupied with the right kind of specialist tasks, when they are to use all their time on this one project.

CHOOSING AN EXTERNAL ORGANIZATIONAL STRUCTURE

Several factors might be taken into consideration when deciding which organizational structure is the most suitable. Some of the most important factors are:

The size of the project

A large project would usually need a pure project organization; the size of the efforts of the project dictates that the project needs a lot of resources on a full time basis.

The duration of the project

Long duration projects are more exposed to the danger of living their own life than projects of short duration. That is an argument for a matrix organization. However, long-lasting projects are often large, which is a factor pointing toward the pure project organization.

The nature of the tasks of the project

Many projects have as their objectives to create changes within the parent organization. Such projects would often benefit from a matrix organization. It is much easier to gain acceptance for changes when people who are affected by them are taking an active part in the preparations. This type of argument for matrix organization does not exist when the project is supposed to deliver a physical product (like a bridge or a road) according to an agreed specification of requirements.

The importance of time, costs and quality

A very time critical project should be organized with full authority to the project manager. A matrix project might be more cost efficient than the pure project organization since it has the advantage of utilising experts from the parent organization at exactly the right time for the project and to the extent necessary. The same reasoning may be applied to the quality factor. We could also add that people from the parent organization would have a better understanding of what kind of quality parameters the project should focus on.

The competence and availability of the personnel of the parent organization

As we have seen, there are many good reasons for establishing the project as a matrix organization with involvement of key people from the parent organization. However, this presupposes that the parent organization has a staff of competent people within the working area of the project, and they are allowed to use their time on the project as agreed upon.

INTERNAL ORGANIZATIONAL STRUCTURES

The internal organization of a project should show how the project manager organizes the work of the project team. A team is a collection of individuals who work together to attain a goal. All their efforts must be coordinated. The project manager must establish the structure of the team, that is the rules of coordination – the rules governing the relationships of team members with the project manager and with each other. The structure and spirit of the team is of great importance for the success of the team.

DIFFERENT INTERNAL STRUCTURES

There are different ways of developing an internal organization structure for a project. One is a traditional, task hierarchical structure. However, I stressed earlier the importance of creating a new spirit, a task oriented culture within the project which is different from the traditional culture of a hierarchical organization. It would not be easy to create this new culture if project organization is structured the old fashioned way. Frame (2003) suggests that a project team might be structured in other ways:

- Isomorphic team structure
- Speciality team structure
- Egoless team structure

- Surgical team structure

I discuss the hierarchical approach and Frame's four structures in turn.

Task Hierarchical Structure

The team may be structured in a hierarchical way. The internal structure of the project would then be rather similar to the organizational structure of many parent organizations. This hierarchical structure might be used in rather large projects where one sees the need for a traditional authority system. It might also be of interest to routine projects, which more or less do the same as previous projects and where the need for creative innovation and variety is small. Each team member should do his or her job without bothering about others.

Isomorphic Team

Figure 18.2 illustrates the isomorphic team structure. Under an isomorphic structure, the project is organized in a way which reflects the physical structure of the deliverable – the thing that is produced. The word isomorphic is a combination of the Greek iso, which means equal or same, and morph, which means form and shape. Two things are isomorphic when they can be said to have the same shape or structure. An isomorphic organizational structure might be used when the task of the project is to implement a new IT-system. A successful implementation requires the installation of the software package, the training of future users and even some organizational changes in the parent organization to better utilize the potentials of the software. We would have an isomorphic structure if the project were organized as three groups: one is dealing with the software, one with training, and one with the organizational changes. All three groups report to the project manager. The isomorphic structure has several advantages. It is organizationally simple. It is easy to see who is responsible for each part of the deliverable. If the different parts are independent, this approach allows for parallel work. In that way it could turn out to be a highly effective organization. However, usually the different pieces of the deliverable are seldom independent of each other and that constitutes the main problem of an isomorphic structure. There is a great risk that the efforts of the different working groups are not well enough co-ordinated. The main task of the project manager would be to secure the co-ordination of the different working groups.

The isomorphic team structure borrows features from the traditional hierarchical functional organization, even if the intention is clearly a flatter structure than we would find in the parent organization. It has at maximum three levels: the project manager, the group leaders and the rest of the team.

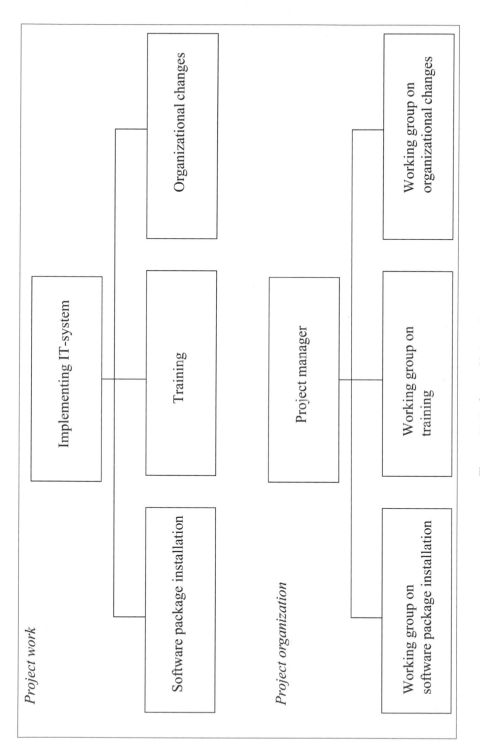

Figure 18.2 Isomorphic team structure

341

Speciality Team

The speciality team structure is illustrated in Figure 18.3. The next internal organizational structure, the speciality team structure, is more like a matrix structure. Under the speciality team, all project members have a speciality or a special field of competence, which is the main reason for their participation in the project. In the speciality team structure, the project team members may work on different deliverables or different aspects of a specific deliverable. Their orientation would therefore tend to be more oriented toward their speciality rather than toward the deliverables. For each project task the project manager would put together a group of specialists who will execute it. The project manager might draw on the same people, the same kind of specialists, for several different tasks. The main advantage would be, as we find in all matrix organizations, the better utilization of the specialists – the sharing of competence between different tasks. The problem, also well known from earlier, is that a certain specialist will have many different assignments which all compete for the limited time available. The efforts of the project manager should be directed towards putting together working groups that have the right combination of specialists and ensure that all the members of the team have an acceptable working load.

Egoless Team

The egoless team structure is illustrated in Figure 18.4. The egoless team structure is as close as you can get to a completely flat organizational structure. There is no obvious leader on the egoless team. The work of the egoless team is a truly collaborative effort. Decisions are achieved through consensus. Project tasks are based on inputs from most of the team members. This structure demands high level of interactivity and communication among project members. The strong point of an egoless team structure is that there is no boss who can impose his or her own subjective beliefs on the work of the project. All decisions are based on the knowledge and experiences of the team members themselves. In a positive and secure atmosphere they should be able to build on each other's viewpoints, which will create a result that is much better than what would be achieved by one person alone. The objection to this structure is that project work will not function without strong leadership. This criticism is certainly not without merit. However, the egoless team may function and achieve good results in some projects. It might be most suitable when the project is confronted with a complex ill-defined problem, and we can put together a small project team with people who know each other well and are creative and opposed to being told what to do. An egoless team is certainly a challenge to all the team members.

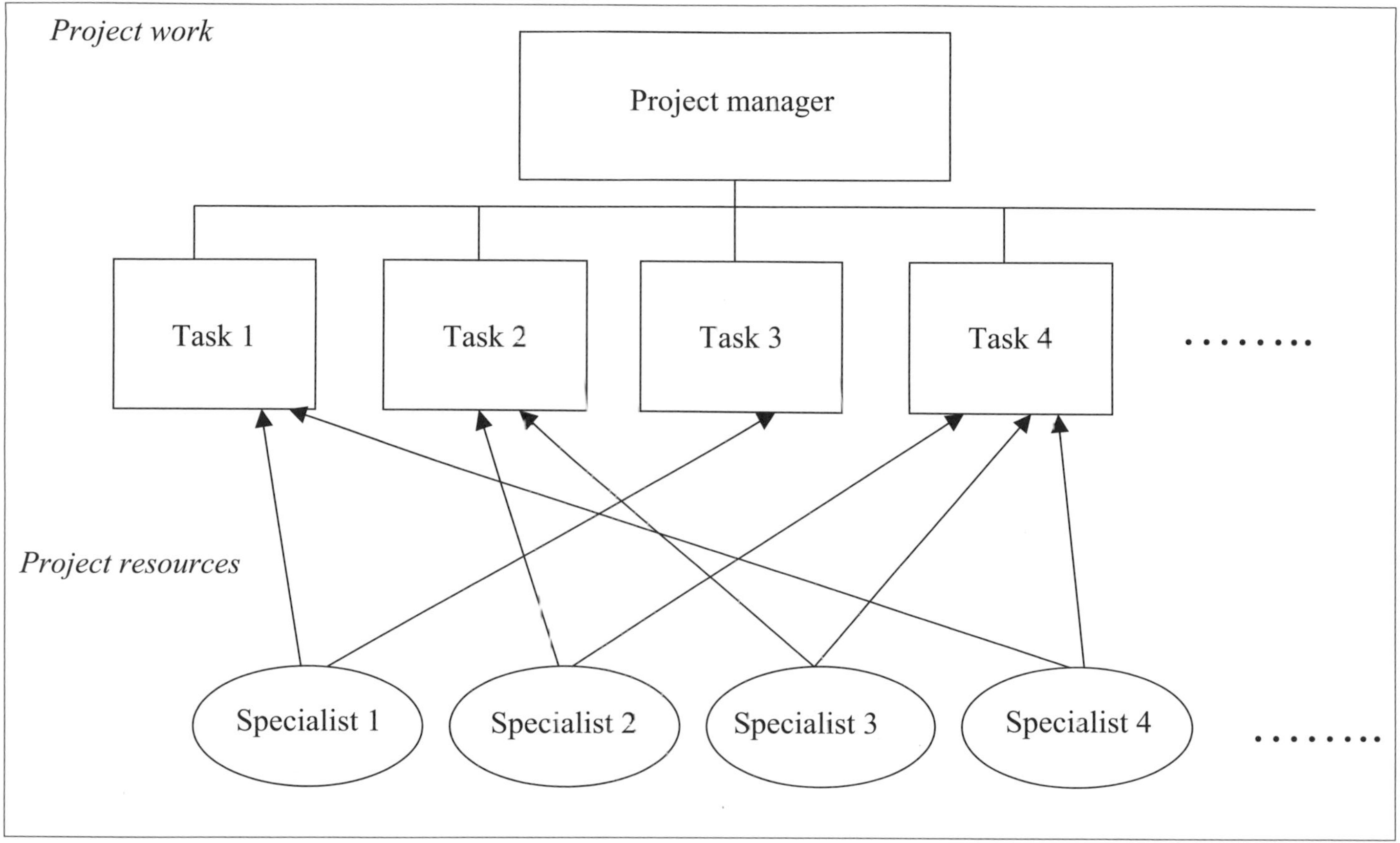

Figure 18.3 Speciality team structure

343

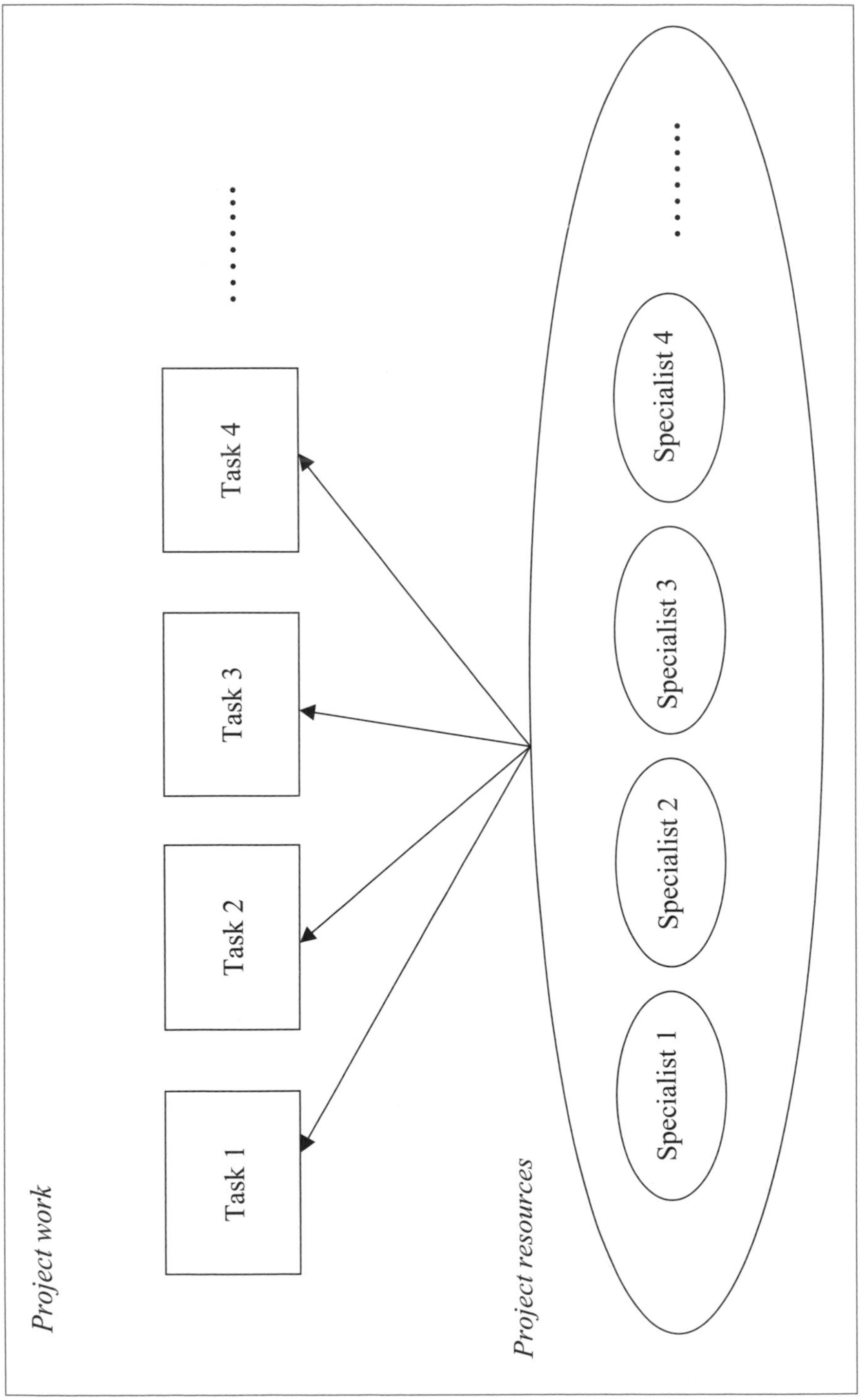

Project work

Task 1

Task 2

Task 3

Task 4

. . . .

Project resources

Specialist 1

Specialist 2

Specialist 3

Specialist 4

. . . .

Figure 18.4 Egoless team structure

Surgical Team

The surgical approach to team structure, Figure 18.5, stands in direct opposition to the egoless approach. In an egoless team, it is the overall group effort that counts. In the surgical approach, one individual is given total responsibility and all focus is on this person and his or her abilities. The term is derived with reference to the situation of a surgeon, who during an operation has full authority in all subject matters and the full responsibility for what happens to the patient. In the surgical structure, the project manager is the most skilled and capable person on the project. The project manager is both managing the project team and at the same time deciding on all professional matters of importance. The instructions to the subordinates are often very detailed, allowing for very little freedom to determine how to conduct the work. The main task of the team members is to support the project manager and work according to his or her detailed instructions. The advantage of the surgical team structure is that one person is in charge of all professional matters and is very capable of handling them; consequently the result of the project will be a very well integrated product. All parts of the deliverable will fit together perfectly. This approach might be of interest to projects which demand a high degree of creativity, for example a design project, and you have access to an extraordinarily talented person to direct the creative process. The disadvantage is obvious; it is very difficult to find a person who can play the role of the master. When we choose this approach, we might find out that the chosen person was not able to handle the challenge. In today's knowledge society, some team members with excellent professional background themselves, may also object to being treated as assistants or helpers.

I have now described five approaches to the internal structuring of a project, the traditional hierarchical organization and the four suggestions of Frame (1995). This is not an exhaustive list. Other alternatives exist. We have shown that there is no one perfect structure. All the structures had advantages and disadvantages. Turner (1999) shows how the different structures suggested by Frame are appropriate at different stages of the project life-cycle, Figure 18.6. Whatever structure we choose, we have to be aware that there are problems not tackled, which will need the special attention of the project manager.

RESPONSIBILITY CHARTS

In a hierarchical organization each person's responsibility is defined by the position in the hierarchy. When we have a flatter organization, or a completely flat organization, the responsibility of each person is not so clear. We need to define the obligations of each project member. The responsibility chart, Figure 18.7, is a

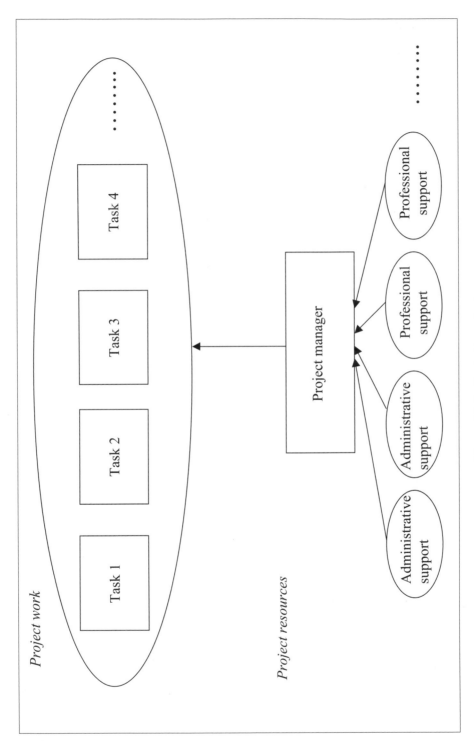

Figure 18.5 Surgical team structure

Life-cycle stage	*Work culture*	*Team type*
Feasibility	Laissez-faire	Egoless
Design	Democratic	Speciality
Execution	Autocratic	Isomorphic
Close-out	Bureaucratic	Surgical

Figure 18.6   Appropriate team structures at different stages of the project life-cycle

useful tool to express what is expected of everybody in a project. It should be considered a necessary supplement to the organizational structure. The organizational structure determines the organizational principles, which are to be applied in substantiating the relationships between all participants of the project. The responsibility chart can be used to make the organization 'tailor made' to the actual project task. Because every project is unique, it is important that an organization be specially formulated for each individual project. The responsibility chart can be used to this purpose.

In its basic version, a responsibility chart is a matrix with activities shown as rows and the people involved in the project as columns. For each activity the chart assigns different responsibilities to the affected persons. The chart may allow for many different types of responsibilities. They should cover most of what is necessary to determine when we discuss what is involved in carrying out a work task. The following set might be sufficient in most cases (each type of responsibility is referred to by a letter):

X   EXecutes the work
D   Takes Decisions solely or ultimately
d   Takes decisions jointly or partly
P   Manages work and controls Progress
T   Provides Tuition or coaching on the job
C   Must be Consulted
I   Must be Informed
A   Available to Advise

Figure 18.7 is an example of a responsibility chart. It is a lot simpler than it would be in a real life project. It here serves the purpose of illustrating the different aspects of a chart. We are looking at one part of a project. The task is to conduct a survey. The rows of the chart are showing the different activities. The columns are showing the people involved in these activities. The chart states the different responsibilities. On each row there must be one, and only one, who has the letter P. There must be one person who is in charge of the activity and has the main responsibility for the progress of the work. This person has the responsibility of ensuring that the activity is done on time and within budget. The person who has

	Ashley – project manager	Ben – manager	Cynthia – production	David – sales	Elisabeth – controller	Frank – consultant
Draw up draft of questionnaire	X/P					T
Gather views on questionnaire	P		C	C	A	X
Determine final form of questionnaire	X/P	D				
Set up mailing list, send out questionnaire	X/P					
Process the replies	X/P					X

Figure 18.7   The responsibility chart

the overall managerial responsibility (letter P) may at the same time do some work (letter X). The combination P and X is quite common in small projects.

Establishing the responsibility chart is a process where all the participants of the project should be involved. This work clarifies the responsibilities of all team members. The responsibility chart serves the role of a contract of what has been agreed to.

Figure 18.7 illustrates that the responsibility chart was used to define the responsibilities for the different activities of a project. It has been shown that it also would be to the advantage of the project to use a responsibility chart on a higher level. Andersen, Grude and Haug (2004) suggest the use of the responsibility chart to clarify the responsibilities of the involved parties to achieve the milestones of the project.

REFERENCES AND FURTHER READING

Andersen, E.S., Grude, K.V. and Haug, T., 2004, *Goal Directed Project Management, 3rd edition,* London: Kogan Page.

Frame, J.D., 2003, *Managing Projects in Organizations,* 3rd edition, San Francisco: Jossey-Bass.

Graham, R.J., 1989, *Project Management As If People Mattered,* Bala Cynwyd, PA: Primavera Press.

Handy, C.B., 1993, *Understanding Organizations,* London: Penguin.

Turner, J.R., 1999, *The Handbook of Project Based Management,* 2nd edition, London: McGraw-Hill.

Turner, J.R. and Müller, R., 2007, *Matching Project Management Leadership Style to Project Type,* Newtown Square, PA: Project Management Institute.

19 Managing the Schedule

Dennis Lock

Most people would agree that scheduling ranks high in the skills needed for successful project management. It is required to:

- ensure that the project is delivered when the customer needs it
- coordinate the activities of the resources working on the project (Chapter 21)
- schedule cash flows: cash out, cash in and net cash balances (Chapter 20)

During the first half of the twentieth century, the principal scheduling tool was the bar chart. These diagrams are often called Gantt charts after the American engineer, Henry Gantt, who developed them for production scheduling in a munitions factory towards the end of the First World War. Bar charts remain popular, mainly as a tool for communicating the schedule to people working on the project (Chapters 21 and 28). However, the amount of information that a bar chart can convey is limited, both in terms of the practical number of project tasks and in the way in which those tasks can be shown to interrelate.

In the 1950s a new family of techniques emerged which overcame the limitations of bar charts. These were all based on the use of diagrams called critical path networks. As with bar charts, the exploitation of these critical path diagrams was accelerated and publicized following their successful use on high priority military projects in America. Several early versions of the critical path method can, however, be traced back to a number of sources in Europe as well as America. Morris (1994) gives a full historical account of all these developments but here we shall concentrate on two versions of the critical path method in common use at the beginning of the twenty-first century.

PREPARATION FOR SCHEDULING

The scheduling process is followed through this chapter using a small project (the furniture project) as a case study. A medium-sized furniture company wishes to embark on a project to add two new items of furniture to its catalogue. These are a kitchen table with a single drawer and a simple but comfortable chair. The table design is expected to be straightforward but the company's marketing manager has asked for an anatomical study to be conducted, using statistical data, to determine the ideal size and shape for the chair. The person assigned to lead this project is a senior design engineer. Finding resources for this small project should present few difficulties because the project leader has considerable authority and is able to ask suitable people throughout the company to join her small team when she needs them, and the team has access to design facilities and a small workshop. The project deliverables are a prototype desk and chair set.

PROJECT WORK BREAKDOWN AND TASK LIST

The project leader knows that one of her first tasks is to create a project schedule. She has started by listing all the known tasks or activities (the words task and activity are used synonymously throughout this chapter). The list, shown in Figure 19.1, divides logically into three parts or work packages that form a simple work breakdown structure:

Activity number	Activity description	Duration (days)	Preceding activities
	Chair		
01	Anatomical study for chair	15	None
02	Design chair	5	01
03	Buy materials for chair seat	6	02
04	Make chair seat	3	03
05	Buy chair castors	5	02
06	Buy steel for chair frame	10	02
07	Make chair frame	3	06
08	Paint chair frame	2	07, 21
09	Assemble chair	1	04, 05, 08
10	Apply final finishes to chair	2	09
	Desk		
11	Design desk	10	None
12	Buy steel for desk frame	10	11
13	Make desk frame	5	12, 15
14	Paint desk frame	2	13, 21
15	Buy wood and fittings for desk	5	15
16	Make desk drawer	6	15
17	Make desk top	1	15
18	Assemble desk	1	14, 16, 17
19	Apply final finishes to desk	2	18
	General activities		
20	Decide paint colours	10	None
21	Buy paint and varnish	8	20
22	Final project evaluation	5	10, 19

Figure 19.1 Task list for the furniture project

ESTIMATING THE TASK DURATIONS

In consultation with her colleagues, the project leader must estimate how long each task is expected to take. Each estimate is for the total time expected to elapse between starting a task and finishing it. That time is irrespective of the number of people needed if, indeed, any people are needed at all. Each duration estimate must include non-productive time, such as waiting for glue to set during assembly. These duration estimates, therefore, serve a different purpose from those made for cost estimating. They are concerned primarily with task times, rather than cost or work content, because collectively they will determine the duration of the whole project.

This furniture is to be made in the company's prototype workshop. The workshop manager should, therefore, be asked to estimate all the workshop task durations. For the times needed to buy all the materials, the project leader should ask the purchasing manager, but she should herself know how much time to allow for the design tasks.

UNITS OF DURATION AND THE PROJECT CALENDAR

A project schedule is likely to be expressed in time units of days, weeks or months, the choice depending on the size and duration of the project. The furniture project is small and simple, so the project leader has decided to estimate every task in days. She knows that her company normally works a five-day week, so that an estimate of five days' duration really means five weekdays (equivalent to a calendar week). If the schedule is eventually entered in a computer for processing, it is likely that the default calendar in the project management software will also assume a five-day week.

Public holidays

If the furniture company is to shut down for public holidays, or for any other general holiday, the weekdays affected will have to be removed from the default calendar to prevent tasks from being scheduled during the holiday period.

Alternative calendars

Most project management software allows the planner to create one or more special calendars (Chapter 21). One of these can be assigned to an activity (or in some cases to a resource group), replacing the default calendar to overcome the following kinds of problem:

- When a task can be allowed to occupy six or seven days a week instead of being limited to the five weekdays in the default calendar

- When a task is to be performed over more than one shift in a 24-hour period
- Where the duration can include passive time that can span a weekend, such as waiting for concrete to cure
- Where the schedule calls for tasks to be done in places where the public holidays, religious festivals or the working week fall on different days than those in the default calendar

Conversion of numbers to calendar dates

Project schedules are often compiled before the start date of the project is known. In those cases it is not possible to put calendar dates on the schedule. All the examples in this chapter use day numbers or week numbers. In practice, day numbers or week numbers are inconvenient and mean little unless they can be related to the calendar. In any case, conversion of times to calendar dates from a schedule containing only numbers is tedious, time consuming and prone to human error. For the furniture project it is assumed that the project leader will eventually use a computer to process the schedule. When the start date has been decided, the computer will base its calculations from that date and convert all day numbers into calendar dates before printing out the various reports.

TASK SEQUENCE

The project leader must decide the sequence in which the tasks are to be done. She must consider each task in turn and note which tasks, if any, precede it. For example, the chair design cannot start until the anatomical study has been completed. Before the chair frame can be painted, two other tasks must have been finished, namely make the frame and buy the paint. These relationships are difficult to show clearly in a simple list. However, all the tasks have been given identification numbers, and this has simplified the project leader's problem. For every task in the furniture project list, she has entered the identification numbers of tasks that must immediately precede it in the extreme right-hand column of Figure 19.1.

SCHEDULING THE FURNITURE PROJECT USING A BAR CHART

SIMPLE BAR CHART

Figure 19.2 shows the result when the furniture project leader attempted to produce a working schedule using a bar chart. The purpose of such a schedule must be twofold:

354

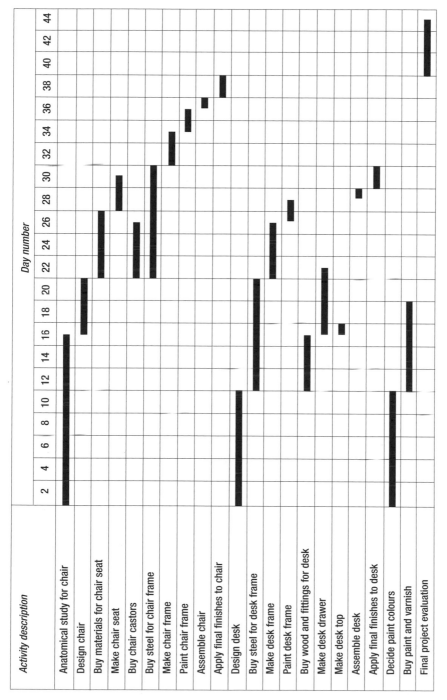

Figure 19.2 Bar chart for the furniture project

355

- To inform her superiors in the company of the intended project timescale
- For use as a progressing tool throughout the short life of this project.

The bar chart will succeed in the first of these two aims as soon as calendar dates can be substituted for day numbers. It is a good visual aid and sets out the intentions clearly. Every task is depicted graphically in its allotted time slot. The chart is easy to understand by project management experts and non-experts alike. From the project leader's viewpoint, however, the chart is of less value. Its most significant failing is that it does not show which tasks have to be finished before others can start.

When the chart is first set up on an adjustable board or drawn on paper, the project leader can observe all the relationships indicated in the final column of the task list. This can be quite a mental challenge, but a person with suitable aptitude can do it, provided that the project is not too big. The real difficulties come when the schedule has to be updated. Then it is easy for errors to creep in.

LINKED BAR CHART

A linked bar chart can be used to indicate task interdependencies. This has been attempted for the furniture project in Figure 19.3. However, even for this small project it has not been easy for the project leader to show every interconnection between different tasks. She did not find it possible in this case to show the link from the end of the task to buy paint and varnish to the beginning of the two frame painting tasks. On a larger project this difficulty would have been more serious. The notation provided by this method is therefore inadequate, or at least extremely limited, even for the small furniture project.

There are many computer programmes which can plot linked bar charts quite well. Microsoft Project is a common example. These solve the problem of inflexibility associated with hand-drawn charts. Their value, however, remains limited because of the visual difficulty in trying to follow the paths of all the link lines on anything except the very simplest project.

The project leader must look for another scheduling method to overcome these problems. Her answer lies in using some form of critical path network. She has two variations from which to choose: activity-on-arrow and activity-on-node. Each of these methods has its advantages and disadvantages. Both will now be described, first in principle and then as the project leader applied them to her furniture project.

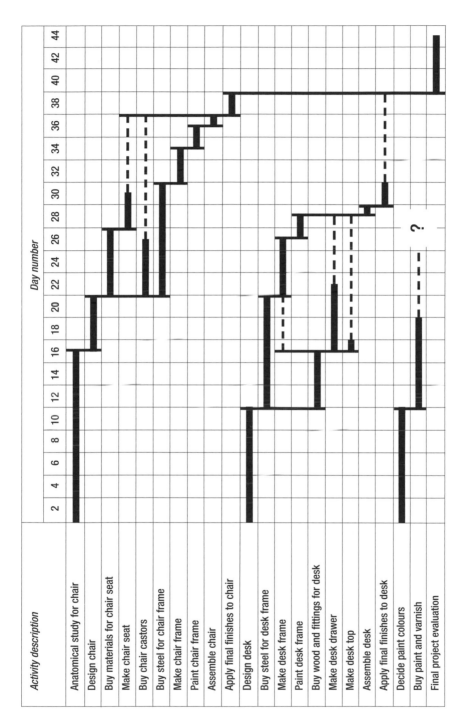

Figure 19.3 Linked bar chart for the furniture project

ACTIVITY-ON-ARROW CRITICAL PATH NETWORKS

THE NOTATION

All the essential notational elements of an activity-on-arrow network diagram are shown in Figure 19.4. Arrow networks (as they are often called) are easier to sketch quickly than precedence networks (described later). They lend themselves to rapid sketching, erasure and resketching on paper or other medium in front of an audience. They are, therefore, ideal tools for developing plans that embody the advice of experts at group brainstorming sessions. Unfortunately they are not supported by any modern computer software. If a computer is going to be used, it will be necessary either to use precedence notation from the start or, as I often do myself, sketch the network as an arrow diagram and convert it to precedence later, when the data are input to the computer. However, small precedence networks can be created quickly and easily using Post-it Notes® on a whiteboard or flip chart in a way that engages the audience interactively.

Every circle in the arrow diagram represents an event in a project, and the number written in it is simply a code or name that identifies the particular event. An event might be the start or finish of the entire project, the start of one or more activities, the finish of one or more activities or some combination of these. Events do not need to be numbered in sequence from left to right but planners usually number them in ascending order because this makes the job of finding a

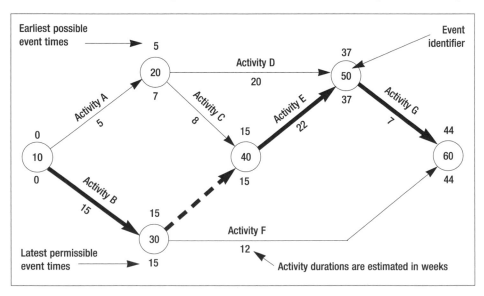

Figure 19.4 Notation for activity-on-arrow networks

particular event on a very large network diagram far easier. The numbers in this example jump in intervals of ten: intervals of five or ten are often used so that, in the event of later activity insertions in the network, the left-to-right numbering sequence can be preserved.

Each arrow represents the activity needed to progress from one event (the preceding event) to the next (the succeeding event). An activity may be an active task (such as designing the desk in the furniture project) or a passive passage of time (such as waiting for materials to be delivered). Each activity takes its identification number from its preceding and succeeding events. Thus the activity from Event 10 to Event 20 would be identified as Activity 10:20. By convention, all network activities must progress from left to right. It is not strictly necessary, therefore, to draw arrowheads unless for some unavoidable reason an arrow has to be drawn running from right to left, in which case the arrowhead must be added to avoid any chance of a mistake when interpreting the logic. Network diagrams do not need to be drawn to scale because neither the length of an arrow nor the diameter of an event circle has any significance.

There are a few computer programmes that can plot networks on a timescale, but the results can disappoint and cover large areas of paper. If a timescaled chart is wanted, by far the better solution is to have the computer convert the finished network to a bar chart.

No activity can start until all activities leading into its preceding event have been completed. Activities 20:50 and 20:40 cannot therefore start until Activity 10:20 has been finished or, in other words, until Event 20 has been achieved.

The dotted line from Event 30 to Event 40 is a dummy activity. Dummies are not true activities and have zero duration by default, but they are real links (constraints) that form part of the logic. In our example, therefore, Event 40 will not be achieved until Activity 20:40 has been finished and, through the dummy, Activity 10:30 has also been finished. Thus network notation can show clearly the interdependencies (constraints) between all the different activities in the project.

TIME ANALYSIS AND THE CRITICAL PATH

Durations in the example in Figure 19.4 have been estimated in weeks and written below the activity arrows to which they refer. Activity 10:20, for instance, is expected to take 5 weeks from start to finish.

The forward pass

The numbers written above the event circles indicate the earliest time at which each event can be achieved. Clearly the earliest times for Events 20 and 30 in Figure 19.4 are at the ends of Weeks 5 and 15, respectively, because these events cannot be achieved until their preceding activities have finished. The earliest times for all other events are found by adding activity durations from left to right throughout the network, a process known as the forward pass.

In each case it is the longest path that will determine the earliest possible time for an event. Dummies must be included in all paths. So, when looking at Event 40, for example, two paths must be considered. One goes through Events 10, 20, and 40 with a total path duration of 13 weeks. The other possible path leading into Event 40 runs through Events 10, 30, and 40 via the Dummy 30:40, with a total path duration of 15 weeks. So the earliest possible time for Event 40 is 15 weeks.

At Event 50, the path from Event 20 through Activity 20:50 is 25 weeks (5 + 20) but the path from Event 40 is the longer, at 37 weeks (5 + 8 + 22). The earliest possible time for Event 50 is therefore 37 weeks. As the earliest possible time for Event 50 is the end of Week 37, Activity 50:60 cannot start until the end of Week 37, which in practical scheduling terms actually means the start of Week 38. The forward pass must end at the final project event, which is Event 60. The earliest possible time for this event is Week 44. This means that (provided the activity duration estimates are correct) this project cannot be completed in less than 44 weeks.

The backward pass

The forward pass through the network has found the earliest possible time for every event and, through those results, the earliest possible start and finish time for every activity. The question now arises, what are the latest permissible times for those events and activities if project completion is not to be delayed? These times are found by a subtraction process known as the backward pass. The principal determinant must be the latest permissible time for the end event. In other words, what is the latest permissible finish time for the project?

It is assumed here that the project must be finished as soon as possible, which is the case for most projects. This means that the earliest possible time at the final event (Event 60) is also the latest permissible time for achieving that event. The result, Week 44, is written below the event circle. Again taking the longest path in each case, we now have to work backwards through the network to find the latest permissible times for all the other events. At Event 50 the latest permissible time must be the latest time for Event 60 minus the duration of the connecting activity. That is, 44 minus 7 which is 37. The latest permissible time for Event 20, for example, is found by looking at the paths from Events 50 and 40. These, respectively give the results 37 minus 20 (17) and 15 minus 8 (7). So Event 20 must be achieved not later than the end of Week 7 if the project finish is not to be delayed beyond Week 44.

The critical path

When both the forward and backward passes have been made through any network, there will always be at least one path in which the earliest and latest times of each event lying along that particular path are the same. These events must be achieved at their earliest possible times if the project is to finish at its earliest possible time. No delay to any one of these events can be permitted. They are critical to the progress of the project. The path linking them from project start to finish is called the critical path. It is not uncommon to find a critical path that branches or a network with more than one critical path. The critical path in Figure 19.4 is shown in bold rules.

Float

Float, otherwise known as slack (particularly in America), is the amount by which any event or activity may be delayed without delaying the whole project completion. All critical activities have zero float. Any attempt to impose a project finish time that is earlier than the earliest possible time calculated from time analysis will drive the system into a hypercritical state, with some or all events and activities having negative float values. For example, if an arbitrary completion target at Week 42 should be imposed on the project network in Figure 19.4, then all previously critical activities would have their zero float reduced to minus two weeks. This, of course, would mean that the schedule is impracticable, and either the target or the network must be reviewed.

If an activity possessing float is delayed for any reason during the actual progress of a project, some or its entire float will be used up. Less float is then likely to remain for all the following activities, but this effect is not quite straightforward and depends on the position of the activity in respect to its surrounding activities. That position will determine the type of float, as explained in the following definitions.

Total float

Total float is defined as the amount by which an activity can be delayed if all its preceding activities take place at their earliest possible times and all succeeding activities are allowed to wait until their latest permissible times. All non-critical activities possess total float. The total float of an activity is calculated by taking the latest permissible end-event time *minus* the earliest possible start-event time *minus* the activity duration.

The amount of time analysis information that can be shown on an arrow diagram is often limited and can be misleading for the beginner. This is seen at Activity 30:60, for example, in Figure 19.4. Events 30 and 60 both lie on the project critical path but Activity 30:60, which joins them, is not critical and does not form part of the critical path. The situation soon becomes clear with a little thought. Event 30 is effectively fixed at Week 15, and Event 60 is fixed at Week 44. So the time separating these two events is 44 minus 15 weeks, which is 29 weeks. Activity 30:60 can be allowed to take place anywhere within these 29 weeks without affecting the project completion time. Since it occupies 12 of the 29 weeks itself, it must possess 29 minus 12 weeks float, which is a total float of 17 weeks. Activity 30:60 is slightly special in another way because it possesses two other kinds of float. These are *free float* and *independent float*.

Free float

Free float is the amount of float possessed by an activity when all preceding activities take place at their earliest possible times and all preceding activities can also still take place at their earliest times. Free float is the earliest possible end-event time *minus* the earliest possible start-event time *minus* the activity's duration. The result for Activity 30:60 is 17 weeks. Free float is far less common than total float. Many planners ignore it.

Independent float

Independent float is the float possessed by an activity if all preceding activities take place at their latest permissible times and succeeding activities can still take place at their earliest times. Independent float is calculated by taking the earliest possible end-event time *minus* the latest permissible start-event time *minus* the duration. The result for Activity 30:60 is again 17 weeks. Independent float is uncommon and is not usually featured in computer reports.

ACTIVITY-ON-ARROW NETWORK FOR THE FURNITURE PROJECT

The project leader of the furniture project, after attending a two-day training course, learned how to draw arrow networks. On returning to her office she converted the tasks listed in Figure 19.1 to the arrow diagram shown in Figure 19.5. This gave her the ability to show all the task interdependencies and to calculate the relative priorities of all the tasks (expressed in terms of total and free float). However, her superiors did not feel so comfortable with the new diagram, and preferred the original simple bar chart.

The dummy connecting Event 13 to Event 15 is not strictly necessary. The additional event created by inserting the dummy (Event 13) does, however, provide space for showing the earliest possible completion time for Activity 6:13. More importantly, without the dummy, the activities for making the desk drawer and making the desk top would both be identified as Activity 6:15. By adding the

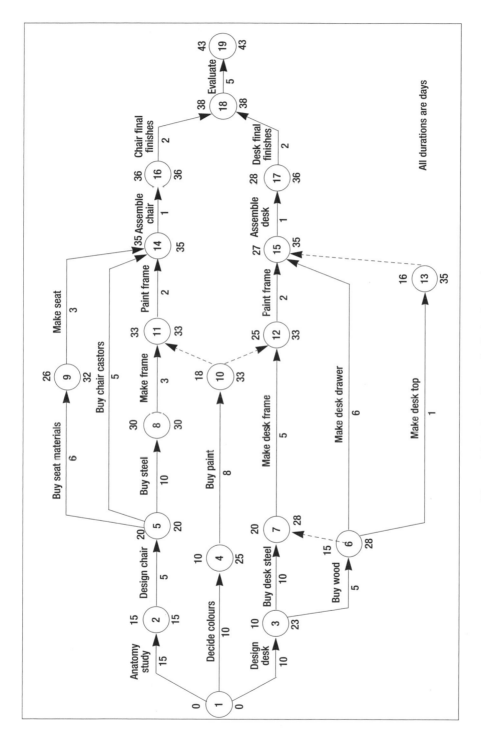

Figure 19.5 Arrow diagram for the furniture project

363

dummy, the project leader has given both these activities different identifier codes. This distinction used to be very important when computer software was available for arrow networks. The problem does not arise with precedence notation.

The time analysis data become more useful for progressing the furniture project when they are set out as the table shown in Figure 19.6, but the project leader would still find the information of little practical scheduling use without knowing the start date for the project. Once that start date has been established the network can be processed by a computer, so that the table shows calendar dates instead of week numbers. The computer can also sort the activities into a more useful sequence. For this project, sorting activities by ascending order of their earliest start dates will be most convenient for issuing and controlling work, the resulting schedule sometimes being known as a work-to or work-to-do list.

The computer brings flexibility to the scheduling process and is able to cope with changes in project scope or with rescheduling for any other reason. Further, the senior managers can still have their beloved bar charts, because modern project management software is able to plot bar charts from the network data. Before the furniture project leader can use the computer, however, she will have to learn how to draw the network using the precedence system.

PRECEDENCE NETWORKS

Precedence networks are now the more common form. Their use became mandatory for computer processing since the computer software industry decided to stop supporting the once far more common activity-on-arrow system. For precedence networks the nodes (drawn as rectangles) represent activities instead of events. There is no special provision in precedence diagram notation for depicting events, although activity nodes with zero or unity duration can be placed to represent key events or project milestones if the planner wishes.

The arrows joining the activity nodes are simply links, indicating the logical constraints and dummies are not needed. Precedence time analysis is carried out by the same process as in arrow networks, using forward and backward passes through the network. People generally find precedence diagrams easier to understand than their arrow counterparts, probably because they resemble flow charts used by engineers and others.

PRECEDENCE NOTATION AND TIME ANALYSIS

The most commonly used elements of the precedence method are shown in the simple example of Figure 19.7. This is for the same project used in Figure 19.4,

Prec. event	Succ. event	Activity description	Duration (days)	Earliest start	Latest start	Earliest finish	Latest finish	Free float	Total float
1	2	01 Anatomical study for chair	15	0	0	15	15	0	0
2	5	02 Design chair	5	15	15	20	20	0	0
5	9	03 Buy materials for chair seat	6	20	26	26	32	0	6
9	14	04 Make chair seat	3	26	32	29	35	0	6
5	14	05 Buy chair castors	5	20	30	25	35	10	10
5	8	06 Buy steel for chair frame	10	20	20	30	30	0	0
8	11	07 Make chair frame	3	30	30	33	33	0	0
11	14	08 Paint chair frame	2	33	33	35	35	0	0
14	16	09 Assemble chair	1	35	35	36	36	0	0
16	18	10 Apply final finishes to chair	2	36	36	38	38	0	0
1	3	11 Design desk	10	0	13	10	23	0	13
3	7	12 Buy steel for desk frame	10	10	18	20	28	0	8
7	12	13 Make desk frame	5	20	28	25	33	0	8
12	14	14 Paint desk frame	2	25	33	27	35	0	8
3	6	15 Buy wood and fittings for desk	5	10	23	15	28	0	13
6	15	16 Make desk drawer	6	15	29	21	35	14	14
6	13	17 Make desk top	1	15	34	16	35	19	19
15	17	18 Assemble desk	1	27	35	28	36	0	8
17	18	19 Apply final finishes to desk	2	28	36	30	38	0	8
1	4	20 Decide paint colours	10	0	15	10	25	0	15
4	10	21 Buy paint and varnish	8	10	25	18	33	7	15
18	19	22 Final project evaluation	5	38	38	43	43	0	0

Figure 19.6 Time analysis data from the furniture project network

and Activity F on the precedence diagram corresponds with Activity 30:60 in Figure 19.4. The key provided on the precedence diagram shows the meaning of the numbers written in each activity box and no further explanation is needed here. There is more room on the precedence diagram to show the time analysis results, so the 17 days' total float of Activity F can be shown, whereas this was hidden in the arrow network.

PRECEDENCE DIAGRAM FOR THE FURNITURE PROJECT

The precedence network for the furniture project is shown in Figure 19.8. Compare this with the arrow version in Figure 19.5. Most people would agree that the precedence version is neater and easier to understand.

COMPLEX CONSTRAINTS IN THE PRECEDENCE SYSTEM

Precedence notation allows the expression of complex relationships between different activities that cannot easily be shown in arrow networks. There are three complex relationships possible in addition to the normal (default) finish-to-start links. All four constraints are explained in Figure 19.9.

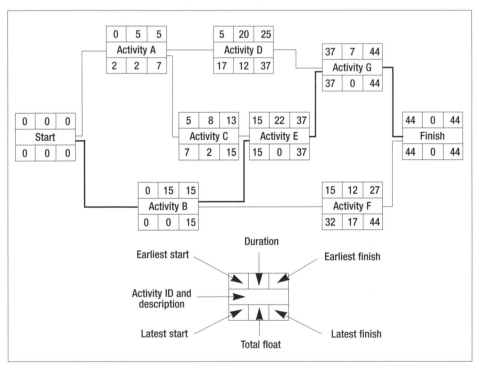

Figure 19.7   Basic notation for precedence networks

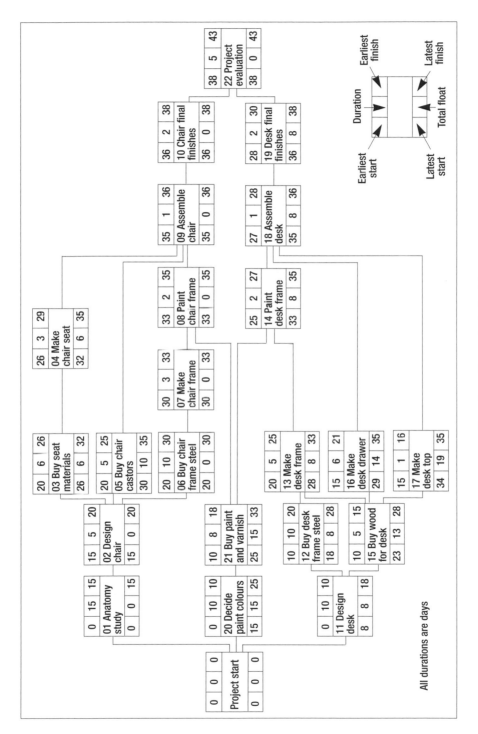

Figure 19.8   Precedence diagram for the furniture project

367

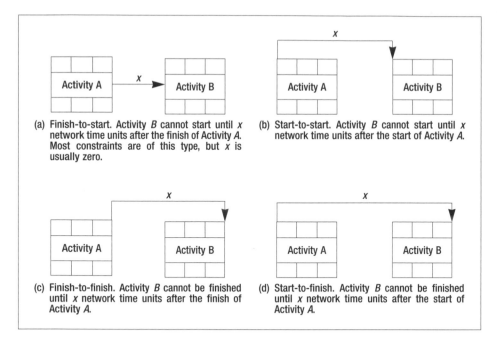

(a) Finish-to-start. Activity *B* cannot start until *x* network time units after the finish of Activity *A*. Most constraints are of this type, but *x* is usually zero.

(b) Start-to-start. Activity *B* cannot start until *x* network time units after the start of Activity *A*.

(c) Finish-to-finish. Activity *B* cannot be finished until *x* network time units after the finish of Activity *A*.

(d) Start-to-finish. Activity *B* cannot be finished until *x* network time units after the start of Activity *A*.

Figure 19.9   Complex constraints

Care must always be taken to avoid leaving any activity that is not a start or finish node as a start or end dangle. A dangle is created when a link is missed out by mistake. So if, for example, the finish-start link from Activity A to Activity D were to be omitted by mistake, Activity A would become an end dangle and Activity D would be become a start dangle. The computer would simply recognize these as start and finish activities, respectively. Dangles obviously cause serious errors in time analysis. The risk of creating dangles becomes greater when complex constraints are used. If, for example, the start-start link from Activity A to Activity B in Figure 19.9 is not complemented by a finish-finish link between these two activities, Activity A will be an end dangle.

CREATING PRACTICAL LOGIC

The furniture project leader used her project work breakdown and its resulting task list as the starting point for her network. This approach is widely taught and used, and is probably best for the beginner. However, the best network solution will result from a brainstorming session led by an experienced planner and attended by the key project participants. The task list remains important, but it has to be regarded as an incomplete checklist.

The brainstorming session will help to identify activities that might otherwise have been forgotten and it should certainly result in more practical network logic. For example, the task list is unlikely to include activities such as waiting for materials to be delivered, or for key stage approvals during design. When tasks do not attract any cost or work effort they need not feature in work breakdowns made with cost estimating in mind. However, they can have great significance for the project timescale and must be included in network diagrams.

So, unless the organization has great experience in very similar projects, a good way to produce an initial network is to call a meeting of all those who will manage or execute work in the key areas of the project. (Project start-up is covered Chapter 26). The planning expert should be in the chair, and he or she should be so familiar with the networking technique that those who have never even seen a network diagram before will quickly absorb the concepts through the expert's example and guidance as the meeting proceeds. The expert will, from long experience, know the kinds of questions to ask in order to reveal tasks that might otherwise have been forgotten; questions that can seem obvious but are easily forgotten:

- Can this chair really be assembled now before the frame has been painted?
- Can you start to dig the foundations for this construction project the instant you arrive on site? How would you know where to dig? Surely you would need to do some marking out first? Will you not need to hire some machinery?

A project network must do more than contain all significant activities: it must link them in a logical and practical way. Ask any two people to draw a network for the same project and you will almost certainly get two different networks. That does not mean one or both are wrong. There is usually more than one practical way of planning and executing a complex project. What is important is to strive for a plan that is seen to be achievable, efficient, practical and expressed in sufficient detail for work to be issued and monitored at regular intervals.

EARLY CONSIDERATION OF RESOURCES

Planners are often faced with the problem of resources when they estimate task durations. How can they estimate the duration of a task when they do not know if sufficient resources will be available at the time scheduled by time analysis? What effect will other activities have where they need the same resources? Suppose that a particular task might take two weeks if one person is employed but only one week if three people are used. Should the duration for that task be estimated as one week or two? There are useful rules to apply when answering these questions. These are illustrated by the following examples.

CASE 1

An activity will need the use of an electrician. So will several other activities in the same network. How can the planner estimate the duration of the activity when he or she does not know whether or not an electrician will always be available? The answer is to estimate the duration for the activity as if an electrician will be available whenever required, irrespective of the demands of other electrical tasks in the project. The planning process then goes through two logical, consecutive stages, as follows:

1. The computer will first establish time analysis data with no reference at all to resources.
2. The computer can now do separate resource scheduling calculations in which it attempts to start each task at its earliest possible time but will only do so if the electrician has not already been allocated to another task. Tasks with highest priority will have first claim on the electrician and are scheduled next. Highest priority usually means least float.

The main point to grasp here is that the network should first be estimated without considering possible resource conflicts. Resource scheduling is a subsequent, quite separate exercise.

CASE 2

A single project activity calls for the use of one or more electricians. The planner knows the electrical department usually has a total of ten electricians available to work on projects. The duration of the activity in question depends on the number of electricians used: it would take six days if two electricians could be found but would extend to 15 days with only one. It is more efficient in this case to plan for two electricians and write six days down as the estimated duration. The planner now sees a problem. No one knows how many of the ten electricians will be available for the activity because that must depend on when it takes place and on what else is happening at that time. The correct approach in this case is to estimate the duration as six days, using the optimum number of electricians and ignoring possible resource conflicts. Subsequent resource scheduling will take care of the actual resource consideration. In other words, the scheduling must be taken one step at a time, which means time analysis first and resource allocation as a quite separate second.

CASE 3

An activity could be completed in 20 days with five electricians but this duration might be reduced to 15 days if eight electricians could be used. The planner knows that the company employs a total of only six electricians. Although the planner must ignore the claims on these electricians made by other tasks in the network, he or she must exercise common sense and avoid planning to use more electricians than the total available to the project. So the duration for this activity must be estimated as 20 days.

NETWORK TOO BIG?

At one time network size was limited only by the length of the drawing paper roll available. Almost invariably drawn in arrow notation, networks containing several thousands of activities were fairly common. Although large networks are still sometimes necessary, modern networks tend to contain fewer activities for two principal reasons:

- Scrolling large networks across computer screens is not particularly convenient
- Planners now recognize that very large networks can be cumbersome and impracticable

Projects, however, have not shrunk. So how do we still manage to include all the important activities with smaller networks? The answer is to break the plan down into a number of smaller, more easily manageable networks. This can often be achieved by drawing a separate network for each major work package from the work breakdown structure. However, the separate networks must be welded into a project whole. This is best achieved by linking them at suitably chosen interfaces. Suppose, for example, that the furniture project scope were to be extended to include setting up a new production facility and also to run a nation-wide marketing campaign. The company management would be unwise to ask for one detailed network for the whole project. Instead, they would probably separate the project into three major work packages, each with its own leader, and each with its own network plan thus:

1. The furniture design and prototype project
2. The furniture factory project
3. The furniture marketing project

Computer software caters for these hierarchical project arrangements. Indeed, software is available that can combine not only subprojects within projects, but also all the projects in a company or even a group of companies. Thus a large project network plan can be broken down into subnetworks of manageable size, each of which allows the manager of a major work package to plan the work for which he or she is going to be directly responsible. Care must be taken, however, never to lose sight of the whole project picture. This is achieved by producing a summary network for the entire project under the direction of the project manager. Each activity in the summary network will represent (and span in time) one major work package. Particular planning care is needed to interface these summary activities so that sensible logic and time analysis data are produced for the whole project.

TIMESCALE TOO LONG?

When time analysis is first carried out on a new network, the result is often a disappointment or even a shock. Taking the furniture project as an example, suppose that instead of the 43 days predicted, the company's management wanted the project finished in only 30 days. What could the project leader do about this? First reactions are likely to be anger or despair and a 'can't be done' response. She can, however, consider three options.

1. She can review all the duration estimates and shorten some of them arbitrarily.
2. She can consider asking for more money and other resources.
3. She can review the network logic.

Options 2 and 3 can be combined for maximum effect in a process known as fast tracking (or in product development projects as reducing the time-to-market).

OPTION 1: REDUCE NETWORK DURATION TIMES ARBITRARILY

This option can usually be dismissed. If the original network was compiled using the best possible assessment of duration times, substituting shorter times without good reason is likely to produce failure. The revised plan might look good on paper and please senior management but, if it is not practicable, it should not be accepted. The result can only disappoint.

OPTION 2: SPEND MORE MONEY

An activity can sometimes be shortened by putting in more effort. Perhaps two people could be used instead of one for a particular critical task. It might be possible to get materials faster, but at more expense, by changing suppliers or by using express freight. Additional equipment might be hired to speed a task. Although the use of planned overtime is never recommended, an exception might be made in the case of a critical activity. All of these actions are collectively known as 'crashing'. To achieve maximum effect at minimum extra cost, only critical activities should be considered for crashing. There is no point in wasting money to crash an activity that has a considerable amount of float. It is usually found, however, that crashing all the activities along the critical path shortens the path to the extent that it is no longer the path with greatest duration. In other words, when time analysis is carried out on the revised network, activities that were previously non-critical have themselves become a new critical path. So, then those activities too can be considered for crashing.

If a network is crashed expertly and the process is repeated until the limit is reached, it is probable that many, if not most, activities will have become critical. That should result in a plan representing maximum time saving at minimum extra cost. Bear in mind, however, that this cost/time optimization is to some extent an artificial concept. The activity duration times are only estimates and it is unlikely that every task will be completed exactly according to plan. The network schedule should, therefore, be kept under constant review as the project proceeds and changed whenever necessary to maintain optimization.

OPTION 3: REVIEWING THE NETWORK LOGIC

A careful review of the original network logic can sometimes lop a considerable amount of time from the planned project duration. It might even be found that one or two activities can be omitted altogether (perhaps an approval stage could be removed, for instance). Although most network constraints assume that no activity can start before all its predecessors have been finished, it is sometimes practicable to allow activities to overlap to some extent.

For example, it might be possible to purchase materials before design is complete, because the designer will be able to tell the buyer what is required before the finished drawings are issued. Similarly, a limited amount of manufacture can sometimes take place before final issue of drawings. If a subcontractor is to be involved, advance notice can sometimes be given that will allow the subcontractor to reserve capacity and, perhaps, start ordering supplies. It might even be discovered that two or more activities can be run completely in parallel instead of sequentially. Such measures can shorten the expected duration of a project considerably, but there is often a price to pay in the form of added risk.

The complex constraints of precedence notation are ideal for depicting overlapping activities. The start-to-start option is particularly useful in this respect (see Figure 19.9). Time analysis becomes more difficult but this is not a problem when the network is processed by computer.

REFERENCES AND FURTHER READING

Lock, D., 2003, *Project Management, 8th edition,* Aldershot: Gower.

Lockyer, K., and Gordon, J., 1996, *Project Management and Project Network Techniques, 6th edition,* London: Financial Times, Pitman Publishing.

Morris, P.W.G., 1997, *The Management of Projects, 2nd edition,* London: Thomas Telford.

Spinner, M.P., 1992, *Elements of Project Management: plan, schedule and control, 2nd edition,* Englewood Cliffs: Prentice Hall.

20 Managing Cost

Dennis Lock

Successful management of project costs is a complex process that cannot be left solely to the responsibility of the project manager. It embraces many aspects of contractual and commercial management that usually fall within the remit of other managers in the project organization. This chapter concentrates on initial cost estimating and budgeting, and on some of the cost analysis tasks that typically fall under the direct control of the project manager.

COST DEFINITIONS

It is generally understood in accounting circles that the word 'cost' should never be used without a qualifying adjective. It must always be made clear what kind of cost is meant. There are many ways in which costs can be described, but it will be useful to outline some of the terms with which the project manager should be acquainted. There is no need to include self-explanatory terms (such as labour costs and material costs) so the following list has been limited to a few that may not be familiar to all readers.

Below-the-line-costs

Various allowances that are added once a total basic cost estimate has been made are often known collectively as 'below-the-line' costs. These might include allowances for cost escalation, exchange rate fluctuation and other contingencies.

Cost escalation

This is the increase in any element of project costs caused by wage and salary awards and inflationary pressures on prices of purchased materials and equipment. It is usually expressed as an annual rate per cent. Where the rate of cost inflation is low it has little importance and may often be ignored, but in economies where high inflation is rife it must be considered and built into any fixed price contract proposal as a 'below-the-line' item.

Direct costs

Costs that can be attributed directly to a job or project task are termed direct costs. If a person spends two hours in the manufacture of a component for a particular project, that person's time can be classed as direct because its cost can be identified, recorded and charged direct to the project. Similarly, the costs of materials, components and expenses directly attributable to a particular project can be classed as direct. Direct costs are also likely to be *variable costs*. Variable costs are those which vary in proportion to the level of work actually taking place on the project. If work stops, so do the direct or variable costs. If the work rate is increased with the use of more resources, then the rate of variable cost expenditure will also increase.

Fixed costs

See *Indirect costs*

Indirect costs (overhead costs or overheads)

Facilities and services such as factory and office accommodation, management, personnel, training, cost and management accounting, administration, heating, lighting, and maintenance all attract costs that must be incurred in running a business. Except in the case of an organization set up specially to fulfil only one project, these general costs cannot usually be allocated directly to one job or project. They are therefore termed indirect costs, often called overhead costs, or simply 'overheads'. Most indirect costs are also likely to be *fixed costs*. Costs are said to be fixed when they remain substantially unchanged and continue to be incurred irrespective of the level of project activity. Indirect management salaries are an example.

Standard costs

Standard costing is a system in which cost data are compiled using standard rates for labour and materials. Standard rates are realistic mean rates. For example, all design engineers in a company might always be charged at the same standard hourly cost, even though individually some engineers might be paid less than that and others more. (In reality the standard cost will be the mean hourly wage plus an overhead recovery rate). In projects, standard costs are typically used in cost estimates, budgets and for subsequent cost collection (from timesheets and material stores issue requisitions). This eliminates the need to consider day-to-day fluctuations in materials prices or salary differences between individual staff of the same trade or professional discipline. From time to time the current cost rates are reviewed by the organization's accountants and compared against the standard rates in use. Any differences will give rise to a set of variances. When these variances become significant (usually as a result of cost inflation) new standard cost rates must be introduced.

Variable costs

See *Direct costs*.

Variance

A variance is any difference (desirable or undesirable) between a planned or budgeted quantity and the quantity actually measured after the event. It is usually used in connection with costs but it can also describe a deviation from the project schedule. Undesirable variances are especially important quantities because, provided they are detected and reported sufficiently early, they highlight problems where corrective action is needed. Variance analysis and reporting therefore satisfy the principle of management by exception.

PRINCIPLES OF COST MANAGEMENT

Project cost management begins long before a project starts. It is a widely misunderstood function. Much of the activity often described as cost control or cost management is really nothing more than historical cost reporting, carried out too late to have any effect on costs that have already been incurred or committed.

CHECKLIST OF COST MANAGEMENT FACTORS

The following list contains some of the factors that contribute directly or indirectly to effective project cost management. Items are not listed in any particular order of significance.

1. Full definition of the project and the scope of work involved before committing expenditure.
2. Careful assessment of technical and commercial risks, with strategies for minimizing their possible effect.
3. Competent project manager.
4. Cost awareness by all project participants throughout the life of the project.
5. A project organization in which everyone is made aware of his or her project responsibilities.

6. A project work breakdown structure which yields work packages of manageable size.
7. Cost budgets, divided so that each work package is given its appropriate share of the total budget.
8. A code of accounts system which can be aligned with the work breakdown structure. As far as possible this should be compatible with other systems, such as drawing numbers and codes used in the organization's management information system.
9. A cost accounting system that can collect costs as they are incurred and allocate them to their relevant cost codes with minimum delay.
10. A prioritized work schedule, sufficiently detailed to allow the assignment and progressing of individual tasks from the work breakdown.
11. Effective management of well-motivated staff, to ensure that progress meets or beats the work schedule.
12. A method for comparing actual and planned expenditure for individual tasks, and for extrapolating the results to cover the whole project.
13. Willingness to commit additional resources or to take other measures promptly to bring late critical tasks back on to schedule.
14. Effective supervision and quality control of all activities to aim at being right first time.
15. Supervision of staff timesheets to ensure that only legitimate times are entered and that the correct cost codes are used.
16. Proper drafting of specifications and contracts.
17. Discreet investigation to ensure that the customer is of sound financial standing, with sufficient funds to make all contracted payments.
18. Similar investigation, not necessarily so discreet, of all significant suppliers and subcontractors (especially those new to the contractor's experience).
19. Effective use of competitive tendering for all purchases and subcontractors to ensure the lowest costs commensurate with quality and to avoid committing costs that would exceed estimates and budgets.
20. Proper consideration and control of modifications and contract variations, including charging all justifiable claims for price increases to the customer.
21. Avoidance of non-essential changes, especially those for which the customer will not pay.
22. Avoidance of unbudgeted dayworks (particularly on large construction contracts).
23. Where dayworks are unavoidable, proper authorization and retention of daywork sheets.
24. Control of payments to suppliers and subcontractors, to ensure that all invoices and claims for progress payments are neither overpaid nor paid too soon.

25. Recovery from the customer of all incidental expenses allowed for in the contract charging structure (for example, special printing and stationery, travel and accommodation).
26. Proper invoicing to the customer, especially ensuring that claims for progress payments or cost reimbursement are made at the appropriate times and at the correct levels, certificated where necessary, so that disputes do not arise which could delay payments.
27. Effective credit control to prevent payments from the customer becoming long overdue.
28. Internal security audits, to detect and deter losses through theft or fraud.
29. Regular cost and progress reports to senior management, highlighting potential schedule or budget overruns in time for corrective action to be taken.
30. Cost effective design, perhaps using value engineering.
31. Strategic use of concurrent engineering, in some cases involving the client, to reduce total project costs (even if that means accepting higher design costs).
32. Prompt action at the end of the project to close off the accounts to prevent unauthorized time bookings and other items being charged to the project.

That long list cannot be guaranteed as complete, but it includes the more important aspects of project cost management.

MINIMIZING INDIRECT COSTS

Indirect costs are a true burden and must be incurred for every day for which the project is live in the organization. If the project overruns on time, it is almost inevitable that the indirect costs will overrun in direct proportion. If an organization is structured and managed so that its indirect cost rates are high, then that organization will be at a disadvantage when it seeks new work against its competitors in a price sensitive market. There are at least three ways in which indirect costs can be minimized.

1. *Reclassify some indirect costs as direct:* Companies differ in their interpretation of direct and indirect costs so, where one might class a particular cost item as direct, another would regard it as indirect. For example, printing and stationery costs are typically indirect but special printing and stationery costs for a project may sometimes be accepted as a direct charge by the client. It might be possible to treat items such as travel costs and other administrative expenses associated with a particular project in such a way that they can be recorded and billed to the client. Whether or not the client will accept all these charges can be a matter for negotiation when the contract is made. Although the amounts for individual items may appear small, in total they can often result in significant saving.

2. *Complete work on or ahead of time:* If work can be completed on time, the associated indirect costs should be within budget. Let the work run late, and additional indirect costs must be absorbed.
3. *Review indirect salary costs and expenses:* Many aspects of indirect cost reduction apply universally and are not restricted to project management. They involve running a 'lean organization' in which every manager and administrative member of staff is seen to fulfil an essential role, with unnecessary layers of management and wasteful administration jobs stripped out. Waste must be eliminated by managing accommodation and other assets.

COST OF MATERIALS AND PURCHASED ITEMS

Purchased materials and equipment typically account for a large proportion of total project costs. Once a purchase order has been issued at a price over the budgeted amount it is too late to do anything about it. When the cost accounting system eventually picks up the costs of these purchases, when the invoices are paid, any over-expenditure will come to light as a nasty delayed shock. The costs of bought-out materials and equipment are committed irrevocably when each order is issued. The cost planning and reporting systems should, therefore, use data based on committed costs. That means considering the budgeted and quoted cost of every purchase at the time when the purchase order is signed.

Procedures should include adequate quality controls for producing accurate and unambiguous materials and equipment specifications. Sound purchasing methods are important. These will almost certainly involve competitive tendering and careful analysis of bids for all significantly expensive purchases. Clear authorization procedures should be in place, so that every purchase order is properly checked before final approval by an authorized signatory.

COST ESTIMATING

The most obvious reason for producing cost estimates is to assist in pricing decisions. However, cost estimates are necessary for all projects, including in-house projects and those sold without fixed prices. They are essential for funding and budgeting, for establishing outline resource requirements and for subsequent cost control.

ESTIMATING ACCURACY

It is clear that the better the project can defined at the outset, the less chance there should be of making estimating errors. It can sometimes be convenient

380

to classify project cost estimates according to the degree of accuracy expected. Different organizations have their own ideas, but here is a typical arrangement.

- **Ballpark estimates**: are estimates made when information or time is scarce. They are valuable for preliminary checks on resource requirements and for screening enquiries for possible tender preparation but are otherwise unreliable. It has been known for a manager to pick up a pile of drawings, weigh them thoughtfully in the hand and declare 'This project will cost £x million'. Some people have an extraordinary gift for that sort of thing, but such estimates are obviously unlikely to prove accurate. A well-reasoned ball park estimate might achieve an accuracy of ± 25 per cent, given a fair wind, a great deal of luck and intuitive judgement.

- **Comparative estimates:** as their name implies, are made by comparing work to be done on a new project with similar work recorded on past projects. They depend on an outline project definition that enables the estimator to identify all the major tasks and assess their size and complexity. The other important requirement is access to cost and technical archives of past projects that contain comparable work packages or tasks. The estimator will adjust costs to allow for the effects of cost inflation since the relevant past projects. Accuracy must depend very much on the degree of confidence that can be placed in the proposed new design solutions, on the working methods eventually chosen and on the closeness with which the new project tasks can be matched with those of previous projects. It might not be possible to achieve better than ±15 per cent accuracy but comparative estimates are often used as a basis for pricing tenders.

- **Feasibility estimates**: can only be derived after the completion of preliminary project design. Quotations must then be obtained from the potential suppliers of expensive project equipment or subcontracts. Material take-offs, bills of material or similar schedules should be available to assist with estimating the costs of materials. The accuracy confidence factor for feasibility estimates should be better than ±10 per cent. This class of estimate is often used for construction tenders. The construction industry has the benefit of published cost tables, which give expected cost rates for a comprehensive range of construction activities based on the quantities involved.

- **Definitive estimates**: cannot usually be made until most design work has been finished, all major purchase orders have been placed at known prices, and work on the project construction or manufacture is well advanced. Estimating accuracy should obviously improve with time as actual recorded costs replace their corresponding estimates. Estimates become definitive when their accuracy can be accepted as ±5 per cent or better. Subject to good cost accounting, the figures for actual project costs and the definitive project estimate should converge at the end of the project.

The degrees of accuracy quoted in these examples are about as good could ever be expected. It is very likely that many organizations will assign wider limits. It is also possible to find asymmetric limits, skewed about zero. A company might, for example, work on the assumption that its ballpark estimates are accurate to within +50 or -10 per cent.

TABULATION

Project cost estimates should be coded and tabulated to conform to the work breakdown structure. This will help to ensure that comparisons can readily be made between the estimates and the cost accountant's records of the actual costs eventually incurred, on a strict item for item basis. This is essential as part of the cost reporting and control functions. As experience builds up over a few years, records of estimates and corresponding costs can be used in comparative estimating for future projects, but only if all estimating and cost data are held in files structured to a common, sensible coding system. Using the work breakdown structure as the basis should automatically place all the cost estimates in a hierarchical structure. One estimating subset can be allocated to each main project work package or group of tasks. All the subsets can then be rolled up to give the estimated net total project cost.

TABULATION FOR MANUFACTURING PROJECTS

A suggestion for a manufacturing project tabulation is given in Figure 20.1. This is just an example; there will, of course, be considerable variations in practice. One page or subset should be allocated to each manufactured assembly, work breakdown package or main component. Each row on the tabulation carries a project task, which might be a design job, the manufacture of a component or assembly, or perhaps the provision of special tooling or a jig. Totalling relevant columns should give the commitment expected from each department, and these results can be used to help with departmental budgeting and in making coarse assessments of resource requirements. A project summary page can then be arranged on which each row will correspond to one work breakdown package or other estimating subset.

The upper headings used in Figure 20.1 are all self explanatory except, perhaps for the item 'Case' at the top right-hand side. This is used when cost estimates have to be made for different proposed versions of a potential project. Each version can be given its own unique case number, so that there should be no

COST ESTIMATE

Project number
or sales reference:

Estimate number:
Case:
Date:
Page   of

Estimate for:

Compiled by:

1	2	3	Labour times and costs by department or standard grade														10	11	12	13	14	15
			4		5		6		7		8		9				Total direct labour cost	Overhead cost %	Standard or net cost	Materials Burden %	Longest delivery (weeks)	Total cost 10+11+ 12+13
Cost	Item	Qty	Hrs	£	Hrs	£	Hrs	£	Hrs	£	Hrs	£	Hrs	£								

Figure 20.1 Tabulation for a manufacturing project cost estimate

subsequent confusion in finding the cost estimate that correctly applies to the project version actually chosen and authorized.

Our example allows six different standard cost grades of labour to be shown. A few more grades might be needed in practice, but the number of columns has been limited here to maintain clarity within the space available.

The tabulation allows for overheads to be recovered as a percentage levy on the direct labour cost. Materials are estimated at cost, but with a small handling charge added to cover the cost of order preparation, storage and other administration. These arrangements will vary from one organization to another.

DETAILED TABULATIONS FOR MATERIAL COSTS

Material cost estimates are often compiled separately from labour costs, perhaps using bills of materials, parts lists, or material take-offs to carry the necessary level of detail. The method depends particularly on the industry. Special attention must be given to purchases where commercial and transport transactions cross national frontiers.

Figure 20.2 is a slightly simplified version of a format used by a company engaged in very large international mining and minerals projects. Arranged in subsets according to main packages of the work breakdown structure, the aim is to show the total cost of each purchase, including all expenses needed to get the materials delivered to the project site. In the example shown, the project contractor always insists that suppliers quote to supply FOB (free on board). This means that the supplier's price in each case includes for packaging the goods and delivering them on to a ship or aircraft. Thereafter the buyer must pay all freight, insurance and agents' charges plus destination port charges, import duties and taxes. Columns have therefore been provided in the tabulation for these items. The column headed 'ship mode' is simply to indicate whether the main part of the journey is to be by sea, air or road. FOB is one of a set of internationally recognized abbreviations for international terms of trade known as Incoterms. These are regulated and published by the International Chamber of Commerce.

PROJECT CURRENCY

Many projects involve transactions in foreign currencies. A glance at Figure 20.2 will show that columns have been allocated for the conversion of foreign exchange rates. A typical situation for a large project is that costs arising in different countries are likely to be quoted or incurred in a variety of currencies. This can greatly complicate the estimator's job and subsequent attempts at using the total estimate for budgeting and cost management. A partial solution to this

COST ESTIMATE FOR MATERIALS
AND PURCHASED EQUIPMENT

Project number
or sales reference:

Estimate number:
Case:
Date:
Page   of

Estimate for:

Compiled by:

Cost code	Description	Spec No. (if known)	Proposed supplier	Unit	Unit cost FOB	Quoted currency	Exchange rate used	Converted FOB cost	Qty	Project FOB cost	Ship mode	Freight cost	Taxes/ duties	Delivered cost

Total delivered materials and equipment costs this page ⟶

Figure 20.2   Tabulation for purchased materials where international transport is involved

385

common problem is to convert all costs into one currency, which is then called the project control currency. This control currency is likely to be the currency that is in circulation in the country of the contractor's head office, but it might have to be a currency convenient to, and specified by, an overseas client. Whether or not the contractor wishes to disclose the exchange rates used in reaching the final cost estimates, the rates used for all conversions must be recorded on all estimate tabulations and similar internal documents.

Forecasting future changes to foreign exchange rates for the life of a project is a matter for skill, careful judgement and foresight. Even the most skilled estimator's efforts can be undone by unforeseeable political and economic events. The contractor might be able to achieve some hedging against these risks by inserting safeguards in the contract or by insisting that all quotations from foreign bidders are, wherever possible, made as firm prices in the project control currency.

SOURCES OF LABOUR ESTIMATES

Records from past projects have already been mentioned as a basis for comparative estimating. In some industries, particularly those associated with construction, published tables can be consulted. The London publisher Spon, for example, publishes pricing and estimating guides and updates them annually. Estimates of labour times where no previous records exist are more difficult to obtain. Theoretically, they are best made by the managers who will eventually be responsible for working within the resulting budget limits. But not everyone has good estimating ability.

PERSONAL ESTIMATING ABILITIES

Project cost estimating is not an exact science. Much of the process, particularly when estimating labour times, has to rely on the subjective judgement of individuals. If any ten people were to be asked separately to judge the time needed for a particular project task, it is hardly conceivable that ten identical answers would be received. Repeat this exercise with the same group of people for a number of different project tasks, and it is likely that a pattern will emerge. Some people will tend always to estimate on the low side. Others might give answers that are consistently high. The person collecting project cost estimates needs to be aware of this problem. In fact, just as it is possible to classify estimates according to confidence in their accuracy, so it is possible to classify the estimators themselves. I evolved the following classifications when dealing with estimates for design and manufacturing times on fairly large engineering projects.

1. *Optimistic estimators* usually understate the time required for tasks. A person asked to estimate the time needed for a design task might, for example, say 'three weeks' when the initial task will actually take four weeks. It is likely that still more work will be needed later on as corrections have to be made to the drawings (sometimes called after-issue work). Most estimators are optimists.
2. *Pessimistic estimators* always underestimate tasks. They demand too much time and too many resources. Such people might be seeking to build empires. Fortunately they are less common than the optimists.
3. *Inconsistent estimators* lack the capability and skill to understand what is required of a task.
4. *Accurate estimators* are too rare to be considered.

The person responsible for compiling the final project cost estimate will learn to recognize these personal characteristics, and associate them with particular people. It might be necessary to apply a correction factor to some of the raw estimates.

BELOW-THE-LINE COSTS

When the costs for every work package have been estimated, adding them all together should give the basic total cost for the project. However, additional costs have to be taken into account for most projects. So a line must be drawn under the basic total cost, and below that line two or three important additions are usually needed.

CONTINGENCY ALLOWANCES

A common source of estimating errors is the failure to appreciate that additional costs are almost bound to arise as the result of design errors, problems in the physical execution of the project, material and component failures, construction site difficulties and the like. The extent of these additional items will depend on many factors but performance on previous similar projects can give an indication of what to expect. For a straightforward project, not entailing undue risk, a contingency allowance of 5 per cent of the net project cost might be appropriate. It might have to be higher, but contingency allowances usually have to be applied with restraint in order to maintain competitive project pricing.

COST ESCALATION

Every year wages and salaries increase, many raw materials and bought-out components cost more, and indirect costs rise in a process that we all know as inflation. The effect on a project that is estimated, quoted and carried out within a short period is not likely to be significant in a country with a stable economy and low annual rate of inflation. In other cases, however, and especially for projects with a life-cycle covering several years, the effects of inflation can be significant. There are three complementary ways in which this problem can be tackled.

1. Validity of quoted prices must be time-limited, say for 90 days, to avoid the risk of cost inflation reducing the intended profit.
2. Another action for countering cost inflation is to write a cost escalation clause into the contract. The contractor should then be able to agree a price addition with the client if there are increases in wages and materials that are recognized as being outside the contractor's control.
3. A cost escalation allowance can be made below the line in the estimate. Depending on the method used, this can be quite a complex calculation. Once a percentage annual escalation rate has been agreed, the most accurate method is to look at each cost element in turn, decide when that cost is likely to be incurred, and then work out the probable additional costs according to the predicted elapsed time and the escalation rate.

PROVISIONAL ITEMS

It often happens, particularly in construction contracts, that the project contractor foresees the possibility of additional expense if certain pre-identified difficulties arise when work actually starts. For example, a client might specify that certain materials salvaged during demolition of a building are to be reused in the construction of a new replacement building. So, the cost of those materials should be free to the new project, they will not be included in the net project estimate and they will not be incorporated in the quoted price. However, the contractor might wish to make provision in case the salvaged materials are subsequently found to be unsuitable for reuse. To allow for that risk, a provisional item can be added below the line to cover the estimated cost of providing new materials. It is not unusual for a project proposal to include several items priced as provisional sums.

COST BUDGETS

The initial project budgets must be derived from the cost estimates used when the tender or internal project proposal was prepared. These denote the authorized level of expenditure for all departments engaged on the project. Ideally the departmental managers, even if they did not provide the cost estimate data, should have had prior opportunity to approve the estimates and accept commitment to them.

BUDGET BREAKDOWN

The total project budget should be distributed over the project work breakdown structure so that there is a specified budget for each work package and, within those work packages, a budget for each task. Each of these budget elements must have a unique cost code against which manpower timesheet data, material costs and all other direct expenses can be collected and accumulated. Now the benefits of a sensible and comprehensive coding system will become apparent, because the data can be filtered and sorted to provide budgets not only for work breakdown packages, but also for project departments and groups.

LABOUR BUDGETS

It is often said, with good reason, that managers should be given their work budgets in terms of man-hours rather than as the resulting costs of wages and overheads. The argument is that a manager should never be held accountable for meeting targets where he or she has no authority to control the causal factors. Project managers are rarely responsible for general increases in wages and salaries or for company overhead expenses. They are, however, responsible for progress and (through supervision) the time taken to complete each task. It is assumed here, therefore, that each manager will be given, and will be expected to observe, the man-hour budget for every work package under his or her control.

BUDGETS FOR PURCHASES AND SUBCONTRACTS

Budgets for purchases and for subcontracts have to be expressed in the appropriate project currency. Relevant packaging, transport, insurance, duties and tax must be included. When these budgets are set out as time-scaled graphs, there are three possible options on how the timing should be determined. Depending on which option is chosen, the graphs will be displaced in time by several months. The options are as follows:

1. The earliest option, with costs plotted at the times when the signing of a contract or the issue of a purchase order irrevocably commits the expenditure.
2. The middle option, timed when payments have to be made against suppliers' and subcontractors' invoices.
3. The final option, timed when the materials are withdrawn from stores for use on the project.

The first of these is most appropriate for cost control. The second is relevant to cash flow prediction and funding. The third is of more interest for historical cost accounting.

BUDGET ADJUSTMENTS FOR BELOW-THE-LINE ALLOWANCES

All budgets should initially be based on net project estimates, with below-the-line allowances excluded. Below-the-line items, especially contingencies, should be regarded as carefully guarded reserve budgets. Subject to an effective authorization procedure, appropriate sums can be 'drawn down' from these reserves from time to time to augment the control budget as legitimate needs arise.

BUDGET CHANGES

Budgets on most projects are not static. They often change through the life of a project. Budgets are amended, for example, each time a customer-requested change results in an agreed change to the project scope, condition and price. Project budgets and their various breakdown elements start from the original baseline condition, before work actually starts. As work proceeds, the budget has to be viewed in two parts, namely the amount released and approved for expenditure (called here the control budget) plus amounts held back in reserve. These reserves equate to the below-the-line items in the cost estimate. At any time it should be possible for the current approved control budget to be evaluated and reported in the following terms:

1. The original baseline cost estimate, excluding all provisions listed below the line.
2. The estimated cost of approved internal changes, funded by drawing down the relevant sums from the below-the-line contingency allowance. If that reserve is exhausted the profit will fall below target.
3. Additions to the original baseline estimates (with corresponding augmentation of the control budget) resulting from changes requested and paid for by the client. On rare occasions client requests can reduce the project scope, price and budgets.
4. Approved amounts drawn down from time to time from other below-the-line reserves, for example to cover cost inflation.

COST MONITORING USING SIMPLE GRAPHS

When project work starts, the project manager and others will want to know whether the rate of expenditure is in line with the plan. One common method is to draw a graph of budgeted costs against time and then compare the actual costs against it periodically.

DRAWING A TIME-SCALED BUDGET GRAPH

The simplest way to draw a budget graph is to consult the schedule to find the project's start and finish dates, assume that expenditure is zero at the start, put a point representing total expenditure on the completion date, and then join the project start and finish points with a straight line budget. That idea can obviously be dismissed at once because it makes the wrong assumption that expenditure will be linear with time. It is necessary, therefore, to examine the elements of a budget in more detail. Each work package or, better still, each task, should first be positioned in the timeframe by reference to the detailed project plan. Then, using a cumulative build up of budgeted costs, a curve can be plotted that should reflect more realistically the planned rate of expenditure.

Whenever authorized changes affect the project budget, the curve should be stepped up or down by the appropriate amounts at the relevant dates. Cumulative project expenditure typically follows an S-shaped curve, starting with a low rate, then moving through a centre period of high activity until, finally, the rate slows down and the curve becomes asymptotic to the final cost.

DATA SOURCES

Two things need to be said about the sources for the budget and actual cost data:

1. Care should be taken to ensure that the budget basis and actual cost basis correspond, so that like is compared with like. This applies not only to the selection of tasks or work packages, but also to the times when the relevant costs are to be considered.
2. The data sources must allow actual costs to be measured as soon as possible in the project life-cycle, so that adverse trends can be picked up in time for corrective action.

Direct labour costs should be considered as soon as the periodical time bookings can be analysed. Common practice is to collect and analyse time bookings weekly. The accounting system should be capable of allocating and costing these with little or no delay, provided there are no communication difficulties in collecting them. Any processing delay, at the outside, must not be allowed to exceed three or four days if the data are to be used effectively. Good project management software packages allow timesheet data to be entered directly for those working on the project, but care must always be taken to preserve the audit trail and ensure that times and cost codes entered are checked and approved.

Claims expected from contractors and subcontractors should be budgeted at the times when they are planned to arrive. This information can be found by comparing the relevant tasks on the project schedule and the terms of payment agreed for the contracts. The collection of actual cost data for these claims should be possible at any time by adding the value of payments already made to claims received but not yet processed. Some contractors, however, can be very late in submitting claims, in which case provisional allowances (accrued costs) will have to be added to the actual cost data to avoid errors of omission.

Purchases of materials and equipment must be budgeted to coincide with the planned purchase order issue dates. For comparison, committed rather than actual invoiced costs have to be collected and accumulated. This means adding the values of all purchase orders as they are issued. Although it is the resulting invoices that will determine the actual final costs, that information will not be available in time for use in any cost control decisions. Indeed, such invoices sometimes continue to arrive after project completion.

A SIMPLE EXAMPLE

The dotted curve in Figure 20.3 is an example of a planned cost curve (a time-scaled budget). This is for a construction project planned to last for 56 weeks with a net budget of £845,000. The curve has been plotted at four-weekly intervals. Now imagine that you are the manager of this project. You want to compare the actual project costs with the budget graph throughout the life of the project.

Your first task must be to establish the sources of your actual cost data. You should expect to receive direct labour cost reports from your cost accountant or your organization's project management information system after prompt analysis of the time booked by the personnel involved. For contractors' claims you will probably have the services of a project cost engineer, a contract administration department or a project support office. Your purchasing organization is likely to be the best source for the total value of materials and equipment costs committed at any given time.

Now consider Figure 20.3. Every four weeks you or, if you are fortunate, your administrative assistant plots the actual cumulative cost of the project on the same axes as your budget graph. It is now just past the end of week 28. You note, with satisfaction, that expenditure is running consistently below budget. The planned expenditure by the end of week 28 is £350,000 and the actual expenditure is only £280,000. There are managers who would be well satisfied with this state of affairs but what can *you* deduce from this? In fact, not a great deal. Only one thing is certain, which is that the project started late. Low spending at the start indicates insufficient input of resources in the very early weeks. To deduce more about the true cost performance at week 28 you need to know what has been achieved.

The significance of the S curve alone for assessing cost performance is, therefore, coarse and very limited. A method is needed that brings some measure

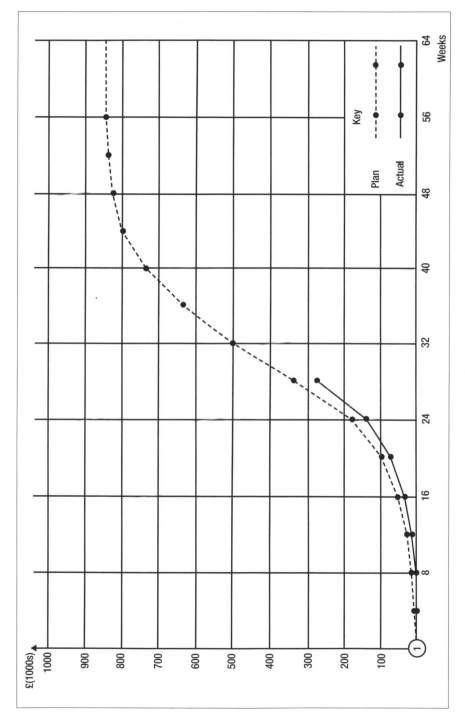

Figure 20.3 Comparison of actual costs against budget using simple graphs

393

of related achievement into the argument and which can provide answers to all the following questions:

- How much have we spent to date?
- What should we have spent to date?
- What have we achieved so far?
- What should we have achieved?
- What implication do the answers to these questions have for the final cost of the project?

Milestone monitoring can provide answers to at least some of these questions.

MILESTONE MONITORING

Milestone monitoring (or milestone analysis) is one of the simpler methods by which managers can compare actual costs and progress with a project budget and schedule of work. The method is neither the most effective nor the most detailed, but it has the merit of needing only a modest amount of effort to set up and maintain. It also has the advantage of being useful where the project plans and work breakdown structure are not available in great detail.

IDENTIFYING MILESTONES

The first step in milestone analysis is to identify the milestones. This is done by selecting certain key activities or events which lie at the boundaries between significant phases of the project. Put another way, a milestone denotes a particular, easily recognized stage in the progress of a project towards completion. The start and finish of the project are two obvious examples. Others might be the customer's acceptance of the final design, the issue of a package of drawings, or the day when work starts on a construction site.

Ideally, milestones should coincide with the completion of packages from the work breakdown structure. That approach will be assumed in the remainder of this discussion. For each milestone, two essential pieces of information are needed. These are:

1. The date for which the milestone is planned.
2. The associated budget cost. In the simplest method (described here) this is taken as the budgeted cost of all the project work and expenditure at the milestone date.

PLOTTING THE MILESTONE GRAPHS

The milestone/budget curve

With milestone data available, the milestone/budget curve can be plotted. There is more than one method for doing this, but the simplest is to start by drawing the time-scaled budget graph in the same way as in the previous example (the S curve in Figure 20.3). Then the date for each milestone can be indicated by placing a symbol at the relevant point on the graph. Graph legibility will be greatly enhanced if all the milestones are identified by simple codes. If, for example, the planned milestones are numbered 1, 2, 3, etc., the corresponding symbols on the graph can use the same numbers, so avoiding the clutter of too much data in a small space.

Plotting the actual results

Actual cumulative costs are plotted on the same axes as the milestone/budget curve. Symbols for completed milestones can be added to this actual cost graph on the dates when the milestones are achieved. To be able to plot these results for comparison against the plan, two facts must, therefore, be established for each completed milestone:

- The date on which the milestone was actually achieved
- The actual project expenditure incurred or committed up to that date

MILESTONE EXAMPLE

The simple example now described uses the same construction project and cost data as that introduced in the previous case. Figure 20.4 illustrates the milestone monitoring process. As in the previous case, the dotted curve represents the time-scaled budget and the solid line is the plotted actual expenditure up to the end of Week 28. Milestones (represented by the numbers in the circles) have been added to the budget curve at their planned times. Milestone achievement dates are shown by the black diamonds on the actual cost curve. The relevant milestone cost and progress data are set out separately in Figure 20.5.

INTERPRETING THE RESULTS

The best way to appreciate the use of this method is to imagine yourself, as project manager, observing the relationship between the planned and actual graphs as the project weeks go by. Your first reaction must be frustration caused by the late start of the project. In milestone language, Milestone 1 has been delayed by six weeks. However, it can be seen from the graphs, and from the table in Figure 20.5,

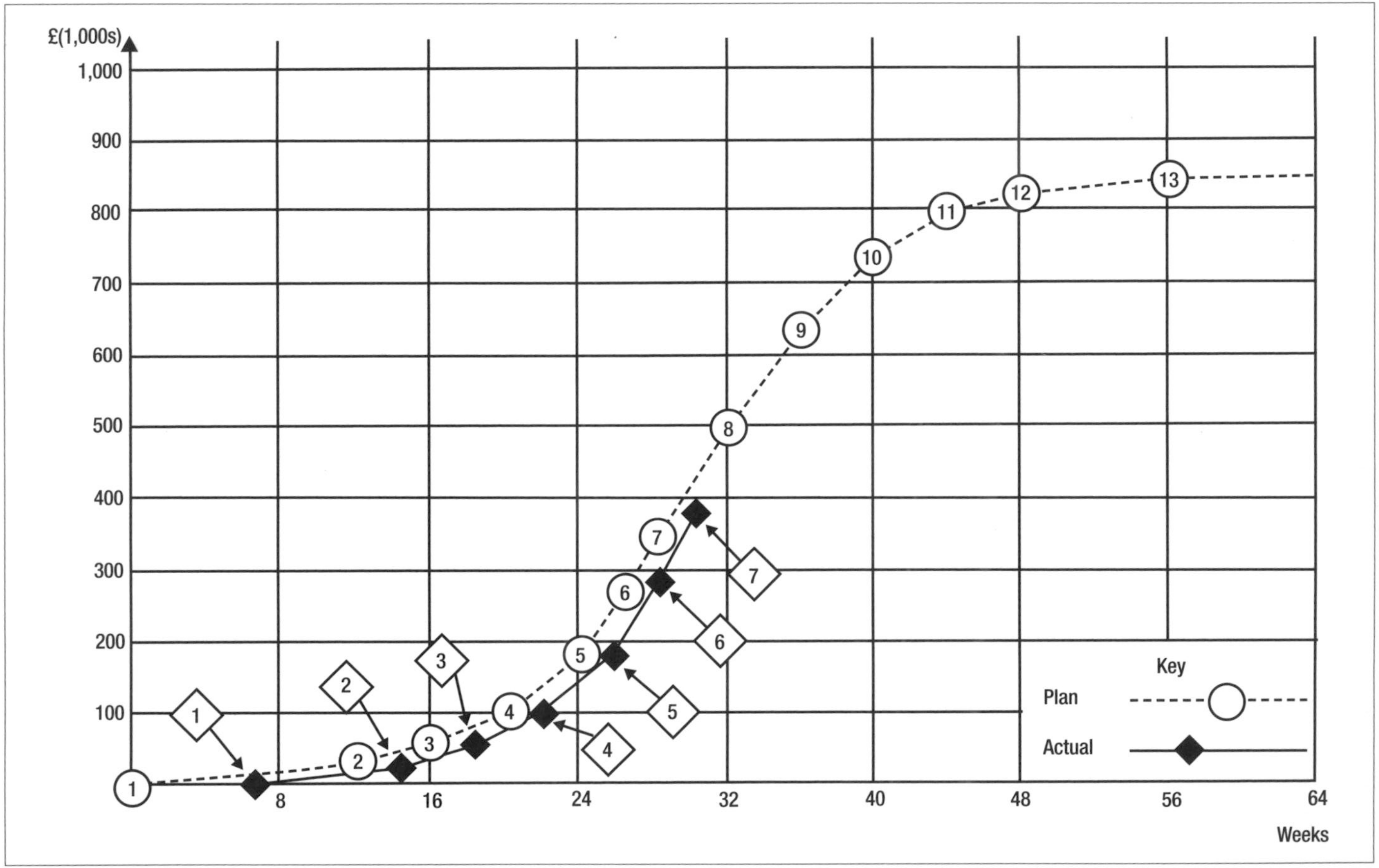

Figure 20.4 Comparison of actual costs against budget using milestones

Milestone description	Schedule (week number)		Cumulative cost £(1000s)	
	Plan	Actual	Budget	Actual
1 Project start authorized	0	6	0	0
2 Design approved	12	14	25	20
3 Drawings issued for building	16	18	60	55
4 Foundations completed	20	22	100	100
5 Drawings issued for services	24	26	180	180
6 All equipment for services ordered	26	28	275	285
7 Walls built to eaves	28	30	350	380
8 Windows and doors finished	32		500	
9 Roof on, building watertight	36		630	
10 Wiring and plumbing finished	40		730	
11 Services installed and tested	44		795	
12 Internal finishes completed	48		825	
13 Site and building handover	56		845	

Figure 20.5 Milestone data measured at Week 28 of the example

that progress has improved as the project proceeds. Four weeks of the initial slippage were recovered, so that milestone achievement dates are now generally falling two weeks behind schedule.

How do these results relate to costs? Although the graph of actual costs is running consistently below the budget line, comparison between the planned and actual milestone performance gives a more revealing picture. Look at Milestone 5. Although completed two weeks later than plan, the budgeted and actual costs are practically in line. The situation has deteriorated somewhat by the time Milestone 6 has been achieved. Now, not only is the programme running two weeks late, but the costs are starting to exceed those budgeted. At Milestone 7, the two-week lag remains and the actual cost to achieve this milestone has been £380,000 against a budget of £350,000. The graphs show that this divergence between planned and actual costs is increasing with time. Unless effective action can be taken to reverse this trend, the project is likely to be completed at no profit or even at a loss.

VALUE OF THE MILESTONE METHOD

The milestone method is not perfect. It is a compromise between attempting no comparison at all between planned and actual cost performance and committing the considerable effort needed for full scale earned value analysis (outlined in the following section of this chapter). The principal disadvantages of milestone analysis can be summarized as follows:

1. The quantities measured tend to be rather coarse, at intervals which might be too infrequent.
2. Analysis is historical rather than predictive, so that results may be obtained too late for the most effective action to be taken to reverse bad trends.
3. Work in progress is not properly considered, or is not considered at all.

However, the method involves comparatively little effort and is a considerable improvement on the simple comparison of actual and budget cost graphs. It may, therefore, be attractive and useful to the project manager who has insufficient time and resources for carrying out more detailed analysis and prediction.

COST REPORTING BASED ON EARNED VALUE

THE CONCEPT OF EARNED VALUE ANALYSIS

Earned value analysis is a method for comparing actual performance against planned performance in considerable analytical detail. As a predictive tool it can be regarded as the missing link between historical cost reporting and active cost management. There is more than one approach, but the procedure generally followed is outlined in Chapter 28.

At each review date the process aims to discover the true earned value achieved for all tasks completed or in progress. The results allow indices of cost and schedule performance to be calculated. The cost performance index (CPI) can be used to factor the baseline cost estimates for all remaining work (costs remaining to completion) on the assumption that the standard of cost performance measured up to the review date will continue unchanged to the end of the project.

REPORT TABULATION

Figure 20.6 shows a fairly typical layout for a project cost report based on earned value analysis. The number of pages in the complete document will depend on the size of the project but they should be grouped logically in sets according to the work breakdown structure. Page totals can then be summarized on a sheet for the total project, at the top level of the work breakdown, and it is only this summary (sometimes called a rolled-up summary) which is likely to be used in project cost reports to the more senior management. A column-by-column examination of the tabulation will explain the procedure in more detail.

Column A

The choice of items listed in this column will depend on where the particular page fits into the work breakdown structure. At the project summary level only the

PROJECT COST REPORT SUMMARY

Project title:

Project number:

Page   of

Report date:

A Item	B Cost code	C Original budget	D Authorized budget changes	E Authorized current budget C+D	F ACWP	G BCWP (assessed)	H CPI G/F	J Forecast costs remaining (E–G)/H	K Forecast costs at completion F+J	L Forecast variance at completion E–K
Sheet summary										

Figure 20.6   Project cost report summary based on earned values

major work packages are listed, but at the lowest level every task might have to be included.

Column B

The preferred choice for this column is to show the cost code for each item using the project contractor's own coding system. However, some clients expect to receive regular cost report summaries, particularly when the project manager and client work closely together in the periodical release of project funding by the client. Clients have an inconvenient habit of expecting to see cost codes from their systems, in which cases it might be necessary to arrange for both coding systems to be used side-by-side.

Column C

The original baseline budget for the project, before any changes, is shown in here. A decision has to be made as to whether this will include any below-the-line allowances. Usually it is safer to exclude these until they are drawn down as authorized budget changes.

Column D

This column is used to show the total budget changes authorized up to the report date. These changes might arise from the release of amounts held in reserve as contingencies or other below-the-line estimates but most usually come from authorized changes requested by the customer or client.

Column E

This column gives the current total authorized budget. This should be the original baseline budget plus amounts authorized by subsequent customer-funded changes and releases of below-the-line allowances.

Column F

The actual cost of work performed (ACWP) is entered here. For each item this usually means all direct labour and expenses used up to the review date, plus the total value of all purchase orders issued, and the value of any contractors' claims paid or awaiting payment. These costs must be entered for all items that have incurred costs, whether or not they are completed. Thus these costs include work in progress.

Column G

The entries in Column G require careful attention. For each item the budgeted cost of work performed (BCWP) is wanted, measured at the review date. For any item, one of three conditions might apply:

1. Work may not have been started, so that no value has been earned and BCWP is zero.
2. The item might be finished, in which case its full value has been earned. The BCWP for a completed item is equal to its current authorized budget (column E).
3. For every item which has been started but not finished, the earned value must be assessed. There are several methods, but one way is to judge the percentage completion for the item. The BCWP can then be taken as that percentage of the current authorized budget.

Column H

This column is optional and is often not used. When the BCWP is divided by the corresponding actual cost of work performed ACWP a cost performance index (CPI) is obtained. This is an indicator of how efficiently money is being spent on each item. A CPI of less than one means that the assessed earned value is less than the costs so far incurred.

Column J

When £40,000 has been spent on a task out of a total budget of £100,000 a reasonable question to ask is 'How much will the work remaining cost? Will it exceed or lie within the £60,000 budget remaining?' This question should be asked for every item and for the whole project. Here are three conditions that could apply to any item.

1. The item has not started. There is no earned value. The costs remaining should, therefore, be the whole of the authorized budget. If, however, the average CPI for the entire project is less than one, indicating overspending, the project administrator might decide to divide this item's baseline budget by the CPI to make a more realistic prediction of the expected cost to complete. This is not, of course, an increase in the authorized budget. It is simply a way of attempting to face and report facts. If current performance on other tasks is taken as the norm, this task too is likely to exceed its budget.
2. The item is finished. In that case there should be no cost remaining.
3. The item is in progress. The first step in deciding the remaining cost is to start with the value earned to date (BCWP) and subtract that from the total value (the current budget). That gives the remaining value to be earned. That figure

401

must be divided by the CPI to adjust the remaining estimate in the light of the cost performance being experienced.

Column K

Adding the forecast costs remaining to completion and the costs actually incurred to date should predict the total final cost.

Column L

This column shows the difference (variance) between the authorized current budget and the predicted final cost.

EFFECTIVENESS OF THE EARNED VALUE METHOD

It is easy to place too much reliance on earned value analysis predictions. Results are likely to be flawed for several reasons. Here are some:

- It is difficult to assess accurately the amount of work achieved on many kinds of task.
- Difficulty is greatest when a task has just started, so prediction errors will be greatest at the time they are most needed, which is early enough for corrective action to be effective.
- The project manager will find it difficult to get everyone's cooperation in supplying complete and reasonably accurate data at the review dates.
- A considerable amount of clerical effort is needed to maintain the database and carry out the calculations. It is unlikely that such effort will be free of errors.
- If a computer is used to process the data, rubbish can easily result. Suppose work on a particular task is scrapped. The BCWP and CPI for that task both revert to zero at the point where the task is stopped and restarted. Dividing the remaining budget by the CPI gives infinity. So the project administrator must choose a different basis for calculating the CPI. One option is to calculate the CPI for the whole project and use that.

These observations are not intended to deter the reader from implementing an earned value system, but the difficulties in making it work should be realized.

REFERENCES AND FURTHER READING

Barnes, M., 1990, *Financial Control*, London: Thomas Telford.
Bull, J.W., 1992, *Life-cycle Costing for Construction*, London: Blackie Academic.
Carter, R., and Wheeler, R., 1995, *How to Cut Costs by 20%*, London: Kogan Page.

Fleming, Q.W. and Koppelman, J.M., 2000, *Earned Value Project Management*, 2nd edition, Upper Darby, PA: Project Management Institute.

George, D.J., (ed), 1988, *A Guide to Capital Cost Estimating,* 3rd edition*,* Rugby: Institution of Chemical Engineers.

Smith, N.J., (ed), 1995, *Project Cost Estimating*, London: Thomas Telford.

Stewart, R., 1991, *Cost Estimating,* 2nd edition, New York: Wiley.

Sweeting, J., 1997, *Project Cost Estimating: Principles and Practices,* Rugby: Institution of Chemical Engineers.

Wearne, S.H., 1989, *Control of Engineering Projects*, London: Thomas Telford.

21 Managing Resources

Dennis Lock

Project planning cannot usually be considered complete until all activities have been scheduled to take account of the organization's resources. The aim should be to plan so that these resources are never impossibly overloaded nor left wastefully idle, while attempting to finish every project on or before its required completion date. This can be a complex process. The ideal schedule may not always be achievable, but this chapter offers some guidelines and techniques that can help to schedule resources sensibly and efficiently.

WHAT RESOURCES TO SCHEDULE

In addition to time, the resources used by most projects include materials, accommodation, cash, plant and labour. A proposed project to redevelop the centre of the Dutch town of Utrecht was not able to proceed, because there was just not enough of one resource, and that was road capacity to remove rubble from the demolition site. We start by considering who needs to schedule resources, and which resources they can and should schedule using the methods described here.

WHO NEEDS TO SCHEDULE RESOURCES?

Responsibility for scheduling resources may belong to the project manager, or it could be a problem for someone else in the management chain. The person who acts only as project management consultant or adviser may be able to leave resource scheduling (with the probable exception of cash flow) to the contractors and subcontractors who directly employ the people to do the work. A managing contractor for a construction project will have to schedule work for the head office engineering staff but, again, can leave the day-to-day scheduling of most direct labour to the relevant subcontractors. In the case of the town of Utrecht mentioned above, it was the project management consultant who was scheduling road capacity, but the project never progressed beyond the feasibility stage.

Companies most likely to benefit from detailed project resource scheduling are those which employ professional or skilled direct labour in significant numbers. If temporary staff with the requisite skills can be engaged readily at short notice, scheduling may simply be a process of assessing future numbers (a crude form of manpower planning). The most complex and difficult resource allocation problems are found in those organizations where the labour force is largely permanent (and, therefore, relatively stable and inflexible) and where the people have valuable skills, training and experience that are peculiar to the company and its work.

RESOURCES THAT CAN BE SCHEDULED USING PROJECT MANAGEMENT TECHNIQUES

Most examples in this chapter are illustrated using direct labour examples, where the resources are people with particular skills. The same techniques can, however, be applied to any other type of resource that is quantifiable in terms of simple units or numbers. These techniques can therefore be used to schedule hire plant, bulk materials, machine time, process plant capacities, or even road capacity. Accommodation is one possible exception because it is not a resource that can always be described and calculated adequately in terms of simple units of area, such as square metres. Area shape, height, means of access, lighting, power supplies and other services, materials handling facilities, floor loading, may have to be taken into account. In planning the use of assembly bays for the assembly and test of large machines, for example, one machine can sometimes be allowed to overhang another. This is just one example of circumstances where different projects may be able to share common floor space. Such problems cannot be solved by simple arithmetic, but may need three-dimensional drawings, physical scale models or a dynamic computer-aided design system.

RESOURCES THAT SHOULD BE SCHEDULED USING PROJECT MANAGEMENT TECHNIQUES

It is usually a mistake to try to schedule every resource to be used on a project. That leads to unnecessary complication, and just one attempt at the monumental amount of work needed will probably be enough to deter the planner from ever trying it again. Consider, for example, an engineering department which designs special purpose machinery. The department is handling a continuous workflow for several projects. The engineering manager knows, from experience, that for every ten engineers working on mechanical design, one instrumentation engineer is needed to design the supporting pipework and lubrication systems. In this case, it may only be necessary to schedule the mainstream engineers. If 100 engineers are going to be needed, the manager knows that ten instrumentation engineers must be provided to support them. This approach, which I have used myself successfully, can be extended to many other types of resources (for example, inspection personnel in relation to machine operators, paint oven capacity in relation to sheet metal machine capacity and so on). Similar arguments usually apply to most indirect staff, such as print room operators, purchasing clerks, and those involved in the more general administrative and management activities. The old expression KISS – Keep It Simple, Stupid – applies. Do not attempt to schedule everything, but concentrate on the scarce or key resources and let their dependent resources fall into place.

RESOURCE SCHEDULING PRINCIPLES

RESOURCE AGGREGATION

The practice of resource scheduling can be introduced by considering the case of just one department within an organization that is carrying out a project to build a chemical processing plant. The department concerned is responsible for pipefitting. The time data for these activities have been derived from a network diagram for the complete project. In practice, of course, all the other activities in the network would have to be scheduled, involving several other departments and resource types.

The upper part of Figure 21.1 shows a fragment of a bar chart. This has been derived from the project network, but has been edited so that it includes only pipe-fitting activities associated with the main plant control panel. For simplicity it has been assumed that each activity on the network will need one pipe-fitter for the whole of its duration. Every activity has been shown starting at its earliest possible time, as determined by network critical path analysis. The hatched extensions shown after some of the bars indicate the amount of total float available. The figures at the foot of the bar chart show the number of pipe-fitters needed each day to fulfil this schedule. This usage requirement is displayed to better effect by the histogram in the lower half of Figure 21.1.

This schedule has been obtained by the simple addition of resources with no regard to their availability. The process is, therefore, known as resource aggregation. It is common for managers to rely on such schedules, hoping optimistically to be able to start each task at its earliest possible time predicted by the network. The pattern of work, however, is going to be far from satisfactory in practice, with alternating high peak loads and relatively idle periods. If the department in our project has only two pipefitters, the schedule is impossible.

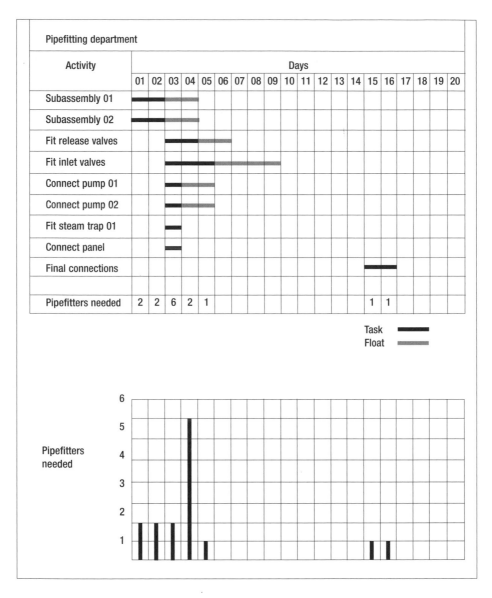

Figure 21.1 Resource aggregation example

RESOURCE SCHEDULING

Figure 21.2 shows the same tasks as those displayed in Figure 21.1. However, some of the tasks have been deliberately delayed by the planner, but not to the extent that their times will exceed the amount of total float available. Now the work pattern expected from the pipefitters has become far more satisfactory. The

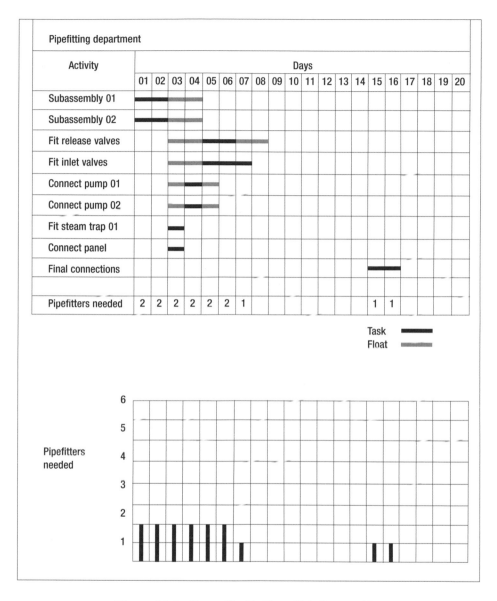

Figure 21.2   The workload in Figure 21.1 after smoothing

peaks and troughs have been smoothed out. Attempts to obtain acceptable resource schedules are variously called resource smoothing, resource allocation, resource scheduling or resource optimization. These terms are not quite synonymous: the smoothing or optimization process aims at a more perfectly smooth result than the simpler scheduling or allocation procedure. Most computer systems will not produce the smoothest possible work patterns but the results are likely to be acceptable and practicable, especially when it is remembered that all planning and scheduling relies at heart on estimates that are largely subjective and, in many cases, open to question.

USE OF CHARTS

It is easy to imagine the scheduling process, at least at the basic level just described, as being conducted by clerical or simple charting methods. An adjustable bar chart can be used, with task strips coloured to represent different resource types. The chart, probably mounted on a wall, allows the positions of all the strips to be adjusted, perhaps using slots, a plug-in grid, or magnetic adhesion. Such charts were once common for planning departmental workloads, both for workpeople and for various processing facilities (such as machines in a workshop). Although charts are still an option to be considered in extremely simple circumstances (departmental holiday charts are an obvious case) they cease to be of any value when the amount of data to be considered is too great. Unlike a critical path network, it is not usually possible to show all the logical constraints between jobs on an adjustable chart and this is likely to lead to scheduling errors. Once the planner attempts to use more than a few different colours for coding, or tries to plan more than about 50 different tasks, the whole thing becomes tedious to set up, difficult to interpret, and exceedingly difficult to reschedule. In the remainder of this chapter it must be assumed that the planner has access to a suitable computer system.

THE ROLE OF CRITICAL PATH NETWORKS IN RESOURCE SCHEDULING

To obtain a smooth resource schedule, it will be necessary to delay the start of some activities beyond their earliest possible times. When a person or a computer attempts to match the planned start and finish dates for any activity with the allocation of resources, there are several questions that must be considered with respect to the project's critical path network:

1. What other activities must be completed before this activity can start?
2. What is the earliest date this activity could start, assuming that resources are available?
3. If there is a shortage of resources, for how long could this activity be delayed without affecting the project completion date?
4. If there are other activities requiring the same scarce resource at the same time, which of these should be started at once and which could be delayed until the resource again becomes available? In other words, which activity has the highest priority?

410

FLOAT AS A DETERMINANT OF PRIORITY

Critical path analysis will determine how much float each activity has at the start of the project. This float information is vital to the subsequent resource scheduling process. Activities with float can be delayed, until their latest permissible dates if necessary, if resources are not available for them. Critical activities must be started at their earliest possible dates if the project is to be finished at its earliest possible time. When two or more activities are competing for the same scarce resource, it is the activity with least remaining float that must be given priority. The term remaining float is not in general use, but it is nonetheless significant and deserves explanation. If, during the resource scheduling process, the planned start of an activity is delayed, the total float of subsequent activities on the same network path will be depleted as a consequence, to become instead the remaining float.

RELATIONSHIP BETWEEN NETWORK LOGIC CONSTRAINTS AND RESOURCE CONSTRAINTS

When a network is first drawn, the planner will have plenty to do identifying all the activities needed, specifying the logical constraints between them, estimating durations and carrying out time analysis. It is not possible to consider all potential resource constraints at that time, owing to the complexity of the task and the unsuitability of critical path networks for that purpose. It is always sensible to defer consideration of resource scheduling until after the network logic has been determined and time analysis has been carried out. A planner who happens to know that a particular resource is scarce might be tempted to introduce special logic constraints to the network logic but that temptation should always be resisted. Suppose, for example, a project organization employs only one instrument fitter, and that ten instrument fitting activities are scattered throughout the network. The planner could ensure that no two of these activities could be scheduled in parallel by the simple expedient of linking them all in series. However, that would indeed be a foolish approach, for the following reasons:

- How can the planner know in advance the best sequence in which all the instrument fitting activities, lying on different paths of the network, should take place?
- What would the addition of extra links, purely for the consideration of resource constraints, do to the main body of the network logic?
- How would the planner be able to remember all those resource constraints if the network had to be changed?
- What would happen if resource availability levels changed? Again the planner would be faced with an impossibly complex rescheduling task.

411

The critical path network is therefore not usually the appropriate place for dealing with constraints arising from resource limitations. However there are exceptions.

EXCEPTIONS TO THE RULE

Although resource scheduling is usually an exercise that follows network analysis as a separate process, there are cases where the allocation and availability of resources will affect the initial network diagram and the estimated durations of some activities.

Consider, for instance, an activity on a project network diagram that requires one or more fitters to assemble a complex piece of electromechanical equipment. Suppose that the planner has been given the options shown in Figure 21.3 to help in estimating the duration of this activity. Which of these options should the planner use? The optimum solution appears to be to plan for the use of two fitters, who should be able to finish the job in three weeks. The use of more than two fitters would shorten that estimated duration, but at the expense of reduced efficiency and increased cost. So the planner should enter an estimated duration of two weeks for this activity and record that it will need two fitters. This is one case where resource considerations have correctly been taken into account at the early stages of network planning.

Number of fitters	Time needed for assembly (weeks)	Works content (man-weeks)
1	6.0	6.0
2	3.0	6.0
3	2.5	7.5
4	2.0	8.0
5	1.5	9.0

Figure 21.3 Scheduling data for a complex activity

We know that other activities in the network are also going to need fitters for various durations at times that are as yet unscheduled and therefore unknown. Quite possibly, two or more activities needing the same fitters will be scheduled at coincident or overlapping times. The planner cannot and should not consider those other demands on the fitters when the network diagram is compiled. The problem of resource overload caused by other activities competing for the resource at the same time can be resolved later, by the quite separate procedure of resource scheduling.

Now suppose that the planner has been told that cost is less important than completing this project in the shortest possible time. If this assembly activity is found to lie on the critical path, it might be thought justifiable to increase the number of fitters planned for this task to be increased from two to nine, regardless of the increase in cost from six man-weeks to nine man-weeks. The planner knows, however, that only five fitters are employed in the entire company and it can generally be assumed that, at any given time, one or other of those will either be absent or doing non-project work. So the planner would be foolish to plan for the use of nine fitters on an activity where it is apparent that only four fitters are available in the whole organization. The planner would, therefore, enter an estimated duration of two weeks for this activity on the network diagram, and note that the number of fitters required for this activity will be four. So, although resource scheduling across the project or the organization cannot be considered when each individual project network plan is made, common sense will determine the number of resources to be allocated to each activity.

SPECIFYING THE RESOURCES NEEDED FOR EACH ACTIVITY

This example illustrates that a preliminary step in resource allocation is to consider each network activity in turn and estimate not only its duration, but also the number of units of each resource type needed to complete the activity within that duration. This means that the planner must (usually in conjunction with the relevant line managers) make a number of tactical decisions in which a balance is struck between planned activity durations and the numbers and types of resource required. These decisions should be recorded on the network diagram so that the data can be used later for input to the computer for resource scheduling and to ensure that the original tactical intentions are followed when the work actually takes place. To save clerical effort and to make best use of the limited space for showing data on the network it is usual to allocate a short code for each resource type. To give an example, BL might be used to indicate bricklayers and BM for bricklayers' mates or labourers. Then if, for instance, an activity is estimated to last for five days, needing two bricklayers and two labourers, the planner need enter only 5D 2BL 2BM on the network diagram.

CONFLICT BETWEEN PROJECT TIME AND RESOURCE LIMITS

During the resource allocation process, it is often found that the resources available will not allow work to take place fast enough to complete the project within its target timescale. (I assume, for simplicity, that this target timescale is equivalent to the duration of the network critical path, the shortest possible time in which the project can logically be finished given ample resources). Figure 21.4 illustrates the problem. The project is depicted as a balloon containing the

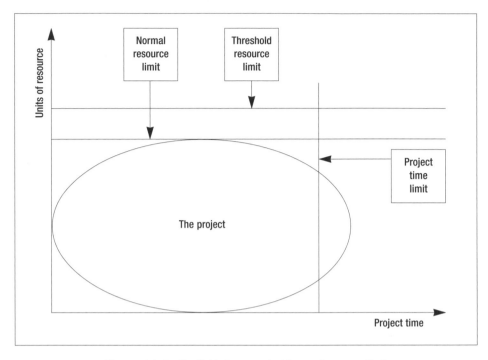

Figure 21.4   Conflict between project time and resource limits

resources. The resources can be regarded as an incompressible liquid so that the balloon can be changed in shape but its volume will remain constant. A project that uses resources is bounded by two principal limits, namely the level of resources available and the required project completion time. If the project timescale is reduced, (for example, if the client wants the project finished earlier), the time limit can be moved to the left until it hits the earliest possible time indicated by the network. However, the balloon will then be squeezed upwards to require a higher rate of resource usage. If, for any reason, the amount of resources available has to be reduced, then the balloon will be squashed flatter, and the project timescale must be extended to accept a later project completion date.

This argument gives rise to the terms 'resource-limited schedule' and 'time-limited schedule'. The planner often has to decide or be told which option is the more important: keeping within available resources at the risk of running late, or running to time at the possible expense of having to hire extra resources. The computer system should prompt the planner to state whether time-limited or resource-limited rules apply before running the programme.

THRESHOLD RESOURCES

The use of threshold resources is one solution to the problem of a time-limited schedule where the known levels of available resources might prove to be inadequate. A simple case will illustrate the concept of threshold resources. Suppose that the number of test technicians normally available for project work is five. The planner will therefore set up the project in the computer system, and specify the availability of test technicians as five. The planner, however, has doubts that this number of technicians will be able to complete a new project in time and these doubts are confirmed when the time-limited schedule is first processed by the computer. The planner knows that three more senior (and therefore more highly paid) test technicians could be called in from another part of the organization to assist at times of crisis. Some computer programmes will allow the planner to specify these additional technicians as a threshold resource. The threshold resource will be held in reserve, and allocated by the computer only when activities would otherwise be delayed past their latest permissible finish times. Other sources of additional labour resources might be from external subcontractors, agencies supplying temporary personnel or by expecting existing personnel to work extended hours or overtime (this last option is not to be recommended except in emergencies).

SPLITTABLE ACTIVITIES

Activities can be specified as splittable or non-splittable. A splittable activity is one that can be interrupted and restarted later to release scarce resources temporarily for another activity that has higher priority. The split activity will be resumed later when resources are again available. The default condition of most software will regard all activities as non-splittable.

SCHEDULING PROJECT RESOURCES WITH A COMPUTER

Practically every project management programme has some sort of useful resource scheduling capability. Many programmes are capable of excellent all round performance and there is generally something to suit every project requirement and every purse. Advertisements announcing improved versions of existing programmes and completely new products are regularly seen in project management journals. However, it always pays to check out the more extravagant claims made in advertising material before committing time and money to a purchase, so that hard facts can be separated from optimistic fiction. For example, one particularly irresponsible software advertisement, appearing in a respected publication, proclaimed triumphantly 'If you can move a mouse you can manage a project.'

415

Most modern programmes operate in the Microsoft Windows environment and therefore share many characteristics. However, these programmes vary greatly in their general approach, method of use, capacity, capability and flexibility. Some are relatively simple and can be put to work almost immediately, while those at the higher, professional end of the market need operators who have had at least some training. The remainder of this chapter must be written in general terms, and some of the features or characteristics described here will not apply to every available software package.

INITIAL DATA PROCESSING

The first significant step in scheduling is time analysis. The computer digests the network input data and, on command, attempts time analysis. Backward and forward passes are made through the network and the computer will log any obvious input data errors and omissions, such as dangles and loops. Dangles are caused when links are omitted in error, so that activities are left dangling, like start or finish activities. Loops are created when the planner inadvertently places a link in the wrong direction, which in some cases can result in a path that is a continuous loop. When all known errors have been cleared, valid time analysis data can be calculated and written to the database. The following information is among that which will now be on file for each activity record:

- The activity ID (from the network)
- Activity description
- Duration
- Earliest possible start
- Latest permissible start
- Earliest possible finish
- Latest permissible finish
- Free float
- Total float
- Resources needed, by type and quantity
- Activity cost (either as a specified activity cost or as a derivative of the number of resource units multiplied by unit cost rates)
- Various codes allocated by the planner for later use in filtering and sorting data for reports

Although resource allocation is a separate, subsequent process after initial time analysis, modern computer systems are so fast in operation that the whole time analysis/resource allocation process can appear seamless.

PRIORITY RULES

The planner may be asked to specify a priority rule to be applied at the activity level. The range of options depends on the software used. A useful choice is to give highest priority to activities with least remaining float. Remaining float is the amount of total float left for an activity after the resource scheduling process has caused its planned start to be delayed.

SPECIFYING AVAILABILITY LEVELS

The input data for any software package will include the establishment of a resources file, which lists all resource types and their availabilities and cost rates. For each resource type, the planner will be prompted to enter normal and threshold availability levels. These levels may vary as time proceeds, so that, for example, 10 instrument technicians might be specified as the number available from 1 January 2008 to 30 June 2008, 11 from 1 July 2008 to 31 December 2008, and so on. A cost rate per unit of time can be given for each resource, with different levels for normal and threshold quantities, and these cost rates can also be varied for different time periods when competent software is used.

Some caution is needed in deciding the availability levels that should be declared. It has to be remembered that not all people in a typical department will be able to work on projects at any given time. Some will be ill, some on holiday, some away on training courses and so on. Others might be working on jobs that could not have been planned, such as rework from earlier projects or small but urgent tasks for customers. In short, there will always be unplanned activities or other reasons why the total workforce cannot be used for project work. My own solution to this problem has always been to reserve a small percentage of each resource for these unplannable activities (it might be 15 per cent) and to reduce the amount available for project work accordingly. If, for instance, there is a department of 60 engineers, all capable of doing similar work, the planner would specify only 51 as being available as the normal resource level for all project work.

Alternative resources

A resource that is in short supply can sometimes be augmented or substituted by specifying a different resource; accepting the alternative would not be the preferred first choice on grounds of cost or efficiency. For example, in a project using both senior and junior engineers, one or more senior engineers might be persuaded to do urgent work that was originally scheduled for junior engineers to ease a temporary overload. Substitution possibilities such as this can be specified in advance with one or two of the higher-level software packages.

417

OUTPUT REPORTS FROM RESOURCE SCHEDULING

Various reports can be produced from the resource schedule.

WORK-TO LISTS

All readers who use project management software will be familiar with the typical time analysis tabulation that can be obtained from computer scheduling, an example of which is shown in the upper half of Figure 21.5. Imagine that this contains all the project activities to be carried out by electricians. The usual practice is to exclude, by filtering, all activities that have no relevance to the electrical department. The electricians' activities can be sorted in one of several ways, earliest possible start dates in ascending sequence being very commonly used. When given such reports, the electrical department manager will attempt to issue work at the earliest start dates, but must hold some activities back if all the electricians are otherwise occupied. Because time analysis reports are calculated with no regard to resource loading, their use as control tools can be a hit and miss affair.

The lower half of Figure 21.5 shows a report format that is typical of a work schedule produced after resource scheduling. The result is, at first sight, similar to the simple time analysis tabulation in the upper half of the figure and it will certainly list the same activities. The important difference is that the manager is given a set of scheduled start and finish dates for all project work for the department. These dates should be feasible and achievable working times because they have been calculated by the computer after consideration of the electricians as a resource. In other words, the computer is issuing work to the department at a rate commensurate with the resources available to the department manager.

OTHER REPORTS

Many other reports, tabular and graphic, can be obtained from a resource scheduling programme, especially if cost rates are given for each resource, and where estimated costs are specified for activities such as the purchasing of materials. Many of these reports can be printed using multiple colours and three-dimensional affects. These reports can include:

- A table listing the quantity of each type of resource needed for the project, spelled out day by day, week by week, or for whichever duration units apply. Such reports can have a column for the daily estimated project costs, and can also show cumulative cost totals that increase with time until they flatten out at

TIME ANALYSIS

Test project.	Project number 1234						Report date	15 Jan 2005	
Department:	Electricians						Time now	17 Jan 2005	
								Page 1	

ID	Activity description	Duration	Early start	Late start	Early finish	Late finish	Free float	Total float	Activity cost

All activities for the electrical department listed here, sorted by order of early start date

WORK-TO LIST

Test project.	Project number 1234						Report date	15 Jan 2005	
Department:	Electricians						Time now	17 Jan 2005	
								Page 1	

ID	Activity description	Duration	Early start	Scheduled start	Scheduled finish	Late finish	Remaining flcat	Resources

All activities for the electrical department listed here, sorted by order of scheduled start date

Figure 21.5 Time analysis and work-to lists compared

419

the scheduled project completion date to indicate the estimated total direct project cost;

- Resource histograms (see Figure 21.2)
- Cash flow schedules (which need special network diagramming skills);
- Time/cost graphs
- Bar charts, using scheduled dates (a graphic form of the work-to lists)

SOME RESOURCE TIMING PROBLEMS

Every project management programme is governed by one or more working calendars. A default calendar is usually applied to every activity, but a different calendar can be specified where this is appropriate for certain activities. Some software also allows different calendars to be applied to resources.

THE DEFAULT CALENDAR

The simplest calendar case is the default calendar. This will probably be specified as five eight-hour weekdays (Monday to Friday), with no work possible at weekends. This means that the computer will not include weekend days in time analysis calculations or reports for any activity, unless a different calendar is specified for that activity. The default calendar means that an activity with an estimated duration of 10 days will be shown as taking two calendar weeks. Weekend dates will simply not appear in any schedule and resource usage will be confined to weekdays. The default calendar can and should be modified by the planner so that, in addition to weekends, public holidays are designated as non-working dates.

USE OF SPECIAL CALENDARS

Adherence to the default calendar is adequate for many projects but it can produce anomalies. One example would be for an activity labelled 'allow concrete to cure'. If the preceding activity were to be timed for concrete to be poured on a Friday, the default calendar would (illogically) not allow curing to begin until the following Monday because weekend days are simply invisible for scheduling. Such problems can be solved by introducing a special calendar that does include all seven days of the week and, for this special case of concrete curing, all public holidays. Every non-default calendar will need a short filing code, so suppose we call this special every day of the year Calendar 02. Then it is simply necessary to assign Calendar 02 when any activity record for concrete curing is created during data input. However, that will not solve every problem, because some activities

420

might need weekend working but no work on public holidays. So another calendar, coded 03, can be created that includes all seven days of each week but not public holidays.

If the organization shuts down completely for an annual holiday (such as during the wakes weeks of some towns in the northern English counties), a special calendar can be created with the relevant weekdays remove, and this calendar would be used only for activities carried out within the organization.

All good project management software allows the planner to set up and file many different calendars, each with its own identifying file code. Some systems allow the creation of separate holiday calendars.

Allowance for public holidays in international projects

An international project will have activities performed in countries with different public holidays and religious festivals. This scheduling difficulty is easily overcome by setting up a special calendar file for each country and then allocating the appropriate calendar to every activity where the default calendar is inappropriate.

Allowance for individual holidays

There are several ways of dealing with the scheduling problem of staff (resources) who will be absent at varying times for their personal annual leave. There is at least one very sophisticated project management software suite that will allow a personal staff file to be set up for every individual in the organization. The file can include all kinds of data, including personal skills (in other words, the resource category), cost rate, employment history and their planned holiday dates. However, that method is far from common, and beyond the capabilities of most project management software. Moreover, it tends to place responsibilities on the project administration function that should more rightly be those of the human resources department. The usual practical approach is to allow for staff holidays as a blanket reduction in the number of resources declared as available.

Shift working

Some organizations operate two- or three-shift working for some of their staff, while other people in the same organization work at normal office hours. This is another case where the introduction of multiple calendars can solve the problem. The planner must set up different calendars for activities that can take place outside normal daytime working hours, and then ensure that those activities are assigned to their correct calendars.

RATE CONSTANCY

The most common method for specifying resource requirements when each activity record is set up in the computer is to regard the application of each resource as constant throughout the duration of that activity. The planner will then be presented with this as the default, rate constant, option. Thus, when an activity has been estimated with a duration of five days and needing one labourer, the assumption is that one labourer will be employed on the activity constantly from start to finish for all five days. Even if the resource usage varies somewhat during the course of the activity, the rate constant option will probably be an acceptable compromise because any slight error would be swamped by all the other labouring activities in the total project.

Some software allows for non rate-constant planning. For example, a ten-day activity for bricklaying might need one bricklayer for the first day, two bricklayers for the next seven days, and one bricklayer for the final two days. However, I have always found this software feature to be unnecessary and avoidable because, unless the number of activities needing bricklayers (or any other type of resource) is very small, the day-to-day variations for individual activities will smooth out in the total calculation.

MULTI-PROJECT SCHEDULING

Most organizations work on several projects simultaneously (see Chapters 3, 4 and 8). The projects might be at different locations and would almost certainly be represented by logically independent network diagrams. Such projects typically require resources to be provided from a common pool. Engineers, designers, laboratory facilities and corporate resources are all examples of common resources. All these projects therefore interact with each other in their demand for resources and this increases the complexity of resource scheduling.

It might be considered possible to schedule an individual project by setting aside resources specially for that project. This, however, would introduce the need for arbitrary decisions and lead to inflexible and wasteful use of resources across the total programme of projects. Multi-project scheduling (part of programme management) is the best approach to solving this problem. A detailed analysis of the way systems are used was given in Chapter 8. Here we focus on the resource scheduling issues. The method involves planning all projects in a computer model of the organization, where all relevant resources are scheduled and allocated to projects according to a set of rules specified by the planner and followed by the software. Provided suitable software is used, the process is relatively straightforward and should not be beyond the ability of any planner capable of scheduling resources for a single project.

PROJECT PRIORITIES IN A MULTI-PROJECT MODEL

When several projects are being scheduled against common resources, the question of the relative priorities of these projects must arise. There are several different ways of assigning priorities to projects. Two are discussed here.

Using target project completion dates as the driver

In the ideal multi-project model, priorities should fall out automatically if each project is given a target start date and target completion date. Then, even though there are unlikely to be any logical network connections between the different projects, all the time analysis data held on the common database can be used by the computer when deciding which competing activity should receive first claim on a scarce resource. It may be enough to consider the total float of the individual activities in the projects as being the criterion upon which they are scheduled. This is adequate if the projects are of roughly equivalent importance, so that a critical item in project A carries the same priority as a critical item in project B which shares the same start date. If this is not so, a process known as 'residual scheduling' may be appropriate.

Residual scheduling

Here, the projects to be scheduled are taken one by one. All activities of the highest priority project are scheduled before any of the second priority project. The second priority project uses those resources remaining after the first project has finished and so on down the list. This tends to produce a resource utilization pattern similar to Figure 21.6. Residual scheduling is the opposite extreme from the strategy of giving each project essentially equal weight.

Which option?

Some managers might find the ideal solution somewhere between the two extremes just described. Compromise solutions can be obtained by allocating only part of the total resource pool to the highest priority project. My own practice has always been to rely solely on the imposition of target start and finish dates for every project. Although many other options might be possible (depending on the capability of the software), I have always considered that the appropriate course is to decide priorities on the basis of delivery dates required by and promised to the customer, leaving the computer to undertake the extremely complex task of scheduling the many hundreds or thousands of activities.

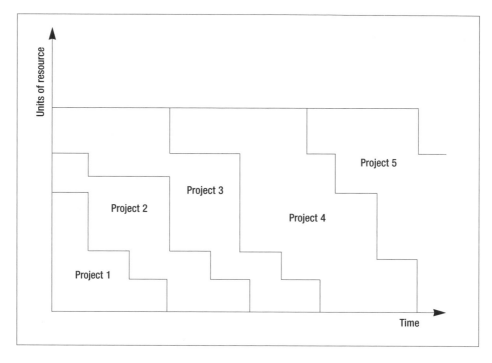

Figure 21.6   Resource usage pattern typical of residual scheduling

MANAGING THE MULTI-PROJECT MODEL

It should be assumed that some form of access to the multi-project model will be available to several project managers and other senior project team members. The level of access allowed needs to be considered with some caution, balancing the great potential benefits against the risk of database corruption. The project management programmes capable of handling many projects in a large multi-project model are themselves complex and need specialist training to achieve their maximum potential. It is unlikely that every person working on every project will have the necessary skills to interact with the software fully without introducing errors and corrupting the model. Some access limitation is therefore desirable.

It might be sensible, for example, to allow project managers and senior staff to have access to the model for interrogation and for the entry of progress data, whilst blocking any action that would change the basic set-up parameters of the model. One useful approach (which I recommend) is to establish a small control or coordination group to act as a system interface (Chapter 8). This group need only be one or two people strong and it could be part of the project support office (Chapter 9). Any authorized project member can have access to the database to

424

enter progress data or time sheet information or to view most of the reports produced by the system. Senior members of management or the sales organization can be given access to a specially created copy of the model in which they can test the possible effects of new project opportunities in 'what-if?' testing at the strategic level. Any data corruption in this process will be limited to the copy.

DETAILED WORK SCHEDULING WITHIN SMALL DEPARTMENTS

Project schedules govern the general rate at which work will reach various departments by providing achievable work-to lists. Each of these work-to lists will correspond to the network activity level of detail. The scheduled start and finish dates for each activity will set priorities that have been soundly based on a combination of critical path time analysis and resource scheduling. Project scheduling from most software packages should not be expected to cope with the finer level of detail needed for allocating work to individual people or for controlling manufacturing operations in a machine shop.

The production manager must rely on production control methods for sequencing machining operations, the routeing of workpieces and timing detailed assembly tasks. But the project schedule will provide the framework within which production control schedulers must work, by recommending start and finish dates for each network activity (where each activity might embrace a number of more detailed production tasks). Project resource scheduling should ensure that work is loaded to the production departments at a rate commensurate with their overall capacity. This should enable the separate production control system to plan all the detailed machining and assembly operations within the overall project target dates.

The allocation of work to skilled individuals in departments according to their particular experience or aptitudes (for example, an engineer with a special flair for gear design) must be left to departmental managers and supervisors. Project resource scheduling does not, therefore, remove or dilute the responsibility of supervisors and managers for allocating tasks within their departments. It is left to managers to decide which of their staff should be assigned to each job on their work-to lists. The purpose of the project schedule is to ensure that no department is ever expected to work beyond its capacity.

BENEFITS

The organization which successfully uses multi-project resource scheduling based on network analysis will enjoy many benefits. The data obtained can help in strategic planning decisions and in recruitment (or redundancy) planning for the whole organization. New project opportunities can be tested in the multi-project model to help management to decide whether or not to bid for them. My own experience has been that greater efficiency, greatly reduced costs, earlier project completion dates and fewer crises can be expected for all active projects.

These rewards can be gained for relatively small cost, provided that appropriate software is chosen and that it is used sensibly by individuals who have been properly selected and trained. It is not necessary to set up a large planning group. One or two specially trained individuals with the appropriate skills and aptitude can cope with many projects. If it is to succeed, however, multi-project scheduling needs total commitment from all project managers and key staff plus unqualified support from higher management.

Top management support must, of course, be asked to authorize funds for the purchase of software and for the provision and training of planning staff. This aspect of management support is, however, of far less importance than the need to motivate, persuade, or (in the last event) command every responsible person in the organization to follow the necessary procedures. The highest and most common risk of failure lies in the lack of this total and continuing commitment from all management levels. The multi-project model can only be established, remain valid, and justify its investment if all project managers produce their project network plans before their project start dates and report subsequent changes and progress to the planning coordinator promptly and regularly.

REFERENCES AND FURTHER READING

Lock, D., 2003, *Project Management*, 8th edition, Aldershot: Gower.

Reiss, G., 1996, *Programme Management Demystified: Managing Multiple Projects Successfully*, London: Chapman & Hall.

22 Managing Risks

Chris Chapman and Stephen Ward

This chapter describes a project risk management process initially drafted for the 1997 edition of the Project Risk Analysis and Management (PRAM) Guide developed by the Risk Management Special Interest Group (SIG) of the Association for Project Management (APM), (Simon et al 1997). The process described here was further developed in the 2004 edition of that guide (APM, 2004), and in two editions of an intervening book (Chapman and Ward 2003). The process described here also draws on other developments, like William's (2002) book on complex projects, Cooper et al's (2005) book on large projects and complex procurements, and three editions of the Risk Analysis and Management for Projects (RAMP) guide (ICE, FA & IA 2005). The PRAM basis of this chapter captures the experience of a large number of organizations which have successfully used formal risk management processes for a number of years. Linking the results of the PRAM working parties with RAMP discussions and the work of other authors has further developed this basis in ways which the authors believe add useful clarification and generalization.

A formal risk management process (RMP) should be applied at all stages in the project life-cycle, by clients (project owners), contractors, and other parties associated with a project, such as financial institutions providing funding. RMPs are most easily understood and explained in general terms when implemented in a comprehensive manner on behalf of a client during the development of a strategic plan. This chapter assumes that this is the perspective and stage of interest initially, revisiting these assumptions later. Figure 22.1 clarifies this later discussion, aspects of the initial RMP discussion, and the current project life-cycle timing assumption – the 'plan development' step in the 'plan' stage is the assumed timing of the initial application of the RMP, 'plan' being an abbreviation of 'plan the execution strategically'.

Most RMPs are described in terms of phases which are decomposed in a variety of ways, some related to tasks (activities), some related to deliverables (outputs/products). The nine phase structure used here is more detailed than

stages	steps
conceive the product of the project	trigger event
	concept capture
	clarification of purpose
	concept elaboration
	concept evaluation
design the product strategically	basic design
	development of performance criteria
	design development
	design evaluation
plan the execution strategically	basic activity and resource-based plans
	development of targets and milestones
	plan development
	plan evaluation
allocate resources tactically	basic design and activity-based plan detail
	development of resource allocation criteria
	allocation development
	allocation evaluation
execute production	co-ordinate and control
	monitor progress
	modification of targets and milestones
	resource allocation modification
	control evaluation
deliver the product	basic deliverable verification
	deliverable modification
	modification of performance criteria
	deliver evaluation
review the process	basic review
	review development
	review evaluation
support the product	basic maintenance and liability perception
	development of support criteria
	support perception development
	support evaluation

Figure 22.1   Project life-cycle stages and steps

most process structures. One consequence of this detail is clarification of the role of aspects of the process which are implicit to various degrees in other RMP descriptions. This includes making explicit several very important aspects which many descriptions ignore.

The methodology described here is comprehensive, encompassing all important aspects of all methods familiar to all the APM SIG authors, and as far as possible, those of other authors. Shortcuts are possible, and more sophisticated processes are also possible, within the framework provided. Both are addressed briefly later in this chapter; in more detail in Chapman and Ward (2003).

Illustrative examples, case studies and supporting detail are provided in Chapman and Ward (2003 and 2002), the PRAM and RAMP guides, and other references listed at the end of the chapter.

THE RISK MANAGEMENT PROCESS, RMP

The nine phases of the risk management process (RMP) are discussed in a start-to-start precedence sequence. Once started all phases proceed in parallel, with intermittent bursts of activity defined by an iterative process interlinking the phases. Each phase is associated with broadly defined deliverables. Each deliverable is discussed in terms of its purpose and the tasks required to produce it. Significant changes in purpose underlie the boundaries between phases. Figure 22.2 outlines the purposes and tasks associated with each phase, providing a useful introductory overview of the RMP. Figure 22.3 indicates in linked bar chart form the way effort expended in each phase of the RMP might be focused over the life-cycle of a typical RMP, and Figure 22.4 summarises the phase structure in flow chart format. Other RMP descriptions can be mapped onto the nine phase descriptions provided here. Some key aspects of comparisons are considered in this chapter, and complete comparisons for three alternative phase structures are provided in Chapman and Ward (2003).

Part of the purpose of the APM PRAM Guide (2004) was the provision of simple standard process descriptions and terminology to avoid unnecessary confusion generated by different descriptions of common concepts, but this goal has proven elusive. The Chapman and Ward (2003) SHAMPU (Shape Harness And Manage Uncertainty) versions have been used here, for clarity and simplicity, with some indications of widely used alternatives. Key differences of immediate relevance are the SHAMPU emphasis on shaping uncertainty at a strategic level as the starting point and the following definitions of terms used and terms avoided.

- 'Uncertainty' is very broadly defined as 'lack of certainty', for any reason, including all sources of ambiguity as well as events which may or may not happen.
- 'Risk' is defined as 'possible departures from expectations which matter', in terms of all relevant aspects of performance, a cumulative or portfolio view of the impact of uncertainty from all sources which can operate at an event level, a project level, a corporate level, or anywhere in between. Risk in this sense at a project level is referred to as 'project risk' in the PRAM Guide (APM 2004).
- 'Event risk' in PRAM (APM 2004) terms, events which may or may not happen, is not worth the confusion of a separate 'risk' label in the authors' view. Some readers may wish to continue to use the term 'event risk' or the

429

phases	purposes and tasks in outline
define the project	Consolidate relevant existing information about the project at a strategic level in a structure suitable for risk management. Fill in any gaps uncovered in the consolidation process, and resolve any inconsistencies.
focus the process	Scope and provide a strategic plan for the RMP. Plan the RMP at an operational level.
identify the issues	Identify sources of uncertainty at a strategic level in terms of opportunities and threats. Identify what might be done about it, in terms of proactive and reactive responses. Identify secondary sources of uncertainty associated with responses.
structure the issues	Complete the structuring of earlier phases. Test simplifying assumptions. Provide more complex or alternative structures when appropriate.
clarify **ownership**	Allocate *both* financial *and* managerial responsibility for issues (separately if appropriate).
estimate variability	Size the uncertainty that is usefully quantified on a first pass. On later passes, refine earlier estimates of uncertainty where this is effective and efficient.
evaluate implications	Assess statistical dependence (dependence not modelled in a causal structure). Synthesize the results of the estimate phase using dependence assumptions that are fit for purpose. Interpret the results in the context of *all* earlier phases. Make decisions about proactive and reactive responses, and about refining and redefining earlier analysis, managing the iterative nature of the process as a key aspect of these tasks.
harness the plans	Obtain approval for strategic plans shaped by earlier phases. Prepare action plans. These are base plans (incorporating proactive responses) and contingency plans (incorporating reactive responses with trigger points) ready for implementation within the action horizons defined by appropriate lead times. Commit to project plans that are fit for implementation.
manage implementation	Manage the planned work. Develop action plans for implementation on a rolling basis. Monitor and control (make decisions to refine or redefine project plans as required). Deal with crises (unanticipated issues of significance) and be prepared to cope appropriately with disasters (crises that are not controlled).

Figure 22.2   RMP overview in terms of an outline of purposes and tasks

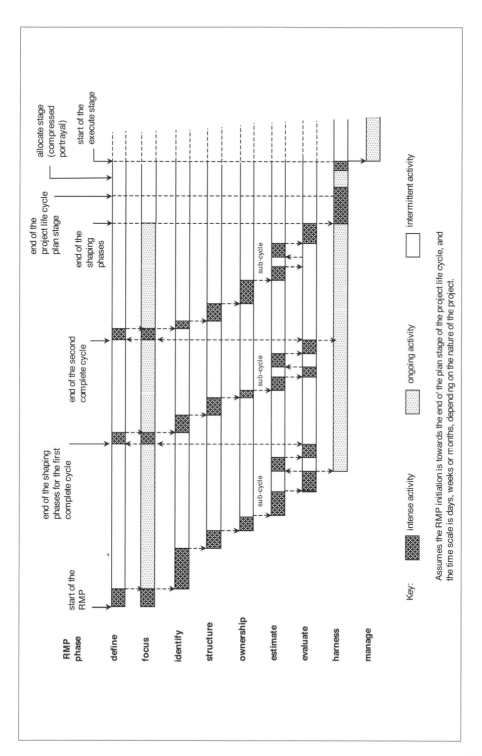

Figure 22.3   RMP Gantt chart portrayal

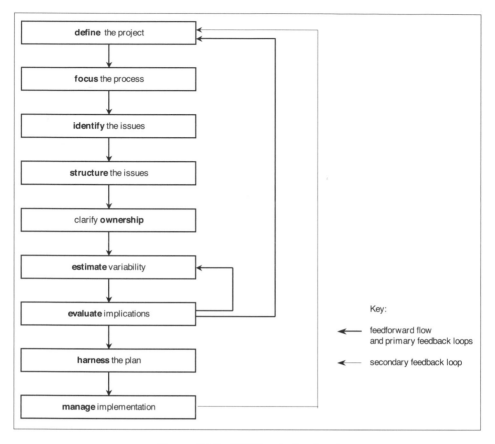

Figure 22.4   RMP flow chart portrayal

term 'a risk' as an equivalent to 'event risk' in the PRAM (APM 2004) sense, but we strongly advise against it.

- 'Source of uncertainty' is a more general equivalent to 'a risk' or 'event risk' which we find useful. One key aspect of the rationale for using 'source of uncertainty' or 'source' is clarification and emphasis of the shift in focus from threats to both opportunities and threats which has been widely adopted recently. Another is the need to address ambiguity as well as variability in explicit and direct terms. However, the principal aspect of the rationale is the need to see both upside and downside risk as departures from expectations, which are the net implications of uncertainty involving threats and opportunities that accumulate over time and other project dimensions, requiring strategic responses as well as tactical responses. The 2004 PRAM guide distinguishes 'event risk' from 'project risk' because the first edition limited the definition of risk to event risk, and some members of the working party still prefer to maintain a focus on event risk. Limiting the focus to event risk is a dysfunctional aspect of 'common practice', a feature of the way many organizations implement RMPs, at least in part because an event risk view of risk has always been central to the widely used PMBOK® chapter on RMPs (PMI® 2004). For a more detailed discussion of the controversy associated with these issues see Chapman (2006).

Using the terms 'uncertainty', 'risk' and 'source of uncertainty' as suggested here both simplifies and generalizes the purposes and roles of project risk management in very important ways. We can consistently focus on the 'big picture' in terms of what drives it, concerning ourselves with 'what matters' without overlooking cumulative and compounding effects of minor contributions when developing an understanding of how major sources of uncertainty combine and interact. We can do this by managing uncertainty first – with a focus on expected outcomes, and risk second – with a focus on those exceptional circumstances when a trade-off between risk and expected performance needs to be considered. Further we can avoid confusing the value and role of quantification of uncertainty and risk with the availability (or not) of data, adopting a modern flexible view of probabilities as inherently subjective, possibly with an objective estimate starting point based on assumptions which never hold precisely in practice, associated 'robustness' requiring judgement.

DEFINE THE PROJECT FOR RISK MANAGEMENT PURPOSES: THE DEFINE PHASE

All RMPs embody aspects of a define phase, but much of it is usually implicit. Its purpose is to define project effort to date in a form appropriate for the RMP, to:

- consolidate in a suitable form existing relevant information about the project which the RMP addresses – for example project objectives should be clearly stated, project scope (including breadth and timeframe) and strategy should be defined, activity plans need to be defined at an appropriate, simple, overview level, associated timing and resource usage implications specified, underlying issues like design and stakeholders' interests defined;
- undertake project management activities to fill in gaps uncovered in the consolidation process – in principle such gaps should not exist, but in practice this is a crucial aspect of the RMP, a form of risk assessment of the project management process to date, and respond to any concerns.

Achieving both purposes of the define phase is essential, a basic foundation for what follows. The deliverables provided by the define phase may be a single document or parts of several documents. Whatever their form, a comprehensive and complete define phase should clarify all relevant key aspects of the project

433

which the RMP addresses, in a manner accessible to all relevant client staff. The target deliverable is this clear, unambiguous, shared understanding of the project. Six tasks are required to provide this deliverable:

1. *consolidate*: gather and summarise in a suitable form relevant existing information
2. *elaborate*: fill in the gaps, creating new information
3. *document*: record in text with diagrams as appropriate
4. *verify*: ensure all information providers agree as far as possible, highlight important differences in opinion , and refer to all relevant providers
5. *assess*: value the analysis to date in context, to ensure it is 'fit for purpose' given the current status of the risk management process
6. *report*: release verified documents, presenting if appropriate

The first two of these tasks are specific to the define phase. The last four are common to all nine phases. Because aspects of the project may not be clearly defined when the RMP begins, and may take some time to be clearly defined, important and central aspects of the define phase may be ongoing. However, the initial concern of the RMP should be making as much progress as possible with the define phase before moving on to later phases. The greater the level of unfinished business from the define phase, the lower the efficiency and effectiveness of the following phases. Figure 22.3 indicates the way effort expended on the define phase might be timed in a typical RMP. The bulk of the effort is at the outset, but there are further bursts of effort at the start of subsequent cycles through the process, three complete cycles being illustrated in Figure 22.3. Ongoing define phase activity throughout the process is another way Figure 22.3 might portray this phase.

Development of this phase is usefully structured around Figure 22.5, which uses an influence diagram to explore the relationships between 'the six Ws'. Ensuring all six, and their interrelationships, are fully understood, provides insight of great value. It allows recognition, for example, that the best way to deal with some sources of uncertainty may be to abandon activities generating these sources of uncertainty and achieve objectives some other way, in the limit perhaps redefining success. Development of this phase is also usefully structured around Figure 22.1. A brief description of the future project life-cycle stages provides a basis, along with the six Ws, for considering sources of uncertainty (both threats and opportunities) which may have upside or downside risk implications. Figure 22.1 associates generic steps with each stage, which need to be given a form specific to the project to trigger identification of sources of uncertainty which may arise in future stages of the project life-cycle. Alternative project life-cycle definitions can be used, but explicit attention to a future life-cycle stage portrayal and a six Ws portrayal is essential in the authors' view.

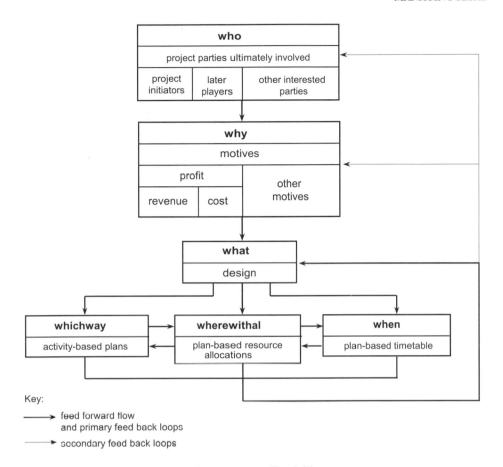

Figure 22.5 The six Ws

The comprehensive framework provided by Figures 22.1 and 22.5 is essential, but a key concern is keeping the basic structure within this framework as simple as possible. For example, about 20 activities is an appropriate target level of decomposition for the 'how' aspect of the six Ws for most large projects, and about 5 activities is an appropriate target for most small projects, with a non-linear scaling in between, anticipating a maximum plus 150% outcome. If several hundred activities are used, common practice in many organizations, the analysis will 'lose sight of the wood for the trees', getting lost in minor tactical details and failing to focus on strategy.

FOCUS THE RISK MANAGEMENT PROCESS: THE FOCUS PHASE

All RMPs should embody a focus phase, although much of it is often implicit, and some of it may be given other titles. Its purpose is to:

435

1. define RMP scope and strategy as distinct from the strategy of the project it addresses
2. plan the RMP in operational terms as a project in its own right

If an RMP is being applied to test the viability of a new project, a purely qualitative approach may be appropriate. However, if an RMP is being used to assess budgets or bid prices, a fully quantitative (probabilistic) approach may be required. These differences have important process and resource requirement implications. Achieving both purposes of this phase is essential, as basic to what follows as the define phase. The deliverables provided by the focus phase may be a single document or parts of several documents. Whatever their form, a comprehensive and complete focus phase should clarify all relevant key aspects of the RMP as a project in its own right in a manner accessible to all relevant client staff. The target deliverable is this clear, unambiguous shared understanding of the RMP. As well as the repetitive common tasks (*document, verify, assess and report*), additional specific tasks required to provide this deliverable include:

1. *Scope the process:* This task addresses issues like who is doing the analysis for whom, why is the formal project risk management process being undertaken (what benefits must be achieved), and what is the scope of the relevant risk.
2. *Plan the process:* This task addresses issues like using what resources over what time-frame, using what models and methods (techniques), what software and so on, and culminates in an operational plan for the risk management process.

The focus phase may be largely concurrent with the define phase initially, but updating RMP plans will be ongoing. Figure 22.3 shows how the effort expended on the focus phase might be timed in a typical RMP, assuming bursts of activity linked to the define phase, and some ongoing activity. The define and focus phases may be thought of jointly as a higher level 'clarify the basis of the analysis' or 'process initiation' phase. They are separated here because they are concerned with very different sets of deliverables, both of which are essential to what follows. Separation facilitates viewing the focus phase as a project in its own right, and applying all we know about good project management to this phase, including the management of uncertainty and risk.

Using a Gantt chart like Figure 22.3 to plan the first pass of the RMP can be a useful part of the first pass of the focus phase, and planning to use about 20% of the time available for the first pass is a useful rule of thumb based on a version of the 80:20 rule (we want to spend 80% of the time available on the 20% which matters most, identifying what matters being the focus of the first pass). However, it is not worth initial planning beyond the first pass in a Figure 22.3 format. The second and third passes shown in Figure 22.3 simply illustrate one possible outcome, and in practice more partial iterations are a more likely outcome.

The key here is keeping the process simple, but not simplistic, with a clear focus on delivering what is required from this particular stage in the analysis. This notion of delivering effective analysis efficiently is extensively developed and illustrated in Chapman and Ward (2002 and 2003) in terms of the related concepts 'constructive simplicity' and 'simplicity efficiency'. The latter involves maximising the insight provided by any given level of effort, and choosing the most appropriate level of effort. The former is about process choices to do so.

IDENTIFY THE ISSUES: THE IDENTIFY PHASE

Most RMPs have an explicit identify phase for sources of uncertainty. Some use a separate later phase to identify responses to these sources. The authors believe it is useful to couple the identification of sources of uncertainty and responses, and to use the term 'issues' to mean 'sources of uncertainty and associated responses'. To manage uncertainty and risk effectively and efficiently we must understand:

1. the scope and nature of the uncertainty, in terms of what positive and negative effects might be experienced, and the mechanisms underlying these effects if they are significant and effective and efficient responses are worth careful consideration;
2. what we might do about uncertainty, in proactive and reactive response terms, at a level of sophistication consistent with the level of threat or opportunity;
3. what significant uncertainty associated with our responses may need consideration – that is, secondary issues.

On the first pass the identify phase should emphasize the identification of sources of uncertainty in broad terms to form a comprehensive overview of what matters. In general a concern for responses and for understanding root causes underlying uncertainty to refine responses is best left until later passes, when it is clear what matters. However, at least one response, even if it is 'do nothing and accept the risk' (which may not be feasible) must be identified and assumed in order to understand the impact of a source of uncertainty later in the first pass (iteration) through the process.

In addition to the four common tasks (*document, verify, assess* and *report*), identifying issues (sources of uncertainty and responses) involves two specific tasks:

1. *Search*: for sources of uncertainty and responses, employing a range of techniques such as pondering, interviewing, brainstorming and checklists;
2. *Classify*: to provide a suitable structure for defining sources of uncertainty and responses, aggregating/disaggregating sources and responses as appropriate.

The deliverables from the identify phase should include lists of sources of uncertainty and associated response lists, indicating at least one assumed response, 'do nothing' being one option. The key deliverable is a clear common understanding of threats and opportunities facing the project. Opportunities may be initiated by event based sources of upside risk like 'unusually good weather' or 'favourable market conditions', or by the accumulation of good luck in relation to ambiguity favourably resolved. Whatever the nature of the source, it is essential to ensure that effective responses will capture the good luck so it does not get lost. Potential opportunities and responses to generate and manage opportunities need to be identified and managed with the same resolve as threats. Often RMPs are successful because the process of generating and reviewing responses leads to the identification of opportunities with implications well beyond the sources of uncertainty which led to their identification.

On the first pass a comprehensive list of sources of uncertainty is the primary concern, with comprehensive sets of potential responses to key sources becoming more important later, as it becomes clear what sources of uncertainty matter most and optimal response choices becomes the concern in the evaluate phase. Secondary sources of uncertainty also need attention on later passes – opportunities and threats associated with responses. For example, transferring a source of uncertainty to a contractor may give away an opportunity but fail to eliminate the threat.

A key concern in the identify phase is keeping the issue structure as simple as possible, adding complexity only when this is useful. The first pass should pool sources of uncertainty (treat sources collectively under one label) which can be managed reactively during execution without prior actions or via a common response, only distinguishing sources which clearly require different reactive or proactive responses, with a focus on sizing the uncertainty involved. Later passes can explore areas where uncertainty matters most to seek greater clarity about effective responses. We want to spend 80% of the time available on the 20% that matters most, the reason we have to use the first pass to size uncertainty, later passes to focus on what matters most. Figure 22.3 indicates the way identify phase effort might be focused in a typical RMP.

STRUCTURE THE ISSUES: THE STRUCTURE PHASE

Providing structure to clarify our understanding of complex issues is central to RMPs. Some aspects of providing this structure are necessarily integrated with earlier phases, like the structure implied by the way issues are defined in the identify phase. Other aspects are necessarily left until this phase. For some RMPs structure is implicit, assuming a simple standard structure by default. In general we want the structure developed by a RMP to be as simple as possible, but not misleadingly so. The basic purposes of the structure phase are testing simplifying assumptions, and providing a more complex structure when necessary. Failure to structure in the full sense of this phase can lead to lost opportunities. For example, some responses to particular sources of uncertainty can in practice deal with sets of sources, possibly all uncertainty up to that point in a project. We refer to these responses as 'general responses', as distinct from 'specific responses' associated with only one source of uncertainty. It is important to recognize the opportunities provided by such general responses.

The structure phase involves three specific tasks:

1. *Refine classifications:* This involves the review and development (where appropriate) of existing classifications, because a 'new' response may be defined because the understanding associated with an 'old' one may be refined, or because a new classification structure may be introduced, distinguishing between specific and general responses, for example.
2. *Explore interactions:* This involves reviewing and exploring possible interdependencies or links between project activities, sources of uncertainty and responses, and seeking to understand the reasons for these interdependencies.
3. *Develop orderings:* An ordering for sources of uncertainty is needed for several purposes, including priorities for project and process planning, and for expository (presentation) purposes. In addition, this step involves developing a priority ordering of responses which takes impacts into account, including secondary issues.

In terms of documentation, the structure phase involves completing the generation of a set of pictures or graphs, and defining associated mathematical models where appropriate, which capture all the key relationships in terms which are as simple as possible. The key deliverable of the structure phase is a clear understanding, on the part of the analysts and all users of the analysis, of the implications of any important simplifying assumptions about the relationships between sources of uncertainty, responses, base plan activities and all the other *W*s.

CLARIFY OWNERSHIP ISSUES: THE OWNERSHIP PHASE

All effective RMPs have an ownership phase, with three purposes, to:

1. distinguish the sources and associated responses the client is prepared to own and manage from those the client wants other organizations (such as contractors) to own or manage;
2. allocate responsibility for managing sources and responses owned by the client to named individuals;
3. approve, if appropriate, ownership/management allocations controlled by contractor(s) and third parties.

The first of these purposes should be achieved on the first pass before moving on to the following phase of the RMP. Some organizations consider this first purpose as a part of project strategy, which the define phase will identify. Deferring achievement of the other purposes until later passes is usually appropriate. This suggests modest effort initially, increasing in subsequent cycles as the first purpose is replaced by the second and third. The deliverables provided by the ownership phase are clear ownership and allocations of management responsibility, efficiently and effectively defined, and legally enforceable as far as practicable. The tasks required to provide this deliverable may be very simple or extremely complex, depending upon contract strategy. For expository purposes assume no fixed corporate contracting policy. In these circumstances the ownership phase involves two specific tasks:

1. *Scope the policy:* This task addresses concerns like what are the objectives of the ownership strategy (the *why*), which parties are being considered (the *who*), and what kinds of risk require allocation (the *what*). This task culminates in a policy for risk allocation issues.
2. *Plan the allocation:* This task considers the details of the approach (the *whichway*), the instruments (the *wherewithal*), and the timing (the *when*). This task transforms risk ownership policy into operational contracts.

Separate identification of this phase facilitates treating it as a project in its own right, and applying to it all we know about good project management.

ESTIMATE VARIABILITY: THE ESTIMATE PHASE

All RMPs have an estimate phase, concerned with cost, time and other performance measures. However, it may be given alternative designations, and sometimes it has separate 'qualitative' (non-numeric) and 'quantitative' (numeric) components (PMI® 2004). It should have two purposes, which are related but important to distinguish:

1. to 'size uncertainty', identifying overall uncertainty and those areas of the project plans which *may* involve significant uncertainty, which need more attention in terms of data acquisition and analysis;
2. to 'clarify uncertainty that matters', clarifying root causes of uncertainty in order to test and develop effective and efficient responses in areas of the project plans which *clearly* involve significant uncertainty requiring careful decisions and judgements by the client team.

A single pass which attempts to achieve both purposes is never a cost-effective approach. We want to minimize the time spent on relatively minor sources and sources with simple response options, to use the time on major issues involving complex response options. To do this a first pass with a focus on the first purpose can be used, looping back until the second purpose can be achieved with confidence. Initial iterations can involve just the estimate and evaluate phases, illustrated in Figure 22.3 by one such loop (sub-cycle) within each of the two complete loops back to the define phase. Later more complete loops are effective, providing more attention to detail and some revisions in relation to the previous phase outputs in those areas where unresolved issues suggest it is worth applying more effort. Attempting to achieve the required outputs via a single pass is not effective because it involves attention to detail which proves unnecessary in some areas, as well as skimped effort in areas where more effort would be productive. Part of the process of managing the RMP as a project in its own right is concerned with responding to those areas where important issues are identified and better solutions required. The RMP has a clearly defined formal structure, but it cannot be applied in a mechanical manner. Most experienced risk analysts understand this, but many formal statements of RMP methodology do not make this important point clearly enough.

The deliverables provided by the estimate phase are usually estimates of parameter probability distributions for cost, duration, or other project criteria identified earlier in terms of base level sources of uncertainty.

When numeric measurement of uncertainty is likely to be useful, the authors strongly advise the use of numeric probability distributions from the outset, initially using simple 'minimalist' approaches. For example, variability associated with 'productivity variations' which were listed in terms of examples but pooled in the identify phase might be associated with a 'plausible maximum' and a 'plausible minimum' which correspond approximately to 90 and 10 percentile values, assuming a rectangular density probability distribution which makes the mid-point the expected value and median, and directly comparable plausible minimum and maximum values can define both the probability and the impact of other sources requiring separate probabilistic treatment (Chapman and Ward 2002 and 2003).

If an organization currently uses probability impact matrices, the authors strongly advise interpreting them as subjective probability estimates in a 'minimalist' framework as a first step towards a more general minimalist approach, avoiding common practice 'qualitative analysis' and associated risk indices as recommended in PMI® (2004), for reasons discussed in detail in Chapman and Ward (2003) and Chapman (2006). Briefly, 'common practice' use of probability impact matrices uses: an inappropriately restrictive framework (inflexible in terms of the range of probability values and impact values defined by a standard grid) for looking at a restricted subset of the sources of uncertainty ('event risk'); this framework is not suitable for sources of uncertainty like 'productivity variations' which always happen; and this framework distracts

441

attention away from the way uncertainty accumulates, based on a restrictive view of risk and a lack of understanding of subjective probabilities.

As explained in Chapman (2006), if an organization is not willing or able to embrace a minimalist approach to quantification, there are better qualitative alternatives to probability impact matrices. For example a simple traffic light scheme can be used. If a source of uncertainty has a clear owner and a plausible response, it can be given a green light. If it has a clear owner but no clear response, it can be given an amber light. If it has no clear owner it can be given a red light. Red lights require senior management attention to resolve ownership issues as soon as possible, the first priority. Amber lights require a lower level of management attention to resolve response choice questions given ownership assumptions, the second priority. When these two priorities have been dealt with, sizing the residual uncertainty and risk can be addressed. Common practice use of probability impact matrices often ignores these first two priorities, in addition to taking an inappropriate approach to the third.

When a quantitative (subjective probability based) approach is used, it is applied only to those sources of uncertainty which are usefully quantified. Assessment of some sources of uncertainty and responses may be best handled by identifying them as conditions, associated with assumptions, deliberately avoiding estimation in the usual sense. If on a first pass the concern is identifying and then managing any 'showstoppers', estimation reduces to looking for showstoppers. The key deliverable of the estimate phase is the provision of a basis for understanding which sources and responses are important, using metrics when appropriate which offer precision adequate for effective and efficient management of the issues involved. Three specific tasks are required to provide this deliverable, as follows:

1. *Select an appropriate issue* – As the basis of a process of successive estimation of a set of issues, select an appropriate place to start, and each successive issue, in terms of initial estimates and refinement of those estimates.
2. *Scope the uncertainty* – Provide a simple numeric subjective probability estimate, based on the current perceptions of the individual or group with the most appropriate knowledge, to 'size' the issue.
3. *Refine earlier estimates* – If the impact of the source being estimated given chosen responses warrants, or the sensitivity of associated response decisions warrants, refine the initial scoping estimate. This may be undertaken in conjunction with refining the response related decision analysis.

EVALUATE THE IMPLICATIONS: THE EVALUATE PHASE

All RMPs have an evaluate phase, although it may be coupled with the estimate phase. Its purpose is the synthesis and evaluation of the results of the estimate phase in the context of the structuring provided by all earlier phases with a view to managing the iterative nature of the RMP and client assessment of decisions and judgements. The deliverables will depend upon the depth of the preceding phases achieved to this point, looping back to earlier phases before proceeding being a key and frequent decision at this stage. For example, an important early deliverable is a prioritized list of issues, while a later deliverable might be a diagnosed potential problem associated with a specific aspect of the base plan or contingency plans, and suggested revisions to these plans to resolve the problem. Specific loops back to earlier phases are not indicated on Figure 22.4, because they could be to any phase. The key deliverable is diagnosis of any and all important difficulties, and comparative analysis of the implications of responses to these difficulties. Tasks other than the three common tasks include selecting an appropriate subset of issues, specifying dependence, integrating the subset of issues, portraying the effect, and diagnosing the implications. On the first pass the diagnoses can focus on sensitivity analysis. Sensitivity analysis should drive an understanding of where more data would be useful, and where careful attention to the root causes of uncertainty and the refinement of decision rules would be useful, comparing alternative responses. This in turn should form the basis of a search for 'risk efficiency', defined as 'a minimum level of risk for any given level of expected performance'.

The evaluate phase should be used to drive the distinction between the two purposes of the estimate phase indicated earlier. That is, a first pass should be used to portray overall uncertainty and the relative size of all contributing factors. Further passes are then used to explore and confirm the importance of the key issues, obtaining additional data and undertaking further analysis of sources of uncertainty where appropriate before moving on to consideration of project decisions and judgements.

Figure 22.6 illustrates a key form of analysis output portrayal for sensitivity assessments. It portrays the effect of six issues associated with the fabrication of a 'jacket' for offshore oil production. The curve labelled '6' represents the combined effect of all six issues. The curve labelled '1' represents the first on its own, the curve labelled '2' represents the sum of the first two, the curve labelled '3' represents the sum of the first three, and so on. The large gap between '4' and '5' indicates issue '5', 'industrial disputes', is the biggest contributor. A search for data, insight about root causes, and insight about effective responses which would avoid the issue and offer additional opportunities was the result. Similar curves can combine lower level sums, building up to overall uncertainty for each attribute (time, cost, and so on).

Figure 22.7 illustrates a key form of analysis output portrayal for testing alternative response options and making decisions. It portrays the effect of changing the assumed barge 'wave height capability' for a 'hook-up' activity,

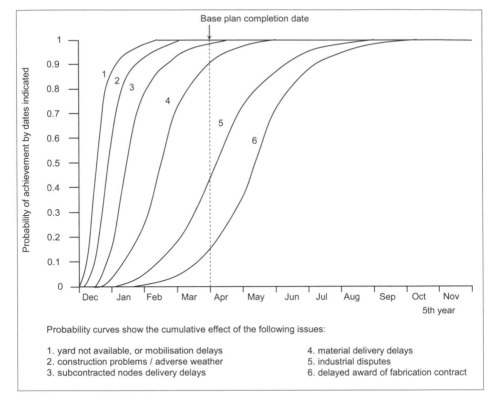

Figure 22.6 Jacket fabrication example of the initial level of output from an offshore project to illustrate sensitivity portrayals

connecting an offshore pipeline to the jacket. The more capable 3 metre barge offered less risk as well as a lower expected cost, an improvement in risk efficiency. The 3 metre barge cost more per day, but it could cope with the winter weather delays to earlier activities made likely, and such delays were likely and costly.

Understanding why a RMP which involves a search for opportunities to improve risk efficiency using portrayals like Figures 22.6–7 can lower cost and risk simultaneously makes it clear that such processes repay the effort spent many times over. They are not an overhead. They are the key to better decisions. Chapman and Ward (2002 and 2003) develop this and other objectives for RMPs in detail.

This framework can help to test and demonstrate (or not) the validity of common rules of thumb, like 'always insure low probability high impact threats', and 'always pass to contractors high probability low impact threats', both forms of uncertainty avoidance which are often counterproductive. Seeking risk efficiency is about seeking best choices in terms of all options identified earlier. A failure to

444

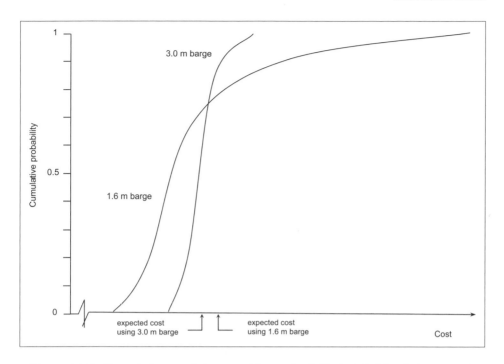

Figure 22.7 Barge choice example from an offshore project to illustrate decision choice portrayals

adopt at least a minimalist approach to quantitative analysis to assist with these choices is a feature of common practice which is very limiting.

HARNESS THE STRATEGIC PLAN SHAPED BY EARLIER PHASES: THE HARNESS PHASE

The harness phase begins by obtaining approval for the strategic plans shaped by the first seven phases. Detailed action plans are then prepared. Action plans involve base plans incorporating proactive responses and contingency plans incorporating reactive responses with trigger points. They need to be prepared over an action horizon defined by critical lead times. A tactical version of the earlier strategic level risk management process may be involved in developing the action plans. Approval of the action plans and commitment to their implementation completes this phase. Ensuring these action plans are complete and appropriate is the end purpose of this phase. The approvals and the action plans are the deliverables. The specific tasks are reasonably obvious in relation to the specific deliverables. Some of the key specific deliverables any RMP Harness phase should provide are:

1. base plans in activity terms, at the detailed level required for implementation, with timing, precedence, ownership and associated resource usage/

445

contractual terms where appropriate clearly specified, including milestones initiating payments, other events or processes defining expenditure, and an associated base plan expenditure profile;

2. risk assessment in terms of threats and opportunities, prioritized, assessed in terms of impact given no response if feasible and potentially desirable, along with an assessment of alternative potential proactive and reactive responses;

3. recommended proactive and reactive contingency plans in activity terms, with timing, precedence, ownership and associated resource usage/contractual terms where appropriate clearly specified, including trigger points (decision rules) initiating reactive contingency responses, and impact assessment.

Proactive responses are built into the base plans, and reactive responses into the associated contingency plans, when they become part of the overall project plans. All phases of the RMP should be closely coupled with project planning in general, but the need for this coupling is perhaps particularly obvious in this phase. Some RMPs suggest a formal separation between base plans (which are owned by the project planning function) and the risk management plans (which are owned by the risk management function). This can be required by organizational constraints, but it is not desirable. It highlights a perceived need to separate project management and risk management in some organizations, but the general desirability is to see risk management as an integral part of project management.

Figure 22.3 indicates the project life-cycle transition from 'plan' stage to 'allocate' stage which the harness phase involves a shift from strategic planning to tactical planning. Some RMPs have a 'response planning' phase after their 'evaluate' phase which is equivalent to the response development aspects of our identify-evaluate phase multiple pass loops, not to be confused with the approvals processes and tactical planning of the harness phase. Some RMPs also have a 'response management' phase which is equivalent to embedding responses into base and contingency plans at a tactical level after these plans have been approved because otherwise the results of the RMP will be ignored. Effective integration of project management and RMPs in a project life-cycle framework renders these additional phases redundant, and it clarifies the important role of the harness phase in the project life-cycle. Alternative life-cycle stage definitions should preserve this relationship whatever the associated approvals structure as early conceptual stages move towards the execution of a detailed plan.

MANAGE IMPLEMENTATION: THE MANAGE PHASE

All RMPs should have a manage phase, ongoing as the project is implemented. One key deliverable is diagnosis of a need to revisit earlier base and contingency plans, the basis of control. Another is rolling development of action plans ready for implementation as the detailed planning horizon rolls forward. Some of the key

446

deliverables that any RMP manage phase should provide on a regular cycle (monthly for example) include:

1. measures of achieved performance in relation to planned progress;
2. a short prioritized list of risk/response issues requiring ongoing management attention, with recent changes in priority emphasized and trends assessed;
3. related lower level more detailed reports drawing appropriate management attention to all issues requiring action;
4. appropriate replanning and exception/change reporting in response to significant events.

ALTERNATIVE PERSPECTIVES

We now consider several alternative perspectives: the application of the RMP earlier or later in the project life-cycle, the sharing of risk between clients and contractors, and possible shortcuts or extensions to the process. All three raise complex issues, and only a few overview comments can be offered here, but the comments provided indicate the nature of what is involved.

RMP EARLIER IN THE LIFE-CYCLE

Implementing a RMP earlier in the project life-cycle is in general more difficult, because the project is more fluid, and less well defined. A more fluid project means more degrees of freedom, more alternatives to consider, including alternatives which may be eliminated as the project matures for reasons unrelated to the RMP. A less well defined project means appropriate documentation is harder to come by, and alternative interpretations of what is involved may not be resolvable. At a very early stage in a project's life-cycle, just after conception, RMP can be like attempting to nail jelly to the wall.

That said, implementing a RMP earlier in the project life-cycle is in general much more useful if it is done effectively. There is scope for much more fundamental improvements in the project plans, perhaps including a risk driven initial design or redesign of the product of the project. The opportunity aspects of RMP can be particularly important for early RMP implementation. It can be equally important to be clear about project objectives, in the limit decomposing project objectives and formally mapping their relationships with project activities, because pre-emptive responses to risks need to facilitate lateral thinking which addresses entirely new ways of achieving objectives. Some broad general features of a RMP earlier in the project life-cycle include characteristics like it is usually less quantitative, less formal, less tactical, more strategic, more creative, and more concerned with the identification and capture of opportunities.

447

More specifically, if a RMP is initiated in the design stage of the project life-cycle as described in Figure 22.1, the focus can be the design aspect of the six Ws, in terms of its strategic development. If it is initiated in the conceive stage of Figure 22.1, the focus can be the concept in more general 'business case' terms. The RAMP Guide (ICE, FA & IA 2005) illustrates an early 'business case' focus.

If a RMP is introduced at the concept stage it must be used again at all subsequent stages with a shifting focus, each successive application building on the earlier applications, in addition to possible multiple or ongoing use within project life-cycle stages, and the iterative nature of each application. As a general rule, the earlier this successive as well as iterative process starts the better. However, organizations which want to introduce a RMP and have some choice about when in the context of a range of possible projects to use as test cases would do well to start with a project which has been well managed to date and is now approaching the approval stage for its strategic plan, as assumed in Figure 22.3 and the earlier body of this chapter. Being thrown into the deep end may prove an effective way to learn to swim, but there are preferable alternatives.

RMP LATER IN THE LIFE-CYCLE

Implementing a RMP later in a project life-cycle gives rise to somewhat different difficulties, without any compensating benefits. Contracts are in place, equipment has been purchased, commitments are in place, reputations are on the line, and managing change is comparatively difficult and unrewarding. A RMP can and should encompass routine reappraisal of a project's viability. In this context early warnings are preferable to late recognition that targets are incompatible or unachievable. That said, better late than never, sometimes.

More specifically, if a RMP is introduced for the first time in the allocate stage of Figure 22.1, common practice involves a tactical level of analysis in the absence of prior strategic consideration of uncertainty. This can be counterproductive. Reconsideration of plans at a strategic level is usually more beneficial. This can be politically difficult. Avoiding these all too common problems is a key reason for using the plan stage of the life-cycle as our initial focus and recommended initiation point for organizations not familiar with RMPs.

If an RMP is introduced for the first time in the execute stage of Figure 22.2, it is arguably too late to take an effective strategic view of risk. It might be argued that an event risk focus is the best that can be done at this stage, and a single pass process using post evaluation phase 'response planning' and 'response management' phases is essential. If this line of thinking is taken to its logical conclusion, it might be argued that RMPs using these phases have been developed to deal with introducing risk management too late, which is why they are not very effective when used earlier in the project life-cycle.

If an RMP is introduced for the first time in the deliver or support stages, an event risk focus may seem inevitable. The important threats that may reveal themselves here are the key target of effective earlier risk management, ideally in the conceive or design stages, no later than the plan stage if proactive responses are to provide cost effective resolution.

ALTERNATIVE PERSPECTIVES: SOME OBSERVATIONS ON CLIENT AND CONTRACTOR RISK

Detailed guidance associated with alternative perspectives is beyond the scope of this chapter, but it may be useful to make the following points:

1. if risk ownership is not clearly defined, a client's risks can be a contractor's opportunities;
2. clients and contractors necessarily have different objectives, but a contract which leads to confrontation is perhaps the biggest single risk most projects encounter, a contract which seeks congruence in objectives being absolutely critical;
3. clients and contractors both need to undertake separate RMPs, but they need to establish a constructive dialogue involving input to each others' RMPs; 'fixed' price contracts mitigate against this;
4. the trend towards 'partnering' and other forms of contracting which facilitate cooperative working is a trend to follow, but not blindly, when developing a comprehensive procurement strategy;
5. a carefully and thoughtfully executed RMP should address all the really difficult and sometimes obscure questions, like how should contracts be structured and defined, as well as the comparatively obvious ones like how much will the project cost, if for no other reason than the fact that the answers to the simple questions usually depend upon the assumptions about the difficult ones.

SELECTING SHORTCUTS

The comprehensive RMP outlined here should be understood as a cohesive, internally consistent, integrated process in full before attempting the shortcuts and modifications which are essential in most practical applications. Practical projects require shortcuts, but explaining how shortcuts should be selected is not a simple matter, and selecting shortcuts requires a clear understanding of what shortcuts cost and deliver based on experience with comprehensive RMPs as well as shortcut versions. Early implementation of comprehensive approaches by organizations should be viewed as investments in corporate learning when assessing the value and cost of processes for simplicity/complexity trade-offs.

449

DEVELOPING DEEPER UNDERSTANDING

The RMP outlined here can use its six Ws – source of uncertainty – response – secondary issue structure to probe root causes of uncertainty and effective associated responses to provide deep levels of understanding of complex issues. However, there are alternative approaches which may prove fruitful in some circumstances. For example, Williams (2002) considers complexity in different frameworks, including positive and negative feed-back loop structures based on systems dynamics models. It is important to be open to alternative approaches to complexity which best suit the nature of the concerns needing attention.

CONCLUSION

This chapter provides an overview. Chapman and Ward (2003) give this overview more operational content, and clarify its nature with examples. The APM PRAM Guide (APM 2004) elaborates usefully in a different manner, including the use of case studies. Further references provided below also elaborate ideas developed in this chapter in various useful ways. Several key issues should be clear from the overview provided here:

1. RMPs are highly structured, but they do not imply a rigid 'paint by numbers' approach. Creativity, lateral thinking and imagination are stimulated by an effective RMP, not discouraged.
2. RMPs are in many important respects largely a formalization of the common sense project managers have applied for centuries. The RMP described here is not a new way of thinking, or the engine of an intellectual revolution which requires a significant change in mind set to be appreciated.
3. The formalization involved in RMPs is central to capturing the benefit of RMPs, as part of the communication processes involved. The level and kind of communication RMP can generate can lead to significant culture changes within organizations. These changes can be quite fundamental, and they can be very complex.
4. Because RMPs can be concerned with very complex issues, it is very important to see 'keep it simple' as a guiding principle, adding complication only when benefit from doing so is perceived.
5. The iterative nature of the RMP is central to 'keeping it simple', using early passes of the process to identify the areas that need more detailed assessment in later passes.
6. A particularly useful insight which the focus phase of the process captures is the need to 'plan and manage the planning' as a project in its own right, using everything we know about 'planning and managing'. The distinction between

'planning the project' and 'planning the planning' is important, and making it explicit is very useful.

7. A particularly useful insight which the ownership phase of the process captures is the need to manage relationships as a project in its own right.

8. An exciting aspect of the direction this RMP definition and development is taking is its 'strategic opportunity' flavour, moving away from 'tactical threat' planning as the starting point. It is driving project 'owners' towards seeing risk management of individual projects as benefit management, and understanding the connections between individual project benefits and requirements as a output of a programme management approach to project management. Further, they are seeing programme management as a basis for strategic management. Finally, to close the loop, they are seeing project selection as an output of strategic management.

ACKNOWLEDGEMENTS

The authors are grateful to members of the APM SIG on Project Risk Management who were involved in the working parties which contributed to the generic process definition described in this paper. We are also grateful to those who contributed to the clarification and generalization described in this chapter. John Wiley and Sons kindly agreed to the use of diagrams and tables from Chapman and Ward (2003) for Figures 22.1–7.

REFERENCES AND FURTHER READING

APM (Association for Project Management), 2004, *Project Risk Analysis and Management Guide,* High Wycombe: APM Publishing.

Chapman, C.B., 2006, 'Key points of contention in framing assumptions for risk and uncertainty management', *International Journal of Project Management*, Volume 24, Issue 4, pages 303–313.

Chapman, C.B. and Ward, S.C., 2002, *Managing Project Risk and Uncertainty: a constructively simple approach to decision making,* Chichester: Wiley.

Chapman, C.B. and Ward, S., 2003, *Project Risk Management: Processes, Techniques and Insights*, Second Edition, Chichester: Wiley.

Cooper, D., Grey, S., Raymond, G. and Walker, P., 2005, *Project Risk Management Guidelines: managing risk in large projects and complex procurements,* Chichester: Wiley.

ICE, FA & IA (Institution of Civil Engineers, Faculty of Actuaries and Institute of Actuaries), 2005, *RAMP Risk Analysis and Management for Projects,* London: Thomas Telford.

PMI® (Project Management Institute), 2004, *A Guide to the Project Management Book of Knowledge: PMBOK® (Project Management Book of Knowledge) Guide,* Upper Darby, PA: PMI®.

Simon, P., Hillson, D. and Newland, K., (eds), 1997, *Association for Project Management (APM) Project Risk Analysis and Management (PRAM) Guide,* Norwich: APM Group Limited.

Williams, T., 2002, *Modelling Complex Projects,* Chichester: Wiley.

23 Managing Health and Safety

Jim Pearce

Safety is defined as the result of controlling work activities to ensure accidents are prevented. An accident is an uncontrolled or unforeseen event that is capable of causing one or more of:

1. damage and other harm, such as ill-health, to people
2. damage to plant, equipment or premises
3. damage to the project such as interruptions
4. damage to the external environment

Although other names are sometimes used for accidents that do not cause actual personal injury (near misses, incidents, etc.) I prefer to use the term 'accident' to include all of these.

The objective of this chapter is to review the role of occupational health and safety (OHS), highlighting the requirements placed upon the project manager in order to meet good practice and legal requirements (see Appendix 23.1). Above all, a positive common sense approach is needed. All concerned with the project may be required to justify their actions and omissions before a court (see Appendix 23.2: Personal Responsibility).

AN INTRODUCTION TO OCCUPATIONAL HEALTH AND SAFETY

Acceptable standards of occupational health and safety (like anything else worthwhile) do not happen by chance. They can only be achieved by a positive planned approach to all work activities. To help ensure high standards are consistently achieved a well established and formal health and safety management system (HSMS) is required. This must ensure that OHS is an integral part of all corporate and hence project activities. It should establish clear responsibilities for the management and further development of OHS standards and procedures to control specific risk activities. In general it will help ensure that the organization:

1. identifies possible loss producing situations, that is hazards, taking into consideration who could be hurt, both employees and non-employees
2. evaluates the risk associated with each identified hazard
3. checks the suitability of existing controls and identifies additional measures required
4. plans the implementation of these control measures
5. monitors and reviews OHS performance
6. ensures that standards are maintained and where possible improved

A hazard is defined as a property of a substance, equipment process or workplace environment that has the potential to harm persons, equipment or the workplace environment. In other words, it is a built-in property, an integral part of that item or situation. The Health and Safety Executive (HSE) in their publication *Successful Health and Safety Management, HSG65* (HSE 1997a) emphasizes the need for an effective HSMS. It says that successful organizations are good at managing OHS while insufficient attention to health and safety in management decisions lead to disasters such as the fire and explosion on Piper Alpha, etc.

THE COST OF HEALTH AND SAFETY

Health and safety can be expensive, but if ignored, the lack of control could prove even more expensive. Sooner or later deficiencies will result in accidents and loss, due to:

1. injuries, damage, business interruption
2. shutdown as a result of prohibition notices
3. criminal prosecutions resulting in potentially unlimited fines or imprisonment
4. costly civil law claims for compensation

The human and economic cost of failure should be a tremendous incentive to improve safety standards. The HSE (1997b) publication, *HSG 96 Cost of Accidents*, identifies that, during a study period, poor OHS performance cost:

- a construction site a loss of over 8% of the original tender price of £8 million
- a NHS hospital losses amounting to 5% of annual running costs
- a transport company losses amounting to 37% of their annual profits

It also revealed that uninsured losses from accidents cost organizations between 8 and 36 times what they are paying in insurance premiums. Therefore, far from all the costs of failure being borne by the insurers, organizations are themselves bearing a substantial portion of the costs. In some cases these can make the difference between profit and loss. In the view of the HSE, investment in loss reduction contributes directly to profits and may yield a better return than a similar investment to improve sales and market share. This view is held not only by safety professionals, but also by more successful organizations. For instance the CBI recognizes that effective OHS management contributes to waste and cost reduction and promotes a positive corporate image. Managers should therefore recognize that OHS management makes a positive contribution to the success of the organization and ensure it has at least the same degree of importance as productivity and quality.

As the cost of failure can be high it makes sense to devise and implement suitable control systems. These must take into account relevant (minimum) legal requirements (see Appendix 23.1: The Legal Requirements). Some legal duties are absolute and must be complied with no matter what the cost or practicality. However, most are qualified by the terms such as 'as far as is reasonably practicable' or 'suitable and sufficient'. This requires an assessment of effectiveness, reliability and cost relative to the scale of the foreseeable loss. The requirement to carry out risk assessments has been made explicit in the Management of Health and Safety at Work Regulations 1999 (MHSW) and other regulations such as the Control of Substances Hazardous to Health Regulations (COSHH) and the Construction (Design and Management) Regulations 1994 (CDM) soon to be replaced by the Construction (Design and Management) Regulations 2007. They also require the introduction of appropriate control measures.

RISK ASSESSMENT

MHSW Regulation 3 requires every employer to assess the OHS risks to which employees (and non employees, such as the general public and the employees of contractors) are exposed as a result of work activities. Identical responsibilities are placed upon the self-employed. Note this requirement does not require an employer to repeat any risk assessments carried out under other legislation, such as COSHH. It is worth noting that increasingly organizations are being prosecuted, and convicted, for not carrying out a suitable and sufficient risk assessment as well as for the breach of a specific Regulation or the Health and Safety at Work Act that has led to a serious accident.

Assessments should be carried out covering workplaces, work equipment and work activities including the use of substances. They should also be carried out as soon as possible during the purchasing process, as part of project planning as well as covering the outputs of an organization's activities. The process should

455

anticipate and take into account possible failures in control measures possibly due to human factors (*see HSE(1999): HSG48 Reducing Error and Influencing Behaviour*) as well as equipment failure.

Each assessment must be periodically reviewed to check its validity. They should also be reviewed when there is reason, such as because of an accident, or because the introduction of new or changed systems puts in doubt the validity of the original assessment. If an employer has more than five employees, the significant findings of these assessments must be formally recorded. When the assessment has been completed, its findings must be communicated to those who need to take control action, i.e. managers, employees and others.

OBJECTIVES OF RISK ASSESSMENT

A risk assessment has the following objectives:

1. to identify the foreseeable hazards that might cause harm to employees or non-employees;
2. to evaluate the tolerability of the risks arising from these hazards;
3. to ensure that suitable measures are in place to protect exposed persons from harm (and to comply with relevant statutory duties); and if necessary
4. to identify the additional or alternative control actions required to minimize these risks. These protective and preventative measures must meet the standards set in current HSE and other authoritative publications.

METHOD FOR RISK ASSESSMENT

Risk assessments should be undertaken by people who are:

1. trained in the assessment process;
2. familiar with good practice and legal requirements relevant to the activity, equipment, etc. being assessed;
3. capable of analysing and evaluating the task, substance, persons, equipment and environmental (both workplace and external) factors;
4. able to identify the need for further information on the risks, or to recognize their own limitations and know when to call for specialist advice;
5. able to draw valid conclusions and make recommendations to improve risk control;
6. able to make a clear record of the assessment. It should be borne in mind that the organization could be challenged by the enforcing authorities or the courts to prove that the assessment was adequate (see Appendix 23.1).

A commonsense and systematic approach is often all that is needed. The extent to which the exercise goes beyond this depends on the complexity of the project and the identified risks. For activities and equipment covered by HSE and other authoritive guidance texts the use of a checklist based on these documents will almost certainly ensure the appropriateness of the assessment and the identified control measures. For complex and potentially high-risk projects quantitative risk assessment techniques and possibly external consultants may be used. These techniques could include failure mode and effects analysis, event tree and fault tree analysis, etc. It can be found to be beneficial if workers required to exercise a significant degree of self supervision also carry out a basic task and environment risk assessment before commencing their work activity; these are some times referred to as 'take 2' or 'dynamic' risk assessments.

A SIMPLE RISK ASSESSMENT TECHNIQUE

Figure 23.1 contains a risk assessment technique, which could be useful. If necessary to guide and prioritize the implementation of control actions the risk potential (R) can be estimated by assigning a rating to the potential loss severity (S), the frequency at which this could occur (F) and the number of persons who could be affected (N) and multiplying these together:

$$R \ = \ S \times (F \times N)$$

This can be used to place the resultant risk within tolerability bands and aid prioritization of any necessary remedial action plans.

RISK CONTROL

Decisions concerning the reliability of control measures must be guided by reference to the preferred hierarchy of control principles established by MHSW Regulation 4 and Schedule 1. This in effect requires:

1. avoiding or eliminating risks, by for example:
   - Avoiding carrying out particular operations by using a contractor (see risk transfer)
2. carrying out a risk assessment on any risks that cannot be avoided and applying appropriate control measures that:
   - combat risks at source using engineering controls giving priority to measures that protect both the operator and anyone else who could be foreseeably at risk, by:
     - ➥ isolating operators from risk of exposure to hazardous substances by enclosing the process;

457

➡ keeping all persons away from the danger zones associated with machinery by the provision of guards;

➡ adapting the work to the individual by designing workplaces, equipment and work procedures;

Step 1:	Identify all the tasks involved in the project. These can then be organized into generic groups, so reducing the overall number of individual assessments needed.
Step 2:	Appoint small teams of trained and experienced people to examine the tasks and identify the associated hazards. These teams should include representatives of operators and supervision. A manager should lead each team.
Step 3:	Identify, in a stepwise manner, how each task is carried out, as this will affect the risk potential. A variant of the hazard and operability studies technique can be used. In this simple flow diagrams are examined to identify possible failure scenarios by asking 'what if ...' questions. (Workplace observation of established tasks is essential in order to identify all relevant activities.) When assessing work equipment and workplaces a checklist based on relevant current HSE or other authoritive guidance should be used. The above should enable required control actions to be identified. Note the affect of proposed control actions should be assessed to ensure that no additional risks have been introduced.
Step 4:	With established tasks evaluate whether the risks associated with the identified hazards are adequately controlled or not. (At this stage it may be possible to identify more effective methods of risk control than those currently used). If control is inadequate additional measures must be identified and subsequently assessed to ensure unnecessary risks are not being introduced.
Step 5:	A formal record should be made of the significant assessment findings. The assessment should be circulated to management and anyone affected by the risk. The formal record will assist in management reviews and subsequent reassessments.

Figure 23.1 A risk assessment technique

➡ as soon as possible, taking advantage of new technology to improve working conditions and methods;

● minimising risk by:

➡ substitution with the inherently less dangerous, i.e. by use of less hazardous substances or equipment;

➡ establishing a coherent overall risk prevention policy and task specific safe systems of work that take into account technology, organization of work, working conditions, human factors, and the influence of factors relating to the work environment;

➡ lowering the number of people exposed and/or the scale of the operation;

➡ adequately supervising work activities. The level of supervision required will depend on the level of the risk and the competence of the employee;

➡ ensuring employees are competent by supplying suitable training, information, and instruction;

➡ the use of appropriate personal protective equipment (PPE) when risks cannot be reduced to acceptable levels by other means – as far as is reasonably practicable the use of PPE should be accepted only as a temporary or emergency response measure.

Low cost temporary actions are often required to establish control until 'permanent' measures can be installed. Remember it is usually necessary to support the above control actions by regular monitoring and maintenance activities.

RISK TRANSFER

Can the cost of OHS be transferred to someone else? If risk elimination is not possible, risk transfer might certainly be an acceptable way of reducing the potential for loss to a tolerable level. However, remember that a level of risk acceptable to management may be significantly different to that which is tolerable to exposed persons. Methods of risk transfer include:

1. subcontracting to a specialist supplier of products or services
2. insurance

For most organizations, Employer's Liability Insurance is compulsory. However while it is possible to insure against the effects of negligence it is neither legal nor possible to insure against fines that the courts might impose.

There have been several instances where the cost of risk transfer has been expensive for the 'innocent' party. What if the damage was due to the negligence of a contractor? Can a claim be made against them? Contract conditions may be drafted so that damage to the occupier's buildings, contents and plant by fire (a common source of loss) is specifically excluded. Sometimes the client is required to purchase insurance in the joint names of itself and the contractor. Contracts with subcontractors or suppliers often state that they accept no liability for loss of business or profit arising out of any damage caused by them. If the contractor accepts liability, it may be limited in extent. The claim may also have to be made within a short period after the supply of the product or service. This is often too short for the damage to be discovered. Even when the specialist contractor has been engaged to supply both specialist plant and operators, the contract can be worded so as to transfer liability for any accidental damage to the client.

Is it, therefore, worth trying to transfer the risk to someone else? Yes, of course it is. The best commercial and technical option may be to use an external supplier. It is, however, necessary to ensure that any contractor used has an appropriate level of OHS competency. It is also advisable to consult a specialist risk manager at the earliest possible stage. Even if no external suppliers are to be-used, it would still be good sense to consult a specialist risk manager to ensure that the project is adequately covered for:

- employers' liability
- occupier's liability
- fire and other damage
- product liability
- consequential business loss
- third party (public) liability
- environmental liability

HEALTH AND SAFETY MANAGEMENT SYSTEMS

The duty to conduct a formal risk assessment is a key requirement and should be the basis for satisfying Regulation 5 of the MHSW Regulations. This regulation requires every employer to make and implement such arrangements as are appropriate for the effective planning, organizing, control, monitoring and review of protective and preventive safety measures. If there are more than five employees, these arrangements must be formally recorded. This is a similar requirement to that of §2.3 of HSWA, which requires the establishment and revision as necessary of an OHS policy (see below). As with the HSWA requirement a HSMS should provide practical organizational and risk control standards. These help an employer or project manager communicate requirements, ensure competency, monitor performance and hence control OHS. It should be recognized that the HSMS is a facet of the organization's overall management system. Specific examples of this requirement are contained in:

1. The tender and construction phase safety and health plans required under the Construction (Design and Management) Regulations 1994 which implements (within the UK) the EU Temporary or Mobile Construction Sites Directive. Note it is intended that these Regulations will be repealed and a revised version issued becoming effective on the 1st April 2007 to take into account experience gained during the operation of the 1994 Regulations;
2. The Offshore Installations (Safety Case) Regulations 2005;
3. The Railway (Safety Cases) Regulations 2000 as amended (These are being replaced by The Railways and Other Guided Transport Systems (Safety) Regulations, which have been developed to implement the EU Rail Safety Directive, and replace some existing rail safety regulations, in particular that dealing with railway safety cases. These new regulations came into force on 10 April 2006; and
4. The Control of Major Accident Hazard (COMAH) Regulations 1999, which require that with respect to a Major Accident Prevention Policy and the preparation of a Safety Case:

Operators who have control of an (specified) industrial activity ... shall at any time provide evidence including documents to show that they have:

1. Identified the major accident hazards; and
2. Taken adequate steps to:
    2.1. Prevent such major accident hazard;
    2.2. Limit their consequences to persons and the environment (by establishing emergency plans); and
    2.3. Provide persons working on the site with sufficient information, training and equipment to ensure their safety.

A possible draw back of these safety cases is they focus on the prevention of major disasters, so it is possible for the organization to neglect more routine hazards. All actions taken to control risk should comply with the preferred hierarchy of control measures identified earlier.

THE ROLE OF OCCUPATIONAL HEALTH AND SAFETY IN PROJECT MANAGEMENT

There are a few basic questions that should be answered before starting any project. These include the obvious:

Can it be done? Is the project technically feasible?
Do we have the technical capacity to do it?
Have we got enough resources to do it?
Is it worth doing? Will it be profitable?

However, there is one other important question, namely:

Can it be done without an unacceptable degree of risk to the OHS of those working on the project or to anyone else who could be affected by it?

Whilst the main objectives of a project may be to get the job done, maximize efficiency, minimize costs and manage for profit; it must be recognized that actions to identify and prevent, or reduce, losses due to accidents are essential. To achieve this OHS must never be regarded as an 'add-on' function or an optional factor as 'add-ons' are too easy to remove or nullify. To achieve acceptable standards, safety must be built in from the design concept stage. If this is done, it is more likely that an optimum mix of control measures and performance standards will be achieved for production, quality and OHS. Please note it is not the role of OHS practitioners to place 'silly' barriers in the way of a project, but

461

instead to aid managers to recognize and evaluate risks and ensure that its aim can be effectively achieved while meeting current good practice and legal standards.

PROJECT DESIGN OBJECTIVES AND RESPONSIBILITIES

The OHS objectives of a project are to ensure that it is, as far as reasonably practicable, safe and free from risks to health during:

- design including any associated research and development
- construction or installation
- commissioning
- setting (for example, tool setting of machinery)
- use
- maintenance and repair
- modification
- removal or demolition
- disposal

The above must not only take into account normal conditions, but also meet any reasonably foreseeable misuse or emergency conditions. Responsibility for this lies with senior project managers, senior user (client) managers and their employees. To achieve this, the roles and levels of authority of all participants must be clearly defined, ideally in writing. In addition to the usual actions leading to project definition (see Chapter 27) the client should appoint a competent person (or organization) to act as (project) co-ordinator (this role, as far as OHS is concerned, is established in the 2007 CDM Regulations and takes over and expands upon the responsibilities previously assigned to the planning supervisor in the 1994 Regulations).

Amongst the OHS project coordinator's responsibilities is ensuring that safety and health considerations are an integral part of the design process and resolving any conflicts arising from various design requirements. As a result, specialist design requirements will be reconciled and translated into a plan that clearly communicates to implementers a set of established OHS performance standards. This plan should also address hazards associated with the environment in which the project is to be carried out. It should also help ensure as many of the client's requirements as are reasonably practicable are achieved in an economical and safe manner. Consequently the product outcome will be of good construction, sound material, adequate strength, be safe to use and without undue risk to health.

HEALTH AND SAFETY FILE

Among the responsibilities specified by the Construction Design and Management Regulations (CDM) is the preparation of a health and safety file appropriate to the characteristics of the project. This duty is similar to the requirements to produce a technical file included in the so-called European Union Product Directives. These set various requirements that must be met before specified types of product can be marketed within the EU. In particular, these items must satisfy relevant 'essential safety requirements' (ESRs). ESRs have been produced to cover a number of cases, including use of machinery and hazardous substances, to name just two examples.

PRODUCT LIABILITY

Managers of projects for the purpose of introducing new products into the market place may have to take into account the effects on OHS of domestic, as well as occupational users. To provide for this, the EU has produced the Directive on Strict Product Liability. This was implemented in the United Kingdom by the Consumer Protection Act 1987. Strict liability means that there is no need to prove that the producer of a defective product was negligent. What has to be proved by the claimant is that:

- there was injury or damage;
- the product was defective; and
- the defect caused the injury or damage.

An article or substance is defective if the safety of the product is not to the standard that the consumer is entitled to expect. This will take into account all the circumstances including user instructions, accompanying warnings, etc. Amongst possible defences is the *development risk defence*. That is the state of scientific and technical knowledge at the time of supply was not sufficient to enable the defect to be discovered. This defence reinforces the need to prepare a product technical file, to keep adequate records and to be prepared to respond in a prompt and positive manner to rectify any defects revealed through user experience. Organizations have been prosecuted for not informing customers when experience has identified previously unknown OHS risks.

SAFETY POLICY

Every employer of five or more persons is required under §2.3 of HSWA to prepare a statement of its OHS policy. The purpose of this policy document is very similar to that of a safety plan required by other legislation. It must state the organization's OHS objectives, define the responsibilities of its management and staff and set performance standards that can be used to guide and control implementation. Above all, it must be a working document reflecting a practical management system that helps all persons in the organization to meet personal and corporate obligations. Successful OHS policies are in three parts:

1. a general statement of policy that outlines the commitment of the organization and its management with respect to OHS;
2. statements of assigned responsibilities to manage the ongoing development and planned implementation of the policy; and
3. specific arrangements for ensuring that adequate standards will be achieved and maintained. These will consist of procedures to:
   - ensure management establishes and maintains (i.e. controls) the system
   - guide co-operation/consultation with employee representatives
   - ensure dissemination of OHS information
   - ensure development and maintenance of employee competency
   - guide the control of specific risks

The last section should be written as internal codes of practice, setting both organizational and technical performance standards. These will aid monitoring, management review activities and modification as required. The safety policy, like a project safety plan, must be specific to the site or project. However in multi-site organizations there is a need for a co-ordinated approach to ensure that high standards are achieved in a similar manner. Every employee must have been thoroughly briefed on their responsibilities and the procedures by which they are to be implemented. The content of the three parts will now be examined more closely.

GENERAL STATEMENT OF OHS POLICY

The purpose of the general statement is to set out a brief but explicit declaration of the organization's commitment to OHS and outline how this is to be achieved. This should include identifying the senior executive responsible for co-ordinating the development and implementation of the policy. It should also include, amongst others, the following commitments:

1. health and safety issues are just as important as any other organizational objective;
2. legal requirements are to be considered as the minimum – not the optimum – standards;
3. the organization is committed to review and upgrade standards on a continuous basis;

4. the commitment to involve all staff in the development and implementation of OHS measures.

DEFINING THE ORGANIZATION

The objective of this part of the OHS statement is to set out the chain of responsibility from executive management through to 'shop-floor' employees. It should also define the role of specialist support staff, such as the safety advisor.

Managers should have their general functions for formulating, planning and implementing the organization's policy clearly identified (see Appendix 2 of HSG 65). These should be, as appropriate, complemented by specific responsibilities for an established set of tasks. They should be described in sufficient detail to give positive guidance and also to aid performance monitoring by the individual's manager. The review of a person's OHS performance should be regarded as a normal activity to be conducted along with the appraisal of other operational responsibilities. It is recommended that job descriptions should make reference to OHS responsibilities.

ARRANGEMENTS FOR IMPLEMENTATION

The objective of this part of the OHS policy is to provide procedures that set required standards of performance and give positive guidance on how to meet assigned responsibilities. It should include the following elements:

1. activities designed to ensure the management team are in *control* of the HSMS. These should include procedures guiding:
   - the formulation and planned development of the system;
   - supervision of work activities taking into account the level of risk and the competence of the operators;
   - proactive monitoring activities, such as planned inspections;
   - reactive monitoring through the reporting and investigation of accidents;
   - systematic audits of the HSMS; and
   - management review of the system covering:
     - an assessment of the degree of compliance with organizational procedures;
     - the identification of activities where procedures are absent or inadequate;
     - an assessment of the achievement of specific objectives;
     - an examination of accident, ill health and incident data, accompanied by the analysis of both immediate and underlying causes, trends and common features.

2. the establishment of formal *cooperation* between the management team and employees by establishing an OHS committee which assists in both monitoring the implementation of the HSMS and its ongoing development;
3. the establishment of systems which guide the acquisition of OHS information and its systematic *communication* both within the organization and outside as required;
4. activities designed to ensure *competent* persons are recruited and the on-going development of their capabilities to meet organizational needs via training;
5. the systematic carrying out of *risk assessments*;
6. the creation of specific *risk control systems* as needed to meet operational needs, such as the use of lift trucks, chemicals, noise, personal protective equipment, control of contractors, permits to work and so on.

These procedures should contain clear statements of required performance standard that specify who is responsible for what, when activities are to be carried out and how. Within all procedures the following features should be evident:

1. A statement that the procedure is part of the organization's policy;
2. A description of its scope of application;
3. Assignment to a senior manager responsibility for their development and monitoring their implementation. This does not detract from the responsibility of those in charge of an area or activity to ensure standards are achieved. Their responsibilities should also be defined;
4. Procedures should then detail the activities and standards needed to achieve adequate control, through consultation, communication and the competence of project personnel;
5. Arrangements for monitoring performance, management reviews and the keeping of essential records.

SAFETY MANAGEMENT SYSTEM AUDITS

It is strongly recommended that regular internal HSMS audits be conducted to ensure existing procedures are satisfactorily implemented. These should be supported by regular (perhaps annual) verification audits to measure performance against HSG 65 and other current good practice requirements including legislation. These audits should be conducted in accordance with the methodology described in BS EN ISO 19011:2002 'Guidelines for quality and/or environmental management systems auditing', by someone independent of the system and the organization's operational activities. This person could be from elsewhere in the organization or from an external consultancy. A number of proprietary audit systems have been developed to facilitate appraisals, including:

- CHASE: The Complete Health and Safety Evaluation System, from Health and Safety Technology Management Limited, Birmingham.
- Five Star System, from the British Safety Council, London.
- ISRS: International Safety Rating System, from the International Loss Control Institute.
- QSA: The Quality Safety Audit, from the Royal Society for the Prevention of Accidents (RoSPA), Birmingham.

Many audits include scoring systems to help evaluate the quality of the HSMS; these are useful as they can help determine priorities. However, care should be taken to ensure that the system chosen examines the detail of the organization's HSMS and not just broad-brush concepts.

REFERENCES AND FURTHER READING

Bird, F.E. Jun. and Germain, G.L., 1996, *Practical Loss Control Leadership*, International Loss Control Institute, Loganville, Georgia., Revised.

BSI, 2000, *OHSAS 18002: 2000: Occupational health and safety management systems – Guidelines for the implementation of OHSAS 18001*, London: British Standards Institute.

BSI, 2002, *BS EN ISO 19011:2002: Guidelines for quality and/or environmental management systems auditing,* London: British Standards Institute.

BSI, 2005, *PAS 79 Fire risk assessment – Guidance and a recommended methodology*, London: British Standards Institute.

Cooper, D., 1996, *Improving safety culture; a practical guide*, Chichester: Wiley.

Department for Communities and Local Government, *Fire risk assessment guidance books*, <http://www.communities.gov.uk/index.asp?id=1162101>

ECI, 1995, *Total project management of construction safety, health and environment*, Loughborough: European Constuction Institute.

Heny, J. and Ford, M., 1997, *Redgrave, Fife and Machin. Health and Safety,* London: Butterworths.

Greenburg, H.R. and Cramer, J.G., (eds.), 1991, *Risk Assessment and Risk Management for the Chemical Process Industry,* New York: Van Nostrand Reinhold.

HSE, 1996, *CD200: Revision of the Construction (Design and Management) Regulations (CDM) 1994, Construction (Health, Safety and Welfare) (CHSW) Regulations 1996, Approved Code of Practice (ACoP) and Guidance,* <http://hse.gov.uk/consult/condocs/cd200.pdf>

HSE, 1996, *Construction (Health, Safety and Welfare) (CHSW) Regulations 1996*, London: The Stationery Office.

HSE, 1997a, *Successful Health and Safety Management, 2nd edition* HSG65, Sudbury: HSE Books.

HSE, 1997b, *The Cost of Accidents, HSG 96*, Sudbury: HSE Books. – Out of print but not superseded.

HSE, 1998, *Managing risk- adding value. How big firms manage contractual relations to reduce risk – A study*, Sudbury: HSE Books.

HSE, 1999, *Reducing error and influencing behaviour 2nd edition* HSG65, Sudbury: HSE Books.

HSE, 2001, *Managing Health and Safety in Construction*, HSG224, Sudbury: HSE Books.

HSE, 2003, *Research Report 151, Good practice and pitfalls in risk assessment, The Health and Safety Laboratory*, <www.hse.gov.uk/research/rrhtm/rr151.htm>.

HSE, 2004, *Investigating Accidents and Incidents, HSG 245*, Sudbury: HSE Books.

HSE, 2005a, *Offshore Installation (Safety Case) Regulations 2005*, London: The Stationery Office.

HSE, 2005b, *The Work at Height regulations 2005*, London: The Stationery Office.

HSE, 2005c, *ING401 The Work at Height regulations 2005*, Sudbury: HSE Books.

Jones, Alan, 1999, *The Health and Safety Factbook*, London: GEE, (with updating service) (CD-ROM).

Ridley, J., 2003, *Safety at Work 6th edition*, London: Butterworth-Heinemann.

Smith, A.J., 1992, *The Development of a Model to Incorporate Management and Organizational Influences in Quantified Risk Assessment*, HSE Contract *614* Research Report, no. 38/1992, London: The Stationery Office.

Stranks, J.W., 2005. *The Handbook of Health and Safety Practice 7th edition*, Harlow: Prentice Hall.

Tolley Publishing, 2005, *Tolley's Health and Safety at Work Handbook 2006, 18th edition*, Croydon: Tolley Publishing.

Wells, G., 1997, *Major hazards and their management*, Rugby:Institution of Chemical Engineers.

APPENDIX 23.1: LEGAL REQUIREMENTS

INTRODUCTION

Traditional United Kingdom safety legislation, such as the Factories Act 1961, the Shops, Offices and Railway Premises Act 1963 and their supporting regulations, was prescriptive in nature. It was a response to persistent serious accidents and concentrated on a 'safe place/safe machine' strategy. Employers were expected to meet minimum requirements based on what was good practice at the time each law was introduced. Unfortunately, as these requirements often did not keep pace with technology, many loopholes were created and many persons were not protected. Recognising the need for a change of approach, and the fact that human factors needed to be taken into consideration the Health and Safety at Work etc Act 1974 was introduced. This brought many aspects of common law into statute law. In particular, it required the provision and maintenance of safe systems of work (these being safe equipment, safe workplace, safe substances, plus safe person strategies linked together into safe working methods). The goal setting nature of this Act has been re-enforced by legislation required by the European Union, such as the Management of Health and Safety at Work Regulations 1999 and the Construction (Design and Management) Regulations 2007.

COMMON LAW

Common law is based upon the duty of care. Failure to take reasonable care that your acts and omissions do not adversely affect your 'neighbours' is negligence. These failures could, if damage to persons, plant, property or business interruption results, lead to claims for compensation. Negligence can be defined as doing something that the reasonable person would not do or failing to do something that the reasonable person would do (in the prevailing circumstances (*Blyth v. Birmingham Waterworks Co., 1856*)). In occupational terms, a 'reasonable person', that is a 'competent person', is one who has sufficient theoretical and practical knowledge, skill and experience to be able to recognize faults and their significance in the particular circumstances and take control actions. He/she is also not too rash or too timid. A 'neighbour' is anyone who could be so directly affected by one's acts and omissions that one ought reasonably to have them in contemplation *(Donaghue v. Stevenson, 1932)*. Overall the doctrines of foreseeability and reasonableness are of paramount importance. In *Walker v Bletchley Flettons Limited (1937)* the judge stated:

> *The fact that an accident has never happened does not necessarily diminish the foreseeability of one, no more than does the occurrence of one accident yesterday increase the foreseeability of accidents in the future.*

THE HEALTH AND SAFETY AT WORK ETC ACT 1974, HSWA

HSWA sets duties on all persons concerned with occupational activities. This means not only the employer, but also employees, the self-employed, manufacturers, suppliers, designers, importers and, potentially, the general public. It should be read in conjunction with the Management of Health and Safety at Work Regulations 1999 and other subordinate Regulations. To fail to meet these

469

responsibilities is a criminal offence that, in some cases, could result in unlimited fines and or up to two years in jail. The largest fine for health and safety up to July 2006 is £10million and the reduction to £7.5million (Balfour Beatty with respect to the Hatfield rail crash).

The main duties lie with the employer (see Appendix 23.2: personal responsibilities). This is to ensure, so far as is reasonably practicable, the health, safety and welfare of his employees (§2.1). In addition, each employer (or self employed person) shall, so far as is reasonably practicable, ensure that their work activities do not adversely affect the health, safety and welfare of other persons (§3). They must also, in prescribed circumstances, supply information. All persons connected with non-domestic premises (§4.2) shall, so far as is reasonably practicable, ensure safe access and egress, and absence of risks to OHS arising from the use of plant or substances to persons who are not their employees. The employer's responsibility to its employees is further expanded in §2.2, by having to ensure that, so far as is reasonably practicable it:

1. provides and maintains safe plant and safe systems of work;
2. provides and maintains safe arrangements for the use, handling, storage and transport of articles and substances;
3. provides each employee with information, instruction, training and supervision as is necessary to ensure OHS;
4. provides and maintains a safe place of work with safe access and egress;
5. provides and maintains a safe and healthy working environment.

§9 requires the provision, maintenance and free replacement of any item specifically required to be provided by OHS legislation.

It should be recognized that all the obligations specified with 1974 Act are absolute duties and must be met (see *Lockhart v Kevin Oliphant 1992*). A permitted defence is that the duty-holder achieved a standard that was as far as was reasonably practicable.

The meaning of 'so far as is reasonably practicable'

When a duty is qualified by the phrase 'as far as is reasonably practicable' the required standard of compliance may be lower than that which is physically achievable (by current technology). It requires the reasonably foreseeable losses arising out of the activity be calculated. These should be compared against the costs of control actions. All calculations must be done before initiating the activity. A control action would be deemed unreasonable if the costs were grossly disproportionate to the loss, that is the risk must be insignificant in proportion to the sacrifice (*Edwards v NCB 1949 1 All ER 743, CA*). That is, there is a strongly implied requirement to conduct risk assessment. Failure to carry out this assessment is trusting to luck and a breach of legislation (see *R v Board of Trustees of the Science Museum 1993*). This assessment must be followed up by suitable control action. There is no obligation to eliminate the risk, only to reduce it to a tolerable (currently acceptable) level and by adequate supervision ensure these standards are consistently achieved.

Self regulation

One effect of HSWA is that employers or project managers can conduct their business in any way they wish, as long as they can justify their actions within the framework set by current legislation. This freedom has been termed self-regulation. It is a demanding requirement and not a soft option. Judges' decisions, e.g. *Walker v. Bletchley Flettons Limited* (*1937*) have determined that there is a duty:

- to identify foreseeably dangerous items and situations;
- to take into account the reasonably foreseeable actions of persons including forgetfulness, and to some extent wilfulness and stupidity; and
- to take into account circumstances that can be reasonably foreseen.

Something is dangerous

Something is deemed to be dangerous if:

> *in the ordinary course of human affairs, danger can be reasonably anticipated from its use not only to the prudent, alert and skilled worker intent upon his task, but also to the careless and inattentive worker whose inadvertent or indolent conduct may expose him to risk of injury or death. (Mitchell v. North British Rubber Company Limited 1945)*

Current legislation sets objectives

HSWA and its subordinate regulations are designed to set objectives, rather than specific standards, as these can easily be rendered redundant by technological progress. These measures are often supported by dedicated approved codes of practice (AcoPs), approved by the Health and Safety Commission (HSC) that, when offered in evidence by the enforcing authority, must be accepted as setting minimum reasonably practicable standards. In addition, the Health and Safety Executive (HSE) has published an extensive series of guidance notes and booklets. These, although not automatically admissible in court, provide official guidance to what is 'reasonably practicable' and have significant persuasive influence. It is worth noting that all recent guidance notes and booklets follow the management approach outlined in HSG65. Additional sources of information on acceptable standards include codes of practice published by various professional institutions, the British Standards Institution and other authoritative bodies.

Interpretation

Managers must to be able to interpret the requirements of legislation. Fortunately, the Acts and Regulations themselves often provide definition clauses, and of course there are the associated ACoPs and various HSE Guidance notes. In general a practical or 'normal meaning' common sense approach is often required. For example, the term 'as applied' in HSWA, §82.2 (dealing with the general interpretation of the Act) requires the application of current technology. Common practice will be taken into account, but beware – common practice is often not good practice. This mirrors the guidance provided in *Stokes v. GKN, 1968* where it was stated that the reasonable and prudent employer would:

1. Use proven, safe and recognized practices;
2. Keep reasonably abreast of developing knowledge; and
3. Not be too slow to apply it.

Although a self-regulatory approach is required there is still a need for specific and prescriptive guidance. This will be supplied by Regulations produced to meet the requirements as identified by EU Directives and the HSC. These will produce an increasing body of common standards throughout the Single European Market.

The burden of proof

The onus of proving what was reasonably practicable does not lie with the enforcing authority. It is up to the accused (HSWA §40) to prove that it was not practicable or reasonably practicable to do more than was done to satisfy the requirement. This is a change from the usual UK criminal legislative position, where it is the responsibility of the accuser to prove guilt once the enforcing authority has established that there is a case to answer. The accused is required to prove that he had exercised due diligence. That is:

1. the hazards and risks had been identified;
2. the best available technology not entailing excessive cost had been employed; and as a result;
3. the residual risk was as low as was reasonably achievable, that is the best OHS option had been implemented.

To prove this there is a need to keep records of significant risks assessments and decisions.

UK IMPLEMENTATION OF EU DIRECTIVES

In the United Kingdom EU directives will be implemented by the HSWA supported by:

- Management of Health and Safety at Work Regulations
- Provision and Use of Work Equipment Regulations
- Manual Handling Operations Regulations
- Personal Protective Equipment at Work Regulations
- Health and Safety (Display Screen Equipment) Regulations
- Workplace (Health Safety and Welfare) Regulations
- Construction Design and Management Regulations
- The Work at Height Regulations 2005, etc.

These Regulations amend and extend previous legislation. Features common to them include:

- the need to identify hazards and carry out a risk assessment
- the need to control identified risks by means of recognized protective and preventative measures
- employers are expected to introduce arrangements for meeting these protective and preventative measures (which means planning, organizing, implementing, control monitoring and management reviews)

It should be noted that the 'due diligence' defence of 'so far as is reasonably practicable' has been excluded from the requirements of these directives and hence the Regulations. Their requirements are absolute and therefore must be met. It is to be hoped that the standard achieved will be interpreted in the light of current technology and what could be considered reasonable considering the circumstances.

ENFORCEMENT

Health and safety requirements are enforced by inspectors managed by the Health and Safety Executive (HSE) or by environmental health officers appointed by local authorities. The HSE inspector most likely to be encountered by project managers will belong to the Factory Inspectorate. All inspectors appointed under HSWA have wide ranging powers to enable them to enforce the requirements of the Act. The most probable outcome of an inspector's visit will be verbal requirements backed up by a *letter*. If necessary, the inspector will issue an *improvement notice*. This will require protective and preventative measures to be implemented within a specified period. When, in the opinion of the inspector, the circumstances give rise to immediate danger or risk of serious injury, a *prohibition notice* will be issued. This will prohibit specified activities until the situation has been remedied. It is possible to appeal against these notices within 21 days to an industrial tribunal. Failure to meet the requirements of an inspector or a notice is an offence. However, when necessary they can initiate prosecution and,

473

depending on the degree of seriousness, cases will be heard either in a Magistrates' Court or a Crown Court (or their Scottish equivalents).

The Offshore Safety Act 1992 (OSA) allows Magistrates (Sheriffs in Scotland) to impose fines of up to £20 000 for a breach of §2-6 of HSWA or breach of an improvement notice, prohibition notice or court remedy order. Individuals may be liable for a term of imprisonment not exceeding six months. It also widens the range of OHS offences for which a Crown Court (or its Scottish equivalent) can impose custodial sentences. These courts can sentence individuals to imprisonment for up to two years and/or an unlimited fine for serious offences or a breach of an enforcement notice or court remedy order, as well as for offences against earlier legislation (explosives, licensing regimes). Offences other than those outlined above will, under the Criminal Justice Act 1991, attract a fine of up to £5 000.

THE MANAGEMENT OF HEALTH AND SAFETY AT WORK REGULATIONS

Figure 23.2 contains a set of Regulations, which together with HSWA, form the framework for all OHS responsibilities.

Regulation 3	Requires all employers and self employed to carry out suitable and sufficient risk assessments. See body of text above. This Regulation also requires the carrying out of fire risk assessments, a duty that has been enhanced by the Regulatory Reform (Fire Safety) Order 2005.
Regulation 4	Establishes the principles of prevention that are to be applied.
Regulation 5	Requires the introduction of OHS arrangements to ensure risks are adequately controlled. See earlier in this chapter.
Regulation 6	Requires the introduction of health surveillance when identified as necessary (by risk assessment) to aid the control of risks to health.
Regulation 7	Requires the appointment of a competent person or group of competent persons to provide OHS assistance. See Appendix 23.4 covering the role of the OHS adviser.
Regulation 8	Requires the establishment of appropriate emergency procedures. These could range from first-aid arrangements to full-scale disaster plans. They should be based on formal assessment, be fully documented, and would form part of the safety plan or safety policy. (It should be noted that, in the United Kingdom, to meet fire emergency situations the Home Office has introduced the Fire Precautions (Places of Work) Regulations 1997.)
Regulation 9	Covers contacts with external services particularly covering first aid, emergency medical care and rescue work.
Regulation 10	Reinforces the requirement of s. 2.2 of the OHS at work act (HSWA) to provide information to employees.
Regulation 11	Emphasises the duties of two or more employers sharing a workplace to co-operate with each other to enable them to meet their duties under the relevant statutory duties.
Regulation 12	Describes responsibility of employers to provide OHS information to employer of any employees from an external organization who are working on his premises.
Regulation 13	Reinforces employers' duties under s. 2.2 of HSWA to provide training, as necessary. It specifies circumstances where training is required and emphasises the need to provide refresher training.
Regulation 14	Reinforces the employee's duty not to interfere with preventative and protective measures. It also adds a new duty: to inform the employer of OHS problems and shortfalls in the protective arrangements of which they become aware.
Regulation 15	Requires the provision of operational OHS information to temporary workers and to any agency providing such workers.

Figure 23.2   The Management of Health And Safety at Work Regulations

APPENDIX 23.2: PERSONAL RESPONSIBILITY

The Health and Safety at Work Act, the Fire Precautions Act, the Environmental Protection Act and recent Regulations place responsibility on both the employer, and on individuals from directors to the shop floor. This is fair, as corporate responsibilities will only be achieved by the efforts of individuals on whom the organization must rely. The employer remains responsible for ensuring managers and others who exercise discretion and judgement:

● Are competent to do so;

475

- Have been provided with clear guidelines; and
- Meet set performance standards.

Responsibility for carrying out these duties is personal and cannot be transferred to any other person, especially the safety adviser. This role (see Appendix 23.3) should be recognized by all as being to advise the organization with authority and independence. In the eyes of the law, the obligations placed on a manager or individual do not extend beyond matters that are, in practice, within their control, or where authority to act has been delegated explicitly by the employer. Figure 23.3 lists four sections of HSWA which deal with personal responsibility.

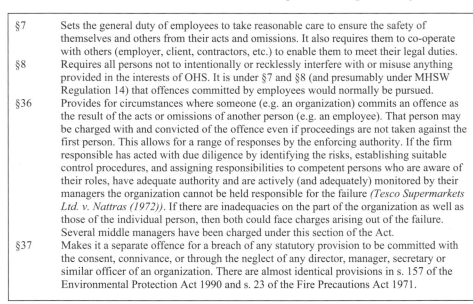

§7	Sets the general duty of employees to take reasonable care to ensure the safety of themselves and others from their acts and omissions. It also requires them to co-operate with others (employer, client, contractors, etc.) to enable them to meet their legal duties.
§8	Requires all persons not to intentionally or recklessly interfere with or misuse anything provided in the interests of OHS. It is under §7 and §8 (and presumably under MHSW Regulation 14) that offences committed by employees would normally be pursued.
§36	Provides for circumstances where someone (e.g. an organization) commits an offence as the result of the acts or omissions of another person (e.g. an employee). That person may be charged with and convicted of the offence even if proceedings are not taken against the first person. This allows for a range of responses by the enforcing authority. If the firm responsible has acted with due diligence by identifying the risks, establishing suitable control procedures, and assigning responsibilities to competent persons who are aware of their roles, have adequate authority and are actively (and adequately) monitored by their managers the organization cannot be held responsible for the failure *(Tesco Supermarkets Ltd. v. Nattras (1972))*. If there are inadequacies on the part of the organization as well as those of the individual person, then both could face charges arising out of the failure. Several middle managers have been charged under this section of the Act.
§37	Makes it a separate offence for a breach of any statutory provision to be committed with the consent, connivance, or through the neglect of any director, manager, secretary or similar officer of an organization. There are almost identical provisions in s. 157 of the Environmental Protection Act 1990 and s. 23 of the Fire Precautions Act 1971.

Figure 23.3 Sections of the Health and Safety at Work Act dealing with personal responsibility

An appeal under the Fire Precautions Act 1971 *(R. v Boal 1992)* clarified the interpretation of the term 'manager'. The Court of Appeal determined there was no intention in §23 of the Act to impose criminal responsibility on anyone but those in a position of real authority in an organization. These were those with the power and responsibility to set corporate policy; there was no intention to 'strike at underlings'. This decision confirms that these sections are designed to deal with offences committed by senior persons, who can be described as being 'of the mind of the body corporate'. A case often quoted is that of *Armour v. Skeen (1977)*. A worker repairing a bridge over the River Clyde fell to his death. Armour, as Director of Roads for Strathclyde Regional Council, was responsible for supervising the safety of council workers while on the roads. It was alleged he had not prepared a written safety policy statement for roadwork and had failed to inform his staff of implications and requirements of the 1974 Act and of the need for adequate training and supervision. His defence, that he had no personal duty to carry out the council's statutory duty under HSWA, §2.3, was rejected. This conviction was upheld on appeal. It is noteworthy that for failing to follow the terms of a prohibition notice, a director (Mr. Rodney Chapman of Chapman Chalk Supplies Ltd.) was not only fined £5,000 under §37, but also disqualified from being a company director for two years under a provision of the Company Directors Disqualifications Act 1986.

As a result of the sections of the Act described here, those concerned with management should note they are always accountable for OHS standards. This cannot be delegated. It will exist even when the manager is not physically present. It is important that they ensure that:

1. Hazards have been identified;
2. The risks have been evaluated;
3. Suitable protective and preventative measures have been established;
4. Operational responsibilities have been assigned to competent persons;
5. Proactive monitoring systems (physical inspections and audits) have been established;
6. Accidents are promptly and thoroughly investigated;
7. Necessary remedial actions are promptly implemented; and
8. The safety management system is reviewed regularly by those responsible for its overall management.

APPENDIX 23.3: SAFETY PRACTITIONER

MHSW Regulation 7 requires every employer to appoint sufficient competent persons to assist in undertaking the protective and preventative measures. In addition Regulation 8 requires the employer to establish emergency procedures and nominate a sufficient number of competent persons to implement the evacuation aspects of these procedures. There is also a requirement to ensure that they are allowed sufficient time and facilities to enable them to fulfil their functions. Although these assistance functions could be done by people who are not in direct employment, it is best if directly employed people are appointed. Persons appointed can only be regarded as competent if they have sufficient training, experience, knowledge or other qualities to enable them properly to assist the employer in his duties. The safety adviser must be competent to advise on the action to be taken or (where so required) to implement such action. This requires suitable training, such as in the National Examination Board in Occupational Safety and Health's Diploma, and appropriate technical expertise.

COMPETENCE AND DUTIES OF A SAFETY ADVISER

The following list has been adapted, from the document *Criteria for a Registered Safety Practitioner,* published by the Institution of Occupational Safety and Health. Note the title Registered Safety Practitioner (RSP) is now redundant since the Institute achieved its Royal Charter. RSPs can now use the designation Chartered Safety and Health Practitioner.

1. Assist management to identify the full range of hazards known and not previously encountered in the workplace by:
   - helping to draw up safety inspection systems and occupational health and hygiene survey programmes;
   - assisting in drawing up procedures for vetting the design and commissioning of new plant and machinery and the introduction of new chemicals into the workplace
2. Assist in the assessment of the extent of the risks to which persons both inside and outside the workplace are exposed by:
   - maintaining an adequate OHS information data base;
   - analysing data on injuries, dangerous occurrences and near misses in the workplace;
   - helping to assess the risks to third parties caused by products, services and pollutants;
   - arranging for quantitative risk assessments when appropriate.
3. Assist in the development of control strategies by:
   - helping the organization make judgements on what is reasonably practicable in minimising particular risks and so ensuring legislative compliance;
   - assisting in the development of a framework of safe systems of work (including permit-to-work systems);
   - helping to set strategies for risk reduction for particular problems;
   - assisting in setting up strategies for assessing health risks as required by, for example, the Control of Substances Hazardous to Health Regulations;
   - contributing to the development of strategies for eliminating or reducing risk, in co-operation with other professional staff and with line management;
   - helping to analyse training needs and develop training strategies.
4. Assist in the implementation of control programmes by:
   - helping in setting safety objectives;
   - helping to set control programmes for the use of personal protective equipment;
   - organizing and reviewing emergency and disaster planning procedures;
   - providing hazard information to managers, workers and others;

- assisting in the organization and running of safety education and training programmes.
5. Assist in monitoring and evaluating the success of control programmes by:
   - helping to set up systems for the regular collection of information on injuries, diseases and dangerous occurrences, near misses and the state of the workplace environment;
   - helping to analyse such information to establish whether objectives are being met, and whether there is improvement or deterioration in performance;
   - assisting in ensuring that the audit, survey and inspection procedures in the organization are carried out;
   - participating in the investigation of injuries, diseases and dangerous occurrences and near misses to see whether improvements to systems of work or equipment are needed;
   - encouraging prompt remedial action to be taken to rectify deficiencies.
6. Help maintain an adequate organizational framework for safety and health programmes by:
   - assisting in the preparation and revision of the organization's OHS policy;
   - helping to establish effective safety committees and effective co-operation with workplace employee safety representatives;
   - managing the work of subordinate safety and health staff (in larger organizations);
   - co-operating effectively with other professional safety and health staff;
   - influencing engineers, architects, buyers, members of elected bodies and others in safety issues;
   - helping to set up and maintain effective safety and health information systems, including access to outside sources;
   - helping to maintain satisfactory relations with safety and health enforcement agencies, and other relevant outside bodies (e.g. insurers, trade associations, etc.).

In addition the employer should ensure that the person or persons appointed has adequate resources and sufficient seniority and independence of action in the organization.

APPENDIX 23.4: CONSTRUCTION HEALTH AND SAFETY

The Construction (Design and Management) Regulations 2007 (CDM) set out the responsibilities of the client, the planning supervisor and the principal contractor. These require the client to appoint a competent person or organization to act as (planning) co-ordinator as well as competent designers and a competent principal contractor.

In its consultative document covering CDM 2007 (Revision of the Construction (Design and Management) Regulations (CDM) 1994, Construction (Health, Safety and Welfare) (CHSW) Regulations 1996, Approved Code of Practice (ACoP) and Guidance), the Health and Safety Commission (HSC) describe the co-ordinator's function as to assist the client, designer and contractor in achieving better health and safety on site. The client responsible for instructing the co-ordinator and is required to ensure he or she carries out his or her duties.

The co-ordinator's tasks are set out in draft regulation 13 and are outlined below. The HSC describes its intention in making these alterations is to position the co-ordinator as the client's *friend*. Responsibility for ensuring the co-ordinator carries out the necessary functions continues to rest with the client.

The (project) co-ordinator is required to:

1. advise and assist the client in carrying out its duties;
2. assist in the selection of designers and the principle contractor advising the client on the competence and resources of their appointees;
3. manage the flow of health and safety information between the client and designers and principle contractors to ensure they are supplied with adequate and comprehensible information relevant to the required project and the surrounding environment to enable them to specify and co-ordinate the measures needed to comply with relevant statutory provisions. This will include:
   - a general description of the work comprised in the project or contract;
   - details of:
     - the time within which it is intended that the project and any stages will be completed;
     - the reasonably foreseeable risks to health and safety of any persons carrying out the work;
       - the reasonably foreseeable risks to health and safety of other persons not carrying out the work and likely to be affected;
   - Any other information that all parties concerned may be reasonably be expected to know in order to carry out the work required and to comply with any requirements placed upon the client and contractor;
   - Advising the client how to fill significant gaps, e.g. by commissioning surveys;
4. monitor and co-ordinate design work, planning and other preparation for construction, where relevant to health and safety;
5. check the suitability of information prepared by designers for contractors;
6. liaise with the principal contractor about design developments during the construction phase that are likely to have implications for health and safety and the construction phase plan;

7. produce or update a relevant, user friendly, health and safety file suitable for future use at the end of the construction phase;
8. notify HSE about the project on behalf of the client;
9. develop effective management arrangements for the project and review and revise them as required;
10. carry out early planning and, sometimes, preparation for the construction work;
11. advise the client on the suitability of the construction phase plan (for the initial construction work) and welfare facilities before construction work starts;
12. monitor the flow of information forming the health and safety file.

The CDM 2007 consultative document emphasizes that designers have considerable potential to reduce the risks associated with construction work, as well as those associated with building use, maintenance, cleaning, and eventual demolition. The HSC's proposals reflect this and are largely unchanged from those established in the 1994 Regulations, clarifying the factors they must take into account when exercising their professional judgement. The aim is to encourage designers to focus on what they can do, in the design, to eliminate hazards, where possible, and reduce the risks resulting from any that remain.

The HSE has recently established a website http://www.hse.gov.uk/construction/designers/index/htm to breathe new life into the CDM designers debate by:

- being clear on what designers do and don't have to do;
- suggesting an alternative to design risk assessments (DRAs) for conveying information;
- suggesting how designers can assess their training needs, and their level of CDM competence;
- introducing the concept of red, amber and green lists as practical aides to designers on what to eliminate/avoid, and what to encourage;
- providing a facility for practicing designers to recommend other sites or reference materials to their professional colleagues.

During project execution the responsibility for OHS rests mainly with the principal contractor and this has not been substantially changed within the draft 2007 CDM Regulations. The only enhancement is to make explicit their duty to plan, manage and monitor their own work.

However, it should be realized that the client has a responsibility to monitor standards to ensure that the project activities are not endangering third parties. Failure to do so can result and has resulted in the client being successfully prosecuted.

The main responsibilities of the principal contractor are to:

1. draw up a 'construction phase' OHS plan
2. select and co-ordinate the activities of sub-contractors ensuring that they have the relevant competencies and information to safely perform assigned tasks
3. monitor and co-ordinate OHS and operational provisions in order to ensure that all persons
    -   apply the preventative and protective principles in a consistent manner;
    -   where required, follow the safety and health plan referred to above;
    -   make, or cause to be made, any adjustments required to the safety and health plan and provide information to the planning supervisor to take into account the progress of the work and any changes which have occurred;
    -   organize co-operation between sub-contractors and the self employed, including successive employers on the same site;
    -   co-ordinate their activities and information flow, with a view to protecting workers and preventing accidents and occupational health hazards;
    -   co-ordinate the arrangements for checking that working procedures are being implemented correctly;
    -   take all necessary steps to ensure that only authorized persons are allowed on the construction site.

For information covering the roles of the HSC and HSE see <http://www.hse.gov.uk.aboutus/hsc/index.htm>

24 Managing the Environment

Zhen Chen, Heng Li and Rodney Turner

Adverse environmental impacts have become a major concern and received more and more attention, especially after BS7750 and ISO 14001 Environmental Management System (EMS) were issued in the 1990s. Although many professionals and academics have put their efforts into environmental management (NAE 1999), most work has only been qualitative in nature focusing on the use of regulations and guidelines. A literature review conducted by the authors in 2003 revealed only 2% of research work provided quantitative methods related to environmental management for the construction industry (Chen and Li 2006). However, it is becoming more important to adopt quantitative environmental management to understand the influence of environmental considerations in business decisions, especially throughout the project lifecycle (NAS 2005). These requirements generally focus on:

- environmental performance and competitive advantages
- customers and investors demands for environmental performance by businesses
- supply chains and production networks
- sectoral standard-setting
- decision factors in industrial ecology
- environmental accounting and disclosure practices
- government policy influences on business decision making

In this chapter, we present qualitative and quantitative approaches to environmental management. We describe how an organization can develop an environmental strategy, and basic principals of environmental management. We then describe methods for pollution prevention, control and reduction, including some quantitative approaches. These quantitative methods are further integrated under a knowledge–driven managerial frame based on a standard EMS process and other processes normally adopted in project management. It is expected that this knowledge–driven approach can be used to effectively support conducting quantitative environmental management throughout the lifecycle of projects.

ENVIRONMENTAL STRATEGY

More and more organizations have put forward their strategies or policies for environmental management, following either the requirements of a standard EMS process or ethical values held by themselves or the public majority. An organization's *Environmental Policy* is a written statement of its missions in relation to managing the environmental effects of its operations (Envirowise 2005). For organizations intending to obtain accreditations to the ISO 14001 or registrations under EMAS, the *Environmental Policy* is essential for the development and implementation of an EMS. Environmental strategy is on the top of specific environmental regulations inside an organization's *Environmental Policy*, and it can be regarded as a theoretical and practical plan for understanding and evaluating various environmental impacts within the framework of future environmental scenarios. In developing and implementing environmental strategies, participants can acquire the skills to anticipate technological, legal and policy trends so as to assist their organizations to plan strategically beyond legislative compliance and stopgap interventions (Envirowise 2005). However, the effective and efficient implementation of environmental policies requires tactical tools using both qualitative and quantitative methods. Figure 24.1 gives an example of an Environmental Policy document.

The environmental strategy is the starting point for project managers to work with their teams in the prevention, control and reduction of various adverse environmental impacts in the project period. It is essential to develop a tailored environmental strategy. For developing an environmental strategy, a four–step process (Pollock 1995) is suggested:

● Develop understanding
● Measure and improve performance
● Maintain positive attitudes
● Review progress and decide next steps

DEVELOP UNDERSTANDING

The first step is to obtain the commitment and the right attitudes of people in the organization to improving environmental performance. There are three frequently asked questions:

TriMagi Plc, 2007

The Opening Statement	In the pursuit of its mission to provide world class tele-communications and information products and services, TriMagi exploits technologies which are basically friendly to the environment. In the sense that use of the telecommunications network is often a substitute for travel or paper-based messages, TriMagi is contributing positively to environmental wellbeing and conserving resources.
Commitment to Pollution Prevention	We recognise however that in our day-to-day operations we inevitably impact on the environment in a number of ways and we wish to minimise the potentially harmful effects of such activity wherever and whenever possible.
Improvement Principle	As part of our continuing drive for quality in all things we do we have therefore developed a comprehensive policy statement which will enable us to set the targets by which our efforts towards sustainable environmental improvement can be measured and monitored on a regular basis.
Communication to Staff Commitment to Continuous Improvement	We have undertaken to help every TriMagi person to understand and to implement relevant aspects of this policy in their day-to-day works through the regular communication of objectives, action plans and achievements. At Board level, the Deputy Chairman has specific responsibility for policy development, coordination and evaluation of performance. TriMagi is committed to minimising the impact of its operation on the environment by means of a programme of continuous improvement.
Setting Specific Policies Commitment to Legislative Compliance	In particular TriMagi will: • meet, and where appropriate, exceed the requirements of all relevant legislation – where no regulations exist TriMagi shall set its own exacting standards; • promote recycling and the use of recycled materials, while reducing consumption of materials wherever possible; • minimise waste in all operations and product development; • work with TriMagi suppliers to minimise the impact of their operations on the environment through a quality purchasing policy; • protect visual amenity by careful siting of buildings, structure and the deployment of operational plant in the local environment; and respect wild life habitats; • include environmental issues in TriMagi training programmes and encourage the implementation by all TriMagi people of sound environmental practices; • monitor progress and publish an environmental performance report on an annual basis.

Figure 24.1   An example of an environmental policy

485

Is it necessary?

Yes! Not only to protect the environment, but for legal, social and commercial reasons. Most of us are aware of the nightmare scenarios that are painted of rising atmospheric temperatures, rising sea levels and rising incidences of skin cancer. Many of the doom mongers have been proved wrong in the past. A report produced in the 1970s by an organization called the Club of Rome predicted the oil would run out in the early 1980s. There are now greater reserves than ever. But even if some of the predictions are just one-tenth right, there is enough to be concerned about. Later two principles are described, the Precautionary Principle and the Principle of Sustainable Development, both of which suggest we should not do something if we are not aware of its impact; and that we have an ethical duty to our grandchildren to leave them a world they can live in. Even if we are unconvinced by those arguments, there is a body of national, European and international legislation that imposes significant constraints on what we can do, Figure 24.2. However, it is also a common principle that public opinion runs ahead

Domain	Legislation
UK	Alkali Act
	Control of Pollution Act 1974
	Health and Safety at Work Act 1974
	Environmental Pollution Act 1990
	Integrated Pollution Control Act 1991
	Water resources Act 1991
	Control of Industrial Major Accident Hazard Regulations 1984
	Town and Country Planning (Assessment of Environmental Effect) Regulations (1998)
	Planning Policy Guidelines
	Building Regulation, 2000
	The Solvent Emissions (England and Wales) Regulations 2004
	The Hazardous Waste (England and Wales) Regulations 2005
Europe	Construction Products Directive
	Emissions Directive
	Environmental Impact Assessment Directive
	Hazardous Waste Directive
	Integrated Pollution and Protection Directive
	Noise Limits Directive
	Single European Act – Polluter Pays Principle
International	US Environmental Protection Agency
	Montreal Protocol, 1989
	Rio de Janeiro Accord 1992
	Kyoto Protocol 1997; Kyoto Accord 2005
	Bonn and Buenos Aires Accords 1998

Figure 24.2 Environmental legislation

of legislation; politicians respond to public opinion rather than lead it. Pressure to improve environmental performance can come from the following:

- government
- pressure groups and green consumers
- local communities and public awareness
- competitors
- employees
- insurers, capital markets and shareholders
- risks and crises
- ethics (Chapter 40)

Do we actually have an impact?

To determine the impact of the organization or a project, you need to consider the inputs and the outputs. The processes tend only to have an impact through the inputs and outputs. Figure 24.3 contains a potential checklist of impacts.

Can we afford it?

Well, 'You have to!' But in fact there is substantial anecdotal evidence that environmental awareness pays. The question reduces to a cost–benefit analysis. The section below on environmental accounting and costing shows how the cost of environmental impact and awareness can be built into project appraisal. There are also other costs associated with conducting environmental impact assessments and the consent process, but those are often required by law. Benefits can come from reduced costs and increased income. Often environmental hygiene reduces waste and other inputs and outputs listed in Figure 24.3, reducing costs and hence making savings greater than the cost of implementing the environmental policies. A Japanese steel company felt it was not attracting the right quality graduate

Inputs	Outputs
Raw materials	Products or services
People	Waste
Water	Sewerage
Energy	Emissions
▪ electricity	Smoke
▪ hydrocarbon	Greenhouse gasses
▪ steam	Noise
	Land use
	Transport
	Internal environment
	▪ sick building syndrome

Figure 24.3 Input–output model of environmental impacts

engineers because of its working environment, so the company improved the environment so people could wear white overalls. Energy consumption dropped 30 per cent. Other benefits can arise from:

- attracting the green consumer
- attracting the green investor
- meeting the environmental requirements of potential clients
- reducing insurance premiums
- improving staff commitment and satisfaction
- being better integrated with the local community
- reducing energy consumption
- reducing waste disposal costs
- avoiding fines

In the early 1980s, Rodney Turner worked with ICI in North East England. There was a proposal to store low- and medium-level nuclear waste in a redundant mine on the site. This would have cost ICI nothing and generated rental income. Local house prices started to fall, so the local population was paying for the proposal, and as the support of the local community was essential to ICI it did not go ahead with the scheme.

MEASURE AND IMPROVE PERFORMANCE

The British Standard, BS7750, suggests a twelve-step process or environmental management system, EMS, for measuring and improving environmental performance.

1. **Initial review:** Review environmental performance and construct an input–output model.
2. **Strategy:** Develop a strategy based, perhaps, on the sixteen-point charter issued by the International Chamber of Commerce (Figure 24.4).
3. **Organization and personnel:** Gain commitment of all people in the organization, from top to bottom. Develop positive attitudes.

1. Integrated management	9. Research
2. Employee education	10. Precautionary approach
3. Products and services	11. Contractors and suppliers
4. Facilities and operations	12. Emergency preparedness
5. Corporate priority	13. Transfer of technology
6. Process of improvement	14. Contributing to the common effort
7. Prior assessment	15. Openness and concerns
8. Customer advice	16. Compliance and reporting

Figure 24.4 Sixteen-point charter for sustainable development

4. **Register of regulations:** Keep a list of relevant regulations, as per Figure 24.2.
5. **Register of effects:** Record your input–output model as per Figure 24.3
6. **Objectives and targets:** Set aims and objectives for improvement. Objectives should be SMART: specific, measurable, achievable, realistic and time–framed.
7. **Management action plans:** Develop project plans for the achievement of each objective, including a milestone plan and responsibility chart (Chapters 15 and 18).
8. **Management manual:** Record everything so far in a manual and put on wide circulation, including the Intranet. Make sure people refer to it.
9. **Organizational control:** Control the implementation of the improvement projects.
10. **Record:** Monitor what is achieved.
11. **Audits:** Audit effectiveness of improvement projects, make appropriate improvements.
12. **Review:** Review progress annually.

MAINTAIN POSITIVE ATTITUDES

The third step of developing an environmental strategy suggests it is important to develop and maintain positive attitudes. This can be achieved by the six steps below:

1. Seek senior management support and involve it in the process.
2. Hold regular meetings of interested people, including environmental hygiene circles.
3. Network with people in other organizations.
4. Run competitions and offer awards for suggestions.
5. Involve the local community.
6. Maintain internal communications.
   - newspapers
   - company magazines
   - notice boards
   - Intranet
   - involve the functions of the organization:
     - marketing
     - finance
     - human resource management

REVIEW PROGRESS AND DECIDE NEXT STEPS

In the annual review, you will want to ask yourself the following questions:

How did we do?

You will obviously review progress against your objectives, but other measures of improvement include:

- environmental initiatives suggested
- environmental initiatives achieved
- staff attending environmental courses
- staff requesting information
- hits on the Intranet page
- support from senior management
- customer satisfaction
- benchmarking against competitors
- feedback from network contacts

Where do we go next?

Again, you will obviously set objectives for greater improvement, but as you move up a learning curve that will be increasingly difficult. Improvements will become increasingly costly. You will need to work to maintain what you have achieved and to maintain positive attitudes, and that may eventually become more important than achieving new improvements. You may start to ask deeper questions like:

1. Why does it have to be like this?
2. How can we change attitudes on a wider stage:
   - the local community?
   - nationally?
   - globally?
3. Are we masters of our destiny or creators of our doom?

ENVIRONMENTAL PRINCIPLES AND IMPACT ANALYSIS

ENVIRONMENTAL PRINCIPLES

In making decisions about what options there are in the design of our projects, and their impact on the environment, there are four principles which can guide our thinking:

- Sustainable development
- The precautionary principle

490

- BPEO, BATNEEC and IPC
- The polluter pays

Sustainable Development

Bruntland (1987) defined the sustainable development as a development that meets the needs of the present generation without compromising the ability of future generations to meet their needs. Recently, the UK Government SDU (2006) gave a widely-used and accepted international definition of sustainable development:

Development which meets the needs of the present without compromising the ability of future generations to meet their own needs

Globally we are not even meeting the needs of the present let alone considering the needs of future generations. The UK has identified four priority areas for immediate action:

- Sustainable Consumption and Production
- Climate Change and Energy
- Natural Resource Protection and Environmental Enhancement
- Sustainable Communities

The UK Government also recognizes that changing behaviour is a cross cutting theme closely linked to all of these priorities. Many of the examples of unsustainable development from both rich and poor nations are of agricultural land taken out of production in ways that mean they can never be returned to agriculture:

- covered in tarmac, housing and industrial sites throughout the western world
- made unusable through poor irrigation practices resulting in soil salinity which cannot be economically reversed in developing nations
- mined for minerals

In the former Soviet Union poor irrigation practices resulted in the Aral Sea halving in size so that former fishing villages were 80 kms from the coast, and the salinity of the sea rising and killing most of the fish. Our grandchildren and their grandchildren need the land for development and so we have a moral duty to use it in such a way that it continues to be reusable. If that increases the cost of our projects, then so be it.

The Precautionary Principles

Sometimes when faced with various options we do not know what the impact of some of them will be. Some people say it is acceptable to carry on doing things until we know for certain that the impact is bad. However, the view that is gaining

491

credence is the opposite, that we should not do things if there is any risk that they may damage the environment until we know for certain what the consequence is, and that we know it is acceptable (sustainable).

BPEO, BATNEEC and IPC

The concepts of best practical environmental option (BPEO), best available technique not entailing excessive cost (BATNEEC) and Integrated Pollution Control (IPC) are defined within the UK's Environmental Protection Act 1990:

BPEO: applies at the strategic level, when governments or companies make decisions about what projects they will and will not do. For instance, in disposing of waste the government may choose between landfill and incineration. In deciding transport policy it will choose between road and rail.

BATNEEC: applies at a tactical level, once a project is underway, when deciding what options will be carried forward for design and implementation. If a design option is likely to have an impact on the environment, then alternative design options should be considered and compared. The difference in cost between the initially proposed option and the next best alternative can be calculated and then the simple question asked, 'Is that extra cost worth spending to protect the environment?' Sometimes the extra cost can be justified not just through the protection to the environment but through the benefits listed above. Sometimes the comparison will result in improvements to the original design which will reduce the impact on the environment. Sometimes the analysis shows that the originally proposed option was the best and the cheapest.

IPC: has as its main objectives:

- to prevent or minimize the release of prescribed substances, and to render harmless those substances which are released;
- to develop an approach to pollution control which considers discharges from industrial processes to all media in the context of the environment as a whole.

Organizations are regularly fined for harmful discharges. This is not so much a technique to help us consider options and then choose the optimum in terms of cost and impact; it lays down minimum requirements for pollution control.

The Polluter Pays

This principle receives a lot of lip-service, but its application falls short. Environmentalists have argued that if the true environmental impact of road transport were taken into account, rail transport would be preferred. A motorway covers more agricultural land than a railway, it consumes more land in the mining of aggregates for its construction, and cars pump out more carbon per passenger mile than trains. In the late 1990s the Labour Government increased the price of petrol year on year, but the money raised was not used to reduce pollution from road transport. They are now levying so called 'green taxes' on air transport, but there is little indication of the money raised being used for reducing CO_2 emissions. If the polluter were truly to pay, it would shift the balance perhaps for BPEO and BATNEEC.

ENVIRONMENTAL ACCOUNTING AND COSTING

In choosing options under BPEO or BATNEEC, we need a way of providing a perceived benefit to environmental protection or disbenefit to the environmental damage we cause, so that cost–benefit analysis can be conducted on the various options. Various methods have been developed to do this, including:

1. *The contingent valuation method* This involves asking people what they would pay for an environmental improvement or accept in compensation for a disbenefit. In the example of ICI and the storing of nuclear waste described earlier, the local population would have wanted compensation for the loss of value of their houses. The fall in the price of houses provided a clear indication of the contingent valuation.
2. *The travel cost method* For national parks and other public amenities which may be damaged we can find out how many people visit per year, and the time and cost of travelling there. The estimated value of people's leisure time (what they would pay for alternatives) and the cost of travelling can provide a guide to the annual value of the site.
3. *The hedonic pricing method* Hedonic comes from the Greek word meaning pleasure. We try to evaluate the pleasure people receive from the environment. How much is their leisure time worth? What is the reduction in perceived pleasure in living somewhere reflected in the reduction of house prices? The latter applies to road and rail schemes as much as the ICI example above.
4. *The least cost alternative method* Sometimes when applying BPEO or BATNEEC you are reduced to comparing the cost of two alternatives and asking, 'Is the environmental damage I am doing worth that much?', thus making a subjective assessment. This could have been applied to the M3 motorway extension over Twyford Down, near Winchester. The damage done can *never* be reversed (sustainable development). (This project is an example of government not subjecting itself to the laws it imposes on the population).

ENVIRONMENTAL IMPACT ANALYSIS

Environmental Impact Assessment (EIA) is used to identify the environmental, social and economic impacts of a project during initiation, UNEP (2003). It aims to predict environmental impacts at an early stage in project planning and design, find ways to reduce adverse impacts, shape projects to suit the local environment and present the predictions and options to decision-makers. By using EIA both environmental and economic benefits can be achieved, such as reduced cost and time of project implementation and design, avoided treatment/clean–up costs and impacts of laws and regulations. The key elements include:

- **scoping:** identify key issues and concerns of interested parties;
- **screening:** decide whether an EIA is required based on information collected;
- **identifying and evaluating alternatives:** list alternative sites and techniques and the impacts of each;
- **mitigating measures:** dealing with uncertainty: review proposed action to prevent or minimize the potential adverse effects of the project; and
- **issuing environmental statements:** report the findings of the EIA.

UNEP (2003) promotes the appropriate application of the EIA process to major projects, and supports practitioners, clients and review agencies through the publication of guidance documents. A recent review of the EIA process recommended that it should consider, and be used during, the entire project cycle from planning through operation to eventual closure. EIA should also be closely integrated with the environmental management systems now used by major companies. There are many reasons why an EIA may be desirable or even essential as part of the feasibility or design process for a project:

1. It is required by law in some instances, especially in the WETT (water, energy, telecommunications and transport) industries.
2. It may be a requirement of obtaining planning permission or consents, or it may facilitate that process.
3. It may help persuade the local community that the project does not have the impact it fears, especially as part of a stakeholder management strategy.
4. It may help you consider various options under BPEO or BATNEEC analysis.

A booklet has been produced in the UK by the former Department of the Environment called *Environmental Impact Assessment – Guide to Procedures*, (DETR 2000) which spells out how and when to carry out an assessment under the Town and Country Planning (Assessment of Environmental Effects) Regulations 1988. It gives guidance on when an assessment is essential or desirable, and how one should be conducted. This booklet reflects a directive issued by the European Union in 1987, which requires an EIA to be conducted for certain types of developments.

The Contents of an EIA

There is no specified requirement of what an EIA should include and who should be involved in its preparation. However, if we examine what should be included in an EIA we can then consider who should be involved in its preparation. It is likely that an EIA will include some or all of the following:

1. A full description of the development, including information about the site, design, size and scale, and other information considered relevant. This may include drawings and artists' impressions.
2. A description of the significant effects of the development on the environment, including its impact on people, flora, fauna, air, water, soil, climate, landscape, cultural heritage and so on. This may include an input–output module for the project prepared as suggested earlier. This should be supported by data and further drawings and artists' impressions.
3. Where significant environmental effects have been identified, a description of measures taken to reduce them. This should include alternatives considered under BPEO and BATNEEC and an explanation why the option chosen was preferred.
4. A summary in non-technical terms of all the above information for the layperson.

This last item is essential. Unfortunately for developers, the public has become more active in its resistance to developments. Although people are better educated, and therefore better able to formulate their position and widely publicize it, they still do not always understand scientific or engineering principles. Objectors are therefore able to cause substantial damage through their ignorance of all the scientific or other facts, or their misrepresentation of them to the public. Examples include:

- Greenpeace stopping Shell from finding the best solution for disposing of the Brent Spar North Sea oil rig.
- Protestors killing a uranium mining project in Canada by asking at the planning enquiry what the level of radiation would be in the waste water. The developers gave an exact answer, and even though the level was less than that in rain water, the protestors argued than anything other than zero (impossible to achieve) was unacceptable.

Conducting an EIA

The preparation of an EIA should be a collaborative exercise involving the project manager, planning authorities, statutory consultative bodies and other interested parties, especially the local community. Depending on the project and its impact, some statutory authorities need to be consulted by law. Others may be consulted.

Obviously the more widely you consult, the more it costs, but the lower risk that there will be a hitch in obtaining consents.

OBTAINING CONSENTS

Almost all developments require some form of consent. The UK's planning regulations define a development as the carrying out of building, engineering, mining or other operations in, on, over or under land, or making of any material change in the use of buildings or other land. Consent will usually be awarded by a local planning authority, a district or unitary authority. However, the Secretary of State for the Environment, Transport and Regions can ask to scrutinize any application, and an applicant can appeal to the Secretary of State against rejection. Sometimes consent is obtained via an Act of Parliament. A Private Members Bill is introduced in November and the result is known 14 months later. For major developments, a public enquiry is also required. A major proposal is defined as: the development proposal is of major public interest because of its national or regional implications, or the extent or complexity of the environmental, safety, technical or scientific issues involved, and where for these reasons there are a number of third parties involved as well as the applicant and the Local Planning Authority. The consent process breaks into two stages:

Stage 1: Pre-consent: The project and consent application are formulated, up to the decision to make the application for consent. During this stage:

- the project is defined
- consent and other key factors are identified
- risks are analysed and reduction strategies are formulated
- mitigators to obtain local support are identified
- a consent strategy is developed
- local consultations are planned and begun
- the potential application is reviewed
- the decision is taken to abandon the application, to redefine the project or to proceed with the application

There are two possible strategies for local consultations:

1. **Define and inquire:** The project formulation is undertaken entirely within the sponsor's organization, only being made public when the consent is applied for.
2. **Consult and refine**: Consultation with affected parties begins early, to obtain their input while significant options remain open.

Stage 2: Consent application: The application is made, and the project team are involved with managing external relationships. During this stage:

- the consent strategy is finalized
- the application is submitted
- the inquiry is planned for and held if necessary
- risk assessment is continued
- local consultations are continued
- the outcome is assessed
- the decision is taken to abandon the scheme, redefine it or to proceed to construction

Risks and Costs

Clearly the above procedures can entail considerable cost and there is always the risk that consent will not be granted. Costs can arise from:

- drawing up the case, including the preparation of an EIA
- the holding of an enquiry, including legal fees, attendance, inspection, etc
- idleness of the project team between the completion of design (required for the consent) and commencement of work (after consent has been obtained) – errors of communication can arise at this time
- conditions attached to the consent
- mitigators (bribes) to the local community to induce their acceptance of the development
- delays as a result of redesigning the proposal to meet the planning requirements; lost commercial value of information disclosed to the public
- delayed return on investment from delay to the start of the revenue stream
- wasted effort if consent is refused

Against this, if consent is awarded, the project will be well scrutinized from many viewpoints and so the chances of error in the design are very much reduced, making the proposal more robust and increasing the chance of success.

POLLUTION PREVENTION

It is important, at the early stage of any project, to identify and plan to prevent any potential, adverse environmental impacts. In general, effective prevention relies on comprehensive qualitative review and consideration during project planning. However, quantitative tools can usefully support the process. We suggest a three step process for pollution prevention:

- identify all adverse environmental impacts potentially generated during the project
- value all identified impacts, and integrate with the project schedule
- evaluate different project options for the most appropriate one to implement

497

IDENTIFICATION

The first step is to identify a group of Key Performance Indicators (KPIs), for the adverse environmental impacts generated by the project. Figure 24.5 gives a list of possible KPIs for a construction project. It is assumed the KPIs can be used by project managers to regulate the environmental performance of processes or operations in their project that may directly or indirectly lead to pollutions and hazards. The identification of KPIs based on relatively objective rules is essential in both pollution prevention and reduction. There are two quantitative approaches for assessing the relative impact of KPIs, Environmental Impact Index (EII) and Energy–Time Index (ETI), Chen and Li (2006).

Environmental Impact Index (EII)

EII measures various adverse environmental impacts that could be potentially generated during a project. The EII can be calculated by adding subjective judgements of different types of pollutions and hazards.

$$EII_i = \sum_{J=1}^{8} EII_{i,j} \qquad (j = 1,2,\ldots,8) \qquad 24.1$$

where

- EII_i is the total environmental impact caused by KPI_i,
- $EII_{i,j}$ is the individual environmental impact leading to one of the eight possible pollutions and hazards
  - soil and ground contamination (j=1)
  - ground and underground water pollution (j=2)
  - waste (j=3)
  - noise and vibration (j=4)
  - dust (j=5)
  - hazardous emissions and odors (j=6)
  - wildlife and natural features impacts (j=7)
  - archaeology impacts (j=8)

Each $EII_{i,j}$ has one of three values:

- -1:   KPIi will intensify the level of adverse environmental impacts
- 0   KPIi will bring uncertain environmental influence
- +1:   KPIi can reduce the level of adverse environmental impacts.

Figure 24.5 gives an example of the use of EII in assessing KPIs. The assumed value of environmental impact of each KPI can then be used to reclassify all KPIs into one of three groups (Figure 24.6):

Cluster	Environmental KPIs	Unit	$EII_{i,1}$	$EII_{i,2}$	$EII_{i,3}$	$EII_{i,4}$	$EII_{i,5}$	$EII_{i,6}$	$EII_{i,7}$	$EII_{i,8}$	$\sum_{j=1}^{8} EII_{i,j}$
								Potential environmental impacts (EII_i)			
Technology	Cleaner technologies and Automation ratio	%	+1	+1	+1	+1	+1	+1	+1	+1	+8
	Constructability	%	0	0	0	0	0	-1	0	0	0
Resource	The amount of electricity use	kWh	0	0	-1	-1	-1	-1	0	0	-4
	The amount of fuel use	joule	-1	-1	-1	-1	-1	-1	-1	-1	-8
	The amount of water use	ton	-1	-1	-1	0	+1	0	0	0	-4
	Wastewater treatment/reuse ratio	%	+1	+1	+1	0	0	0	0	0	+3
	Material serviceability	%	0	0	+1	0	0	0	0	0	+1
	Material durability	%	+1	+1	+1	0	0	0	0	0	+3
	Cargo packaging recycling ratio	%	0	0	+1	0	+1	+1	0	0	+3
	Generative material use ratio	%	0	0	0	0	0	0	0	0	0
	Waste generating rate	%	-1	-1	-1	0	-1	0	0	0	-4
	Waste reuse and recycling ratio	%	+1	0	+1	0	0	0	0	0	+2
	Health and safety risk to staff	%	0	0	0	+1	+1	+1	+1	0	+4
	Required skills on staff	%	0	0	+1	0	+1	0	0	0	+2
Time	Construction duration	day	-1	-1	-1	-1	-1	-1	-1	-1	-8
	Transportation time	hour	0	0	0	-1	-1	-1	-1	-1	-5
	Construction delay risk	hour	0	0	-1	0	-1	-1	0	0	-3
Cost	Construction cost	$	-1	-1	-1	-1	-1	-1	-1	-1	-8
	Environmental control cost	$	+1	+1	+1	+1	+1	+1	+1	+1	+8
Management	ISO 14001 EMS adoption	%	+1	+1	+1	+1	+1	+1	+1	+1	+8
	ISO 9001 QMS adoption	%	0	0	0	0	0	0	0	0	0
	Computerizations	%	+1	+1	+1	+1	+1	+1	+1	+1	+8
	Cooperativity/Unionization risk	%	+1	+1	+1	+1	+1	+1	+1	+1	+8
	Site layout suitability	%	+1	+1	+1	+1	+1	+1	+1	+1	+8
Society	Public health and safety risk	%	-1	-1	-1	-1	-1	-1	0	0	-6
	Waste disposal price	$	+1	+1	+1	+1	+1	+1	+1	+1	+8
	Legal involvements	%	+1	+1	+1	+1	+1	+1	+1	+1	+8
	Public traffic disruptions	day	0	0	0	-1	-1	-1	-1	0	-4
	Cargo transportation burden	ton-mile	0	0	0	-1	-1	-1	-1	0	-4
Nature	Temperature affection risk	%	0	-1	-1	0	-1	0	0	0	-3
	Storm affection risk	%	0	0	-1	0	0	-1	0	0	-3
	Earthquake affection risk	%	-1	-1	-1	0	-1	-1	0	0	-5

Figure 24.5 Environmental KPIs and their potential environmental impacts on a construction project (Chen and Li 2006)

Classification	Environmental KPIs	Unit	EII_i	Plan Alternatives		
				Plan A	Plan B	Plan C
1 EA Factors	1.1 Fuel consumption amount (FCA)	Mjoule	-8	36k	45k	49k
	1.2 Construction duration (COD)	Day	-8	500	560	450
	1.3 Construction cost (COC)	M$	-8	30	31	29
	1.4 Public health and safety risk (PHS)	%	-6	10	20	25
	1.5 Transportation time (TRT)	Hour	-5	4.0k	4.5k	4.8k
	1.6 Earthquake affection risk (EAR)	%	-5	0.01	0.01	0.01
	1.7 Electricity consumption amount (ECA)	kWh	-4	30k	45k	50k
	1.8 Water consumption amount (WCA)	ton	-4	3.1k	3.8k	4.1k
	1.9 Waste generating rate (WGR)	%	-4	1.2	3.0	3.5
	1.10 Public traffic disruptions (PTD)	day	-4	39	60	70
	1.11 Cargo transportation burden (CTB)	ton-mile	-4	450k	500k	550k
	1.12 Construction delay risk (CDR)	hour	-3	150	200	220
	1.13 Temperature affection risk (TAR)	%	-3	10.0	8.9	8.7
	1.14 Storm affection risk (SAR)	%	-3	2.0	1.8	1.8
2 EU Factors	2.1 Constructability (COB)	%	0	100	100	100
	2.2 Generative material use ratio (GMU)	%	0	20	10	8
	2.3 ISO 9001 QMS adoption (QMS)	%	0	100	100	100
3 EF Factors	3.1 Cleaner technology/automation ratio (CTA)	%	+8	80	50	40
	3.2 Computerizations (PCA)	%	+8	80	80	80
	3.3 Environmental control cost (ECC)	M$	+8	0.8	0.5	0.5
	3.4 ISO 14001 EMS adoption (EMS)	%	+8	0	0	0
	3.5 Cooperativity/Unionization risk (COP)	%	+8	100	80	60
	3.6 Site layout suitability (SLS)	%	+8	80	60	50
	3.7 Waste disposal price (WDP)	M$	+8	0.10	0.25	0.29
	3.8 Legal and Responsibility risk (LRR)	%	+8	0.10	0.23	0.32
	3.9 Health and safety risk to staff (HSR)	%	+4	0.10	0.21	0.28
	3.10 Wastewater treatment/reuse ratio (WTR)	%	+3	90	50	40
	3.11 Material durability (MAD)	%	+3	100	80	80
	3.12 Cargo packaging recycling ratio (CPR)	%	+3	100	50	0
	3.13 Waste reuse and recycling ratio (WRR)	%	+2	90	30	35
	3.14 Required skills on staff (RSS)	%	+2	80	60	60
	3.15 Material serviceability (MAS)	%	+1	100	80	80

Figure 24.6 Environmental KPIs and their values of construction plan options (Chen and Li 2006)

1. adverse environmental impact factors (denoted as EA factors) (EII_i <0),
2. favourable environmental impact factors or environmental-beneficial factors (denoted as EF factors) (EII_i >0)
3. uncertain environmental impact indicators (denoted as EU factors) (EII_i =0)

These reclassified environmental KPIs are ready to be used by managers for effective planning and control of their projects in order to fulfil both external and internal requirements on environmental-friendly performance.

Energy-Time Index (ETI)

ETI is a quantitative measure of the use of energy and time by a project. Energy and time are used by all project processes and operations. Embodied energy is an important measurement. Embodied energy refers to the energy used in all procedures associated with the completion of a project, which covers all stages of a project lifecycle from the acquisition of natural resources to product delivery, including mining, manufacturing of materials and equipment, transport and administrative functions (CMIT 2002). For example, previous research into the Life Cycle Assessment (LCA) of the cost and/or the environmental impacts of construction projects focus on the embodied energy of products such as material, component equipment and building, and the processes such as construction, installation and maintenance, (Chen and Li 2006). The time factor in project management, which can be regarded as the speed of energy use, has been disregarded in previous LCA research. However, it is important to measure the speed of energy use in all project processes and operations. A high energy use in a long period may not be more adverse to the natural environment than a relatively low energy use over a short period because the environment itself has the power to eliminate pollutants (Stephens 2005). Thus, ETI has been put forward as a means of measuring the rate of use of embodied energy:

$$ETI_i = (\sum_{j=1}^{2} SEU_{ij} / \sum STU_{i,j}) \times 100 \qquad 24.2$$

where

- ETI_i is the *ETI* of *KPI_i*;
- $SEU_{i,j}$ is the Score of Energy Use (SEU) of *KPI_i* relevant to *Indicator Cluster j* (*j=1 or 2,* corresponding to the two *Indicator Clusters: Products Cluster (j=1)* and *Processes/Operation Cluster (j=2)*)
- $STU_{i,j}$ is the Score of Time Use (STU) of *KPIi* relevant to *Indicator Cluster j*.

The $SEU_{i,j}$ are based on consideration that energy embodied into a product covers a period of time during a process and/or an operation, which is highly specific to the *KPI_i*. To further regulate the evaluation of *KPI_i*, fundamental scales for scoring $SEU_{i,j}$ and $STU_{i,j}$ can be subjectively defined (see Figure 24.7). Figure 24.8 contains the ETI for a range of KPIs.

PLANNING

Process pollution prevention refers to industrial processes by which resources such as materials and energy are efficiently utilized to achieve the end product(s) while reducing or eliminating the creation of pollutants or waste at source (Das 2005). The US EPA (1992) proposed a seven-level pollution prevention hierarchy:

Scales for scoring	The Patterns of Energy/Time Use	
	Products (Embodied Energy/Time Pattern)	Processes/Operations (Operational Energy/Time Using Pattern)
The Score of Energy Use (SEUi,j) 1 = Extremely low 6 = High 2 = Very strongly low 7 = Moderately high 3 = Strongly low 8 = Strongly high 4 = Moderately low 9 = Very strongly high 5 = Low 10 = Extremely high	Energy embodied in products and/or materials in manufacture, transportation and/or installation.	Energy used in processes and/or operations depending on specific requirements.
The Score of Time Use (STUi,j) 1 = (0, 1 day] 4 = (1 month, 1 year] 2 = (1 day, 1 week] 5 = >1 year 3 = (1 week, 1 month]	Time embodied in products and/or materials in manufacture, transportation and/or installation.	Time used in processes and/or operations depending on specific requirements.

Figure 24.7   Fundamental scales of the scores and relevant descriptions of energy/time use

1. minimize generation
2. minimize introduction
3. segregate and reuse
4. recycle
5. recover energy value in waste
6. treat for discharge
7. safe disposal

The first three of these provide the greatest opportunity for reducing the waste to be treated (Mulholland and Dyer 1999; Das 2005). The other four lead to a better construction management environment.

PPI

The Project Pollution Index, PPI, and Process Pollution Index, PPI_i, provide quantitative measures of the adverse environmental impacts of projects and individual processes respectively. They are defined as follows:

$$PPI_i = p_i \ D_i \ 100\% \qquad\qquad 24.3$$

$$PPI = \sum_{i=1}^{n} PPI_i \qquad\qquad 24.4$$

where

KPIs	$SEU_{i,1}$	$SEU_{i,2}$	SEU_i	$STU_{i,1}$	$STU_{i,2}$	STU_i	ETI_i
Electricity and Electrical services	7	5	12	1	5	6	200
Heating services	7	9	16	3	5	8	200
Ventilation and air-conditioning	6	9	15	3	5	8	188
Building services automation system	9	7	16	4	5	9	178
Construction materials	8	8	16	4	5	9	178
IT&C facilities and services	8	6	14	3	5	8	175
Thermal comfort and indoor air quality	5	8	13	3	5	8	163
Lifts/escalators and controls	5	8	13	3	5	8	163
Security and safety control	6	5	11	3	5	8	138
Reserve electric power	7	3	10	3	5	8	125
Green materials	5	5	10	3	5	8	125
Flushing water system	6	4	10	3	5	8	125
External decoration	5	6	11	4	5	9	122
Building architectural design	4	2	6	4	1	5	120
Lavatory accommodation	4	5	9	3	5	8	113
Refuse collection	5	4	9	3	5	8	113
Circulation for the disabled	5	5	10	4	5	9	111
Computer aided construction/installation	2	8	10	4	5	9	111
Waste Disposal	1	2	3	1	2	3	100
Flexibility for renovation	4	3	7	2	5	7	100
Internal decoration	4	4	8	3	5	8	100
Structural monitoring and control	4	4	8	3	5	8	100
Computer aided manufacturing	8	1	9	4	5	9	100
Potable water system	5	3	8	3	5	8	100
Green design	6	2	8	4	5	9	89
Lighting	4	3	7	3	5	8	88
Fire detection and resistance	4	3	7	4	4	8	88
Cleanliness	4	3	7	3	5	8	88
Property management	1	5	6	2	5	7	86
Computer aided design	5	2	7	4	5	9	78
Carpark/transportation facilities	2	3	5	2	5	7	71
Entertainment facilities	1	4	5	2	5	7	71
External landscape	2	3	5	2	5	7	71
Extensive use of artificial intelligence	4	2	6	4	5	9	67
Electromagnetic compatibility	3	1	4	2	5	7	57
Environmental friendliness	1	2	3	1	5	6	50
Conference and meeting facilities	1	3	4	3	5	8	50
Drainage	2	1	3	2	5	7	43
Existence of green features	1	1	2	1	5	6	33
Access sign and directory	1	1	2	1	5	6	33
Maintainability	1	1	2	1	5	6	33
Usable areas	1	1	2	2	5	7	29
Means of escape	1	1	2	3	5	8	25

Figure 24.8 ETI for selected KPIs

- PPI is the pollution index of a specific project
- PPI_i is the pollution index of a specific process or operation i
- p_i is the magnitude of pollution and hazards generated by a specific process or operation i per unit of time

503

- D_i is the duration of the process or operation i that generates pollution and/or hazards
- n is the number of processes or operations for the specific project

The core calculation of PPI and its PPI_i is the p_i, which is a relative value to measure the magnitude of adverse environmental pollution and hazards generated by a particular process or operation in a unit of time. Although the magnitude value can be calculated based on the amount of actual energy use in a process or operation, the p_i is currently measured by subjective judgments (Chen and Li 2006). The value of this subjective judgment is limited in the range [0.00, 1.00]. If p_i=1.00, it means that the level of pollution and/or hazards may cause fatal damage or generate a catastrophe to people and/or properties nearby. For example, if a construction operation can generate some noise and the sound level at the receiving end exceeds the 'threshold of pain', which is 140 dB(A) (McMullan 1993), then the value of p_i for this particular construction operation equals 1.00. On the other hand, if p_i=0.00, then it indicates that no pollution and hazards could be detectable from a process or operation. In practice, the initial value of each p_i depends on experience and experts' opinions. However, this treatment can not give an accurate value to each p_i because it relies on subjective judgments. Values of p_i are given for some standard processes in Figure 24.9.

The values of p_i can be treated like a quasi resource, and scheduled in the project plan along with other resources. Thus using resource smoothing, (Chapter 21) it is possible to smooth out the environmental impact of a project.

EVALUATION

A project plan is normally evaluated through criteria such as cost, time, quality, and safety. Since a project plan has considerable influence on the successful completion of a project, project management professionals need to be familiar with tools for preparing and evaluating their plans. Although the PPI method is an effective and efficient approach to indicating, reducing or mitigating pollution during project planning, the problem of how to select the best or the most appropriate plan from the different options, which are all based on distinguishing the degree of their potential adverse environmental impacts, is still an issue. The major premise of the PPI method is that each PPI_i and its p_i can be linearly aggregated. This hypothesis does not directly reflect the complicated nonlinear causal relationship of environmental impacts among diverse processes and operations. Thus, a nonlinear multicriteria decision-making method may be a more useful way to evaluate different plan options for environmental impact. The Analytic Hierarchy Process, AHP (Saaty 1994) is a powerful and flexible decision making process which can help people set priorities and make the best decision

Process	p_i
Demolition	0.70
Site preparation	0.70
Cast-in-place reinforced concrete pile	0.50
Excavation & support system	0.70
Foundation base plate	0.30
Reinforced concrete framework	0.50
Steel framework	0.20
Roof works	0.50
Water supply & sewerage works	0.10
Power supply system	0.10
Lighting system	0.10
Air conditioning	0.10
Local area network	0.10
Floor finish & polishing	0.70
Internal wall finish	0.40
External wall finish	0.20
Internal partition wall	0.10
Ceiling work	0.20
Site improvements	0.20
Landscaping work	0.10

Figure 24.9 Pollution index, p_i, for some standard construction processes

when both qualitative and quantitative aspects of a decision need to be considered. The AHP method is recommended for its stronger mathematical foundation, its capacity to gauge consistency of judgments, and its flexibility in the choice of ranges at the subcriteria level.

A limitation of AHP is that it does not deal with interconnections between factors at the same level as the model is structured. However, this can be overcome by using another multi-criteria analytical technique known as Analytic Network Process (ANP). The ANP is more powerful in modelling complex decision systems than AHP because it can be used to model very sophisticated decisions involving a variety of interactions and dependencies. These advantages are embodied in a lot of examples of applications of the ANP (Saaty 2005). For example, Saaty (1996) recommended the ANP to be used in cases where the most thorough and systematic analysis of influences needs to be made. In addition, the ANP method has been successfully applied to the strategic evaluation of environmental practices and programmes in both manufacturing and business to help analyze various project, technological or business decision alternatives, and it also has been proved to be useful in modelling dynamic strategies and systemic influences on managerial decisions related to environmental management (Chen and Li 2006). As a result, the ANP is selected to evaluate project plan options in regard to the criteria of environmental-friendly performance in the project period.

Above we introduced two indexes, EII and ETI, to identify KPIs to evaluate potential adverse environmental impacts of projects. We now show how the KPIs can be used with the ANP approach to construct decision-making models for the assessment of project plan options. This method aims to integrate important considerations such as time, cost, quality and safety in project planning with the evaluation of diverse environmental impacts indicated by KPIs, and as a result the most suitable plan can be identified. ANP is a general theory of relative measurement used to derive composite priority ratio scales from individual ratio scales that represent relative measurements of the influence of elements that interact with respect to control criteria (Saaty 1996, 2005). An ANP model comprises a coupling of two parts, including a control hierarchy or network of criteria and sub-criteria that control the interactions (interdependencies and feedback); and a network of influences among the nodes and clusters. Moreover, the control hierarchy is a hierarchy of criteria and sub-criteria for which priorities are derived in the usual way with respect to the goal of the system being considered. The criteria are used to compare the components of a system, and the sub-criteria are used to compare the elements of a component. Steps of the ANP approach in decision-making can be summarized as follows:

- model construction
- paired comparisons
- supermatrix calculation
- selection

We show how this can be applied to the project in Figure 24.10.

Model construction

First we construct an ANP model for the evaluation based on determining control hierarchies such as benefits, costs, opportunities, risk, and corresponding criteria for comparing the components (clusters) of the system. The ANP model for the assessment of project plan options focuses on the evaluation of potential diverse environmental impacts and the target of this evaluation is to select the most appropriate plan options based on their priority weights.

Figure 24.10 shows a model which has been set up using ANP. The decision environment includes exterior environment and internal environment. In the exterior environment, a downward arrow indicates the process of transferring data required by the ANP, an upward arrow indicates the process of feedback with evaluation results from the ANP, and the feedback process (loop) between the

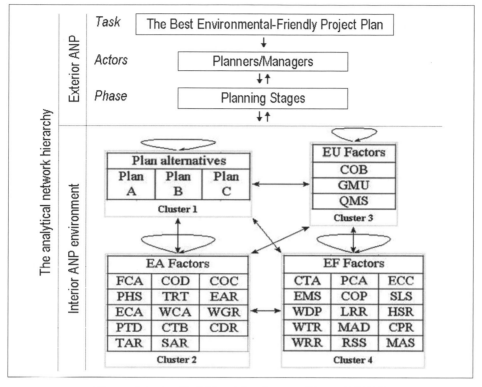

Figure 24.10 The ANP model environment (Chen and Li 2006)

exterior environment and the internal environment indicates a circulating loop for environmental priority evaluation of project plan options. In the internal environment, connections among four clusters and 35 nodes (see Figure 24.10), including three plan options, are modelled by two-way and looped arrows to describe the interdependences existed. The four clusters are:

C1: plan alternatives
C2: EA factors
C3: EU factors
C4: EF factors

We can inspect the model for interdependence between any two clusters or any two nodes, looking for feedback loops. However, there will be no control model, because environmental impact is an implicit control criterion, by which all judgments (paired comparisons) are made within the model. For example, when comparing the cluster of EA factors to the cluster of EF factors, the latter will obviously have greater impact in reducing the environmental impact of a project.

Similarly when the node comparisons are done (see below), the relative importance of one node over another can be identified. Figure 24.10 gives a list of 32 KPIs and 3 plan alternatives used in constructing the model. From these we can construct two decision-making models, a complicated model containing all 32 KPIs and a simplified model containing 15. We can then use these two models to evaluate the degree of potential adverse environmental impacts of the three plan options for a construction project.

Pairwise comparisons

We now conduct pairwise comparisons of paired clusters and paired nodes, and the relative importance is determined by using a scale of pairwise judgments, where the relative importance weight is valued from 1 to 9, see Figure 24.11. The weight of interdependence needs to be determined by a skilled estimator, with suitable experience.

Pairwise judgments		1	2	3	4	5	6	7	8	9
$KPI_{1.1}$	Plan A	✗	✗	✓	✗	✗	✗	✗	✗	✗
	Plan B	✗	✗	✗	✗	✓	✗	✗	✗	✗
	Plan C	✗	✗	✗	✗	✗	✗	✓	✗	✗
$KPI_{1.1}$	$KPI_{1.1}$	✗	✗	✗	✗	✓	✗	✗	✗	✗

Figure 24.11   Pairwise judgements for $KPI_{1.1}$

Figure 24.11 shows the pairwise comparisons for KPI1.1, fuel consumption amount (FCA) (EA Factor 1). The fuel consumption in Plan A is the least among the three plan alternatives, whilst the fuel consumption in Plan C is the highest (Figure 24.6). Quantitative pairwise judgments are also conducted in order to define priorities for each plan option. Weights of all interdependences based on pairwise comparisons among all KPIs are then aggregated into a series of sub-matrices. For example, if the cluster of plan alternatives, includes Plan A, Plan B and Plan C, and each of these plans is connected to nodes in the cluster of EF Factors, pairwise judgements of this cluster can thus result in relative weights of importance between each plan alternative and each EF Factor. The aggregation of the weights thus forms a 3×14 sub-matrix, *W21* in Figure 24.12. It is necessary to note that pairwise comparisons are necessary for all connections (clusters and nodes) in an ANP model to identify the level of interdependences which are fundamental in the ANP procedure. The series of sub-matrices are then aggregated into a supermatrix, the left hand side of Figure 24.12.

Supermatrix   Sub-matrix

$$
W = \begin{bmatrix}
W_{11} & W_{12} & W_{13} & W_{14} \\
W_{21} & W_{22} & W_{23} & W_{24} \\
W_{31} & W_{32} & W_{33} & W_{34} \\
W_{41} & W_{42} & W_{43} & W_{44}
\end{bmatrix}
$$

$$
W_{IJ} = \begin{bmatrix}
w_1\big|_{I,J} & \cdots & w_1\big|_{I,J} \\
w_2\big|_{I,J} & \cdots & w_2\big|_{I,J} \\
\cdots & \cdots & \cdots \\
w_i\big|_{I,J} & \cdots & w_i\big|_{I,J} \\
\cdots & \cdots & \cdots \\
w_{N_{I_1}}\big|_{I,J} & \cdots & w_{N_{I_n}}\big|_{I,J}
\end{bmatrix}
$$

$Cluster:$ $\quad C_1 \quad C_2 \quad C_3 \quad C_4$

$Node:$ $\quad N_{1_{1\sim3}} \quad N_{2_{1\sim14}} \quad N_{3_{1\sim3}} \quad N_{4_{1\sim15}}$

I is the index number of rows; and J is the index number of columns; both I and J correspond to the number of cluster and their nodes (I, J∈ (1, 2, …, 35)), NI is the total number of nodes in cluster I, n is the total number of columns in cluster I. Thus a 35×35 supermatrix is formed.

Figure 24.12   Formulation of matrices for the model (Chen and Li 2006)

Supermatrix calculation

Thus we synthesize a super matrix which illustrates the interdependences between the elements (nodes and clusters) of the ANP model, Figure 24.12. At first, an initial supermatrix of the ANP model needs to be created. The initial supermatrix consists of local priority vectors obtained from the pairwise comparisons among clusters and nodes. After the formation of the initial supermatrix, a weighted supermatrix is created. This process is to multiply every node in a cluster of the initial supermatrix by the weight of the cluster, which has been established by pairwise comparison among the four clusters. The last step is to compose a limiting supermatrix from the weighted supermatrix, by raising the weighted supermatrix to powers until it converges/stabilizes when all the columns in the supermatrix have the same values.

Selection

We now select the most appropriate plan based on the computation results from the limiting supermatrix. The most appropriate plan should have the highest value of a synthesized priority weight, equation 24.5, (Figure 24.13).
where

$$
Wi = \frac{W_i}{\sum_i w_i}
\tag{24.5}
$$

ANP Model	No. of KPIs	Synthesized priority weight Wi			Selected Plan
		Plan A	Plan B	Plan C	
Simplified Model	15	0.58229	0.19072	0.22700	Plan A
Complicated Model	35	0.59351	0.21926	0.18723	Plan A

Figure 24.13 Comparison of the three plans using priority weights calculated by the simplified and complicated ANP models

- W_i is the synthesized priority weight of plan alternative i ($i=1, ..., n$) (n is the total number of plan options, $n=3$ in this study)
- w_i is the limited weight of plan i in the limiting supermatrix

Here both the simplified model and the complicated model result in a preference for Plan A. This plan uses the least fuel and water, produces the lowest ratio of wastage, and has the has the highest ratio of recycle and reuse on materials and packaging. This indicates the ANP model can provide quite a reasonable comparison result for the target of environmental-conscious construction and therefore can be applied into practice.

Recommendations

The ANP model can be used to conduct an environmental analysis on all types of projects using the following steps:

1. Identify a group of KPIs
2. Set up an ANP model selecting either the simplified model or complicated model
3. Conduct an assessment of plan options on all KPIs using Figure 24.5
4. Conduct pairwise comparisons of all KPIs using Figure 24.11
5. Calculate the supermatrix as shown in Figure 24.11
6. Calculation the limiting priority weight of each plan option, Figure 24.13

For a more detailed description refer to Chen and Li (2006). If none of the plan options meets environmental requirements, adjustments can be made. The PPI method provides necessary support and re-evaluation of the plans by repeating the procedure from the second step.

POLLUTION CONTROL

During any project, it is crucial to control environmental performance. This requires the project manager to consider all the external issues that may impact on their project. Relevant documents may include:

- planning documents such as laws and regulations, environmental issues, and stakeholders analysis
- control documents such as environmental reports

In this section we suggest a Group-oriented Incentive Reward Programme (GIRP) for tracking materials and equipments being used by work groups on the project. This encourages all workers to minimize avoidable wastes of materials and unnecessary use of equipment by rewarding them according to the amounts they may have saved.

GIRP

It is important to manage materials and equipment to reduce unnecessary wastage. We have observed in our site surveys (Chen and Li 2006) that materials are often taken from on-site storage without any effective tracking mechanism;they are used with poor regard to reducing unnecessary wastage, and residual materials are seldom returned. Furthermore equipment is often used without attention to saveing fuel and electricity, and with little attempt to improve productivity and reduce idling and misuse. Thus project managers need effective tools to track on-site materials and equipment usage, and to motivate workers to reduce and even minimize wastages. GIRP is designed as a Financial Incentive Programme, to meet the demand of on-site materials and equipments management with regard to reducing wastage.

Fairness

Fairness is an important consideration in designing a GIRP. Before a GIRP is implemented, its fairness should be examined carefully. There are two aspects of fairness in the GIRP:

- **Fairness to the project:** This is easy to investigate, because the GIRP relates to the amount of materials and energy used for final products and if the overall amount of waste is reduced, then the project can get benefit; and in return the project should share the benefits (saved money) with the contributors – workers.
- **Fairness to workers:** This, on the other hand, is complex. Workers are normally organized into gangs, crews or groups according to their trades or types of work. Materials and equipment are normally shared by all workers in the group. If an amount of material waste and/or energy waste is detected, who should be punished, or, if there is a reduction of wastage, who should be rewarded: the person who is responsible for shifting materials or equipments from storage, or the leader of the group? Following discussions with the project managers and workers involved in the projects we surveyed, it was

finally deccided to adopt a GIRP. For the GIRP, all members of a group have to be rewarded or punished equally should there be any reduction and increase of materials and/or equipment wasted. The group-based reward can provide a common or shared goal for all group members and therefore encourage collaboration and cooperation among members to achieve a higher-level working performance, which can be expected with higher productivity and less adverse environmental impacts, and it can avoid the difficulty in determining an individual's contribution.

Calculation of Rewards

According to the GIRP, each work group has a group leader who is responsible for withdrawing all the materials and equipment needed by his group from the storekeeper. The storekeeper records the amount of materials and equipment taken by each group. When a group finishes its work, the group leader is also responsible for arranging any unused materials to be returned to the storekeeper as well as the equipment for updating the records of materials and energy use. Once a process or an operation has been finished, the project manager can measure the environmental performance of each group by comparing the actual amount of materials and energy used by the group with the estimated amount. The actual amount of material and energy used is tracked and recorded by the storekeeper, while the estimated amount of materials and energy use is prepared by the quantity surveyors or project managers. The estimated amount may include a wastage percentage, which is considered as a normal amount of waste on site. The percentage is determined based on the levels of wastes according to experience and/or statistics from past projects. At the end of the project, the overall performance of the group in minimizing adverse environmental impacts such as waste, noise and hazardous gases, can be measured, and the group rewarded with an agreed percentage of the savings, typically 40%.

IMPLEMENTING GIRP

Barcode system

Barcode systems have been used for materials and equipment management, plant and tool control in project management (Chen and Li 2006). The primary function of such a bar-coding system is to provide instant and up-to-date information on quantities of materials and equipment exchanged between storage keepers and working groups. Specifically, the bar-coding system can provide the following automatic functions to implement GIRP for reducing adverse environmental impacts:

- tracking real-time data of new materials and equipment on site
- tracking real-time data of unused materials and equipment on site
- tracking real-time data of packing of materials and equipment
- tracking real-time waste debris of materials and equipment on site
- recording data of materials and equipment used in the project period
- monitoring materials and energy used by working groups
- transferring real-time data to project management systems on site
- transferring real-time data of materials and equipments to head office via the Internet

RFID system

The Radio Frequency Identification technique (RFID) is an automatic identification method, relying on storing and remotely retrieving data using devices called RFID tags or transponders. An RFID tag is an object that can be attached to or incorporated into a product, animal, or person for the purpose of identification using radio waves. Chip-based RFID tags contain silicon chips and antennae. Passive tags require no internal power source, whereas active tags require a power source. They allow data to be acquired quickly and automatically using radio frequency. Unlike bar-coding, RFID technology enables the reading, writing and recording of data on the applied tag irrespective of location, type of environment, contact or visibility. Thus RFID opens up new opportunities in the areas of identification logistics, material management, production and service. An RFID system essentially consists of the following coordinated single components:

- transponders (tags, smart labels or mobile data storage)
- readers (read/write units)
- communication module (connection module)
- software for the system integration

RFID systems have been applied in numerous projects in the trend to replace barcode techniques across the world, and have been regarded as a powerful technique to maximize competitive advantages in real-time enterprise circumstances (Tabrizi 2006).

On-site Materials and Equipment Management

The architecture of an on-site materials and equipment management information system based on GIRP and bar-code/RIFD utilization is illustrated in Figure 24.14. The figure shows that when the group leader goes to the store to withdraw new material or equipment, or return surplus materials or equipment, the storekeeper scans the barcode labels or reads the RFID tags of the materials or equipment as well as the ID card of the group, so that the amounts of materials or equipment

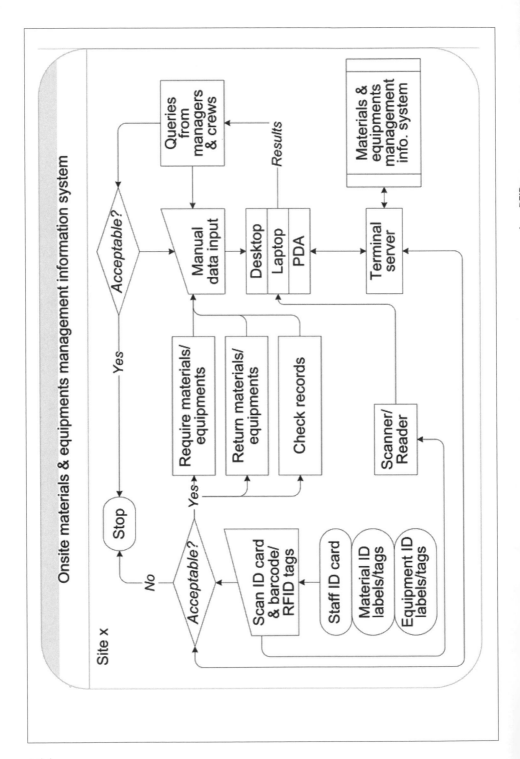

Onsite materials & equipments management information system

514

taken or returned by the group is recorded. In this way, the total amount used by the group can be calculated.

POLLUTION REDUCTION

At the later stages of a project, it is crucial to reduce any permanent adverse environmental impact that may have been generated. For example, project managers are encouraged to pay attention to long term land and water contamination such as solid and liquid waste. Project managers may also need to think about reused and recycled materials and equipment in their on-going projects to reduce pollutions generated from the different sectors. However, you need to be careful that the cost of pollution reduction does not increase adverse environmental impacts from other sources.

One method for reducing permanent pollution is waste exchange, and web-based information systems can effectively facilitate waste recycling. The concept of waste exchange systems for exchanging industrial residues and information and for reducing the waste volume was introduced in the 1970s (Middleton and Stenburg 1972). In recent years, web-based services for waste materials and equipment trade and information exchange have been developed because the web supports effective multimedia communication. There are a number of websites related to waste exchange, and some of them provide for quality salvaged materials and equipment at reasonable prices. Websites for waste exchange are generally regarded useful and effective in reducing total industrial waste. For example, since 1992 more than 650,000 tons of materials have been diverted from landfills and over $US5.5 million have been saved through the Californian material exchange system. However, it has been also noticed that either the information about some waste or the number of managers who actually dealt with second-hand materials is very limited. In addition, a process simulation (Chen and Li 2006) indicated that web-based waste exchange may actually increase transportation, which can directly increase adverse environmental impacts due to extra transportation, although the use of landfills can be decreased. As a result, it is recommended that project managers pay much of their attention to decreasing pollution before it is generated, and meanwhile, using recycled materials and equipments if this may bring benefits to their projects.

KNOWLEDGE-DRIVEN EMS

Besides the status of implementing an EIA and ISO 14000 EMS across diverse industries, there has been an emerging interest in knowledge management. The growing consciousness, requirements and initiatives of knowledge management are being used to manage the intellectual capital and get benefits from experience in both previous and on-going projects. For example, the C-Sand project (c-sand.org.uk) has been conducted for the UK construction industry to foster organizational practices which aim to enable knowledge creation for subsequent sharing and re-use, and to promote sustainable construction (Khalfan et al 2003). The Centex Construction Group (centex-construction.com), which is one of the largest contracting companies in the United States, faces some knowledge-related business challenges that are not always associated with the construction industry. They have a technology infrastructure in place where all professionals in the company have access to computers; and all offices and job sites are connected to a nationwide WAN via dial, ISDN and Frame. Thus, remote access is web-based and available from anywhere to increase knowledge sharing and provide better information access across the company's diverse landscape (Velker 1999). The progress of knowledge management across all industries also reflects the trend of enterprises away from traditional pure blue-collar operations towards a more knowledge-driven engineering and management in projects.

On the other hand, according to some survey results, the implementation of an EMS requires a practical approach, such as the EIA, that is popular and easy to use by practitioners. Thus, although government regulations have been identified as a major factor influencing the implementation of an EMS and EIA in diverse industries, individual industries are still unconvinced if there are not enough technical conditions to support implementing EMS, especially the techniques or tools which can help managers to conduct environmental management in their projects. Even for those with a high willingness to implement environmental management, effective, efficient and economical tools are essentially required. Nevertheless, the requirements of reusing experience also exist (Chen and Li 2006). Quantitative tools and techniques for environmental management in projects are currently not as regularly adopted as qualitative ones such as administrative regulations and practical guides because of the raw on-site information and data transformation to perform the necessary computations. Thus, it is necessary to power an EMS accredited or under accreditation with adequate support from quantitative tools or techniques and their background knowledge warehouse, which is the essential component of an enterprise's Knowledge Management System (KMS), Chapter 33. Based on all these considerations, this section presents a knowledge-driven EMS approach, called E+, which integrates several environmental management tools and an ISO 14001 EMS based dynamic EIA process into the process of knowledge management, for effectively, efficiently and economically supporting environmental management in the dynamic environments of various projects. To amplify this holistic objective, there are four sub-objectives:

- to illustrate an integrative knowledge-driven system to capture and reuse data, information and knowledge for dynamic environmental management;
- to specify individual tools that can be integrated into the knowledge-driven system for dynamic environmental-conscious projects management;
- to describe the interaction among all individual tools for the knowledge-driven system in regard to processing and reusing information, data and knowledge for dynamic environmental management in diverse projects; and
- to demonstrate the best practice of the knowledge-driven EMS through case studies.

E+ MODEL

Although individual approaches to environmental management have been proved effectively, efficiently and economically applicable at corresponding stages in the project period, it has also been noticed that those tools can be further integrated for a total environmental management purpose in projects based on their interrelationships. It is believed that this integration can bring about not only a definite utilization of current tools but also an improved environment for project managers to maximize the advantages of utilizing each of those environmental management tools due to sharing relevant data, information and knowledge in projects management. Figure 24.15 illustrates an integrative knowledge-driven EMS called E+ for the capture and reuse of data, information and knowledge in order to facilitate processes in dynamic environmental management in the project period. The E+ model comprises three main sections, including

- E+ EM Toolkits entity, which consists of three kinds of tools, including the Toolkit A for pre-project stage, the Toolkit B for mid-project stage, and Toolkit C for post-project stage, which are corresponding to the three phases of the project period
- The E+ KMS entity, which is the knowledge engine of the E+, which consists of five knowledge-related sub-entities;
  - knowledge source sub-entity
  - knowledge capture sub-entity
  - knowledge classification and evaluation sub-entity
  - knowledge storage sub-entity
  - knowledge reuse sub-entity
- The EMS-based EIA entity, which is the essential structural frame of the E+ in regard to implementing EMS in projects, and the entity consists of six EMS-related sub-entities:
  - environmental policy sub-entity
  - EM planning sub-entity
  - EM implementation and operation sub-entity

517

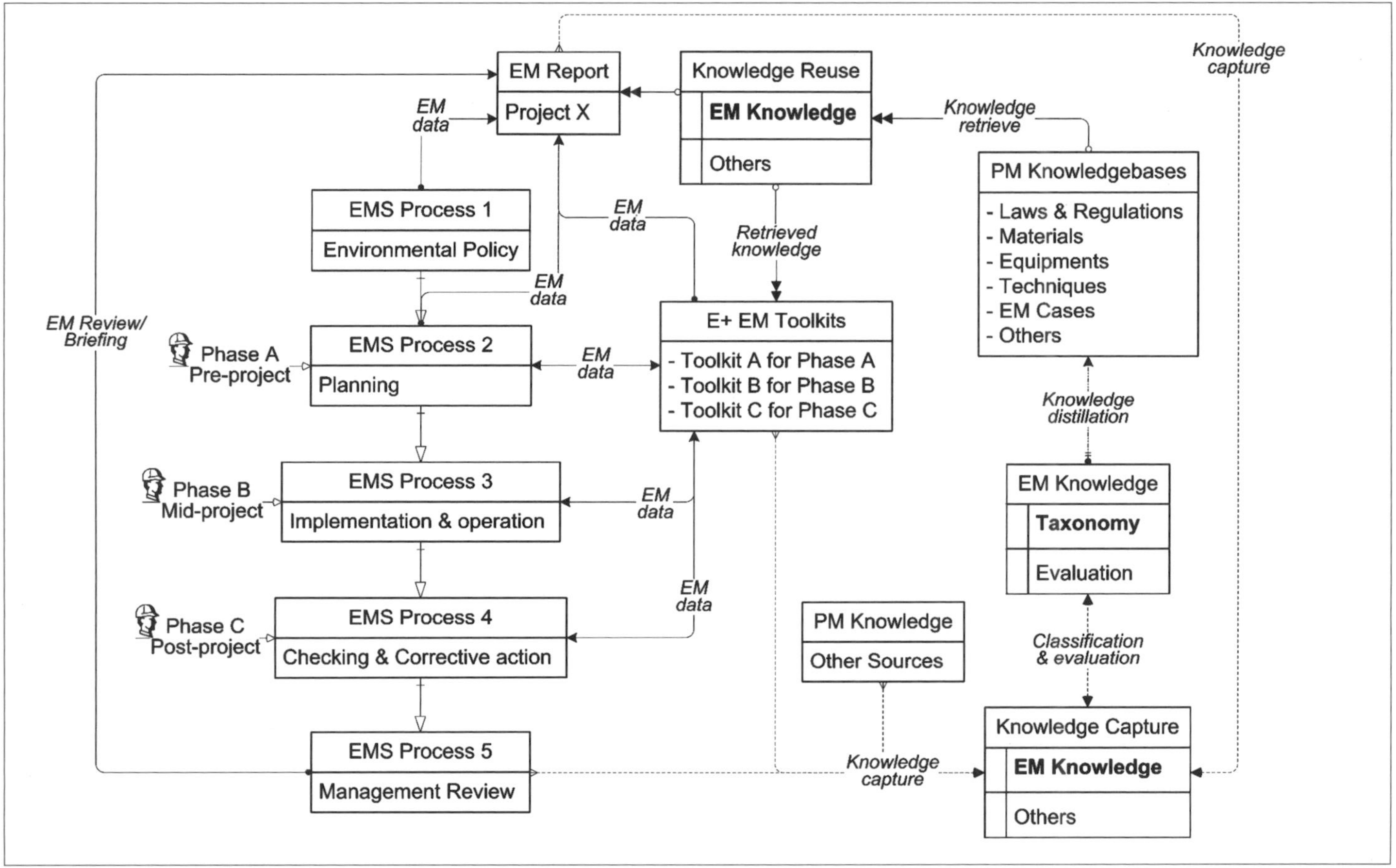

Figure 24.15 Knowledge-driven EMS

- EM assessment sub-entity
- EM review sub-entity
- EM report sub-entity

All these sub-entities belong to a standard EMS process normalized by the ISO 14001 EMS.

IMPLEMENTATION

The implementation of the E+ in project management needs a computer environment in which various E+ entities and their sub-entities can work together with the EMS process to accommodate both intramural and extramural evaluation and decision-making related to environmental management. The general process of knowledge management, including knowledge planning, creation, integration, organization, transference, maintenance and assessment (Rollett 2003) and the general process of computer software development, an E+ system (software environment) can be realized through three main steps: E+ system feasibility study, E+ system analysis and development, and E+ system evaluation; detailed contents in regard to these steps are described below:

- **Feasibility study:** The feasibility study is conducted not only prior to the establishment of the E+ model, but also before the system analysis and realization of the E+ software environment. First of all, it is important to analyze whether such an E+ system is necessary for the EMS-based dynamic EIA process to fulfil specific requirements in all projects, and this is to be done prior to the establishment of the E+ model. Next, if the E+ system is necessary, it is required to search for enough qualitative and quantitative tools to support the E+ system, and this is to be done before the system analysis and development of the E+ system. The feasibility study is essential for both a practicable E+ model and E+ system.
- **System analysis and realization:** The system analysis and realization are conducted after the E+ model has been established and a number of relevant tools have been identified for the E+ system. The aim of this step is to realize the E+ system from a model to a software environment with computer programming. Being limited to the length of this chapter, no further discussion is presented here to illustrate the development of the E+ system.
- **System evaluation:** The system evaluation is a trial process for the developed E+ system in regard to its capacity in fulfilling specific requirements in environmental management. There is also no further discussion related to this step due to the under-construction of the E+ system, although there has been an experimental case study (Chen and Li 2006) to facilitate the system analysis and realization of the proposed E+ system.

519

SUMMARY

Environmental management in the project period needs both qualitative and quantitative methods to enable managers to effectively, efficiently and economically achieve the diverse objectives of their projects. For qualitative environmental management, this chapter focuses on environmental strategy and environmental principles; meanwhile, for quantitative environmental management, this chapter focuses on various methods for pollution prevention such as EII, ETI and PPI and for pollution control such as GIRP. To facilitate environmental management in the project period, information and communication technologies such as barcode and RFID are introduced. In addition, a knowledge-driven EMS model is introduced in regard to conducting a total environmental management based on the capture and reuse of relevant information, data and knowledge in the dynamic circumstances of diverse projects.

REFERENCES AND FURTHER READING

Berge, B., 2000, *The Ecology of Building Materials*, Oxford: Architectural Press.

Bruntland, H.G., 1987, *Our Common Future*, Oxford: Oxford University Press.

Chen, Z. and Li, H., 2006, *Environmental Management in Construction*, London: Taylor & Francis.

CMIT, 2002, *CSIRO Sustainable Built Environment Online Brochures: Embodied Energy,* CSIRO Manufacturing & Infrastructure Technology (CMIT), Commonwealth Scientific and Industrial Research Organization (CSIRO), Australia. <http://www.cmit.csiro.au/brochures/tech/embodied/> (31 May 2005).

Das, T.K., 2005, *Towards Zero Discharge: innovative methodology and technologies for process pollution prevention*, New York: John Wiley & Sons.

DETR, 2000, *Environmental Impact Assessment – Guide to Procedures,* London: Thomas Telford.

Envirowise, 2005, *How To Write An Environmental Policy,* Envirowise, USA, <http://www.envirowise.gov.uk/page.aspx?o=Ref012> (16 December 2005).

European Construction Institute, 1995, *Total Project Management of Construction Safety, Health and Environment*, 2nd edition, London: Thomas Telford.

Khalfan, M.M.A., Bouchlaghem, N.M., Anumba, C.J. and Carrillo, P.M., 2003, 'Knowledge management for sustainable construction: The C-SanD Project', in Molenaar, K.R. and Chinowsky, P.S., (eds), *Winds of Change: integration and innovation in construction (Proceedings of the 2003 Construction Research Congress, Honolulu, Hawaii, March 19–21, 2003)*, Reston: American Society of Civil Engineers.

McMullan, R., 1993, *Environmental Science in Building*. 3rd Edition, London: Macmillan.

Middleton, F.M. and Stenburg, R.L., 1972, 'Research needs for advanced waste treatment', *Journal of the Sanitary Engineering Division*, 98(3), 515–528.

Mulholland, K.L. and Dyer, J.A., 1999, *Pollution Prevention Methodology, Technologies and Practices*, New York: AIChE Press.

NAE, 1999, *Industrial Environmental Performance Metrics: challenges and opportunities*, Washington, DC: National Academy of Engineering and National Research Council.

NAS, 2005, *Decision Making for the Environment: social and behavioral science research priorities*, Washington, DC: National Academy of Sciences (NAS).

Pollock, S.E., 1995, *Improving Environmental Performance*, London: Routledge.

Rollett, H., 2003, *Knowledge Management: processes and technologies*, Boston, MA: Kluwer Academic Publishers.

Saaty, T.L., 1994, *The Fundamentals of Decision Making and Priority Theory with the Analytic Hierarchy Process,* Pittsburgh, PA: RWS Publications.

Saaty, T.L., 1996, *Decision Making with Dependence and Feedback: the analytic network process*, Pittsburgh, PA: RWS Publications.

Saaty, T.L., 2005, *Theory and Applications of the Analytic Network Process,* Pittsburgh, PA: RWS Publications.

SDU, 2006, *What is Sustainable Development?*, The Sustainable Development Unit (SDU), Department for Environment, Food and Rural Affairs (Defra), UK. <http://www.sustainable-development.gov.uk/what/index.htm> (9 January 2007).

Stephens, T., 2005, 'Impact of earlier global warming long-lasting: new findings show a slow recovery from extreme global warming episode 55 million years ago', Currents Online, UC Santa Cruz. <http://currents.ucsc.edu/04–05/06–13/ocean.asp> (16 June 2005 and 9 January 2007).

Tabrizi, B., 2006, *Becoming a Real-time Enterprise: harnessing the power of RTE to maximize competitive advantage,* New York and London: McGraw-Hill.

Turner, J.R., (ed), 1995, *The Commercial Project Manager,* London: McGraw-Hill.

UNEP, 2003, *Environmental Impact Assessment (EIA),* United Nations Environmental Programme (UNEP). <http://www.unep.fr/pc/pc/tools/eia.htm> (11 January 2007).

US EPA, 1992, *Facility Pollution Prevention Guide*, U.S. Environmental Protection Agency, Office of Research and Development, Washington, DC, EPA/6OO/R-92/088.

Velker, L., 1999, 'Caution: KM under construction – challenges and solutions from a geographically diverse contractor', *KMWorld Magazine*, 8(5).

Wathern, P., 1988, *Environmental Impact Analysis, Theory and Practice,* London: Unwin Hyman.

Part III
Process

INTRODUCTION TO PART III

In Part III, we consider processes by which the project's products or facility are delivered. We describe what the life-cycle is, why it is an inherent part of project management, and its implications. We then describe three stages of the life-cycle: start-up. definition, and implementation and control.

CHAPTER 25: THE PROJECT LIFE-CYCLE

In Chapter 25, Chris Dawson describes the project life-cycle. He tells how the modern approach is to view the life-cycle as a process; the project is a process to convert inputs into desired customer outputs. He differentiates between two life-cycles: the project management life-cycle, the process by which the project is planned and executed; and the product life cycle, the process by which the inputs are physically converted into the outputs. He describes the sub-processes in the project management life-cycle, and describes the overlap between the project and product life-cycles. He ends by discussing extended models of the life-cycle and project management techniques.

CHAPTER 26: PROJECT START PROCESS

In Chapter 26, Roland Gareis describes project-start. A project is a social system, which exists in its context, and it must be integrated into that context. Roland Gareis considers how the project start process can help achieve that. He considers the need for a professional project start process, its design and the use of different types of start process for different types of project.

CHAPTER 27: PROJECT PROPOSAL AND INITIATION

In Chapter 27, Lizz Robb describes the project initiation process. The chapter explores the diligence and the approach best practice suggests should be invested into project proposal and initiation. Lizz explains how to develop the governance structure and the project plans, and how to establish document control and configuration management.

CHAPTER 28: PROJECT MODELLING

Terry Williams describes Project Modelling in Chapter 28. Projects are complicated entities, and managers cannot generally analyse all the aspects of a project in their head. Modelling is needed to help managers understand their projects, so it lies at the heart of project analysis and planning. Terry Williams considers what sort of models are used in Project Management, and why modelling is needed particularly for complex projects. He discusses the role of the project modeller, and how modelling can contribute to the project through the life-cycle.

CHAPTER 29: MANAGING IMPLEMENTATION

In Chapter 29, Dennis Lock describes implementation and progress monitoring and control. He introduces an essential framework for implementation and progress measurement, and then discusses the need to communicate the plan. He describes key issues of start-up as they relate to implementation and progress measurement. He then describes how to manage progress in several functions. He also discusses higher levels of progress measurement and some special cases. He then describes methods of progress measurement and control covering the *earned value method*, change control and progress reporting.

CHAPTER 30: PROJECT CLOSURE AND AFTERMATH

There was no chapter on Project Close-out in the 3rd edition, as a protest that nobody was researching or writing about it. I had several offers for a chapter for this edition and chose Mark O'Callaghan to write it. Project closure requires that all elements come together on the final project completion date. Mark O'Callaghan describes the three major phases in the process of closure: finishing the work; handing over the project; winding up project management; and project aftermath. He describes the finishing of the work as a continuation of the project until completion, but the handing over the project as a sub-project in itself. He describes how the project management process itself must be wound down during this period. At the end he suggests there should be an evaluation and review of the project.

25 The Project Life-cycle

Christian W Dawson

A project is a temporary endeavour undertaken to create a unique product, service or result, (PMI® 2004).

The above definition succinctly captures the essence of two main characteristics of all projects; their *uniqueness* and their *temporary existence*. The term 'temporary' in this definition necessarily implies that projects occur within a finite time frame – that is they have a particular start and end point. During their existence between these two points, projects progress through a *life-cycle* which consists of two main sets of processes – project management processes and product development processes. This chapter discusses the project life-cycle with these two sets of processes in mind.

The chapter begins by defining three management perspectives on projects, it moves on to discuss the two life-cycle processes involved (product development and project management) before finishing with an example of how projects are managed through their life-cycle using appropriate techniques. It is worth noting that some of the terms used within this chapter differ from those used elsewhere in this book (for example, Chapter 5). However, while there is no definitive definition of these terms (authors use them interchangeably and with different meanings) this chapter goes some way to defining their use.

THREE PERSPECTIVES

All projects are managed from three different perspectives. They are managed at different *levels* (for example, from short-term day-to-day management to longer-term strategic management); they are managed through a series of *stages* – the life-cycle; and they are managed by controlling and trading-off five *elements* that are inherent in all projects.

(a) **Levels**. A project can be viewed from the different management levels at which the project is planned and controlled. These levels focus on either short-term or long-term goals which include ways in which projects integrate into organizations, business areas and markets. Viewing projects from this perspective enables one to see their broader environmental impacts and their industrial context.

(b) **Life-cycle**. All projects progress through a series of steps or stages. While this perspective can be rather complex, it is possible to visualize the project process in simple terms using diagrammatical project management techniques. These techniques include familiar activity networking techniques (such as PERT and CPM), Gantt charts, breakdown structures, organizational charts and so on (See Part 2). The life-cycle is the focus of this chapter.

(c) **Elements**. From the third perspective a project is seen to be composed of five elements that require managing and controlling throughout the entire life-cycle: time, cost, quality, scope and resources. While scope is sometimes interpreted as an aspect of quality and subsumed within it, identifying scope as an element in its own right enables it to be managed and controlled more easily. All projects contain these five elements to a greater or lesser extent. Tradeoffs and attention to these elements vary throughout the project life-cycle, and also from one project to the next.

A factor subsumed in each of these perspectives is that of risk. Because of the unique nature of projects, risk is inherent throughout all levels of a project, all elements of a project and within the life-cycle processes themselves. Managing risk is described in Chapter 22.

AN HOLISTIC PROJECT OVERVIEW

At an holistic level, the project life-cycle can be represented by a simplistic process model. Such a model shows the life-cycle as a process that takes a set of inputs, acts upon these inputs through a coherent set of activities, and produces a consequential set of outputs. This process is well represented by the *Meliorist model,* Figure 25.1 (adapted from Dawson 2005,4). The Meliorist model shows how a project transforms an existing situation, S_A, into a desired situation, S_B, by performing a set of actions that represent a project. This desired situation S_B may mean different things to different people; the project's sponsor, the project manager, the users and so on. The desire to move to S_B might stem from the fact that situation S_A is currently unacceptable and a project is seen as a solution to this problem. This problem may not yet exist but may be anticipated in the future. Before the problem arises something, a project, must be done to avert it. Alternatively, while situation S_A may be satisfactory, there may be a more

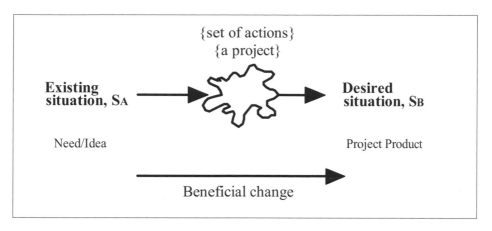

Figure 25.1 The Meliorist model interpretation of the project process (adapted from Dawson 2005)

appealing situation at S_B to which people are drawn. In this case there is a 'pull' towards an appealing situation S_B rather than a 'push' from an unsatisfactory situation S_A. Whichever the case, a project's objective is to bring about some form of beneficial change, whatever this happens to be.

PROJECT LIFE-CYCLES

Projects progress through a number of stages from their initial conception as a project idea through to their eventual completion and termination. This *project life-cycle* is defined in many different ways by authors who identify different numbers of stages in the cycle at different levels of detail. Gardiner (2005), for example, identifies four steps in the project life-cycle; initiation and definition, planning, execution and control, and closure. Weiss and Wysocki (1992) identify five distinct stages as definition, planning, initiation (organize), control and close; and Lock (2003) identifies 5 phases of project management and six phases in a typical product life history.

These definitions of the project life-cycle encompass two types of activity – those concerned with planning, managing and controlling the project – *the project management life-cycle*; and those directed towards the development of the project's product – the *product development life-cycle* (this is referred to as the *project life-cycle* in Chapter 5). In this section these two aspects of the project life-cycle are separated and presented as distinct staged processes. In the following section these aspects are further refined into process models.

PROJECT MANAGEMENT LIFE-CYCLE

For the purposes of this chapter the project management life-cycle is defined as a five stage process based on Weiss and Wysocki (1992). The five stages through which all projects progress from a project management perspective are *definition*, *planning*, *organization*, *control* and *close*. Figure 25.2 provides an overview of this staged interpretation of the project management life-cycle. In this figure the stages have been shown to overlap somewhat. This is intentional as project management stages are not independent of one another but inter-dependent and project managers will often have to re-work documents and plans produced earlier in a project as new information is obtained and the project progresses.

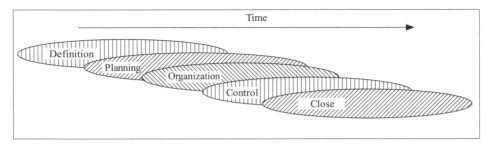

Figure 25.2   The project management life-cycle stages

More detail is provided on the activities performed during each of these stages later, but, broadly speaking; definition involves the initial identification of the project as a need or desire and the production of a project definition report that sets out precisely what the project hopes to achieve. Planning involves deciding how the project will be performed in order to meet the requirements outlined in the definition stage. Organization (sometimes referred to as *initiation*) involves mobilising the workforce, obtaining resources, assigning work (sometimes identified as a distinct activity in its own right and referred to as *implementing* as in Chapter 5), and getting the project started. Control encompasses all the project management tasks that are ongoing throughout the development of the project's product – monitoring, motivating, re-planning, correcting, controlling etc. Finally, *close* refers to the project management activities of closure such as disbanding the project team, completing final reports and budget accounting. This form of closure is in contrast to the *close-out* of the project life-cycle defined in Chapter 5 which covers the handover and implementation of the project's product.

PRODUCT LIFE-CYCLE AND PRODUCT DEVELOPMENT LIFE-CYCLE

The product life-cycle is much broader than the project management life-cycle and product development life-cycle. The project management life-cycle manages the development of the project's product (or a single phase of this development within the product development life-cycle), while the product life-cycle also covers the product's implementation, its use and its eventual retirement and replacement. This is a similar interpretation to that of Lock (2003) who refers to the product life-cycle as the *full life history* and identifies the *project management span* (covered by the project management life-cycle here) as a subset of this.

Sometimes it is difficult to determine when a product is 'finished' but it can also be difficult to define just when its development started. Does one, for example, include in the product life-cycle activities such as the development of the initial product idea? For example, Field and Keller (1998) discuss whether a feasibility study is part of this cycle. Towards the latter stages of the project process it is arguable whether a project would encompass operation, maintenance and retirement of the project's product. However, many projects exclude these activities as they occur after the project is signed off. For example, when building a bridge, while the project's sponsor may be concerned with future maintenance, the project manager would only be concerned with completing the bridge. The problem arises because of confusion between the project management and product life-cycles. A product life-cycle can span several years – from the time the idea for the product is formed to the time it is finally phased out, retired and replaced. A project, on the other hand, progresses through a series of phases that occur within a much more limited period. A project is unlikely to encompass the broad life-cycle of the product and is usually focused on the product's initial development.

Here a broad set of product life-cycle stages is presented that encompass the entire spectrum of activities that occur in a product's life time. Such a definition is shown in Figure 25.3. This definition covers operation and eventual retirement of a product. Analysis refers to the initial investigative work on a project's product: its idea and its feasibility. Synthesis encompasses the work on the product itself – its development. Operation represents the implementation, use and maintenance of the project's product and retirement represents the final withdrawal and replacement of the product. These stages are not mutually exclusive and common activities occur at the overlaps between each stage. For example, between operation and retirement, a phased implementation of a new system would lead to a reduced operation of the existing system and the initial pilot running of the new one.

The *product development life-cycle* is embodied within the first two stages of the product life-cycle – Analysis and Synthesis – and it is this development that is typically managed by the project management life-cycle. The product development life-cycle varies from project to project as it depends on the nature of the product that is being developed. This life-cycle comprises those activities that are performed to develop the project's product. This does not embody the

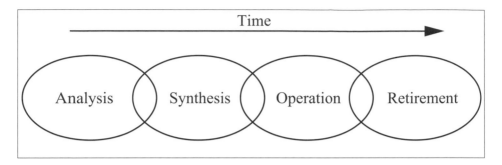

Figure 25.3 The product life-cycle

operation or eventual retirement of the product covered by the overarching product life-cycle but it does consist of the *phases* through which a product is developed. Phases are elements of a product's work breakdown structure. They identify the actual work that will be performed to achieve the project's objectives. While the product life-cycle represents abstract categorizations that attempt to classify work in particular time frames, phases represent key developments of the actual work itself. For example, a project to develop a railway across a country might be split into a number of phases; Phase 1: build railway linking towns A and B; Phase 2: build railway linking Towns B and C, etc. Each of these phases is a project in its own right and would be planned and managed as such. There is some confusion in the literature between the terms phase and stage. It is worth emphasizing here that a stage is a step in the project management life-cycle, while a phase is a step in the product development life-cycle.

PROJECT MANAGEMENT AND PRODUCT DEVELOPMENT INTERACTION

Although the project management and product life-cycle have been defined separately it is important to be aware of the relationship between them. A project can be a small part of a larger product development – representing the development of one phase of the product. Alternatively, a project may wholly encompass the entire product life-cycle. Each phase of a product development should be managed as a mini-project and consequently should be managed through the five stages of the project management life-cycle. Figure 25.4 provides an interpretation of this issue. In this figure:

(a) Project A represents a small project to complete the initial feasibility study and design for a system – Phase 1 of the product's development. This project is managed and pursued just like any other project. The project's product in this case would be the completed analysis, design and feasibility documentation for the larger product.

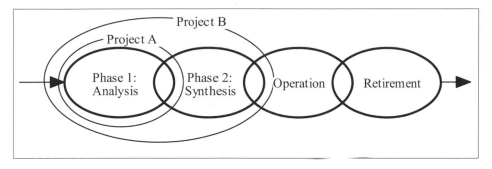

Figure 25.4 Projects as part of the product life-cycle

(b) Project B is a medium-sized project to investigate, design, develop, and implement a system. This project would be concerned with integrating the system into its working environment and setting up operational procedures. This project encompasses Phases 1 and 2 of the product's lifecycle.

This interpretation of project and product can be compared with Boehm's (1988) spiral model within the software development industry. In this model the product is seen to develop through a series of phases; Requirements, Development, Integration and Maintenance. Each phase is completed in turn through a four stage management-type process; Determine Objectives, Evaluate Alternatives, Develop, Plan Next Phase. Thus, each step in the development can be interpreted as a mini-project with its own budget, goals, and time scales.

PROJECT PROCESSES

> *A process is a set of interrelated actions and activities that are performed to achieve a pre-specified set of products, results or services* (PMI® 2004)

While the Meliorist Model introduced earlier provides an interesting academic interpretation of the project process, it provides little information, explanation or technique that can be utilized. It is the sub processes within this model that are more valuable and require closer scrutiny and explanation. The PMI® quote provided above succinctly defines the important aspects of a process. There is more to a process than a mere collection of tasks or functions. A process is a *coherent* (*interrelated*) series of activities that takes a collection of inputs (i.e. *pre-specified*) and creates a set of outputs (i.e. *products, results or services*). A process should be capable of improvement, it should be supported by tools, it should be measurable and it should be repeatable (Down et al 1994). It is by its inputs and outputs that a process is identified and defined. In project management terms, these inputs and outputs are represented by either documents or documentable

533

items. No item should be produced from such a project process without being documented in some way or another.

The input to the Meliorist Model introduced earlier would be either a documented idea for a project, a documented problem that requires resolution, or a set of documentation from a previously completed product phase. The output from this holistic model is the project's documented product. A project's product is not necessarily a physical object but a product in the most general sense of the word. This product might be a new organizational structure, a software system, a new set of management procedures, a change in working practices, the restructuring of a department, a new process or service, an industrial plant, a bridge, a set of aircraft designs, a set of quality standards, etc.

While inputs and outputs are crucial to the understanding of processes another of their key features is that they must consist of a *coherent* series of activities. The key term within this definition is coherent. A process **must** consist of activities that interrelate and combine effectively with one another and it must be understood and manageable. A process that is merely identified as a number of connected activities will be inefficient, difficult to manage and unrepeatable. This is not to imply that projects are repeatable. Projects are unique endeavours that bring about beneficial change. The project management process that is used to manage a project that achieves this aim should itself be repeatable and be applicable in many project scenarios. In this way project success through successful project management processes can be achieved again and again.

THE PROCESSES INVOLVED

Figure 25.5 (adapted from Dawson 2005,55) provides a generic view of the project process and shows the five elements inherent in all projects – *time, resources, cost, scope* and *quality*. The diagram shows that all projects consume *time, resources* and *money* (cost) in order to produce a product which has its own *scope* and *quality*. This product can be something tangible or intangible (supported by appropriate physical documentation). There are two aspects to this product – it will have a certain *scope* (what it covers, what it does – i.e. what it achieves) and a certain level of *quality* (how well it does it).

The project itself consists of two main activities – *project management processes* and *product development processes*. Project management processes are those processes that deal with managing and controlling the project as a whole. That is they represent the work a project manager performs to hold a project together on a daily basis; defining work, organizing resources, planning, scheduling, controlling, motivating, delegating, etc. These processes are 'common to most projects most of the time' (PMI® 2004).

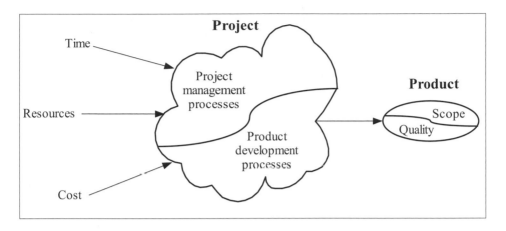

Figure 25.5   Project overview (adapted from Dawson 2005)

Product development processes are involved with the actual project work itself i.e. developing a project's product. These processes vary from project to project; for example, developing a programme, writing reports, preparing a requirements document, meeting clients, clearing land, building foundations, etc. These are the processes performed by the project's resources, which are managed and controlled by the project management processes. A project's resources cover everything used in a project, predominantly those resources used to develop the project's product. These resources include staff, contractors, equipment, machinery, computer access time, rooms, consultants, plant, software, hardware, etc.

Generally speaking, project management processes represent no more than around 10% of overall effort on the project. This 10% of project management effort is not distributed evenly throughout the life span of the project. A lot of project management effort will be expended towards the start of a project, planning how it will be performed for example, while less effort will be expended on project management as the project progresses during control.

PROJECT MANAGEMENT PROCESSES

Classifying project activities into stages, as we did earlier, can confine them to temporal frameworks and can ignore interrelationships, interactions and possible repetition of work. Defining a project from a process perspective overcomes this issue and it is this view that we will now look at. Project management processes represent the series of actions that are performed to bring about a project's result (PMI® 2004). In reality project management activities occur in parallel with each other, they might be repeated and they might occur at different stages of the

535

project process. By classifying activities from a process perspective the temporal problem of the staged interpretation diminishes. There are six project management process groups that occur within a project's life-cycle. These are shown in Figure 25.6. Rather than looking at the activities that are performed within a particular stage of the project life-cycle, and at the order in which these activities are performed, the process perspective classifies the processes into groups that are performed irrespective of project stages. These processes are repeated for each phase of a product's development.

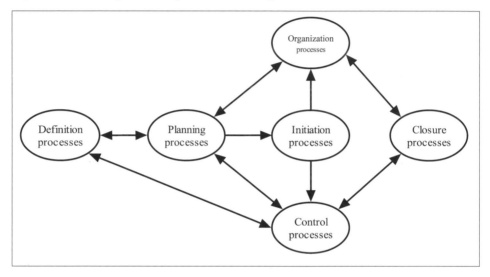

Figure 25.6 Project management process interaction

Definition processes

Definition processes are those used to investigate the feasibility of the project or product phase, clarify the problem that needs resolving, define goals and objectives, submit a project proposal and obtain project go-ahead. They might also involve arranging finance, planning permission, sorting out environmental issues and contracts, negotiating legal problems, defining the project in specific and general terms and committing to the project.

Planning processes

Planning processes are those used to prepare workable plans and identify how the project will fulfil its business needs. Project planning involves identifying the work that needs to be performed to complete the project successfully, deciding on how to approach this work, estimating and scheduling work and resources, budgeting and planning cash flows for the duration of the project and defining standards that

536

need to be maintained. This stage also involves preliminary risk management work involving the identification and quantification of risks and contingency planning. Planning processes also involve scope planning and definition, activity planning and sequencing. It is during these processes that project management tools and techniques are applied with enthusiasm. These include techniques such as Gantt charts and activity networks, work breakdown structures, organization structure charts, responsibility matrices and so on.

Initiation processes

Initiation processes relate to a project's set up and start up. They are important as they include motivating staff, communicating the plan, arranging staff and resources into a work routine, setting up communications strategies, allocating rooms and work areas, assigning work to resources and starting the project with a kick-off meeting or launch workshop. They have a particular impact on the motivation, confidence and understanding of a project's work force. Failure to motivate staff and provide them with a clear view of the project's goal may well lead to a poor team performance that is difficult to rectify later.

Control processes

Control processes focus on the four elements: time, cost, quality and scope as the project progresses. Control processes are those concerned with monitoring these elements with respect to project plans, trading them off against one another, identifying variances and taking corrective action where necessary. Any changes introduced through a project's control processes must be communicated and coordinated across the project as a whole.

Organization processes

These concentrate on coordinating and organizing the fifth project element – the resources that do the work to develop the product. While control processes focus on abstract project elements, organization focuses on the project's resources and actually getting the work done.

Closure processes

The final set of processes relates to closure activities. These processes are concerned with winding down the project, completing any final documentation, disbanding and reassigning resources, completing any budget requirements, closing the books etc.

PROJECT MANAGEMENT PROCESS INTERACTION

This process interpretation identifies the interactions between processes through the transfer of documents and documentable items. In Figure 25.6 the interconnecting arrows between the processes represent this flow of items. Thus, the output from one process serves as an initiating input to another. For example, from a project's definition processes a product definition document will be produced. This will form the initial basis from which project plans can be drawn up by appropriate planning processes.

What Figure 25.6 appears to imply is that each process group is discrete and occurs only when another set of processes within another group have completed. This appears to return to the idea of distinct project management stages. However, this is not the case as process groups overlap with one another and occur simultaneously. Figure 25.7 shows an interpretation of this overlap. In this figure it is clear that project management processes do not happen in isolation but overlay one another and occur simultaneously throughout the project life-cycle. For example, while definition processes start well before anything else, there is a time when they are performed simultaneously with planning processes. Planning processes in turn continue until almost the very end of a project (its closure). This happens because re-planning may be necessary as schedules are missed or resources change.

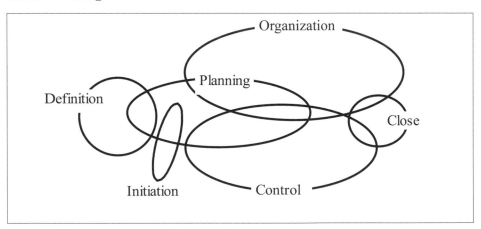

Figure 25.7 Overlapping project management process groups

While Figure 25.7 shows the overlap between process groups, Figure 25.6 shows the interaction between them. For example, Figure 25.6 shows there is interaction between the initial definition processes and planning processes. This interaction can stem from certain planning processes highlighting potential difficulties, risks or bottlenecks that were not apparent during earlier definition processes and feeding this information back. The organization and control processes also interact with the planning process groups as the project is re-planned when information emerges from these two groups.

PRODUCT PROCESSES

PMI® (2004) defines an additional process group to those outlined in the previous section – the Executing Process Group. This group encompasses those activities 'used to complete the work defined in the project management plan to accomplish the project's requirements'. These processes clearly vary from project to project and are dependent on the scope of the project's product. The executing process group embodies those processes outlined in the organization process group outlined above. By separating out the actual product development processes in this case we are able to show more clearly the actual product development life-cycle and how this relates to the project management life-cycle.

In this case, Figure 25.8 provides an overview of the relationship between product development activities and the project management process groups outlined earlier. Notice that the product development processes act beyond the project as product refinement, improvement, and maintenance usually continue long after a project is completed. In this diagram, while product development overlaps most of the project management processes, project definition processes and initiation processes can (and do) take place before any product development is undertaken. Similarly, it is possible for closure processes to occur after product development is completed (for example, it might take some time to reassign staff to new projects), although, as noted earlier, product development may continue long after this.

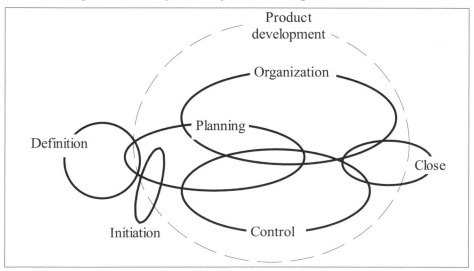

Figure 25.8   Product development processes occurring during the project management life-cycle

539

PRODUCT PROCESS ACTIVITY

The level of effort directed towards developing the actual project's product only picks up during the central 80% of the project life-cycle. This is shown in Figure 25.9, which reveals the level of activity directed towards the development of the product by the project resources. During a project's definition and planning stages no product development activities are performed. It is only when a project's initiation, organization and control processes are performed that resources focus on getting the job done. Once underway, work on the project's product intensifies. This work is completed before the project's final closure which remains the concern of the project manager. Notice that the curve is not symmetrical. There is more intense activity on product development towards the end of the project than in the project's earlier stages, as critical deadlines approach.

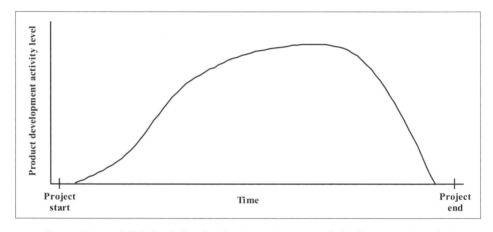

Figure 25.9 Activity level of product development processes during the course of a project

EXTENDED LIFE-CYCLE MODELS

The previous sections aimed to set within context project processes. This has been achieved by a moving away from the 'stages' interpretation of projects. The move towards a process interpretation can be likened to the ideas introduced by business process re-engineering (BPR) during the 1990s in which organizations are viewed from a process rather than a functional perspective.

PROJECT LIFE-CYCLE PROCESS MODELS

The project management process model in Figure 25.6 is stable at this top level, because the processes involved with project management should be clear and follow a repeatable model such as this. On the other hand, the product development process is not fixed. This process is product dependent as the product might well be difficult to define; for example, in research and development projects. Some flexibility in the product development process is therefore required. This flexibility can be introduced and managed in two ways: by identifying alternative routes through the product development process, or by using flexible planning techniques that allow plans to evolve as projects progress. Rolling wave planning is just such a technique. Rolling wave planning (Turner 1999; OGC 2005) provides a broad plan that the project will follow, leaving any details until each phase of the product life-cycle is tackled. Thus, project planning activity ebbs and flows like a rolling wave throughout the entire life-cycle of the project. In this case what happens to the project's product at each stage of the product life-cycle is unclear at the initial stages. Rolling wave planning allows plans to be firmed up as a project progresses and more is learnt about the product.

HYBRID PROCESS MODELS

The alternative is to attempt to identify any potential routes through the product development process at a much earlier stage. This technique can be achieved by using hybrid models that combine all potential development routes into one model at the start. This has an advantage over rolling wave planning in that potential trouble spots, repetition and alternatives are explicitly identified early on. Thus, contingency plans can be put in to effect sooner and more accurate assessments of risks can be made.

One of the main characteristics of projects that separate them from ordinary day-to-day operations within a company is that they are *unique*. The uniqueness of projects introduces problems for project management as it implies that a repetitive, consistent product process model cannot be used 'off-the-shelf'. Such a process would need adopting and adapting to each new project situation. An alternative is to use hybrid processes that implicitly incorporate flexibility into their structure. Hybrid processes combine several product process models. They identify complex process structures at several levels. These are models that can be relatively flexible in their lower levels but can be relatively stable at the top.

EXAMPLE

As an example, a software development life-cycle model is presented. Figure 25.10 shows a simplified version of this life-cycle. This model is an extract from the broader life-cycle steps of the software development process:

- *Requirements definition* is the documentation produced by the users identifying their needs for a system.

541

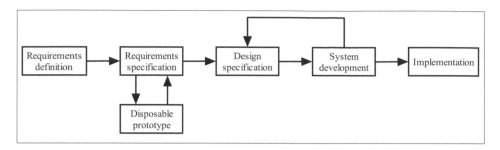

Figure 25.10 A software development process model

- This is interpreted by the software developer (systems analyst) to produce a *requirements specification*. A *requirements specification* aims to remove any inconsistencies and ambiguities from the users' requirements definition in order to provide a firm, clear specification of what the users need from the system. This is sometimes referred to as a *functional specification* or a *system specification*.
- Now that the users' needs have been clearly specified it is possible to put together a detailed design for the system that will address those needs. This results in the *design specification*.
- From this design the system can be developed and implemented (*System development* and *implementation*).

Looking more closely at this process it is clear that feedback and repetition may take place as indicated by the arrows. Figure 25.10 actually identifies a hybrid process. In this model the conventional software development life-cycle has been combined with a throw-away prototyping model and an evolutionary prototyping model. The process now consists of potential alternative development routes. For example, once the requirements specification has been drawn up the systems analyst may wish to check that these are a fair representation of the users' needs by producing a disposable prototype. This prototype is presented to the users to confirm their satisfaction with the proposed system and confirm that their needs have been correctly identified. This may result in modifications to the requirements specification and the development of another throw-away prototype.

The evolutionary prototyping model is represented by the feedback loop from the *System development* to the *Design specification*. A subset of the final system will be developed from the initial design. This is presented to the users to obtain feedback. The users may or may not be satisfied with this system. If they are not, changes are made to the design (the design specification is revisited) and the system is redeveloped in line with these changes. Once again repetition within the process may or may not occur. Depending on the nature of the customer and system being developed, there will be more or less chance of this repetition taking place.

PROJECT MANAGEMENT TECHNIQUES

To manage the project management process it is necessary to represent this process in some way. The most common way of visualizing projects is through the use of Gantt charts (bar charts) and activity networks. While Gantt charts are useful for managing and controlling time and resources, activity networks provide a useful means of managing project activities by identifying their relationships and sequencing. Figure 25.11 summarises the different kinds of activity networks available. PERT and CPM are terms commonly used to refer to such networks. This is highlighted in Figure 25.11 which shows how PERT and CPM apparently refer to a number of different representations and complexities. CPM* and PERT* highlight the extended use of these terms when referring to more complex activity networks.

	Representation		
	AoA	**AoN**	**PDM**
DANs	CPM	CPM*	CPM*
PANs	PERT	PERT*	PERT*
GANs	GERT/VERT	-	-

Figure 25.11 Activity network representations

Since their inception in the late 1950s activity networks have become an invaluable aid to planning and managing all kinds of projects throughout industry. At that time the activity network originated in two very similar forms: PERT (Programme Evaluation and Review Technique) and CPM (Critical Path Method). Activity networks began initially by representing the tasks in a project by arrows connecting nodes or events. Consequently these networks are sometimes referred to as Activity-on-the-Arrow (AoA). An alternative representation soon developed in which the activities were represented by nodes and their relationships were represented by interconnecting arrows. This representation is called Activity-on-the-Node (AoN) and is logically equivalent to the AoA representation. In both these cases it is implicit within the network structure that all tasks must finish in sequence for a project to complete successfully. It is possible to extend the logic of the AoN representation by introducing constraints between the finish times and start times of connected activities. The Precedence Diagram Method (PDM) does this by introducing finish-to-start delays, start-to-finish delays, start-to-start delays and finish-to-finish delays (for example, when laying foundations there is at least a 24 hour delay between pouring concrete and being able to start any further building work, while waiting for the concrete to harden).

Not only can activity networks be split according to their representation but they can also be classified according to how they represent the characteristics of tasks. CPM belongs in the simplest of these three categories – the Deterministic Activity Network (DAN). DANs are used to manage projects in which the tasks are well understood and complete in recognized times. Thus, each task is represented by a single cost/duration estimate. However, in many projects it is difficult to accurately predict the duration (or cost) of certain tasks. Probabilistic Activity Networks (PANs), such as PERT, assist in these situations. In these cases activity durations are represented by probability distribution functions that are usually based on three time estimates (most likely, optimistic, and pessimistic durations). Due to the stochastic nature of the activity durations, PANs tend to be difficult to analyse unless Monte Carlo simulation is employed or probability distributions are replaced by simple derived summaries. It is usual, therefore, for managers to focus on the critical path of these networks – the path which has the longest duration.

To take these networking techniques one stage further requires their logic to be redefined. Generalized Activity Networks (GANs) represent this advancement. Development of GANs began in 1962 and the most common form is the Graphical Evaluation and Review Technique or GERT (Pritsker and Happ 1972). More recent developments include the Venture Evaluation and Review Technique or VERT (Moeller and Digman 1981; Kidd 1991) and an AoN GAN developed by Dawson and Dawson (1995). GANs differ from other activity networks in their definition of task input and output characteristics. PERT and CPM networks insist on a deterministic structure which implies that all activities must occur, in sequence, for a project to complete successfully. GANs, on the other hand, allow either deterministic or probabilistic branching to be defined. An interesting facet of GANs is their ability to handle loops. If loops are formed in ordinary networks, activities appear to be unable to begin until after they have completed. The probabilistic nature of the GAN, on the other hand, allows feedback from activities to earlier stages in the project life-cycle.

EXAMPLE

As an example of the application of GANs, take the hybrid process model of the software development life-cycle introduced earlier. On the surface this might appear as a linear process with each phase succeeding the previous one. At this top level this can be planned using conventional project management techniques such as PERT and Gantt charts. A simple example of this plan is presented in Figure 25.12. Unfortunately, as discussed, ordinary activity networks cannot plan for the repetitive loops identified in this process. These loops would have to be implicitly planned using the probability distribution functions of PERT. In this case the throw-away prototype used to elicit the requirements specification at

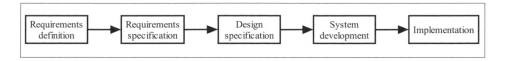

Figure 25.12 Standard activity network representation of example software development process

stage two has been implicitly planned into this phase of the life-cycle. The PERT network might include an optimistic estimate of no prototype being developed, an expected estimate of one prototype development and a pessimistic estimate of two prototype developments.

Figure 25.13 provides a GAN interpretation of this hybrid process model. Now it has been possible to explicitly identify probabilistic branches and loops. These loops may now have their repetitions defined. For example, within a certain department only one disposable prototype is ever developed. Alternatively, it may be unclear how many times each of the loops might be performed and each loop may have, say, a 40% chance of occurring each time. This figure may be calculated from experience of past projects and may be adjusted each time the loop is performed. Figure 25.13 is a much more accurate representation of the software development process model. Loops can now be clearly identified and some form of analysis can be made to predict likely results from this project. Such analyses are likely to include Monte Carlo simulation that will provide probability distributions indicating the likelihood of completing the project within particular time limits. Even if it is difficult to attribute appropriate figures and probabilities to this form of plan, it still provides a more honest interpretation of the proposed project. Managers can explicitly see where uncertainties exist and identify appropriate review points where decisions need to be made.

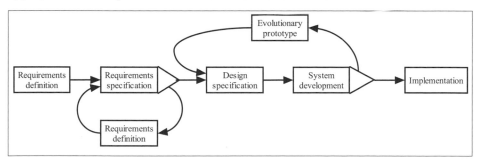

Figure 25.13 GAN representation of example software development process

SUMMARY

Projects can be viewed from three perspectives; their elements, their levels and their processes. These processes are concerned with either product development or project management. While project management processes are consistent and should be repeatable from one project to the next, the product development process is not. Managing the product process can thus be improved by incorporating flexibility into project plans. This might be achieved by rolling wave planning techniques or by combining several product models into one hybrid process. Such a process is difficult to manage using conventional project management techniques such as PERT and CPM. A more flexible technique such as GANs can cope with these uncertainties.

REFERENCES AND FURTHER READING

Boehm, B.W., 1988, 'A spiral model of software development and enhancement', *Computer*, May.

Dawson, C.W., 2005, *Projects in Computing and Information Systems*, Wokingham, UK: Addison Wesley

Dawson, C.W. and Dawson, R.J., 1995, 'Generalized Activity-on-the-Node Networks for Managing Uncertainties in Projects', *International Journal of Project Management,* 13(6).

Down, A., Coleman, M. and Absolon, P., 1994, *Risk Management for Software Projects*, London: McGraw Hill.

Field, M. and Keller, L., 1998, *Project Management*, London: Thomson Business Press.

Gardiner, P.D., 2005, *Project Management: a strategic planning approach*, Basingstoke, UK: Palgrave.

Kidd, J.B., 1991, 'Do today's projects need powerful network planning tools?', *International Journal Production Research,* 29(10).

Lock, D., 2003, *Project Management*, 8th edition, Aldershot, UK: Gower.

Moeller,G.L. and Digman,L.A., 1981, 'Operations planning with VERT', *Operations Research,* 29(4).

OGC, 2005, *Managing Successful Projects with PRINCE2®,* 2005 edition, London: The Stationery Office.

PMI®, 2004, *A Guide to the Project Management Body of Knowledge,* 3rd Edition, Newtown Square, PA: Project Management Institute.

Pritsker, A.A.B. and Happ, W.W., 1972, 'GERT: graphical evaluation and review technique part i. fundamentals', *Journal of Industrial Engineering,* 17.

Turner, J.R., 1999, *The Handbook of Project-Based Management, 2nd edition*, London: McGraw-Hill.

Weiss, J.W. and Wysocki, R.K., 1992, *5-Phase Project Management, A Practical Planning and Implementation Guide*, Reading: Addison-Wesley.

26 Project Start Process

Roland Gareis

Project management approaches can be differentiated by the way in which projects are perceived. Traditional, method-oriented project management approaches are based on the perception of projects as tasks with special characteristics. A systemic project management approach is based on the perception of projects as temporary organizations and social systems. The design of the project start process according to a systemic project management approach requires not only the development of the project plans, but also the establishment of the project as a social system, the development of a project specific culture and the establishment of relationships of the project to its relevant social environments. Having these objectives for the project start in mind, we recognize we need to manage the application of project management methods, standard project plans, and adequate project communication forms, and possibly the involvement of project consultants.

PERCEPTIONS OF PROJECTS AND PROJECT MANAGEMENT APPROACHES

In project management research, as well as in the practice, various definitions of projects are used. This is important because different perceptions of projects lead to different project management approaches. The definition of projects as tasks rather than the definition of projects as temporary organizations and as social systems, results in a different understanding of the objectives of project management, of the project management tasks, of the objects of consideration of project management and of the project management methods used.

PERCEPTION OF PROJECTS AS TASKS WITH SPECIAL CHARACTERISTICS

Traditionally, projects are defined as tasks with special characteristics. These special characteristics of projects are the 'complexity' of the content, the relative

547

uniqueness, the high risk and the high strategic importance for the project-oriented organization. Projects are understood as goal-oriented tasks since the objectives in terms of the scope, the schedule, the required resources, and the costs are planned, agreed on and controlled. A proponent of this understanding of projects is PMI®, the American Project Management Institute. PMI® (2004) defines a project as '... a temporary endeavor undertaken to create a unique product or service. ... Temporary does not necessarily mean short in duration; many projects last for several years.' PMI® (2004) further defines project management as 'the application of knowledge, skills, tools and techniques to project activities to meet project requirements'.

PERCEPTION OF PROJECTS AS TEMPORARY ORGANIZATIONS

According to organizational theory, projects can be perceived as temporary organizations for the performance of processes which are limited in time. As with other organizations, a project has a specific identity, which is characterized by its specific project objectives, project organization, project values and project environment relationships. A project is a temporary organization (see also Chapter 5). Through this temporary character the establishment of the project in the project start process, as well as the dissolution of the project in the project close-down process, attain a special meaning.

PERCEPTION OF PROJECTS AS SOCIAL SYSTEMS

The perception of projects as temporary organizations also makes it possible to view them as social systems. According to social systems theory organizations, and therefore also projects, can be viewed as social systems which have clear boundaries to differentiate themselves from their environments. But they are also related to those environments. The specific characteristics of social systems, such as their social complexity, their dynamics and self-reference, are management topics in projects as well. This understanding of projects results in a systemic project management approach which matches the complexity and dynamics of projects. Social systems are complex, self-referencing and dynamic. Luhmann (1996) defines the grade of complexity of systems in terms of the following influence factors:

- The number of elements in the system
- The number of possible relationships between these elements
- The diversification of the relationships
- The development of these three factors over time

On the formation of a social system, complexity may increase or decrease. The ability of a social system to survive is determined by its ability to develop an appropriate complexity of its own and use it to deal with the complexity of the environment.

PROJECT PERCEPTION ACCORDING TO ROLAND GAREIS PROJECT AND PROGRAMME MANAGEMENT®

A project is a temporary organization of a project-oriented organization for the performance of a relatively unique, short to medium term, strategically important process of medium or large scope (Cleland and Gareis 2006; Gareis 2005). Projects are used for the performance of relatively unique processes. The more unique the objectives and deliverables to be fulfilled are, the higher the associated risk. Information from past experiences which can be used as reference is often only available to a limited extent. Projects are used for the performance of processes with short to medium duration. These should be performed as quickly as possible, in other words in several months. One exception is the performance of infrastructure projects (construction or engineering projects) which can have a longer duration. Processes for which projects are used have a medium to high strategic importance for the company performing them. The performance of contracts contributes to, for example, the short- to medium-term survival of the company. The development of new products and the establishment of a new strategic alliance have, however, long-term consequences and are, therefore, strategically more important. Projects are used for business processes of medium to large scope. The scope of a process can be described by the tasks, the resources required, the costs occurring and the organizations involved.

TRADITIONAL PROJECT MANAGEMENT

The traditional perception of projects as tasks with special characteristics promotes the planning orientation in project management, as reflected in the bodies of knowledge (PMI® 2004; APM 2006; IPMA 2006), and in the works of Kerzner (2006). The main focus is on how an assignment is to be performed. Methods for work planning and work organization, such as the REFA methods (Čamra 1976), or methods of operations research (Hillier and Lieberman 2001), represent the theoretical basis of traditional project management. For decades, project management was understood as the use of project scheduling methods, such as CPM and PERT (see Chapter 19), used for scheduling projects as well as supporting resource and cost planning. Because of the CPM-based risks tied to unique tasks traditional project management uses methods for risk management as well as for controlling the project progress, project schedule, project resources and project costs. Only through the definition of non-technical projects, such as marketing and organizational development projects, and the consideration of additional disciplines (such as organization, marketing, controlling), were methods introduced which were easy to use and to communicate, such as the work breakdown structure (Chapter 6).

Organizationally, it appears the most important element in traditional project management is the division of formal authorities between the project manager, the immediate supervisor of the project team member, and the team member. As possible solutions to this the pure project organization, the matrix project organization and the influence project organization are offered as standards (see Chapter 18). The project management tasks are defined as the planning, the controlling and the organizing of projects. In traditional project management the objects of consideration of project management are the scope, the schedule and the costs. The relationships between these objects of consideration are depicted as the 'magic triangle'.

SYSTEMIC PROJECT MANAGEMENT

The influences of organization theory

The perception of projects as temporary organizations promotes the awareness that every project requires a specific organizational design which goes beyond the definition of the formal authority of the project manager. In addition to project planning, a situational design of the project organization should contribute to the success of the project. The organizational design of projects includes the definition of project-specific roles, the development of project organizational charts, the definition of project-specific communication structures and the agreement on project-specific rules. Through the temporary character of projects the designing of the project start and the project close-down obtain a special importance. Relatively new management approaches, such as customer orientation, 'empowerment', flat organizational structures, team work, organizational learning, process orientation and networking, can be implemented in projects to contribute to project success. The management approaches 'learning organization', 'lean management', 'process management' and 'total quality management' are therefore to be seen as an additional, new theoretical basis for project management. The perception of projects as temporary organizations also promotes the development of a project-specific culture. Such project management methods are, for example, the choice of the project name, and the formulation of the project mission statement and of project-specific slogans.

The influences of social systems theory

The perception of projects as social systems enables the use of views and models of social systems theory for project management. A 'systemic' project management builds not on traditional project management, but puts its methods into a new framework, interprets them and promotes the development of new project management methods. Because of the need to manage the boundaries and the context as well as the complexity and dynamics of projects, new potential and challenges arise for project management. A new understanding of the project management tasks to be fulfilled is enabled: instead of planning, controlling and organizing the project the tasks of constructing the project boundaries and the project context, building up and reducing the project complexity and managing the dynamics of the project become relevant. The construction of the project boundaries and context ensures an holistic view of the project. The definition of the project boundaries should enable an integrated consideration of technical, organizational, personnel and marketing objectives in the project.

For a detailed management of the project boundaries the following project management methods are available: project objectives plan, objects of consideration plan and work breakdown structure, project schedule and project resource plan, project costs and project income plan, project organization, etc. For an analysis of the project context and the design of project context relationships the project environment analysis, the analysis of the pre- and post-project phases, the business case analysis, as well as the analysis of the relationship of the project to other projects and to the company strategies can be used.

Projects require a certain amount of complexity in order to be able to relate to the (infinitely) complex environment. The building up and reducing of complexity is a project management task. An holistic project view, creativity in the project and the acceptance of project-related decisions can be ensured through adequate communication structures. The performance of project workshops at the project start process, at milestones and at the close-down process of the project, as well as the performance of project team and project owner meetings, promote the building up of complexity in a project. The differentiation of project roles, the definition of the relationships between the roles as well as the inclusion of different specialist disciplines and hierarchical levels in the project team are further organizational possibilities for the building up of complexity in a project. By using different project management methods different perspectives for designing a project are chosen. Only the linking up of these different views in a 'multi-methods approach' enables appropriate consideration of the project complexity.

To ensure continuity in a project, redundant structures should be created. A reducing of project complexity is achieved by the agreement on the project objectives within the team. Furthermore, the use of project management standards, the establishment of project-specific rules and norms, the development of project plans as well as the performance of integrative project team meetings gives repeated orientation for the project work. The dynamics of a project result from the interventions of relevant environments as well as through the self-reference of the project. Examples of interventions from relevant project environments are new legal requirements from public authorities, a change in scope by the customer, cancellations from suppliers, an unexpected media response, a demotivated project team, etc.

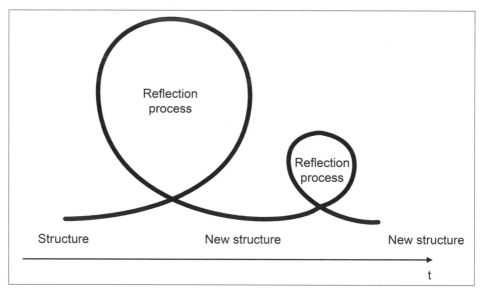

Figure 26.1   Management of the dynamics of a project

The formal communication structures of a project enable its self-reference. Project management methods, such as the work breakdown structure, the milestone plan and the project environment analysis can support the communication in the project. The possibility of change in a project is dependent upon its relationship to relevant environments. Only when the functionality of the (relative) project autonomy is recognized and, therefore, the interventions of the permanent organization in the project-oriented organization are limited, is there a possibility of self-reference. In order to promote change in a project, reflections and meta-communications, that is communications about communications, are necessary. Time, space and the corresponding know-how are all necessary for reflection. In a cyclical process the structures necessary for the performance of a project are formed, questioned and possibly adapted according to the new requirements.

Self-referencing processes in a project, or interventions from project environments, can lead to continuous or discontinuous changes in a project. Continuous changes in projects are considered in project controlling. Continuous changes in projects take the form of adaptations in the project structures, such as new project slogans, new formations of relationships to relevant environments, new definitions of project roles, new demands on the project team members, new planning of the scope and the project schedule, etc. A discontinuous development in a project comes about when a change in the project identity takes place. This can result from a substantial deviation from the project objectives. A project discontinuity can take the form of a project crisis, a project chance or a structurally determined change in the project identity.

THE PROJECT MANAGEMENT PROCESS

ROLAND GAREIS Project and Programme Management® (Gareis 2005), as a systemic project management approach, defines project management as a process of the project-oriented organization and focuses on its sub-processes, Figure 26.2. The project management personnel require competencies for managing the sub-processes: project start, continuous project coordination, project controlling, project close-down and possibly resolving a project discontinuity. The success of project management is assessed on the basis of the professional performance of these processes, not only on the basis of a project handbook that meets all formal demands.

For the performance of the project management sub-processes the corresponding project management methods are used. Their importance does not get lost. The definition of the sub-processes of project management adds an integration level for ensuring the professional application of project management methods. Producing an optimal project schedule cannot be an objective in itself, but it must be an overall integrative objective to start the project in an optimal way. The management of project objectives, the management of the project schedule, the management of the project cost planning, and so on, cannot be accepted as project management processes (PMI® 2004, p47), since only an integrated consideration of all methods of project management can lead to optimal results. The management of project plans as 'processes' cannot ensure an holistic management.

In functional terms, project management is a process of the project-oriented company which contains sub-processes project start, continuous project coordination, project controlling and project close-down. It may also contain the resolution of a project discontinuity (project crisis, project chance and structurally determined project identity change).

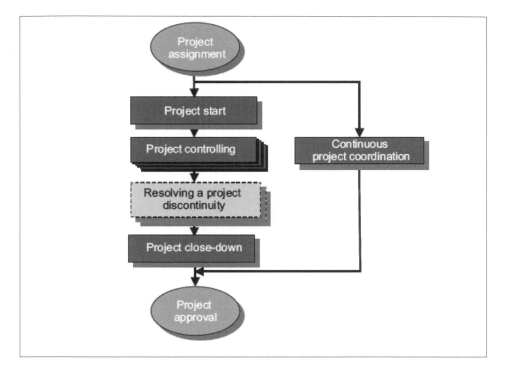

Figure 26.2   The project management process

DESCRIPTION OF THE PROJECT MANAGEMENT PROCESS

The process objectives, the process boundaries and the rough process structure can be described for the project management process as a whole, Figures 26.2 and 26.3. The objectives, tasks, responsibilities and results can be presented in detail in the descriptions of the project management sub-processes. The objective of the process of project management is the professional management of projects. A prerequisite for the realization of the project objectives is the professional fulfillment of the sub-processes of project start, project coordination, project controlling, (possibly) resolving of a project discontinuity and project close-down.

The objects of consideration of project management as defined by traditional project management, Figure 26.4, are to be added to the perception of projects as temporary organizations and social systems. The objects of consideration of project management are the project objectives, the project scope, the project schedule, the project resources, the project costs and project income, the project risks as well as the project organization, the project culture and the project context. The project management process is to be differentiated from the business processes for the fulfilment of project deliverables. Therefore, project

---

Objectives of the project management process

- Assuring the realization of the project objectives
- Efficient performance of the project start, project controlling, project close-down and the continuous project coordination
- Possibly: Efficient resolution of a project discontinuity
- Management of the social-, time- and content-related project boundaries
- Management of the relationships of the project to the project context
- Building up and reducing of project complexity
- Management of the project dynamics
- Non-objective: Realization of the content work of the project (Note: This is an objective of the project and not of project management)

Time boundaries of the project management process

- Start: Project assigned
- End: Project approved

Structure of the project management process

See Figure 26.2

Figure 26.3   Objectives, time boundaries and structure of the project management process

content-related processes such as procurement, the engineering of components and the testing of software, for example, are not management tasks.

RELATIONSHIPS BETWEEN THE PROJECT MANAGEMENT SUB-PROCESSES

From a systemic point of view, it is the objective of the project start process to establish the project as a social system, the objective of project controlling is to promote the evolution of the project and the objective of the project close-down is to dissolve the project as a social system. The objective of resolving a project

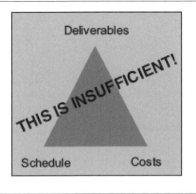

Figure 26.4   Objects of consideration of project management

555

discontinuity is to develop a new project identity to resolve the discontinuity. The objective of continuous project coordination is to ensure the project's progress. The project coordination process is performed continuously. The performance of the other project management sub-processes is limited in time. By definition, the project start and the project close-down are each performed only once. Project controlling is performed several times in a project and takes place either periodically or at project milestones. The necessity of resolving a project discontinuity depends on the situation.

The benefit of a common view of the project management processes lies, on the one hand, in ensuring the uniformity of the project management approach used and, on the other hand, in considering the relationships between the sub-processes of project management. The application of a uniform project management approach ensures that uniform terminology and methods are used in all sub-processes. A professional project management considers the relationships between the sub-processes in order to optimize the project management results. The following relationships between the project management sub-processes exist:

- At the project start, the structures for project controlling and project close-down are planned
- The criteria for evaluating the project success at project close-down are determined at the project start by defining the project objectives
- At the project start the working methods to be applied during project controlling and during project close-down are established (such as project meetings, project workshops, developing minutes, reflections)
- Through the application of the scenario technique and the development of alternative plans at the project start, potential measures for the resolution of a project discontinuity are provided
- The management of any structurally determined change of identity of the project is planned at project start
- In project controlling the project plans developed at the project start will be controlled and possibly adapted
- When managing a project discontinuity the alternative plans developed at the project start and/or the current project plans from the latest project controlling can be used
- At project close-down the plans which were developed at the project start and adapted during project controlling form the basis for evaluating the project success and for ensuring organizational learning, and
- Project marketing is performed in all sub-processes of project management based on a uniform project marketing strategy.

THE CONTEXT OF THE PROJECT MANAGEMENT PROCESS

The context of the project management process in terms of time is the project assignment and the investment controlling processes. In terms of content these are the content-related business processes. The content-related business processes depend on the project type. For an ICT-conception project, the following content-related business processes have to be performed, according to the project phase structure: gathering information, analysis of the current situation, definition and description of alternative solutions, implementation plan for each alternative, decision-making. For a contracting project the engineering, the procurement, the production and the logistics, the construction and the installation as well as the training and the commissioning make up the content-related business processes. To increase the efficiency of projects in the project-oriented company the processes for the performance of the project contents are to be documented and standardized. Standards can be adapted for each project by considering individual project requirements. Content-related processes are performed during a project parallel with the project management process. The relationship between the project management process and the processes for the performance of the project contents is immediate, as it is an objective of the project management process to develop appropriate structures for the fulfillment of the project contents.

The project assignment process is performed before the project start, while that of the investment controlling process is performed during the project and after the project close-down. The project assignment process is especially important for project management because in it the basic structures for the project are determined. The definition of the project objectives, the planning of the project organization and the drafts of the project plans are roughly worked out. Project management is important for the investment controlling process since the project documentation constitutes an essential foundation for the controlling.

THE PROJECT START PROCESS

DEMAND FOR A PROFESSIONAL PROJECT START

Due to the time pressure of projects once they are assigned it is tempting to start the content-related processes immediately, without having performed the corresponding project start process. This lack of willingness to perform the project planning and the design of the project organization together with the project team often results in:

- Unrealistic project objectives and unclear definitions of roles
- Project plans which are inadequate and not binding

● Unclear agreements regarding the design of project environment relationships and missing organizational rules

A professional project start must be performed in order to ensure adequate project management quality.

DESCRIPTION OF THE PROJECT START PROCESS

Figures 26.5 and 26.6 describe the project start process with regard to its objectives, time boundaries, tasks and responsibilities as well as the organizational tools to be used. The project start process in common with the other project management sub-processes can be structured into the phases planning, preparation, performance and follow-up. The planning of the project start process includes a brief situation analysis based on existing project documents (such as project assignment, initial project plans), minutes of meetings and interviews with members of the project organization and representatives of relevant environments. The design of the project management process is to be developed, i.e. the use of project management methods and of standard project plans, the selection of communication forms, the use of ICT, the

---

Objectives of the project start process

- Information transfer from the pre-project phase into the project,
- Definition of expectations regarding the post-project phase,
- Development of adequate project plans for managing the project objectives, scope, schedule, resources, costs, income and risks,
- Design of the project organization, adequate integration into the permanent organizations,
- Development of the project culture,
- Establishment of communication relationships between the project and other projects and relevant project environments, initial project marketing,
- Communicating the 'big project picture' to all members of the project organization,
- Planning of measures for discontinuity management,
- Definition of the structures for the following project management sub-processes,
- Developing the documentation 'Project start' and
- Efficient design of the project start process

Time boundaries of the project start process

- Start: Project assigned
- End: Documentation 'Project start' filed
- Duration: 2-3 weeks

Tasks and responsibilities in the project start process

See Figure 26.6

Figure 26.5   Description of the project start process

Tasks / Responsibilities	Project owner team	Project manager	Project team	Project team members	Project management consultant	External	Documents
Planning the project start							
• Checking the project assignment and the results of the pre-project phase		P					
• Selecting start communication form		P					
• Selecting project team members (and a PM consultant)		P					
• Selecting PM methods and PM templates to be used		P					
• Agreeing with project owner	C	P					1)
Preparing the project start communication							
• Hiring of a project coach (possible)		P			(C)		
• Preparing the start communications I, II, etc.		P			(C)		
• Inviting participants		P					2)
• Documenting the results of the pre-project phase		P		C	(C)	C	
• Developing drafts for planning, organizing and marketing the project		P		C	(C)	C	
• Developing information material for start communication		P		C	(C)	C	3)
Performing the project start communications							
• Distributing information material to participants		P					
• Performing start communication I	C		P		(C)	C	
• Developing draft of PM documentation "Project start"		P			(C)		
• Performing start communication II, etc.	C		P		(C)	C	
Follow-up to the project start communications							
• Completing draft of PM documentation "Project start"		P			(C)		
• Agreeing with project owner	C	P					4)
• Project marketing: Initial information	C			P	(C)	C	
• Distributing PM documentation "Project start"		P					
• Filing of PM documentation "Project start"	C			P		C	
Performing first work packages (parallel)				P		P	

Legend:	Documents:
P ... Performance	1) List of project management methods to be used
C ... Contribution	2) Invitation of participants to the project start workshop
I ... Information	3) Information material for the project start workshop
	4) Project management documentation "Project start"

Figure 26.6 Tasks and responsibilities of the project start process

use of a project management consultant and/or project management coach have to be decided on.

To prepare the project start communications the results of the pre-project phase are to be documented, the initial project plans are to be developed and the project marketing is to be planned. Project crisis-avoiding and/or project chance-promoting measures are to be planned and provisional measures for the management of project discontinuities are to be taken. A structurally determined change of a project identity may possibly have to be prepared.

The participants in the individual communication situations are to be selected and invited. The performance of the project start communications is usually a combination of individual meetings with project team members, a kick-off meeting and a project start workshop. For projects of high complexity several workshops and also joint social events may be necessary.

The follow-up work to the project start communications includes the development of the documentation 'Project start' and its distribution to the members of the project organization, as well as the performance of initial project marketing.

DESIGN OF THE PROJECT START

ORGANIZATION OF THE PROJECT START PROCESS

The project owner team, the project manager, the project team and the individual project team members are responsible for the performance of the project start process. The project manager may be supported in the documentation work by a project management assistant or a project controller. In a socially complex project start process, a project management consultant or a project management coach can be called in. When a project-external consultant takes over the moderation and documentation tasks the work loads of the project manager and the project team members are reduced. In small projects the preparation of the project start communications can be developed by the project manager alone. In projects of high complexity the project manager can perform the task in cooperation with 2–3 selected team members. The project owner team, and possibly representatives of relevant environments, can be presented with the results of the project start workshop in authentic form with the help of developed flip-charts, graphics, and so on at the end of the workshop. The resources (personnel, equipment, ICT, external consultants, etc.) and costs required for the project start process should be determined and assigned to the work package 'project start' in the work breakdown structure.

USE OF PROJECT MANAGEMENT METHODS

The use of project management methods in projects is to be laid down in the organizational guidelines of project-oriented companies. In accordance with the structure of the project management process, the project management methods to be used in the project start, in project coordination, in project controlling, in resolving a project discontinuity and in the project close-down, are to be differentiated. As regards the use these methods, a distinction is to be made between those that 'must' be used and those that 'can' be used (Figure 26.7). Decisions regarding the use of 'can' methods and regarding the degree of detail in the use of methods are to be made according to the project.

Each new project plan resulting from the use of a project management method is a model of the project and serves to construct the project reality. The use of several different project management methods enables the development of a management complexity that complies with the complexity of the project. The quality of the project plans is to be ensured by applying multiple methods. The completeness of the project plans can only be ensured by relating the project management methods with each other and by cyclical revisions of the project plans. For example, insights from the project environment analysis can be incorporated in the work breakdown structure and/or in the project cost plan. The degree of detail of project plans is to be determined in relation to the complexity of the project.

Project plans should be developed jointly by the project team in a project start workshop. Thereby the creativity of the team can be utilized and the identification of the project team members with the results is promoted. The initial development can be prepared by a small group of selected project team members. The use of moderation techniques ensures target-oriented and efficient teamwork. Visualization techniques promote communication in the project management process and support the documentation of the results.

Project plans are often understood to be instruments used exclusively for documentation. In fact, however, project plans are also instruments for decision-making (decision on alternative strategies), instruments of leadership (basis for agreements on objectives, establishing commitment) and instruments of communication. Adequate IT support (project management and graphics software) serves to design and communicate recipient-specific information.

USE OF STANDARD PROJECT PLANS

Standard project plans can be used for managing repetitive projects. If a project-oriented company repeatedly performs certain types of projects (such as contracting projects of an IT company or product development projects of a pharmaceutical company), standard project plans can be developed for these

561

Methods for the project start	Project
Project planning	
Project scope planning	
Project objectives plan	Must
Objects of considerations plan	Must
Work breakdown structure	Must
Work package specifications	Must
Project scheduling	
Project milestone plan	Must
Project bar chart	Must
CPM schedule	Can
Project resources, project costs, project income	
Project resource plan	Can
Project cost plan	Must
Project income plan	Can
Designing the project context relationships	
Project environment analysis	Must
Business case analysis	Must
Project – other projects analysis	Must
Pre- and post-project phase analysis	Must
Project presentations, project vernissage	Can
Designing the project organization	
Project assignment	Must
Sub-project assignment	Can
Project organization chart	Must
Project role descriptions	Must
Project responsibility matrix	Can
Project communication plan	Must
Project rules	Must
Developing the project culture	
Project name	Must
Project logo,	Can
Project-specific "social" events	Can
Project risk management and project discontinuity management	
Project risk analysis	Must
Project scenario analysis and alternative planning	Can

Figure 26.7 Project management methods for the project start process

types of projects. This kind of standardization represents an instrument of organizational learning and of knowledge management in the project-oriented company. Project plans which can be standardized are, for example, work breakdown structures, work package specifications, objects of consideration plans, milestone lists, project organization charts and project responsibility matrices. The efficiency of the project management processes can be considerably increased by the adequate use of standard project plans. Standard project plans are to be adapted according to the respective project conditions, that is they are to be complemented, labeled project-specifically.

USE OF ADEQUATE PROJECT COMMUNICATION FORMS

In the project start process, the communication forms of meetings between the project manager and individual project team members, team meetings and start workshops can be combined, Figure 26.8. Project workshops are to be performed to assure the appropriate project management quality.

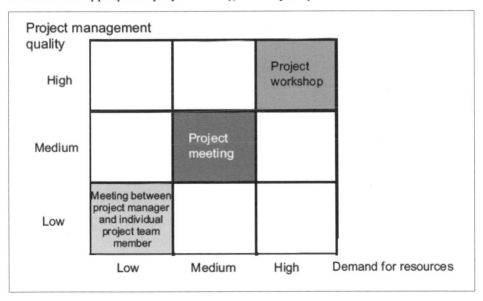

Figure 26.8 Communication forms in a project

The objective of a meeting between the project manager and individual project team members in the project start process is to exchange information regarding the project and mutual expectations regarding the cooperation in the project. This general orientation forms the basis for the participation in project team meetings and in the project start workshop.

563

The objective of a 'kick-off meeting' is that the project owner and the project manager inform the project team about the project. It usually takes place in the form of 'one-way communication', is 2 to 3 hours in length, with little opportunity for interaction.

The objective of a project start workshop is to develop jointly the 'big project picture'. By interaction of the team members in the workshop an important contribution to the development of the project culture is made. A project start workshop lasts 1 to 3 days, is moderated and generally takes place outside the usual workplace, possibly in an hotel. The number of participants in a project workshop should not exceed fifteen. The project team members should attend the whole workshop, representatives of relevant project environments can attend selectively as guests. The most important results of the workshop should be presented to the project owner team at the end of the workshop. Involving representatives of relevant project environments and all members of the project organization in good time considerably contributes to project marketing. A checklist for designing a project start workshop is depicted in Figure 26.9. In projects of higher complexity a combination of several kick-off meetings and project start workshops with different target groups at different locations may be necessary.

DESIGN OF THE PROJECT-RELATED INFRASTRUCTURE

Professional project management requires the use of an appropriate information and communications technology (ICT) infrastructure as well as of an appropriate

Project start workshop: Design for one day
Morning
Introduction: Ideas, objectives, agenda Information about the project and results of the pre-project phase Expectations of the project owner team, the project team, the partners, the suppliers, the consultants, etc. regarding the project Clarification of the project objectives and of the objects of consideration
Afternoon
Completion of the project plans: Work breakdown structure, project cost plan, project risk analysis, etc. Review of the design of the project organization Presentation of the achieved results to the project owner team Planning of further course of action

Figure 26.9   Checklist: design of a one-day project start workshop

spatial infrastructure. Especially in virtual project organizations, with project team members working at different locations, the planning of the software and telecommunications to be used in the project poses a challenge. The use of a uniform project management and office software is to be ensured, the appropriate hardware is to be provided. Decisions have to be made regarding the use of new communication tools, such as project management portals, collaboration software, telephone conferences and video conferences. A spatial infrastructure is to be planned and provided for holding meetings, for performing project presentations and, possibly, a project home page as well as for creating a workspace for a Project Office.

USE OF PROJECT MANAGEMENT CONSULTANTS

Projects, project managers and project teams represent new 'objects' for consulting. Project management consulting can be defined as management consulting of a project. Project management coaching is the management consulting of the project manager and/or of the project team. Project management consulting and/or project management coaching serve to assure and increase the quality of the management of a project. Due to the social complexity of projects the use of a project management consultant or a project management coach is recommended especially in the project start process. The decision regarding the use of a project management consultant or a project management coach should be taken jointly in the project team. As a project-external role, the role of the project management consultant and project management coach can be assumed either by an adequately qualified employee of the project-oriented company or by an external consultant.

QUALITY OF THE PROJECT START PROCESS

The quality of the project start process can be measured by an evaluation of the results and the duration and the costs of the project start process. The results of the project start process are, above all, the developed project plans and the established project as a social system. The project plans can be evaluated in terms of their existence and their quality (completeness, level of detail, fulfilment of formal criteria, etc.). The project start process is to be documented in the meeting and workshop minutes. It must be an objective of the project to maintain the high level of project management quality achieved by a professional project start process. Therefore, analogous to the project start, regular project controlling meetings and/or workshops are to be performed, Figure 26.10.

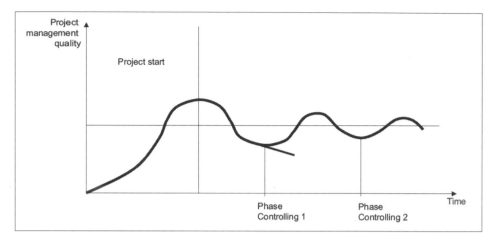

Figure 26.10   Project controlling for maintaining the project management quality

PROJECT START WITHOUT A FORMAL PROJECT ASSIGNMENT PROCESS

For the performance of a professional project start the results of the project assignment process, i.e. a formal project assignment document, a business case analysis and the initial project management documentation, are required. In practice, however, these ideal prerequisites are not always available. When no formal project assignment process has been performed before the project start, the definition of the project objectives, the development of a business case analysis, the selection of a project owner team and the development of the initial project management documentation, are to be made up during the project start in a cyclical process of concretization. In the case of starting a project without having performed a formal project assignment process there is a high risk that the project will not be performed at all. By developing a business case analysis it may become apparent that the investment to be initialized by the project is not profitable.

DIFFERENT PROJECT STARTS FOR DIFFERENT TYPES OF PROJECTS

Different types of projects lead to different demands and potentials for the project start:

- A conception project and a realization project are an example of a chain of projects. In a conception project drafts of project plans are developed for the realization project which might follow. These constitute an essential basis for the project start of the realization project.

566

- For repetitive projects project plans can be standardized. For unique projects, however, new solutions are needed. Therefore, specific working forms and creative techniques are to be used in the project start. Unique projects usually attract a great deal of attention at the project start. The project start process for repetitive projects can be upgraded, for instance, by inviting external participants to the project start workshop.
- In contracting projects representatives of the customer are to be actively involved in the project start process. They may become members of the project owner team and/or members of the project team.

REFERENCES AND FURTHER READING

APM, 2006, *APM Body of Knowledge,* 5th edition, High Wycombe, UK: Association for Project Management.

Čamra, J.J., 1976, *REFA-Lexikon*, 2nd edition., Berlin, D: Beuth.

Cleland, D.I. and Gareis, R., 2006, *Global Project Management Handbook*, 2nd edition, New York, NY: McGraw-Hill.

Gareis, R., 2005, *Happy Projects!,* Vienna: Manz Verlag.

Hillier, F.S. and Lieberman, G.J., 2001, *Introduction to operations research*, Boston, MA: McGraw-Hill.

IPMA, 2006, *ICB: IPMA Competence Baseline*, Zurich. CH: International Project Management Association.

Kerzner, H., 2006, *Project Management: a systems approach to planning, scheduling and controlling*, 9th edition, New York; Wiley. (2003 is the 8th edition).

Luhmann, N., 1996, *Social Systems,* Stanford, CA: Stanford University Press.

PMI®, 2004, *The Guide to the Project Management Body of Knowledge,* 3rd edition, Newtown Square, PA: Project Management Institute.

27 Project Proposal and Initiation

Lizz Robb

Running a project can be likened to playing a game of football. If the objective is to win the game, then every move, right from the start, needs to be carefully calculated and should be in line with the game strategy to ensure a successful outcome. The team will require skilled coaches and players, excellent teamwork and communication, structured planning, tactics, training, preparation, support and resources, as well as effective management of time, cost, quality and risk. The more critical the outcome, the more thought and planning need to go into the game from the outset.

The commencement of a project is usually triggered by a mandate from programme management or by a directive from a higher authority. At this point it is often far more exciting to jump right in and get things happening rather than sit back and build a firm foundation for the project, via sound start up and initiation processes, before any serious work is commenced. Depending on the industry they work in or the type of projects they are involved with, project managers have varying ways of starting and initiating projects. Some require a formal process. Others may be driven by an urgency that does not allow for structured planning during project initiation. This chapter explores the diligence and the approach best practice suggests should be invested into project proposal and initiation.

BEGIN WITH THE END IN MIND

Stephen Covey (1989) suggests that:

> ... all things are created twice. There's a mental or first creation, and a physical or second creation to all things.
>
> Take the construction of a home, for example. You create it in every detail before you ever hammer the first nail into place. You try to get a clear sense of what kind of house you want. If you want a family-centred home, you plan to put a family room where it

569

would be a natural gathering place. You plan sliding doors and a patio for children to play outside. You work with ideas. You work with your mind until you get a clear image of what you want to build.

Then you reduce it to blueprint and develop construction plans. All of this is done before the earth is touched. If not, then in the second creation, the physical creation, you will have to make expensive changes that may double the cost of your home.

The carpenter's rule is 'measure twice, cut once.' You have to make sure that the blueprint, the first creation, is really what you want, and that you've thought everything through. Then you put it into bricks and mortar. Each day you go to the construction shed and pull out the blueprint to get marching orders for the day. You begin with the end in mind.

In discussing 'Habit 2, Begin with the End in Mind', Covey could be describing project start up and initiation when he says:

To begin with the end in mind means to start with a clear understanding of your destination. It means to know where you're going so that you better understand where you are now and so that the steps you take are always in the right direction.

Covey further adds, 'We may be very busy, we may be very *efficient*, but we will also be truly *effective* only when we begin with the end in mind.'

While there is often a temptation to get the technical work of the project underway, upon receipt of the project mandate some basic preparation work needs to be done before the project commences. It is recognized that the opportunity to add value is far greater at the outset of a project, when the cost to change is relatively low (Chapter 16). However, as the project progresses the opportunity to add value diminishes, while the cost to change can increase significantly. If the preparation work is done well and any value added up front, where it belongs, the cost to change should be minimized and the likelihood of delivering a successful project increased. Essential preparation work for a project conducted during proposal and initiation should include some or all of the following:

1. defining the governance structure
2. developing the plans
3. establishing essential project controls
4. initiating document and configuration management

Each of these is discussed in turn.

DEFINING THE GOVERNANCE STRUCTURE

In Chapter 5, Rodney Turner suggested that there are at least four roles required for the governance of a project. In discussing Benefits Management in Chapter 13, Terry Cooke-Davies identified the need for similar roles. The roles are:

- **The Project Sponsor or Project Executive:** Somebody from the business, who convinces the organization that this investment is worthwhile and can provide value to the organization. The sponsor owns the business case and is ultimately responsible for benefits realization.
- **The Steward or Senior Supplier:** Somebody from the technical department, who says what technology is available to meet the business need, and who works with the sponsor to develop a technical solution.
- **The Project Manager:** Responsible for managing the work of the project, and delivering the new asset in accordance with the defined requirements (Chapter 14).
- **The Owner or Senior User:** Somebody from the business or operations departments, who is responsible for benefits management (Chapter 13), that is, ensuring the new asset is used to achieve the desired business benefit (or better) as laid out in the business plan.

The sponsor should be an optimist, seeking the best possible outcome from the project. The steward should be a pessimist, who brings a touch of reality. This tension is essential, not something to be avoided. The ideal solution for the project will be a compromise between the two. The sponsor and owner may be the same person. On larger projects the steward and manager will be the same person, but on smaller projects they will be different. On programmes the steward may be the programme manager. The people fulfilling these roles need to be defined during project initiation.

PROJECT MANAGEMENT TEAM

General management theory and practice support the importance of identifying and documenting people's job descriptions, at the time of engagement, to clarify their roles and responsibilities. Yet somehow this concept doesn't always flow through to project management, where it is just as important to have clearly defined role descriptions and responsibilities drawn up, understood, agreed to and signed off for all project management team members. Failure to comply with this requirement can lead to lack of clarity and ownership of responsibility and accountability, often with disastrous consequences. In the event of project failure, if there is a search for the guilty, this measure can help protect the innocent.

A project executive, as key decision-maker, and a project manager, as the project planner/manager of the day-to-day work, need to be appointed at the very outset and should be appointed by senior management. If the project is being run as part of a programme, it is preferable for someone from programme management to take on the role of project executive. As the roles of project executive and project manager are the two key roles of the project, it is important to get commitment from these individuals on their documented roles and responsibilities before they take the project mandate through to the initiation stage and kick off the project in a structured and planned fashion.

Thought needs to be given to other individuals who should be on the project board (sometimes called a project steering committee) and the individuals who will do project assurance for them. The role of project assurance is to independently verify that what the project manager says is happening is actually happening and to ensure throughout the project that the needs of the business, the user and the supplier are being met. Programme management may well perform this role.

The rest of the project management team should be designed to whatever degree it is possible to do so at this early part of the project. Where it is possible, individuals may be appointed to their project roles. At this stage, it is not usually desirable to appoint people to all the roles as the project itself may be unclear and it may not be possible to identify all the specific resources who will be required. Team managers should be appointed as and when the project manager is able to hand them work packages to produce products of a technical nature.

In line with the PRINCE2™ methodology (Chapter 7), at project start-up it is a good idea to appoint at least a senior user and perhaps a senior supplier to the project board in an informal capacity to get the initial input from these roles. The senior user should be a senior manager who is capable of representing the needs of those who will be impacted by the project's major deliverables or outcomes. The senior supplier is usually someone at a senior level who will represent the group or organization delivering the solution.

If the project is to involve some procurement, then it may be advisable to appoint the organization's procurement or contract manager to the role of senior supplier initially, especially if it is assumed that once a contract is signed, the external party or consulting group will provide a resource for the senior supplier role.

Consideration should also be given to whether or not project support will be required and who will take on the role of configuration librarian. If a project management office exists, it may be possible to delegate the work of project support and configuration management, and even perhaps change control, to appropriate individuals in the project management office.

At this early planning time, the project management team structure should be reviewed to ensure there are no gaps in responsibilities. There should be a clear understanding by all parties in terms of various accountabilities, responsibilities and the authority to make decisions. The importance of appointing the right people and appointing them at the right time cannot be stressed enough. Sound governance, leadership and decision-making are essential for the effective functioning of the project. After all, it's people who get the work done. The soft skills of the people involved will make a major contribution to project success or project failure, as the case may be.

VARIATIONS RESULTING FROM MANAGEMENT ISSUES

Governance issues can contribute to inadequate planning during initiation. Even where there is an experienced project manager, who is aware of the pitfalls of poor planning, working in an environment where either through inexperience in governing projects, lack of understanding by senior management of the project management discipline or through complacency in applying diligence to clear initial planning, there is a risk that poor work in the initiation stage will contribute to poor product delivery. Experienced project managers, who have had to deliver products to customers who are not satisfied that the final deliverable is fit for purpose (as a direct result of poor planning in the initiation stage), will be wary of being pushed through the planning process without ensuring that all factors are considered and investigated.

DEVELOPING THE PLANS

Throughout Project Initiation, the project is planned in increasing detail. But before initiation starts it may be necessary to conduct a feasibility study.

FEASIBILITY STUDY

If a project needs a feasibility study to be undertaken, best practice suggests that the feasibility study be conducted as a project in its own right. The feasibility study should analyse various ways in which the stated problem or opportunity could be addressed. The outcomes of the feasibility study will be a number of recommendations for the way to conduct the project. Each option should have its own business case, budget, timeframe, project plan and set of risks. These options need to be measured against a set of criteria and a recommendation made on the way ahead. If a decision is made to run a project based on the recommended option, best practice suggests that it should be done as a new project. This essentially gives a clean break between the feasibility study and the actual project to deliver a solution or bring about required change. Composition of the project team may well change for the project following the feasibility study. The outcome of the feasibility study determines the project approach.

BUSINESS CASE

With projects it is all too easy to be caught up in identifying and/or developing a solution without looking in sufficient detail at the reasons why the project is required and the justification for the project. Ideally the project executive should write the full business case but unfortunately in real life this tends to be delegated to the project manager. Consideration needs to be given to the developments that have taken place in the project so far. The basic business case created in the project brief will need to be further developed and/or updated.

A comprehensive business case will clarify the justification for the project and the desired benefits. It should also indicate likely costs and timeframe (based on information contained in the project plan); together with major risks and cost-benefit analysis. This document should become the driving force of the project, telling the business, the customer, the supplier and the project team why the project is being undertaken and what benefits it needs to deliver. The benefits need to be stated in measurable terms. The business case should stipulate how the benefits can be measured or evaluated at a future point in time (normally some time after the project has been closed out) when it is possible to evaluate whether or not the required benefits were delivered. The business case does not need to be a lengthy document. It could be a relatively succinct document as long as it contains all the required information.

Best practice suggests the business case be regularly updated and reviewed to ensure the project is still viable and on track to deliver benefit. There is a close relationship between the updated project plan and the updated business case. At a minimum, elements of the business case which require updating as the project progresses are cost, timescale, risk and investment appraisal, if there are significant changes to the projected cost and timescale. If at any stage, the business case indicates the project is no longer going to deliver value for money, it should trigger the project board to consider whether or not the project should continue or be terminated. Under these circumstances, premature closure does not necessarily reflect project failure but perhaps reflects that further work on the project is not deemed to be viable.

PROJECT APPROACH

The project approach needs to be defined to clarify the various ways in which the solution could be delivered – options such as outsourcing the work, modifying an existing product, developing a customized solution or buying something off-the-shelf. The selected approach should be documented and evaluated against applicable criteria. The project approach document justifies the way the solution or result will be delivered and will therefore influence quality of the project's deliverables and the work outlined in the project plan.

PROJECT BRIEF

Attention can now be turned to understanding at a high level what the project is about and why it is needed. A project brief or a project charter should be drawn up to communicate the vision for the project. It should contain the background to the project, the reasons for the project, the project's objectives, how they map to corporate strategy, the customer's quality expectations, the acceptance criteria, the scope of the project, major risks and the benefits that the project should deliver. The project brief is a major input to the project initiation document developed in the project initiation stage.

INITIATION STAGE PLAN

As initiation represents the first stage of the project, approval must be given by the board for the work to be done to prepare the project initiation document. The work to be conducted during the initiation stage, how it will be done, who will be involved and how much it will cost should be reflected in a detailed plan, called the initiation stage plan.

AUTHORITY TO PROCEED TO INITIATION

As soon as the project management team structure, the project brief, project approach and initiation stage plan have been developed, the project board should meet to determine whether or not they wish to give the project manager approval to proceed into initiation. The work involved in the initiation stage will require resources and the board need to commit to deploying these resources.

INITIATION

Once the authority to proceed is given, the project manager is commissioned to work to the approved initiation stage plan to uncover in greater detail the requirements for the project and to plan how these requirements may be met. The purpose of initiation is to develop a project blueprint to give the project a firm foundation and to enable the project board to make an informed decision on whether or not they wish to commit to the actual work of the project. The effort required by initiation safeguards against the temptation to get on with the technical work at the expense of putting the right structures and planning in place before the technical work commences. Significant expenditure will be required after initiation so it is worth while sitting down and first counting the cost before commencing the specialist work to ensure that what was begun can be completed and will deliver the required benefits. This meanss that the work of initiation should be mandatory on every project; however, the scale to which it is applied may vary from project to project. The final output of initiation will be a project initiation document, forwarded to the board, to provide them with detailed information on the project so they can make a clear decision to proceed with the project or to terminate it.

PROJECT QUALITY PLAN

In beginning with the end in mind, consideration should be given not only to the benefits to be realized by the project (Chapter 13), but also to the requirements of final acceptance and the transitioning of the final solution into an operational environment (Chapter 14). In line with best practice, agreement should be reached and documented on the customer's quality expectations and appropriate acceptance criteria before the work of the project is even planned (Chapter 17). Any planning from that point on should ensure that the work, and only the work, of the project is done, and that it is done to meet precise stated quality requirements. Quality measures need to be established and agreed to in order to prevent any unnecessary and potentially costly rework in the project, resource wastage or the possibility of the final deliverable not being fit for purpose. The project quality plan should assist with this.

The project quality plan should specify the overall quality requirements, such as any quality standards, procedures and processes that need to be adhered to. The customer's quality expectations and the acceptance criteria need to be fully fleshed out as these will then form the basis for developing the solution or result. Beginning with the end in mind, the diligence required to develop an effective project quality plan should help avoid any unnecessary work, resource wastage or the possibility of the final deliverable not being fit for purpose.

Other elements of the project quality plan are identification of configuration management (Chapter 15) and change control approaches and processes for the project (Chapter 7). Quality responsibilities, both within and outside the project, need to be identified and assigned to individuals. Many projects fail to address quality in enough detail to allow the project team to understand exactly what the customer's requirements are. This could be a major contributor to project failure. On the other hand, it could necessitate extensive rework further down the track, often at much greater expense. During the handover process, it may also result in misunderstandings, unhappy customers and frustrated project teams. The Project Quality Plan is a contributing factor to understanding the quality requirements of the project's deliverables and/or outcomes/results.

PROJECT PLAN

The project plan should draw on information contained in the project brief, the project approach and the project quality plan. The project plan itself should be created as a high level plan covering how the project should run from start through to finish. It should include timeframes and costs for the major deliverables of the project. Unless the project can be planned completely in detail at the outset, it is unwise to spend too much time developing a detailed plan. The project plan should cover the totality of work for the project and cover all aspects, including things like cultural change in an organization which may need to be brought about in order for the product, service or result of the project to be successful. The project plan should define and identify major products and associated activities, estimate the amount of effort and resources that will be required, clarify project constraints, identify and address countermeasures for both project and business risks, while also identifying milestones and key decision and review points.

The PRINCE2™ methodology requires that product-based planning be used for the development of project, stage and team plans. Essentially this means that the products to be delivered and their components are identified first, product descriptions (similar to specifications for each product) are developed and the sequence that the products are required in is agreed, prior to planning the actual work to produce the products. While this approach requires a planning overhead, it is a proactive measure to ensure the work required by the project, and only that work, is done.

The work of the stage following initiation should be detailed so that once the project is authorized, the project manager has a detailed stage plan to work to. Detailed plans for each subsequent stage will be drawn up, consistent with the project plan extract for that stage, towards the end of the preceding stage. Any prerequisites for the project should be stated, as should any assumptions and external dependencies.

Key outputs of the project plan will be a more accurate estimate of how much the project should cost, how long it should take, what it will deliver and what resources will be required. The project plan will become a major component of the project initiation document as it will give project board members essential information to assist with decision-making when the project arrives at stage gates. The project plan therefore needs to be a living, breathing document that is updated towards the end of a stage with actuals and the detailed plan for the next stage. It is an important control document for the project board, who can review updated versions of the project plan against the original project plan to ascertain whether or not the project is on track to meet its key deliverables and whether or not it is still viable.

RISKS

A complete risk analysis (Chapter 23) should be done and the project risk log updated with details of all risks, their analysis and suitable ways of addressing those risks. The risk analysis should assess the likelihood of every risk occurring, together with the impact that the risk could have on the project and/or the business. Depending on the type of project and the industry, a risk analysis can be a simple list with a 3x3 matrix addressing the impact and likelihood of the risk

577

event, right through to complex documents used in line with national or international risk standards.

Risk countermeasures are likely to cost money and need to be resourced accordingly. Often special contingency budgets are allocated for risk management actions. Some organizations have formulas that they use to calculate contingency budgets, while others may have more of an ad hoc approach to calculating the contingency budget.

Ultimately the project board will be responsible for the management of risk on the project and will make decisions on the major risks. However, at a more practical level, the project manager takes care of risk analysis and risk management on behalf of the project board. Best practice suggests that the project board should own the risk log but in essence it is usually the project manager who creates, maintains and updates it on a regular basis. The project manager should regularly report on risks to the project board and consult the board on the management of major risks. Risk identification and analysis for risks internal to the project are often the domain of the project manager. Identification of risks external to the project and management thereof should be the responsibility of the project board. For example, if there is a risk that the project may have some negative reporting in the media, this is a risk that the project board, rather than the project manager, should address. Where risks impact or affect the programme or other projects within the programme, the project executive should take responsibility for communicating with programme management about these risks.

STAKEHOLDER MANAGEMENT PLAN

In project terms, a stakeholder may be anyone who has an interest in the project or its outcomes (Chapter 36). Inadequate stakeholder management can cause numerous challenges for the project. A stakeholder analysis involves identification of stakeholders, their needs and levels of influence within the organization and on the project itself. Strategies need to be developed and plans made to manage stakeholders throughout the project life-cycle.

COMMUNICATIONS PLAN

The stakeholder analysis should lead to development of the communications plan (Chapter 37 and 38), which records details of the communication requirements for all parties both internal and external to the project. Effective and timely communication is the lifeblood of a project. The goal of the communications plan is to identify all the communications requirements and to ensure that, by executing the plan, all parties' communications needs are effectively met throughout the project life-cycle. This includes all forms of communication such as meetings (whether face-to-face or virtual, formal or informal), emails, newsletters, letters, surveys, telephone calls, minutes, reports, teleconferences, web blogs, podcasts and web pages or web sites. Development of the communications plan will lead to an update of the project plan to ensure that all communications management activities are scheduled and resourced.

PROJECT INITIATION DOCUMENT

The purpose of initiation is to give the project a firm foundation. The project initiation document contains detailed information on the project to assist with management decision making for the rest of the project life-cycle. The information base provided by the project initiation document forms a sound communication mechanism, detailing the 'who, when, what, where and why' of the project. It comprises the project brief, together with other project management documents created so far, such as the project approach, project plan, project quality plan, risk log, communications plan, project organization structure, business case and project controls. It is not usually a single document but often has a covering document with some narrative. The other documents are attached or affixed as appendices.

The project initiation document and accompanying documents are usually created by the project manager under the guidance of the project board. Once compiled, it is advisable for the project manager to run the draft project initiation document past individual project board members (and perhaps project assurance) for review before the project initiation document is finally presented to the project board for authority to proceed with the project in concept but more particularly with the next stage, as per the detailed next stage plan that accompanies the project initiation document. As the project initiation document forms the blueprint of the project, once approved, it should go under change control to prevent any unauthorized changes to it.

INITIATING DOCUMENT AND CONFIGURATION MANAGEMENT

When looking at the range of documents required to complete the project initiation document, it is understandable that where the management group or the project team consider there is a risk of document overload for the scale of the project, there will be some pressure to proceed without developing some of the documents. Therefore it is important to understand why each document exists, and why and how each one should be used. As a methodology is bedded down in a project environment, it is important to review the specific requirements for the

579

documentation and to consider when and how some documents can be combined and where some content requirements can be reduced, if this is warranted.

There is no one simple way of doing this. A regulated government department may be constrained to work through a gateway process that requires extensive documentation and adherence to all of the documents within the methodology. Therefore, in line with the maxim that 'what gets rewarded gets done', the project executive and the project manager will need to ensure compliance with this requirement. Alternatively, a fast-to-market commercial organization, working with a lean workforce, will not be able to produce the amount of documentation required. No-one will possibly read it anyway. The challenge for them is to modify the methodology to ensure that the minimum requirements are in place to ensure due diligence, then proceed with developing their products, recognising that in some industries, second to market means project failure. The business case may be about getting there first, but if the project team is not resourced to develop all the project documents in accordance with a structured methodology, the project manager should not despair. The methodology should be tailored so that the level of documentation required is minimized, without compromising the integrity of the methodology. This is especially the case with project initiation, where haste in the planning process may result in project failure, even if the project team is first to market.

It is preferable for an organization to have standardized templates for project documents. Consistent documents contribute to a common understanding and facilitate a better grasp of what is required for each documented process, especially for the project manager, project board members, project assurance and team managers. Martina Huemann discusses the need for standardized project documentation in Chapter 11, and how that can be checked through a project audit.

FILING SYSTEM

In line with the project management maxim that 'if it's not written down, it was never said', it is important to document information and file documentation away so that it can be easily retrieved at any point during the project life-cycle or, for audit and other purposes, perhaps even after the project has been decommissioned and closed out. Initiation is the ideal time to devise the filing system for all project documentation. There is probably little filing to be done as the technical work of the project is not yet underway. Consideration should be given to devising a system that will support the easy retrieval of project management and technical documentation for audit purposes once the project has been completed. The filing system should form the repository for the storage and retrieval of documentation on the products produced during the project, information on quality checks conducted on each product and, where appropriate, the products themselves. The agreed filing system forms an input to the project initiation document and should interface with the configuration management system. The filing system should include the following documents:

RISK LOG

In conjunction with developing the project brief, an initial risk analysis should be carried out to identify risks facing the project (Chapter 22). Details of risks identified, their status and agreed countermeasures should be detailed in a risk log. A risk owner should be identified for every risk. The role of the risk owner is purely to keep an eye on the risk. Risk identification, analysis and management should be done on a regular basis by the project manager from this point onwards through to the very end of the project. Project board members will be responsible for identifying risks external to the project. In consultation with the project manager, the project board will determine which risks they would like to make decisions on and which risks they will leave to the project manager to mitigate.

Daily Log

The project manager needs to create a daily log in which to record day-to-day happenings on a project, such as details of meetings, telephone calls, events, problems, concerns and questions. The daily log is like a diary or journal. It may be used to maintain the project manager's to-do list. Basically, the daily log contains information not captured in other project documentation. It is filed with other project documentation at the end of a project.

Issue Log

Files to be set up include the issue log and the lessons learned log. Details of all project issues, their analysis, status and actions to address them should be recorded in the issue log. The issue log should be reviewed and updated on a regular basis, starting from initiation.

Lessons Learned Log

Best practice in both knowledge management and project management suggests that a great deal of knowledge gained from projects is tacit knowledge, in that it stays with the individuals concerned (Chapter 32 and 33). When they leave, the tacit knowledge they have goes with them. It is therefore in the interest of the organization to have this knowledge documented and captured to form a vital part of its explicit corporate knowledge. From a project perspective, the project management team needs to reflect on which management processes are working

581

well and which aren't working so well, issues encountered on the project, together with various aspects of the technical work of the project.

The lessons learned log forms a repository for this information so that at the end of the project a lessons learned report can be compiled from the lessons learned log and disseminated to other people within the organization who may benefit from them. This will assist the organization with continuous improvement. Attempts are sometimes made to collect lessons learned at the end of the project. However, on a more practical basis, many of the lessons learned earlier on in the project may not be remembered towards the end, project personnel may move on and often battle-weary project staff may be more interested in other things such as a taking a holiday break or their next project. The effective documenting of lessons learned may suffer as a result. Developing the lessons learned log at the start of the project, promoting a learning culture within the project and documenting lessons learned on a regular basis, will assist with garnering valuable corporate and project knowledge.

ESTABLISHING ESSENTIAL PROJECT CONTROLS

Without appropriate measures in place, it is easy for a project to get out of control. Lack of appropriate control can result in a project suffering from serious issues such as cost overruns, poor stakeholder management, unnecessary delays and non-delivery of products. By establishing appropriate levels of control and reporting by the various levels of management within the project, problems can be dealt with objectively and proactively. As a guide, the complexity of the project and its risk exposure may be useful in determining project control measures. It should be noted that there is a fine line between too much control and too little. It is important for the project board to clarify the controls required of the project manager as they essentially delegate the day-to-day running of the project to the project manager. The project manager needs to be empowered and have the authority and responsibility for running each stage of the project without undue interference once the board has signed off a stage plan. However, this needs to be done within established control limits, with tolerance levels set on things such as cost, time, scope, risk, quality and benefits, where appropriate.

AUTHORITY TO PROCEED WITH THE PROJECT

A great amount of effort is expended to this point, as initiation is a major project control. All the effort is based on clarifying the precise requirements, establishing how the project will be executed and determining if it is worthwhile committing the resources the project requires. Beginning with the end in mind is a proactive approach to safeguard against nasty surprises at the end. If the authority to proceed is given, terms of reference are agreed and the project progresses from initiation into the first specialist stage. Work packages can be handed out to team managers and the project can swing into action mode, with all parties being clear on:

- **why** the project is being run
- **who** will be involved
- **what** the project is to deliver in each stage and what quality requirements must be met both for the project overall and for individual products to be developed
- **when** things should happen and when products should be delivered
- **how** the work should be done, how long it should take and how much it should cost

SCALABILITY

In an organization, a project manager or management group can find reasons for not applying all the established processes and templates to their particular project. The delicate relationship between the project executive, the project manager and the project office or keeper of the methodology and templates, as well as the level of maturity of the project environment, will determine how effectively a methodology can be scaled to suit a particular project. Project managers who don't like to work with appropriate documentation can be in danger of missing some of the key measures if they proceed without ensuring, for example, that all potential risks are identified. If there is a risk that scope changes will result in external scrutiny of the project, and it could be identified that there was inadequate planning in the initiation stage, the project manager must factor this in and plan accordingly. Project executives, who are minimalists in the development and maintenance of project documentation, may also seek to circumvent some of the project initiation processes. Where they direct project managers to commence the projects without some of these processes, the project managers should identify and record this as a project risk. A mature approach recognizes that a small project lasting three months and involving four part-time resources, resulting in some process changes to a small workgroup, should be managed differently to a business project that re-engineers the operating environment of 20,000 staff across 25 buildings servicing three million customers.

So both groups may ask, 'How do we scale our project and what can we omit' and they do, often with dire consequences if the wrong decisions are made based on a misunderstanding of key requirements for project planning in the initiation stage. Using best practice again, the question should not be, 'What can I leave out?' but rather 'How extensively do I apply this process or template to my project?' Scalability should be about reducing requirements for the planning overhead to suit the size, complexity, scope or risk profile for the project. On a very small and straightforward project, the project initiation document could be a summary document with the business case as a paragraph in the project plan, and a simple project schedule with a list of the products to be produced. In the same way, the corollary document in the Project Management Body of Knowledge (PMBoK®) world, the project management plan, could be a much simpler document.

It is desirable that all processes should be addressed in the initiation stage, and included at the level of detail that is appropriate to the project. For example, there should always be a risk log and an issue register. There should always be an up-to-date business case. The project approach should always be defined. The project manager should maintain a communications plan and understand the needs of the key stakeholders. There should be an agreed and defined reporting process using some form of documentation that is appropriate to ensure management has an understanding of progress against the plan. There should always be a documented change control system to ensure that where changes are made, they are recorded and approved to ensure the project team can demonstrate compliance and due diligence.

Project managers who work in commercial environments where each project or initiative must be justified by a formal investment appraisal process may be surprised to know that a public sector project can be initiated without this step. It should be noted that major projects in the public sector may be required to go through a formal development and approval process, but this is often tempered by a political mandate that deems that the need to deliver the project will take precedence over the financial appraisal. This should be recognized as a normal part of the process for public sector projects and some commercial projects with a political imperative. It is recommended that the appraisal still be done by the project manager to ensure that those delivering the project maintain a clear understanding of the driving force for the project. Project management is about managing uncertainty and, while the project plan may not be able to address all possible futures, inadequate planning will almost certainly guarantee increased challenges for the project management team.

CONCLUSION

A well-run project is like a symphony orchestra, which calls on the ability of a number of proficient individuals with varying skill sets, all working together in harmony, towards a common goal. The audience cannot see the planning, hours of practice, the challenges, the crises and the preventative measures that culminate in what seems like an effortless performance. Project proposal and initiation is all about ensuring that a firm foundation is laid to proactively ensure the smooth delivery of a successful project.

ACKNOWLEDGEMENT

The author would like to highlight the support and insights provided by Brian Phillips of Yellowhouse Consulting.

REFERENCES AND FURTHER READING

Covey, S.R., 1989, *The 7 Habits of Highly Effective People,* New York: Fireside.
OGC, 2005, *Managing Successful Projects with PRINCE2™,* 4th edition, London: The Stationery Office.
Turner, J.R., 1999, *The Handbook of Project-based Management: improving the processes for achieving strategic objectives,* 2nd edition, London, UK: McGraw-Hill.

28 Project Modelling

Terry Williams

Projects are complicated entities, and managers cannot generally analyse all the aspects of a project in their head. Modelling is needed to help managers understand their projects, so it lies at the heart of project analysis and planning. This chapter looks at what sort of models are used in Project Management, and why modelling is needed particularly for complex projects. The chapter discusses the role of the project modeller, and how modelling can contribute to the project through the project life-cycle.

Rodney Turner's *Handbook of Project-Based Management* (1999) describes five functions of management:

- planning the work to be done to achieve the defined objectives
- organizing the team of people to do the work
- implementing by assigning work to people
- controlling progress
- leading the team of people

In at least the first, second and fourth of these, in a complex project, basing decisions on intuition and simple breakdown structures runs the risk of badly inefficient or even counter-productive plans. In order for the project team to carry out rational, coherent decision-making, modelling is important to enable the consequences of decisions to be understood, the current status of the project to be comprehended, and sensible forecasting to be carried out.

A modeller's organizational position in the project depends upon the type and size of the project, sometimes reporting directly to the Project Manager, sometimes as Risk Manager and so on. Where there is a Project Support Office (Chapter 9), given that the PSO maintains the project plan and provides advice on proposals for change or implications of events, this can be a natural place for the modeller to ensure that models inform and advise. As a unified office, the PSO also enables the modeller to influence where appropriate the whole spread of the project management function, from planning and cost-control through to contract administration, purchasing, and material management.

WHAT IS A MODEL?

What is meant by the word 'a model' or 'to model'. This section will address models generically, before going on to discuss modelling our specific interest – the behaviour of projects.

There are clearly many different sorts of model – human, plastic, and so on. In this chapter we're interested in 'management science' models, models of human or operational systems (which could be 'hard' quantitative or 'softer' qualitative models). These models are built of concepts and mathematics. A good definition of a model is taken from Williams (2002):

A model represents or describes perceptions of a real system, simplified, using a formal, theoretically based language of concepts and their relationships (that enables manipulation of these entities), in order to facilitate management, control, or understanding of that system.

This definition has a number of ideas which can be unpacked separately:

- A model 'represents' or 'describes' the world. Not everything that represents or describes the 'real' world would be termed a model in this sense, the difference lying in the words 'in order to': we want to manipulate a model to tell us something useful, such as to explore alternative realities or to explain how differences between realities occur. A model not only defines parts or conceptual elements of the whole, it must also define the relationships between concepts.
- Since we wish to manipulate these definitions, they must be formal, theoretically based definitions of reality that can be manipulated. This means that the 'language' of the model will need to be as consistent, unambiguous and precise as possible, often – but not always – implying using some form of mathematics.
- Modelling can be used to represent the whole breadth of reality as we see it (subject to caveats below), and although one technique may be more useful than another, modelling must be available to model any aspect of our project.
- What is a system in the 'real world'? In practice the modeller gains much of his knowledge about the reality he or she is seeking to model through human actors, such as the project team, who will each have their own world-views. This means that often we are modelling our subjects' perceptions of the real world rather than the reality itself.
- A model is a simplified representation of reality. This enables the modeller to analyse the model and come to some simplified conclusions about the real

world which would be impossible to come to if he or she had to deal with all the richness, complexity and detail of the real world. The degree of simplification that we impose on reality to produce our representation depends crucially on the purpose for which we are building the model.

A good model (Williams 2002) should:

- be empirically based, and informed by data that is objective
- be theoretically sound
- be coherent, facilitating coherent, consistent decisions;
- simplify to a requisite degree (see below)
- address the complexity of the system
- add value
- impact decisions.

As well as a providing a model, the process of modelling itself has benefits. Schultz and Sullivan (1972) list:

- confrontation: facing and testing vague generalities to be aired
- explication: assumptions must be made explicit
- involvement: motivating the modeller to try to fill in gaps in knowledge
- dialogue: between the analyst and people from various disciplines involved in the project

implying also a fifth:

- learning throughout the modelling process

Once the model is built:

- the model can show how inputs combine
- the model can enable scenario analysis and 'what-if' studies
- having a project-wide model can help project management to visualize the whole project, or to understand how the project as a whole entity behaves
- the model can help management to prepare the project plan, allocate contingency, and make the necessary pre-project planning
- the model is auditable, and having a model makes the planning process auditable
- effective use of a model enables management to understand why projects have behaved as they did, and thus learn from experience

WHY DO WE NEED TO MODEL – THE COMPLEXITY OF PROJECTS

For simple, easy projects we might not need to use modelling at all. But most projects in which we are involved are *complex*. We need to understand what complexity is if we are to model and manage this complexity. The failure to comprehend and thus deal with complexity either of the product or particularly of the project can lead to significant problems.

Simon (1982) says that a complex system is essentially:

> ... one made up of a large number of parts that interact in a non-simple way. In such systems, the whole is more than the sum of the parts, not in an ultimate, metaphysical sense but in the important pragmatic sense that, given the properties of the parts and the laws of interaction, it is not a trivial matter to infer the properties of the whole.

Thus while standard project management techniques, that decompose a project in a structured way into manageable sub-sections, which together encompass all of the content of the project, have proved very successful, if used in a simplistic way they can form a significant hindrance to effective modelling of complex projects, whose behaviour is beyond the sum of its parts and whose reaction to changes in inputs is difficult for the human mind to predict.

I defined complexity (Williams 1999) in two parts:

The first, termed 'Structural Complexity', is taken from Baccarini (1996), who defines complexity as 'consisting of many varied interrelated parts', entailing differentiation – the number of varied elements – and interdependency – the degree of interrelatedness between them (or connectivity). These measures apply to many different project dimensions, such as organizational complexity (in which 'differentiation' would mean the number of hierarchical levels, number of formal organizational units, division of tasks, number of specializations etc; and 'interdependency' would be the degree of operational interdependencies between organizational elements) or technological complexity (where 'differentiation' would mean the number and diversity of inputs, outputs, tasks or specialities, and 'interdependency' would be the interdependencies between tasks, teams, technologies or inputs).

A major source of project (structural) complexity is product (structural) complexity, where the product is the physical deliverable (the product being designed and manufactured, or the building being built, etc). A project to develop a more complex product must normally be a more complex (in this sense) project, but it is useful to distinguish the cause and effect of product type of complexity first. Product (structural) complexity is the number of subsystems of a product and their interrelationships (where an inter-relationship can mean, for example, that changes in the design to one subsystem produce cross-impacts and affect the design of the other system). When modelling or analysing a project that is producing such a product, measures of complexity can be propounded in order to quantify these interrelationships (such as sequential complexity or feedback complexity). Having measured the product complexity, such measures can then be used to investigate project complexity. For example, to evaluate the effect of a client change on a project, it is important to consider how many changes to other systems are likely to be required, or how many system-designs hitherto considered as 'frozen' will need to be re-designed.

Simply counting interdependencies within the project structure is clearly not sufficient; the nature of those interdependencies is also important. Thompson (1967) defines three types of interdependency:

1. pooled: in which each element gives a discrete contribution to the project
2. sequential: one element's output becomes another's input
3. reciprocal: in which the inputs feed back

It is this last type of interdependency that particularly intensifies complexity, particularly as it causes feedback effects (Williams et al 1995). These reciprocal effects can clearly be seen in the case of a set of designers designing a product subject to cross-impacts; but less easily modelled reciprocal interdependencies occur, for example when there are functional aspects affected by, and affecting, many activities (such as safety issues, Williams 2002), or when events occur which affect many project elements (such as a change in regulations). In addition, it needs to be remembered that most projects are by definition multi-objective, which adds (structural) complexity, as the effects of activities on all goals has to be assessed and traded-off. The complexity within the set of stake-holders also needs to be considered.

The second constituent element of complexity is *uncertainty*. This is defined by Rodney Turner and Bob Cochrane (1993) in two parameters: how well defined the goals are, and how well-defined are the methods of achieving those goals.

Uncertainty in the methods used to carry out a project will add complexity. Turner and Cochrane point out that if methods are uncertain, the fundamental building-blocks of project management defined in other chapters of this book will not be known: the work break-down structure, WBS, the tasks required to complete the job and their sequence, the organizational break-down structure, OBS, etc; and even when they are planned, the plan will be subject to change. This will cause characteristics of Structural Complexity: as the team structures the work and refines the methods, there will be interdependencies between project sub-teams; and as methods are tried and re-planned, feed back loops will naturally occur, and so on.

Added complexity also comes about when there is uncertainty in goals – typically found in software development projects. Changes or lack of freeze in requirements and specifications will mean that interfacing elements also need to change, and again we have cross-impacts, re-work, feedback loops – an increase in the features of structural complexity. Furthermore, changes to goals mid-project add to the project's (structural) complexity, and also generally combine to increase the product complexity (and thus project complexity).

591

Both uncertainty in methods and uncertainty in goals tend to be difficult to operationalize into quantifiable parameters.

The two sub-dimensions of structural complexity lead to a complex system in which the whole is more than the sum of the parts. In these systems, as in Simon's (1982) definition, it is very difficult intuitively to infer their behaviour from the behaviour of the sub-elements – indeed, the systems can be shown to be likely to exhibit counter-intuitive behaviour. One example would be Cooper's well-known '$2000 hour' effect (Cooper 1994), in which it is shown that the influence of management on the rework cycle can generate vicious circles of cause and effect, reducing productivity and quality, and thus mean that each hour of *effective* work becomes very expensive. When uncertainties arise, either in the goals or the methods, they can cause perturbations and dynamics to be set up within the structurally complex systems causing complex dynamic behaviour. Uncertainty in goals, on its own, might not cause complexity – but add uncertainty in goals to a product development project which is already structurally complex, and changes and perturbations cause cross-impacts, feedback, dynamics effects and behaviour much too complex for a simple intuitive understanding – in fact, we need models to comprehend what is happening (or might happen).

It seems accepted (Williams 2002) that project complexity has been increasing over recent decades. Laufer et al (1996) characterized the last four decades of project management by an evolution of models appropriate to changing dominant project characteristics: they characterize the 1960s by scheduling (control), for simple, certain projects; the 1970s by teamwork (integration) and the 1980s for reducing uncertainty (flexibility), as projects became complex and uncertain, and the 1990s by simultaneity (dynamism) for complex, uncertain and quick projects – the very elements defined as 'complexity' above, and for which effective models are needed.

PRACTICAL ISSUES

Three practical issues are discussed here. First we need to consider the status and meaning of data used to populate our models. Modellers are often modelling not the objective world but their client's perceptions of the world, relying on the clients for data. If that data is filtered before it gets to the client, or if the client takes underlying data and interprets it or overlays additional understanding, then the modeller must seek to understand these processes in order to understand the degree of validity of the data. Thus, where data purports to represent a particular parameter, it must be ensured that this is indeed what is being measured. For example, when performing (say) Earned Value Analysis (Chapter 20), each activity is assessed to see how far it has proceeded: but this is of course not a concrete reality which can simply be measured but an individual's interpretation of the state of the activity. A model must therefore include consideration of the causes of attitudes and biases, and thus start to capture the socially constructed nature of 'reality' in a project (Bredillet 2004).

The second practical issue is, how complex or how simple should a model be? There are two key balancing principles generally accepted:

1. The principle of 'Ockham's razor' states that that if a few entities or reasons are sufficient to explain a phenomenon, this is a preferable explanation to one using many entities or reasons. The simplest models appropriate to the task should thus be used. This is to avoid needlessly over-complicated models, which can cause needless work, possibly emergence of false or misleading results, unrobust models, and accusations of 'fiddling'.
2. The principle of 'requisite variety' (Ashby 1956) states that a model must be able to represent the features in the system that the modeller needs to be interested in, thus must have sufficient variety. Thus again requisite variety is not an intrinsic feature of the phenomena being modelled, rather it derives from the purpose of the model. A model of a complex project which does not have requisite variety will not display the essential features of a complex project as described by Simon above.

Finally, a major issue in modelling is validation, checking that the model is a good representation of reality. There is a large literature on this topic. Much work has developed in the field of System Dynamics (a method popular among some project modellers), based on the ideas of Forrester and Senge (1980), who set out a list of 'Confidence Tests', with the idea that as a model passes these tests we gain confidence in its validity. These tests consist of 'Tests of model structure', 'Tests of model behaviour', and 'Tests of policy implications'. The second of these has a key test

- Behaviour-reproduction. How well does the behaviour of the model match behaviour that can be observed in the real system?

Subsidiary to this come:

- the model should reproduce symptoms of the system of interest
- the model should reproduce typical characteristics of the real system's behaviour
- the model should predict reasonable patterns of behaviour in the future
- if a model generates behaviour which is unexpected or different from what has been experienced within the real system, then the causes of this behaviour should be traced
- when the model is run under extreme conditions, behaviour should be consistent with what is considered would actually occur in the real system

- the sensitive parameters in the model should be identified, and it should be considered whether the real system would be similarly sensitive

WHAT MAKES A GOOD MODELLER?

The client-modeller relationship is critical to the success of any modelling exercise. The modeller who engages with his client and develops a rapport, will be the one whose model is accepted and is used. If this is so when modelling a well-defined situation, it is even more so when the client's objectives, data and the relationships within the data are only vaguely understood. In this 'complex' situation, the modeller must journey together with the project team to look further into the problem facing them. The modeller in this situation is acting as a problem-finisher rather than a problem-solver to use Colin Eden's (1987) language: 'Problem-finishing as a description of working on a problem directs attention to the 'management of meaning' and thus the role of the consultant intervening in the act of deliberation'. The project-team thus has to form part of the problem-structuring, the search for alternatives, implementation and monitoring, and the modeller and project team must work together in developing understanding and facilitating the decision-making process.

A key attribute of the modeller is the perception of neutrality: he or she is seen to be objective and bringing no pre-conceptions or partiality to the decision-making process. The PRAM Guide, (Simon et al 1997), here gives useful advice for the risk analyst – but which is equally true for any modeller advising or forming part of a project team: the modeller needs to be able 'to elicit and capture data about risk in an impartial manner, and to reflect information in a controlled and structured way. In reality, the risk analyst's relationship with the project team can have a major bearing on the outcome of the PRAM [Project Risk Analysis & Management] process. The project team will need to trust the risk analyst's judgement and take his/her guidance during the PRAM exercise.' It then goes on to highlight four aspects of the relationship between a modeller in a project-context and the project-team.

- Modellers having a dual role can cause a problem, where they also hold authoritative positions on the team so that their neutrality comes into question.
- Any previous relationship between the modeller and the team will affect the process.
- Domain knowledge. A modeller does not need to be an expert in the project work – indeed, much of his or her data comes from eliciting the expert opinions of others. However, some domain experience is important for a modeller to gain and maintain credibility with the project team.

- Interpersonal skills of the modellers, that is 'their abilities to develop sound and trusting relationship with individuals within the project, are crucial to the effective implementation' of any modelling process. This is a key requirement: within the project context, where team-work and application are so highly prized, a modeller who likes to stay in a back room could not operate at all.

MODELLING IN THE PROJECT LIFE-CYCLE

The modeller has an important role throughout the project life-cycle, and this continuing role is essential in giving continuity to the models developed. Four stages of the project can be identified.

Before the project

Before the project starts, estimating and risk analysis are clearly two important roles. The supporting role to estimators is fairly clear, and the use of models in estimating is discussed in Chapters 19 and 20. Chapter 22 deals with some of the risk analysis role also, but it is worth noting:

- risk modelling provides a firm basis for the project bid, taking into account the (correlated) distributions of all cost uncertainties and under-achievement penalties
- risk modelling informs the contract; in particular, risks often should not be treated independently, but systemic modelling can show the effects of combinations of risks
- risk modelling can help choose or define the contract type (for example see Chapman and Ward 1994)

There is an increasing emphasis on projects where the contractor takes on more than the responsibility for simply delivering a facility, such as BOO(T) (Build-Own-Operate-(Transfer)) or DBOM (Design-Build-Operate-Maintain) projects. Here the modeller has to look at a more integrative level. On these types of project, the contractor is interested in the (discounted) through-life cost (TLC) of the asset. This means the modeller must build models which include through-life costs such as the distribution of costs of maintenance and loss of availability through unreliability, and for BOO(T) projects the expected costs of ownership and the expected income from the market. (See Blanchard 1998 for work in this area).

At the start of the project

Chapter 26 describes Project Start-up. Modelling underlies many actions in this process. A model needs to be specified for the project at the integrative level

595

(Turner 1999 calls this step 'developing the project model'). This will show the effects on the organization beyond the project of, for example, later or earlier completion. But at the tactical level at which modellers are normally working there are many more aspects requiring modelling, such as:

- exploring possible options for implementing the project; costing them and evaluating their multi-criteria benefits and disbenefits
- analysis of the factors influencing success and their inter-relationships
- establishing the feasibility of resource-constrained plans (both budgetary and temporal)
- deepening the analysis of project risks and understanding the effects of planned actions to counter such risks if they arise
- identifying project-control metrics and understanding the meaning of those metrics

Project start-up is often effected by a start-up workshop followed by the production of a project start-up manual (Turner 1999). At the Workshop stage, the modeller must be able to contribute to negotiations and discussions with support and advice, requiring the use of rapid-analysis high-level models. The modeller must also be able to understand the implications and shortfalls of those models so that caveats and warnings can be issued; this means that, where further analysis is necessary, the post-workshop negotiation stage can be used to ensure the models are available to support the decisions. The key here is timeliness: a rough-and-ready, robust but requisite model which is available when decisions are being made is much preferable to a more correct model which is not available until irrevocable decisions have been taken.

Models developed in the pre-project stage are further developed and used in this stage, and form a useful link between the phases. Explanatory models that show the types of effects, albeit at a high-level without all of the data in the models fully evaluated, are used to give rapid support to team decisions. The project start-up phase is a rapid ramping up of the project, and this can be the time at which the modeller is most in demand.

During the project

During the project, the modeller supports the team in two main tasks

1. The first is decision-making. There are frequent points within a project where significant decisions have to be taken. At these points, the modeller's support is similar to that in project start, where he or she provides firstly increased understanding (such as why does the 90% syndrome happen? how does the $2000 hour occur?) and secondly models of specific decision-situations. One example could be where events imply delay to a project, the modeller is able to

advise on whether simply to accept Liquidated Damages and not try to deliver on time, or whether to accelerate the project, with all of the causal implications of acceleration (Howick and Eden 2001). A second example could be the attitude of the project team to Change Orders. Chapters 15 and 29 give advice on the need to evaluate the cost and time effect of proposed Change Orders, but in a complex project, the implications of Change Orders are impossible to evaluate without a project model (Eden et al 2000); the implications are often greater than intuition would suggest, and project models can be very useful also in educating (and negotiating with) the customer as to the implications of a proposed Change Order.

2. The second role for the modeller is in supporting project monitoring and re-planning. There are standard metrics that every project measures (Dennis Lock describes some in Chapters 19, 20, 21 and 29), and the project management team monitors progress, and bases its control actions, upon these measures. Some of these might be uncontroversial: for example, while digging a tunnel, if the team has completed 200 feet of tunnel, that might be a measurable fact (although even with this simple example there might be problems). However, as discussed above, some metrics might be uninformative or even misleading. The use of project models can suggest metrics to use (such as productivity over time, engineering re-work rate and so on); can explain the implications of metrics (such as when work appears to be x% complete, then hidden rework implies that y% will need some reworking); and can explain how measures change over time if behaviour appears counter-intuitive. Some of these metrics might be subjective but can be useful in showing at least how perceptions change over time.

There are two areas of project monitoring in which models are particularly useful. The first is in Earned Value (EV) calculations (Chapter 20): if estimates of work completed are significantly over-estimated, or if processes underlying the project are going to cause significant extra work or re-work to happen downstream, then the EV calculations will be misleading. So a project making significant use of EV can be helped if a model describing the systemic effects within the project is available to explain and adjust the EV results. The second area is in risk-monitoring: the project team needs to understand the impact of risks, and the meaning of collected metrics, and the likely effect of mitigation actions, and in a complex project these all require the project team to have the support of a modeller, with models to explain, analyse and estimate.

After the project

The role of the modeller is not complete after the project has finished; two tasks remain. While this is a separate section in this description, the models should be operational during the project, so the post-project work is simply a continuation of the use of the models from the stages above.

The first task is supporting post-project reviews and feeding this into on-going organizational learning, (Chapter 33). Organizations need to be 'learning organizations' (Senge et al 1994), and there is a particular need for project-based organizations, if they are to flourish, to learn from one project to the next. But in practice, project review processes are often not in place, project failure and success are rarely analysed, and learning often does not happen – maybe due to lack of time, or lack of standardised methods, or lack of previous experience of finding post-project reviews helpful. For complex projects, data don't always give understanding. It is not easy to learn the deep lessons of why a project behaved as it did. Often causal chains that led to the results are not obvious: 'The performance that matters is often a result of complex interactions within the overall development system. Moreover, the connection between cause and effect may be separated significantly in time and place. In some instances, for example, the outcomes of interest are only evident at the conclusion of the project. Thus, while symptoms and potential causes may be observed along the development path, systematic investigation requires observation of the outcomes, followed by any analysis that looks back to find the underlying causes' (Wheelwright and Clark 1992). Thus we need to be able to trace complex sets of causal links from actions taken by parties through the dynamic behaviours set up within the project and to understand and quantify the resulting effects.

As well as capturing facts and causality underlying the facts, interviews and workshops can enable the stories of the project to be captured. 'The most valuable learning about past projects often comes from listening to those few individuals that assume the role of storyteller. One absorbs the context, nuances, and rationale (or lack thereof) behind the project documentation from them. Combining objective project documentation with subjective perceptions about a project is the leap between historical data and historical information' (MacMaster 2000); and these stories can be taken and developed into qualitative explanatory models (Williams 2002). Project post-mortems should naturally feed into pre-project risk analysis of succeeding projects. Post mortems should be structured to enable this. As well as specific circumstances of the individual project, running the final models can help to develop generic rules which can contribute towards understanding risks and particularly the likely impacts of risks upon the project to contribute towards later risk analyses.

The second task in which the modeller might be involved is post-project claims, which can be a major task. Sometimes claims, particularly Extension of Time claims, can be based on simple network methods (see Chapter 19). However, this is often too simplistic for complex projects, and influence diagrams and a technique such as System Dynamics (SD) are needed to answer questions such as the effect of a delay, or a set of delays, upon a project. Models in claims need to:

- show causality: the systemic inter-relationships which caused the various ramifications of the events to build up
- show responsibility: show the party causing the initial causes of the events
- calculate the quantum of the effects – in other words, show the size of cost- and time-overrun resulting from a particular delay or set of delays
- do all of these transparently

Williams (2002) proposes:

- using simple Gantt charts to find out what actually was the out-turn in the project
- if there are a limited number of disruptive events, using standard network-based methods
- otherwise, for the parts of the project displaying complexity, to seek to understand the out-turn, and to trace causality from the triggering effects, using causal maps and SD
- in practice, using a combination of methods for different parts of the project

These models then show both time-effects and the reasons for cost-overruns; in a complex project which has been disrupted and thus accelerated, time and cost are closely related, and an analysis must be done of the two together.

CONCLUSION

Modelling underlies much of the analysis of projects, and indeed is assumed in much of the work described in Part II of this book. This chapter has given some underlying rules for how to model projects, and the role of the project modeller.

REFERENCES AND FURTHER READING

Ashby, R., 1956, *An Introduction to Cybernetics*, London: Chapman and Hall.

Baccarini, D., 1996, 'The concept of project complexity – a review', *International Journal of Project Management*, 14(4), 201–204.

Blanchard, B.S., 1998, *Logistics Engineering and Management*, 5th edition, Englewood Cliff, NJ: Prentice-Hall.

Bredillet, C.N., 2004, 'Understanding the very nature of project management: a praxiological approach', in *Proceedings of the PMI® Research Conference 2004*,

London, July, ed D.P. Slevin, D.I. Cleland and J.K. Pinto, Newtown Square, PA: Project Management Institute.

Chapman, C.B. and Ward, S.C., 1994, 'The efficient allocation of risk in contracts', *Omega,* 22, 537–552

Cooper, K.G., 1994, 'The $2,000 hour: how managers influence project performance through the rework cycle', *Project Management Journal,* 25(1), 11–24.

Eden, C.E., 1987, 'Problem-solving or problem-finishing', in M.C. Jackson and P. Keys, (eds), *New Directions in Management Science,* Aldershot: Gower.

Eden, C.E., Williams, T.M., Ackermann, F.A. and Howick, S., 2000, 'On the Nature of Disruption and Delay (D&D) in major projects', *Journal of the Operational Research Society,* 51(3), 291–300.

Forrester, J.W., and Senge P.M., 1980, 'Tests for building confidence in system dynamics models', in Legasto, A.A. jr, Forrester, J.W. and Lyneis J.M., (eds), *TIMS Studies in the Management Sciences 14,* New York:North Holland.

Howick, S. and Eden, C. 2001, 'The Impact of Disruption and Delay when Compressing Large Projects: Going for Incentives?', *Journal of the Operational Research Society,* 52, 26–34.

Laufer, A., Denker, G.R. and Shenhar, A.J., 1996, 'Simultaneous management: the key to excellence in capital projects', *International Journal of Project Management,* 14(4), 189–199.

MacMaster, G., 2000, 'Can we learn from project histories?', *PM Network,* 14 (July), 66–67.

Schultz, R.L. and Sullivan, E.M., 1972, 'Developments in simulation in social and administrative science', in Guetzkow, H.S., Kotler, P. and Schultz, R.L., (eds), *Simulation in Social and Administrative Science: overviews and case-examples,* Englewood Cliff, NJ: Prentice-Hall.

Senge, P.M., Kleiner, A., Roberts, C., Ross, R. and Smith. B., 1994, *The Fifth Discipline Fieldbook: Strategies and tools for building a learning organization,* New York: Doubleday.

Simon, H.A., 1982, *Sciences of the Artificial,* 2nd edition, Cambridge, MA: MIT Press.

Simon, P., Hillson, D. and Newland, K., 1997, *PRAM: Project Risk Analysis and Management Guide,* High Wycombe, UK: Association for Project Management.

Thompson, J.D., 1967, *Organizations in Action,* New York: McGraw-Hill.

Turner, J.R., 1999, *The Handbook of Project-Based Management,* London: McGraw-Hill.

Turner, J.R. and Cochrane, R.A., 1993, 'The goals-and-methods matrix: coping with projects with ill defined goals and/or methods of achieving them', *International Journal of Project Management,* 11(2), 93–102.

Wheelwright, S.C. and Clark, K.B., 1992, *Revolutionizing Product Development: quantum leaps in speed, efficiency, and quality*, New York: The Free Press.

Williams, T.M., 1999, 'The need for new paradigms for complex projects', *International Journal of Project Management*, 17(5), 269–273.

Williams, T.M., 2000, 'The risk of safety regulation changes in transport development projects', *International Journal of Project Management*, 18(1), 23–31.

Williams, T.M., 2002, *Modelling Complex Projects*, London: Wiley.

Williams, T.M., Eden, C.L., Ackermann, F.R. and Tait, A., 1995, 'Vicious circles of parallelism', *International Journal of Project Management*, 13(3), 151–155.

29 Managing Implementation

Dennis Lock

This chapter starts with the assumption that progress needs managing. The importance of delivering all project commitments on time should be obvious. Quite apart from inconvenience caused to the customer, late delivery of any project is likely to involve the contractor in excess expenditure through financing work in progress and suffering the fixed costs that accumulate relentlessly with time for as long as a project remains unfinished on the premises. Late completion of a project will have knock-on effects that disrupt the schedules for subsequent projects. Project time is a vital, irreplaceable and expensive resource. All project resources should be managed effectively and time is emphatically no exception.

ESSENTIAL FRAMEWORK FOR MANAGING PROGRESS

To give a project some chance of being carried out according to the client's wishes, the management methods and organization structure have to be suitable. If any of the following conditions is not met, progress will be difficult or impossible to manage effectively. Some of these conditions may seem very obvious but they are not always fulfilled in practice.

Project definition (Chapters 14, 15 and 27)

The project specification and objectives have to be clearly defined. The project manager must be in no doubt about what he or she is expected to deliver and those deliverables must be feasible given the resources and time available.

Control of changes (Chapter 15)

Uncontrolled changes can wreak project havoc. They must be properly considered and controlled if delays and overspending are to be avoided.

Organization (Chapters 18, 21 and 35)

The project organization must be led by a competent project manager and should be appropriate to the size and nature of the project, with effective downward, upward and lateral communications.

Supportive management (Chapters 34, 35 and 36)

The project manager does not stand alone. He or she cannot operate in isolation. Backing from higher management is essential, in terms of both material provisions and moral support.

1. Material support includes the authorization of funds necessary for managing and executing the project. The project must not be allowed to fail through lack of essential resources and facilities (such as people, equipment and accommodation).
2. Moral support is at least as important as material support. It can take many forms. Here are some examples:
   - Appropriate and generous delegation of authority and responsibility to the project manager
   - Enforcement of project management procedures and systems
   - Interceding with managers inside the organization in support of the project manager, for example to resolve arguments over conflicting priorities
   - Interceding at higher management level outside the project organization – a common example is seen when a project manager has no success in obtaining essential materials from a key supplier; dialogue between the two organizations at higher management level can sometimes produce results
   - Encouragement of individual development through training and further education
   - Physical presence – occasional attendance at progress meetings and visits to workplaces or a project site to lend encouragement

Customer partnership

The customer (or client, or owner) must act responsibly and cooperate with the project contractor. This means:

- paying valid claims for payment promptly
- avoiding unnecessary changes
- giving design approvals without delay
- generally appreciating the problems that face the contractor

There should be an atmosphere of partnership rather than confrontation. Concurrent engineering is a good example of such partnership, where customer and contractor work together in a search for mutually beneficial project strategies.

Competence of people in organizations (Chapter 32)

The success of a large project depends on the competence of many people throughout the organizations of subcontractors, suppliers of equipment and materials, service companies, government departments, the customer and the project contractor. Some of these people will be competent. Others might be less so. We have to assume that most are capable of performing their jobs properly if project progress is to be assured. Although the project manager will not have direct control over the people in external organizations, control can be exercised by the careful choice of those organizations.

Allocation of responsibilities (Chapters 15 and 18)

People must know what is expected of them. One tool that can assist the project manager to allocate responsibilities is the linear responsibility matrix (Chapter 18). The responsibility matrix is best suited to deal with task categories rather than listing all the detailed tasks. For example, it can show the person or body responsible for approving new designs in general, but it is not the place in which to list all the drawings that carry those designs.

Workable schedule (Chapters 19 and 21)

The project schedule is key for managing progress. Here are some characteristics of the ideal plan for a project or, a larger project, each subproject or work package, all significant tasks:

- Tasks placed in logical sequence, preferably as a critical path network
- Estimates of duration as realistic as possible
- Scheduled to use resources at feasible rates
- Flexible to authorized changes and progress, so that it can be kept up to date
- Divided into separate work-to lists for departments or work groups

IMPOSSIBLE?

With all these imposed conditions perhaps it is a wonder that any project ever gets finished on time. And, so far, we have not even thought about all the other things which can go wrong accidentally, as seen in any insurance company's catalogue of disasters: fire; storm; civil commotion; war (civil or otherwise); strikes; lockouts; objects dropped from aircraft; other natural disasters; unnatural disasters; and so on ad infinitum. What chance does any project ever have of being finished on time? Many do, of course, finish late.

Progress management seeks to start and finish every task in accordance with the project plan. It should foresee and forestall possible risks, monitor work in

605

progress, identify current problems and (above all) must take corrective and timely action against significant delays.

COMMUNICATING THE WORK PROGRAMME

Consider a contracting organization which has received a prized order for a new project. Possibly over one hundred of the contractor's staff are going to be working on the new project for a prolonged period. All good news. But how do they know when to start and what to do?

PROJECT AUTHORIZATION

The first official document used in many companies to start a new project is a works order or project authorization. This gives key information about the project in summary form. Apart from giving information about the project, the works order carries the signature of a director or senior manager which authorizes the start of work and other expenditure on the new project. The following items are among those likely to be included:

- Name and address of the customer or client
- Project site or delivery address (if different)
- Project title
- Project number (which should provide the root of the code of cost accounts and work breakdown structure)
- Name of the customer's project manager or key contact person
- Number and date of the customer's purchase order or contract
- Project description and scope of supply
- Serial and revision numbers of key documents, such as the project specification
- Pricing details and agreed terms of payment
- Key dates in the project life-cycle
- Departmental budgets
- Name of the project manager

WORK-TO LISTS

While the works order or other project authorization document gives instructions across the organization in broad management outline, it does not carry enough detail from which to issue and control work down to the level of separate jobs in all the separate departments and groups. The most effective and convenient tool for that function is the work-to list (Chapters 19 and 21), derived from the project network and resource scheduling. This provides each manager with a list of all project tasks for which he or she is responsible together with essential schedule information. Ideally, the computer should filter tasks so that reports can be specific and relevant to each departmental manager.

Giving every activity a departmental code will facilitate departmental filtering. The computer should sort and print the list for each department in ascending order of activities' scheduled start dates. The earliest possible start dates from time analysis will have to suffice if resources have not been scheduled. Other sort sequences may be more appropriate for some departments. The person responsible for expediting purchase orders might, for example, find it more convenient to have all the lead time activities for purchased goods listed in order of their planned completion (delivery) dates. Work-to lists provide managers or their delegates with valuable schedules and checklists from which to issue tasks and manage their progress.

STARTING UP

Project start-up is covered in Chapter 26. Key issues for implementation include the following:

KICK-OFF MEETING

When the contract has been won and work authorized, the kick-off meeting is a good way to get things started. The project manager, having first been thoroughly briefed on all known aspects of the project, must call together the principal participants and brief them in turn. This is the time and place to explain the project's general technical and procedural requirements, warn of specific risks, quantify deliverables, obtain everyone's agreement and commitment, and generally encourage all concerned get their forces mobilized and motivated.

STARTING EARLY

One of the biggest risks in managing progress is failure to start a project on time. A project which starts late is likely to finish late. It can be difficult for an organization to activate a new project at the time and rate of working envisaged in the schedule. Delay in signing the project contract can be one reason for delay, perhaps while a few final details are negotiated or for the more mundane reason that one of the authorized signatories is temporarily unavailable. No work should be allowed to start on a commercial or industrial project until a firm contract exists between contractor and client. This is an inviolate rule that should be ground into

607

every self-respecting manager from birth. However, as with most rules, there is an exception.

In most projects, the rate of working and expenditure follow a well-known pattern, the characteristic S-curve results (Figure 20.3). The rate rises slowly at first, while preparations are made and the resources are mobilized. Expenditure is at its highest rate near the middle of the project. Work and expenditure then tail off towards the end, and the curve converges on the final cost. In an engineering project, for example, the first weeks of the active project life-cycle might be used for planning, investigating standards, resolving queries with the client, establishing procedures, and so on. Some companies use checklists for controlling this preliminary work, and put the checklist in the form of a standard preliminary network diagram. All these early activities are likely to need no more than one or two people. It can be seen from Figure 20.3, that this early work is unlikely to account for a significant part of the total expenditure. Yet this work must be done before the main project activities can start and many of these early tasks will lie on the project critical path.

If the time available for the project is tight, or a company wants it finished quickly, it might be advantageous to commit commercial heresy and allow some activities to go ahead, and to incur some costs, before the contract with the client has been signed. There are risks. In the event that the contract is not awarded, the preliminary expenditure will have to be written off. There is a danger that the contractor's price bargaining position will be weakened if the client discovers work has already begun. The contractor can limit the risk by issuing a preliminary internal works order that releases only a very restricted budget, specifies the work allowed and names individuals authorized to carry it out. The risk has to be evaluated and weighed against the benefit of bringing the project completion forward by one or more months.

MANAGING PROGRESS IN THE VARIOUS PROJECT FUNCTIONS

A simple control cycle can be described for accomplishing each activity. The steps are:

1. Prompted by the work-to list, the manager responsible allocates the work to the appropriate person, group or other resource as near as possible to the scheduled time.
2. The responsible manager ensures that all necessary facilities and information are provided and that the task requirements are fully explained and understood.
3. Work is monitored against schedule so delays are identified as soon as possible.

4. If any potential problem is identified, corrective action is taken immediately. The severity of such action is in inverse proportion to the amount of float remaining for the activity

5. At set intervals, and on completion of the task, progress information is fed to the project manager and to the computer so that the project schedule can be updated and kept valid.

PROGRESS CHASING

In the ideal modern system, it should be possible for all progress information to be reported and entered into the computer control system by the responsible managers or their delegates, using the local area network. Project managers, being ultimately responsible, may not rely entirely on other managers for progress monitoring and control. Partly for this reason and to ease the administrative load on all managers, routine progress monitoring can be delegated to one or more specially assigned people, who may have job titles such as progress clerk or progress chaser. These people should cooperate with the various departmental managers to gather information against work-to lists and report as necessary to the project manager and the relevant computer system. (The role of the project office is described in Chapter 9).

OBTAINING DESIGN INFORMATION FROM EXTERNAL SOURCES

Engineering design activities very often depend on information from outside sources. In the case of a large construction project, for instance, this can include considerable correspondence with the client, suppliers and subcontractors. Engineering and other work can be held up while waiting for information from these external sources, or for the client to approve documents such as key drawings, specifications and purchase documents. The project manager must ensure close monitoring of these information exchanges and see to it that no external organization is allowed to put the success of the project at risk by avoidable delays.

On larger projects it will probably be necessary to impose office procedures on all correspondence and document transmissions, whether these are by mail or electronic means. All important communications need to be monitored to make certain that every message needing an answer gets that answer promptly. These transmissions may need to be given serial numbers and subject codes so that they can be filed for future reference.

SUBCONTRACTED ENGINEERING DESIGN SERVICES

Engineering companies sometimes offload work to external design offices, either at times of overload or as a more permanent policy to maintain staffing flexibility. It is not unknown for a company to operate with a small core of permanently employed professional engineers, and to have a substantial amount of detailed design work being performed in several external offices. The two most apparent risks to project deliverables introduced by this practice are:

- dilution of company standards or quality
- loose control of progress

The quality aspect can be covered to some extent by ensuring that the external offices are certificated to relevant quality standards (Chapter 17). A practical measure is to arrange for one or more supervising engineers from each regularly used external office to be trained in the company's own offices so they absorb the host company's standards and culture. When these engineers return to their own offices they become an effective extension of the company's own engineering management. A useful arrangement for controlling progress in external offices is to appoint a qualified and experienced person as a subcontract liaison engineer. This person can visit each external office at frequent, regular intervals to deliver and collect work, monitor progress and give on-the-spot answers to some technical queries.

PURCHASING

Purchased materials and equipment can take months or even years to obtain and purchasing activities often lie on the critical path. Engineers and designers must be encouraged to release purchasing information for critical items as early as possible, without waiting for the issue of parts lists or bills of materials and purchase schedules. That should enable the purchasing department to place orders as soon as possible for long delivery items, such as castings and bearings. Even in cases where final design details cannot be given with confidence, the release of outline information will allow external manufacturers to reserve capacity.

Once a purchase order has been placed, expediting becomes important to keep each supplier reminded of their contractual obligations and give early warning of any difficulty. Items ordered from the supplier's catalogue usually require only one check during the waiting period. For major purchases, especially for bespoke goods, it might be necessary to send expediters and inspectors to the manufacturer's premises to see progress for themselves and, in some cases, to carry out inspection and witness tests.

MANUFACTURING

The timely movement of machined parts, subassemblies and other production jobs between work stations is particularly important for progress. If a job requires, say, 10 operations from raw material to completely finished component, and if it takes a day to move that job between each work station, then the part will spend two weeks of its time in the factory sitting on racks or trolleys. Delays in work transit (and therefore in work in progress inventory) can be reduced by the use of Kanban or just-in-time methods, although these may not always be appropriate for special project work. All good manufacturing establishments will have their own methods for production control and detailed progress management, and these are outside the scope of this handbook. The principal role of project management in manufacturing should be to provide work-to lists, from the project schedule, that give the required start and finish times of each manufactured assembly or subassembly. The manufacturing managers should be relied upon to work within those limits, but that is not to say that the project manager should be shy of making spot checks on progress. Given the acquisition of the necessary skills, project planners can use resource scheduling to ensure that, in overall terms, work is fed to the manufacturing departments in line with their normal overall capacity.

A project manager with access to the manufacturing facilities employed on the project can spend profitable time walking through the factory regularly (perhaps once a day). Just ten minutes is often sufficient for the project manager to note whether any job is held up. A stack of steel piled in a corner for a few days might be an indication that the production management have downgraded the priority on this project work to the advantage of some other project manager who is able to shout louder.

CONSTRUCTION

At a construction site (which may be thousands of miles removed from the project manager and the home office) it is customary to establish a management team to control work on the spot. The size and organization of this team can vary, from just two or three individuals on a small project to a substantial management and administration team for a larger job. Adequate communication facilities must be established between the project site and the contractor's head office. This used to be a serious problem with some international projects and remote sites before the days of communication satellites.

Organizational arrangements can have a marked effect on the degree of day-to-day control that the site manager must exercise on the work of the various trades. A managing contractor which employs no direct labour but relies instead on subcontractors would need less day-to-day involvement than one which employed its own direct labour.

It is obviously essential that all materials are delivered to site at the right time and in good condition. Thus the project purchasing organization has a prime responsibility towards maintaining construction progress. The site manager will report any shortages, preferably when they are foreseen rather than waiting for them to happen, and the purchasing organization will be expected to take urgent action to get the goods to site.

No less important than the flow of materials and equipment to site is the supply of construction information. This takes the form of drawings, equipment suppliers' installation instructions, take-off lists, engineering standards, specifications and erection instructions. Construction often starts before engineering design is completely finished. Thus there is a danger of construction work outstripping the supply of drawings and other engineering information. Drawings sent to a construction site are usually stamped to show they have passed the necessary checking and approval stages. 'Released for construction' is a typical legend for this purpose. Design engineers are sometimes unable to release drawings fully for construction. They might be awaiting final details of bought-out equipment before power supply requirements and fixings can be added to the drawings. In these circumstances the incomplete drawings may be released provisionally for construction, perhaps with a rubber-stamped legend reading 'Released for construction with holds'. A drawing released with holds can often allow some planning and limited work to take place on site.

The use of network float is another point worthy of mention. It is easy to allow all float to be taken up in the engineering design phase, so that the construction site team are left with no remaining float and therefore find themselves squeezed for time. One way out of this difficulty is to add a special final activity to the project network which does not represent work, but which adds an artificial delay of, perhaps, four weeks to the end of the programme. This has the effect of driving float away from the front (engineering) end of the network, and provides a safety buffer for construction activities. This is not unfair to the engineers. Most project difficulties, at least most of the excusable ones, occur on site. Engineers are not likely to be affected by ice, snow, floods, running sand, strikes, fights, thefts, or any of the other unforeseen problems faced by the site manager.

SPOT CHECKS AT HIGHER LEVELS

When attempting to manage progress at the level of individual activities it is easy to lose sight of the big picture. An example based on the engineering design function illustrates this point. Consider a project on which the engineering design effort is expected to need 100 people during (say) the tenth week. The project manager should have access to this figure from the resource schedule, (Chapter 21). Whether the detailed feedback on progress is good or bad, the project manager would be advised to ask, 'How many engineers are actually working on my project this week?' The answer might produce a shock: not 100 engineers, but only 60.

I once carried out a similar check myself. An external, subcontracted, drawing office was supposed to be making numerous detail drawings, based on overall layouts and specifications produced by our in-house engineers. At the time of the check the schedule showed that 30 external staff should be busy on the project. Our check found only six. Yet engineering progress was confidently being reported by our internal managers as being in step with the plan. Urgent investigation found the in-house engineers were reporting their layouts as completely finished, but were not releasing them to the external office for detailing. They were reluctant to let their work go, perhaps through some lack of confidence in their designs or so that they could give a few late tweaks to move their work nearer to absolute perfection. Firm action from the engineering director put this right, but the problem would not have been revealed in time without the independent, overall global check on the rate of working.

SPECIAL PRIORITY CASES

It is generally not good management practice to attempt the allocation of priorities to work outside the normal scheduling sequence. Manufacturing, for example, is a function in which attempts to allocate priorities are fraught with risk of failure. Labelling work as priority A, B or C might seem a good idea, but eventually all work becomes Priority A. However, there are occasions where special action is needed. The cost to a project of a failure which delays the production of one small item can be out of all proportion to the cost of obtaining that item. Particularly disastrous is the case of an assembly, possibly containing complex electronic or electromechanical gadgetry, which fails catastrophically on its final test. Possibly some single component has broken down, causing other components to be lost. Situations such as this are even more difficult to resolve when it transpires that the failures were caused by design errors, so that the whole cycle of design and manufacture has to be repeated.

There is a procedure which can cope well with such problems. It depends on the issue of an immediate action order (IAO). The usual documents seen in the factory or engineering offices are printed on ordinary plain paper, so one document looks much like another. The first thing which strikes one about an IAO is it is anything but an ordinary piece of plain paper. These top priority documents are printed on paper with brilliantly coloured diagonal stripes (fluorescent if possible). They cannot fail to be seen on a desk or worktop.

Another feature of IAOs is that, because they are so special, they have to be authorized at general manager or managing director level. They are so special that their use has to be restricted. They must not be allowed to proliferate or their impact will be lost. The rule, therefore, is that no more than one IAO may be sanctioned at the same time.

Once authorized, there is no limit placed on the expenditure allowed to get the job done. If the offices or factory must remain open all night, or over Christmas, then so be it. If materials are only available in Sweden and the factory is in Cornwall, then those materials must be obtained by the quickest route regardless of cost. An IAO commits all departments so that, in the case of a design fault, the engineering department must correct the relevant drawings without delay. Normal quality standards must still be respected, but those responsible for carrying out inspection and testing will be bound by the urgency of the order. The IAO is carried from department to department by a progress chaser, who date- and time-stamps its arrival and departure times at each departmental manager's desk. The progress chaser remains with the IAO until the job is done.

In companies where this system operates, managers learn to fear IAOs. They are a nuisance. They carry risk of criticism or rebuke from higher management if they are not properly obeyed. They command priority over all other work – even to the extent of stopping a machine in mid-cut, removing the workpiece, and resetting the machine to take the immediate job. The logic is seen when by spending perhaps £15 000 to finish a job which should only have cost £1000, a project delay of several weeks is avoided. The cost of the immediate action is likely to be very small in relation to the savings in overall costs and reputation.

Immediate action orders get dramatic results. A tiny prototype 5000 volt transformer for military equipment burned out on test. It had taken six weeks to manufacture and was difficult to make, being encased in an intricate electroplated copper gauze screen and then encapsulated in epoxy resin. Manufacturing operations were subject to numerous quality checks against a stringent military specification. The successful replacement took three days from the start of redesign to final test.

PROGRESS MEETINGS

Progress meetings provide a forum in which progress difficulties and risks can be discussed, and actions agreed. Each meeting should be managed efficiently from the chair, with the aid of a sensible agenda, so that it deals effectively with all matters related to keeping the project on schedule but is not side-tracked into technical and other issues that should more properly be dealt with elsewhere. Progress meetings should also be kept as short as possible, given that those attending are probably busy, short of spare time, highly paid, and needed back at their own departments for actually doing work rather than simply discussing it. It is not a bad plan to arrange that progress meetings, at least those attended only by in-house staff, are started at a fairly late hour in the working day. Then there is a real incentive to get the business done quickly. Of course, this argument would not apply where the client had travelled thousands of miles to attend the meeting.

FREQUENCY

The frequency of progress meetings depends on the duration and complexity of the project. For a highly intensive project carried out at feverish speed over just a few weeks or months it might be deemed appropriate to hold a short progress meeting every week. Monthly is a more usual interval for most projects. One company in my experience managed its projects well without regular progress meetings. All project departmental managers were issued with work schedules from a multi-project model, and a project coordination group controlled progress against these schedules on a day-by-day basis. As soon as any activity seemed in danger of running late action was taken to bring the work back on schedule. No specific decision was taken to abolish the traditional progress meetings: they simply became unnecessary. However, a project manager has no alternative but to call progress meetings when the participants come from different departments or organizations and must meet face-to-face to resolve their genuine difficulties and so keep the programme on course.

COMMITMENTS

During progress meetings it is common for individuals to be asked to make estimates, or to give promises of fresh dates by which late or additional jobs can be finished. The chairman ensures promises with vague wordings such as 'the end of the week', or 'sometime next month' or (worst of all) 'as soon as possible' are not allowed. He or she must insist on firm, measurable commitments. If any member of the meeting feels the promises being made by others are unrealistic, he or she should (politely) say so, so that all possible consideration is given in advance to likely problems. All promises and commitments must be realistic. How often have we attended progress meetings where, from one meeting to the next, the same item keeps cropping up with the only result being that a new, later, promise is given each time?

MINUTES

Progress meetings are a waste of time when the agreements reached are not followed up to ensure that promises are kept. The control document for this purpose is that containing the minutes of the meeting. The minutes should be:

- concise, giving short statements of actions agreed
- annotated to show those persons required to perform or manage the agreed actions
- issued promptly, as soon as possible after the meeting
- distributed to all those present plus any other person listed as having to take action

PROGRESS MEASUREMENT

Progress measurement is not the same thing as progress management because, by itself, it does not imply the taking of action. Measurement is, however, necessary for several reasons. The most important of these are:

1. To provide an equitable and certifiable basis for interim claims for payment. Thus the work of subcontractors has to be measured to establish when and how much they can bill the main contractor (or the client) for work done. A main contractor's own work should be measured for similar reasons. The inclusion of key events or milestones in the plan is a good way of identifying the timing and amounts of interim payments.
2. To provide data for inclusion in reports to senior management and the client.
3. To allow comparison of actual costs and progress with the current schedule and budgets. Such comparisons give early warning of possible overspending or late completion.

If a computer schedule is used which is updated and reissued at intervals, all new data and progress information must be related to the next 'time-now' date. This is the date (decided by the planner) that the project management software uses as the start date from which to calculate and report the next revised schedule. Most computer programmes allow the progress of an activity to be assessed in a number of different ways. Here are some of the possibilities:

1. Report that the activity has started, or will be started, by time-now. This information should prevent the computer from rescheduling activities which are already in progress.
2. An assessment of progress achieved. This might be expressed as one of the following:

- estimated duration remaining to completion after time-now;
- estimated percentage completion achieved at time-now; or
- an estimated completion date for the activity.

3. Report that the activity has been completed, or will have been completed at time-now.

ASSESSING PROGRESS ON SOFTWARE TASKS

Estimates of activity durations usually tend to be optimistic. The project manager finds that when the work actually takes place, some activities take longer to finish than the time allowed in the plan. It is common practice to judge progress on software tasks (such as engineering, drawing and computer software design) in terms of percentage completion. Thus, if a particular design job were to be estimated as taking four weeks, the progress might be reported as (say) 75 per cent complete, from which the project manager and any other interested person would conclude that one week's work remained. It is, unfortunately, true that most people tend to be optimists when making assessments of their achievements. Thus, the project manager with several years' experience should not be surprised when this particular job is finished not one week later, but after three weeks, and then with questions still to be answered on some finer engineering point or other.

MILESTONE TRACKER DIAGRAMS

Variations between the estimated and actual completion times can be predicted and highlighted for most tasks using a milestone tracker diagram (Figure 29.1). These are sometimes known as milestone slip diagrams, but that title is unsatisfactory because it reflects a negative attitude and assumes that milestones will always slip.

Tracker diagram: preparation

The milestone in the example used in Figure 29.1 is for a gearbox design, but the method could be applied to any other software activity, whether for mechanical design or computer software. The estimated duration for this gearbox design activity was first judged to be 20 weeks (the baseline estimate). Preparation of the tracker diagram requires the following steps:

1. Draw two axes at right angles to each other, and scale these axes in weeks. The total period allowed should be at least as long as that which the milestone could take under the worst possible conditions. The axes should be equal in value. Note that the scaling of the y (vertical) axis is in the reverse direction from that expected in a normal graph, with zero at the top instead of at the

617

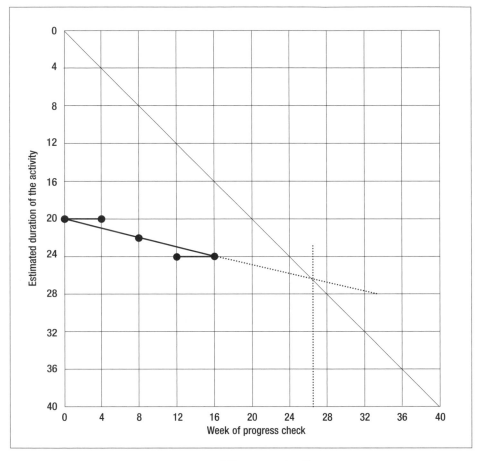

Figure 29.1 Milestone tracker diagram

origin. (The diagram can also be drawn rotated about the diagonal, that is with the planned date along the top, and actual down the vertical axis).

2. Draw a diagonal line from the zero on the y axis to the maximum possible duration point on the x axis (which is 40 weeks in this example).

3. Plot the estimated delivery date of the milestone (week 20) at week zero on the time-now axis.

TRACKER DIAGRAM: APPLICATION

After the gearbox designer has been at work for four weeks, her supervisor asks how things are going. She replies that all is going well and she expects to finish in the 20 weeks originally estimated. This is plotted on the diagram, as shown in Figure 29.1. After a further four weeks, at week eight, a new progress check shows the designer to be less confident. She thinks she will need a further 14

618

weeks before she finishes. This is equivalent to a revised total duration estimate of 22 weeks, and this result is plotted on the diagram at week eight. During further checks at weeks 12 and 16 the designer has revised her estimates again and now expects the total duration to be 24 weeks. Again, these results are plotted on the diagram. At any time during these progress checks the project manager can draw the best possible straight line to connect these revised estimates. If that straight line is projected to the right, it will intersect the diagonal line at a point which can be taken to predict the delivery date of the milestone.

All project milestones can be put on a single tracker diagram to give an overall view of progress, although earned value analysis, described later in this chapter, is the method generally preferred.

ALMOST FINISHED

A problem facing the manager trying to get a project designed on time is the frequency with which engineers and software designers report work as 90 or 95 per cent complete, leaving that last tantalising 10 or 5 per cent just out of reach. The shrewd manager learns to apply a few simple rules to elicit progress. The first requirement is to identify a set of milestones or key events that allow no compromise in interpreting whether or not they have been achieved. These events, which should appear on the project network (and therefore have a scheduled date) must be chosen at close intervals. A good general rule when planning targets is to choose events where jobs pass from person to person, or from department to department. Thus the handover of a manufacturing drawing from designer to checker, or the release of a particular set of fully checked and approved drawings might be real indicators of progress.

CONSTRUCTION INDUSTRY TASKS

Procedures are well established in the construction industry for monitoring and measuring progress by the various trades on construction sites, including the work of subcontractors. Quantity surveyors work with people from the site management team to ensure that work is progressing at the planned rate. Much of the work can be measured in terms of physical quantities, such as tonnes of earth moved, amount of steelwork erected, and so on.

EARNED VALUE ANALYSIS

Earned value analysis (Chapter 20) is a methodology for comparing the achieved value of work in progress against the project schedule and budget. It can be performed at the single activity level but its maximum benefit depends on looking at all activities and rolling the results up through the hierarchy of the work breakdown structure. As with any measurement technique, earned value analysis is not a progress control tool in itself. It can only highlight a need for corrective action by indicating trends. The method does, however, have the advantage of being able to show trends fairly early in the project life-cycle. It depends on the existence of a sound framework of planning and control, including:

- A detailed work breakdown structure
- A correspondingly detailed cost coding system
- Hierarchical and complete tabulation of all project tasks with their approved budgets
- Inclusion of all authorized changes to the project at the appropriate times
- Timely and accurate collection and reporting of cost data
- Regular progress reviews
- A method for quantifying the amount of work done at each review date;
- Inclusion of work in progress in all reviews
- A competent administrator

The basic principles can be described using the milestone tracker diagram (Figure 28.1). The original estimate for the task in that example was 20 weeks. Suppose that this work is costing £1 000 per week, so that the corresponding total budget is £20 000. Assume, for simplicity that the expenditure rate is linear. Consider a reporting date of week 16. At this time the activity should be 80 per cent complete, for which the budgeted cost would be 80 per cent of £20 000. In earned value analysis terms, this would be expressed as follows:

BCWS = £16 000

where BCWS is the budgeted cost of work scheduled to be complete at the reporting date. Here we are looking at just one activity, but BCWS would usually have to include all project work scheduled to be complete at the reporting date. BCWS must include not only all work actually finished, but also the completed portion of all work in progress. Returning to the single package of work in Figure 28.1, we know, that this activity is running late and the latest estimate from the milestone tracker chart shows a likely total duration of 25 weeks. If the activity expenditure is at the expected level of £1 000 per week, the likely cost will be £25 000 instead of £20 000. It could be said that, at week 16, the percentage of work achieved is not 80 per cent, but only 64 per cent. The earned value analysis expressions which describe this state of affairs are as follows:

ACWP = £16 000

where ACWP is the actual cost of work performed to date;

$$BCWP \quad = \quad £12\ 800$$

where BCWP is the budgeted cost of work performed (budget cost appropriate to the amount of work actually achieved). These results can be used to produce the following indices:

$$\text{Cost performance index, CPI} \quad = \quad \frac{BCWP}{ACWP}$$

$$\text{Schedule performance index, SPI} \quad = \quad \frac{BCWP}{BCWS}$$

For the single task in the tracker diagram in Figure 28.1 the CPI and SPI are both 0.8. Values greater than unity point to performance better than plan. Values less than unity, as here, indicate negative variances and the need for action to correct the trend. When the measurement takes into account all the project's work, the CPI can be used to calculate the estimated costs remaining to completion or the predicted final project cost, as described in Chapter 20 and illustrated in Figure 20.1. Similarly the SPI can predict the probable completion date, although this factor is not used nearly as often as the CPI.

CHANGES

Change to an active project can threaten progress and increase costs. It is true that there are companies which welcome their client's requests for changes, since these can provide reasons for levying additional charges and extending the timescale at the client's expense. Once the project is active, any change can be an increase in project scope which the contractor can sell at a price unrestricted by external competition. Project managers, however, usually view all changes as nuisances.

CHANGES WHICH NEED CONTROL PROCEDURES

Changes can obviously occur at any stage in a project. Some are relatively insignificant, because they happen early, cause little wasted effort, and do not affect the project as it was originally defined in the sales specification and contract. For example, a designer may have to make several attempts at a difficult design problem before a drawing can be produced that is suitable for release to the production or construction organization. It would not be reasonable or practicable to expect the designer to seek formal approval every time he or she wiped the computer screen and started again. There is a way to decide whether or not an action should be regarded as a change needing formal management approval. This is to ask whether or not the proposed change would alter any information on a document that has already been issued to authorize work. This definition means that a formal procedure should be applied whenever a proposed change would affect:

- the contract document or any of its attachments (in which case the controlling change document would probably be called a project variation order or contract variation)
- an issued purchase order (the change would probably be called a purchase order amendment)
- any drawing or specification which has previously been issued for manufacture, purchasing or construction

These changes can be interactive, so that a contract variation originated by the client (for instance) might result in a series of engineering changes and purchase order amendments.

CONTROL PROCEDURES FOR ENGINEERING CHANGES

Before a proposed engineering change is allowed to go ahead, it is usual to assess its risks, examining the possible effects carefully in all respects (technical, manufacturing or construction methods, commercial, safety, reliability, timescale and costs). Because no one person can usually be found in the organization who is capable of assessing all these factors, a committee of departmental managers or other experts, which might be called the change committee or change board, is often formed for the purpose. A change committee might contain a senior representative of key company functions. A typical composition might be:

1. The chief engineer, acting as design authority
2. The quality manager, acting as the quality authority (or the inspecting authority)
3. The manufacturing manager, as the manufacturing authority
4. The commercial manager
5. The purchasing manager

All requests for engineering changes should be submitted to the change committee in a suitable standard format. The procedure should ensure change requests are dealt with properly, without undue delay, and that actions decided by the committee are followed up. Not least of these actions is the updating and reissue of drawings and other affected documents.

The change control procedure should be centred on a technical clerk or project coordinator, who can serial number and register each request and then use the register to control its progress. The project support office is an ideal home for this function (Chapter 9).

Monitoring must continue until each change request is either rejected by the committee or fully implemented. The coordinator must keep those who are likely to be affected (including the request originators) informed of the committee decisions. In a typical arrangement, the change committee will meet at regular intervals (perhaps weekly or every two weeks) to consider change requests in batches. The committee will consider each change on its merits and potential risks.

In one multinational company the view was taken that all changes would initially be classified as either 'essential' or 'desirable'. Essential changes would include those necessary to guarantee safe and reliable operation of plant, or to correct errors. These might be approved without comment, sent back to the originator for more information or an alternative proposal, given approval in a modified or limited form, or rejected altogether. Changes requested by the customer would also fall into the essential category; most of these resulting in additional revenue. Changes classed as desirable would always be rejected. The slogan was 'If it's essential we must do it, if it's only desirable we won't'.

DESIGN FREEZE

Sometimes project organizations recognize that there is a point in the design and implementation of a project after which any engineering change would be either particularly inconvenient or unacceptably damaging to costs and progress. This leads the organization to announce a 'design freeze' for the project. In some companies this is called 'stable design'. The idea is to deter anyone from having the temerity to suggest any further change. The change committee will refuse approval for any change request once design has been frozen, unless the originator can show compelling reasons such as safety or a funded customer request. Ideally the customer should also be bound by the design freeze, or at least should be made to pay heavily for the privilege of breaching it.

OTHER PROCEDURES RELATED TO ENGINEERING CHANGES

There are at least three procedural systems that are similar in many respects to engineering change procedures, especially in manufacturing companies. These procedures deal with:

1. Engineering queries: requests for advice from manufacturing departments where drawings and specifications are unclear or appear to contain errors.
2. Production permits and concessions: requests from the manufacturing departments for permission to depart from design or process instructions in one or more respects.

623

3. Inspection rejection reports, where there the degree of rejection is marginal and the design authority must rule whether or not to allow a concession.

Change procedures and their related systems are described more fully in Lock (2003).

PROGRESS REPORTING

Progress reporting takes place at many levels, formally and informally, on any project of significant size. At the simplest level reporting is person to person when, for example, a supervisor performs the daily rounds and asks how individual jobs are progressing. There follows an ascending hierarchical structure of reporting, involving other departments, subcontractors, purchasing and shipping organizations, finally reaching the level of regular, comprehensive cost and progress reports to the client. The lowest and most detailed level of reporting is concerned with collecting data from which to keep the schedule up-to-date. This was discussed earlier in this chapter.

EXCEPTION REPORTING

Strictly speaking, the more senior a person in the management structure of the project, the less detail he or she should be given about progress. Those managers responsible for taking action when things look like going wrong should not be given a long list of jobs that are on course, so that potential problems are hidden among them. It is necessary to pick out the problem activities and highlight them. Then managers' time can be focused on resolving the problems. Every item in danger of running late or of exceeding its cost constitutes an exception that should be reported. Accountants have known and followed this principle for many years, but they call exceptions variances, a term that has since gone into wider use.

When a computer is used for scheduling, it is possible to edit lists so that only late or critical activities are shown. There are also techniques, such as the allocation of report level codes to activities, for reducing the number of activities in reports to individual managers still further on a need-to-know basis. These methods can be combined to produce effective exception reports and target them to the managers who should get them and take action.

Material shortage lists are a good, if specialized, example of exception reports. They list all items of purchased materials and equipment that are urgently needed to maintain or regain work momentum. The purchasing department is then able to concentrate the efforts of its expediting section on dealing with these exceptions and getting the goods delivered.

PROGRESS REPORTS TO THE CLIENT

If the project is large in terms of time and cost, the client will want to know how the project is progressing at any time. This information is usually presented in the form of a progress report (typically issued monthly). It is usual to combine progress reports to the client with cost reports and statements showing how project funds are being used. The main contractor of a large international project might include the following items in regular reports to the client:

1. A written account of progress achieved to date, with special emphasis on progress achieved since the previous report;
2. Photographs showing physical progress;
3. Some form of quantified evidence to back up the progress claimed. This might include, for example, a table of drawing achievement showing:
   - total number of drawings required for the project;
   - number of drawings issued during this reporting period;
   - total number of drawings issued to date;
   - number of drawings in progress;
   - number of drawings not started;
   - percentage of total engineering design and drawing finished;
4. A statement of the position regarding purchased equipment, possibly with detailed lists in the form of purchase and order schedules;
5. A cost report, showing in tabular and graphical form the expenditure to date on main areas of the project and a summary. The cost report should include the latest predictions of total final project expenditure, and would also give the client up-to-date cash flow forecasts;
6. A short summary of the work planned for the next reporting period;
7. A list of problems caused by the client in holding up the supply of information, approvals or funds. That is a schedule of actions which the contractor requires from the client;
8. A summary of project variations, separated into those which have been approved and those which are undergoing appraisal;
9. A summary of documents and correspondence communicated during the reporting period, highlighting as exceptions those which still have to be satisfactorily answered.

Project managers or their superiors should edit reports for clients carefully to ensure that the contents represent a true picture of the project progress. It is not necessary, obviously, to tell the client of every silly mistake made during design or manufacturing, provided that such mistakes are correctable within the time and cost constraints of the contract. The client must, however, never be misled or intentionally misinformed. If a problem is foreseen which poses a real threat to the timescale, to the budget, or to the technical performance of the finished project, then the client must be told. A client who is left to find out such problems by default will not feel that the project manager has acted to protect his best interests. The client should feel justified in asking how the contractor felt able to ask a fee for managing the project when, at best, there appears to have been no awareness of the problem and, at worst, deception.

REFERENCES AND FURTHER READING

Harrison, F.L., and Lock, D., 2004, *Advanced Project Management: a structured approach*, 4th edition, Aldershot : Gower.

Fleming, Q.W. and Koppelman, J.M., 2000, *Earned Value Project Management*, 2nd edition, Upper Darby, PA: Project Management Institute.

Lock, D., 2007, *Project Management*, 9th edition, Aldershot: Gower.

Rosenau, D.R. Jr., 1998, *Successful Project Management*, 3rd edition, New York: Wiley.

Webb, A., 2000, *Project Management for Successful Product Innovation*, Aldershot: Gower.

30 Project Closure and Aftermath

Mark O'Callaghan

As a long project nears its end there is a danger that energies will diminish at one of its most critical phases: close-out. The problem may be compounded if the project team are already thinking about the next project. Much of the good work carried out over the rest of the project can be undermined at this stage. Rodney Turner (1999, p329) warned, 'This is the second most critical stage of the project. Nobody remembers effective start-up, but everyone remembers ineffective close-out; the consequences are to be seen for a long time.' Yet the previous edition of this book contained no chapter devoted to this subject. This stage requires that all elements come together on the final project completion date. Maximum vigilance is required when, due to fatigue and other interests, the project team may not be at its most alert. There are four major phases in the process of closure:

- finishing the work
- handing over the project
- winding up project management
- project aftermath

Finishing the work is a continuation of the project until completion, whereas handing over the project can be regarded as a sub-project in itself. In addition, the project management process itself must be wound down during this period, (Figure 30.1). Finally, there should be an evaluation of the project and review of the lessons learned during it; parts of project aftermath.

The Project Manager is responsible for obtaining formal project acceptance from the project sponsor and/or users, presenting the final product and ensuring that the sponsor and/or users agree that the project has been completed to their satisfaction. The Project Manager should prepare a draft of the final project status report, documenting the completion of the project and any outstanding issues. The sponsor and any required users should carefully review the final status report and work with the project team to address issues that must be resolved before the product can be accepted. The Project Manager should update the final status

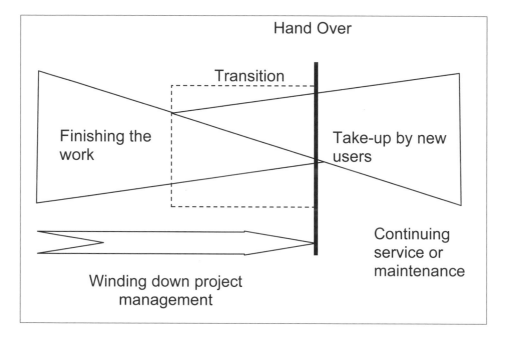

Figure 30.1 Project closure

report and obtain a formal sign-off from the project sponsor and any required users.

FINISHING THE WORK

IDENTIFYING WORK TO BE DONE

At some stage of the project there needs to be a plan about how the close-out of the project will occur. This usually arises out of a review meeting, but it must be planned in order for the close-out to be successful. The first stage of the close-out process is to identify what work remains to be carried out in order to complete the project. Close-out resembles the last half-an-hour before a major banquet is put on the table. All the separate elements have been prepared and are cooking separately, but there needs to be a check as to what needs to be done to ensure that they all arrive on the table at the same time. Adjustments may need to be made to some elements to assist in the timely delivery of the meal. A close-out planning meeting identifies what remains to be completed and who will be responsible for ensuring that it is done. Whilst some elements may be identified as a result of the review meetings, the transfer of the project is a new and separate sub-project. Rodney Turner (1999) recommends the use of checklists to help produce the lists of outstanding work.

PLANNING THE CLOSE-OUT

Once the work to be done has been identified, the plan for completion of the project and transfer should be drawn up with responsibilities assigned. The work needs to be planned with considerable detail to ensure that the project deadlines will be achieved. Given the possibilities of shortfalls in some of the project elements, additional resources may be required to assist completion. At this stage an inventory of resources available and those required should be carried out so that the suppliers and subcontractors can be informed of what is still needed and when contract will be closed. This is to ensure that sufficient resources will be available to finish the project without incurring unnecessary cost due to excess supplies. As part of this process the phasing out of the project team should be planned. Given the amount of work involved, especially in large projects, Rodney Turner (1999) recommended that a special task force be created to complete any outstanding work. In addition, he proposed that a deputy with finishing skills should support the project manager.

IMPLEMENTING THE CLOSE-OUT

Great flexibility is required during this stage in order that the project is completed successfully and additional resources may be required. Close-out has different effects on the three constraints of project management. Quality should have been maintained throughout the project, although during this last phase any lack of attention may give rise to problems. Whilst most of the overall budget has already been spent during the rest of the project, failure to achieve close-out can incur penalty costs if the project over-runs its completion date. Time is the most precious resource during this phase since as the completion date nears the opportunity to redress any shortfalls is extremely limited compared with other phases.

CONTROLLING THE CLOSE-OUT

Given the crucial nature of this phase more frequent meetings should be held, as at the start of the project. Count-down techniques together with checklists help manage the burden.

TRANSFERRING THE ASSET

Parallel with finishing the work is the process of transferring the project's product. Transition is rarely achieved on a single day. In long-term projects this transition phase can last months or years. For example, the new general hospital project in Malta has taken almost ten years in construction until the first occupation by its eventual users; there is a further transition of six years before the whole facility is fully completed and occupied. Clearly, such lengthy transition periods are unusual, but on other projects they can still involve weeks or months. During this stage both the deliverers of the project and the end users need to be involved.

PLANNING FOR THE TRANSITION

End users of the project should have been more heavily involved at the start of the project, especially during the planning process. They are then occasionally consulted during the implementation phase. During the final phase of the project they need to be more heavily involved again. The project team needs to ensure that the benefits that were envisaged by the project will occur. There is the possibility that while the needs of the project may not have altered, external or internal circumstances may have changed. For example, during a long hospital construction programme, changes in service delivery or policy (greater introduction of day surgery, or alterations in the configuration of accident and emergency services) may require modifications to the project. These cannot be made too early otherwise the project might become outdated before it is commissioned. Joint commissioning teams composed of members of the project team and end users can assist in the process of ensuring that the project delivers the benefits required.

IMPLEMENTING THE TRANSITION

Much of the work of this phase is directed towards ensuring that the project does meet the users' requirements.

SIGN OVER

This step involves agreeing the paperwork for the project. The first document that requires signing is the completion certificate that stipulates that the project has been completed to the appropriate specifications. The term 'appropriate' rather than 'original' is used to indicate that changes may have been agreed by both parties to ensure that the project meets the needs of the user. The latest details of the as-built design must be recorded to help the end-users make best use of the facility as well for legal requirements in case of problems. In addition to these plans, operating manuals should be prepared and discussed with the end users.

TRAINING

In complex projects the users may need training in how to use the facility or service. In some projects, which require cultural changes, this may be carried out in parallel with the construction of the facility. In the United Kingdom the perceived failure of 'Care in the Community' was because of the concentration on the 'bricks and mortar' issue of hospital closure and reprovision. In many instances there were little or no cultural or organizational changes that were needed to make the policy a success. The greater the cultural change, the more training and organizational development is required to achieve the goals of the project. For example, in Malta the construction of the new hospital was envisaged as part of widespread reforms in the health sector. Training and staff development as well as policy changes were all carried out at the same time as the new facility was being constructed. In other projects the training may just concentrate on how to use the facility or service as well as how to conduct basic maintenance.

HANDING OVER THE PROJECT

At some stage the project's product must be formally handed over to its owners. This is to ensure that payments are effected appropriately. It also delineates clear responsibility in terms of health and safety for the site for construction projects.

CONTINUING SERVICE OR MAINTENANCE OF THE FACILITY

Training, details of the as-built design and operating manuals may be sufficient to enable the end users to run the facility or service on a day-to-day basis. However, in more complex projects these may not be sufficient. In some cases the involvement of the organization responsible for delivery of the project does not end at hand-over, but continues afterwards in the form of maintenance or service agreements. Information Technology projects often involve such arrangements and these need to be clearly defined.

OBTAINING THE BENEFITS

Any transfer must ensure that what is expected from the enterprise is indeed realized and this is easier if at the start of the project there is a clear definition of the project's purpose and benefits (Turner 1999). As previously stated, there may be a tendency to concentrate on the easier, more visible or quantifiable, aspects of the project. It is easier to envisage a bathroom in a new hospital, for example, rather than what would happen in the case of an emergency at two o'clock on a Sunday morning. Many projects can only be judged as a success not when the new facility is constructed but when the new service is running smoothly.

If there is no adequate vision of the service to be provided then it will be difficult to measure project results. It once again depends on the definition of the project. In the case of 'Care in the Community' the measure of success was seen as the number of old psychiatric hospitals closed rather than the number of former patients successfully living in the community. The project could have been judged a success in terms of the original objectives set rather than the original need or purpose underlying it. Some projects can only be judged a success after many years. For example, changes in defence provision can only be really judged in the event of war or crises. Once again, the greater the cultural change associated with the project the harder it will be to measure the results and the longer it might take to reap the benefits.

As part of this process Rodney Turner (1999) suggests that an investigation be carried out to determine the differences between expected benefits and those obtained. He concentrates on measuring the revenue stream and profitability of the project. However, other variances between the expected and actual benefits should be examined. Gap analysis can help indicate whether expectations were too high or whether what was delivered did not conform to what was planned (Speller & Ghobadian 1993). As Rodney Turner suggests, it may be that the end user is not using the facility or service correctly. In projects involving cultural change this is more likely to happen. Such resistance can be unconscious but it can be deliberate, even extending to sabotage. In one reorganization of an orthopaedic facility involving complete refurbishment, the expected benefits of faster throughput were not obtained because it was not in the interests of staff concerned who were expected to work harder.

If there are any variances then action must be taken to overcome these. Given that projects are unique and a reflection of their original context, it would be hardly surprising if some modification were not required. Training or alterations in procedures may be required. As Turner (1999) noted, a further project may be required. He introduced the notion of the problem-cycle. There is a danger that staff in the new facility or service might regard the problem as solved once handover has been completed. Continuous monitoring of changes of the external and internal environment is required to ensure that the new service is altered to match them.

WINDING UP PROJECT MANAGEMENT

An important task of Close-out is to wind up project management. This is sometimes referred to as 'project wind-down'. The danger with using this latter term is that it might imply a slowing down of energy and motivation. Project wind up is a difficult task for a number of reasons. First, there are still many important tasks to be completed. Second, there is a danger that whilst winding up the project management team, the staff may have their attention focussed elsewhere. Finally, the process of closure, especially in long projects can be quite emotional and affect the project team adversely. The project team must be disbanded in an efficient manner but in such a way as to maintain their motivation. In the rush to work towards reprovision, members of the project team often have mixed and contradictory feelings towards the end of the project. On the one hand they look forward to the successful completion of a job well done, but on the other they may be concerned about their own futures. It can be described as 'turkeys waiting for Christmas'. Such feelings are natural and not ignored but taken into account. The project team will have undertaken new responsibilities and learnt different skills; these need to be valued and taken into consideration for their new career. The problem may be less severe if the project team have jobs to go to in the organization.

PLANNING THE WIND UP

The phasing of the project must allow for consideration of the project team itself. If the project team have new posts or are returning to former positions then this must be phased, so that they are able to see the project through to the end. A problem may arise if good project management members leave before the project is finished. In the case of psychiatric hospital reprovision, for example, good staff may be more likely to get jobs first and so leave before close-out. Given that the most challenging patients are usually left until last there is a danger that they will be left in the care of the less able staff. In such instances agreements should be reached to enable key staff to remain with the project until closure. Planning for staff dispersal should take place at least at the very initial stage of project close-out.

RETURNING PROJECT STAFF TO THEIR SUBSTANTIVE ROLES

Project staff must be allowed to move promptly to their post-project positions. This helps them be useful to the new service especially given their knowledge of the project. It also enables them to adjust to the change to life after the project.

HOLDING END OF PROJECT PARTY

Taking account of the psychological aspects of project management can greatly assist a project's success. Rodney Turner (1999) suggests holding of an end of project party for the staff. This can be extended in major projects by marking the achievement of crucial milestones by parties or events as part of the process of rewarding project staff as well as providing a psychological adjustment to the eventual end of the project. Inviting media to these events can give an opportunity to present a positive image of the project. If handled properly in politically sensitive projects, such as hospital reprovision, it can also help reduce any lingering opposition. A year after the hospital closure party at South Ockendon Hospital outside London, an anniversary party was held for staff and former residents to help them renew old acquaintances and adjust to the hospital closing.

HOLDING A DEBRIEFING MEETING

A debriefing meeting can serve practical, technical purposes as well as to allow staff to vent their feelings about the project. It helps complete the project cycle. In some instances these debriefing meetings can act as almost therapeutic encounters, especially in emotionally charged projects such as hospital reprovision. In addition, formal counselling for some project staff may even be necessary as they experience a form of bereavement process.

EVALUATING PROJECT STAFF

Project staff should be assessed as to their performance in project management both individually and as part of the team. Formal and informal appraisals give feedback on performance. With all the issues and problems the project team members may not be able to assess their own performance adequately. As a result motivation may be compromised. These help appraisals provide indications as to whether the appraisees should be involved in project management in the future as well as what they may need to improve their performance. The appraisal round also provides a forum for rewarding good performance as well as, if appropriate, disciplining underachievement. Given the difficulties of a major project it is all too easy to ignore or excuse underachievement or poor performance in the commotion of finishing the project. This sets a bad precedent for new projects.

PROJECT AFTERMATH

Traditional project cycles are usually described as a circle with a number of stages. Rodney Turner (1999), for example, provides a four-stage project life-cycle:

1. Proposal & Initiation   - Start
2. Design & Appraisal   - Plan
3. Execution & Control   - Do
4. Finalization & Close-Out   - End

The first of these starts the cycle and the last one completes it, (Figure 30.2). In reality project management is more like a spiral (Figure 30.3). The project arises out of a previous context and hands over to a new one. The experience of preceding projects enhances the present, which in turn should improve subsequent ones.

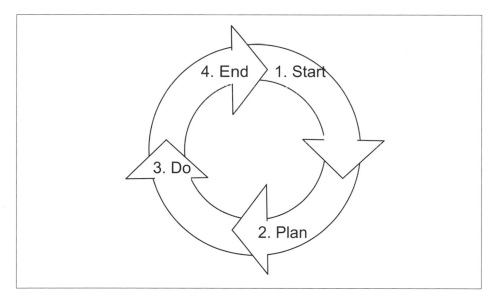

Figure 30.2   Traditional project life-cycle

Project Aftermath completes the project cycle and hands over to the next one. There are three sub-steps in Project Aftermath:

- Evaluating the Project
- Learning the Lessons
- Archiving the Project

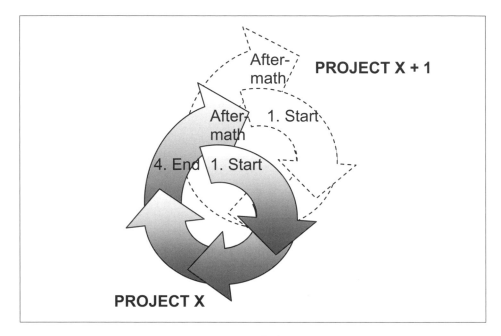

Figure 30.3   Project spiral

EVALUATING THE PROJECT

The Project Manager is responsible for preparing, conducting and distributing the project evaluation. Project Evaluation serves three purposes. First, it acts as an audit of the project and provides a record of what happened compared to what was supposed to happen. Second, it provides information about changes in project design. Finally, it helps in adjusting the project management process for future projects: the lessons learned. The Project Manager must first convene the Project Evaluation Meeting(s) and then prepare and distribute the Project Evaluation Report.

Project Evaluation Meeting(s)

The project manager organizes the meeting(s) at which all the project management team should be present as well as any key stakeholders and other important participants in the project management process. During the project's lifetime the project manager should ensure that recording of progress is carried out on a regular basis. Review meetings can provide much of the data for the final Project Meeting, although the final Close-out meeting will give the final status of the project.

Adequate preparation for the meeting(s) is essential since there is much information to be shared. Information from plans, maps, charts and Review

Meetings should be made available in advance of the meeting(s). The meeting needs to be well facilitated and may require the services of an interested but outside facilitator since the role of the project manager and the team will also be under scrutiny. There is a danger that the meeting could degenerate into one of finding fault, with the various parties blaming each other for any problems encountered during the project. For large projects more than one meeting may be necessary. The actual detail of the items to be discussed is presented in the next section.

The Project Evaluation Report

The Project Report provides a record of what happened against what was planned. It is important since it can provide a record for the future maintenance of the project. Records of alterations in building design as well as the underlying reasons for such changes will help architects or engineers know where, how and why to make any necessary adjustments in the future. Similarly recording changes in the non bricks and mortar issues of a health care project also helps future providers of health care maintain the system or care better for their patients. The project report helps to identify lessons for the future. As Rodney Turner (1999) has noted, 'Project management is fractal management' (p. 15). Therefore the overall project evaluation report should be composed of individual contributions from the various departments and functions that made up the project. The Project Report can be divided into three parts:

- Objectives
- Project Process
- Lessons Learned

The first of these enquires whether the project completed the circle, that is achieved what it was meant to accomplish. The second investigates the process of how this was accomplished. The third uses the experience of both to hand over to the next project.

OBJECTIVES

Evaluation of Overall Purpose and Objectives

The fundamental question underlining any project evaluation is whether the project met its overall purpose: to solve a problem or exploit an opportunity. Although it is useful to restate the original objectives, it should be remembered that these might have changed. There is a danger of confusing the achievement of goals with the achievement of purpose. A project may meet the original

637

specifications, but not the need underlying them. For example, a long-term project such as a new defence capability may reach its original technical goals, but fail to provide adequate protection given a changing world. This is where the concept of project management in the context of strategy is important. Adjustments in strategy arise out of changes to the external and internal environment. The project may also need to be altered in the light of such changes. The areas that should be covered are whether the project:

- delivered the benefits
- satisfied the (priority) stakeholders

At his workshops Rodney Turner asks four questions of the participants when preparing their project objectives:

1. What do you think is the last day of the project; when will it be finished?
2. On the last day of the project what will the project team deliver?
3. When the project team delivers that how will their success be judged?
4. Who gets to vote on questions 1, 2 and 3?

A related issue is whether the project satisfied those who were contracted to deliver the project: the project managers.

Evaluation of Constraints

The report should present an evaluation of the three major constraints of a project: time, quality and cost. For each of these the items or metrics for measuring the success of the project should be stated as well as the extent the project achieved these.

Time: In terms of time the report should present the project's performance against the original schedule. The original schedule together with the key milestones should be listed. It is helpful to present a visual display of the actual project plan against the original intention. This makes it easier to detect where overruns or shortages took place and their consequences on elements of the project as well as on the whole. Timing in terms of so many weeks or months late or early should be listed.

Quality: At the outset of the project certain specifications were established. These should be restated with any modifications and reasons for the changes. The items or metrics devised to measure quality should also be presented and how far the project managed to achieve them. This helps establish whether the time, cost and quality configuration was realistic. The Configuration Management Reviews should give an indication as to whether the original specifications were realistic or whether the project management process was at fault. Any adjustments should be recorded.

Costs: Projects are notorious for overrunning budgets, although there are limits to the extent that this is acceptable. The original budget should be presented and any modifications. The reasons for changes should be identified. The actual costs and expenditure limits should be presented against the original cost targets. Reasons for failure to achieve the targets should be presented or, if targets were achieved, what alterations had to be made to time or quality specifications. These should help in developing more accurate financial forecasts.

PROJECT PROCESS

Each stage of the project should be examined to compare what actually happened with what was planned. Recommendations for improvement should be made which will be carried over into Lessons Learned.

Project Planning

The planning of a project is often where problems develop during implementation. A description of the planning process should be stated together with what actually happened. Areas for examination involve:

Project planners

The report should identify who was responsible and who was involved and whether they were the right people.

Project plan

The report should have the formal written plan as an attachment, if there was one, with comments on whether it was sufficiently well defined and well communicated. An evaluation should be made on whether the plan was good enough for the project, whether it was realistic and whether there were any key elements missing. Details of any changes to the plan should be recorded as well as whether these were planned or evolved. The effects on the project (good as well as bad) should be noted.

Project Management

The roles and competence of the Project Manager and the Project Team should be recorded. Whether the team worked well together and with the stakeholders as well as with contractors. Communications within the team and with the

639

stakeholders as well as with contractors should be examined in terms of their timing and frequency, who was involved, what means were used, and if they were effective. Similarly, meetings within the team and with the stakeholders as well as with contractors should be examined in terms of their timing and frequency, who was involved, what means were used, and if they were effective. Details of the forms, charts and procedures used should be provided together with an assessment of how well they worked. The processes used for change control, quality and configuration management should all be examined.

Execution

The resources consumed should be noted as well as whether these were sufficient in terms of staffing numbers and skills as well as materials. The process for identifying, deciding, communicating and tracking changes should be stated and improvements noted.

Risk

The risks associated with the project were identified at the planning stage. These should be restated as well as whether they or others that had not been foreseen occurred and whether the actions taken to avoid, pass on or manage risks were successful.

Control

The project report should detail what control mechanisms were put in place for the project and whether they were effective.

LESSONS LEARNED

Whilst not strictly necessary for the project itself, identifying and recording lessons learned are important in improving the project design and project management process. These should be carried out throughout the project but may also be done as part of the final project evaluation phase. The lessons learned should indicate good points about the project (what went well and therefore should be retained) as well as points for improvement (what went wrong and should be avoided or managed better). Lessons Learned provide the double-loop learning necessary for project design and project process improvement.

Good Points: What Went Right

It is useful to identify and record in bullet-point form key things that went right with the project. It is helpful to provide concrete examples such as 'the weekly feedback forms were useful' rather than use generalizations such as 'the feedback system was good'. The Project Manager should identify any charts, forms or procedures that should be used again.

Points for Improvement: What Went Wrong

Similarly, it is useful to identify and record in bullet-point form key things that went wrong with the project. Once again it is helpful to provide concrete examples such as 'the monthly meetings between the project team and the stakeholders were unfocussed' rather than 'communication between the project team and the stakeholders was poor'. The Project Manager should identify any charts, forms or procedures that should not be used again or that should be modified. In addition, the non-easily quantifiable aspects of the projects that led to difficulties should also be recorded. However, rather than merely list the problems, the Project Manager should record the way the project team managed them as well as any successful solutions. In cases of failure an attempt should be made to suggest remedies.

Recommendations for the Future

From the lessons learned the project manager should record any recommendations that will be crucial for future projects of this size, complexity and type. These may be written under the various Project Management headings (such as Stakeholder Analysis, Project Risk Management).

There are a variety of ways to distribute the learned lessons, depending on the nature of the project. Commercial projects may wish to retain these within the project team so as not divulge information that may assist their competitors. Public projects may need to publicise the Lessons Learned especially in controversial issues. The closure programmes for hospitals in the United Kingdom received quite extensive publicity so that other institutions might learn from their mistakes. Distribution can be through reports, published articles or even conference talks or workshops. Publicising the Lessons Learned can be a form of advertising should this be needed.

ARCHIVING THE PROJECT

Once the project is over all its records need to be carefully archived. Apart from serving as an historical record as well as to help with successive projects, the archives may be needed in case there is a problem with the project in the future or for audit purposes. Whilst most documents may be handed over to the commissioners of the project, copies as well as some originals will be retained by the Project Team. In some instances various documents may be located elsewhere. For example, in the case of hospital closure in the United Kingdom,

641

certain records must be transferred to the local Public Records Office for storage for at least twenty years. The types of record that need to be archived naturally vary with the project but can include:

- original project plan
- original project specifications
- contract documents
- technical documents
- notes of Review and Evaluation Meetings
- project correspondence
- progress and status reports

REFERENCES AND FURTHER READING

Speller, S. and Ghobadian, A., 1993, 'Change for the public sector', *Managing Service Quality*, 5 (3), 29–32.

Turner, J.R., 1999, *The Handbook of Project Based Management,* 2nd edition, London: McGraw-Hill.

Part IV
People

INTRODUCTION TO PART IV

In Part Four, we consider the soft skills of project management, that is the management of the people. We consider Human Resource Management in the project-based organization and competence development, both of the people and of the organization. We consider many issues associated with the management of the people on the project team, and other stakeholders. We describe how to make effective teams, and the role of the manager as leader. We consider the stakeholders, how to communicate with them, and the management of conflict that can arise. We also describe the impact of different cultures, and ethical standards of project managers.

CHAPTER 31: MANAGING HUMAN RESOURCES IN THE PROJECT-BASED ORGANIZATION

In Chapter 31, Anne Keegan, Martina Huemann and I describe how the management of human resources differs in a project-based organization from the old functional, hierarchical, line management organization. We identify that new HRM practices are required specific to the project, including assignment of people to the project, appraisal, development and reward of people in the project, and dispersement of people from the project. We also show that the parent organization needs to adapt the standard processes of selection, appraisal, development reward and release to deal with the temporary nature of the work processes and the dynamic nature of the work environment associated with project-based working.

CHAPTER 32: DEVELOPING INDIVIDUAL COMPETENCE

In chapter 32, Lynn Crawford explains how to develop the project management competence of individuals. She describes how competence and its components

645

are defined, the standards that exist for the assessment and development of project management competence, how assessment can be used in the development of project management competence, and what approaches are used by organizations for assessing and developing competence.

CHAPTER 33: DEVELOPING PROJECT MANAGEMENT CAPABILITY OF ORGANIZATIONS

In Chapter 33, Lynn Crawford and Rodney Turner describe how to develop the project management capability of organizations. First they describe why organizational project management capability is important, and its components. Then they explain how an organization can use innovative practices to improve its enterprise-wide project management capability.

CHAPTER 34: MANAGING TEAMS: THE REALITY OF LIFE

In Chapter 34, Tony Reid describes the management of project teams, and how to make high performing teams. He gives practical guidelines on the development of high performing teams, and describes several other techniques for improving their performance.

CHAPTER 35: LEADERSHIP

In Chapter 35, David Partington considers the leadership role of the project manager, whether there is a difference between managing and leading, and whether leadership is something which can be learnt. Certainly good leaders can make themselves better by improving on the behaviours that work, and to that end David sets out some of the theories of leadership. He describes trait and behavioural theories (two one size-fits-all theories), and contingency and visionary theories (two situational approaches).

CHAPTER 36: MANAGING STAKEHOLDERS

Stakeholders are all the people who have an interest in the outcome of the project. Some can be for you, some against. In Chapter 36, Bill McElroy and Chris Mills describe how to manage the project's stakeholders. They describe a stakeholder management process and gives hints and tips.

CHAPTER 37: MANAGING COMMUNICATION

In Chapter 37 Ralf Müller describes how people communicate and how to develop a strategy for project stakeholder communication. He presents communication as a five layer model, from motivation, through interpretation, understanding, choice of frequency and media, up to the transfer of messages from sender to receiver. Subsequently a process for managing communication is introduced, which describes the identification of stakeholders' communication needs, development of communication strategy, matrix and schedule, as well as implementation and control. Finally typical practices are described for communication between project manager and sponsor, in different cultures, or in virtual teams.

CHAPTER 38: MANAGING CONFLICT

Sometimes the stakeholders will be just plain difficult, or they may have a truly different opinion of the project from other members of the team. That can lead to conflict. In Chapter 38, Bob Graham describes the management of conflict. He describes how to avoid conflict, and resolve it if it occurs. He also describes the power of information in avoiding conflict, and a strategy for a project information system as a tool, to avoid conflict.

CHAPTER 39: MANAGING CULTURE

Parties to a project can come from a range of backgrounds, from different professions, or different countries. Their different backgrounds can lead to different cultural traditions. In Chapter 39, David Rees describes the impact of culture on business and how it can be managed.

CHAPTER 40: MANAGING ETHICS

Finally, in Chapter 40, Alistair Godbold describes business ethics, particularly as they relate to projects. Evidence shows that in the long run, it is better to behave ethically, as in the long run it leads to better performance of your business. Alistair describes different ethical approaches, how they differ around the world, and offers some practical tips.

Managing Human Resources in the Project-based Organization

31

Anne Keegan, Rodney Turner and Martina Huemann

This handbook is based on the premise that we live in a world in which projects and multi-disciplinary working are key vehicles for delivering corporate strategy, (Chapter 2), and the increasing use of projects over the last forty years reflects rapid change in the nature of markets and technologies (Gareis 2005). Projects are spreading from their traditional strongholds of construction, aerospace and shipbuilding to all kinds of industries including the software, insurance, banking and education industries. All industries are now benefiting from project-based working. The widespread use of projects as a way of organizing work has managerial implications for organizations embracing it in areas such as governance and operational control (Turner and Keegan 2001), and the management of knowledge and learning (Love et al 2004). It also impacts directly on the human resource practices of organizations. Every time a new project starts, or an old one ends, the human configuration of the organization must change, demanding adaptability and flexibility from employees and managers.

Human resource management (hereafter called HRM), has a long and distinguished history stretching back more than eighty years. However, up until the early 1980s, the industrial scene was characterized largely by manufacturing firms organized along bureaucratic lines and managed through functional hierarchies carrying out operations which were stable and routine by design. This model dominated HRM thinking, with prescriptive models that put the organization's interests ahead of the individual's (Fombrun et al 1984).

In recent years, researchers have investigated new concepts in HRM applicable to different branches of industry and in different types of organization, (see Flood et al 1996). In the last thirty years, the introduction of new technologies and materials led to a huge increase in innovation in industry. The scope of activities

649

undertaken by firms has widened considerably as firms have sought to respond to changing consumer preferences. Innovation has become a normal part of business activity, a pre-requisite to survival instead of a fancy addition. Projects are frequently established to carry on this novel work. In the beginning these projects were isolated from operations and designed to produce something outside the normal stream of work (Burns and Stalker 1961), but now many organizations are perceiving themselves as project-oriented and adopting that as their normal way of working.

Unlike operations, projects are transient. Unlike operations, projects are always novel and therefore, to varying degrees, unpredictable in their outcomes (Turner 1999; Gareis 2005). Operations set the status quo and rely on its being maintained for their survival while projects upset the status quo because they are unique, novel and transient. And unlike many operations that are capital intensive and rely on standardised skills, projects are heavily dependent on the specific human inputs in the form of project team members who bring skills together in unpredictable ways. A cursory reading of recent management literature reveals that projects are no longer the isolated entities they once were. They are no longer the skunk works placed discreetly in the parking lot, or the odd group of researchers working alone in an office far from normal workers and normal activities. Projects now pervade most organizations and are accepted as a regular feature of doing business. In many cases, projects are the core activity of organizations and the centre of value added activity.

The HRM literature argues that all organizations should align their HRM practices with organizational strategy (Lengnick-Hall and Lengnick-Hall 1998), and so if an organization chooses to be project-oriented, it should adopt HRM practices and processes that support that choice. Our work shows that project-based organizations need to adopt new HRM practices and processes to deal with the temporary organizations that are projects that they create to undertake their work, and different HRM practices to deal with the associated dynamic environment. In this chapter we describe HRM practices and processes we have observed used for managing people in project-based organizations. We start by defining the project-based or project-oriented organization, and explore the nature of the work environment in such organizations that creates the need for new and different HRM practices and processes. We then describe the new HRM practices required to deal with the temporary organization that is the project, and the different HRM practices required to address the dynamic work environment that project-based working creates. We are also concerned about the ethical treatment of employees in project-oriented organizations, and so we also consider the issues there, and how project-based firms can address them.

HRM CHALLENGES IN THE PROJECT-BASED COMPANY

In essence, what defines a company as project-oriented is that it perceives itself as being project-oriented and shapes its policies and practices for working, for organizational culture and for strategy towards the challenge presented by management by projects. Turner and Keegan (2001) defined a project-based company as one in which

> the majority of products made or services delivered are against bespoke designs for customers.

This implies that it is project-based perforce because of the customized nature of the demand from their customers. Martina Huemann and the Austrian school (Gareis 2005) suggest that the project-oriented organization is such by choice. The project-oriented organization is one which:

1. defines *'management by projects'* as their organizational strategy
2. applies projects and programmes for the performance of complex processes
3. manages a project portfolio of different internal and external project types
4. has specific permanent organizations like a project portfolio group or a project office to provide integrative functions
5. views the organization as being project-oriented

In reality both these views are different perspectives of the same idea. No organization is purely project-based or purely routine. All organizations lie on a spectrum between the two extremes, but many organizations, usually towards the project-based end of the spectrum, make the strategic choice to be project-oriented because it suits the nature of their business and gives them competitive advantage. Project-oriented organizations need to adopt HRM practices which support this strategic choice, and so we need to understand the specific pressures they face which create the need for new and different forms of HRM. These are summarized in Figure 31.1.

TEMPORARY WORK PROCESSES

Project-oriented organizations use projects and programmes to perform work. Projects and programmes are temporary organizations, (Chapter 5). Every time a new project or programme starts or an old one finishes the human resource configuration of the parent organization changes. Thus not only will the organization require HRM practices in the parent organization, Figure 31.2a; it will need to apply practices specific to the temporary organization that is the project, Figure 31.2b. This creates the need for new HRM practices like assigning personnel to projects, assessing, developing and rewarding their work on

Specific features of the project-oriented company	HRM challenges
Temporary nature of projects	<ul><li>The HRM configuration of the organization changes every time a project starts or finishes</li><li>Appraisal, development and reward need to be linked to projects</li><li>Project assignments need to be linked to career development</li></ul>
Dynamic work environment	<ul><li>Future resource requirements difficult to predict</li><li>Temporary workers are employed to respond to fluctuating resource demands</li><li>Individual workloads can peak as project demands peak together, or clients make unexpected demands</li></ul>
Project-portfolio resource and role demands	<ul><li>Different and conflicting role demands</li><li>There is a need for HRM practices to assign people to several projects simultaneously, and to smooth the demands between projects</li><li>Individual workloads can peak as project demands peak together</li></ul>
Specific management culture and management paradigm	<ul><li>A clearly adopted project management culture as a strategic choice</li><li>Staff require specific competencies for working in this environment</li><li>This may require new and different training structures</li></ul>
Employee well-being	<ul><li>Employee well-being marginalized as client and project needs take priority</li><li>Individuals uncertain about their future work assignments and the colleagues they will work with.</li><li>Project assignments need to be linked to career development</li></ul>

Figure 31.1   HRM challenges in the project-based company

projects, dispersing them on project completion, and linking project assignments to careers. These practices will need to be applied every time a project or programme starts or finishes, Figure 31.2b.

DYNAMIC WORK ENVIRONMENT

The temporary nature of the work creates dynamic work boundaries and contexts. The number and size of projects performed constantly changes, making

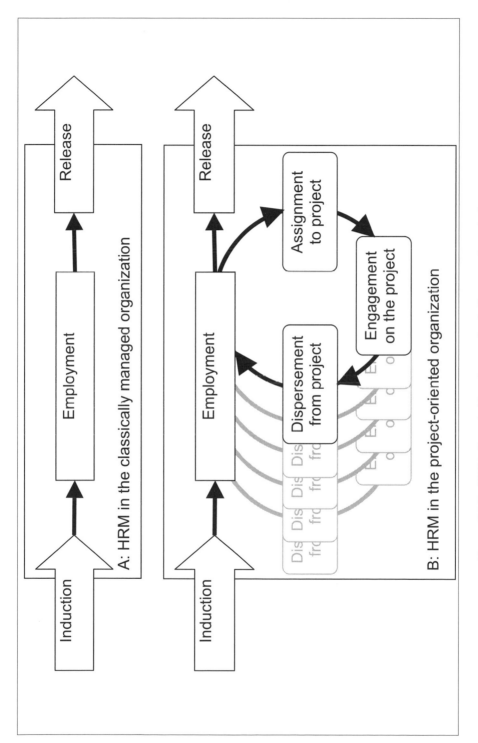

Figure 31.2 HRM in the project-based versus classically managed organization

A: HRM in the classically managed organization

Induction — Employment — Release

B: HRM in the project-oriented organization

Induction — Employment — Release

Assignment to project

Engagement on the project

Dispersement from project

predictions of future resource requirements difficult. Many organizations respond to the fluctuating resource demands by employing temporary workers, (Keegan and Turner 2003). In a dynamic environment in which the HR configuration is constantly changing, the challenge of ensuring employee well-being is important. In this environment, individual workloads can peak as project workloads peak together. When the demands of clients for immediate organizational response become felt in the project, there may be a requirement for HRM practices to guide the response and ensure that employees are not confronted with excessive levels of stress, and demands for working long hours.

PROJECT-PORTFOLIO RESOURCE AND ROLE DEMANDS

At any time a project-oriented organization holds a portfolio of internal and external projects (Chapter 3). A person can work in different projects and different project roles at the same time. In one project he or she may be a project manager, in another a project team member or sponsor. Or a person can simultaneously carry a role in a project and one in the permanent organization. The organization also needs HRM practices to assign people to several projects or programmes simultaneously, and to smooth the demands between projects and programmes.

SPECIFIC MANAGEMENT PARADIGM

The ideal POC has a specific management culture expressed in the empowerment of employees, process-orientation and teamwork, continuous and discontinuous organizational change, customer-orientation, and networking with clients and suppliers (Gareis 2005). Therefore specific competences and skills are needed by the project personnel to successfully work together in projects. This may require project-oriented organizations to adopt training and development practices to develop employees capable of working in the project environment, which in turn may require them to adopt specific HRM practices in these areas matched to the management paradigm adopted.

WELL-BEING OF EMPLOYEES

In the dynamic work environment where the HR configuration is constantly changing, the challenges of ensuring employee well-being and ethical treatment are important but may be overlooked. The temporary nature of the work and the dynamic nature of the work environment can create specific pressures on employees. These may include the following:

Achieving a work life balance

Employees can find it difficult balancing their workload in the face of peaks in project work, especially against unpredictable demands from customers. This in turn creates problems in managing their work-life balance. Recent case studies have shown that companies have problems in grasping the work and emotional situation of the individual and multi role assignments that may lead to burn out for younger employees, or in managing the damaging consequences of role overload and role conflict.

Uncertainty of future work assignments

It is also likely that temporary projects bring a degree of uncertainty for employees who cannot be sure what kinds of projects they will be assigned to or what kinds of colleagues they will work with. Noe et al (2004) suggest that both tasks and roles, and managers and co-workers, are core aspects of employee work experience. From an organizational and managerial perspective, failure to address the role conflict of project work may damage efforts to retain workers as both can cause job dissatisfaction and in extreme cases physical, psychological and behavioural withdrawal and voluntary turnover.

Linking project assignments to career development

Finally there is a need to link project assignments to career development, both from an organizational and individual perspective. The organization needs to develop staff for its future projects, but if staff members do not feel that their project assignments offer them the development opportunities they aspire to, they may look elsewhere.

We have seen that when it comes to considering the effects of HRM polices and practices, the organizational or managerial perspective dominates and the effect on individual employees can be marginalized. Failure to consider the specific requirements of HRM in project-oriented companies may mean theorists overlook these issues, and fail to consider the effects, positive and negative, of project-oriented work practices on individuals. However, we have also observed that project work does seem to be inherently more interesting than routine work. Project-oriented companies have greater success in retaining their employees doing project work than those doing routine work.

Against this background we have found that project-oriented organizations need to adopt new HRM practices and processes to deal with the HR issues on the temporary organizations that are projects and programmes, and they need to adapt HRM practices and processes to deal with the dynamic work environment. We discuss each of these in turn. We also consider what project-oriented organizations do to help employees manage their work-life balance.

HRM PRACTICES FOR THE PROJECT-BASED COMPANY

We would expect the HRM practices and processes required by any organization would include the following, (Fombrun et al 1984):

- induction into the organization
- appraisal of performance
- assessment of competence
- development in the current role and for the next role
- reward for performance and competence
- release from the organization

As we have seen, Figure 31.2, in the project-oriented organization these need to be applied both within the parent organization, and specifically to the temporary organizations that are projects and programmes, Figure 31.3.

ADDITIONAL PRACTICES SPECIFIC TO PROJECTS AND PROGRAMMES

The project-oriented organization requires the following additional HRM practices applied specifically to its projects and programmes, Figure 31.4.

ASSIGNMENT TO THE PROJECT

This is the process of assigning project personnel (programme and project managers, and team members) to new projects and programmes. It is similar to recruitment of people to the parent organization, but has substantial differences, even when appointing external contractors to be peripheral workers on a project. The assignment processes usually start in the parent organization, often managed by the project sponsor and perhaps also the steward (Chapter 15), but then are taken over by the project manager. We have observed different methods adopted depending on the nature and size of projects being undertaken.

In companies with very large projects, the assignment of personnel to projects may be planned as part of the annual budgeting cycle. At the start of the project, a small project team will be created, but the project is of such duration that the resource requirements can be predicted over several years, and incorporated into the annual resource plans for the parent organization. Which people are actually assigned to the project when they are required can be determined by negotiation between the project manager and resource manager, taking account of:

- the competencies required
- the organization's need to develop people
- the individual's career aspirations

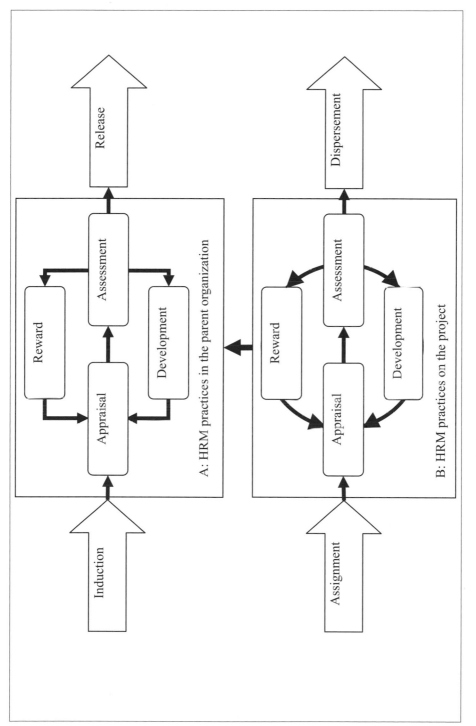

Figure 31.3 HRM practices in the parent organization and on the project

A: HRM practices in the parent organization

B: HRM practices on the project

▪ Assignment to projects	Usually managed by negotiation between project and line Companies with large projects manage through the annual budgeting cycle Few companies have company-wide resource planning tool Assignment to account for individual career development needs
▪ Appraisal, assessment, development, reward	Project appraisals are conducted in most organizations, and some require them at project milestones Sometimes they are conducted only in response to the need for the routine appraisal in the line In most organizations project appraisals are used as input to routine appraisal in the line Project start methods to include team building and briefing Knowledge transfer is necessary as team members need briefing on the designs, plans and technology of the project Project specific training rare, except as part of project induction Project specific rewards are rare
▪ Dispersement from projects	In organizations with very small projects dispersement is not necessary as people are working on several projects simultaneously In organizations with large projects, this is planned as part of the annual budgeting cycle In organizations with medium sized projects dispersement is necessary to manage the transition from one project to another or return to the line In companies aiming to maximize utilization employees may be responsible for reassigning themselves Under dispersement a project team member may be: 1. immediately assigned to a new project 2. held in abeyance for a project about to start where his or her skills are needed 3. sent on training 4. given development work

Figure 31.4   Additional HRM practices adopted specific to the project

For organizations undertaking shorter projects, particularly against unpredictable client requirements, assignment needs to be more ad-hoc. The organization will retain a pool of potential project personnel, and assign people from that pool at the start of a project. A list of criteria similar to the above will be used, but an individual's availability will now also need to be considered more carefully. On very small projects, the entire project team, including the project manager may be appointed by negotiation between the project sponsor, the steward and resource managers. This will particularly be the case where the project is part of a programme, and the steward role is fulfilled by the programme manager. On larger projects, the project manager will be appointed, and he or she will determine additional resource requirements, and obtain them by negotiation with resource managers. A very small number of organizations have a company resource plan, to track staff competence and availability and their and the organization's development needs, for use at project assignment.

If there are insufficient people within the pool of project personnel to staff current projects, then it may be necessary to use peripheral or freelance workers. Many organizations find this is the only way to deal with the fluctuating resource demands. Anne Keegan and Rodney Turner (2001) reported that companies from both the high-tech and engineering industries typically are using between 20% and 40% of peripheral workers at any one time, and even had one client who was using 80% of peripheral workers. Many organizations have a pool of people who regularly work for them, like the pool of internal staff. Others need to recruit peripheral workers to work on new projects, and that has to be handled as part of the recruitment practices within the parent organization, but takes much longer.

Two key criteria when assigning staff to projects are their and the organization's development needs. This does need to be taken account of. The issue keeps arising where an individual has an identified development need and a project starts that would satisfy that need but he or she is currently working on another project. Are such people taken off their current projects, or do they miss the development opportunity? Enlightened organizations will move them for at least two reasons:

- the organization wants to develop people of appropriate competences for its projects and so wants to maximize opportunities
- if people feel their development needs are being ignored they will look for them elsewhere

HRM PRACTICES ON THE PROJECT

Organizations may also need to apply HRM practices on the project, delegating responsibility to the project manager.

Appraisal on the project

Most organizations require some form of appraisal on the project. Usually this is conducted at the time of the regular performance appraisal in the parent organization. The project manager is asked to conduct appraisals of project team members and the information is given to the line or resource manager who uses it as part of the main appraisal. Some organizations conduct 360° appraisals, and so seek information from project managers, the client or sponsor, and other project team members. Some organizations require project appraisals to be conducted at key project milestones, particularly project completion. Such appraisals are then gathered and used as part of the main appraisal. This is usually done where the duration of projects is shorter than the appraisal cycle in the line and they wish to gather information from all projects the individual has worked on. Finally, in organizations undertaking very large projects the responsibility for the main appraisal is transferred to the project manager. This usually only happens if the duration of projects is typically longer than one year. In one organization we talked to, people could not be seconded onto projects lasting more than one year, they had to be transferred, and the project manager became their line manager for the duration of the project.

Competence assessment on the project

Competence assessment on the project is rare, except as part of appraisal as described above. A person's competence to work on a project will be shown as part of the assignment. However, on longer projects, or complex projects, competence assessment may be necessary as the project develops in ways that were not foreseen at initiation, to determine whether the current project team members are still the best people for the job, and whether they need any project specific training for the project as it moves on. A project audit (Chapter 11) may identify the need for further development of the competence of project staff.

Development on the project

As we have seen, projects are often viewed as important steps in the development of an individual's experience. Organizations need to develop individuals with the competence necessary to perform current and future projects. As part of the annual appraisal cycle, the line manager and the individual together need to be assessing the individual's development aspirations, and identifying what sort of projects will provide the appropriate experience. Some organizations supplement that with career development structures. Turner et al (2003) report that companies in the engineering industry often have career committees with the responsibility for forecasting the future needs of projects and formulating development plans for the current pool of project staff. This may be done as part of the knowledge management practices through the project management community practice (Chapter 33), or by making it the responsibility of the project office (Chapter 9).

Project specific training for competence development is not uncommon. For instance people may need cultural or language training for an overseas assignment, or, as we saw above, they may need training if the project develops in unexpected ways. Some organizations pay for this training out of the project budget. Other organizations insist all training is paid for by the line and the project manager needs to negotiate with the line manager for the release of monies for training.

Project specific training which is necessary on every project is not for the development of competence, but for the induction of project team members into the project, and for briefing them about the current state of the project, and about any specific technologies that may be required. This will usually be done as part of the project start process (Chapter 26). This form of project specific training can sometimes be a bottleneck to the rate at which a project team can be ramped up. We worked with one company with a client who wanted the project team on an out sourcing assignment increased from 32 to 96 people in the space of two weeks. But the contracting company felt they could not induct more than 8 people per week and maintain quality, so it would take eight weeks to ramp up the project team.

Reward on the project

Again reward in the form of pay and rations is usually done as part of the line. If a bonus is due for good project performance that will be paid by the line organization. However, most organizations will allow project managers to make small gifts to project team members to reward them for project progress, particularly in the form of social events, or project mementos (containing the project name, Chapter 34). A very small number of organizations do allow the project manager to make a monetary award, especially on larger projects.

DISPERSEMENT FROM THE PROJECT

This is a process whose need is not widely recognized in the literature on projects or on HRM. It has similarities to, but also substantial differences from, the release from the parent organization. At this point the organization needs to decide whether the employee will be:

- immediately assigned to a new project
- assigned to a project starting sometime in the future where their skills will be better used
- held in abeyance because there is no project for them to be assigned to, (colloquially called 'sitting on the bench', from the sporting analogy)
- released from the organization in the case of temporary or peripheral workers

What we have observed is that dispersement is only an issue in organizations undertaking medium-sized projects. In organizations doing small projects, people tend to be working on several projects at once. Thus their workload is made up of a steady stream of projects, with old ones ending and new ones starting on an almost continuous basis. In organizations undertaking large projects lasting several years, then, as we saw above, peoples' assignment to projects is planned as part of the annual budgeting cycle. So their transferral from one project to another, or from a project back to the line, is planned in the annual corporate plan.

Thus dispersement is only an issue in organizations where people usually only work on one project at a time, and the typical project duration is a few months. As a project comes to an end, the organization needs to decide if the project team members have projects they can be immediately assigned to. If they do not, they can do one of several things:

- sit on the bench
- attend training or other personal development
- be assigned to do technical or process development

One company we have worked with gave an example of a project team member on a project that was about to finish who had a specific skill that was needed on a project that was going to start in two weeks time. They did not want to assign him to a project that was about to start because he would not be so effectively used there. So they used him in development work for two weeks. A similar situation could arise if you had identified that somebody needed a particular project experience for him or her career development and an appropriate project was going to be starting in two or three weeks time. Again it might be better to leave him or her sitting on the bench for that time rather than assigning them to a less appropriate project. Several consultancy companies we have worked with make dispersement the responsibility of the individual. Individuals are judged in their appraisals on their rate utilization, and so the responsibility for finding their next assignment is put on the individual.

It is at the end of a project that core workers are most vulnerable to leaving the organization, especially if faced with a period of sitting on the bench. At the end of the project, core workers should be debriefed about their experiences and counselled about the future. This period is one in which we might expect project personnel to be more anxious, and having practices in place to recognize and manage that is clearly important for both individual and organizational wellbeing. The choices made about what to do with project personnel at the end of the project need to be made in consultation with them to ensure employee well-being and procedural fairness in project allocation decisions, and from an organizational perspective to avoid valued personnel leaving. Peripheral workers also need to be counselled and debriefed. If they have performed well, the organization may like to retain them. The organization can advise them on training, even involve them in training, invite them to attend social activities, and work at keeping them with the network of potential peripheral workers.

Capturing learning in project close-out

Turner et al (2003) have also identified the need to capture knowledge during but particularly at the end of projects. As temporary organizations, projects come to an end, and if the learning from the project is not captured by the end, it is lost forever. It is especially important in the case of peripheral workers who may be released from the project at the end of the project that their learning is captured for the parent organization. This should be made part of the knowledge management practices (Chapter 33).

Many firms try to use project standards, reviews and project close-out as opportunities to capture learning. The idea is that people recall what they have learnt during a project and share this with others. On project standards and project reviews, there is overwhelming evidence that project members, in general, neglect this responsibility. This means that improvements made during the project are often lost. Time pressures at the end of projects often preclude the effective writing up of lessons learned or even face to face review between project team members or their colleagues. This is rendered even more difficult because at the end of projects, the energy of project team members is at its lowest level. This is why if people have a gap between one project ending and the next starting it can be useful to engage them in development work rather than sitting idly on the bench. Some firms call into question the usefulness of project end review processes because of the argument that technical knowledge changes so much that an end project wrap up is often not adequate.

Despite all this, firms are also adamant that operating amidst a largely project environment requires special attention to be paid to capturing the advances made by people on projects and ensuring the knowledge is less transient than the projects from which it emerged. To overcome these difficulties, some firms place formal processes for capturing learning on a corporate basis and hand responsibility for that to groups not directly involved with projects on an operational basis. An ICT vendor we have worked with has *centres of excellence* working to develop best practices internationally. This helps to explain why local offices have been able to move towards a fully project-based way of working. The loss of functions as repositories of knowledge is ameliorated by corporate-wide efforts to nurture learning and develop excellence in strategic areas. Learning and knowledge sharing, although vital for the success of project-based firms, are among the thorniest issues managers and employees deal with. Practical suggestions include:

1. The continued use of practices which capture and share knowledge, including project review procedures and project standards used as broad but flexible guidelines

2. The strengthening of informal networks and opportunities for 'talk' within the company
3. Greater attention paid to giving personnel the basic resource they need to capture and record their own learning for the purposes of externalization and socialization – people given time within the lifespan, and at the closedown, of projects
4. And finally, the maintenance of functions as centres of excellence, or the creation of corporate wide resources to ensure that learning is developed within and between parts of the organization on strategic issues

Lynn Crawford and Rodney Turner deal with learning and knowledge management further in Chapter 33.

DIFFERENT PRACTICES WITHIN THE PARENT ORGANIZATION

Project-based organizations also need to apply some of the standard HRM practices differently to cope with the dynamic work environment, Figure 31.5.

HRM Practices	Methods used
Induction	Organic selection methods are used by many companies Many firms have high levels of contract staff. 20% to 40% is typical People may be offered a position initially as contract staff, but retained if their face fits Recruitment agencies do not understand the nature of projects so their recommendations need to be treated with caution
Appraisal, assessment, development and reward	The spiral staircase career is evident with people being given experience in a range of job roles People are rewarded according to the amount of risk they manage Career development objectives need to identify project experiences required Training needs to train people for project work, and this may require different approaches than training for other functions
Release	Knowledge management practices need to capture learning from temporary workers leaving the company on project completion Some companies maintain a network of temporary workers who return to work on future projects They need to be debriefed on leaving the company on completion of one project to assess their appreciation of working for the company and identify their desire to return

Figure 31.5 HRM practices adapted to meet the needs of the project-based company

INDUCTION INTO THE PARENT ORGANIZATION

The selection of people is a major issue for project-based firms. Differences in selection practices are evident according to whether the skills and knowledge of potential employees are core to the firm and not easily substituted or peripheral and easily found on the labour market. In many areas of project work, particularly traditional areas such as engineering and construction, employees are substitutable with standard skills acquired through relatively short training. For example, several categories of construction worker and administrative, security and catering personnel can be considered here. Project-based firms often utilize these workers on a contract by contract basis or outsource this work to specialist service providers. In these industries, project management is the key core competence. In other areas, particularly high technology industries, employees are far less substitutable and constitute the core competence. Programmers in proprietary technologies, project managers and client liaison personnel are three of the categories of personnel less easily substitutable in the short or even medium term and who represent key contributors to value added. Where employees are potentially core members of the firm, more time is taken to ensure they are going to 'fit in' with the turbulent nature of project work. Selection of core staff – including technical experts and particularly project managers, leaders and supervisors – is conducted in a highly organic manner, meaning that emphasis is placed on informal methods of assessing people for employment. The main practices used for selecting people to work for a project-based organization differ quite markedly from the functional, hierarchical organization, and include:

- the use of headhunting both directly and through agencies
- the use of personal contacts and 'the grapevine' in finding prospective employees
- the hiring of personnel on project trials and work experiences
- liaison with personnel at universities and technical schools, often for many years

The goal of selection: the right people at the right time?

In project-based firms, we often observe informal selection practices. That is, companies have informal practices for managing selection, as shown in the list above. For most of the firms we have observed, finding *the right people at the right time* is not the most important goal when it comes to selecting personnel. People we have spoken to are on the whole cautious about the precision that can be attained in a transient client led environment with respect to what it means to find *the right people*, and how sustainable such a definition might be. They indicate a more open attitude towards finding suitable candidates for their organizations, and lay emphasis on the importance of supporting those people to grow with the organization, and change as it changes. They tend to avoid go/no go decisions in selection and emphasize selection by project, trial and work experience. Specific skills and knowledge sets are not as important as the adaptability of people to the changing environment within project-based firms, and the willingness of organizational members to adapt as projects change and clients demand new approaches. Most of the firms we have observed avoid the use of selection tests in hiring decisions. They argue that decisions based on observing people at work, over time, and in interaction with colleagues and clients, are far more valuable than a go/no go decision strategy based on once-off selection and assessment exercises.

Project-based firms as flexible firms

In addition to hiring people 'gradually' through projects and trials, most firms we have observed use contracting as a way of coping with qualitative and quantitative uncertainties in their business. This is a type of selection for the short term. In a major engineering and construction contractor in the process plant industry, estimates of temporary employees range from 20% to 40% depending on the workload. A supplier of bespoke systems to the telecommunications industry estimates that at least one third of personnel, including project personnel, are employed on temporary contracts to work on projects. Similar estimates were given for the other organizations we have visited. This mirrors the ideas of free-lances and core peripheral workers. In both these models, the use of contract labour is a central feature. Numerical flexibility can also be attained by the increased use of part-time labour. As a twist on this theme, we have observed evidence of *more than fulltime* labour usage as distinct from 'part-time' labour usage as a strategy to cope with uneven workloads of projects.

One implication of the use of high levels of contract labour in project-based firms is the importance of melding disparate groups of temporary and permanent employees into effective project teams. The successful achievement of this depends largely on how successful employees and managers are at coping with the disintegrative tendencies of project work, and whether they display an emotional adaptability to new faces, new leaders, new colleagues and new conditions. Many firms use this as a strong indication of whether a new member will contribute to their organization, or whether the relationship should be terminated early. In many companies, there is a pattern of newcomers leaving early in their probationary periods, whereas those with whom the company forges a stronger connection tend to stay for a long time. Although flexibility can be attained by surrounding a core of workers with a more flexible and dispensable periphery, the benefits may be illusory given the disenchantment of those in the periphery and attendant costs of training, selection and specialization required to maintain such an arrangement. However, project workers, especially those in the construction and oil, gas and petrochemical industries, have always worked in a transient environment. Project-based firms are transient firms because projects have a finite lifespan.

The potential difficulties of project-based ways of working are more relevant for those sectors experiencing a greater demand for innovation and higher levels of complexity. Resolving the tension of project-based work in terms of transience of employment is already a focal point for firms we have visited in the government and financial services sectors. In particular, the question of how to combine the machine bureaucracy with project-based ways of working remains a taxing issue. For those firms where this is relevant, there is an emphasis on instituting culture change, training and socialization programmes to make the transition to a transient environment of project work easier for all.

HRM PRACTICES IN THE PARENT ORGANIZATION

Development

One of the clearest results from our work in project-based firms is the rapidly changing nature of career development and career profiles. Project-based firms in established industries such as engineering and construction are accustomed to shorter term careers and the mobility of personnel. Organizations who have more recently adopted projects as an important form of operational control are faced with the reality that lifetime and long-term employment patterns are increasingly a thing of the past. Bastions of long-term employment such as universities and the civil service, as well as specific organizations like Phillips, Shell and Hewlett Packard, have all in recent years shifted towards shorter term contracts and an emphasis on 'employability of staff' rather than employment guarantees.

We have introduced the metaphor of the spiral staircase as the image that best describes the career patterns in project-based firms. Spiral staircases sweep upwards rather than ascend in a narrow ladder-like manner. The sweeping element of the spiral staircase represents the breadth of expertise and knowledge required in a multi-disciplinary project environment that people must gather through a range of appointments as their career develops. This differs markedly from climbing the ladder up the functional silo, where people are developed in a narrow specialism. In six years with ICI, Rodney Turner had six jobs, covering the complete life-cycle of process plant from feasibility, to design, construction, and maintenance. This is essential of the competence development required for the project-based firm, not narrow specialization up the functional silo.

In conceptualising careers in the project-oriented firms, we are also inspired by Dutch artist, Escher, and his representation of the monk's staircase that is

667

constantly ascending and descending at the same time. Escher's staircase captures for us the challenge in the modern versatile firm that people must always learn and unlearn, both ascending the staircase of knowledge, as they master one set of skills and knowledge and then descending to the lower level of a new learning challenge only to ascend once again. Career development in the project-based firm is also clearly dependent on the initiative of employees and their willingness to master new skills often at short notice. In this environment, employees must take responsibility for managing their own careers and use their own knowledge and initiative to advance. Our work with project-based firms suggests that the reframing of career expectations is a vital aspect of the support firms can offer their employees in coping with the reality of customized problem solving and project-based work.

Lynn Crawford describes development in detail in the next chapter.

Rewards

Project-based firms are coping with a tension in their reward systems. This tension arises in the shift from traditional rewards, especially promotion 'upwards', to new forms of reward and recognition. It is becoming harder to reward people with promotion 'upwards' (and the prestige it affords) because hierarchies are flattening under cost pressures and under evidence that more organic forms of managing are appropriate in innovative, project-based firms. Project-based firms are placing emphasis on different types of rewards, and encouraging employees to see development, and the prestige that normally went with promotions to a 'higher rank', in a new way. A Dutch firm of engineering designers and constructors in the process plant industry with whom we have worked are a good example of this career reframing. They have developed a culture in which career development is couched in terms of projects of increasingly greater responsibility, complexity and challenge as opposed to taking a step up the clearly defined career ladder from junior to more senior roles. This firm is trying to break the long-established link between number of subordinates and the value placed on a member of the organization. Instead of the number of subordinates, the amount of risk a person manages, and the strategic importance of the projects on which they are working, is given emphasis. The company stresses the importance of people moving across projects, to different areas within functions. It rewards people who take on new roles in order to expand their skills even if it is not an upward move in a traditional sense.

In several organizations, from the engineering, electronic and financial services industries, we have met people who moved from senior positions within departments, to new roles which provide development of their skills and knowledge, and more responsibility for adding value for the organization and for clients, but which are not a move 'upwards' in the traditional sense of more subordinates or a 'higher' rank. A Dutch consultancy firm with whom we have worked is also committed to the broad based development of people, and to the elimination of barriers to development including the shortening of hierarchies and the creation of a culture in which greater responsibility is taken as a hall mark of career development. In these firms, the spiral staircase career is widely evident.

Developing new managers for the new environment

Many companies point to the strongly held beliefs of managers as a barrier to changing career expectations. Two companies from the telecommunications industry, one Dutch and one Austrian, offer training to help managers deal with a new environment with flattened hierarchies where managers need to secure the co-operation and consent of project team members in order to operate effectively. There is a shift from viewing careers in terms of promotion and subordinates to viewing careers as continuous processes of learning and successful completion of projects. They concentrate on training and development practices to meet the new needs that arise in a changing world. For that reason, team building and coaching are an integral part of their training to help employees manage new career demands. Project managers are learning that the goal is not to manage subordinates, but to lead experts and technical specialists in knowledge work.

Dual or multiple career strategies

Dual career strategies have long been used by professional firms as a way to overcome the dysfunction of promoting technical experts to senior managerial and administrative roles. Many firms have career paths for line and functional managers as well as technical experts and team managers. The Dutch telecommunications company above propounds a 'Competence Model' where the competence of staff is seen as a triangle. Each of the three sides of the triangle represents a specific type of competence: Human Competence, Technical/ Professional Competence and Business Competence.

Not all of the firms we have worked with have tackled this issue with equal success. In an electronics firm, technical people cannot advance as far as traditional line managers and this is a challenge the firm recognizes must be addressed if they are to continue carrying out effective projects utilising highly knowledge intensive personnel. Respondents report losing valuable personnel as a consequence of their leaving when forced into line and departmental managerial roles as part of their progression. This loss has promoted a reorganization, only recently commenced, with the solution of this problem one of the major goals.

We have also found a strong tendency towards the creation of more diverse career ladders, breaking away somewhat from dual ladders emphasising technical versus line management careers. Microsoft have career ladders for project managers, programme managers, consultants, and technical experts as well as line managers. However, an unresolved issue which emerges from our research is the tendency for the uppermost layers of governance still to be drawn from one stream, generally that of line managers, as opposed to the other streams of career development. This may act as a barrier to the development and retention of experts in non-traditional management roles and seeking to create a more open environment.

The elimination of functions

The traditional functionally organized firm has a strong benefit for people: they have well defined functional homes to which they belong, and through which they develop careers. In the project-oriented firm, those functional homes are less important to the way people work because projects provide the main source of operational control. In some companies, the project orientation has gone so far that the functional structure has all but been eradicated.

Take the example of the Austrian subsidiary of a major IT vendor, a company providing bespoke computer and information technology systems. They employ approximately 200 people in Vienna and serve the needs of mainly Austrian clients. They have abandoned the functional departments in the largest and most strategically important area of its activities, the ISG (Information Systems Group), and adopted a fully project-based way of organizing. Employees within ISG are allocated to projects, which when completed are disbanded. The employee is immediately allocated to another project. There are no functional departments to which people belong and around which they form an identity. At the end of projects, there are no functional homes.

The elimination of functions and the creation of the project-based firm have advantages for firms like this one. One benefit is the reduction of costly overhead structures in the form of functional departments in which people physically have desks and a place to return to between projects. Indeed, there is no real 'between projects' with this approach to organization. Highly educated and skilled personnel are constantly moved between one project and another. As if to reinforce the 'movement' inherent in this approach to organization, companies also adopt a policy of hot desking in which people yield their traditional workstation and share desks with others on an as needs basis. One reason is that IT firms and other knowledge intensive firms work so closely with clients that many workers spend much of their time in the client organization and not in the employing organization.

Having eradicated functions, the goal is to keep people utilised and so have a stream of new projects coming on line. For knowledge based firms, keeping highly educated and expensively trained professionals working on projects is a key issue. Many companies experience this pressure. However, there are very few firms where we find the total elimination of the functional structure. In the Dutch telecommunications company above, members are organized according to clients and also according to traditional areas such as operations, marketing and sales. In the engineering design and construction companies, functions are retained as centres of expertise and efforts are made to encourage co-operative and non-segmentalist approaches to projects. This can be seen as vital to the organization, and regarded as providing crucial services to the value-adding heart of the firm, the projects. Many firms allude to the tension between projects and functions. Some see the tension as helpful and regard the maintenance of project and functional elements as essential to the development of knowledge and expertise as well as the effective carrying out of projects. Project-based firms have lived with tension between project and function for a long time. However, although the project orientation is a strong feature of these firms in general, there are disadvantages to be considered when functions are de-emphasized or entirely eliminated. People may feel somewhat lost, lacking a 'place' to hang their hat, or constancy in terms of the people with whom to work. We call this 'no home syndrome'. This is a drawback of the temporary organization in general, and also of the much vaunted virtual organization.

No home syndrome and the issue of learning

The *no home syndrome* has another serious drawback in that when functions are eliminated, so too are repositories of organizational knowledge. There are only projects and project groupings which, because transitory, are not the best vehicle for capturing and sharing, let alone disseminating, knowledge. Although there is no doubt that a fluid project-based environment can speed up the response to client needs, the potential loss of knowledge, or transfer of learning from project to project, must be overcome for the benefits to be realized. The challenge for project-based firms is to try and nurture a learning environment in the absence of secure employment. Some lessons emerge as to how project-based firms are managing the challenge of learning and knowledge management.

By way of illustration, given that the IT vendor mentioned above has adopted a highly project-focussed way of working in Vienna, how does it cope with the drawbacks of the loss of a functional structure in its ISG? Their management, both locally and internationally, acknowledges that the loss of functional repositories of knowledge is a serious concern. They have practices in place to try and ameliorate these disadvantages in order to maximize the benefits including trying (where possible) to ensure that there are additional people on a project so that two people are available to do the same job (two systems administrators/two programmers). The rationale here is to allow people to work together on similar tasks, especially new ones, so that each person can learn alongside another and the knowledge can be captured through the communication of the two people. In a supplier of business and financial data products, we have uncovered a pattern of innovation that relies heavily on the simultaneous and unplanned creativity of employees. This pattern of innovation and learning is shaped by the complex and unpredictable nature of the firm's markets for which there are few standards, and even fewer guidelines.

In the absence of 'Nellies'

The practice of pairing people on projects that we found reflects another feature of project-based firms. While 'sitting next to Nellie' has been a classic training and learning practice for decades, there are very few Nellies in the ICT industry. So rapidly changing are the technologies and solutions that these firms offer their clients, there are very few people experienced enough in the organization with whom newcomers can be paired in an effort to provide mentoring and coaching opportunities. 'Nellies' are created by seating next to each other people who learn from one another through experimentation, rather than the transfer of learning from an experienced individual to an apprentice. Although there may be some redundancy, there is a greater chance that the knowledge will be captured more effectively than if a person works alone. This system also ensures that knowledge is developed and learning captured continuously over the timescale of the project instead of simply at the end. The widespread use of mentoring as a form of training in recent years reflects the importance of ongoing learning and development in a changing environment.

RELEASE FROM THE PARENT ORGANIZATION

There are three key elements of the release process:

- organizational learning as temporary workers leave at the end of projects
- maintaining contact with temporary workers
- individual review and feedback

The most significant problem faced by many project-oriented organizations is loss of knowledge as temporary workers leave at the end of projects. Projects are temporary organizations, and as a project comes to an end there is a risk that any learning on the project will be lost as temporary workers leave. Rodney Turner worked with an aid agency that did all its projects using contract staff. At the end of every project they left, and the agency never improved its performance from one project to the next. Many organizations have knowledge management practices to try to capture knowledge on project completion (Turner et al 2003, and see Chapter 33), and permanent workers will retain their learning experiences, adding to the organization's tacit knowledge. But temporary workers will take their knowledge with them, and it will be lost to the organization for good. Very few organizations have solved this problem. An ICT vendor we have worked with has instituted a process of debriefing temporary workers leaving to attempt to capture knowledge.

The other issue with temporary workers is whether you attempt to remain in contact with them. If you accept that you need between 20% and 40% of temporary workers working for you to smooth project demands, there is a need for a constant stream of temporary workers. It can be expensive to recruit new people from scratch at the start of every project; it is much more effective to reemploy people you are familiar with. Some organizations have a network of temporary workers they continue to use on projects. Others, larger organizations that tend to use more traditional recruitment techniques, do recruit new people for every project requiring additional resource.

Some organizations also have formal release processes, including exit forms that all staff, both permanent and temporary, must complete on leaving. They also conduct exit interviews and formal knowledge transfer sessions for departing staff. While exit forms are always distributed to staff that are leaving, exit interviews may be planned on the basis of the results of these forms. With the release of freelance workers it can be important to find out how they appreciated their experience of working for the firm, because if you need to use temporary workers you want to remain an attractive place for them to work. Further, as we discussed earlier it can be useful to remain in contact to maintain the organization's network and to make future cooperation possible.

EMPLOYEE WELL-BEING

As we have seen, the dynamic work environment in the project-oriented organization creates issues for employee well-being and ethical treatment, Figure 31.6.

WORK-LIFE BALANCE

The temporary nature of projects and the dynamic nature of the work environment can lead to peaks and troughs in an employee's workload. Very high peaks can result if the work for several projects peaks together, or if customers make sudden unexpected demands. It is not uncommon in contracting

673

HRM Practices	*Methods used*
Work-life balance	The dynamic work environment in project-oriented companies can lead to peaks in work-load that overload employees This is particularly severe in companies undertaking small to medium-sized projects By and large companies are not very good at smoothing these peaks in work-load Companies undertaking large projects usually assign people to one project at a time, and project work is more easy to smooth Working away from home can create additional pressures for employees which needs managing
Matching projects to career development	Identified career paths for project management personnel are needed, with clearly defined skill sets at several levels Project assignments required for career development need to be identified in the routine appraisals Career development needs must be taken account of during assignment to projects If a project arises which matches an individual's development needs, enlightened companies will transfer the individual to the new project. If not individuals start to look for projects outside to match their development needs
Enjoyment of project work	People working on projects often have longer periods of tenure with the organization than people working in the routine parts of the organization, and express greater job-satisfaction Project work appears to be inherently more interesting that routine work

Figure 31.6   HRM practices to ensure employee well-being in the project-oriented company

organizations in both the engineering and high-tech industries to be working regularly 60 hours a week or more. Very few organizations have been able to solve this problem, and indeed some, especially contracting companies, do not want to because it would lead to an increase in costs, making them less competitive. Rodney Turner and Ralf Müller (2006) report interviewing a Swedish company which said a criterion for selecting a project manager to manage a project was his or her ability to maintain a work-life balance. However, that was in a back office department doing development work for a front office whose work was fundamentally routine. Thus the back office department was not working in competition with other contractors, and so cost was less of an issue.

MATCHING PROJECTS TO CAREER DEVELOPMENT NEEDS

We have also emphasized the need to match project assignments to career development needs. Since projects are temporary work processes, employees have an opportunity at the end of every project assignment to review their current aspirations, and if they are not receiving the project opportunities they want, they can seek such opportunities in projects with other companies. We have suggested that development needs should be identified in the regular appraisal process, and the types of projects that will satisfy those needs also identified. The issue then is what to do if such a development opportunity arises while the staff member is already assigned to another project. Enlightened organizations move them to the new project which provides the development opportunity. Nobody is indispensable on their current project, and the current project may provide a development opportunity for somebody else. Further, moving the person is both good for the individual and good for the company. The organization needs to develop people with the competence to deliver its projects, and so wants to maximize the opportunities from development opportunities. But also, as we have seen, if you show commitment to people's development, you are more likely to retain the best people.

PROJECT WORK IS ENJOYABLE

The evidence from our work is that by and large project work is enjoyable, and more so than the routine work of organizations. Project professionals show great commitment to their work, and often have longer periods of tenure with organizations than people from the routine parts of the business.

REFERENCES AND FURTHER READING

Burns, T. and Stalker, G., *The Management of Innovation*, Tavistock, London. 1961.

Flood, P.C., Gannon, M. J. and Paauwe, J. (eds.), 1996, *Managing Without Traditional Methods: international innovations in Human Resource Management.* Cambridge: Addison-Wesley.

Fombrun C.J., Tichy N.M. and Devanna M.A., (eds.), 1984, *Strategic Human Resource Management*, New York: John Wiley.

Gareis, R., 2005, *Happy Projects!,* Vienna: Manz Verlag.

Lengnick-Hall, C.A. and Lengnick-Hall, M.L., 1998, 'Strategic human resources management: a review of the literature and a proposed typology', *Academy of Management Review,* 13(3), 454–470.

Love, P., Fong P.S.W. and Irani, Z., 2004, *Management of Knowledge in Project Environments,* Oxford: Elsevier.

Keegan, A.E. and Turner, J.R., 2003, 'Managing human resources in the project-based organziation', in Turner, J.R., (ed.) *People in Project Management,* Aldershot: Gower.

Noe, R., Hollenbeck, G. B. and Wright, P., 2004, *Human Resource Management,* 5th ed, McGraw-Hill.

Turner, J.R., *The Handbook of Project-based Management, 2nd edition,* McGraw Hill, London, 1999.

Turner, J.R. and Keegan, A.E., 2001, 'Mechanisms of governance in the project-based organization: the role of the broker and steward', *European Management Journal,* 19(3), 254–267.

Turner, J.R. and Müller, R., 2006, *Choosing Appropriate Project Managers: matching their leadership style to the type of project,* Newtown Square: Project Management Institute.

Turner, J.R., Keegan, A.E. and Crawford, L.H., 2003, 'Delivering improved project management maturity through experiential learning', in Turner, J.R., (ed.) *People in Project Management,* Aldershot: Gower.

32 Developing Individual Competence

Lynn Crawford

The competence of project management personnel is a subject of concern to businesses and individuals. Businesses realize that the competence of their employees is vital to corporate performance. When coupled with an increasing recognition of the importance of projects in achieving business goals, organizations become concerned with the project management competence of their people. For individuals, job opportunities in project management and increasing demand by business for evidence of project management competence fuels concern for professional development in the interests of employability, career development and job satisfaction. Further, project management professional associations see the certification of the competence of practitioners as an important part of their role. Associations around the world have devoted considerable effort to the definition of a body of project management knowledge and development of guides and standards for knowledge and practice as a basis for education, training and associated certification or qualification.

Whether it is project management practitioners concerned with personal competence development, or organizations concerned with the assessment and development of project management competence, it is important to have an understanding of:

- how competence and its components are defined
- what standards exist for the assessment and development of project management competence
- how assessment can be used in the development of project management competence
- what approaches are used by organizations for assessing and developing competence

APPROACHES TO DEFINING COMPETENCE

DEFINITION OF COMPETENCE

Most of us have a general understanding of what is meant by competence. When someone is described as competent to do a particular job it is taken to mean that they know how to do it and have the ability to do it and to do it well. Generally, competence is accepted as encompassing knowledge, skills, attitudes and behaviours that contribute to effective performance of a task or job role. However, over the last few decades, considerable attention has been focused on competence and the term has acquired specific meanings for groups of people who understand and approach competence in different ways. In considering project management competence, it is useful to be able to break competence down into component parts that can be measured or assessed and therefore developed. It is also useful to understand what different people are thinking and the approaches they are taking when considering the assessment and development of competence.

THE TRADITIONAL APPROACH TO COMPETENCE

The traditional approach of employers seeking to promote or select competent staff has been to look for the 'right' technical qualifications and a proven track record of doing the same job within their organization or a similar one. Using this approach, appropriate qualifications and a resumé summarising relevant experience, generally supported by a face to face interview, are the basis for assessment of competence. A number of factors have led to dissatisfaction with this traditional approach and have driven the search for a new way of selecting and developing human resources. First, the value of traditional academic aptitude and knowledge tests in predicting job performance has been questioned, as has the equity of such tests for minorities, women and disadvantaged groups. Secondly, this traditional approach often just doesn't work, particularly in project management, for a number of reasons, including:

- demand for such people may exceed supply
- the new project may be one that has not been done before by the organization
- the new environment may differ from that which supported past successes
- there may be factors in the individual's private life – health, family, other commitments – which impact on performance

A further factor in project management is that many people with experience in project management do not have supporting academic qualifications in the field. Project management is a relatively new discipline in which there are relatively few academic courses and associated qualifications and these are primarily at postgraduate level. Many project management practitioners have degrees in another field or discipline and have 'accidentally' found themselves involved in project management.

Two streams of thought, one in the United States and one in the United Kingdom, have given rise to different approaches to competence. The *competency model*, or attribute-based competency approach, has been most prevalent in the United States, while the *competency standards*, or demonstrable performance-approach, has formed the basis for national qualifications frameworks in the United Kingdom, Australia, New Zealand and South Africa.

THE COMPETENCY MODEL OR ATTRIBUTE-BASED APPROACH

The work of McClelland and McBer in the United States, beginning in the 1970s and reported by Boyatzis in the early 1980s (Boyatzis 1982), established what is referred to as the competency model, or attribute-based approach. Followers of this approach define a competency as an 'underlying characteristic of an individual that is causally related to effective and/or superior performance in a job or situation' (Spencer and Spencer 1993). Five competency characteristics are defined by Spencer and Spencer. Two of these are known as surface competencies, namely knowledge (the information a person has in specific content areas) and skill (the ability to perform a particular physical or mental task), and are considered to be the most readily developed and assessed through training and experience. The other three are core personality characteristics, motives, traits and self-concept, and are considered difficult to assess and develop. Thus, according to the competency model, or attribute-based approach, competence comprises several competencies, as follows:

Competence = *Knowledge (qualifications)*
    + *Skills (ability to do a task)*
    + *Core Personality Characteristics (Motives + Traits + Self-Concept)*

Inherent in the competency model approach is the concept of threshold and high performance or differentiating competencies. Threshold competencies are units of behaviour that are essential to do a job, but which are not causally related to superior job performance (Boyatzis 1982). The competency model approach is mainly concerned with high performing or differentiating competencies, those 'characteristics that are causally related to effective and/or superior performance in a job' (Boyatzis 1982). For an approach to be used effectively in selection, promotion and development, employers need to know what personal characteristics, behaviours, knowledge and skills are causally related to superior job performance. Even when research has identified desirable attributes for a particular job role (Boyatzis 1982; Spencer and Spencer 1993), these attributes may be difficult to assess and develop. The competency model approach, used extensively as the basis for numerous corporate competency development programmes worldwide, sees competencies as clusters of knowledge, attitudes, skills, and in some cases personality traits, values and styles that affect an individual's ability to perform. Human resource professionals, in the United States and elsewhere, are most likely to think about competence from the competency model or attribute-based perspective.

THE COMPETENCY STANDARDS OR PERFORMANCE-BASED APPROACH

While the competency model or attribute-based approach assumes identifiable personal attributes will translate into competent performance in the workplace, the competency standards approach assumes that competence can be inferred from demonstrated performance at a pre-defined acceptable standard (Gonczi et al 1993). The competency standards approach has not attracted the same degree of support in the United States as it has in the United Kingdom, Australia or South Africa. In the UK, it is the basis for NVQs (National Vocational Qualifications) (Weightman 1995) and in Australia, New Zealand, and South Africa, it underpins government endorsed national qualifications frameworks. Under the competency standards approach, competence is defined as 'the ability to perform the activities within an occupation or function to the standard expected in employment' (National Training Board 1991). Performance-based competency standards are essentially concerned with threshold performance, the minimum level of performance acceptable in the workplace, according to predefined criteria. Thus, according to the competency standard or performance-based approach:

> *Competence is demonstrable performance in accordance with occupational/ professional/ organizational competency standards.*

Reflecting the emphasis on performance in an occupational role, competency standards were intended to be developed by industry lead bodies representing the employers and employees in the relevant sector, occupation or profession. In Australia, these are called Industry Training Advisory Boards, and in South Africa, Sector Education Training Authorities.

The Competency Standards approach has developed its own terminology, including:

- *Units and elements of competency:* describe what is done in the workplace, profession or role

- *Performance criteria:* describe the required standard of performance
- *Range indicators:* describe the context of performance

Competency Standards are written at a number of different levels corresponding to the demands of occupational roles and /or educational requirements. In these qualification frameworks levels start at the equivalent of secondary school and move through to post graduate qualifications, from entry level to chief executive officer. As an example, the Australian National Competency Standards for Project Management have been written at three levels, generally corresponding to the following job roles:

1. Project team member
2. Project manager
3. Project director or programme manager

This approach has been particularly attractive from an equity viewpoint. It provides a basis for recognition of the competence of those who can demonstrate ability to perform but have not had the opportunity to gain qualifications required for entry to particular jobs, occupations or professions. This makes it particularly useful in areas such as project management where many jobholders do not have formal qualifications relating to that job. It is also being used by larger organizations as a way of identifying those project personnel who have demonstrated ability to manage particular types of projects.

The performance-based competency standards approach is supported by national governments in the United Kingdom, Australia, New Zealand and South Africa and includes well documented processes for assessment against the standards. Assessment is done by registered Workplace Assessors, and individuals are required to gather evidence of competence against the standards from their workplace.

The Global Alliance for Project Performance Standards (GAPPS) includes members from government standards and qualification bodies, professional associations, academic institutions and industry and has developed performance based standards for two levels of Project Manager as a basis for transferability and mutual recognition between existing standards (refer www.globalpmstandards.org).

AN INTEGRATED MODEL OF PROJECT MANAGEMENT COMPETENCE

Attribute-based and performance-based approaches to project management competence place emphasis on different aspects of competence and therefore a combination of both approaches may be more effective (Heywood et al 1992). It is useful, for purposes of assessment and development, to consider project management competence as comprising:

- the underpinning project management knowledge and skills (input competencies)
- the enabling behavioural characteristics (personal competencies)
- the demonstrated ability to perform or use project management practices, at a pre-defined standard in the workplace (output competencies)

Figure 32.1 suggests a framework which brings together the competency model (attribute-based) and competency standards (performance-based) approaches to competence, and provides a useful framework for identifying and measuring aspects of competence as a basis for assessment and development. According to this integrated approach:

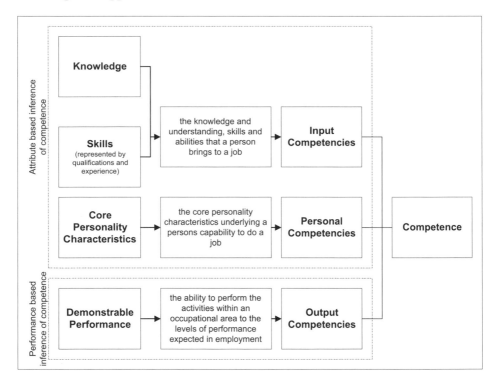

Figure 32.1 Integral Model of Competence identifying key components of competence

Competence = *Knowledge (qualifications)*
+ *Skills (ability to do a task)*
+ *Behaviours and Core Personality Characteristics (Motives + Traits + Self-Concept)*
+ *Demonstrable performance in accordance with occupational/ professional/organizational Competency Standards*

STANDARDS FOR THE ASSESSMENT AND DEVELOPMENT OF PROJECT MANAGEMENT COMPETENCE

Assessment of competence requires standards or guides against which measurement can be made. Knowledge (input competencies) and demonstrable performance (use of project management practices, or output competencies) are the two aspects of competence identified in Figure 32.1 that are most widely addressed in project management standards or guides produced by project management professional associations or standards setting bodies. The ICB – IPMA Competence Baseline, Version 3.0 (IPMA 2006) does however include a section (4.2) on behavioural or personal competence elements associated with project management, the other elements being technical and contextual competence. A number of organizations have developed corporate competency models, identifying the behaviours that are considered desirable and associated with superior performance within a specific corporate context. However these are usually applicable across the organization and not project management specific. The Project Management Institute's Project Manager Competency Development Framework (Project Management Institute 2002) includes personal competencies, but these are derived from the work of Spencer and Spencer (1993) which was developed for general rather than project management.

KNOWLEDGE AND SKILL-BASED COMPETENCE STANDARDS

Several project management professional associations have developed guides to the body of knowledge of project management, including:

- the UK's Association of Project Management, APM (Dixon 2000)
- the International Project Management Association, IPMA (IPMA 2006), whose international competence baseline (ICB) has been adapted into national competence baselines by its national associations
- the Project Management Institute, PMI® (Project Management Institute 2000), whose PMBOK® Guide has been approved as an American National Standard (ANSI/PMI® 99–001–1999) and adopted as an IEEE Standard (1490–1998)
- the Project Management Association of Japan, PMAJ (ENAA 2002)

These standards and guides focus primarily on management of individual projects, although the 2006 versions of the APM and IPMA guides mention programme and portfolio management as aspects of context. PMAJ's *P2M: A Guidebook of Project and Programme Management for Enterprise Management* (ENAA 2002) stands out as an exception. The P2M, developed with support of the Japanese government, specifically extends the focus beyond the management of single projects to management of programmes of projects in the context of corporate strategy implementation and enterprise innovation and management. Each of these guides is the basis for a project management certification programme:

- IPMA has developed a four level programme (Pannenbacker et al 1998). The entry level to this certification programme, Level D, is a knowledge test based on the ICB or National Competency Baseline, which in the case of the United Kingdom is the APM Body of Knowledge.
- APM (UK) offers an Introductory Certificate, APMP (IPMA Level D), Practitioner Qualification (IPMA Level C) and Certificated Project Manager qualification (IPMA Level B) all based on the APM's Body of Knowledge.
- PMI® has developed a single level, Project Management Professional (PMP®) certification which includes a multiple-choice, knowledge exam plus project management experience requirement.
- PMAJ offers a three level certification programme which includes interviews, essay tests and project management experience.

There is growing recognition of the role of the Programme Manager. The Project Management Institute has produced standards for both Programme and Portfolio Management (Project Management Institute 2006a, 2006b) and is planning to offer a Programme Manager qualification. It is important to recognize, however that Programme Management is not just a higher level of Project Management. Many Programme Managers come to the role as part of a general management rather than project management career path. The Office of Government Commerce in the UK was one of the first organizations to recognize the programme manager role and produced a guide titled Managing Successful Programmes (Office of Government Commerce 2003). The Chartered Management Institute and the APM Group Ltd have jointly developed a Diploma in Programme and Project Management. Project management standards, assessment processes and qualifications are presented in Figure 32.2.

PERFORMANCE-BASED COMPETENCY STANDARDS

Demonstrable performance or use of project management practices is represented by performance-based competency standards. These include:

- the Australian National Competency Standards for Project Management (IBSA 2006)
- the UK's National Vocational Qualification (NVQ) framework (ECITB 2003)
- those developed under the auspices of the South African Qualifications Authority (PMSGB 2002)
- those developed by the Global Alliance for Project Performance Standards (GAPPS 2006)

Standard or Guide (Development Body)	Level	Description	Form(s) of assessment
PMBOK® Guide (Project Management Institute)	PMP®	Project Management Professional	Record of education plus Record of experience leading & directing projects plus Multiple choice exam
	CAPM®	Certified Associate in Project Management	Record of education plus Record of experience working on project team or 23 hrs formal PM education plus Multiple choice exam
	PgMP^SM	Program Management Professional	Record of education (degree) plus Record of project management experience plus Record of program management experience plus Multiple choice exam plus Multi-rater assessment (raters selected by candidate)
ICB: IPMA Competence Baseline (International Project Management Association, and member National Associations eg AFITEP, APM)	Level A	Certified Projects Director	CV, project list, references, self-assessment Project report Interview
	Level B	Certified Senior Project Manager	CV, project list, references, self-assessment Project report Interview
	Level C	Certified Project Manager	CV, project list, references, self-assessment Written exam plus Workshop, Short project report (optional) plus Interview
	Level D	Certified Project Management Associate	CV, self-assessment Written exam
P2M (ENAA, JPMF)	PMA	Program Management Architect	Interview and essay tests Experience of at least three projects required
	PMR	Project Manager Registered	Interview and essay tests Experience of at least one project required
	PMS	Project Management Specialist	Written examination

Figure 32.2 Knowledge-based project management standards, assessment processes and qualifications

Assessment against government endorsed performance-based competency standards is undertaken by registered workplace assessors. Candidates are required to gather evidence of the use of practices in accordance with performance criteria specified in the standards. The workplace assessor works with candidates, advises and assists them in achieving recognition of competence. Candidates are assessed either as competent at a particular level, or 'not yet competent'. If assessed as competent, a candidate may be awarded a qualification recognized within a government endorsed framework. The Australian Institute of

685

Project Management (AIPM) has a professional registration process aligned with the Australian National Competency Standards for Project Management and the Australian Qualifications Framework. Requirements for this process are available from AIPM's website (http://www.aipm.com.au). The equivalent project management role, and professional and government recognized qualifications for Australia are shown in Figure 32.3.

PM Role	Australian Qualifications Framework (AQF) (www.aqf.edu.au) Qualification	Australian Institute of Project Management (www.aipm.com.au) Award Title	Post Nominals
Project Team Member	Certificate IV	Qualified Project Professional	QPP
Project Manager	Diploma	Registered Project Manager	RegPM
Project Director / Program Manager	Advanced Diploma	Master Project Director	MPD

Figure 32.3   Project management professional and government recognized qualifications in Australia

The Global Alliance for Project Performance Standards (GAPPS) has developed performance based standards for two levels of Project Manager referred to as Global Level 1 (G1) and Global Level 2 (G2) based on the level of management complexity of the projects they have worked on (refer www.globalpmstandards.org). The GAPPS does not award qualifications. It audits and endorses assessment processes and standards as a basis for mutual recognition and transferability of project management and related qualification.

THE ROLE OF ASSESSMENT IN DEVELOPMENT OF PROJECT MANAGEMENT COMPETENCE

Lifelong learning is becoming increasingly important for project management practitioners, operating at the leading edge of technology, who must be able to engage in critical thinking and reflection to transform existing knowledge, through creative responses and enhanced decision making, to meet unfamiliar situations. Professional standards and qualifications can provide baselines for knowledge and practice but it is the responsibility of each individual to reflect on his or her practice and seek opportunities to develop competence, raise benchmarks and improve performance. A model for assessment and development of competence is presented in Figure 32.4. This model is useful for individual practitioners as a basis for professional development. It is equally useful as a guide for corporate programmes for assessment and development of project management competence. It clearly demonstrates the role of assessment in the development of project management competence.

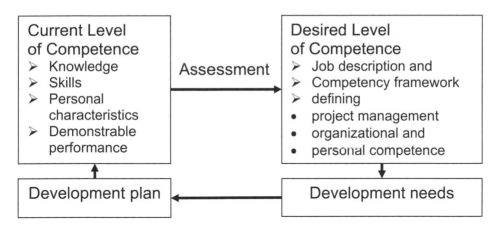

Figure 32.4 A model for assessment and development of workplace competence (developed in consultation with Carol Townley, Caliper, UK)

As a first step, current competence needs to be assessed or measured. Guides and standards such as P2M, PMBOK® Guide, Australian National Competency Standards for Project Management, or IPMA's ICB can be used as a basis for this entry level assessment and can be supplemented by using a range of personality, behavioural and other tests to form a picture of current levels of competence. Organizations such as NASA make a wide range of assessment tools available to their personnel to provide them with feedback on their own knowledge, performance, attitudes, behaviours and motivations. In corporate competency development programmes assessment of current levels of competence of project personnel can provide a baseline for evaluation of improvement.

Requirements of the job role form the basis for identifying the desired level of competence. This will ideally be documented in the job description, although comprehensive job descriptions for project management roles are rare and individuals may need to develop their own detailed job descriptions as a basis for competence development. In identifying job role requirements it is important to recognize that the project management guides and standards referred to earlier relate only to generic or widely accepted project management knowledge and practices and may only form part of the requirements of a job role. A full job description may need to include aspects of competence relating to the following:

- generic project management (represented by PM guides and standards)
- organization specific project management (relating to corporate project management methodology, tools and techniques)
- organizational (relating to processes and systems specific to the organization such as financial management systems, occupational health and safety, etc)
- interpersonal skills (eg negotiation, communication, leadership, teamwork)

687

- personal competence (attitudes, behaviours, motivation, values etc)
- technical (dependent upon type and scale of project eg IT, engineering, product development etc)
- business environment (eg market awareness)

Developmental needs are represented by the gap between current and desired levels of competence. For individuals this can form the basis for a professional development plan. For corporate project management development programmes the difference between current and desired levels of competence of project personnel forms the basis for a gap analysis, the identification of corporate project management development needs and the planning and resourcing of corporate project management development programmes.

In the spirit of lifelong learning, reflective practice, career progression and changing workplace requirements, assessment and development of project management competence, according to this model (Figure 32.4), should be an ongoing developmental process. In corporate development programmes the process should be supported by:

- learning and development policies and resources, including opportunities for
- self-managed learning
- computer and web-based learning resources
- work experience opportunities
- mentoring and coaching
- in-company and off-site training
- professional and academic qualifications
- internal accreditation (matched to project types and external standards)
- performance appraisal and management systems
- career paths
- rewards and recognition

CORPORATE APPROACHES TO ASSESSING AND DEVELOPING PROJECT MANAGEMENT COMPETENCE

Organizations can play an important role in motivating and supporting performance improvement. There are several aspects to this. One is the provision of a supportive environment – a project management culture, top management support, methodologies, systems, tools, recognition and rewards – that encourages effective project management performance. The other is the design and implementation of corporate project management competence development programmes. Design of these programmes should consider the need to ensure that all project personnel have minimum levels of competence required for effective performance as well as providing opportunities for identification and development of superior performance.

Standards for knowledge and use of project management practices such as the PMBOK® Guide and Australian National Competency Standards for Project Management provide corporations and practitioners with guidelines as to the knowledge and practices required for effective workplace performance. Corporate performance can be enhanced if project management personnel are familiar with and follow such standards, thereby having a shared understanding of project management terminology and practices and the ability to deploy corporate project management methodology.

Research done by the author has demonstrated that assessment of levels of project management knowledge and use of practices against standards does not differentiate between threshold and superior performance. It does not provide a good indicator of those project management practitioners who are likely to be top performers. This is not surprising, as factors contributing to successful workplace performance are both complex and shifting. There are factors relating to individuals that cannot be effectively captured in standards or measured in examinations, resumés or in interviews, such as personality and behavioural characteristics, values, ethics and motivation. There are also factors relating to context, such as the nature of the project, the nature of the role, resource availability, competence of the project team, and extent of organizational support.

A practical approach for organizations is to use a standards based approach to assessment and development of threshold competence of project personnel, and to use other methods for assessment and development of differentiating competencies or the identification and development of potentially superior performers. Brief case studies of these two approaches are provided here.

PERFORMANCE-BASED COMPETENCY ASSESSMENT AND DEVELOPMENT: THRESHOLD COMPETENCIES

The Project Management Research Unit at the University of Technology Sydney has developed a process for assessment and development of threshold competencies in project management. This is based on work with several organizations, and the results of research into project management competence using the PMBOK® Guide and the Australian National Competency Standards for Project Management. The process, illustrated in Figure 32.5, involves identifying current project management competency levels of staff through a web based competency assessment process, which includes a knowledge test and self assessment of use of project management practices followed by an interview with a registered workplace assessor. The interview with the assessor is intended to verify the initial self assessment against the standards and provide feedback as an

689

input to preparation of a personal professional development plan which may include progression towards internally and externally recognized professional qualifications. These assessments provide a baseline for development and are related to roles and responsibilities, classification of projects and an internal accreditation system to identify development gaps. Individuals, in consultation with supervisors and supported by detailed guidelines, provided via the corporate INTRANET, develop plans to address the identified developmental gaps and work towards their own career goals. Once project management professional development plans are approved, it is the responsibility of individuals to implement their plan and to report on progress. Developmental resources available include reading and study guides, web based support, mentoring and coaching, education and training, and work experience opportunities.

Figure 32.5   Process for Project Management Development

ATTRIBUTE-BASED COMPETENCY ASSESSMENT AND DEVELOPMENT: DIFFERENTIATING COMPETENCIES AND SUPERIOR PERFORMANCE

We saw above how a firm can identify baseline competency levels of the majority of project personnel in terms of knowledge and use of project management practices, and then identify gaps to encourage staff to develop their competence. Having done this, an organization may wish turn its attention to differentiating competencies and the recognition and development of superior performance. This may involve moving beyond reliance on generic standards for knowledge and project management practices to development of guidelines specific to the specific environment. These may include project management competency models identifying attitudes, behaviours and values that are considered to be associated with superior performance in that organization (such as the NASA Competency Framework).

The most widely used approach to attribute-based competency assessment and development and the fostering of differentiating competencies, is the assessment or development centre (Woodruffe 1990). This is not a place but a process, usually designed to last one to five days, during which participants undertake a series of rigorous individual and group experiential exercises including presentations, interviews, problem-solving and simulations. Participants have an opportunity to complete and receive feedback from instruments that measure performance and effectiveness on different levels and from multiple perspectives, usually related to a defined corporate project management competency model. An important aspect of such centres is the involvement of highly regarded representatives of the senior and project management communities as assessors who observe participants during all activities, usually on a one to one basis, and provide informed and objective feedback and guidance for development. Effectiveness of the assessment and development centre is largely dependent on the willingness, dedication and commitment of the senior personnel, and their recognition that the process is a developmental opportunity for them as much as for the organization and its management personnel. Assessment and development centres are highly resource intensive and expensive to design and operate. It therefore makes sense for organizations to offer opportunities for assessment and development of threshold competences, aligned to standards, for most project personnel and to offer more in-depth, attribute-based approaches such as assessment and development centres, to project personnel in most senior or responsible positions or who are identified by their managers as having most potential for development.

CONCLUSIONS

Increasing recognition of the potential contribution of project management to enhanced business performance and the achievement of business goals focuses attention of individuals and organizations on the assessment and development of project management competence.

Competence encompasses knowledge, skills, attitudes and behaviours that contribute to effective job performance and can be assessed and developed. Competence can be inferred from attributes (knowledge, skills and underlying and enabling attitudes and behaviours) or from evidence of ability to perform in the workplace in accordance with specified standards. Attribute-based inference of competence is generally associated with competency models and assessment and development of differentiating competencies, or those characteristics that are considered to be causally related to superior performance. Performance-based inference of competence is primarily associated with performance-based competency standards and with threshold competence, or the minimum required for effective performance in a job role. The most effective assessment and development of project management competence will include both attribute and performance-based approaches.

Project management standards for knowledge and use of practices have been developed by project management professional associations and government supported industry training and qualification bodies. These provide guidance for assessment and development of threshold competencies, those aspects of competence (knowledge, skills, use of project management practices) that are essential to performing project management roles but are not causally related to superior job performance. A wide range of personality, team role, attitude and behavioural assessment instruments and assessment centres are available to assist in the assessment and development of differentiating competencies but are most effectively used in association with competency models developed by organizations to suit their specific environment, project types and job roles. Development of project management competence will be primarily the responsibility of the individual but will be most effective when complemented by organizational support and recognition.

REFERENCES AND FURTHER READING

APM, 2006, *APM Body of Knowledge,* 5th edition, High Wycombe, UK: Association for Project Management.

Boyatzis, R.E., 1982, *The Competent Manager: a model for effective performance,* New York: John Wiley and Sons.

ECITB, 2003, *National Occupational Standards for Project Management,* Kings Langley, Herts, UK: Engineering Construction Industry Training Board.

ENAA, 2002, *P2M: A guidebook of project & programme management for enterprise innovation,* summary translation, Tokyo: Project Management Association of Japan.

GAPPS, 2006, *A Framework for Performance Based Competency Standards for Global Level 1 and 2 Project Managers,* Johannesburg: Global Alliance for Project Performance Standards. <http://www.globalpmstandards.org>.

Gonczi, A., Hager, P. and Athanasou, J., 1993, *The Development of Competency-Based Assessment Strategies for the Profession,* Canberra: Australian Government Publishing Service.

Heywood, L., Gonczi, A. and Hager, P., 1992, *A Guide to Development of Competency Standards for Professions,* Canberra: Australian Government Publishing Service.

IBSA, 2006, 'Volume 4B: Project Management', in: *BSB01 Business Services Training Package Version 4.00,* Hawthorn, Victoria: Innovation and Business Skills Australia.

IPMA, 2006, *ICB: IPMA Competence Baseline,* Zaltbommel, NL: Van Haren Publishing.

National Training Board, 1991, *National Competency Standards Policy & Guidelines,* Canberra: National Training Board.

Office of Government Commerce, 2003, *Managing Successful Programmes,* Norwich, UK: The Stationery Office.

PMSGB, 2002, *South African Qualifications Authority Project Management Competency Standards: levels 3 and 4,* Pretoria: South African Qualifications Authority.

PMI®, 2002, *Project Manager Competency Development Framework,* Newtown Square, PA: Project Management Institute.

PMI®, 2004, *The Guide to the Project Management Body of Knowledge,* 3rd edition, Newtown Square, PA: Project Management Institute.

PMI®, 2006a, *The Standard for Portfolio Management,* Newtown Square, PA: Project Management Institute.

PMI®, 2006b, *The Standard for Programme Management,* Newtown Square, PA: Project Management Institute.

Spencer, L.M.J. and Spencer, S.M., 1993, *Competence at Work: models for superior performance,* New York: John Wiley and Sons.

Weightman, J., 1995, *Competencies in Action,* 2nd ed, London: Institute of Personnel and Development.

Woodruffe, C., 1990, *Assessment Centres,* London: Institute of Personnel and Development.

33 Developing Project Management Capability of Organizations

Lynn Crawford and Rodney Turner

Much of the focus of project management development to the late 1990s has been at the level of the individual project and project manager as evidenced by the many resources and standards available that provide support for the management of individual projects (Chapters 1, 5, 7 and 32). Interest in the management of multiple projects, programmes of projects, delivery of corporate strategy through projects and therefore the associated development of organizational project management capability is a more recent phenomenon (Chapters 2, 3, 4, 9 and 10). In some ways this is surprising, as the majority of the factors that have been identified as critical to the success of projects (Chapter 6; Cooke-Davies 2001; Hyvari 2006) even at the level of the individual project, such as resourcing, availability of tools for planning, monitoring and control and communication, are highly dependent upon organizational support. Significantly, top management support is regularly reported as vital to the success of projects, (Pinto and Slevin 1988).

In the realm of multiple projects and programmes, the need for organizational capability becomes obvious if only because the management of outcomes is no longer within the confines of a single project or the responsibility and authority of a single project manager. When an organization recognizes that business change and corporate strategy can be delivered through projects, there is realization that project management capability needs to be able to support doing the project right, doing the right projects and doing this consistently across all the organization's projects (Cooke-Davies 2004b). Organizational project management capability is therefore increasingly seen as a key to competitive advantage (KPMG 1997; Nieto-Rodriguez and Evrard 2004) and therefore worthy of investment in its development.

This chapter presents some of the key issues and steps involved in developing project management capability of organizations. In the next section we explore the need for organizational project management capability. We then describe its individual components, and explain how an organization can improve its ability to

695

consistently manage projects, after first setting a baseline for current performance.

THE NEED FOR ORGANIZATIONAL PROJECT MANAGEMENT CAPABILITY

The extent to which an organization needs project management capability is related to the number and size of projects it undertakes and the importance of those projects to corporate success. The nature of corporate project management capability required is influenced by corporate strategy and the types of projects undertaken (Crawford et al 2005).

Where an organization is primarily process based, in a fairly stable industry requiring only occasional business changes, the number of projects undertaken may be relatively small. Under these circumstances it may be possible to rely upon a small number of proven and capable individuals to manage these projects or to outsource project management capability. When the number of projects is relatively small, coordination and reporting is not a major issue. Often organizations will start to recognize and manage projects in this way, but as the number of projects they undertake increases and as projects become more important to effective corporate performance and strategy delivery, they are likely to run out of intuitive 'heroes' and find that outsourcing is too expensive or is not addressing their needs. At this stage they need to find a way of resourcing projects which is effective but accommodates a range of skill and experience levels. They will also need to introduce standard methods of project management and reporting, and other supporting systems that will allow for coordination between projects and strategic alignment to ensure effective resource utilization. As the application of project management to the various activities of the organization increases, a more sophisticated and flexible approach may become necessary, with varying governance requirements and methodology applied to different types of projects and more careful assignment of resources(Payne and Turner 1999). Programme and portfolio management become important in ensuring effective resource allocation, alignment with strategy, coordination between projects and delivery of business benefits (Chapters 2, 3 and 4).

This raises another issue. In practice, the importance of different aspects of project management capability is likely to vary relative to the types of projects and the relationship with clients (Crawford et al 2005). Organizations that deliver projects on behalf of external clients, usually under contract, are likely to place more emphasis on cost control, contract and value management than organizations where the primary project delivery function is for internal clients. Such organizations are likely to be more concerned with governance and benefits management. In the case of projects for external clients conducted under contract, the contract itself provides a governing structure.

Focus on corporate governance, with requirements for increased regulation and accountability, also raises interest in the development of organizational project management capability. In the past, many senior managers had little interest in project management, considering it to be tactical rather than strategic. Others disliked or were suspicious of project management because it fosters visibility, transparency and accountability and this can make it difficult to hide mistakes. As legislation such as the Sarbanes Oxley Act, 2002, requires company directors to take personal responsibility for ensuring 'accuracy and reliability of corporate disclosures' their attitude to transparency is changing and project management can be seen as directly assisting senior management in meeting and fulfilling their legislated obligations. Development of organizational project management capability is becoming increasingly important as a way of ensuring visibility and control and demonstrating corporate responsibility in the utilization of corporate resources.

Having discussed a number of the key reasons for interest in organizational project management capability, we now identify some of its main components.

COMPONENTS OF ORGANIZATIONAL PROJECT MANAGEMENT CAPABILITY

Figure 33.1 illustrates the components of organizational project management capability. As identified at the start of this chapter, the focus of project management has traditionally been on the bottom, on the development of methodologies, tools and techniques to manage individual projects. But as explained in Chapter 2, there is a growing awareness of the need to link projects with corporate strategy. Organizational project management capability is a key component in forging that link. However, there are lynch pins which bind them together:

- top management support
- an effective project management and knowledge management community
- project management competency and career development
- repositories of data

These basic components are further supported by wider organizational processes of Governance, Leadership and Communication, Knowledge Management and Human Resource Management. Figure 33.1 illustrates that organizational project management capability operates at several levels which can be thought of as strategic, operational and tactical equating to three levels of responsibility:

697

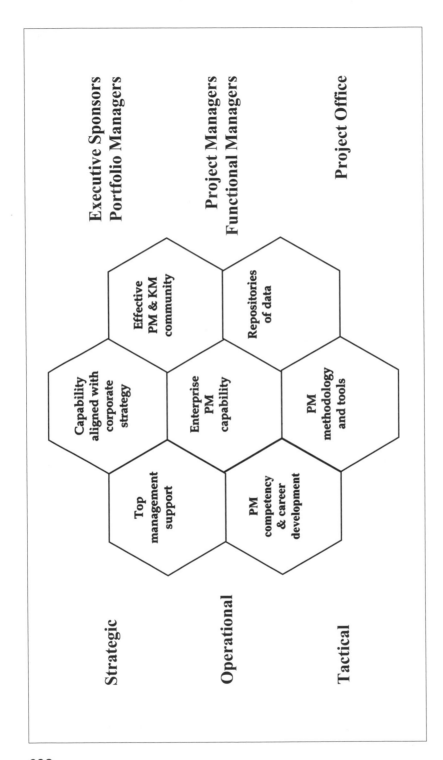

Figure 33.1   Basic Building Blocks of Organizational Project Management Capability

- **project sponsors and senior managers:** who ensure projects are aligned with corporate strategy, provide sponsorship for projects, take responsibility for resources and funding, ensure delivery of benefits, and manage integration through programme structures
- **project and programme managers:** responsible for managing and delivering individual projects and programmes and the new assets and capabilities they provide the organization
- **project team members and the project office:** who use the project management methodologies to plan the work and monitor and control progress

These three levels may also be considered as relating to portfolio, programme and project management processes (Chapters 2, 3, 4, 7 and 9).

We now describe the elements of organizational project management capability:

CAPABILITY ALIGNED WITH STRATEGY

Fundamental to this component of capability is the existence of a corporate strategy. Strategy is delivered through projects and programmes (Chapter 2, Crawford et al 2005), which in turn should only be funded if they support the corporate strategy. The project management capability required by an organization will also be influenced by the corporate strategy. For instance, if an organization identifies project management capability as a core corporate competence they will place a higher priority on development of and investment in that capability. An organization that does not have a high reliance on projects and does not see project management capability as central to their strategy may choose to outsource it. An organization that only does projects for internal clients is likely to be more concerned with ensuring realization of benefits and control through governance than an organization whose strategy is the management of projects for external clients, which may invest more in cost and contract management. The context or external environment will influence the degree to which an organization invests in risk management.

Whatever the emphasis, however, an organization needs to have processes in place to ensure the alignment of capability, and of projects and programmes, with corporate strategy. These processes may include those which ensure that:

- shared vision and corporate strategy are clearly stated and communicated
- portfolio selection and prioritization processes align project and programme investments with the strategic plan
- projects and programmes are either fully funded and resourced, or not started, ensuring genuine corporate commitment to achieving project outcomes

- projects are categorized in terms of strategic importance, as a guide to managerial approach, assignment of resources and as a basis for useful performance metrics
- project selection processes result in a balanced corporate risk profile
- business changes are managed as projects
- projects are monitored throughout their life cycle so that projects no longer consistent with strategy are cancelled
- expected business benefits from projects are identified, aligned with strategy and tracked
- approval processes, reporting relationships, authorities and roles are defined, communicated and accepted as part of good governance

Typical tools associated with strategic alignment are those related to portfolio management, such as project selection and prioritization processes and gateway review processes, that subject projects and programmes to predetermined review and approvals and provide executive owners with a mechanism for oversight, monitoring and control.

TOP MANAGEMENT SUPPORT

Managing projects and developing project management capability is much easier in organizations where top management have a good understanding of and appreciation for the contribution that project management can make to their organization. They value project management as essential to corporate delivery capability and are consequently more likely to consistently fund project management improvement initiatives. A key indicator of executive level support is a serious approach to sponsorship of projects. Sponsors should be members of the executive, who understand and accept their role and are capable of effectively (Dinsmore and Cooke-Davies 2006):

- governing the project
- owning the business case
- harvesting benefits
- being a 'friend in high places' to the programme or project manager
- championing the project

Management usually requires a high level of reporting on projects and programmes. Supportive top management will be careful not to place too heavy a burden on those providing the information, by only requesting that which is necessary and by ensuring supportive infrastructure and systems. They will also monitor the data provided, and indicate their understanding through perceptive questioning and guidance. An aspect of this is understanding the nature of risk and estimates; recognizing risk levels will vary throughout the life of the project, that estimates provided in the early stages of a project are subject to variation in definition and scope, and that confidence levels of estimates will increase as the project progresses. This understanding may be embedded through tolerances defined in a gate review system. Further demonstration of top management support is the active involvement of executive and senior management in the project management community.

EFFECTIVE PROJECT MANAGEMENT COMMUNITY

To reap sustainable benefits in terms of project management capability and outcomes, it is necessary to identify the internal project management community and engage its support in simultaneous development of the project management competence of the organization, and project team. The enterprise must develop an environment and capability that fosters effective project management, and team members must have both competence to lead and manage projects, and commitment to continuing development, if projects are to be consistently successful. Characteristics of an effective project management community include:

Enthusiastic and dedicated leadership

Establishment and maintenance of an effective project management community requires visible and enthusiastic leadership from a respected member of the community who is senior enough within the organization to provide top management sponsorship. It is more likely to be provided by a charismatic individual, than to be one element in someone's job description.

Determination by the community to act as a community

Regardless of the form a community takes, a prerequisite for its effective functioning is that all its members have a desire to be members of the community. This is often far from being the case where project managers are concerned as project managers tend to be more task focused than socially oriented.

Availability of budgets and resources

Although the 'organic, spontaneous, and informal nature of communities of practice makes them resistant to supervision and interference' (Wenger and Snyder 2000, p139), they can be nurtured and encouraged. The organization can therefore assist by providing funding and resources to support the activities of the community. In particular the PMO can have an important role if it sees itself as serving rather than dictating the direction of the community.

Conduct of regular conferences for all project and programme community

Conferences, forums or workshops should reflect community needs and be structured to encourage participative learning. Executive leadership should attend the conferences to demonstrate support for the community.

Cross-fertilization of ideas and experience through regular network activities and communications

This should be supported by clear leadership infrastructure, and technology (such as Intranets) which is adequately resourced for sustainability.

Links to the wider professional and corporate community

Links with project management professional organizations may be established by encouraging community members to join professional associations, or through corporate membership; by attendance at professional association functions; submission of entries for awards; by encouraging community members to contribute as speakers at professional association functions. Benchmarking and knowledge network activities with other organizations provide excellent opportunities for bringing in new information to forums and workshops, and attendance of community members at benchmarking functions widens their horizons, is excellent personal development and enables them to bring new ideas back and share them within the organization. Visits to other organizations also help to widen the perspective.

As noted above, communities are not simple to support or maintain. The trend is always towards apathy or fragmentation. For this reason, a project management community requires a fully-funded resource, skilled in community-building and knowledge management, to facilitate and support the community.

PROJECT MANAGEMENT COMPETENCY AND CAREER DEVELOPMENT

The competence and motivation of project management personnel is central to organizational project management capability. The assessment and development of project management competence of individuals is dealt with in Chapter 32. Although much of the responsibility for competency development rests with the individual, the organization is responsible for providing an environment and infrastructure that supports, encourages and provides direction for that development. It is much easier for an individual to develop and demonstrate competence where the organization provides not only career paths and development opportunities but a corporate project management methodology and tools to guide practice.

An important aspect of corporate project management capability is providing personnel with clarity in terms of expectations. People will be more highly motivated to put effort into development and to remain with the organization if career paths, development opportunities, timely feedback, recognition and rewards and project assignments are conducted in a manner which is open and transparent and enables them to plan their careers without ambiguity.

Project Management Career Paths

Although strongly project based organizations offer specific project management career paths (Chapter 31), most large organizations have career structures that are more generic and do not provide for any specialized formal pathways, let alone those for project management. However, it is possible within generic career structures to provide support and guidance to those involved in projects. Some organizations specifically encourage personnel to move between technical, general and project management positions as a contribution to a more rounded development process (Turner et al 2003).

Project Management Role Descriptions

Clear definition of roles and responsibilities is an aspect of good governance. It is also a factor in organizational project management capability. Role descriptions should be linked to governance in terms of authority and responsibility; should relate to the project type; and identify the accreditation and competency requirements expected for the role. They should recognize generic and organization specific project management competencies required, as well as technical, general and behavioural requirements and developmental expectations.

Project Management Competency Development

Processes for assessment and development (as outlined in Chapter 32) should be in place. Support in the form of learning materials, training, mentoring and coaching should be available. One of the most effective forms of competence development is work experience yet this is often the most difficult to achieve. Corporate processes, an appropriate culture and top management support are necessary for work experience opportunities to be provided to support development. Too often managers are unwilling to release staff for developmental work experience. For work experience to be effective it must also be supported by mentoring and coaching.

Performance Assessment, Feedback and Rewards

Performance assessment should be timely and project based, as feedback motivates effective performance and development. Rewards need to be clear and

703

transparent but may take a number of forms directed at both teams and individuals including social events and recognition, as well as financial rewards. (In Chapter 31, Anne Keegan, Rodney Turner and Martina Huemann discuss the balance between assessment and reward in the line and assessment and reward on the project.)

INTERNAL ACCREDITATION – MATCHING PROJECT MANAGERS AND PROJECTS

Categorization of projects is one requirement for effective allocation of personnel. Having good and reliable information on the competence of personnel is another. Much of this information may relate to qualifications and past work experience and may be difficult to use as a basis for comparison and assignment. Internal accreditation programmes have a number of advantages for organizations. They satisfy the requirement for equity, transparency and clarity in terms of expectations for individuals; they are specifically designed to suit the requirements of the organization, the types of projects they manage and the context, both internal and external, within which they are managed; they are within the control of the organization; and they provide a clear basis for reward, recognition and assignment of personnel. It makes sense for internal accreditation programmes to be aligned to external standards for competence for a number of reasons. Firstly this ensures that the development efforts of individuals can be recognized not only within the organization but externally thereby providing greater value and therefore motivation. From the organizational perspective, alignment with external standards is of assistance in recruitment, and in working in partnership and sharing of personnel with other organizations by increasing the likelihood of shared terminology and practices.

REPOSITORIES OF DATA

Ready access to controlled and reliable data is vital for effective project performance. This should include information on:

- all company processes
- contracts and procurement details
- all project personnel including grade, competence, experience, availability and aspiration
- all projects and programmes throughout the organization
- post implementation reviews and lessons learned.

Having this available saves time in searching for the appropriate information and by reducing the need for re-work due to use of out of date information. It provides the necessary basis for solid capability and continuous improvement. Data on company processes is important in ensuring consistency in conduct and documentation of projects across the organization. Effective resource allocation is dependent upon having up to date information on personnel. Data on project performance are essential as a basis for improving the accuracy of estimating, and accurate estimating is fundamental to reliable delivery in accordance with expectations. Post implementation reviews provide guidance for the planning and estimating of new projects, for risk identification, and for improvement of processes. They are also the primary although ideally not the only source of lessons learned and easy access to these is important for continuous improvement.

Organizations should not, however, confine themselves to data from their own organization. It is important that they make a practice of regularly comparing their own performance on various dimensions with that of other organizations both similar and different in order to avoid staleness, complacency or failure to perform at as high a level as possible. Benchmarking of project management processes and specific aspects of performance at both organizational and project level is a key to development and maintenance of leading edge project management capability. When undertaken internally it enables the pin-pointing of pockets of good practice and the dissemination of this to improve overall corporate practices and performance. When conducted externally it enables the organization to learn from the good practices of other organizations in similar and dissimilar fields.

Comprehensive, user friendly, accessible, controlled, reliable and therefore trusted repositories of data which are also externally referenced are central to effective knowledge management and a critical building block of organizational project management capability.

CORPORATE PROJECT MANAGEMENT METHODOLOGY AND TOOLS

Central to organizational project management capability is a corporate project management methodology and toolset. This may take many forms from the use of an off the shelf methodology such as PRINCE2™, or PROPS (developed by Ericsson); a methodology developed or customized for the organization by consultants; or a completely home-grown methodology devised by the project management community. The latter may not be perfect but will often enjoy a greater sense of ownership and therefore greater usage.

While many project managers complain about having to use a specific corporate project management methodology and being required to limit themselves to the tools approved and provided, having a methodology of some sort does make their lives easier, saving them from having to reinvent the wheel. Such methodologies provide templates and guidance for the project management processes that need to be undertaken. As long as the methodology is sensible and not overly bureaucratic, it will save time and increase efficiency. Importantly, from the organizational viewpoint, if the methodology is followed and the use of tools is controlled, it will ensure consistency of project management practice across the organization which in turn improves the useability and accuracy of reporting and the ability to compare performance between projects and across the organization as a basis for improvement.

There needs to be some process in place to control both the quality and use of the methodology and toolset. This may be through governance or a quality assurance process but by far the most effective approach is for the methodology and toolset to be the responsibility of a Project, Programme or Portfolio Management Office (see Chapter 9), having the added advantage of providing a single point of reference for information and support on methods and tools. Although the project governance structure and project management methodology may allow for different application models for different project types (eg Governance Lite for less complex, more routine, shorter duration projects), consistency of application is vital. Another important consideration is provision of training to introduce people to and to support the use of the methodology and tools.

Having identified some of the key elements of organizational project management capability, the next steps are to baseline the current level of capability, decide what level of capability is right for the organization, identify the gaps and plan and implement an improvement programme that is consistent with the corporate strategy and resource availability.

SETTING A BASELINE FOR DEVELOPMENT

Once an organization decides that it wishes to develop or improve its project management capability it should establish its current baseline and targets for development. This enables the organization to track its development and demonstrate improvements. Such demonstration will be valuable in ensuring ongoing funding of the development process or for reassuring stakeholders of improved capability. General management is familiar with 'Business Excellence' models such as the European Foundation for Quality Management (EFQM) Excellence Model and Baldrige Award which they use to identify, describe and then improve business processes. Similar models, focusing on project and programme management, can be used to assess the current status of organizational project management capability, to guide development and for periodic re-assessment to determine and demonstrate progress (Chapter 11). A number of models are available for this purpose and they tend to be in the form of 'Excellence' or 'Maturity' models. The IPMA International Project Excellence Awards and the Corporate Practices Questionnaire which has been continuously developed over the last fifteen years by the companies that are members of the

Human Systems knowledge networks, are 'Excellence' models developed on principles similar to those driving the EFQM and Baldrige awards. The aim here is to identify and assess those working practices that lead to improved performance (Cooke-Davies 2000)

The large number of available 'Maturity' models have been strongly influenced by the Capability Maturity Model (CMM) developed by the Software Engineering Institute (SEI) of Carnegie Mellon University for the software development process (Humphrey and Sweet 1987; Paulk et al. 1995). Many of these have combined the concept of maturity as established by the SEI CMM with the view of project management presented in the Project Management Institute's PMBOK®Guide which tends to present a specifically project centric or tactical view. Others such as Gareis (Chapter 10) and Kerzner (2001) take different views of organizational project management maturity.

In 2003 the Project Management Institute released its Organizational Project Management Maturity Model (OPM3®) which identifies more than 600 'best practices', more than 3000 'capabilities' and more than 4000 relationships between capabilities. They have since developed an OPM3® Product Suite and a process for certification of assessors. The OGC has also developed a Project Management Maturity Model (PMMM) in recognition that maturity questionnaires provide a simple tool for identifying areas where an organization's processes may need improvement (Cooke-Davies 2004a).

As mentioned at the start of this chapter, different organizations in different industries will place emphasis on different aspects or components of project management capability. Each organization should therefore choose the model and process best suited to their need as a basis for establishing their current baseline, formulating and implementing an improvement plan and conducting periodic re-assessment.

PLANNING AND IMPLEMENTING A PROJECT MANAGEMENT IMPROVEMENT PROGRAMME

Once an organization has established its current level of project management capability, and determined the level of capability that is appropriate to meet its specific needs (such as to serve internal or external clients, address specific regulatory requirements, or deliver tangible or intangible end products) it is in a position to develop an improvement programme that will take it from where it is now to where it wants to be. It is important to recognize that such an endeavour is in itself a project or programme which should be managed accordingly. It is also an organizational change project and both planning and implementation should take this into consideration.

707

As an organizational change project, communications and stakeholder management will be extremely important. The project will need a project or programme manager, a senior sponsor, and ideally one or more champions. Engagement of the project management community and of senior management will be vital to the success of the improvement programme. It will also be important to ensure that the programme is planned to take account of the organization's capacity and appetite for change. Usually a significant element is the need to change the organizational culture – at all levels – to develop an understanding of project management and an appreciation of what it can do to assist the organization in achieving its goals and in making life easier rather than more difficult. Very often organizations may have had previous unsatisfactory encounters with project management and these can act to inhibit the success of the improvement programme if not carefully managed.

A useful approach is to use a framework such as the elements of capability provided above, or one of the many project management excellence or maturity assessment models that are available to establish the current project management capability footprint of the organization. Then use the same model to determine what level of capability it makes sense for the organization to aspire to. The difference between the two, Figure 33.2, provides the basis for a plan of action. Use of such a model as a basis can be very helpful in focusing the effort, in engaging the general and project management communities, in inspiring the effort required to move from one level of capability to another and in demonstrating progress. A two- to three-year period is a practical time frame for an initial project management improvement programme and it makes sense to set annual or bi-annual targets for improvement. The excellence or maturity

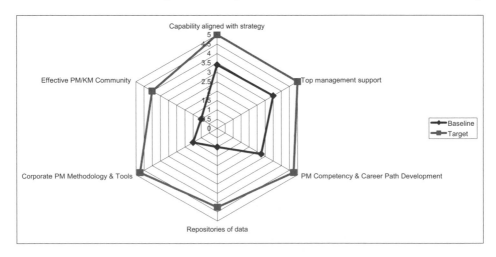

Figure 33.2   Setting baseline and targets for organizational project management capability

frameworks can be used at each stage as a basis for re-assessment and to illustrate and generate interest around achievement.

Having set the improvement programme up as a project, with executive sponsor and project manager and a staged plan for improvement, adequate resources need to be allocated and committed. Strong and consistent senior management support is a significant factor in the success of such a programme. Unfortunately experience demonstrates that support or resources are often withdrawn from corporate project management improvement programmes for a number of reasons. One is financial pressure on the organization. For instance, when telecommunications organizations suffered financial difficulties in the early 2000s, a number of them significantly reduced their investment in project management capability. Another common reason is internal politics often combined with financial pressure. A very successful project and programme management initiative in one major financial institution was completely removed from the organization for a number of reasons. A new CEO who didn't believe in project management was appointed, the head of the initiative had successfully implemented a major cost control programme that had made him and project management unpopular with other senior managers, and the organization had to demonstrate to shareholders a commitment to cost reduction. Hence the importance of communications and stakeholder management.

In conducting the improvement programme there are two key aspects. One is the formulation of the approach which may be relatively easy if adequately resourced. Much of the approach may be documented in a corporate project management methodology. Policies and procedures can be written and put in place. Governance structures can be established. The other aspect is deployment and this is usually far more difficult as it involves the consistent application of the documented approach across the organization.

Project, Programme and Portfolio Management offices (Chapter 9) can play an important part in the planning and implementation of a project management capability improvement programme. A PMO provides the focus and ideally the resources necessary to implement the programme. The PMO can also monitor and encourage the deployment of the approach across the organization.

Once the initial organizational project management improvement programme has been successfully completed, and the capability goals achieved, the next challenge is to maintain that level of capability. It is much easier to move from a low base to a moderate to high level of capability than it is to maintain that level. One way of maintaining the level is to aspire to continuous improvement and this is a common requirement of the highest level of most maturity models.

The next section deals with continuous improvement of project management capability through learning and knowledge management.

CONTINUOUS IMPROVEMENT OF ORGANIZATIONAL PROJECT MANAGEMENT CAPABILITY

LEARNING

Rodney Turner and Anne Keegan (2004) suggest a four step process for continuously improving organization project management capability:

1. **Variation:** through trial and error, and practical experience, you need to identify new ways of managing and delivering projects
2. **Selection:** through review processes, you need to identify those new practices which provide benefit through improved performance, and those which don't
3. **Retention:** through data repositories and knowledge management, you need to store the selected new ideas where they are accessible
4. **Distribution:** through project management procedures and the project management community you need to get the selected new ideas to project managers on projects where they can be used to improve performance on future projects

The first three steps of this cycle were first described by people working on the evolution of species, explaining how new genes arise by random mutation, are selected through survival of the fittest and retained in the gene pool. They was subsequently adopted by the management learning literature. In a functional organization the new ideas are generated in the functional hierarchy, selected and retained there, where they are immediately available for use by managers. But Rodney Turner and Anne Keegan identified that in a project-based organization there is the essential fourth step, distribution. In a project-based organization, new ideas are generated on one project which is going to come to an end, and so need to be transferred to a central pool where they will be held and from there go to managers working on new projects, where they can be used.

Figure 33.3 illustrates how some of the things we have discussed so far support the four learning practices.

VARIATION

In project management new ideas are generated on one project. The project management community and top management can help in this process by identifying weaknesses in the current approaches and encouraging people to try new ideas. We discuss competency traps below, but you need to avoid a blame culture and encourage people to try new ideas, and accept the occasional mistake,

Learning practice	Organizational support
Variation	Project management community Top management support Reviews and Audits
Selection	Project management community Reviews and audits Benchmarking
Retention	Project management community Project management procedures Data repositories
Distribution	Project management community Project management procedures Career development

Figure 33.3 Organizational support for the four learning practices

for the long term benefit of finding a better way of working. Audits and reviews can also help pinpoint weaknesses and point to a need of variation.

Selection

The best new ideas are then to be identified and selected through appropriate reviews:

- project control reviews (Chapter 29)
- health checks or audits (Chapter 11)
- post-completion reviews (Chapter 31)
- gateway reviews (see above)
- benchmarking (see above)

Retention

The selected new ideas then need to be retained centrally, perhaps by the Project Office (Chapter 9), perhaps through knowledge management processes (see below), perhaps through story-telling in the project management community. They cannot be retained on a project, because the project is going to be disbanded. That is the problem of projects as temporary organizations, they cannot own and retain knowledge; it has to be owned and retained separately from the project, and thus the need for the fourth step.

Distribution

The new knowledge needs to be distributed to project managers starting new projects so it can be used on those new projects. There are two main ways that the new knowledge can be distributed on a project-based organization:

- through the project management procedures
- through the project management community

Rodney Turner and Anne Keegan have identified two issues with the four-stage learning practice identified above, attenuation and delay.

Attenuation

There is a loss of learning at each step of the process. Terry Cooke-Davies (2000) has identified that there is a 25% loss of information at each step, meaning that less than one third of the good new ideas that a project-based organization generates actually end up being used on new projects. There are many ways suggested to overcome that problem:

- make project reviews mandatory
- make the project office responsible for collating the results of reviews
- use the Intranet to store and distribute the good ideas
- ensure the project management community is working effectively

The first three of these all tend to add to the bureaucracy of the organization, and so you have to balance the benefit of the knowledge management and innovation against the cost of processing the data.

Delay

Rodney Turner and Anne Keegan (2004) also identified that there tends to be a delay between each step. Traditionally there has been an emphasis on post-completion reviews, and then there may be a delay before ideas are selected and retained; it may be two years before the next edition of the project management procedures are issued, and the project manager at the coal face may be too busy to read the new procedures until the start of his or her next project. There is a concept of the viscosity of information. Some information oozes through an organization like treacle, taking years to go from new idea to use on a new project. But other information zips through, like gas through a vacuum. This is especially true of information entered into the Intranet. It is immediately available for use, and so if there is no control on what information is entered, yesterday's hearsay can become today's received wisdom. We suggest that the ideal is that there should be some delay with variation and selection, perhaps three months, allowing for ideas to be properly tested and distilled. But then chosen ideas could be entered into the Intranet, where they would be immediately available for reuse on future projects. The Project Office can manage this process. Other organizations are using the ideas of discussion rooms or 'wiki' space. In a wiki space, individuals can enter ideas they have, describe how they solved a problem, or describe a new management approach they used. Other people can then comment on that idea, say whether they tried it, what experience they had, and how valuable they found it. The new ideas are then tested and selected through trial and discussion. New ideas can also be tested through the project management community in the same way.

The Learning Cycle

Figure 33.4 illustrates Nonaka and Takeuchi's learning cycle which shows how the project management community can aid organizational learning. It shows how tacit knowledge can be converted to explicit knowledge, and then re-internalized through practice to be made tacit again. Explicit knowledge is knowledge that can be codified and recorded. It is obtained through formal instruction. Tacit knowledge is internal knowledge we have but are not aware we have. It is inherent. It is obtained through practice. It is tacit knowledge which mainly enables high performance. We could not drive a car without relying on tacit knowledge. But in order for the organization to learn and improve, the tacit knowledge of individuals must be made explicit, shared, and then re-internalized and made tacit through further experience. To explain the cycle, it is normal to start in the top left-hand quadrant and work clockwise.

	To	
	Tacit knowledge	Explicit knowledge
Tacit knowledge	*Socialization* Sharing-creating tacit knowledge through experience	*Externalization* Articulating Tacit knowledge through reflection
Explicit knowledge	*Internalization* Learning-acquiring new tacit knowledge in practice	*Combination* Systematizing explicit-knowledge and information

From (appears at left side, between the two rows)

Figure 33.4   Nonaka and Takeuchi's learning cycle

1. *Socialization:* First, through meetings of the project management community, tacit knowledge is shared
2. *Externalization:* It can then be articulated and made explicit
3. *Combination:* The new explicit knowledge can be systematized and recorded in the procedures
4. *Internalization:* People can then start to use the new explicit knowledge, and it will be reinternalized, or internalized by apprentice project managers, and made tacit again.

KNOWLEDGE MANAGEMENT

A key step in the above processes is the storing of new knowledge. This is known as knowledge management. There are four types of knowledge:

- that you know you have
- that you don't know you have
- that you know you don't have
- that you don't know you don't have

Conventionally knowledge management has focused on storing the first of these. But we believe it should also focus on discovering the other three.

Know-you-know

This is explicit knowledge you know you have. There is a four-step process for developing a knowledge management system:

1. *Where are we?* You need to establish an inventory of your current knowledge management practices.
2. *Where do we want to be?* Next you need to consider your knowledge management needs. You need to identify your business context and drivers, and the success factors and key performance indicators relevant to your projects. Then you need to identify the characteristics of the knowledge to be managed. What are the sources, who are the users, and what are the enablers and inhibitors?
3. *What is the gap?* This will identify a gap between your current knowledge management practices and those you need.
4. *What is the migration path?* So you can then plan the project to develop the knowledge management systems you need.

The knowledge management system needs to consist of five processes

1. Knowledge generation:
   - what is the knowledge, where does it come from and how is it captured?

2. Knowledge propagation:
   - how is data converted to information, information to knowledge and knowledge to wisdom?
3. Knowledge transfer:
   - how is data distributed from where it is generated to where it is used?
4. Knowledge location and access
   - where is it stored in repositories of data?
   - how is transferred to those who need it?
5. Knowledge maintenance and modification
   - who has the right to add to it?
   - who has the right to change it?

Don't know you know

There are two types of knowledge that fall into this category: tacit knowledge and X-files. Figure 33.5 explains what I mean by X-files. I described above how to use Nonaka and Takeuchi's cycle, coupled with the project management community to make tacit knowledge explicit and thereby make it known. This can also help identify knowledge through random connections, perhaps resulting in two seemingly unrelated ideas being put together. The X-files need to be found by data mining or careful archiving, indexed so that files can still be found by the search engine on the Intranet.

In the first episode of the *X Files*, Mulder and Sculley think they have found evidence of aliens. In particular they find a person with a device implanted in his ear. This device is conclusive proof, so they send it to FBI headquarters. In the last scene, a man is seen walking in the depths of the FBI basement past all the archive (X) files. He reaches a row, pulls out a box, and throws in the device, and there are already five or six in the box. The knowledge (truth) is not 'out there', it is in the X-files in the basement of the FBI where nobody knows about it. Don't know they know.

Figure 33.5 X-files

Know you don't know

This is easier. Research can be done in the normal places: the Internet; Wikipedia and Google; research journals; books. Bench marking and reviews can also help. Organizations also conduct research workshops to improve their own understanding of a particular situation. Project start workshops (Chapter 26) are in fact an example of such a workshop.

Don't know you don't know

You don't know to look for it and it is difficult to discover in structured normative ways. It requires random searches and random interconnections.

COMPETENCY TRAPS

Competency traps are things that stop us learning. There may be a better, more efficient or more effective way of working, but competency traps either stop us finding it, or stop us trying it even if we know it exists. In project-based organizations competency traps include:

The desire for safety and reliability

You only have one shot at a project, and so there is often a preference for safety and reliability over efficiency and effectiveness. For instance you may have two ways of doing something, one guaranteed to work but with efficiency 100%, and the other with 80% chance of success but efficiency 300%. The second way is on average two and a half times better. But managers in project based organizations often prefer the way that offers guaranteed success for the one time they are going to do it. If in a functional organization you are going to do it 100 times, then with the 300% method the first 10 times you get it right eight times and wrong twice, but you are two and a half times better off. The next 10 times you will have learnt from your mistakes and get it right nine times and wrong once. From then on you will get it right every time and be three times better off. But in a project you only do it once and want it right that one time.

Blame culture

This is related to the previous trap, but now look at the decision from the perspective of the persons making the decision, not the organization. If they work in a blame culture they will have an overriding preference for the safe, reliable option. Their assessment of the situation is different. If they choose the first option they have a certain chance of a quiet life. Nobody will notice. If they choose the second option they have an 80% chance of a quiet life, nobody will notice if it works. They won't get praised for the extra efficiency. But if it goes wrong they will get blamed when it goes wrong, so they have a 20% chance of being hounded. They will choose the safe option. A few years ago, Rodney Turner worked with the British Museum. They lived in fear of the tabloid press. What makes news is public sector organizations making mistakes and so wasting public money. If they choose the first option the tabloid press won't notice. If they choose the second there is an 80% chance that they won't notice, but there is a 20% chance that they will, and the person making the decision will be ridiculed.

The tabloid press won't say it was the better decision. They will just trumpet the waste of public money. In the early 1980s, Rodney Turner worked for ICI. There the attitude was if you don't take risks, you don't make profits, but if you take risks you make the occasional mistake. They therefore liked people who made the very occasional mistakes, and didn't like people who never made mistakes. People who never made mistakes weren't making profits. It was the exact opposite of a blame culture. Of course if you always made mistakes you got put on 'special duties'.

Contracting practice

Standard contracting can be a competency trap. Don't expect a contractor on a remeasurement contract without a bonus to suggest a process improvement. They are going to lose profit. If you want your contractors to suggest improved ways of working you need to offer them a bonus to do it.

Fear of competitors stealing your innovations

Some organizations don't innovate for fear that their competitors will steal their new ideas. It is a similar reason to why some organizations don't train their staff, for fear that they will leave and their competitors will get the benefit of the training. People are actually more likely to stay if they are properly developed. Enlightened organizations train their staff; enlightened organizations find ways of improving their processes. Yes their competitors will eventually adopt the ideas as well, but it will take them about two years, so the organization that does the research and development will always have two years lead.

Non linearity and coupling of projects

Projects are non-linear coupled systems. To make improvements requires not just one bit to be changed on its own but the whole project to be changed. That can sometimes create complexity as it is difficult to design a new, integrated solution. Or it can create competition where all stakeholders want to optimize the project outcome for themselves, resulting in an inferior outcome for the whole project. Rodney Turner discussed this in Chapter 6, when he advocated the need to obtain a balance of all the stakeholders' different objectives.

Traditional project management thinking

One of the worst competency traps of all is traditional project management thinking. It preaches rigid control and certainty of estimates. Closing the estimates early can often lock you into high cost solutions. Often, to find the best solution for the project requires you to keep options open for as long as possible, and that requires you to maintain uncertainty of the outcomes longer than you may be comfortable with. Further rigid plans, with rigid control, can also lock you into high cost solutions at an early stage.

REFERENCES AND FURTHER READING

Cooke-Davies, T.J., 2000, *Towards improved project management practice: uncovering the evidence for effective practices through empirical research*, PhD Thesis, Leeds Metropolitan University available at <http://www.dissertation.com>

Cooke-Davies, T., 2001, 'The 'real' project success factors', *International Journal of Project Management,* 20(3), 185–190.

Cooke-Davies, T.J., 2004a, 'Project Success', in Morris, P.W.G. and Pinto, J.K., (eds.), *The Wiley Guide to Managing Projects*, New York: Wiley.

Cooke-Davies, T.J., 2004b, 'Project management maturity models', in Morris, P.W.G. and Pinto, J.K., (eds.), *The Wiley Guide to Managing Projects*, New York: Wiley.

Crawford, L.H., Hobbs, J.B. and Turner, J.R., 2005, *Project Categorization Systems: aligning capability with strategy for better results*, Newtown Square, PA: Project Management Institute.

Dinsmore, P.C. and Cooke-Davies, T.J., 2006, *The Right Projects Done Right!: From business strategy to successful project implementation,* San Francisco, CA: Jossey-Bass.

Humphrey, W.S. and Sweet, W.L., 1987, *A Method for Assessing the Software Engineering Capability of Contractors: CMU/SEI–87–TR–23, ESD/TR–87–186*, Software Engineering Institute, Carnegie Mellon University.

Hyvari, I., 2006, 'Success of projects in different organizational conditions', *Project Management Journal,* 37(4), 31–41.

Kerzner, H., 2001, *Strategic Planning for Project Management: using a project management maturity model*, New York: Wiley.

KPMG , Editors, 1997, *What Went Wrong? Unsuccessful information technology projects,* <http://audit.kpmg.ca/vl/surveys/it-wrong.htm> (19 March 2002).

Nieto-Rodriguez, A. and Evrard, D., 2004, *Boosting Business Performance through Programme and Project Management: first global survey on the current state of project management maturity in organizations across the world*, PricewaterhouseCoopers International Limited.

Paulk, M.C., Weber, C.V., Curtis, B. and Chrissis, M.-B., 1995, *The Capability Maturity Model: guidelines for improving the software process*, Boston, MA: Addison-Wesley Longman Publishing.

Pinto, J.K. and Slevin, D.P., 1988, 'Critical success factors in effective project implementation', in Cleland, D.I. and King, W.R., (eds.), *Project Management Handbook,* 2nd edition, New York, NY: Van Nostrand Reinhold.

PMI®, 2003, *Organizational Project Management Maturity Model,* Newtown Square, PA: Project Management Institute.

Turner, J.R., and Keegan, A.E., 2004, 'Technology Management', in Morris, P.W.G. and Pinto, J.K., (eds.), *The Wiley Guide to Managing Projects,* New York: Wiley.

Turner, J.R., Keegan, A.E. and Crawford, L.H., 2003, 'Learning by experience in the project-based organization', in Turner, J.R., (ed), *People in Project Management,* Aldershot, UK: Gower.

Wenger, E.C. and Snyder, W.M., 2000, 'Communities of practice: the organizational frontier', *Harvard Business Review,* 78(1), 139–146.

34 Managing Teams: The Reality of Life

Tony Reid

Everyone agrees that project teams are a good idea: true or false? Most teams start out full of energy, with good intentions and often offers of support. Unfortunately, fairly quickly things begin to look less certain. The consequence is that, instead of a surge of energy, there is a feeling of being alone, neglected, attacked even. The goals that were clear now seem conditional on all sorts of other priorities, while the sources of authority are joined by more shadowy influencers who appear to be the ones who really call the shots. The next move is that team members are reassigned back to their home base or to higher priority projects, often halfway through the assignment. Deadlines become immovable and unachievable, overtime and exhaustion sets in. Management reorganizes the project team in exasperation, and de-motivated people begin to fulfil every prophecy. At this moment you may be nodding your head as you recognize this as a familiar experience. The key questions are why and what can be done to avoid it happening?

It is with those thoughts in mind that this chapter of the handbook sets out to provide some basic, proven guidelines to help you create a capable project team. The guidelines do not require you to be a team development specialist, only a well informed manager who has a clear understanding of the purpose of the project and the ability to manage a team of people – not always easy requirements as has been indicated. A warning for you: *management has good intentions but often poor follow-through due to pressures to produce quick results.*

In reality many organizations are poor at project management and project leaders equally poor at team building. In the former instance, it is usually because there is insufficient discipline and effort at pre-commencement, and in the latter the project leader does not see the creation of the team and a team culture as a priority: responding to the client, leaping into action, often with no apparent direction, is more likely to be the norm.

RESULTS THROUGH TEAM WORKING

The evidence of high performing teams is all around us. Here are just three examples:

1. the Formula 1 Racing Teams are a clear example, with at least three key roles:
   - a star place for the individual driver
   - an operational sub-team performing the changes as the vehicle comes in for service
   - behind the scenes a support team to provide the race strategy
2. soccer teams: often made up of outstanding individual performers but working together towards a common goal on the day of the match
3. organizations realizing their business objectives, business improvement and rapid growth using project teams to manage change

Already perhaps there is a lesson to learn from the two sporting examples: what do they do that makes them different from many other project teams? *They spend 90% of their time practising, rehearsing and developing their strategies and processes before they attempt the project.* You may say that is not possible to do that in business, construction or IT; well there is a school of thought that says *'we don't know what we are capable of until we try!'*

PRACTICAL GUIDELINES

PURPOSE

The amazing thing is that very often in the case of an emergency we experience the ideal characteristics of teamwork – a willingness to get involved, to take any role, to work cooperatively together, all driven by a desire to rescue and to save others from pain or disaster. It is this *power of purpose* that seems to provide the direction, resource strategy and key roles of the team, often to great effect. So how can this principle be applied to every project? This is the first most important task for the project leader:

> *To define the purpose of the project, clarify the definition with the client, and then share that purpose with the project team*

It sounds easy of course. Unfortunately, very often the client cannot articulate the purpose so this is the time when the project leader really needs courage to explore, to question and to challenge the client for measured definition. In addition, it is the time to involve other key team members in seeking additional clarification from their professional counterparts in the client organization. This is the first collective team task.

Having sought clarity of definition and tested the interpretation with the key stakeholders now is the time to go public; it is the achievement of the purpose of the project that must become the dominant driver and measurement of success. It is the *power of the purpose* that will drive the project forward and enable the project team to perform through all adversity.

> The purpose acquires power when it is made visible.

This should become the project logo (a drawing of the intended building, a map of the intended system, a group of people sharing the new hospital resources). In addition, a similar but enlarged picture should be placed about the project site, office, locations – including with the client, consultants, suppliers, plus other key stakeholders. Alternatively this 'picture' could become the progress map gradually making the transformation from the existing circumstance to the final vision as it is duly updated as the project progresses. (This is focusing the attention of the stakeholders on the success criteria, Chapter 5.) It is the *purpose* that provides the *meaning of life* for the period of the project and so enables project team members to identify a framework within which to determine their three most important needs:

1   What is expected of me?
2   Where do I fit in?
3   And how am I getting on?

When these fundamental requirements of purpose and personal needs are satisfied you might ask yourself, 'Do I need to spend special time at all on team-building?' The answer may well be no!

PROJECT TEAM SELECTION

If a group has cohesion, spirit and a sense of purpose, they can accomplish any project task, from installing a new IT system to raising money for the Red Cross. We believe that in order to achieve this magical balance you need to seriously consider the make up of personalities in your prospective project team. Your reality may be that the team is composed of 'whoever is available at the time', hardly the way to select the team for the 'premier division', so fight this stance tooth and nail. One of the key merits of deciding to have a team is the possibility of a wide variety of talents and capabilities, so it is worth thinking about the nature of the project, the project needs and the character of the other stakeholders who will need to be managed. The results of this examination will lead you to consider the best mix for the team; professional expertise is never enough. The results of your deliberations are likely to lead you to consider the merits of some of these key traits as essential requirements for your team:

- those who seek to accomplish the task
- those who will be concerned with the quality of working relationships
- those who strive for closure and control
- those who seek the ideal solution
- those who want to leap into action immediately
- those who would prefer to ponder on the option and think things through
- those who excel at detail
- those who love the concepts and the possibilities

Metaphorically, the project leader is the *scrum half*, who hands off an assignment to a package leader (*back row*), who uses support staff (*forwards*) to move a project ahead to a final goal (the try line). In practical terms there is a need to select a team to match the demands of the project. Many projects require extroverts to sell the project to the client and the support units in their own project organization. Equally there is a need for more imaginative personalities who will generate alternative means for raising the money, plus a balance of others who will pound the pavement and follow through on commitment plans.

It's worth compiling key criteria for your project and drawing up a balance card to ensure you select those team players that bring the skill, knowledge and experience with the personality to match the demands of the project, Figure 34.1. Take time to interview potential team members who have been chosen for their functional expertise to determine how they fit with the management style and demands of the project. These are some questions you may ask:

1. Tell me about the best project leader you've worked for.
2. Why was he or she a good leader?
3. What was your least favourite leader like?
4. How did you handle things you didn't like about him or her?
5. Tell me about a disagreement you had with a previous boss. How did you resolve it?
6. What actions are necessary to make a high performance project team?

If you were responsible for selecting a professional sports team then the elements would be: clearly defined roles for team members, an explicit purpose uniting the team, an agreed game plan, and a coach. So in addition to thinking about the team selection, consider whom you will choose as your personal or team coach or mentor.

Project Role	Technical or functional expertise	Personality Profile (Problem-solving and decision-making capability) Emotional Intelligence or Capability	Key Project Demands

Figure 34.1 Balance card for project team selection

CONDITIONS FOR TEAM WORKING

Perhaps the most basic conditions for good team working would be too obvious but frequently they are not considered. They are: size, purpose, goals, skills, approach, and accountability. Paying rigorous attention to these is what creates the conditions necessary for high team performance. Listen to successful teams, you will find that they are committed to their purpose, goals and approach. By applying rigorous attention to performance measurement requirements and conditions for team working, most groups can deliver the goods.

FOCUSING ON TEAM BASICS

Katzenbach and Smith (1993) suggest that managers should focus on team performance and team basics issues, Figure 34.2. It is through disciplined action, much the same as following a diet, that true teams are born. They shape a common purpose, agree on performance goals, define a common working approach, develop high levels of complementary skills and hold themselves mutually accountable for results. Integrated with this basic approach real teams always find ways for each individual to contribute and gain distinction.

TEAM CHARTER

This commitment might take the form of a *Team Charter* that sets out the common approach the team have adopted for themselves. The elements of such a charter might constitute these:

- Purpose of the Project
- Key Performance Goals
- Project Team Values
- Roles and Responsibilities
- Managing Issues and Conflict Resolution
- Assessment and Team Effectiveness

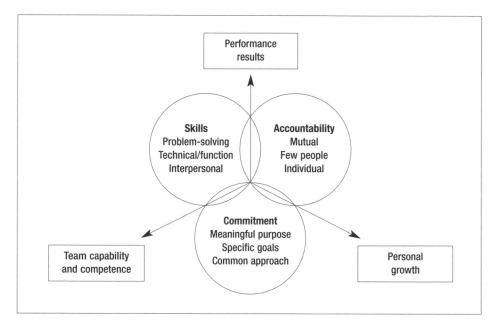

Figure 34.2   Focusing on team basics

The purpose

We have already mentioned that it is purpose that will have the most significant influence on the progress of the project and therefore the team, the key word being *visibility*.

The key performance goals

The goals must be aligned with the project purpose and the organizational-wide goals. The goals serve as benchmarks for which the project sponsor and each stakeholder group, those parties that have a vested interest in the team's success, will hold the team accountable. Some necessary groundwork will be required here to develop a clear understanding of the sponsor's and stakeholder's needs and expectations. The goals should be aligned to:

- Organizational measures for return on investment and profits
- Qualitative and quantitative goals that measure the project outputs (Chapter 14 and 15)
- Individual goals that measure the results of team members, (assigned through the responsibility matrix, Chapter 18)

The goals are likely to reflect the *success criteria* and *success factors* (Chapter 6) that have been agreed with the client for a reengineering project team the critical success criteria might be cycle time, costs, and customer service. Others might be revenue enhancement, market share gain, and employee satisfaction. A matrix that identifies accountability for goals should be created, Figure 34.3 and Chapter 18. The goal leader must ensure that the goals, when translated into workable objectives, must be SMART maybe even SMARTIES, Figure 34.4.

Goals	Goal Leader	Team members who will provide support	Key Project Demands

Figure 34.3   Goal Matrix

Project team values

Goals define what we seek to achieve; our values indicate how we 'behave' to achieve them. Establishing these ground rules of agreed team behaviour is vital to success. Often we discover what works by learning what does not work. Behaviour is so crucial to team success or failure that a willingness to abide by agreed values and norms should be a qualification for membership. Making that expectation non-negotiable sends a strong message. When people refuse to abide by expectations they are, in effect, deciding not to be on the team. Typically, values and norms evolve over time and often remain unspoken and unwritten unless they are violated. In practice there are some basic ground rules that can be defined at the outset:

- share all relevant information
- focus on interest and not position
- be specific and use examples to illustrate the point
- disagree openly with other members of the team
- invite questions and comment
- expect all team members to participate
- make decisions by consensus

S	Specific
M	Measurable
A	Achievable
R	Realistic
T	Timely
I	Involvement of the appropriate team members
E	Environment standards are met
S	Success orientated

Figure 34.4   SMART(IES) goals

727

- explain the reasons behind the words
- respect and value each others time
- conduct self-critique

A fundamental requirement that you will need to seek is that of trust within the project team and this feels an appropriate place to suggest some ways of building it:

- convey consistent principles
- give team members plausible explanations for actions
- offer status reports and forecasts
- make realistic commitments
- showcase what you know
- protect the interests of people that aren't present
- show compassion
- verify understanding

Roles and responsibilities

The functional roles and responsibilities for the project should be clearly defined within the team with a balanced load spread between the players on an equal basis. In addition to the conventional expert functions there are a number of other key duties that will need to be fulfilled; here are some of the most important:

1. *Customer/client service contact:* who monitors the client's expectations?
2. *Liaison with head office:* who builds collaboration?
3. *Mr or Ms Integrity:* who provides the role model of behaviour?
4. *Community and interface developer:* who monitors how the project will impact on the community?
5. *Team motivator:* who provides that extra burst of enthusiasm when all is down?
6. *Challenger and supporter of the workforce:* who ensures that all views are taken into account?
7. *On-the-job educational developer:* who seeks out novel ways of keeping people informed and up-to-date?
8. *Crazy idea and innovation challenger:* who challenges the conventional behaviour?
9. *Fun generator and celebration king:* who generates celebration and makes sure that the team honour individual and group accomplishments?

Managing Issues and Conflict Resolution

Managing project team issues should constitute a regular feature in the weekly review programme. One process that works effectively has five stages:

1. Ask team members to identify, without comment, the issues the team needs to address. These issues are listed on a flip chart without any attempt to order or prioritize. Typically they will be related to team issues to do with procedures, practices, project strategy or roles and responsibilities, and sometimes morale and commitment.
2. Agree with the team the issues that should be challenged; there may be some that can be resolved very quickly, for example when information is needed; prioritize the remainder and decide how many can be adequately examined in the permitted time.
3. The individual team member who raises the issue is then given the opportunity to present it in more detail and the other members are given the opportunity to ask questions for clarity. This part of the process often requires strong direction to ensure that the focus remains on clarification and not solution generation.
4. The issue presenter is then asked to affirm the definition of the issue; sometimes it might have changed out of all recognition from the original statement.
5. The other team members are then asked, in turn, to present their idea of a solution to the revised issue. The project leader then has the task of deciding if further discussion and consensus agreement is necessary particularly if the issue has wider implications.

When teams are composed of strong independent, diverse thinkers, it is inevitable that differences will arise (Chapter 38). Establishing the ground rules as we have indicated will help. In addition it helps to agree on a process for managing conflict and identifying trained facilitators who can support positive conflict resolution.

1. Establish ground rules on how to manage one-on-one and team conflict
2. Adopt a step-by-step model for conflict resolution based on:
   ● Questioning the situation
   ● Identifying the problem
   ● Determining the implications of the problem
   ● Identifying the needs
   ● Developing alternative forms of resolution to meet the needs
   ● Evaluating the alternatives against the needs to determine the best choice
   ● And generating appropriate action plans

Sometimes you might deliberately encourage dispute or productive conflict; it can lead to magic when team members express their opinions, no matter how disagreeable they may seem. A Defiant Attitude can trigger immense energy (Lean Thinking – the Toyota Experience, Womack and Jones 2003). More ideas are put on the table, which can lead to more discoveries, which in turn leads to quantum leaps in improvement and innovation. Agree on an internal or external third party facilitator the team can use to assist with more complex conflict.

Assessment and Team Effectiveness

An important feature of team development is team effectiveness and measuring the 'well-being' of a team is one way of determining team progress. Figure 34.5 gives a structure which works well and is recommended for use from the start of a project and conducted on a regular basis during the initial days, weeks or months depending on the duration of the project. The model identifies seven key measures of team success and asks individual team members to make their own judgement against each measure before then sharing their results with the other members of the team. It is then up to the team to discuss any differences and to seek to find understanding and ways to resolve them.

Item	1	2	3	4	5	6
Purpose – the team members understand the purpose and commit their energy to achieving it.						
Role – all the team members have a common understanding of the team's role						
Strategy – the team members understand the team's strategy and use it to guide their day-to-day activities						
Processes – the teams processes are optimal for its role and purpose						
People – the team members feel well utilised and valued						
Feedback – the team constructively uses the feedback it receives						
Interfaces – the team's key relationships with others are productive						

Figure 34.5 Audit of team effectiveness

FURTHER OPPORTUNITIES FOR GROWTH

THE THIRD COMPETENCE

Why is it that some project teams have succeeded where others have not? The answer lies in another basic – the basic assumptions that we bring with us to every project problem and decision (Chapters 39 and 40).

> *You need to think of yourself as an immigrant. Then you are not hung up with what you believe the rules to be and you make no assumptions as to what is possible or not*

Perhaps these are some of your assumptions:

- We can't speak directly to the client!
- The suppliers are looking for ways to rip us off!
- The project team members are not willing to give it what it takes!
- Doing it the way we've always done it is the best way!
- People are not willing to change!
- You know your boss's goals!

The truth is that very often people have not been asked to contribute; they would be willing to change if you showed them how; the suppliers are looking for continuity and would be happy to join your 'think tank' if you asked them. You do it your way because it's comfortable not because it's the best.

COMMUNICATION

'Guys, we're in this together!' How often do you hear this? A plea when the walls seem to be finally caving in or a rallying cry to keep the team focused? To quote experience on a large engineering contract:

> *There was always a lot of disagreement, different ideas, different priorities. But there was always self-respect and respect for others*

So what constitutes enough sharing and communication? Here's one example:

- Meeting as a team every morning from 08.00 to 08.20
- A meeting each week to review the progress, performance and process of relationships on the project – for a *maximum* of two hours
- A shared lunch break on Wednesdays in the project leader's office, simple buffet lunch, open house meeting to which all are invited, including key suppliers and support staff from the parent organization; no minutes taken, but mountains of information exchanged
- When issues cannot be resolved at the weekly meetings, the full team to gather at the project leader's home on Sunday. All to demand candour and objectivity.

The outcome of these practices, a fanatical belief in what the team is trying to achieve; the consequences, a significant impact on each individual, the project and the parent company. They really believe they can make a difference.

Some other practical ideas that come to mind:

- Humour board for jokes and stories
- Regular 'snapshots' of the team at work and play
- Go to the cinema, theatre, sports game together
- Continue to seek out novel ways of sharing and developing understanding.

CREATING YOUR OWN REALITY

Every project offers the project team members the opportunity to create their own new reality. An example of this is Russian Olympian Vasily Alexeev. He was trying to break a weight-lifting record of 500 pounds. He had lifted 499 but couldn't, for the life of him, lift 500. Finally his trainers put 501.5 pounds on the bar and rigged it so it looked like 499 pounds. Of course, you can guess the result, he lifted it easily. Once he created this new reality, other lifters went on to break his record. Why? Because they now knew it was possible to lift 500 pounds. The British athlete who broke a similar barrier was Roger Bannister when he first ran the mile in under 4 minutes and as a consequence many others followed. The limits we set ourselves exist in our mind. Sometimes if we let our hearts do the talking and believe in our ability to overcome perceptions, we can create another reality. Just imagine the possibilities when the project team truly believe in the *purpose*.

TEAM DECISION MAKING

Increasingly team members bring unique experience, knowledge and skill to a team, as well as cultural and language differences, perhaps an international partnering team for example, and in these circumstances decision-making can become extremely onerous. One approach to this is the Delphi technique. How does it work? It consists of collecting successive (usually two or three) rounds of inputs from team members, submitted without consultation between them. As each round is completed, individual inputs are consolidated and circulated back to the members for review before they provide the next input. Thus individuals see consensus developing, but without knowing who is adopting a given position, and without the potential biasing effect of face-to-face interaction. The resulting decision should reflect a position everyone can live with. This approach is particularly useful when contentious issues have to be resolved, or when you need to minimize the likelihood that, because of their style or personality, certain individuals will have an undue influence on the team's decisions.

TEAM GROWTH AND DEVELOPMENT

The classic model for the journey that teams experience together as they get to know each other seems to hold good:

- Forming   – competent individuals
- Storming   – competitive individuals
- Norming   – competent team
- Performing   – achieving team
- Mourning   – appreciating team

This model provides a frame of reference for judging the growth and strength of the team-working process and warrants periodic evaluation as part of the agenda at the project review meetings. The questions to ask might be:

1. What stage of the model are we at the moment?
2. How does that fit with the project life-cycle?
3. What actions are being taken to move the team to the next stage?
4. What are we learning from our collective experience?
5. How are we sharing that knowledge with other project teams?

If you were in the theatre you would similarly find all of the elements of project teambuilding, plus more. There would be the common goals, defined roles, interdependence, firm deadlines, plus coaching and feedback. The uniqueness in this list is coaching; a responsibility for every leader, the situation in the theatre where you would experience the greatest degree of coaching would be during rehearsal, perhaps the secret weapon of the most astute project leader. Consider when rehearsal could truly add value in the project process:

● pre-commencement period
● testing understanding of goals
● potential problem analysis
● risk analysis
● presentation and meeting the media
● project completion

And working and learning together to develop the team and personal skills in:

● process improvement techniques
● problem solving
● group-conflict management
● interactive skills
● consensus and compromise
● process methodologies

The team must learn to find their own solutions, they must realize that they are in control and no one else is going to tell them what to do or how to do it. The team ideally shares authority, and decision making; perhaps ideally there should be no team bosses.

PERSONAL DEVELOPMENT

Perhaps a starting point is to introduce individual self-assessment to identify expectations and the personal attributes which could be developed through the experience of the project. This process can be reinforced by:

1. Asking each team member to privately assess his/her own contributions to the team
2. Discussing how to encourage/support increased contributions from all members
3. Brainstorming how to make members feel more included, confident or engaged

To learn by experience, one has to experience first and then reflect on that experience to extract the learning. 'Learning Boards', closely located adjacent to or within the project environment, to encourage project team members to share their learning experiences: perhaps a database to be similarly introduced to build a knowledge base related to the project.

Personal development is primarily the responsibility of the individual, just as much on projects as in organizations. In this age of rapid change, skills can become obsolete very quickly. You have to keep pushing the envelope of your own experience and competence, if you hope to keep up with the evolving needs of your job and profession. Perhaps these few practical tips can help your own capacity to stay ahead of change:

1. Learn to be a better listener – 'You don't learn when you're talking.'
2. Read professional journals and business magazines from different industries – once a week take time out to find two new things that relate to your project
3. Let your children tutor you – they know more than you about a lot of day-to-day matters
4. Volunteer – in most voluntary activities everyone is the same. It changes your perspective on hierarchy and authority
5. Read what has stood the test of time – Aristotle, Plato, Shakespeare, Adam Smith

QUICK WINS

Developing high quality project teams is as much about public profile as it is about output and performance. Acknowledging the team members at an early stage can establish a commitment that will have endurance. What are some of the possibilities?

- Establish a project team base with its own identity on the door
- Develop a challenging identity, logo or name to add character to the team. In Chapter 26 Roland Gareis said this is a 'must'
- Select an identity, which in some way characterizes the nature of the project; for example, is it about speed of completion, high image or quality, innovation or originality?

- Turn the logo into a lapel badge, a car sticker, or attach it to documentation to share with other project partners
- Involve all stakeholders at the pre-commencement stage so they can contribute to project strategy
- Meet other stakeholders such as the client, in-house support teams, suppliers, investors, local community influencers, statutory services that have some potential assessment role or function
- Involve in-house or outside press agents as part of the project marketing machinery
- Ensure basic resources are quickly on board so that individuals can make an immediate contribution on their arrival
- Start a Cartoon Board
- Create an information board giving three vital pieces of information, Figure 34.6 – there may be several boards located about the site, offices or buildings, of a size to ensure the best visibility.

TEAM LEADERSHIP

The project team leader today carries many roles; those of marketeer, team facilitator, coach, performance evaluator, as well as leader are the most apparent (Chapter 35). Experience says that many project leaders survive by accident rather than design, perhaps the case for many organizations. Surviving by design means starting by taking stock of all stakeholders who have an interest in your project and determining who has influence and how they will benefit from the project, and don't forget the hidden stakeholders – some of whom may be people who may have personal reasons for not wanting this initiative of yours. Your analysis will reveal a surprising number of players: rate them as positive (supportive) or negative (a resistance) and ask yourself these key questions about each of them:

1. Why have they been appointed as stakeholders: to provide funding, lend their name to the project?
2. Consider the stakeholder's goals, values and needs
3. Consider what concerns or interests he or she might have that would cause resistance
4. Determine what actions could address these concerns
5. Consider the stakeholder's possible objections. How will you respond?
6. Determine the approach that is likely to work the best with this person or organization – fact-based, value-based, participative, or collaborative?

The role is similar to that of an orchestral conductor, allowing each talented individual to have his or her moment of distinction, cultivating the teamness of

New Members	Project Purpose	Member Achievements
A welcome to new members of the team (individuals or other companies), with a definition of how they will be contributing, some personal history and a photograph	A picture of how the project will be when completed. Or a before progress framework (Bar chart) and expected result.	An acknowledgement. As the project progresses this panel might be a grateful 'thank you' to the departing member or organization. Or this could be an opportunity to feature the contribution and performance of a member or organization.

Figure 34.6   Project information board

each group in the orchestra and similarly allowing them their moment of glory whilst maintaining a direction and symbiosis that presents a complete and whole picture.

REFERENCES AND FURTHER READING

Briner, W., Hastings, C., and Geddes, M., 1993, *Project Leadership*, 2nd ed, Aldershot: Gower.

Katzenbach, J.R., and Smith, D.K., 1993, The *Wisdom of Teams,* Cambridge, MA:Harvard Business School Press.

Womack, J.P. and Jones, D.T., 2003, *Lean Thinking,* Free Press.

35 Leadership

David Partington

What makes an effective leader? Are leaders born or can they be taught? To what extent does the effectiveness of a leader depend on the specific situation? How does leading differ from managing? What do effective managers and leaders do? Attempts to answer questions such as these have made the subject of leadership of central interest to managers and social scientists since the beginning of the formal study of management. The reason for this is the obvious link, in theory and in practice, between leadership effectiveness and business success.

In addition to its general importance to the business world, leadership has a special significance for project managers. One reason for this is that notions of leadership are central to that most fundamental project management principle – the project manager as single, integrative source of responsibility. Very small project groups – those with fewer than seven or eight members – can sometimes function without a leader, either one who is formally designated or one who emerges naturally. In all but the smallest groups, however, the operation of some sort of formal or informal leadership hierarchy is inevitable, and is necessary for the group to achieve its goals.

For some, the titles 'project leader' and 'project manager' are synonymous. Indeed, from the viewpoint of many people in organizations, leadership and management are indistinguishable. But another reason why leadership is taking on a new importance for many project managers lies in an emerging key *difference* between leadership and management, especially in the context of the implementation of planned change in organizations. A comparison of traditional definitions of leadership with more recent ideas illustrates this difference. Defining for managerial purposes a word which is in common everyday usage is never straightforward. In common with words like power, control, and politics, leadership is a potent word which has different meanings for different people. However, most traditional meanings combine three common elements, emphasized in the following definition:

> *Leadership is the ability to influence the activities of a group of followers in their efforts to set and achieve goals.*

This defines *transactional* leadership: the influence on a group of followers in the pursuit of defined, rational goals. This influence is normally achieved through the explicit or implicit offer of some form of reward, which may not always be wholly, or even partly, financial.

Theories of transactional leadership focus on the job of the leader as clarifier of role and task requirements, and as monitor and rewarder of task-related activity. Using definitions of transactional leadership like the one above, there is little to distinguish leadership from management, since most traditional and widely-cited attempts to define management have tended to emphasize similar transactional roles. Fayol (1951) for example, defined the five roles of the manager as commanding, organizing, planning, controlling and implementing. Although some of Fayol's terms today sound unfashionably bureaucratic and militaristic they nevertheless present a strong parallel to the essential elements of transactional leadership. Mintzberg (1973) also emphasized the rational side of leadership, although in less belligerent fashion, defining the role in terms of eight skills: communication skills, information skills, people-management skills, disturbance-handling skills, decision-making skills, resource allocation skills, entrepreneurial skills and reflecting (ie planning) skills.

In contrast with these traditional ideas of leadership and management, more recent perspectives of leadership tend to emphasize the *transformational* role of the leader in bringing about change. Transformational leaders 'change the way people think about what is desirable, possible and necessary' (Zaleznic 1977). Transformational leadership has a distinctive orientation towards identity, purpose and change. This subtle alteration in meaning not only sets leadership apart from the relatively ordinary concerns of day-to-day management, but also underlines why the concept of leadership is of special importance to project managers. Increasingly project managers are concerned not only with setting and pursuing goals, but also with managing meaning and changing the way people think, as part of the complex influencing process inherent in project leadership.

This chapter examines the main strands of transactional and transformational leadership theory and discusses their implications for project management professionals.

THEORIES OF LEADERSHIP

In pursuit of the holy grail of managerial performance there have been many attempts to distil the essence of effective leadership, and to communicate that essence as information. The underlying idea is that this information can be absorbed and applied by anyone who is interested in becoming a leader, or in appointing people to positions of leadership. Things are never that simple. Like all fundamental human issues, leadership reveals itself to be complex and multi-faceted. Attempts to pin it down have proved difficult and have led to conflicting answers. Indeed, few management concepts have incited as much controversy. Consider this quotation, attributed to Confucius:

'Of bad leaders, the followers say, "they were bad leaders".
Of good leaders, the followers say. "they were good leaders".
Of the best leaders, the followers say, "we did it ourselves".'

This presents the view, currently popular in management thinking, that effective leadership comes from the involvement, participation and empowerment of followers. The notion of employee empowerment is associated with many positive modern ideas of management and leadership, including the flattening of hierarchies, the project team approach, employee productivity and satisfaction, and the harnessing of individual creativity to the pursuit of organizational goals. However, experience shows that attempts at employee empowerment can have negative outcomes, including lack of direction, alienation, over-work and stress.

This reveals the other side of the leadership coin to that suggested by the quote. On the one hand, few would disagree that leadership is participation. On the other hand, one may argue equally credibly and forcefully that leadership is accountability and creating structured responsibility within a body of rules. Further, one may argue that leadership is *doing*.

So how do managers and leaders create appropriately structured conditions in which they and their followers can perform to the best of their abilities? There have been several major schools of thought, or approaches, to the study of leadership. Five of the most significant of these may be labelled:

1. the **trait** school
2. the **behavioural** school
3. the **contingency** school
4. the **visionary** school
5. the **competency** school

Each of the five has its own research tradition, its own underlying assumptions and its own purposes. An overview of the five schools follows, with a discussion of some of their principal ideas in relation to project management.

THE TRAIT SCHOOL

The idea behind the trait school of leadership research and theory is that effective leaders share the same inherent personal qualities and characteristics. The trait school thus assumes that leaders are born, not made. The purpose of trait theories is the *selection* of leaders, by matching supposedly desirable generic traits to the traits of individuals. Attempts to identify and isolate leader traits have focused on three main areas:

1. *abilities*, for example communication skills and technical know-how
2. *personality variables*, such as self-confidence and introversion/extroversion
3. *physical traits*, including size and appearance

The trait school was prominent until the late 1940s. Although it has been challenged and supplemented by later ideas, it still attracts significant attention, and is currently enjoying revival in the study of new approaches to leadership (see the *visionary* school). Researchers, mostly psychologists, have been concerned with identifying the common traits of leaders who have proved to be effective, by comparison with non-leaders. This is a tall order, since a cursory examination of the traits of a selection of well-known contemporary leaders such as Tony Blair, the Pope and Bill Gates shows that they are individuals with very *different* characteristics. Nevertheless, trait research has produced some valid findings. For example, one relatively recent study of the characteristics of real-life successful leaders found six consistent leadership traits (Kirkpatrick and Locke 1991). These six traits and their implications for project managers are discussed below.

Drive and ambition

Effective leaders are ambitious in their work and careers. The possession of drive is clearly an important attribute for project managers, since the success of many projects depends on the relentless, energetic and focused pursuit of difficult goals, in highly uncertain and volatile circumstances. Personal ambition is a significant characteristic of project managers. Anne Keegan and Rodney Turner (see Chapter 31) reported that when they asked a senior project director how his firm identified those 25 year olds who would make good project managers and directors in 20 years time, he said: 'Those who are vocal with their ambitions.' Most people who move into project management take a bold step away from the relative security of a line or technical function. Unlike some jobs where it is relatively easy, in the short term at least, to rest on one's laurels, project managers' ambition must be sustained. Establishing and maintaining career success in project management hinges on the highly visible outcomes of a manager's recent project assignments.

The desire to lead and influence others

Effective leaders have a strong desire to lead and influence others. For project managers, such a desire is essential, since a key, defining role of a project manager is exerting influence in many ways, at many levels and in many directions. Good project managers have a strong ability to lead and motivate their team. They must also be skilled at building a winning relationship with their clients, ensuring the right level of senior management and external support for the project, and getting the best from technical managers and specialist experts. In order to be able to lead and influence others, good leaders must be good communicators (see Chapters 36, 37 and 38).

Honesty and integrity

Effective leaders exhibit above-average levels of honesty and integrity. Unlike some other important leadership traits, these are widely perceived as desirable and valued personal attributes in their own right. Their opposites, dishonesty and lack of integrity, oppose society's norms of acceptable behaviour. Because of the pioneering, multi-agency nature of many projects, there are frequent opportunities for the project manager to purposefully mislead factions who are associated less centrally with the project and its information processes, or to manipulate situations for personal advantage. Good project managers know that they are under the spotlight, and that any benefits of less than total honesty and integrity will be short-lived, at best.

Self-confidence

Effective leaders have a belief in their own abilities that goes with feeling in control of change. As a result, they are more likely to actively seek information, to act confidently and decisively on the basis of information which may necessarily be incomplete, and to have the courage to change course if necessary. All of these behavioural attributes find strong resonance with the project manager's role.

Intelligence

Effective leaders tend to have above average intelligence and problem-solving ability. Project managers are faced with a constant need to find creative solutions to unprecedented problems, both managerial and technical. Their superior intelligence is often revealed by their unusual ability for breadth and depth of thinking.

Technical knowledge

Effective leaders usually have in-depth technical knowledge of their area of responsibility. Some observers have claimed that project management is a generic ability, and that good project managers are able to apply their skills to any project, regardless of technology. To a limited extent this is true, since the unique quality of many projects will embody at least some element of technical novelty which must be learned or discovered. Indeed, there is some evidence of transferability of successful project managers from one industrial context to another. Nevertheless, few successful project managers would argue against the obvious benefits of possessing adequate technical knowledge relating to their project.

The shortcomings of the trait school lie in its search for a common set of traits possessed by all leaders, regardless of what they are leading. The personal qualities needed to lead a nation, or a religious order, or a multinational corporation are clearly different. In the field of project management it is easy to argue that different project leadership characteristics are required at different phases in a single project, let alone from one project to another.

THE BEHAVIOURAL SCHOOL

The second school of thought about what makes an effective leader, the *behavioural* school, signalled a move away from the trait school. For a period of twenty years, starting in the late 1940s, the focus of attention turned towards the preferred behavioural styles of effective leaders. The basic premise underlying the behavioural school is that effective leaders behave in the same ways. Research has been aimed at identifying the behavioural styles of effective leaders. Do they tend to use a more democratic style or are they more autocratic? A number of studies of behavioural styles were carried out between the late 1940s and the late 1960s. Using subordinates' descriptions of the behaviour of leaders, including both successful and unsuccessful leaders, the studies attempted to identify the principal dimensions of leadership behaviour, and to relate these to measures of performance. The broad finding was that much of leadership behaviour could be distilled and expressed on two dimensions, broadly relating to *task* and *people*. The dimensions are given a variety of different labels; typical are the two axes of the Blake and Mouton (1964) 'managerial grid'. Blake and Mouton's two dimensions, scored on the grid from 1 to 9, are:

Concern for production: Leaders with a strong concern for production emphasize technical and task aspects of work, including the organizing of work, work relationships and goals.

Concern for people: Leaders who are strong on this dimension emphasize interpersonal relationships and consideration for subordinates' needs.

Using the grid, managers are rated according to the concerns which dominate their particular style in their pursuit of results. Their combined rating on the two dimensions expresses their behavioural style. The extreme styles are labelled and described by Blake and Mouton as follows:

1,1 Impoverished management (low concern for production; low concern for people): Exertion of minimum effort to get required work done is appropriate to sustain organization membership.

9,1 Authority-Obedience (high concern for production; low concern for people): Efficiency in operations results from arranging conditions of work in such a way that human elements interfere to a minimum degree.

1,9 Country Club Management (low concern for production; high concern for people): Thoughtful attention to needs of people for satisfying relationships leads to a comfortable, friendly organization atmosphere and work tempo.

9,9 Team Management (high concern for production; high concern for people): Work accomplishment is from committed people; interdependence through a 'common stake' in organization purpose leads to relationships of trust and respect.

Unlike the trait school, which assumes leaders are born not made, the underlying rationale of the behavioural school is that leadership behaviour can be learned. The purpose of behavioural theories is teaching people how to change the assumptions that control their behaviour, in order to become more effective leaders. Blake and Mouton concluded the best performance was obtained by managers who scored high on both dimensions (a 9,9 style).

The clear implication of behavioural leadership theories for project managers is that they must possess both 'hard' and 'soft' project management skills, since neglecting either will result in sub-optimal project performance. This hard versus soft dichotomy is well-known to experienced project managers. Although the majority of basic project management text books concentrate on the 'hard' tools and techniques for planning and controlling cost, schedule and quality, the writers are usually at pains to point out the need for attention to the more elusive, 'soft' side of managing projects.

Like the pure trait school, the simple behavioural school suffers from problems of over-simplification, and the one-size-fits-all approach. We all know that different styles are often appropriate in different circumstances. These shortcomings were addressed in the next stage in the story of the study of leadership effectiveness, the *contingency* school, which dominated the leadership research arena from the late 1960s to the early 1980s.

THE CONTINGENCY SCHOOL

Towards the end of the 1960s there was a growing tendency for management theorists to move away from universal theories which would apply in every situation towards contingency theories, based on the idea that 'it depends'. In the area of leadership effectiveness, as it became apparent that neither trait theories

745

nor behavioural theories would work in every set of circumstances, the search was on for situational variables which moderated the effectiveness of different leader characteristics or behaviours. The contingency school focuses on isolating critical situational influences on leadership success, for example the clarity of the task, the degree of conflict in the group, or the culture of the organization. Several important contingency theories of leadership effectiveness have been developed, some more complex than others. Although the various theories differ in their underlying assumptions regarding what is important about leaders' characteristics and situational variables, the way in which these contingency schools are applied tends to follow the same pattern:

1. Assess the characteristics of the leader.
2. Evaluate the situation in terms of key contingency variables.
3. Seek a match between the leader and the situation.

One contingency theory of leadership which is currently the subject of a lot of interest, and which has important implications for the project environment, is the path-goal theory (House 1971). The theory is based on the idea that the role of the leader is to provide support and/or direction in providing a *path* which will help the followers to achieve their *goals*, at the same time ensuring that these match the goals of the group's task. Following the three steps listed above, the path-goal theory works as follows:

Assess the characteristics of the leader

Path-goal theory identifies four leadership behaviours which contribute to the satisfaction and motivation of subordinates. Any combination may be exhibited, depending on the situation.

- *Directive leaders* define tasks, schedules and processes.
- *Supportive leaders* are friendly and concerned for followers' needs.
- *Participative leaders* involve followers in decisions.
- *Achievement-oriented leaders* set challenging goals and expect high performance.

Evaluate the situation in terms of key contingency variables

Path-goal theory has two classes of contingency factors which affect the relationship between leader behaviour and performance, as follows:

1. *Environmental* contingency factors
   - Task structure
   - Formal authority system
   - Work group

2. *Subordinate* contingency factors
   - Locus of control (the extent to which people feel that they control their own destiny)
   - Experience
   - Perceived ability

Seek a match between the leader and the situation

In path-goal theory, leader behaviour should be congruent with both environmental and subordinate contingency variables. Robbins (1997) lists eight ways in which path-goal theory works, which have tended to be supported by empirical evidence. These are described below, with examples of their implications for project managers.

1. Directive leadership gives greater satisfaction when tasks are ambiguous or stressful than when they are highly structured and well laid out. When a project has the combined characteristics of high uncertainty and high importance, for example in the early stages of a key development initiative, subordinates will welcome more direction and guidance.
2. Supportive leadership results in high employee performance and satisfaction when subordinates are performing structured tasks. On projects which involve the routine application of established processes, for example in the later, detail stages of engineering projects, subordinates will appreciate and be motivated by a friendly, caring leader.
3. Directive leadership is likely to be redundant among subordinates with high ability or with considerable experience. Project managers who over-emphasize cost, schedule and quality objectives to self-believing experts will be wasting their time.
4. The clearer and more bureaucratic the formal authority relationships, the more leaders should exhibit supportive behaviour and de-emphasize directive behaviour. Effective project managers with a high degree of formal authority acting within a highly proceduralized environment, for example on longer-term public sector projects, should have less need to emphasize a style of direction and guidance and more need to counter the possible alienating effects of bureaucracy by adopting a sympathetic approach.
5. Directive leadership will lead to higher employee satisfaction when there is substantive conflict in a work group. Conflict is often unavoidable, and under certain conditions may be beneficial to the project by avoiding apathy and keeping the team alive and creative. Whether conflict is functional or dysfunctional to the project, however, it will be less a source of dissatisfaction to individuals if the project manager exhibits directive behaviour.
6. Subordinates with an internal locus of control (those who believe they control

their own destiny) will be most satisfied with a participative style. People who naturally feel in control of their world will find project managers who seek appropriate involvement in project decisions more agreeable as leaders.

7. Subordinates with an external locus of control (those who believe they have little control over their own destiny) will be most satisfied with a directive style. People who generally feel powerless over their environment will have a tendency to resign their futures to fate, and to avoid seeking out information for improved decision making. They will derive satisfaction from project managers who let them know what is expected of them.

8. Achievement-oriented leadership will increase subordinates' expectations that effort leads to high performance when tasks are ambiguously structured. The motivational effect of setting challenging goals will be heightened on projects which are executed in organizations with a dual power channel, such as the project/functional matrix in a project engineering firm, or the management/clinician structure of a hospital.

One of the features of path-goal theory which makes it especially relevant to the project environment is its simultaneous focus on the needs of (i) the task, (ii) the team and (iii) the individual. There can be a tendency for inexperienced project managers to over-emphasize the first one or two of these, and to make false assumptions about the alignment between the motivation and satisfaction of individuals and the project's objectives.

LEADER GENDER

Recently, much attention has been directed towards issues of gender in management and leadership, mostly in the form of debates and research on women in management. What is known about gender as a contingency factor in relation to leadership effectiveness? Studies show that the leadership styles of men have much in common with those of women. This is not surprising, given that those who occupy positions of formal leadership are both self-selected and selected by organizations on the basis of their self-confidence, intelligence, desire to lead, and so on. But apart from the conclusion that similarities outweigh differences, it is apparent that women tend to employ a more participative leadership style, relying more on inter-personal skills such as negotiation and information-sharing to influence subordinates. Men tend to favour a more directive, command-and-control style, depending more on their formal authority. As the requisite styles of organizations and projects increasingly emphasize values of team work, participation, trust and co-operation, one may conclude that conditions for project leaders in many sectors are changing in favour of women.

THE VISIONARY SCHOOL

We have seen how the ideas which influenced the study of leadership until the 1980s moved through three overlapping stages, the trait, behavioural and contingency schools. The successive influence of these schools has been one of emphasis rather than exclusivity, and today all three traditions live on in various forms, building on their origins and adapting to the changing conditions of society. In the 1980s a new focus to the study of leadership emerged. It became apparent that many successful organizations had been subject to the influence of a 'visionary' or 'charismatic' leader. Therefore, attention turned towards the identification of the personal abilities and characteristics of leaders who were clearly capable of a form of leadership which went beyond traditional ideas about the transactional role of the manager.

Transactional leadership, which emphasizes tasks, goals and performance, is limited by the explicit and implicit contracts between leader and followers. Visionary, 'transformational' leaders, on the other hand, are able to unite leader and followers in the pursuit of a higher purpose which transcends individuals' self-interest. Bryman (1996) illustrates the differences between these two conceptualizations of leadership, listing their components as follows:

1. Components of transactional leadership
   - *contingent rewards*: rewarding followers for meeting performance targets
   - *management by exception*: taking action mainly when task-related activity is not going to plan
2. Components of transformational leadership
   - *charisma:* developing a vision, engendering pride, respect and trust
   - *inspiration*: motivating by creating high expectations, modeling appropriate behaviour, and using symbols to focus efforts
   - *individual consideration*: giving personal attention to followers, giving them respect and responsibility
   - *intellectual stimulation*: continually challenging followers with new ideas and approaches

Most studies of visionary business leaders have been concerned with people in the highest positions of seniority, especially chief executives. However, experience shows that many attempts at bold organizational change which go beyond normal rational goals, and which depend on the articulation of an extraordinary vision of the future, are originated by leaders in less senior positions of formal authority. Many examples of visionary change arise from managers of important technology-related business improvement projects, where visions of the future are more immediate, and problems with existing business processes are more apparent. Others occur in subsidiaries of multinationals or

749

other dispersed organizations, when finding imaginative ways of surviving and dealing with present and expected future local conditions is more pressing than implementing the latest head office fad.

These kinds of change initiative are usually dependent for their success on a high degree of senior management or head office support, or at least non-interference. However, when senior managers have little to gain personally from the success of a transformational change project, and often a lot to lose, this can be too much to expect. For these reasons successful attempts at radical change which are driven from the middle of organizations are likely to be difficult to sustain.

Despite these problems, efforts at initiating and leading organizational innovation from lower down the management ranks are becoming more common. This is partly due to the increasing exposure to unsatisfactory aspects of the status quo which is experienced by managers of more routine internal projects of change. A common example of this phenomenon is the widespread perception at non-senior levels in many organizations of the need to establish a stronger culture of project management. Moving towards a project culture for dealing with change has become a pressing need for many organizations. It is often driven by project managers, who have experienced frustration with barriers to change, which were caused by departmental hierarchies and perpetuated by senior management.

STAGES OF VISIONARY LEADERSHIP

There are four stages of visionary leadership. They represent clearly the distinctive life-cycle of the kind of project or programme of change which, for an increasing number of people, has become a necessary feature of organizational life, and the new challenge for transformational project leaders.

1. The leader identifies the opportunity and the need for change, and formulates a vision of a future state that relates to those needs.
2. The leader communicates the vision, by pointing out the unacceptability of the status quo.
3. The leader builds trust in the vision. The achievement of trust may be helped by building links with other powerful individuals and institutions with similar values, or by showing followers what has been achieved by other organizations with related aims.
4. The leader leads by example and by empowering followers. Sometimes disempowering non-followers is also effective.

Some visionary leaders are better at forming and articulating visions than they are at implementing them, and some prominent visionaries have proved incapable of leading change successfully through the four stages. The factors which commonly lead to failure in implementing transformational change are:

(a) Moving at the wrong pace. Problems can arise either from trying to achieve too much too quickly, resulting in change overload and intolerable employee stress, or from missing opportunities by not taking swift enough advantage of instability and dissatisfaction with the status quo.

(b) Inappropriate use of management consultants. The right consultants can add value to a radical change initiative, especially in the early stages when the leader may need help and outside expertise in selling the need for change to those with the power to block it, and in formulating the detail. However, if the prolonged or excessive use of consultants makes them seem too central or crucial to the change, the vision's underlying values can become distorted, and followers may become disillusioned.

(c) Failure to put enough effort into communicating the opportunity and the need for change. It is apparently too easy for leaders to forget or become distracted from the need for tireless efforts to communicate the vision of a better future. This is especially true in difficult times when general enthusiasm for the change is flagging.

(d) Inadequate scheduling. Excessive formality and detail in planning and communicating change can be demotivating for followers who must own and implement the plans. On the other hand leaders sometimes cause unnecessary confusion by avoiding scheduling the stages of the change. Sometimes this happens because leaders fear that formal plans may set them up for failure if the plans are not met. Another scheduling problem is tackling the easiest parts of the change first, whilst allowing the more intractable aspects to become even more entrenched.

(e) Inappropriate participation. There is a trade-off between seeking too much involvement of followers in difficult decisions, especially when their advice is not used, and not allowing an appropriate level of involvement. The latter problem is especially likely to arise when one of the objects of the change is to establish a culture of increased participation.

THE COMPETENCY SCHOOL

The focus of leadership research has now shifted towards understanding the *competencies* of leaders. Following this school Dulewicz and Higgs (2003) identify 15 leadership competencies (grouped into *intellectual*, *managerial* and *emotional*) and three leadership styles that combine as shown in Figure 35.1. The competency school combines some elements of the four other schools discussed in this chapter. In particular the competency school has clear parallels with the contingency school, with its focus on different leadership styles (and therefore different sets of competencies) being appropriate in different situations. The implications for project managers may be seen in Figure 35.2, which shows how different leadership styles relate to different types of change project.

Group	Competency	Leadership style		
		Goal-oriented	Involving	Engaging
Intellectual (IQ)	Critical analysis and judgement	High	Medium	Medium
	Vision and imagination	High	High	Medium
	Strategic perspective	High	Medium	Medium
Managerial (MQ)	Engaging communication	Medium	Medium	High
	Managing resources	High	Medium	Low
	Empowering	Low	Medium	High
	Developing	Medium	Medium	High
	Achieving	High	Medium	Medium
Emotional (EQ)	Self-awareness	Medium	High	High
	Emotional resilience	High	High	High
	Motivation	High	High	High
	Sensitivity	Medium	Medium	High
	Influence	Medium	High	High
	Intuitiveness	Medium	Medium	High
	Conscientiousness	High	High	High

Figure 35.1   Fifteen leadership competencies and the competency profiles of three leadership styles after Dulewicz and Higgs (2003)

MULTI-LEVEL COMPETENCY MODELS

A further strand of leadership research seeks to identify leadership characteristics arranged in a multi-level hierarchy of competence, or capability. An example of a five-level model is Collins's (2005) study of organizational leaders who are able to sustain superlative performance. The research presents a strong challenge to the popular notion that CEOs should be charismatic, larger-than-life figures. Collins found that 'Level 5' leaders were strong willed but with a high degree of personal

Leadership style	Context		
	Relatively stable	Significant change	Transformational change
Goal oriented	Good fit	Moderate fit	Poor fit
Involving	Moderate fit	Good fit	Moderate fit
Engaging	Poor fit	Moderate fit	Good fit

Figure 35.2   Relationship between leadership style and context in three different types of change project, after Dulewicz and Higgs (2003)

humility, never blaming failure on others, the environment or bad luck. Level 5 *Executives* also possessed the capabilities of lower-level leaders, including Level 4 *Effective leaders,* Level 3 *Competent managers*, Level 2 *Contributing team members*, and Level 1 *Highly capable individuals.*

Research in the context of project and programme management has added to the growing body of literature addressing hierarchies of leadership competence. A multi-level, multi-attribute study of the competence of programme managers in the UK private and public sector (Partington, Pellegrinelli and Young 2005) identifies 17 key behavioural and attitudinal competencies, each mapped at four levels. Level 1 represents the way many effective project managers see their world. Level 4 represents the approach to their work taken by expert leaders of large programmes. Levels 2 and 3 are intermediate and distinct. Figure 35.3 shows the primary concern of managers at each level, and details of the 17 attributes.

CONCLUSION

This chapter has traced the evolution of ideas about business leadership effectiveness through five stages, the trait school, the behavioural school, the contingency school, the visionary school and the competency school. We have seen that all five schools have important implications for project management. In particular, the growing emphasis on leadership research that combines intellectual, managerial and emotional competencies reflects the growing recognition that all three are important. Multi-level approaches offer both an explanation for superior leadership performance and a framework for personal development.

As for the future, it is possible to foresee that, more than ever, project and programme managers will be faced with two significant leadership challenges. First, they will be required to cope with greater flux and uncertainty. Second, they will need to manage relationships in which they are not formally in command.

Just as traditional views about the transactional role of the manager are becoming increasingly out of date, leading-edge ideas about project and programme management are aligning with newer conceptions of leadership. The basis of the world economy is moving towards finite alliances, partnerships and contracts to deliver specific outcomes. The need to lead such relationships through the different contextual phases of their life-cycle places effective leadership skills at a premium.

		Level 1 Concern for delivery of programme scope	Level 2 Concern for wider organizational impact of programme	Level 3 Concern for achievement of high-level programme outcomes	Level 4 Concern for development of strategic capabilities
Relationship between self and work					
S1	**Granularity of focus**	Well-planned detail	Summary plan and broad understanding of internal impact outside project	Level 2 plus personal involvement in selected detail when deemed necessary, for stakeholder benefits	Level 3 plus strong future orientation and understanding of external context
S2	**Emotional attachment**	Detached, factual	Need to be associated with successful delivery of organizational benefits	Passionately committed to achievement of programme outcomes	Committed to delivery of external outcomes; Able to disconnect
S3	**Disposition for action**	Trouble-shooter; Procedural	Proactive, analytical; Procedural	Experimental, reflective; Flexible approach to programme rules and procedures	Intuitively reconfigures and realigns the organization; Makes the programme rules
S4	**Approach to role plurality**	Adopts a focused, single role	Fulfils multiple roles, but is uncomfortable with role conflict	Copes by adopting a clear position when roles potentially conflict	Takes on multiple roles to integrate divergent interests
Relationship between self and others					
O1	**Relationship with team**	Supportive and responsive to requests for help	Seeks detachment; Uses 'need to know' approach to interaction	Social, inclusive, paternal, but prepared to drive hard	Confidence-inspiring leader with charisma and credibility who can get people to modify their natural behaviour
O2	**Approach to conflict and divergence**	Not considered legitimate – seeks procedural solution	Considered legitimate – seeks procedural solution	Considered legitimate – seeks negotiated solution	Encourages creative solution through subtle facilitation
O3	**Education and support**	Helps others solve their problems	Directs others where to look to solve their problems	Coaches in how to influence	Coaches in context to enable influence

Figure 35.3   Attributes and levels of program management competence after Partington, Pellegrinelli and Young (2005) *continued*

O4	Use of questions	Own clarification	1 + challenge others	2 + encourage creative thinking	3 + redefine problem; reframe purpose
O5	**Expectations of others**	Expects contracted effort	Expects special effort when required	Exploits individuals' talents	Extends individuals' talents

Relationship between self and programme environment

E1	**Adaptive intent**	Do what has worked in the past	Adapt self to suit environment	Adapt environment to suit self	Adapt environment to suit purpose
E2	**Awareness of organizational capabilities**	Assumes departments can deliver	Aware of shortcomings. Pushes for delivery	Aware of shortcomings, prepared to go outside without hesitation	Aware and prepared to go outside after exploring internal possibilities
E3	**Approach to risk**	Analyze, report, monitor. Manage out internal risks	Attempt to manage out all risks	Prepare extreme contingency	Be ready for the consequences of failure
E4	**Approach to face-to-face communications**	Report objective facts in consistent style	Provide analysis and opinions in consistent style	Level 2 plus sell vision of outcome in style more sensitive to audience	Level 3 plus cultural sensitivity
E5	**Approach to governance**	Use standardized reporting hierarchy	Create stable support structures both ways	Adapt/create control procedures to specific/dynamic situations	Embedding program in organizational management structures
E6	**Attitude to scope**	Defined until changes authorized	Influences scope through cost benefit analysis	Chooses among trialed alternatives	Shaped to meet emerging and changing needs
E7	**Attitude to time**	Schedule driven; Reschedule when necessary	Planning for possible work, recognizing mobilization time	Aware of the rate at which the environment can absorb or accommodate change	Conscious of issues of timeliness and maturity
E8	**Attitude to funding**	Budget driven	Points out consequences of under funding	Aware of budget ambiguities and financial uncertainty	Creates budget from achievement

Figure 35.3 *Concluded*

755

REFERENCES AND FURTHER READING

Blake, R.R., and Mouton, J.S., 1964, *The Managerial Grid,* Houston: Gulf.

Bryman, A., 1996, 'Leadership in Organizations', in Clegg, S.R., Hardy, C. and Nord, W.R., (eds) *Handbook of Organization Studies*, London: Sage.

Collins, J., 2005, 'Level 5 leadership: the triumph of humility and fierce resolve', *Harvard Business Review*, Jul/Aug 2005.

Dulewicz, V. and Higgs, M.J., 2003, 'Design of a new instrument to assess leadership dimensions and styles', Henley Working Paper HWP 0331 Henley-on-Thames, UK: Henley Management College.

Fayol, H., 1950, *Administation Industrielle et Générale*, Paris: Dunod, (first published 1916).

House, R.J., 1971, 'A path-goal theory of leader effectiveness', *Administrative Science Quarterly*, September.

Kirkpatrick, S.A. and Locke, E.A., 1991, 'Leadership: do traits matter?', *Academy of Management Executive*, May.

Mintzberg, H., 1973, *The Nature of Managerial Work*, Prentice Hall, Englewood Cliffs, NJ.

Partington, D., Pellegrinelli, S. and Young, M., 2005, 'Attributes and levels of programme management competence: an interpretive study', *International Journal of Project Management*, 23(2).

Robbins, S.P., 1997, *Essentials of Organizational Behaviour,* New Jersey: Prentice-Hall.

Turner, J.R. and Müller, R., 2005, 'The project manager's leadership style as a success factor on projects: a review', *Project Management Journal*, 36(2).

Turner, J.R. and Müller, R., 2006, *Choosing Appropriate Project Managers: Matching their Leadership Style to the Type of Project,* Newtown Square, PA: Project Management Institute.

Zaleznik, A., 1977, 'Managers and leaders: are they different?', *Harvard Business Review*, 55.

36 Managing Stakeholders

Bill McElroy and Chris Mills

The Bible describes how the success of one of the earliest examples of a major construction project, rebuilding the walls of Jerusalem in 52 days, depended on how the project manager, Nehemiah, identified and managed the key stakeholders (his sponsor King Artaxerxes and disruptive officials from other provinces). Little has changed in the ensuing twenty four centuries. Regardless of how well you define and achieve the tangible deliverables of your project, failure to adequately *manage* the project *stakeholders* may cause your project to fail. This is not to say that project managers should disregard the need to satisfy the time/cost/performance objectives defined for their projects. Rather they should strive to achieve these objectives while also ensuring stakeholder satisfaction with the project and its outcome (Chapter 6). This requires the project manager to view stakeholder satisfaction as a key project deliverable. As such, the project manager needs to be able to:

- identify stakeholders, and in particular *key* stakeholders
- define what will constitute satisfaction for each
- plan appropriate actions to ensure their satisfaction
- monitor the effect of these actions
- be prepared to implement corrective actions if the desired outcome isn't being achieved

To help the project manager achieve the above, this chapter attempts to explain why stakeholder management is important. It defines stakeholders, provides a framework for identifying key stakeholders and outlines how to manage stakeholders.

PRINCIPLES

WHY IS STAKEHOLDER MANAGEMENT IMPORTANT

Many of the factors which influence a project are not only external to it, but also often lie outside the sponsor organization. For example:

- change of Government
- change of public opinion
- regulatory requirements
- economic performance – both within the sponsor organization and nationally
- change of business environment
- change of business direction
- competitor performance

Because such factors are external to the project it could be argued that the project manager should simply ignore them as they are a 'distraction'. But these distractions can have a major influence on whether the project will be a success. For example, the cost of dealing with pressure groups protesting against a new by-pass can add up to 15% to the cost of the project. So effective project managers need to adopt a proactive approach. The key element of this is the identification of those who embody the external influences on the project (the project stakeholders), and managing that influence which they will bring to bear to the overall benefit of the project (stakeholder management). This influence need not be detrimental to project success. Many stakeholders can assist the project manager by using contacts, trust and knowledge not available to the project team.

Stakeholder management is particularly important when dealing with 'soft' business critical projects. In such projects the success criteria defined by the sponsor are often very subjective, and any subversive efforts of the stakeholders will be less obvious than on those with a high profile capital spend. An example of such criteria would be a desire to increase sales through a more 'proactive' response to customer enquiries. The achievement of such a goal would rely heavily on effective management of the project's stakeholders.

It was stated in the introduction to this chapter that the project manager should view stakeholder satisfaction as a key project deliverable. It should certainly be used as one of the measures of project success. However, as shown in Figure 36.1, whatever outcome is desired by individual stakeholders it will always be essential to safeguard support for future projects. The key point to remember is; don't jeopardize future projects through poor relations now – effectively manage the project stakeholders not only to ensure success of the current project but also the future ones as well!

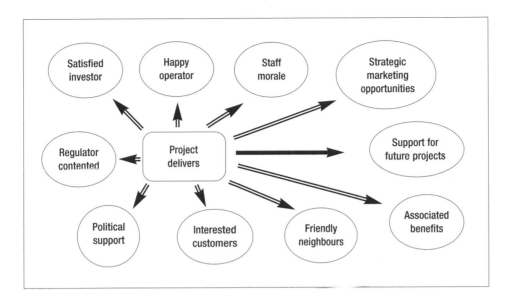

Figure 36.1 Stakeholder satisfaction

WHO IS A STAKEHOLDER?

The term 'stakeholder' is a relatively recent introduction to the project management vocabulary. As such it is difficult to identify a definition which is widely used and accepted. BS 6079–2:2000 Guide to Project Management – Part 2 Vocabulary contains the following definition:

 Stakeholder: A person or group of people who have a vested interest in the success of an organization and the environment within which the organization operates

The Association for Project Management (APM) *Body of Knowledge* (BoK) 5th Edition contains the following definition:

Stakeholders are all those with an interest or role in the project or who are impacted by the project.

In the authors' view these definitions, although robust, deal with stakeholders at too high a level. In the case of the BS 6079 it addresses organizational stakeholders rather than project stakeholders. It is therefore proposed that the BS 6079 definition be slightly modified, as follows, in order to incorporate the essence of the APM definition and to help identify stakeholders at a project level:

A project stakeholder is a person or group of people who have a vested interest in the success of project and the environment within which the project operates

There is however, a further problem with this definition. Potentially there will be lots of people and groups with a vested interest in your project and the environment within which it will operate. Stakeholders are everywhere! Stakeholders may have a vested interest because they are:

- investing in the project
- competitors
- competing for resources
- regulators
- affected by the project implementation
- affected by the project deliverables

This is by no means an exhaustive list! Project managers therefore have to focus on those stakeholders who really matter for their project. That is, they need to identify the key stakeholders. To clarify this, it is proposed the definition used above is expanded as follows:

A key project stakeholder is a person or group of people who have a vested interest in the success of project and the environment within which the project operates and who have an influence over its successful outcome

Expanding on this definition, project managers have to focus on those individuals or groups who are interested, and able to actually prevent or help them (influence) deliver a successful outcome for the project. This also reflects the fact that the vested interest of certain stakeholders may not always be a positive one – they could be interested in seeing the project fail rather than succeed!

WHAT IS STAKEHOLDER MANAGEMENT?

As with the term stakeholder it is difficult to identify a common and widely used definition for 'stakeholder management'. Again, when preparing this section reference was made to BS 6079 and it was found that even in the 2000 update there was no definition given for stakeholder management. *The APM Body of Knowledge* 5th Edition does though contain the following definition:

Stakeholder management is systematic identification, analysis and planning of actions to communicate with, negotiate with and influence stakeholders

Using the authors' definition for stakeholders and incorporating the essence of the APM definition for stakeholder management the following definition is proposed:

Stakeholder management is the continuing development of relationships with stakeholders for the purpose of achieving a successful project outcome

As highlighted there are three key features of this definition. Firstly, this is not a 'one-off' exercise (it continues throughout the project life-cycle). Secondly, it is a two-way process (a relationship), not just telling stakeholders what you are going to do – you have to listen and negotiate as well. Thirdly, stakeholders will make subjective assessments of project success (Chapter 6). It is these assessments which will be remembered, long after compliance with the more objective success criteria of time, cost and performance have been forgotten.

Role of the project sponsor

Throughout this chapter we have made reference to the 'project manager' when indicating who should be taking the lead in the management of stakeholders. However, this is often not the right person to deal with the key stakeholders. In our experience the 'project sponsor' (owner or client) should take the lead role in managing and making the personal contact with the key stakeholders. Why? Well the project sponsor will:

- normally have more stature in the organization, and therefore his/her actions, decisions and agreements will be seen as more important by the stakeholders
- typically have authority over the project business case, and as such will be able to make decisions in order to move stakeholder views, that will impact on the business case
- have a wider appreciation of how the project fits in the organization's overall strategy, and therefore will know the boundaries for any negotiation
- be able to focus on the often ad-hoc nature of stakeholder meetings and forums, allowing the project manager to focus on management of the overall stakeholder process, as well as the project overall

THE STAKEHOLDER MANAGEMENT PROCESS

The stakeholder management process is illustrated in Figure 36.2. The key steps in this process are as follows:

IDENTIFY PROJECT SUCCESS CRITERIA

The project definition process should define the sponsor's success criteria in terms of time, cost and performance. Think beyond these, although they could be influenced by stakeholders. Consider those issues which are likely to affect or concern stakeholders directly. These are likely to be the softer issues surrounding the project, such as marketing, training or changes to working practices. Also, the environmental impact of construction projects, and associated project objectives to mitigate these, are increasingly attracting the interest of stakeholders.

761

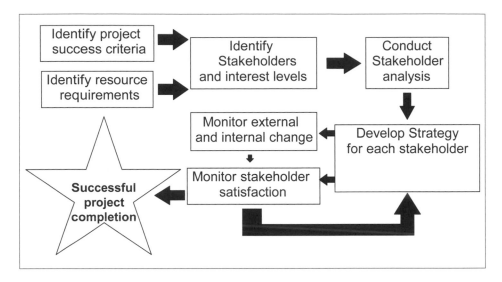

Figure 36.2 Stakeholder management process

IDENTIFY RESOURCE REQUIREMENTS

A project manager needs access to many resources in order to effectively execute a project. As shown in Figure 36.3 'resources', as used in this context, are not confined to tangible items such as *materials* and *finance*. They also include intangible 'resources' such as *support* and *emotion*. The majority of these resources will not be under the direct control of the project manager, but will be supplied by a stakeholder. As such, access to resources will be at the discretion of the stakeholder. This is relatively obvious when considering a stakeholder external to the organization undertaking the project. Some of these stakeholders can be bound by contract, although those supplying 'permissions' will be bound by statute and their decisions can be influenced by political expediency.

Also, the availability of resources supplied by internal stakeholders should never be taken for granted. Particularly where a project is being carried out within a matrix-based organization – the sponsor may well be committed to the project, but line managers might still be able to refuse to release key staff from operational responsibilities. For example, operator training may require the Operations Manager to identify trainees and make them available at the right time – but the Operations Manager might be always able to find more pressing issues to address with current operations. This last example illustrates the importance of 'support' (internal and external) as a key resource provided by stakeholders. This relates both to the stakeholders' direct support (or opposition) for the project, and the support (or opposition) they can generate amongst other individuals and groups.

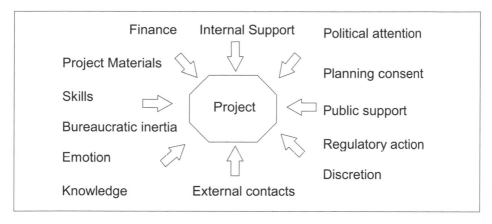

Figure 36.3 Stakeholder resources

As illustrated in Figure 36.4, stakeholders should be viewed as having a vital role to play as *change agents* – positively changing the way others view the project.

As a general rule, the role of key stakeholders as change agents will be more crucial on soft projects. However, as indicated in Figure 36.4, the need for stakeholders to be incorporated as change agents is appropriate for both hard and soft projects. For example the role of stakeholders as change agents on hard projects might include:

- marketing a new road
- explaining how to get the best results from new plant
- getting users to think differently about software

And their role as change agents on soft projects might include:

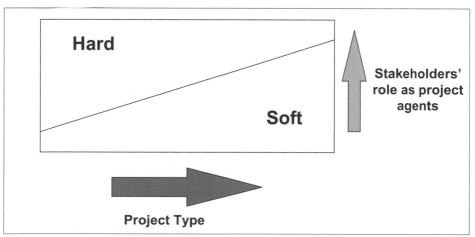

Figure 36.4 Stakeholders as change agents

763

- persuading people to change working practices
- getting staff to think differently about profit
- asking customers to purchase in new ways

As we have already highlighted, and will see further below, it is naïve to think that all stakeholders will want to promote the change being delivered by the project. Also, there is a need to be clear on how the key project stakeholders will influence others, and who will influence the key project stakeholders (see D'Herbemont and César 1998).

IDENTIFY STAKEHOLDER GROUPS AND INTEREST LEVELS

Brainstorm a key stakeholder list from the following classes:

- employees
- senior management
- customers (internal and external)
- suppliers (internal and external)
- neighbours (physical and within the supply chain)
- resource providers (people, time, finance, consents)
- government (local, UK, EU)
- opinion formers (media, commentators, industry pundits, unions, internal departments)

Record these stakeholders on a register. An example of a stakeholder register is given in Figure 36.5.

For each one, identify what, to them, constitutes a successful project. Their idea of project success may be totally different from yours or your sponsor's. For example, a landowner may have no interest in the benefits a pipeline across his land will bring to a community several miles away. His idea of project success will be to attract maximum compensation for the use of his land. Stakeholders' objectives may not always be obvious to the project manager or those close to delivery of the project and may need further research.

When developing the key stakeholder list ensure it incorporates 'secondary' stakeholders. These are stakeholders who do *not* have direct influence over the project, but who are able to change the attitudes the key stakeholders ('primary' stakeholders).

However, these groupings are often far too coarse to identify key stakeholders and allow precise targeting of actions. It is may be far more important to identify the principal:

- motivational drivers for these stakeholder groups
- individuals within each key stakeholder group

764

Scheme	Rural sewerage scheme		Review Date	24 Feb		Reviewers	
Stakeholder Name / Group	Objectives	Awareness H/L	Support H/L	Influence H/L	Strategy		
Project Manager	Meeting project success criteria of time, cost, performance	H	H	H	Ensure company and line manager support		
Sponsor	Remove problem of failures and customer complaints. Minimise disruption and compensation payments	H	H	H	Obtain active support. Keep informed of progress proactively		
Local Residents	Minimal noise and mess As quick as possible No more flooding	H	L	H	Face to face contact, agree local contact, provision for compensation		
Local Authority	Be informed	L	L	L	Involve from start, keep informed		
Environment Agency	Stop incidents, environmental improvements, close communication	H	H	H	Maintain close communication		
Woodland Trust (Environmental Pressure Group)	No environmental detriment	H	L	H	Early communication and involvement. Encourage relationship with Environment Agency		
Landowners	Maximum compensation for land take	H	L	H	Isolate by negotiating compensation and access details early. Document before and after positions very carefully		

Figure 36.5   An example of a stakeholder register

Classification of stakeholders using motivational drivers

In order to effectively target and manage the influence of key stakeholders the project manager must understand the drivers behind their vested interests. Stakeholders can therefore be classified as follows:

Beneficiary Stakeholders: These stakeholders are motivated because they will benefit in some way when the project achieves its objectives. As such these stakeholders can be used as a source of promoters for the project. However, their support should not be taken for granted. If they don't know or understand what benefits they will gain, they will at best be non-committal, and at worst be misguided opposers to the project. Therefore the project manager needs to ensure that communications with such stakeholders set out, and reinforce, the specific benefits to them. A common difficulty arises where key stakeholders in an organization have been set internal targets, often related to bonus payments, which conflict with the aims of the project.

Loss Stakeholders: In line with the laws of physics, gains in one area mean there will be losses in others. Obviously there is the principle of win-win that is the ideal. But in the real world this is an ideal that doesn't often apply to project stakeholders. Projects are designed to cause change. For the losers, this may be a tangible loss (for example a competitor may lose market share; a neighbouring property owner may lose ease of access or property value), or an intangible loss to a powerful personal value (such as loss of status, influence or, in terms of infrastructure projects, environmental benefits). Project managers are often by their nature optimists who are only focused on achieving the benefits to be derived by their project. Identifying loss stakeholders may be particularly difficult for them. However, a period of playing devil's advocate will enable project managers to identify the loss stakeholders and develop strategies to manage them. In developing such strategies project managers must recognize that they are often dealing with issues of personal value and beliefs. An individual's desire to retain the status quo is often more powerful and strongly defended than a desire for beneficial change for the majority. As such, it may prove impossible to move loss stakeholders to a point of support for the project. But they must either be moved to a position of neutrality or the influence they can bring to bear must be stifled.

Regulatory Stakeholders: These stakeholders are motivated by ensuring that the project execution complies with defined regulations and standards, and/or that the resulting outputs from the project will not contravene defined regulations and standards. Generally such stakeholders are not concerned with the success of the project per se, only that it complies with those regulations and standards of

766

which they are guardians. As such they will never be active supporters, but if they believe their requirements are not being met they can become active and very powerful opposers. The project manager must therefore ensure that these requirements are clearly defined and understood, and through communication with these stakeholders clearly show they are being met.

Targeting and influencing principal individuals within each key stakeholder group

These classifications are focused on groups. However, although this is a good starting point when identifying key stakeholders, it is too coarse an approach for determining actions. We therefore focus on principal individuals within each stakeholder group. Such individuals not only influence the group's views, but also represent these to other key stakeholders. These individuals can be the project manager's greatest allies in the management of primary stakeholders, or the greatest hidden enemy. Project managers must determine what measures are required to at least maintain these key individuals at a point of non-commitment or passive support, and never take this for granted. Such an influential stakeholder who is not actively engaged can often be also targeted by the Loss Stakeholders with devastating effects for the project. This is often a difficult area for project managers to deal with. We are generally more comfortable in de-personalising issues, and use phrases such as: '*They* are against it'. But how do we target our actions to influence this impersonal 'they'? We normally can't, but we can target actions to influence individuals. This requires us to understand what motivates these individuals to behave the way they do. So, in addition to the various tools and techniques project managers have to develop an understanding of human motivational and behavioural drivers, and how to influence them. This will take many of us into new areas that will not always sit comfortably with our engineering / technical backgrounds. However, do this we must if we find ourselves managing projects with complex stakeholder issues.

As a starting point we must look beyond the behaviours exhibited by individual stakeholders. We must recognize that these are driven by personal values, beliefs and needs that have been shaped and nurtured by the individual's experiences. Therefore to change these behaviours to ones which will not have a negative influence on our project, we must try and determine what it is about our project that is at odds with the individual's values, beliefs and needs. From this we must either minimize, in the stakeholder's view, these negative features, or increase the features that they view positively so as they outweigh the negative.

Frankly, not many project managers have the necessary skills and expertise to effectively achieve such identification and influence. But it would be arrogant to assume they should. We are experts at what we do. Part of this expertise is to know what other expertise is required on our projects and effectively bring that expertise onto the project – is it not? We quite happily welcome specialist planners, lawyers and cost consultants to the project team – why not psychologists and sociologists? Therefore it is not proposed that project managers have to be trained in psychology or sociology, but rather that they are aware that such expertise may well be required to support them and be ready and willing to draw on this.

CONDUCT STAKEHOLDER ANALYSIS

Stakeholders' attitudes to the project will vary. They will range between:

- Complete Opposition (roads protesters, threatened internal audiences)
- Complete Support (landscaping waste industrial areas, new office building for overcrowded staff)

The stakeholders' attitudes may also vary over time, particularly if the stakeholders are being exposed to effective management by the project team. The actions associated with this effective management need to be focused on the key stakeholders. But knowing who these people are is not enough. The project team needs to base its actions on:

1. A more refined assessment of the stakeholders' current attitude and that required to ensure project success
2. An awareness of the knowledge base upon which the stakeholders' current attitude is based
3. An understanding of the stakeholders' own objectives and how these can, if possible, be aligned with those of the project.

This sub-section provides guidance on mapping and analysis techniques which will support the first two elements listed above. The next subsection outlines steps to be taken to deal with the third element. The first step in the analysis is therefore focused on assessing the current level of support (or *commitment*) for the project amongst the key stakeholders. But in order to provide information to guide effective stakeholder management this needs to be assessed against the commitment levels required in order to achieve success. This combined analysis can be incorporated in a tabular format such as that in Figure 36.6. The characteristics and behaviours of each level of commitment are:

- **Active Opposition:** Will not accept change as proposed by project. Will expend time and energy telling others the project is 'wrong', and will try and turn supporters against the project. Will withhold resources from the project, either overtly or covertly.
- **Passive Opposition:** Not happy with change as proposed by project, but will reluctantly accept it. When asked will voice opposition, but will not seek out

Stake-holders	Active Opposition	Passive Opposition	Not Committed	Passive Support	Active Support
Suppliers			(XO)		
Executive Directors				X ——→ O	
Staff	X ——————→ O				
National Politicians				(XO)	
Finance Director				O ←—— X	
Local Politicians		(XO)			

Key:
X = Current Position
O = Required Position

Figure 36.6 Stakeholder commitment map

opportunities to raise opposition to the project. Will provide resources to the project but may require coercing.

- **No Commitment:** Will accept change. Not opposed or supportive of the project. Happy to see it proceed but not concerned if it succeeds or fails. Will provide resources, but only if it does not impact their own operations.
- **Passive Support:** Wants change as proposed by project. When asked will voice support, but will not seek out opportunities to gather support for the project. Will provide resources to project when asked, but may require prompting.
- **Active Support:** Eager for change proposed by project. Will expend time and energy telling others the project is 'right' and will try to change opposers' views – without prompting from the project team. Will ensure resources are available to the project as and when required.

There are a number of key features to note from this table. In particular:

- Changing a stakeholder's commitment level will require effort by the project team. This will have to be balanced with all of the other activities the project

769

team need to carry out – as outlined in the other chapters of this handbook. Therefore the team should not be over ambitious with regards to how far it tries to move stakeholders, particularly, as in the case of 'Staff', if they are currently actively opposed. Focus on the key stakeholders, those with the most influence to affect the success of the project, and achieve the minimum commitment level needed to ensure project success.

- Where the stakeholders' current commitment matches their required commitment level (as in the case of 'Suppliers') they must not be ignored. It is all too easy for an ignored stakeholder to misinterpret the lack of communication from the project team as disinterest in their objectives. They may respond in a like fashion when required to deliver resources or support. Worse still, they may be swayed by active opposers and change their attitude to the project as a result.

- As in the case of the 'Finance Director' there can be stakeholders whose *active support* may actually have a disruptive effect on the project. This is often due to their active support raising or reinforcing negative attitudes in other key stakeholders.

- The impact of stakeholder commitment on provision of resources to the project needs to be carefully considered by the project team when developing project plans. Especially where the analysis indicates resources may not be readily available, have contingency plans ready.

This commitment analysis will help to focus development of an appropriate strategy for managing each key stakeholder. A summary strategy can be entered on the Stakeholder Register, as shown in the example at the end of this chapter. In developing these strategies it is worth remembering the definition of stakeholder management given above, and in particular: 'the need for the continuing development of relationships'. Therefore the strategies developed need to incorporate actions which will continue throughout the project life-cycle and involve two-way communications.

These communications will be most effective if they are based on an awareness of the stakeholder's knowledge base. Stakeholders' commitment levels will, to a large extent, be based on their level of knowledge of the project. And based on this knowledge, stakeholders will make judgements of how the project will help, or hinder, them in meeting their own objectives. It is these judgements which will determine the stakeholders' satisfaction referred to in the introduction to this chapter. The stakeholders' level of knowledge will range from:

- *full awareness:* They have gained knowledge of the project by detailed research, focusing on those aspects of the project which will help them meet their own objectives, to

- *total ignorance:* They have gained knowledge of the project by hearsay not fact, and are therefore basing their attitudes towards the project on assumptions. Their decision on whether to increase their knowledge will depend on whether they believe they can use the project to further their own objectives.

These two attributes of stakeholders, commitment and knowledge can be mapped on to a chart, such as that in Figure 36.7, to illustrate the knowledge base across the key stakeholdcrs. To populate this chart plot each of the key stakeholders listed in Figure 36.6. Initially you will have to make certain assumptions regarding the knowledge base of each stakeholder. Be prepared to test these assumptions and revisit this chart throughout the project. There are a number of key points to note regarding where stakeholders lie on this chart:

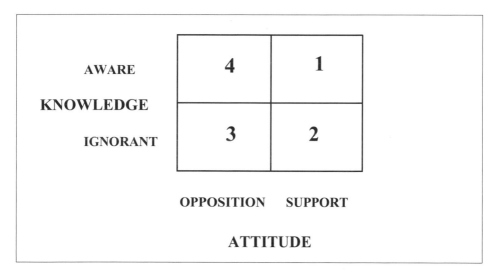

Figure 36.7 Plotting stakeholder knowledge base

Quadrant 1 – Support/Aware: These supporters must not be taken for granted. In order to retain their support they need to be assured that the project will indeed help them meet their own objectives.

Quadrant 2 – Support/Ignorant: This *support* is vulnerable and could easily be lost, particularly if the gaps in these stakeholders' knowledge base are filled by the views of *opposers* to the project. The project team will therefore need to ensure that this support is protected and reinforced.

Quadrant 3 – Opposition/Ignorant: This is a key target area for the project team, especially if the commitment mapping (Figure 36.6) indicates there are stakeholders in this quadrant whose commitment needs to be increased. This chart indicates that it may be possible to achieve this by filling the gap in the stakeholders' knowledge base with positive messages regarding the project.

Quadrant 4 – Opposition/Aware: These can be difficult stakeholders to manage. As they are already *aware*, and are basing their opposition on this, it may never be possible to move them to support the project.

DEVELOP STRATEGY FOR EACH STAKEHOLDER

The analysis outlined just above focused on determining current and required stakeholder commitment levels, and the knowledge base giving rise to these attitudes. Building on this analysis stakeholder management strategies should be developed which focus on achieving the required future commitment levels by influencing the knowledge base. The respective movement in commitment level will therefore be driven by communications between the project team and the key stakeholders. As can be seen from Figure 36.6, gaining stakeholders' commitment to change is often vital to achieving project success. Unfortunately project managers rarely appreciate the scale and complexity of the communication tasks involved in gaining commitment, as shown in Figure 36.8.

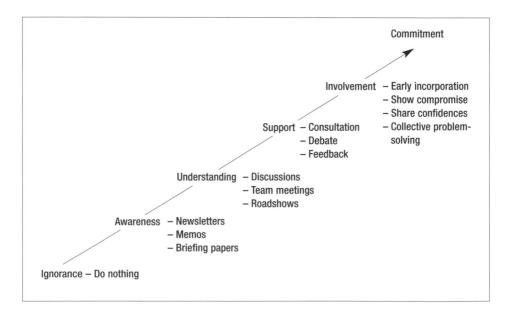

Figure 36.8 Tasks involved in gaining commitment

Project managers must avoid merely focusing on the preparation and circulation of newsletters and briefing papers (i.e. raising awareness). As can be seen above they have to follow this up with more direct actions if they are to gain widespread commitment to the change proposed by the project. Also, if they do not check the stakeholders' understanding they can find opposers use this raised awareness as a basis to attack the project. For ease of reference, the principle features of the various strategies that may need to be adopted has been outlined below in relation to the current knowledge base (Figure 36.7) and commitment levels (Figure 36.6).

Quadrant 1 – Support/Aware

There are three key communication strategies for this group

Raising Commitment: This can generally be achieved by highlighting the role of stakeholders in achieving project success, particularly through ready access to resources and influencing the attitudes of other stakeholders. Prepare for these discussions by developing scenarios showing the effect of, say, late access to resources. Also, if seeking to increase commitment to **active support** you need to build on the stakeholders' awareness, and their desire to see the project succeed, in preparing them for discussions with other (opposing) stakeholders.

Maintaining Commitment: Reinforce the stakeholder's positive view. This is best achieved by repeatedly stressing the alignment between the project and the stakeholder's objectives. Obviously to do this the initial step needs to be finding out what their objectives are.

Lowering Commitment: This can be a particularly sensitive situation to deal with. After all these stakeholders want you to succeed, indeed they want to actively help you. So how do you tell them that their active support may actually help the project to fail! A possible way out of this tricky situation is to stress the need for the project team to co-ordinate the actions of the stakeholder in order to ensure maximum benefit for the project. This can then be expanded to include the project team directing the stakeholder's actions. Even where the above strategy is well implemented there is always a risk that the stakeholder concerned will see an opportunity to help the project and do, or say, their own thing – with perhaps unforeseen and negative results. This risk can never be fully removed and as such needs constant monitoring.

Quadrant 2 – Support/Ignorant

As noted earlier, this support is vulnerable and could easily be lost, even if these stakeholders are initially actively supportive of the project. This could be brought about by opposers raising doubts as to whether the project will indeed help these stakeholders achieve their objectives. The project team must discover why these stakeholders are supporting the project. What is in it for them? Remember these stakeholders are ignorant of the details of the project. They are therefore basing their support on assumptions they have made regarding the project. These assumptions need to be checked.

Let's first look at where the stakeholder's assumptions are found to be valid. The project team need to reinforce the stakeholder's support by showing them that the project is indeed what they have assumed. Such confirmation can in itself often result in an increase in the stakeholder's commitment level – from *passive* to *active support*.

Now let's look at where the stakeholder's assumptions are not valid. Here we have a potential problem. If active opposers discover this they could use it to change these stakeholders' attitudes. However, this change in attitude could just as easily happen if the project team's communications with the stakeholders merely highlights that the project is not what they thought. So should the project team avoid this problem by trying to keep these stakeholders ignorant? There are two main weaknesses in such a passive strategy:

1. You cannot guarantee that the opposers will not fill the resulting communications void with negative messages.
2. You cannot increase commitment level (for example. from *passive* to *active support*) if you don't communicate with the stakeholders (Figure 36.8).

We therefore recommend a proactive strategy is adopted. This must itself be based on an assumption. That is, once the stakeholders are made aware of the project's details their support will turn to opposition. This opposition must then be quickly addressed through the strategy proposed below for Opposition/Ignorant (Figure 36.7: Quadrant 3).

Quadrant 3 – Opposition/Ignorant

As noted in Section 2.5 this is a key target area for the project team. If the project team do not take the time and effort to communicate with these stakeholders they will be targeted by the active opposers. This could result in a strengthening of their attitudes (from *passive* to *active opposition*). You therefore need to start to find out why they are opposed and be prepared to negotiate in order to move them to, as a minimum, *passive opposition* – that is they may not like the change but will reluctantly accept it. To achieve acceptance of change it is helpful to understand what influences this. Figure 36.9 provides an outline of factors which need to be considered and addressed in order to influence someone's acceptance of change.

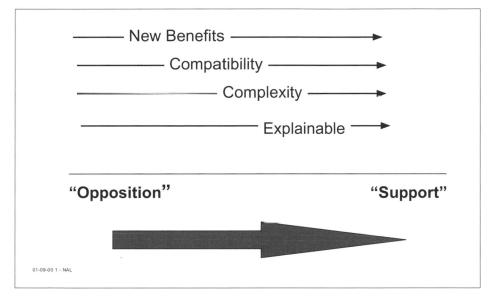

Figure 36.9 What affects stakeholder position?

1. *New Benefits:* Relative advantage – how much better does the new arrangement appear?
   - Will the new IS set-up really help?
   - Will the by-pass really save much time?
2. *Compatibility:* How much the stakeholder has to change:
   - Does the office move mean I'll have to relocate?
3. *Complexity:* How easy is it to adopt the new system:
   - Can I get it in one go or do I have to go through a dozen different processes?
   - How many times will you be digging up my road?
4. *Communicability:* How simple is it to explain it all:
   - Exactly how loud is a decibel?
   - How smelly is a sewage farm?

Therefore the key elements of this strategy are:

- discovery of what is influencing the stakeholder's view of the project
- discovery of what changes would be required to influence the stakeholder's acceptance of the project
- framing propositions to the stakeholder in respect of the factors outlined above

- negotiating with the stakeholder to achieve acceptance while minimising the changes required

Quadrant 4 – Opposition/Aware

This can be a difficult situation to deal with. You are starting with stakeholders who, on the analysis carried out, have knowledge of your project and based on this are opposed to what you are trying to achieve. Initially the same strategy should be adopted as for Opposition/Ignorant outlined above. However, there needs to be recognition that there may be little or no possibility of moving these stakeholders to a position of support for the project. This should not though stop you from trying a process of negotiation. A visible, positive, change in attitude of one of these stakeholders will greatly enhance your chances of increasing or maintaining the commitment levels of other stakeholders.

A note of caution needs to be raised. A lot of energy could be wasted trying to change these stakeholders' attitudes, energy which would probably be better used on stakeholders in one of the other quadrants. Therefore be prepared for the possibility (probability) these stakeholders will never change their attitude. As they have been identified as key stakeholders they therefore, by our definition, have power over the project through the control of resources. So what are you going to do if these resources are not available? The development of contingency measures to deal with this eventuality has to be a priority task for the project team and is indeed the key feature of the management strategy for these stakeholders.

MONITOR AND REVIEW

The position and level of commitment of various stakeholders with regards to the analysis carried above will constantly change, as their knowledge base regarding the project changes. Also, new stakeholders may appear. Therefore the various steps outlined above may need to be revisited at regular intervals. A question to ask in these regular reviews is: are the various stakeholders where you want them to be at this point in time? Remember that you can't win them all. Focus on gaining the support of those who control key resources and those with the highest influence on project success or failure.

HINTS AND TIPS

Here are some key points in a stakeholder management strategy:

1. avoid helping to build opposing coalitions
2. become known as the monopoly supplier of information

3. respond quickly and appropriately to negative impressions
4. encourage supporters to meet and reinforce each other
5. don't abdicate responsibility for dealing with objectors outside the project team
6. use supporters to convert waverers. People are often less suspicious of an intermediary than the company or organization promoting the project
7. stress benefits not features
8. be prepared to change
9. plan ahead
10. be sensitive to changes in the business or political environment

Remember the following:

1. stakeholders must be identified
2. important stakeholders have power AND an interest
3. stakeholder analysis and management is vital for project success
4. stakeholders' attitudes change throughout the project life-cycle
5. dealing with stakeholders is often an intuitive process

CONCLUSION

Effective project management requires effective management of project stakeholders. Project managers and project sponsors need to understand the overall principles, process and techniques that should be applied if they are to ensure project success. They must also clearly define who will do what in order to ensure the appropriate level of representation, and avoid conflicting messages.

However, stakeholder management is not a magic cure for all project management ailments. It should be an addition to the project manager's overall toolbox, not a replacement for any of the other techniques already in there.

REFERENCES AND FURTHER READING

APM, 2006, *APM Body of Knowledge,* 5th edition, High Wycombe, UK: Association for Project Management.

BS6079, 2000, *A Guide to Project Management,* British Standards Institute, London.

D'Herbemont, O. and César, B., 1998, *Managing Sensitive Projects: a lateral approach,* London: Macmillan Business.

37 Managing Communication
Ralf Müller

Communication is the *operating system* of a society. Just like a computer needs an operating system to make the computer's resources available to the programs, so does a society need communication to provide its resources to the individuals in the society. Accordingly communication is a wide subject that touches on almost every aspect of life, be it politics, religion, business, family, or leisure time activities. What applies to societies also applies to projects. Efficient and effective communication between the project manager, the project team, sponsor, steering committee and other stakeholders is crucial for project success. It links the project's requirements with the stakeholders and the final outcome. Effective communication builds trust between the project's stakeholders and allows for mutual understanding of the project objectives and the approach to achieve those objectives. That forms the basis for a collaborative working relationship between the parties in the project.

Communication in projects needs to be thoroughly planned, implemented and controlled in order to provide the right information, at the right time, to the project's stakeholders. How to accomplish this is described in this chapter. It starts by describing how project managers communicate in projects, followed by an overview of the different modes of communication available to project managers. Then the process steps for managing communication in projects are described as:

- identification of communication needs of different stakeholder groups
- development of a communication strategy and matrix
- development of a communication schedule
- implementation, control and continuous adjustment

Examples show how the process steps are executed in practice. Communication in projects can be defined as the sending and receiving of information as part of a social intercourse. Management of this communication consists of a process for identification of communication needs of project stakeholders, as well as the development, implementation and continuous adjustment of communication strategies to meet these communication needs.

A MODEL FOR COMMUNICATION ON PROJECTS

A minimum requirement for communication to take place is a sender and a receiver of information, as well as a motivation for them to communicate with each other. However, that alone does not ensure that the parties understand each other. Many more aspects must be taken into account, among others the language to be used, the media available and the depth of information required to communicate. All this is not done arbitrarily by people communicating. They follow a series of steps, which are first applied by the sender of information to ensure that the receiver can receive and understand the information. Subsequently the receiver uses the same steps to check the appropriateness and contents of the information received. These steps constitute layers in the communication at which a receiver either accepts or rejects the communication. Figure 37.1 shows the five layers that build upon each other in the sequence of:

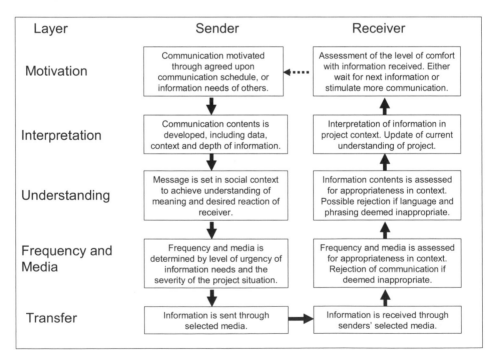

Figure 37.1 Project manager communication model

1. Motivation for communication
2. Interpretation of project situation and context
3. Ensuring understanding of communication contents
4. Selection of communication frequency and media
5. Transfer of information

Senders of information process these layers top-down, while receivers do it bottom-up. The communication flow between sender and receiver through these layers is described.

MESSAGE SENDER

Motivation

A prerequisite for communication to occur is a relationship between the people intending to communicate, for example given through a joint project. The sender's motivation for communication is either externally triggered, for example through existing communication schedules or questions from stakeholders, or it is internally triggered by the desire to have another person behave in a certain way, for example start working on a project task.

Interpretation of project situation and context

Following the motivation for communication, the sender starts to develop the information contents. Here the current situation of the project (eg a technical problem), the project's context (eg pending deadline) and the receiver's existing knowledge about a subject is taken into account to decide on the depth of information to be provided.

Understanding of communication's contents

At this layer the right language and phrasing for the receiver is chosen, so that he or she can interpret the correct meaning from the information and react as expected by the sender. A typical example is the use of English language in international projects, as well as using business terms when talking to managers, as opposed to technical terms when communicating with specialists. Furthermore the phrasing is impacted by the situation within which the communication occurs. This results either in a clear order, a tactful 'politically correct' message, an exchange of opinions, or a question for clarification.

Frequency and Media Selection

This layer determines how often and with which medium the communication should take place. Typical media include email, telephone or face-to-face meetings. Urgency of information needs and severity of the project's situation, together with availability and appropriateness of media for both sender and receiver impact this decision.

Message Transfer

At this layer the message is transferred through the media from sender to receiver. No matter which medium chosen, communication between people always requires the sender of information to encode the information in either spoken or written words, which are then converted into a format suitable for the chosen medium (for example email, telephone etc.) before it is forwarded to the receiver. During the transfer to the receiver the encoded information can be distorted by different disturbances, such as noise in verbal communication or firewalls blocking data transfer in electronic communication. Once the receiver end is reached, the information is decoded back to its original type.

MESSAGE RECEIVER

Receivers process messages in the opposite direction, that is from message transfer layer, through frequency selection, understanding and interpretation, up to motivation.

Message Transfer

At this level the message is received through the communication media selected by the sender and decoded to a format that can be processed by the receiver.

Frequency and Media Selection

Here the receiver assesses the appropriateness of communication frequency and media choice. If the choice is acceptable for the recipient then the information is further processed at the next layer. Communication with unacceptable frequency or media is rejected or ignored. For example daily phone calls of a project manager to a senior level project sponsor, reporting that the project progresses according to plan, even though the sponsor only wants to be notified when the project is in an exceptional situation.

Understanding the Meaning of Communication Contents

The received message is assessed against its appropriateness in the current situation. Assessments differ by the way information is perceived and include appropriateness and effectiveness in the current situation, as well as sincerity and truthfulness. Accepted information is passed on to the next layer.

Interpretation of Project Situation and Context

Messages at this layer add to the receiver's existing perception about the subject of communication. Information that can be integrated with the existing knowledge is added to existing knowledge and new knowledge is formed. Information contrary to existing knowledge and beliefs may be questioned or rejected.

Motivation

Based on the comfort level achieved through the communication the receiver may wait for the next information in accordance with the agreed upon communication schedule, or becomes mentally more involved in the subject and raises further questions. This then stimulates the motivation to become a sender of information, which then triggers again the process described above.

MODES OF COMMUNICATION

PROJECT MANAGEMENT INFORMATION SYSTEMS

Ultimately, project related communication takes place between people. To that end, Project Management Information Systems (PMIS) support project communication through their storage and retrieval capabilities, which allow for timely information access by the project's stakeholders. PMISs can range from a simple paper-based filing system of project documents, up to complex project web-servers using different databases with hierarchical access rights, to allow for global online access to the project's real-time data at any time (see Chapter 8). No matter how sophisticated a PMIS is, its purpose is to support stakeholders with sufficient information for them to feel comfortable in their planning, control and decision making. The type and complexity of the PMIS should therefore be determined by the number of stakeholders needing access to the PMIS, their particular information needs, and the associated security requirements. Projects with strong public interest often use Internet based web-servers to meet the information needs of the public, plus project internal web-sites with confidential project related information. Smaller projects are often served through a hierarchical filing system in a company's Intranet.

PMISs can hold information on any of the widely known communication modes of formal and informal, internal and external, as well as horizontal and vertical communication. These are described in the following sections.

FORMAL VERSUS INFORMAL COMMUNICATION

Formal and informal modes of communication are complementary to each other. Both modes are needed for stakeholders to feel comfortable about the level of information they have about a project. Formal communication provides credible information to the receiver, and informal communication allows for a feedback to clarify questions and build trust between the project manager and other stakeholders. Formal communication is often impersonal, deliberate and to the point, but at a slow speed. Commitment is higher for the topic than for the relationship with the communication partner. This communication mode often uses official reports, presentations or reviews. Therefore formal communication is often perceived by the receivers as credible and accurate.

Informal communication is more casual and spontaneous, with a higher commitment to the relationship between sender and receiver, than to the accuracy of the information. It often takes place in ad-hoc conversations, memos etc. Therefore informal communication is perceived as being less accurate and less credible than formal communication. Whether a communication is formal or informal is often a matter of perception and determined by the situation within which the communication occurs. What constitutes an informal communication in one national or organizational culture can be perceived as formal communication in another culture. The situation should therefore be assessed from the perspective of the sender of the information, that is, whether the sender perceives this communication as formal or informal.

INTERNAL VERSUS EXTERNAL COMMUNICATION

Internal communication includes information exchange between the project team members, plus the project manager. The project's sponsor is sometimes also perceived as part of a project's internal communication, but only if the sponsor is strongly involved in the project and the project manager and sponsor collaborate extensively. Internal communication is often at a detailed level and related to the day-to-day activities in the project. It often requires intimate knowledge of the project's activities and would therefore provide little or no value to recipients outside of the project team. Examples for internal communication include project team members updating the project manager on the achievements of their individual activities. While this is important information for the project manager to help determine the status of the project, it is usually communicated to external stakeholders only on a summary level in order to reflect the entirety of accomplishments in the project.

External communication refers to information exchanged beyond the borderline of the project team. This could include line managers providing resources to the project, as well as Steering Group members, or the public.

Information for external communication must be carefully assessed to prevent confidential or other information not intended for the recipients leaking out and potentially harming the project. External communication should be under strict control of the project manager, to ensure consistency in the messages sent to the project's environment. In cases where the Project Manager has to rely on other stakeholders to communicate externally about the project, the project manager has to review in advance the information contents of the intended communication, the timing, and its suitability for the targeted audience.

HORIZONTAL VERSUS VERTICAL COMMUNICATION

This refers to the direction of communication within the organizational hierarchy. The direction of communication impacts the use of professional terminology and level of detail in the information exchanged.

Horizontal communication includes peer-to-peer communication, such as between project team members, or project managers of several projects discussing the availability of shared resources. This communication often uses specific terminology or jargon which is only sufficiently known to members of a particular profession (such as project managers talking about specific planning techniques). This can make it difficult for others to understand the communication's contents. However, the use of specific terminology within a particular group of peers often adds to the quality of their communication and contributes positively to the project.

Vertical communication can be either upwards or downwards in the organizational hierarchy. From a project manager perspective downward communication relates to information exchange with the project team, suppliers or others reporting to the project manager as part of the ongoing project. Upward communication refers to the project manager's information exchange with the project sponsor, Steering Group or other hierarchically higher institutions in the organization. Communication upwards and downwards in the hierarchy should be carefully assessed for unnecessary jargon or technical details that may be misunderstood by the recipients, in order to avoid a possible breakdown in communication over time. These problems typically arise when project managers use the detailed technical descriptions of issues, as reported by the specialists in their team, and copy them into the status report for the Steering Committee or sponsor. Managers like sponsors or Steering Group members are often unaware of the technical details of a project's product and are more interested in the business use of the final product. While one party in the communication talks technical terms, the other expects business terms. If such a situation lasts for a long period the communication between the parties will cease and the subsequent lack of collaboration will threaten the success of the project. Vertical communication must therefore be as simple as possible, avoid too much jargon, and should be phrased in a way that the receiver understands.

SUMMARY

The six modes of communication described above can occur in any combination. Combinations should be chosen by the project manager to ensure that:

- the receiver understands the information communicated
- the receiver feels comfortable with the level of information provided
- the mode of communication is appropriate for the formality of the situation within which the communication occurs
- the efforts to communicate and the importance of contents are balanced

It is often said that 'you cannot communicate enough in projects'. This is wrong. Managing communication in projects is not a matter of quantity. It is a matter of communication quality. By providing stakeholder groups with the appropriate level of information they require for their decisions and roles in the organization – not more, and certainly not less – the efficiency and effectiveness in project communication is assured. But how can that be done? This is addressed in the next section.

THE PROCESS FOR MANAGING COMMUNICATION

Providing stakeholders with appropriate information at the right time is achieved in a four step process, shown in Figure 37.2. It starts with the identification of communication needs of the different stakeholder groups, followed by the development of an appropriate communication strategy for each of these groups, depending on their attitude and knowledge about the project. The next step is to develop a communication matrix, which outlines, among others, *what* and *when* to communicate with each stakeholder group. This matrix is subsequently transformed into a communication schedule which becomes part of the overall project schedule. Finally, the scheduled communication must be executed in the daily work of the project, controlled by the project manager, and continuously adjusted to the changing information and communication needs of the various stakeholder groups. The steps are described in turn.

STEP 1: DETERMINING THE COMMUNICATION NEEDS OF DIFFERENT STAKEHOLDER GROUPS

Communication needs of stakeholder groups differ according to their roles in the project. We can identify the following:

786

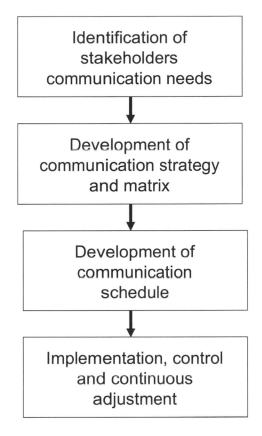

Figure 37.2 Process for communication management

- external stakeholders, such as sponsors, steering groups and investors
- internal stakeholders, such as the project manager, the project team, suppliers and contractors
- users of the project outcome, such as end-users of IT Systems or consultants using a newly developed methodology

Project sponsors' communication needs

In the next chapter, Bob Graham suggests that sponsors, Steering Groups and funding organizations etc are especially interested in:

1. Information about the project's *outcome and process*. They want to know about the project's product or service and the way this is accomplished:
   - whether the project will deliver a product or service that will meet their performance requirements, for example, to generate the revenues expected of it. For that the project outcome must conform to the requirements.

787

- whether an appropriate project process has been designed that will deliver the correct product or service, and that it is being followed. Configuration management data (see Chapter 36) will be a key element of satisfying this communication need.

2. Information about *project performance*. They want to know about the project team's chances of delivering the project in accordance with the plan:
   - is the project progressing at a rate such that the product will be ready at a time and cost that the investment in it will be repaid?
   - are adequate resources being applied to make appropriate progress, in a timely and efficient manner?

These stakeholders look for analytical data, which give statistical or other quantitative evidence of project progress. Earned value (see Chapter 20) or specific, agreed upon metrics, can be used by the project manager to meet these communication needs.

3. Information to build *trust* and ensure *surprise avoidance*. They want to know that the project manager can be trusted to undertake the work competently and ethically and in the owner's best interests. For that they look for information indicating that the project manager is credible and trustworthy. This is often achieved by:
   - the project manager showing that he or she understands the requirements of the project, and takes decisions in the best interest of this stakeholder group.
   - the project manager providing sufficient information, so that these external stakeholders know 'what's going on on the other side' and are not faced with sudden surprises.

This level of trust is often established through a balance of formal and informal communication, where formal communication is used to meet the control needs and reporting requirements of an organization, whereas frequent informal communication is used to build up trust between the external stakeholders and the project manager.

Project managers, teams, suppliers and contractors' communication needs

This group's information needs change over the life-cycle of a project.

- During the early stages, the project manager and project team need to know the project business case, existing requirements, and project context. This information is needed to create a 'big picture' of the endeavour. It allows developing an overall approach to the project at the early stages of the endeavour. At later stages it allows making decisions in the best interest of the project sponsor through a good understanding of the overall strategic or business objectives that are to be accomplished.

- Information about project objectives, specifications, priorities and possible constraints is needed during the planning stages. That allows the team to develop a realistic project plan that can be executed within the constraints imposed by the sponsor or investors. During this stage the team needs answers to their technical and business questions. Furthermore they need feedback from the sponsor that the plan is realistic and acceptable from the sponsor's and the users' perspective.

- Throughout the implementation of the project the information needs of this group of stakeholders changes towards feedback through reviews and acceptance of deliverables, as well as possible changes to the project plan. This is typically provided by the sponsor, or the users acting on behalf of the sponsor. Other information needs include early warnings if a party in the project can not fulfil their obligations stated in the project plan.

- At the close-out of the project the sponsor should provide information about the degree to which the overall business objective was achieved through the project. That includes how well the project outcome did fulfil the expectations. That allows the project manager, users and sponsor to draw lessons learned for future projects and provide adequate information to the project team and other stakeholders.

End-users' communication needs

This group of stakeholders provides input to the initiation and planning stages of projects in the form of requirements, process steps, or handling descriptions for the project's outcome. During project execution this group needs to be updated on project progress, especially:

- Deadlines and availability of deliverables, to allow the users to plan and prepare the introduction of new products or services developed as part of the project.

- Requirements and timings for tests and reviews, to give users lead time to prepare their timely and relevant testing or review of project deliverables.

- Any changes to the project plan or deliverables, to allow users to adjust their expectations and identify possible issues resulting from a change.

- Periodic presentation of project results to foster their trust and support for the project.

Summary

The above list can not cover all the information needs, but should show the minimum communication between the key stakeholders that is needed in a project. Depending upon the different types of projects, the communication needs in the areas outlined above may be much more detailed or at a summary level only.

An initial determination of stakeholder communication needs should be done at an early stage of a project, such as the planning stage. The identified communication needs change over the life-cycle of a project and need to be adjusted, depending on the stage and the status of a project. Communication needs should be requested from the different stakeholder groups. However, not all stakeholders know in advance which communication they need over the course of the project. The project manager should therefore establish a feedback loop with the stakeholder groups to assess their satisfaction with a project's communication and then adjust it accordingly. Often it is helpful for project managers to anticipate special information needs of stakeholders and provide additional information as anticipated. How to develop such a communication strategy is described in the next section.

STEP 2: DEVELOPMENT OF A COMMUNICATION STRATEGY AND MATRIX

Communication strategies should be linked to the stakeholders' communication needs. However, the project manager should also take the stakeholders' knowledge and attitude towards the project into account before defining the breadth and depth of information provided to them. Using the Knowledge vs. Attitude matrix, Figure 36.7, allows for the development of four different communication strategies, depending on the stakeholders' awareness or ignorance of the project and their support or opposition to the project:

Quadrant 1 – Support/Aware

This group should be kept informed at the detailed level, including current or anticipated project issues. This group often includes the stakeholders listed above and uses open communication to foster collaboration.

Quadrant 2 – Support/Ignorant

A suitable communication strategy for this group should foster further trust and support of the project. Information should be provided to increase project awareness, preferably by linking the project outcome positively to the objectives of this stakeholder group. Feedback should be collected periodically to assess the stakeholders' knowledge and attitude level towards the project, and possibly adjust the communication strategy.

Quadrant 3 – Oppose/Ignorant

Communication with this group may be politically sensitive. Care must be taken that information provided to this group cannot be interpreted incorrectly. However, the group should be monitored and informed sufficiently – especially with positive messages – so that their stakeholders have a chance to develop a more supportive attitude and higher awareness of the project over time.

Quadrant 4 – Oppose/Aware

Communication to this group should seek for a solution of the issues between the group and the project. A defensive information strategy often develops, but should be avoided. Instead a steady dialogue should be established which allows overcoming the issues in a constructive manner.

At this stage the stakeholders are identified and grouped, and appropriate communication strategies are developed. It is now possible to implement the communication strategy by developing a communication plan for the different stakeholder groups. The plan consists of a matrix which outlines how to communicate with each stakeholder group. The matrix format provides a summary of stakeholder communication and works as a reference document for all communication internal and external to the project. Figure 37.3 shows the layout of the communication matrix.

Entries in the communication matrix are made for different stakeholder groups, or individual key stakeholders. Examples for stakeholder groups could be those identified in the Attitude vs. Awareness matrix. Examples for key stakeholders include a project's sponsor or end-users of the project outcome. The stakeholder groups and key individuals with particular communication needs are listed horizontally in the top row of the matrix. For each of them the following entries are made vertically:

Stakeholder group -------------------- *Communication*	Stakeholder group A	Stakeholder group B	Stakeholder group C	Stakeholder group D
Objective				
What				
When				
How				
Feedback				
Responsible				
Notes				

Figure 37.3 Communication matrix

791

OBJECTIVE

This summarizes the overall communication strategy developed for this stakeholder or stakeholder group. Examples include: *build collaboration* (for Quadrant 1 stakeholders), or *maintain support* (for Quadrant 2 stakeholders). For particular key stakeholders, such as the project sponsor or Steering Committee, this field should describe the level of information required. Examples could include *keep up-to-date using milestone plan,* or *only involve in case of plan deviation.*

WHAT

This field describes the information contents provided to the stakeholder. This includes:

- *Status and achievements:* what has been accomplished in the project compared with the project's plan. This is the traditional triple-constraints reporting, comparing budget, time, and functionality accomplishments in the reporting period with the plans for this period. It often lists the milestones accomplished and the deliverables finished at this time. It is the most basic form of project status reporting.
- *Changes to the project:* any filed or already agreed upon change in project scope, plan, risks, quality requirements, etc, which requires a re-baselining of the project plan is listed here. An example would be a new request for added functionality, handed in by the project's sponsor for evaluation by the project team.
- *Issues or open items list:* a continuously maintained list of current issues and 'open items', listed to show progress on the resolution of these issues, their impact on project results, and the potential need for further resources.
- *Next steps in the project:* a summary of the near term activities within the next reporting period. It is the forward looking information and complements the backward looking status and achievement reports.
- *Quality and progress measures:* this lists the accomplishments against the agreed upon quality metrics, for example *defect measurements* on the rate of software defect discovery and total defects. It also comprises integrated project performance measures, such as *earned value management* (see Chapter 20*)*, which integrates scope, schedule and resource for performance measurement.
- *Trends in the project:* any tendencies detected within the project should be listed here. These are typically identified through analysis of project progress over time, such as increasing schedule deviation over time. These trends are often calculated from the project's time and costs measures, as well as quality and other progress measures.

WHEN

This shows the frequency with which the communication occurs. In well performing projects the project manager's formal communication to external stakeholders, such as the project sponsor, is often done once or twice a month; and formal project team meetings are held once a week. Informal communication is more frequent in internal communication and less frequent in external communication. Informal communication is often not scheduled.

The frequency of communication is also an indicator for the status of the project. Sponsors or Steering Committees requesting very frequent status reports do this because they have lost trust in the project and now increase their control over the project. Alternatively, very infrequent communication between the project and the sponsor may indicate that at least one party has lost their interest in collaborating towards a joint objective. Here a risk of diverging objectives arises, that is the development of differences in the project supplier's and the project buyer's objectives over time. Both cases are indicative of problems between the project and its environment and should be assessed for root cause.

If the project is in serious trouble, or a threatening situation for stakeholders or the public occurs, the communication frequency must be increased. In these cases the need for increased information frequency should be coupled with face-to-face interaction between the project managers and the stakeholders. This is done to provide stakeholders with the required information so they feel in control of the situation, and also to allow them to trust the project manager through interpretation of his/her body language and general appearance.

HOW

This refers to the medium used to transfer the information in a communication, such as telephone, email or face-to-face meetings. As described under the frequency heading above, media usage changes from lesser to higher interactive media depending on the project situation. If projects are progressing according to plan and with no serious issues, then less interactive media like paper or web-based status reports are used. If problems emerge, then phone calls and emails are increasingly used. Projects in serious trouble, or causing trouble for their stakeholders, often require project managers to communicate face-to-face in meetings or through video conferences. This is because interactive media allow transfer of more information at any point in time. Difficult discussions or reviews are executed faster and with a better mutual understanding of the subject if more interactive media are chosen. This interactivity, however, comes usually at a higher price for the medium chosen and therefore increases communication costs.

Due to possible disturbances during transmission through some media, but also potentially because of a lack of clearness on the side of the sender, received information is often not interpreted as intended by the sender. Therefore it is necessary for the sender to gain feedback on what the receiver has understood from the communication.

FEEDBACK

One of the fallacies in communication is for senders to assume the receiver has read and even understood what has been communicated. Especially written status reports are frequently only browsed through by the recipient or immediately filed without further reading. Even if the information is read by the receiver, it is not certain that it is understood correctly. The receiver may interpret the information in his or her particular understanding of the project context, which can be different from that of the sender. In these cases the same words on both ends of the communication convey different meanings. This is solved through feedback – a deliberate check by the sender that the receiver has correctly understood the communicated information. To prevent that the feedback being subject to the same disturbances as the original information an alternate medium is often used for feedback. Examples include:

- The interpretation of formal written reports should be checked through phone calls from the sender. That allows for formal correction of misunderstandings, but also for building trust between the communication partners due to the informal nature of a phone call.
- Reading and correct interpretation of emails can also be checked through informal phone calls or periodic face-to-face meetings.
- Feedback in face-to-face meeting is provided immediately by body language and questions, or meeting protocols. The same applies to feedback in phone calls or telephone conferences.

This alternate feedback channel also allows balancing formal and informal communication, which typically improves the level of comfort the parties have with the information exchange.

RESPONSIBLE

This refers to the person responsible for the communication with a particular stakeholder group. Frequently it is not only the project manager who communicates about the project, but also the lead technical resources talking to their peers in the organization that sponsor the project, or senior managers of selling organizations talking to their peers in the organization buying a project. No matter how many people are responsible for communication to certain stakeholder groups, it is necessary that the project manager knows what these resources are communicating. While it may not be necessary to know all the technical details discussed between the specialists, it is certainly necessary for the project manager to know how the results of technical discussion impact the project results and the adherence to plan. Similarly, the project manager may not be able to attend all project related communication between higher level managers and their peers. However, project managers must ensure that they give sufficient briefing to their senior executives, so that they can successfully communicate to their peers. After that, the project managers must be updated with the information exchanged and possible decisions made during the senior managers' communication. Accountability for communication about project progress and results remains at the project manager level, independent of the other organizational layers included in carrying out the communication.

NOTES

This field allows capturing the particularities of certain stakeholder groups and making them visible for those planning to communicate with them. Figure 37.4 shows an example of a communication matrix. Only five stakeholder groups are listed for clarity. The example project is the delivery of an ICT project from a selling organization to a buying organization. The communication matrix is for the selling organization's management and its project team. By using the approach outlined above, the stakeholder groups were identified and associated communication strategies developed. The information needs of the different stakeholder groups were assessed and the contents, frequency, media, feedback and responsibility entries determined in a way that the project manager remains the focal point of all information exchanged. That requires careful timing of the project communication events, so that information can be accumulated from the detailed level to summary levels in the shortest period of time. This is necessary to keep all levels of management up-to-date on project's progress.

STEP 3: DEVELOPMENT OF A COMMUNICATION SCHEDULE

Once the communication matrix has been finished the schedule of communication events can be established. This schedule outlines how the various information exchanges link together for a consistent information flow through the project's organizational hierarchy. In the example in Figure 37.5 the information is accumulated from the very detailed level (Thursday and Friday) to summary levels (every second Friday and Monday), which allow for adjusting the depth of information and the language used to the targeted recipients of the information.

Stakeholder group	Sponsor & Steering Committee	Project team	Project Manager of buying organization	Lead technical specialist of buying organization	Vice President of buying organization
Objective	Collaboration	Collaboration	Collaboration	Involvement	Monitoring
What	Progress using milestone plan, budget, functionality achieved, changes and issues	Task achievements against plan, planned tasks for next week, issues & open items, risks	Progress against plan, resource requirements for next period, interface and process issues	Software architecture issues and their solutions	Summary of project progress, anticipated and current project context issues
When	Every second Friday	Friday morning, 10:00AM	Friday afternoon, 3:00 PM	Thursday afternoon, 3:00 PM	Every second Monday 10:00 AM
How	Formal report, attached to email	Team meeting in project room	Face-to-face meeting in buyer's PM office	Phone call	Phone call
Feedback	Phone call to sponsor five working days after report was sent	Immediate check with individuals, and meeting minutes	Immediate check, email with summary of meeting contents	Immediate check, email summarizing decisions	Email summarizing the call and asking for confirmation
Responsible	Project Manager	Project Manager	Project Manager	Software Architect	Director Selling organization
Notes					Politically sensitive

Figure 37.4   Example of communication matrix

STEP 4: IMPLEMENTATION, CONTROL AND CONTINUOUS ADJUSTMENT

The communication schedule becomes part of the overall project schedule to ensure time, budget and resources are allocated to project communication. Subsequently the communication schedule and the relevant parts of the communication matrix are distributed to the resources involved or responsible for communication events.

Over the life-cycle of the project, the communication needs of stakeholders are likely to change. The communication matrix and schedule need to be adapted in case of changing circumstances. Stakeholders' satisfaction with the communication strategy, as well as anticipated changes in their information needs should be assessed at a minimum at the beginning of each phase in the project. Depending on the results of this assessment the communication matrix and schedule might be adjusted to the new requirements.

Day	Time	Purpose	Initiator	Communicator
Thursday	3:00 PM	Software issues	Software Architect	Lead Technical Specialist
Friday	10:00 AM	Project Team meeting	Seller PM*	Project Team
	3:00 PM	Project Manager meeting	Seller PM	Buyer PM
Every second Friday	4:00 PM	Status report for sponsor and Steering Committee	Seller PM	Sponsor
Every second Monday	9:00 AM	Director briefing	Seller PM	Seller Director
	10:00 AM	Senior Manager update	Seller Director	Buyer Vice President
	11:00 AM	Project Manager update	Seller PM	Seller Director

Figure 37.5   Examples of communication schedule

TYPICAL COMMUNICATION PRACTICES

Research has identified some frequently used communication practices in projects. These are outlined below.

BETWEEN PROJECT MANAGER AND SPONSOR

Project managers prefer four different ways of communicating with their sponsors or Steering Groups (Turner and Müller 2004). These are:

- *Personal project reviews:* these are face-to-face meetings with in-depth discussion of all the different content listed above
- *Project analysis:* information on quality metrics and project trends, provided through all media (face-to-face, verbal and written)
- *Written status reports:* written formal information about current status and achievements, issues, changes, next steps and other items needing communication. These other items are potentially followed-up through telephone or face-to-face communication
- *Verbal updates:* less formal, but brief and timely updates over the phone. Here the project manager provides information on status and achievements, issues, changes, and next steps in the project

External stakeholders' expectations for communication might be influenced by the national culture within which a project is executed. This is described next.

IN DIFFERENT CULTURES

Preferences for communication media, contents and frequency differ between national cultures. This should be taken into account when developing the communication matrix and plan. As a starting point for assessing the communication preferences of stakeholders in more detail the following should be considered (Müller and Turner 2004):

- Project sponsors in English speaking countries and Scandinavia prefer frequent updates over the phone, at least once a week. Written reports are only seen as a necessity to fulfil legal requirements. Informal contact over the phone is more important.
- Sponsors in countries like The Netherlands and Germany expect monthly or fortnightly reports with a high content of analytical data about the project status, including quality measures and trends. Communication over the phone, through face-to-face meetings, or through written report is equally appreciated.
- Sponsors in countries like Hungary or India have a strong preference for written reports at fixed times, like monthly or fortnightly.
- In Asian countries like Taiwan and Japan, as well as in Brazil the sponsors do not like informal updates over the phone or written status reports. Rather than that they prefer personal face-to-face reviews with detailed analysis of the project when a milestone or phase end is achieved in a project.

This has implications for project managers working in foreign cultures. Those project managers from the US, Canada, or UK, for example, should adapt their communication behaviour to the local preferences when working in Japan or Brazil. The practice of verbal updates from their home culture is most likely not appreciated in their host country. Personal communication at milestone or project end, as well as at fixed intervals is recommended for these countries. Project managers from The Netherlands or Germany managing projects in the US, Canada, UK, Australia, or Scandinavia should be aware that their preferences for detailed analytic assessment at regular time intervals is not appreciated in their host culture. They should adapt to the continuous verbal update practices via telephone to keep their project sponsors informed.

The preferences listed above are, of course, only country averages. Communication preferences can differ widely within a culture. The above listed recommendations should therefore not be blindly applied, but thoughtfully tested in each individual project.

IN VIRTUAL TEAMS

Constant improvement of communications technology fosters the increased use of virtual project teams, especially in international projects. Communication in successful virtual teams has some specific attributes:

- a high level of open communication among peers and subordinates
- more communication related to the team's tasks and less related to the relationships and authorities of individuals within the team
- e-mail, telephone, and teleconferencing are the top three media choices

Telephone is more often used to establish a two-way communication, for sharing experiences, relaying incidents or stories about the project or its members in an informal manner. E-mail is most often used for one-way business communication or social interaction with other team members, but less often with the two mixed.

A frequent risk in virtual teams' communication lies in forgetting to obtain feedback on the information sent. That increases the chances for misunderstandings and lowers the overall quality of the communication. Unambiguous communication, plus a deliberate action for using a feedback channel, is required for good communication in virtual teams.

CONCLUSION

Communication brings together the minds of the people in a project. It starts with alignment of people's expectations with possible results, which is manifested in the project plan. Once the project plan is accepted the stakeholders assume the project is executed as planned. By then project communication shifts towards avoidance of surprises for the stakeholders. This is accomplished through communication about plan adherence at a level of detail required by each stakeholder group. Deviations from plan and other risks to the project need to be communicated at the earliest possible time to avoid sudden surprises for the stakeholders.

To ensure the provision of timely, correct and sufficiently detailed information to the project stakeholders it is necessary to manage the communication in projects. Two related processes were introduced in this chapter. The first process showed *how people communicate* in projects and the second process explained *how to manage this communication*. A communications model showed the layers that information has to pass in order to be sent and received correctly. It also showed the potential risks for misunderstandings at each of these layers, which could lead to an incorrect interpretation of the information or even breakdowns in communication. The development of a communication plan, including, among others, a communication matrix and schedule, was shown to be of central importance for a structured and controlled communication in projects.

Different modes of communication were discussed as formal and informal, internal and external, as well as horizontal and vertical. Each of these modes contributes differently to the development of stakeholders' perceptions about a project. The best performing projects show a fine balance of these modes in order to make stakeholders feel comfortable with the information they have about the project.

REFERENCES AND FURTHER READING

Dingle J., Topping D., and Watkinson M., 1995, 'Procurement and contract strategy', in J.R. Turner (ed), *The Commercial Project Manager*, Maidenhead: McGraw-Hill.

Müller, R. & Turner, J. R., 2004, 'Cultural Differences in Project Owner – Manager Communication', in Slevin, D.P., Cleland, D.I., and Pinto, J.K. (eds), *Innovations: Project Management Research, 2004*, Newton Square, PA: Project Management Institute.

Turner, J.R. and Müller, R., 2004, 'Communication and co-operation on projects between the project owner as principal and the project manager as agent', *European Management Journal*, 22(3).

38 Managing Conflict

Bob Graham

Managing a project is, almost by definition, managing conflict. This is due to the fact that the success of a project is often measured by the conflicting goals of producing a quality product at a low cost and with a quick deadline. These very goals are in conflict because a quality product often requires a higher cost and a longer deadline. A project can be done faster, but that often requires an increase in budget or a decrease in quality. You can save money on the budget, but that usually results in a decrease in product quality or an increase in project duration. In addition, the project stakeholders are often in conflict. The project represents something new and thus upsets the status quo. The departmental directors who supply the project team members might well want those people working on departmental rather than project work. In fact, the department directors may be fighting each other for headcount and so not want to send anyone over to a project that may be associated with another department. Thus it seems that project management is conflict management as projects are built on conflicting goals and priorities. Managing all these conflicts often becomes the chief job of the project manager.

Managing this conflict requires the ability to persuade others in the organization to act in ways that will benefit the project. The concepts of persuasion and negotiation are used in project management because the project leader typically does not have the command relationship of authority that is present in most departmental organizations. I do not know how many times I have heard a statement like 'the problem in this organization is that the project leaders have all of the responsibility, but none of the authority.' To this comment I usually respond, 'Welcome to the world of project management.' That is, in the process of project leadership, the lack of direct authority over project team members, and other project stakeholders, is considered the normal state of affairs. Successful project leaders discover that they must develop their powers of persuasion and negotiation in order to get the project completed.

This chapter will discuss some of the strategies the project manager can use to avoid and resolve conflict. We begin by discussing the sources of conflict for if these sources can be eliminated much potential conflict can be avoided. This is followed by discussion of some techniques for resolving those conflicts that cannot be avoided. Finally, the importance of information in the conflict process is discussed.

AVOIDING CONFLICT

UNDERSTANDING SOURCES OF CONFLICT

Prevention of conflict is the first step in managing conflict. It is therefore important first to understand the sources of conflict and work to eliminate those sources so they do not affect the project team. Most conflicts on projects arise from differences about the project goals, or the utilization of resources on project teams, or are a result of departmental differences or grudges. They arise because a person, or a group of people, feel frustrated in their ability to achieve their goals. Additional conflict can arise due to interpersonal differences or opposing points of view. The conflict develops out of a basic failure or unwillingness to understand the other party's position (Pinto 1996). Thus, to prevent conflict we begin by examining the sources of conflict, the various people involved in conflict and their point of view.

There are a variety of people in the organization that need to be influenced in favour of the project. One important group is the members of the project team. As these people typically do not report to the project leader, they must be influenced and motivated to devote their best work to the project effort. However, these people come from different departments and may have different work styles and values. In addition, people from one department may have stereotypes of people from other departments and may treat team members as the stereotype rather than the person. Also, it is natural to see one's own departmental aspect as most important for success of the project, and thus feel that most resources should be allocated to that aspect. For example, people from Production, who come to meetings on time, may be irritated by people from Marketing, who may be late. All team members may feel that those from Accounting are just bean counters to be ignored, and those from Engineering may feel that is the most important aspect of the project and should get most of the resources allocation. The potential for conflict in these situations is high.

Another important group of stakeholders is the departmental directors; those people who supply the resources to complete the project. Your project is only one of many projects that they must consider, so they too must be influenced to supply good people for the project, as conflict can occur in the allocation of people for the project. In addition, departmental directors may be fighting among themselves over organizational priorities, and this will be reflected in your project. An important department is Finance, which supplies the monetary resources for the project. Project managers and team members usually feel that not enough financial resources are allocated, and this is a continuing source of conflict.

The group of senior managers must also be influenced to support this project, as projects are seldom successful without top management support (Pinto and Slevin 1987). Many times one or more government agencies must also be included on the stakeholder list. The goals of both these groups could be quite opposed to those of the project team.

Finally, there are the end users of the project, the people who will benefit most from the project completion, but who often give only lukewarm support as the project progresses. The needs of this group are often hard to pin down, and they often change as the project progresses. The moving target of 'satisfying end user expectations' often frustrates team members who may be used to more static job specifications. The pool of potential conflict is wide and deep here.

MOTIVATING CONFLICTING PARTIES

The second step in managing conflict is to ensure that all parties to any conflict or potential conflict are motivated to find a solution or prevent the conflict from occurring. This occurs when people see it as being in their best interest to solve or prevent conflict. People can change their opinion and even see another's point of view if they see it as being in their own best interest. People do not usually continue behaving in a way that is detrimental to achieving their own interests. The same is true for other project stakeholders such as your peers and superiors, as well as functional managers (department directors) who will be supplying the members of your team. The successful project manager will develop an influence strategy for these stakeholder groups as well as for team members in order to show them that conflict is not in their best interest.

DEVELOPING AN INFLUENCE STRATEGY

The first step in developing an influence strategy is to produce a list of potential stakeholder groups, as done above. The next step is to develop a list of key people in these stakeholder groups. For example, within the project team, the core team members are probably the most important. Within the senior management group, the top manager who proposed this project and those that are ultimately supplying the manpower for the project, are probably the most important. There may also be one customer that is more important than the others.

The next step is to ask yourself why these individuals should support your project. That is, what benefit will they derive from a successful project. If you are unsure of the benefit that key individuals might derive, you might want to discuss it with them. From understanding who benefits from this project you can develop a list of potential allies, along with the knowledge of the benefits you need to deliver in order to develop and maintain their support. These benefits are an important element in resolving conflict. An important complement to the list of 'allies' is a list of 'enemies', that is a list of key individuals who do not initially support the project. Although these people are not really 'enemies', they may not see the benefit of the project, or may see it as detrimental to their success or that of the organization. It is important to understand why people do not support the project, and then work to overcome their objections as the project progresses. Remember that all enemies are potential allies, if they can see the project as being in their best interest. Chapter 36 gives advice on identifying stakeholders. Figure 36.2 shows a way of viewing enemies and allies:

● those who are in favour of the project, and those against
● from these two groups, those who can influence the outcome and those who cannot

THE REWARD/RISK FACTOR IN MINIMIZING CONFLICT

The key factor in influencing anyone to do anything, including resolving a conflict, is to ensure the rewards for doing it are greater than the risks involved. The assumption is that if people understand and value the rewards for being on your project, and if you have taken steps to minimize the risks involved in gaining the reward, they will see project work as being in their best interest. This way you can influence them to work on or to otherwise support the project and to minimize any potential conflict because it will be in their best interest to do so.

Reward – perception of value

Most projects will have value to the organization, as well as value to the individual. The project manager must think clearly through the questions of 'why are we doing this project?' and 'what are the potential benefits for the people who work on or support this project?' The project manager must then ensure that the potential team members and other stakeholders fully understand the nature of these benefits.

Risk – perception of loss

Most projects will also have potential risks to the organization and to potential project participants. The nature of these risks is very subjective, and the evaluation of these risks is often a function of the individual's risk preference profile. To begin to understand these risks, the project manager must ask the question 'what will the organization or the individuals potentially lose if they participate in this project?' Once this list is developed, the project manager must work to ensure that the potential losses are minimized. This information must then be told to potential project participants and stakeholders. Thus the key to developing influence is to maximize the value while minimizing the risks. If the perception of value exceeds the perception of risk, the individuals will be motivated to work on or support the project. If the perception of risk exceeds the perception of value, the individuals will not be so motivated, and may work against the completion of the project.

INFLUENCING TEAM MEMBERS

When some managers think of value for team members, they think of money. Many project leaders then lament that they have little control over the salaries of the project team members. However, experience indicates that money is only one part of motivation. Indeed, there are many aspects of projects that people find inherently rewarding and of value. The project leader must use these non-monetary aspects to maximum benefit. Some of these values are:

Satisfying customer requirements

This is the *raison d'etre* for any project. It is also one of the principal benefits to all project stakeholders. This is also one of the most useful levers to use for managing conflict. Whenever two parties are in conflict over product features it is often useful to focus on customer requirements and take the discussion away from focusing on which party is 'right'.

Doing something new/learning a new skill

By definition, a project is something new in the organization. People generally enjoy variety in their work, and thus find value in doing something new and different. Most projects involve developing new technology or developing a new application for old technology. Either way the team members often learn some new skill. This aspect enhances people's self worth, and also their future marketability. Learning and applying the latest methods or technology is rewarding for many people. In addition, learning a new skill often helps people to add value to the organization, enhancing the organizational skill set.

Networking and travel

Most projects cut across departmental lines, and this gives people exposure to other departments. These contacts can increase individuals' organization network, as well as general knowledge about what they do in other parts of the organization.

Developing a unique product

Most work in organizations involves repetition. Being on a team doing something new and unique can be rewarding. People also find much satisfaction to be able to point to a finished product and say, 'I was on the team that made that product.'

Positive visibility with senior management

This is an important reward for many people. In fact this may be one of the most important rewards held by project team members. People often feel it is to their advantage to be viewed positively by upper management. A conflict can often be managed by reminding conflicting parties that their conflict will not look good to upper management and that they should resolve it quickly.

However, there are also many risks associated with something as uncertain as a project:

Negative visibility with senior management

The project leader must remember there are two sides to the visibility coin. Sometimes, being associated with a failed project is a step closer to the exit door. A good track record helps to recruit project team members. However, if the project leader is new to the job, he or she must display a lot of enthusiasm at the beginning of the project; obvious enthusiasm about the potential success of the project will encourage potential team members to feel there is a higher chance of success (which, of course helps to actually lead to success, thus becoming a self-fulfilling prophesy). If the project leader is not enthusiastic, the potential team members will feel there is little chance for success and will thus not be motivated to join that project team.

No reward for project work

This is a typical problem in organizations that are new to project management. Reward systems and performance appraisals are typically departmentally based, as they should be. This means that organization members typically see their future, promotions, salary and the like tied to their performance in the departments. The project leader, however, is attempting to get these people to join project teams, and there will be little motivation to do so unless the work on the project is also appraised and is counted as a part of the performance appraisal and review. The project leader must work to ensure that the project work will be used in performance appraisal, and complete appraisals for all members of the core team as major inputs to the departmental appraisals.

Out of sight, out of mind

This is an associated risk. Potential team members may feel that if they are not working at all times on department work, then the department managers will 'forget' them, and perhaps overlook them if a promotion is available. Thus the project leader must have a plan for continually informing departmental managers about the work of their department members.

A more exciting project may come along

There is not much the project leader can do about this fear, except be certain that the potential team members are fully aware of just how exciting this project is going to be.

The project leader must take steps to maximize the perceived benefits and to minimize perceived risk. In addition, team members must be made aware of the potential risks and rewards. This is an important part of the conflict resolution process.

INFLUENCING OTHER STAKEHOLDERS

Numerous studies of successful projects point to the need for top management support, as well as the support of other project stakeholders (Turner 2002). Thus a part of the task of project leadership is influencing others to support your project. Influencing upper management and other stakeholders is very similar to influencing team members.

To begin with, the project leader must realize that influencing project stakeholders is a process, not an event. That is, some project leaders will hold stakeholder influencing events, such as a project start-up workshop, and feel that the influence has been set for the project. They often feel that their project will maintain a constant, high priority. However, priorities change, and stakeholders' feelings about and attention to a given project also change over the course of time. So while a project start-up workshop is an excellent way of gaining support for a project, it must be seen as just one event in a long and continuous process of developing and maintaining project support.

The process of developing project support begins by identifying the major project stakeholders, as was done above. For the next step the project leader must determine what value these various groups will obtain from a successful project. And for those that are not initially supportive of the project, then what loss they feel the project will bring them. Common values received from projects are shown for the stakeholder groups as follows:

Senior Management

The common value for upper management is that the project will help to support a corporate strategy, such as entering a new market. If the strategy is successful, then the project will ultimately help to lead to higher profitability, and other corporate goals. It is important that the project leader realizes just what strategy it is that the project is supporting. As projects unfold they are often scrutinized as to their expense, and are often felt to be expendable at budget review time. It is important that the project leader remind upper management what strategy will suffer if the project does not receive continued support.

Customers/End Users

The customers and end users are the people who will gain benefit from the use of the end product. To satisfy the customers the project leader must be continually in touch with what the customers want from the product, as well as what they really expect from it. Experienced project leaders understand that what customers say they want, and what they really expect, are often two very different things. It is thus a task of the project leader to continually probe to discover what it is that the customers and end-users really expect from the end product.

There are two parts to discovering customer expectations. One is to develop a mindset of continuous exploration. This means the project team expects and welcomes a sequence of constant changes and suggestions from the customers and end users. In the past, these changes were seen as irritants that delayed project progress. Now they should be seen as additional information that helps to ensure project success. The second part is using a series of prototypes to evoke responses. It is a fact of life that most people cannot really tell you what they expect from a product until they have experience of it. Developing prototypes allows them to have this experience and to say the classic line 'well how come it doesn't do this or that.' Of course, the customers never asked for it to do 'this or that', but the experience of the prototype will uncover that they expected it. Obtaining customer reaction early and often can eliminate potential conflict at the end of a project.

Department Directors

This is the group of stakeholders that will be supplying the people to complete the project work. It is assumed that all of the people working on a project will be 'on loan' from various departments in the organization. It is thus important that the project leader consider the needs and desires of the managers of those departments.

Department managers are also trying to implement corporate strategy, so a knowledge of how the project supports corporate strategy is also important to gaining their support. However, department managers are occupied with the more immediate task of scheduling people to perform the tasks of the department, as well as supporting other projects. Thus the more immediate questions run along the lines of 'What people do you want, for how much of their time, and when will they be finished?' It is thus important that the project leader review project plans, schedules and progress with department managers on a regular basis. The more complete and accurate information they have from you, the better they will be able to schedule people to meet the other demands that are placed on their department. This will help to develop and maintain their support for your project.

Other stakeholders

There may be some groups or individuals, even among those mentioned above, who will not initially support the project. With these people it is important that the project leader determine what they have at risk, or what they feel they have to lose from successful completion of the project. Many times this feeling of risk and/or loss is due to misinformation or false assumptions about the project. Thus to gain the support of these groups or individuals, the project leader must discover what their assumptions are, and work to inform them. In fact, to do more than inform, as talk is cheap. It must be demonstrated that the results of the project will not result in the loss the others expected. This is a long process, and it often takes place over the life of the project. But it has many rewards.

When I became project manager it was at a college that did not have a computer when I walked in the door. Part of my job was to computerize the registration, billing and housing function. At that time it was assumed by most employees that when things went onto the computer that everyone would lose their jobs. Gaining cooperation was difficult as everyone treated me like the grim reaper. I seemed to be in conflict with everyone until I understood the source of their perception of risk. When I was able to convince them they would not lose their jobs, and also demonstrated the value of the computer, much of the conflict evaporated.

RESOLVING CONFLICT

Despite our best efforts, conflict happens and must be resolved. Pinto (1996) suggests three methods of resolving conflict which he classifies as confrontation, diffusion, and avoidance.

Confrontation

Confrontation methods seek the sources of the conflict so that conflicting parties can discuss the sources and work to resolve the conflict. A typical technique is a problem solving meeting where the conflicting parties and the project manager meet and discuss conflict causes and possible resolution. This is a long process, frequently accompanied by high emotions in the parties concerned. If the meeting is not handled well, it can solidify conflict and ill will, making possible resolution much more difficult. As many project managers do not have the skill or the time to do this, obtaining outside help is recommended for this method.

Diffusion

Diffusion tries to diffuse the conflict so conflicting parties can work it out. One diffusion technique is to appeal to the common goal, emphasizing that 'we are in this together'. Another is compromise, 'give and take' in which parties cease conflict because they get something they want while they give something the other party wants. While diffusion techniques address the conflict directly they do not require discovering deep root causes.

Avoidance

Avoidance methods avoid directly addressing the conflict source while seeking to resolve it. One technique is for the project manager to send signals that the conflict is not a good idea. This is an attempt to show people it is not in their best interest if they continue the conflict. Another technique is forced separation, in the hope that the conflict will go away if parties are physically separated. However, this is not good for project management, which relies on close interaction of team members. A third technique is forced togetherness where the project manager gives two conflicting parties a task where they must work harmoniously together to be successful. In this way both parties see conflict resolution a being in their best interest.

AN EXAMPLE OF FORCED TOGETHERNESS

In a large telephone company there were two groups, among others, who were responsible for installation of PBX switches for corporations. Two particular groups were in conflict, and had been in conflict for quite some time. One group had a marketing orientation; the other was old line telephone engineers. The first group was responsible for determining customer requirements. The second group was responsible for designing and installing the equipment to solve the customer problems. This meant that the second group got their instructions from the first group. The marketing function, and many of the members of that group, was new to the corporation. The engineering function and most of the engineers, had been a part of that company since the dawn of time. Both departments were very suspicious of the other and had various derogatory terms to describe one another. They did not like to work with one another.

A recent switch installation had gone badly. The telephone users claimed the switch did not meet their needs. They were furious and threatened to change companies for the next switch. Senior management of the telephone company demanded that this important customer be satisfied with the next installation. Marketing blamed Engineering for not correctly designing a switch that met customer needs, while Engineering blamed Marketing for not correctly determining user requirements. Both sides pointed to the other and said, 'we would not have this problem if those guys would just do their job correctly!' Obviously the level of conflict was getting in the way of understanding the true source of user dissatisfaction.

A project team with members from both departments was formed for the next installation. We began conflict management with departmental managers, convincing them that since senior management was interested in this customer, it was in their best interest to help resolve this conflict. As above so below, we convinced all team members it was in their best interest to work together. At project meetings we focused on understanding end users' requirements. We initiated a process of forced interaction where two team members, one from either department, went together to interview end users. They could understand together what the system requirements were. While doing this they discovered the source of the problem was simple communications errors. By focusing on eliminating these errors and truly understanding customer and end user requirements, the conflict was resolved for that project.

THE POWER AND VALUE OF INFORMATION

One of the final sources of conflict is lack of reliable information. Project leaders need to see themselves as the ultimate disseminators of information. Because of the uncertainty that surrounds most projects, they tend to generate much anxiety among the stakeholders, and this can be a potential source of conflict. This anxiety is usually concerning the outcome, cost, final schedule and resource requirements of the project. Information is the only tool that the project leader has to relieve this anxiety. The project leader will find that he or she can have a large influence on the members of the organization by providing timely and complete information regarding the salient aspects of the project.

The first step in developing a project management information system is to determine what information it is that the stakeholders need in order to help them achieve their objectives. Some texts would advise the project leader to begin with a list of stakeholders and proceed to ask each of them what information they need to know about the project. However, experience has shown that the response to such a question does not reveal all that is needed. Many people find it difficult to answer a question about what data they need. They will give you an answer, but when the data are presented, they typically answer that it is not what they wanted. This often leaves the project leader puzzled and frustrated. The fact is that most people do not think in terms of data, but rather in terms of questions. Therefore, instead of asking 'what data do you need?' it is better to ask 'what questions do you have about this project?' Then the project leader and the stakeholder can work together to develop a set of information that answers those questions. Good information is that which answers stakeholders' questions, is easy for them to understand and is there when they need it. This requires that the project leader understand the questions and associated information from the stakeholders' points of view. The PMIS should then be developed to satisfy their needs, in much the same way that the entire project is developed to satisfy the needs of the customer/end users.

QUESTIONS ON OUTCOME

The questions about outcome are normally of three types:

Functionality

The first type is concerned with the functionality of the final product as stakeholders will want to know what it will do when it is completed (Chapter 14). This is a question for the project leader as well as the project stakeholders as the product specifications will be changing as the project proceeds. The project leader must guard against the mistake of suggesting that a certain function will be available before it is certain that it will indeed be in the final product. So answers to questions about outcome should be in two parts. The first contains features that have definitely been decided. The second contains a list of features that are being considered. This list should be updated regularly and be distributed automatically to all stakeholders.

The project manager should tread carefully here. Publishing a list of potential product features may actually generate conflict and anxiety as each stakeholder, customer group and even project team member will argue the necessity of their favourite feature. The project manager can be caught up in some fierce battles between project stakeholders as the 'feature wars' escalate. One way to minimize the conflict in this area is to use a common measure for the value of any potential feature, a measure which all of the project stakeholders agree upon.

One common measure could be the influence of the feature on potential sales; however, this measure may be misleading as the cost of the potential feature could be more than the revenue of the potential sales. This would point to the need for a more inclusive type of measurement such as return on investment. With this type of measure the project manager can reduce conflict by showing that a stakeholder's favoured feature might actually reduce the project's return on investment. A calculator for determining the project's return on investment can be obtained from www.projectmanagersmba.com and is explained in Cohen and Graham (2000).

Success

The second type of question about outcome is of the 'will it be successful?' variety. Stakeholders want to know how this product compares to the competition, and its probability of market acceptance. The best way to answer these questions is to summarize the information gleaned from the customer or end user representatives, show how the product is being designed to address those expectations, and pass this to the stakeholders. If this cannot be done for competitive reasons (secrecy), then the stakeholders should be assured that it is indeed taking place.

Market

A third type of outcome question is of the 'market segment' variety. Stakeholders often want to know what market the product is aimed to satisfy. Thus the project leader needs to be continually aware of and searching for potential applications and markets for the product, and passing this information on to the stakeholders.

QUESTIONS ABOUT THE SCHEDULE

Of course, the classic schedule question is 'when will it be ready?' Associated questions concern availability of prototypes and milestone reviews. This means that an updated schedule should be always available to stakeholders to answer these questions.

QUESTIONS ABOUT RESOURCE REQUIREMENTS

Projects have a way of using up countless hours of resources, much of which is usually said to be unexpected. This often frustrates the department directors who are supplying those resources and is a continuing source of conflict. Their questions normally revolve around how much of the resource you are going to need, and when the resource will be again available to the department. Project leaders are understandably hesitant to answer such questions, as plans for requirements are difficult to make when you are doing something for the first time. In addition, initial estimates have a quality of being 'cast in stone', so that future changes in requirements cause friction with the department directors. Thus the requirements should be presented with a 'here is what we know so far' quality. The project leader should not just produce an estimate and send it to the department directors; it is better to personally go and explain all of the assumptions that went into making that estimate, and indicate all of the factors that could cause that estimate to change.

Department directors, as with other humans, are much more amenable to change if they understand the reason for the change. It is up to the project leader to ensure that they know the reasons for all changes. Often just knowing the reasons for a change can eliminate a potential conflict. In addition to providing information that answers their questions, good information should also be there when it is most needed. Having the information available to stakeholders is often not enough. The project leader should attempt to determine when it is that the information will most likely be needed. Some simple questions to stakeholders like 'when do you usually discuss this project?' or 'what meetings do you go to where questions about this project come up?' can often reveal the best time to provide the information. For example, if there is a regular meeting where the project is discussed, it would be good to provide the information the day before that meeting. In that way the stakeholder could arrive at the meeting with the latest information. Timely information is current information that arrives just before the person needs it.

As a final note, it is important to remember that timely, accurate information is useless unless the person who is using the information understands what is being presented. Many people are not comfortable with information presented on Gantt charts and network diagrams. Thus the first few times that information is supplied, the project leader may need to personally review the format with the stakeholders in order to ensure that they fully understand what they are being presented. If they cannot work with network diagrams and the like, then a different format should be developed that they are comfortable with.

Always remember that the information is being produced in order to relieve anxiety and avoid or resolve conflict. If the people cannot understand the information, it will actually increase the very anxiety it was designed to reduce. So the information should be made to conform to the person, rather than expecting the person to conform to the information. In summary, good information answers their questions, is there when they need it, and is easy to understand.

SUMMARY

It has been shown in this chapter that the task of running a successful project requires conflict avoidance and resolution. This requires leading by influence rather than authority. The keys to developing this influence lie in understanding individuals' risk/reward relationship, as well as the power of information. It was argued that the project leader can manage conflict and influence individuals to do their best on a project if team members perceive that it is in their best interest, and that the benefits outweigh the risks. The project leader must use information to show people the potential rewards, as well as the way risks are being addressed.

Developing influence is a process, not an event. In everyday terms, this means that the project leader can never really order team members to complete a task, but must persuade them, over and over again. The approach is for the project leader to ask him or herself 'what is the benefit in doing this task?' and then approach the team members by first stressing the benefit. The project leader should then listen carefully to their response, as their perceived risks are often contained in these responses. If the project leader can give information that shows how he/she is addressing those perceived risks, while continuing to show benefit, then that is leading by influence.

Such influence is normally much more effective than authority. However, it takes more time. The project leader will often feel the urge to just say 'Do It' in order to get things done quickly. This approach may often be seen as a short run necessity, but it often leads to a long run disaster. Use it sparingly.

REFERENCE AND FURTHER READING

Cohen, D. J. and Graham, R. J., 2000, *The Project Manager's MBA: How to Translate Project Decisions into Business Success,* San Francisco: Jossey-Bass.

Pinto, J.K., 1996, *Power & Politics in Project Management,* Sylva, NC: Project Management Institute.

Pinto, J.K. and Slevin, D.P., 1987, 'Critical success factors in effective project implementation', in Cleland, D.I., and King, W.R., (eds), *Project Management Handbook,* 2nd edition, ed. New York: Van Nostrand Reinhold.

Turner, J.R., 2002, 'Project success criteria', in Stevens, M. (ed), *APM Project Management Pathways,* High Wycombe: Association for Project Management.

39 Managing Culture

David Rees

Earlier in this handbook we read of the increasing significance of project management as a business discipline and corporate strategy. Various studies, many of them empirically-based, have suggested that the success of such organizational and managerial approaches is heavily dependent on aligning business strategies with an appropriate 'corporate culture'. A project management strategy can only be implemented effectively if it is supported by the right culture. In turn, senior management needs to ensure that people have the right competencies for managing the cultural elements of the organization. This, of course, includes project managers. As a start point, we can loosely define a culture within a business entity as 'the way we do things around here'. When we discuss corporate culture, therefore, many aspects of organizational life are embraced in such discussions – values, relationships, leadership styles, people management and behaviours. Furthermore, most project managers are now operating at an international level, through cross-border deals, multi-national corporations, global projects and transnational partnerships. Our understanding of culture needs to encompass this additional complexity.

This chapter integrates corporate and international dimensions of culture as we evaluate how project management performance can be enhanced through managing culture effectively. In doing so, we seek to address two key questions:

1. How can organizations improve the delivery of projects through a better understanding of cultural environments?
2. What culture-specific competencies do individual project managers need to manage such projects?

DEFINITIONS AND CONCEPTS OF CULTURE

A useful point to begin our understanding of managing culture in projects is to consider how the concept of culture has been defined. The origin of the word 'culture' can be traced to 'kultura' from the ancient Greeks meaning 'to act upon nature', or the Latin form 'cultura' meaning 'cultivating or tilling'. The general concept here is one of status or growth and can be applied in both a physical sense (agriculture) or a development mode (enlightenment, refinement). Two key researchers in this field have provided contemporary descriptions of what culture may be:

> 'Culture is the collective programming of the mind, which distinguishes the member of one group or society from those of another.' (Hofstede 2001)
> 'A fish only discovers its need for water when it is no longer in it. Our own culture is like water to a fish. It sustains us. We live and breathe through it.' (Trompenaars 1993)

Further, there are varying contexts in which the term and its derivatives are used. We talk of personal tastes, manners and social etiquette as being 'cultured'. Groups whose focus is on intellectual and artistic activities are often classified as 'cults'. Organizations and their subsets may take on identifiable 'corporate cultures'. A project-management culture is an example of such a subset. We can think of a range of culture-bound factors that may affect success as a project manager – personal status in terms of technical qualifications, age and gender; the organizational climate and management style under which we operate; the whole concept of project management as a business philosophy; the local and cross-border environments in which we work. Additionally, we have to manage a number of 'cultural' issues related to the project stakeholders. Does the customer understand the approach to service delivery? Do project team members view time management in the same way? Is project planning seen as a valuable tool for effective performance?

CULTURE IN BUSINESS

Consider the simple scenario in Figure 39.1, and the questions accompanying it. Our artist probably saw something compelling to sketch or paint, our lumberjack may realize the potential profit in the quality of the timber, and our botanist could be interested in identifying the sustainability of the flora species. Could there be a

A French artist, a Brazilian lumberjack and a Chinese botanist were walking together through a forest in Sweden one spring afternoon.

What did each of them see, how did they interpret what they saw, and what business ideas could be generated from their observations?

If we could get them to work together as a new project team, what attractive product could they create and how could they market this?

How could our team achieve synergies through working together on this project? What could be potential barriers to this team working effectively?

Figure 39.1   An afternoon walk in the forest

business opportunity to turn some aspect of this forest scene into a viable global product – such as a piece of furniture? Given the consumer trends towards ethically-sound goods and services would this project team be able to produce a uniquely designed chair in natural colours using renewable woods and sold at a profit to various markets around the world? If our team can build respect for each other based on understanding their individual talents, experiences and knowledge they could use their specialist strengths to create a superior and novel product. However, if they do not develop positive relationships and rapport our project team could fail miserably.

Cultural influences pervade every aspect of this scenario and the potential consequences. Our previous experiences, our perceived status, our approach to innovation and our values can strongly impact on the initiation and outcomes of projects. How we manage such cultural variables in business situations becomes a critical success factor. Some would argue that in projects spanning multicultural environments the management of culture is of pivotal importance.

ANALYSING CULTURES IN BUSINESS ENVIRONMENTS

The first step in understanding how culture relates to business is to construct an appropriate framework of analysis. This is not so easily done, given the strong emotional overtones that dominate most discussions on culture. Many of us have very personalized views on values, attitudes and behaviours at both individual and group levels so any analytical process of culture will need to overcome subjectivity, prejudices and stereotypes.

Attempts in the academic world have led to a number of concepts and theories being proposed to explain and codify cultural norms. Over the years the study of culture has become a multidisciplinary activity:

- Anthropologists have been interested in the physiological development of the human species and the associated rituals, myths and beliefs that parallel these growth stages
- Sociologists tend to focus on the study of humans as social creatures in their attempts to explain how communities and societies evolve
- Psychologists concentrate on mental processes and behaviours within the individual and their impact on others
- Political scientists examine power, authority and control structures within geographic, territorial and societal boundaries
- Economists attempt to understand the systems of exchange that enable resources to be developed and utilized in a range of human groupings

Until quite recently an interlocking model bringing together these disciplines to help us understand business culture has been missing. The 'cultural iceberg'

(Figure 39.2) addresses this and provides an opportunity to understand and manage our project organizations more effectively. If we imagine the iceberg at sea we can only physically see about ten per cent of its mass. We are not immediately aware of what supports and shapes it beneath the waves. The iceberg tip is a straightforward way of depicting the 'touchables' of a society. What we do not see are the 'untouchable' (or hidden) elements. Yet these elements are the very building blocks upon which our societies and organizations are based, providing the superstructure and cultural 'fabric' from which behaviours in business will surface.

Let us take another look at the construction of the iceberg model to help us acquire a better understanding of how business and project culture develops.

(a) At its base we have the cultural bedrock. These are the foundations of the culture and are reflected in the evolution of the political and economic systems

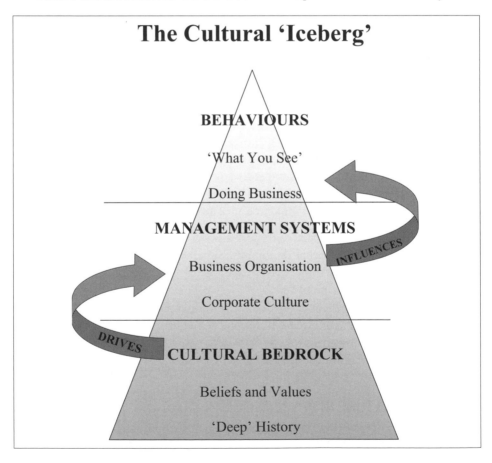

Figure 39.2 Iceberg model of culture, based on Garrison (2006)

that pertain to that cultural environment. Garrison calls these policonomy factors. The ways in which these systems themselves have evolved are sometimes extremely hard to trace. Often the very source of the bedrock has disappeared. Liken this to the discovery of the source of the River Nile – very difficult to find! To penetrate the policonomy of a particular societal culture we may need to go back a long way in history to discover the storyline. Some of it gets lost in the mists of time. Sometimes we arrive at a stage of investigation where seeking further evidence or proof becomes pointless – we are trapped in time. What becomes more important and relevant is how we can then work forward to the present day cultural situations we wish to understand better. Historical policonomy gives us some great clues!

(b) Social frameworks are created reflecting the key value and belief sets born out of the bedrock. These form the superstructure features from which our management and work systems emerge. So, for example, if we have a society which is based upon unquestioning obedience to rulers endowed with 'divine rights', we can expect rigid structures of management control and a management culture which will not tolerate dissent.

(c) At the top of the iceberg we are at the behavioural output level. This is our experiential arena where we physically and mentally interact with cultural artefacts. We touch, taste, feel, smell and see culture. Our intuitive sense – the sixth sense – could be likened to raising the state of cultural sub-consciousness to a level of consciousness – emotions, attitudes and beliefs that are there but can't always be rationalized. We move from the systems level of culture to the individual level – the personal experience. And this is where project managers really feel the impact of culture on their day-to-day activities.

Project managers are, of course, in a unique pivotal position. They themselves are products of the cultural bedrock and the resulting organizational systems. In turn, their task is to manage projects within the prevailing cultural norms of the enterprise. In other words they have a responsibility to administer the activities of the company according to prescribed sets of rules, regulations, processes, procedures and systems. But they also have an opportunity to influence and implement change depending on a variety of factors including their ability to challenge the prevailing corporate culture. This brings us to the heart of our topic – the management of cultures and the particular challenges for project managers.

MANAGING CULTURE IN PROJECT ORGANIZATIONS

The challenges and pressures for organizations to deliver large-scale successful transnational projects are intense. Complexities such as cross-cultural stakeholders, socio-political environments and managerial philosophies increase the demand for organizations to be suitably equipped with the skills and knowhow to execute projects against required specifications. Project management as an organizational strategy and work design is itself culturally influenced. Rodney Turner (1999) consolidated fieldwork undertaken by Svein-Arne Jessen and concluded that project management sits most comfortably as a management philosophy in western cultures. Many features of project team management, communication styles and conflict resolution are culture-bound.

The story of Oticon (a Danish hearing aid enterprise) is one of revolutionary cultural change that took the company from the brink of liquidation to market leadership through developing a strong project management culture. Oticon and another Danish company, Novo Nordisk, built organizational cultures that were embedded in a 'spaghetti' project structure, where project team members needed to be highly adaptive and flexible. Usually, this meant team members would be working on different projects simultaneously, using a range of skills and competencies, and playing various roles throughout the life-cycle of the project. Such flexible and low power-distance structures may not be readily assimilated into country or regional cultural business environments.

It is probably true to say, based on various metrics such as the growth in project management training world-wide, that project management is becoming more recognized as a global management discipline. Whilst project management may be becoming mainstream in regions hitherto dominated by bureaucratic hierarchies (such as China, for example), this does not dilute the importance of having a range of skills, tools and techniques to manage the cultural interfaces of project stakeholders effectively. Our 'iceberg' analysis demonstrates how this may be done, Figure 39.3.

CULTURE AS PART OF THE PROJECT ORGANIZATION'S CAPITAL

The contribution that people and culture make to the organization's value has attracted growing practitioner and academic interest and research. People, stakeholder relationships, company reputation and so forth are value-adding assets that form part of the organization's capital base. Often, these have been termed the organization's 'intangible assets'. Each project team member brings individual capital to the project in the form of knowledge, experience, skills and expertise. These individual assets can be enhanced or diluted by a number of factors – the way team members interact with one another and relationships inside and outside the team. This means getting the right team and organizational culture. Finally, these individual and team assets have to be made to work effectively and efficiently through appropriate styles of leadership. Such leadership should motivate individuals and teams towards the performance goals that the project has to achieve.

Let us imagine that an American organization is about to set up a new oil extracting facility in an overseas country. It adopts classic project management approaches and techniques that are reflective of the management style and philosophy of an American way of doing business. This project would be executed in a highly pragmatic manner where speed of implementation is considered a critical success factor and the operationalization of the new facility should be achieved as quickly as possible. This is what Trompenaars and Hampden-Turner (2004) would term the 'Guided-Missile' type of culture. A quick return on investment from the project may be uppermost in the company's mindset.

Here, the bedrock elements of the cultural iceberg would feature a money-oriented, individualistic and entrepreneurial set of values within the society. This focused attitude towards 'getting things done' breeds a natural orientation towards organizing business tasks as projects – this is an essential part of the management philosophy. In turn, a task oriented perspective may mean that time for dealing with people's needs – such as building long-term social relationships – may not be seen as a priority. Inevitably, the accusation of applying stereotypes to a country's business culture can be rightly levelled at such an analysis but the research from several studies confirms many of these characteristics as a predictive indicator of the likely behaviours to be found in American business.

In contrast, a high context culture – such as may be found in Asia – would place great emphasis on relationship-building as a mandatory pre-cursor to getting a project contract. Therefore, at the behavioural level of the iceberg model, it would be necessary to engage in various forms of extensive protocol and etiquette that low-context cultures, such as the USA, may find superfluous to the main goal of getting things done. We can track the organizational forces driving such behaviours in our Asian organization down to the systems level where a more hierarchical form of organization may encourage the establishment of bureaucracy rather than projects. This greater comfort with hierarchy could then be traced back to the bedrock elements of family importance, respect for elders and wisdom, and a longer-term perspective.

Quite clearly, the potential for conflict is apparent and the management approach to the oil-extracting project needs be sufficiently modified to work effectively within the new business environment.

Figure 39.3   Example of Iceberg Model applied to Project Management, quoted from Rees (2005a)

Figure 39.4 captures the concept of culture as part of the project's capital assets. It can be seen from the model that all three triangulation points have cultural influencers. Personal performance, working together and motivation are inherently stimulated by the internal and external cultural environments of the project. If the project manager can manage this human capital triangle effectively then he/she is well on track to achieving project performance excellence that can be sustained beyond just the immediate project requirements. (Measuring human capital is a complex quasi-science and the interested reader is invited to consult Rees and McBain (2004) further to gain a wider understanding of the principles involved.) The remainder of this chapter is focused on how the cultural aspects of this framework can be exploited and managed for project success.

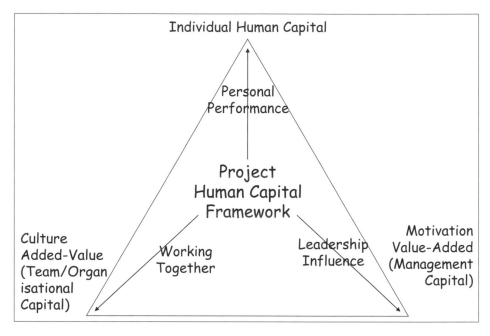

Figure 39.4   Human capital framework components, modified from Rees and McBain (2004)

THE CULTURALLY-FLUENT PROJECT ORGANIZATION

Organizations face a new challenge – how to build organizations that can rapidly adapt their cultures to changing business environments. Many commentators on the developments in global business trends suggest that the scale, pace and complexity of change is quickening. New markets may open up at short notice and technological developments are occurring rapidly, thus exposing laggards to a higher risk of failure. We discussed previously how project strategies will need to be ever more flexible in order to respond to changes and influences. As proposed in earlier sections, these strategies will need to be accompanied by culture shifts. This gives rise to a project organization that has both organizational and managerial properties that enables it to move quickly – technically and culturally. The latter aspect is our focus, here, and we can describe such a feature as the 'culturally-fluent project organization'. The key elements of such an organizational profile are depicted in Figure 39.5.

This is an organization that is aware of its own culture, knows what its culture should be to succeed, and has the capabilities for cultural change. The figure illustrates a conceptual model for such organizational capabilities.

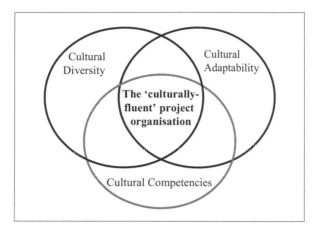

Figure 39.5   The 'culturally-fluent' project organization

BUILDING THE 'CULTURALLY-FLUENT ORGANIZATION'

First, we need an evaluation of the organization's culture as it is now. This is difficult. There is a lack of common methods for calibrating cultural positions against such models and there is no universally accepted process. Furthermore, it is distinctly unsafe to rely on measurements representing just one stakeholder group; there has to be a broad range of perspectives.

Then, a specification of the 'right' culture needs to be developed. The 'right' culture is the aggregation of appropriate values, structure, systems and behaviours that will support future business, operational and project strategies. To meet the criteria for a 'culturally-fluent organization' the 'right' culture has to permit, encourage and facilitate cultural adaptability according to the environment and tasks that it faces.

The 'culturally-fluent organization' will also recognize the cognitive linkages between the underpinning values, beliefs and ethics of a particular culture, the subsequent systems of work organization and management (including project management), and the resulting behaviours between organization/project stakeholders that an observer is likely to witness.

CULTURAL MEASUREMENT

In order to determine whether a team – or project – has the right culture, some form of calibration process needs to be established. To comprehensively describe and plot a corporate culture (and its many cultural sub-sets) a wide range of organizational factors needs to be specifically measured. The 'Strategic Culture Audit Tool' (Rees and McBain 2004) identifies the following factors as worthy of evaluation when conducting a cultural analysis.

Corporate Spirit: is this organization cold and contract-driven, or warm and relationship-driven?

Organizational Cohesiveness: how strong is the social glue?

Time Horizons: now and short-term, or future and long-term?

Responsiveness: introverted and internal focus, or extrovert and external focus?

Management Style: mechanistic/administrative, or charismatic/influential?

Management Competencies: emphasis on 'hard' technical expertise or 'soft' interpersonal skills?

Structure: is this rigid and hierarchical or decentralised and flexible?
Investment in People: positive or negative?

Me or Us: Do individual needs take preference over team/organizational needs?
Performance Management: is performance laissez-faire and unmanaged, or is it strongly monitored and controlled?

Interpersonal Behaviour: is this passive and closed or emotive and open?

Corporate Dynamics: is this an apathetic, low-energy environment or an active, energetic one?

Results can be plotted to form a 'culture map' of the project partner organizations, for example. Figure 39.6 shows how a map could look. The map can then be used to determine if the culture is properly aligned with the strategy (or a project partner). The degree of cultural consistency throughout the organization can be evaluated. Mapping can also be used to benchmark project competitors' cultures, to establish the cultural match between project partners, and to compare internal sub-cultures.

THE CULTURALLY-FLUENT PROJECT MANAGER

We now consider the attributes and abilities needed by individual project managers to work effectively in the culturally-fluent project organization. The culturally-fluent project manager model is shown as Figure 39.7:
- The 'Awareness' circle identifies an individual as a member of one or more cultural groups, and recognizes that other individuals and groups may be culturally different.

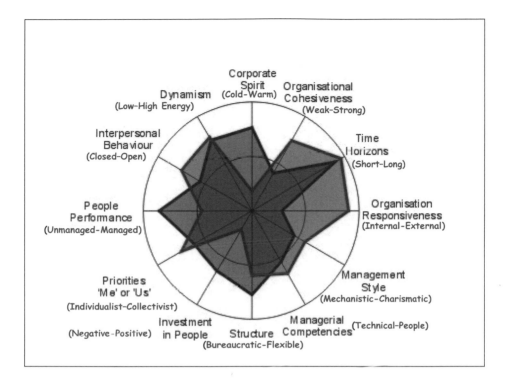

Figure 39.6   Example of a culture radar map, © Cultural Fluency T&D Ltd 2007

- 'Knowledgc' implies the need to understand how and why cultures are different.
- 'Skills' embrace the capabilities required to work effectively in and between different cultures and cultural environments.

PERSONAL CULTURAL FLUENCY LEVELS OF APPLICATION

Cultural fluency competencies can be deployed in strategic, operations and team/individual situations.

(a) At the strategic level, project managers need a deep grasp of the significance of the organization's culture and how this links to business results. They need to ensure this culture enables operations and projects to be run smoothly and in accordance with organizational values and codes of conduct. Managers also need to possess exceptional skills in dealing with a variety of culturally-diverse stakeholders. These could be, for example, customers, trade unions, government agencies, banks and suppliers.

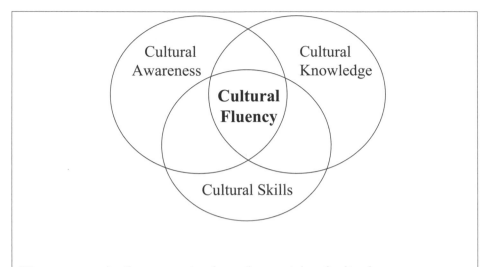

We can summarise these competencies as the repertoire of cultural awareness, knowledge and skills needed by people to perform effectively across different cultural environments".

Figure 39.7 The culturally-fluent project manager

(b) In the project environment, managers need to assimilate the cultural expectations from senior management and ensure these are met through their roles as project leaders. Cultural fluency competencies are required in managing customer and supplier relationships, managing across functions, and managing culturally-diverse project teams.

(c) At the personal transactional level, managers and team members need to acquire skills for effective day-to-day operational working in different cultural environments and within culturally-diverse groups.

CULTURAL FLUENCY COMPETENCIES

There are several competencies that can support a project manager's cultural fluency:

Rapport

An essential competency is the ability to build rapport with others. Rapport is all about developing effective relationships and is achieved through careful observation and active listening. A platform of mutual trust and respect with another party needs to be established. This can be demonstrated by tangibly showing others you understand how and why they see things as they do through skilled inter-personal behaviours.

Leadership Styles

Project managers ideally should possess a repertoire of leadership styles rather than just one style, (Turner and Müller 2006). These styles can be applied to various situations involving people from different cultures. In some cultural situations a highly directive style may be entirely appropriate; in other situations a strongly supportive style may be better.

Conflict-handling/negotiation

Similarly, a range of strategies and tactics that can be easily and quickly accessed to help solve conflicts and ensure successful negotiations are valuable competencies for the project manager to acquire (Chapter 39). Various positions can be adopted to manage cross-cultural conflicts and the aim for the project manager is to achieve win-win positions as often as possible.

Emotional Intelligence

Emotional maturity to deal with situations where the behaviour and attitudes of others are divergent with one's own is a valuable project leadership attribute (Turner and Müller 2006). Putting personal feelings aside can be a most demanding skill. Moving from one cultural position to another will often require a high level of EQ and this can now be more formally assessed using new instruments.

Communication

Linguistic and interpersonal styles and skills can make tremendous differences to project manager effectiveness. The methods and approaches we use to communicate have a major impact on how we influence situations. In transformational situations such as new overseas work placements and structural change this could necessitate the learning of a completely new language or way of thinking and behaving.

ASSESSING YOUR LEVEL OF CULTURAL FLUENCY

You may like to assess your own levels of cultural fluency from an international perspective. Considering Figure 39.8, which box would you fit in?

MANAGING CULTURAL DIVERSITY IN PROJECT TEAMS

At the international level, cultural diversity is being driven by a number of factors, including:

	Total Non-Cultural Fluency	Some Awareness	Active Awareness	Some Understanding	Active Understanding	Some Skills	Culturally Skilled	Culturally Fluent
Understanding how, when and where to apply the awareness, knowledge and skills I have								GLOBAL ROAMER
I love travelling, got lots of experience and like to communicate in the way they do							SEASONED TRANS-NATIONALIST	
I enjoy multi-cultural experiences and I try to 'act local'						RAPPORT-BUILDER		
The reasons for cultural differences are understood					LEARNED TRAVELLER			
I can clearly see cultural differences, I know some of the reasons for this				WILLING LEARNER				
Cultures are different, I don't understand why but I'm interested			INQUISITIVE TOURIST					
I know people are different but I don't see the need to change my behaviour		DAY TRIPPER						
No knowledge, awareness or skills for dealing with other cultures	STAY AT HOME							

Level of Cultural Fluency Competence

Figure 39.8   Assessing your level of cultural fluency, based on Berger (1996)

- greater workplace mobility – such as found in the enlarged European Union – that offers project managers greater choice of project personnel
- demographic change, particularly where working populations are growing, will also influence the degree of diversity in project team membership
- new market opportunities increase the need for including team members with specific knowledge of foreign customer locations and profiles
- outsourcing, off-shoring, and the development of global supply chains mean greater diversity of cultures involved in project delivery
- technological developments create infrastructures that enable projects to be run and managed using highly diversified virtual and distributed teams

Every society in the world is open to influence from other cultural norms. Take two of the most multicultural nations – Britain and the USA. These countries have a strong tradition of absorbing people, language and culture from a wide range of overseas sources (see Bryson 1990). Equally, these same countries have had a powerful impact on other societies, exporting their ideas, knowledge and creative talents around the world.

It can be proposed, therefore, that project-based organizations could gain competitive advantage through proactively viewing cultural environments as new sources of creativity and innovation. Rather than allowing creative ideas and innovations to be transferred by 'accident' or in a random way, it is proposed that organizations can gain substantial benefits by creating the right conditions for cultural influence to form part of the organization's creative resource base. To exploit such opportunities, organizations need to develop internal corporate cultures that welcome national cultural influences. In this paradigm, the company does not stubbornly defend the status quo or seek to block external influences. Rather, the organization makes every effort to selectively absorb cultural influence, placing a high value on diverse thinking and behaviours.

If an organization wishes to take advantage of such opportunities, it needs to be able to identify these diverse resources, develop a system for facilitating knowledge transfer, and possess strong management capability to turn culturally-based ideas into winning products and services. We can term this 'flexible' diversity in contrast to 'imposed' diversity. 'Imposed' diversity refers to schemes usually formulated by national governments that aim to promote social inclusiveness or a defined balance of ethnic representation in a workforce, a geographical area or career progression. Positive discrimination and affirmative action programmes that have been seen in countries such as the USA and South Africa are examples of forced diversity. These are given constraints or parameters that project organizations may have to work within.

Whether diversity is voluntary or imposed there are opportunities for organizations to exploit the potential advantages of diverse project teams. An

831

appropriate context for this discussion lies within the framework of what Ghoshal and Bartlett (1998) describe as the 'Transnational' organization. Their empirical research was aimed at gaining an understanding of the tasks facing managers in worldwide companies at a time of substantial global competition. As a result of their investigations these two scholars suggested that the successful international organization of the future had to achieve national responsiveness, global-scale efficiencies and worldwide knowledge transfer. The way in which project teams can be organized within a transnational structure can be seen in Figure 39.9.

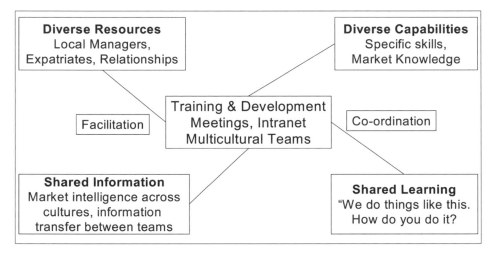

Figure 39.9   Transnational Project Team Organization, based on Ghoshal and Bartlett (1998)

In order to achieve transnationalism the organization needs to develop effective HR strategies to facilitate global learning, legitimise cultural diversity and promote sharing of ideas. By implication, Ghoshal and Bartlett would advocate that new internal cultures need to be developed within the organization.

TRANSNATIONAL COMPETENCE

In their discussions on building competences across cultures, Hampden-Turner and Trompenaars (2000) propose that wealth can be created from conflicting values. Conflicting values produce 'dilemmas'. They see human creativity and innovation as infinitely variable and opposing cultural values as both complementary and reconcilable. By understanding this, better decisions can be made and wealth created. Drawing upon Scott Fitzgerald's famous test of first rate intelligence as 'the ability to hold two opposed ideas in the mind at the same time and still retain the ability to function' the authors propose cross-cultural competency as a focus for the reconciliation of dilemmas. These dilemmas are formatted against the six dimensions of cultural diversity from Trompenaars' earlier work (1993) and can be reversed to provide a large number of ways of looking at a particular problem. Thus, the six dimensions create twelve different logics that can be combined differently to provide up to 64 variations. Assuming a third integrative position, Hampden-Turner and Trompenaars argue that the number of variations possible rises to 729. This is a compelling line of analysis to support the notion that human creativity and innovation in a cross-cultural context is almost infinitely variable. The manifestations of these competencies have been identified earlier as 'cultural fluency'.

PROJECT TEAM ROLES

Further, the roles that project team members play will need to be aligned appropriately. A number of team role models exist and Figure 39.10 illustrates the

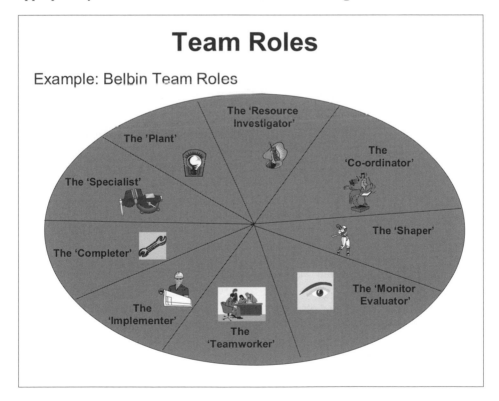

Figure 39.10 Team roles proposed by Belbin (1982)

833

roles that Belbin (1986) proposes for effective team working. However, these roles reflect personal attributes of each team member, and to some extent these are culturally-oriented. The development of transnational organizations requires managerial skill in selecting people for roles and developing them for new/additional roles.

MULTICULTURAL PROJECT LEADERSHIP

Effective leadership of multicultural project teams requires the project manager to understand the stage the team has reached in its development, what cross-cultural difficulties and benefits can be expected at these stages, and what style of leadership is appropriate for the team. Drawing upon Tuckman's (1965) model for team formation (form, storm, norm, perform), we can predict the likely multicultural relationship stages. By overlaying these with Hershey and Blanchard's Situational Leadership (1988) styles a leadership framework for the multicultural project can be proposed. This composite framework is shown below as Figure 39.11.

Figure 39.11   **Multicultural team leadership**

We are now in a position to consolidate these building blocks of managing culturally-diverse project teams into a framework that links corporate, business strategies and HR strategies with multicultural project team management. This is presented as Figure 39.12.

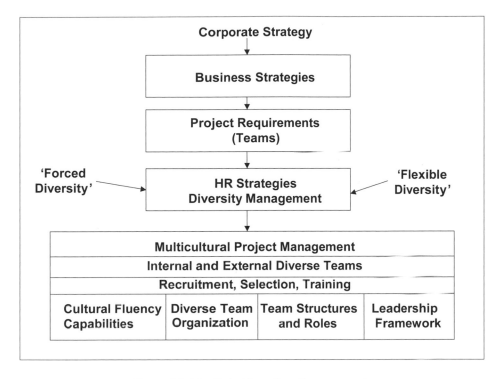

Figure 39.12   Project team diversity management

ORGANIZATIONAL STRATEGIES FOR LEVERAGING CULTURAL ASSETS

These strategies can usefully be classified at three levels:

1. Corporate level
2. Team level
3. Individual level

CORPORATE LEVEL STRATEGIES

The project organization needs to develop a corporate culture that views cultural diversity as a positive attribute. Top management should live out and promote the values of diversity, ideas sharing, transparency and innovation. There is a key role for HR professionals in promoting such a culture. If creativity and innovation is sincerely held as a key organizational competence then HR should be seen as a strategic function and thus appropriately represented at senior management levels.

If the added value created by the organization's people assets (including employees, managers, partners and external networks) is more than the value of the company's tangible assets, then the capitalisation of the organization is increasingly underpinned by human resource assets. As is the case with many companies that rely on human ingenuity for their survival, growth and profitability, this will require effective systems of human capital management. Such systems should be managing the cultural assets of the organization, too.

HR strategy needs to initiate various programmes and processes that support the leverage of cross-cultural innovation and creativity. These could include, for example, developing a diverse pool of talent from which to recruit, select, promote and train human resources. Other strategies could encourage ideas and innovation sharing through appropriate rewards and incentives systems.

PROJECT TEAM LEVEL STRATEGIES

The organization needs to consider the most effective way of organizing people in such teams and creating structures that promote cross-cultural sharing of ideas and innovations. Often, there is no formal vehicle for coordinating project innovations that take place in one part of the company with other projects. Informal networks are fine and should be encouraged but this alone does not capture the total potential benefits of creative outputs. The transnational model is one possible approach to team and functional structures. Other ways of organizing people could be to create the multiple project team concept where employees are members of several project teams simultaneously, continually receiving and offering ideas to their team members who in turn will go on to share these ideas with other teams.

INDIVIDUAL STRATEGIES

Managers and their individual team members need to develop distinct competencies in being able to leverage ideas and innovations between themselves at a personal level. Some writers have termed this competency 'cultural intelligence'. Cultural intelligence picks up where emotional intelligence leaves off (Earley and Mosakowski 2004). Someone with high emotional intelligence understands what makes us human and what makes us different from one another. High cultural intelligence is the ability to distinguish universal and idiosyncratic behaviours within groups. A critical element that both emotional and cultural intelligence share, however, is 'a propensity to suspend judgement – to think before acting' (Goleman 1996). The term 'the culturally-fluent project manager' is used to describe the capabilities of cross-cultural awareness, understanding/knowledge, and skills. Within this framework of individual competence there is a notion of fluid adaptation, similar in concept to the competency of language fluency. As one moves into a new cultural environment or engagement the challenge is to re-orientate perspectives on the 'foreign' culture to create a climate of positive disposition. In so doing, rapport is built between the giver of ideas and initiatives and the recipient.

THE MANAGEMENT OF CULTURE IN YOUR PROJECTS?

As we conclude this chapter you are encouraged to consider how the cultural aspects of project working are managed in your organization:

- Does the management of culture have a high priority, is it taken seriously and are project managers sufficiently well-equipped with suitable competencies?
- Where do the organization's cultural fluency strengths and weaknesses lie?
- What could be done to improve the management of culture in your projects?
- Could your organization develop its culture to produce competitive advantage in future projects?

REFERENCES AND FURTHER READING

Belbin, R.M., 1986, Managing Teams, London: Heinemann.

Berger, M., 1996, Cross-Cultural Learning Curve, New York: McGraw-Hill.

Bryson, W., 1990, Mother Tongue, London: Penguin Books.

Earley, P.C. and Mosakowski, E., 2004, 'Cultural Intelligence', Harvard Business Review, 82(10), 139–146.

Hampden-Turner, C. and Trompenaars, F., 2000, Building Cross-Cultural Competence, Chichester: Wiley.

Hershey, P. and Blanchard, K.H., 1988, Management of Organizational Behaviour, 5th edition, Englewood Cliffs, NJ: Prentice Hall.

Hofstede, G., 2001, Culture's Consequences: Comparing Values, Behaviors, Institutions and Organizations Across Nations, 2nd edition, Thousand Oaks, CA: Sage Publications.

Garrison, T., 2006, International Business Culture, 3rd edition, Huntingdon: Elm Publications.

Ghoshal, S. and Bartlett, C., 1998, Managing Across Borders: The Transnational Solution, 2nd ed, London: Random House.

Goleman, D., 1996, Emotional Intelligence, London: Bloomsbury Publishing.

Lewis, R.D., 2000, When Cultures Collide, 2nd edition, London: Nicholas Brealey Publishing.

Rees, D. and McBain, R., 2004, People Management: Challenges and Opportunities, Basingstoke: Palgrave Macmillan.

Trompenaars, F., 1993, Riding the Waves of Culture, London: Economist Books.

Trompenaars, F. and Hampden-Turner, C., 2004, Managing People Across Cultures (Culture for Business), London: Capstone Publishing.

Tuckman, B.W., 1965, 'Development sequence in small groups', Psychological Bulletin.

Turner, J.R., 1999, The Handbook of Project-based Management, 2nd edition, London: McGraw Hill.

Turner, J.R. and Müller, R., 2006, Choosing Appropriate Project Managers: Matching their Leadership Style to the Type of Project, Newtown Square, PA: Project Management Institute.

40 Managing Ethics

Alistair Godbold

Interest in business ethics has grown in reaction to well publicised scandals of the 1990s and 2000s, including donations to political parties, the fraud related collapse of former 'blue chip' companies such as Maxwell Communications, and more recently Tyco, Enron, WorldCom, and a host of other scandals. The globalisation of companies and their anonymity can add to the perceptions of mistrust. All of these companies and their stakeholders lost money as a result of their unethical actions and in some cases went out of business altogether, and the political parties suffered damage to their reputations. The above are the infamous and the large scale; there are many more that impact on a local scale or have yet to come to public notoriety. On the other hand, it is important when considering ethics in business, and more specifically in project management, not to become puritanical, and to remember that you are in business. The aims of the business, or a project, are not somehow rendered more profound or acceptable by attaching to them a spurious social or philosophical dimension. All that achieves is to remove the clarity that ensures people do what is right in business and projects. Business and projects must be seen and managed in the wider context of all of the stakeholders, not just the narrow pursuit of a commercial aim, cost and timescale.

The ethical content of an organization's actions is only significant when there is a transaction with a stakeholder. Where there is no such transaction, there is no basis to judge the ethical content of an action. Business today is becoming more complex, and more interrelated with other social phenomena. It is also international, operating in a world of complex social and economic interdependencies. Pressure groups are becoming more powerful, exercising legitimate power, and representing the views of large sections of society. This was the case when Greenpeace mounted a campaign against Shell's plans to sink the Brent Spar oil platform in the North Atlantic, and organizations such as Transparency International who maintain a world corruption perception index, and lobby for the removal of corruption from governments of the world. The actions of the company came under public scrutiny through the interests of the pressure groups, the media, the general public and parliament.

In the first paragraph I recalled some of the more obvious ethical issues, those that 'the person on the Clapham omnibus' would recognize as being an ethical decision. However there are many more decisions in our every day careers that individually may be considered a matter of style, but when taken together project an image of the way a person, and so a company, behaves, ethically or unethically. This can be thought of as an iceberg, Figure 40.1.

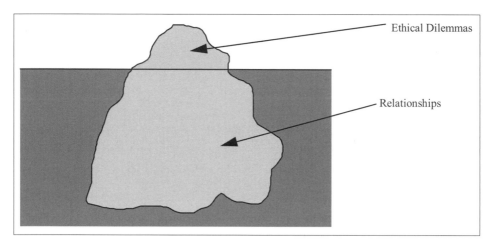

Figure 40.1 The ethical iceberg

The ethical dilemmas are those everyone can recognize, insider share dealing, accepting or offering bribes, funding of political parties etc. However, today's business and projects are composed of relationships with stakeholders, employees, members of the project team, customers, suppliers, users and people affected by the secondary impact of any change process. These are not one-time relationships; we may have to continue doing business with these people as customers, suppliers or partners in the future. In the short term it can pay to be unethical, you may win the contract by spotting a loop-hole in the specification, and choosing to exploit it, you may improve your cash flow by paying your suppliers late or gain prestige by taking credit for the actions of a subordinate. These are all short-term advantages paid for by loss of long-term gains. The company's, or individual's, reputation in the market place precedes them and there are a finite number of players in any market. If we do not have a successful relationship with any of them then it may affect the competitive position of the company and the flexibility that any stakeholder is prepared to accept in this relationship. Business is about people, the relationships the people in business have with each other and the way in which they interact. Projects are a micro-environment of these relationships; project manager to team, project to customer, to user etc. The management of these relationships is vital to the continuing success of the project, or the parties taking part in them.

Dealing with these issues for the majority of people working under pressure of deadlines and budgets needs to be actively managed. These ethical issues are likely to occur more frequently and the ability to recognize them, or resist their attractiveness is that much more difficult. The principles for managing this kind of issue are similar to those needed to manage 'ethical dilemmas'. The application of these principles needs to be considered on a smaller scale than that described here.

ETHICS AND PROJECT MANAGEMENT

In Chapter 5, it is described how a project is a temporary organization different from the steady state of the parent organization. Projects may be undertaken by companies with temporary teams to achieve a set task, by groups who will work on one project, then move on to work on the next, or companies that specialize in projects for clients. All of these temporary teams have to work with each other and with other companies whom they may not have dealt with before. In order to quickly establish a relationship, and start to work together an important element is that there is a cultural fit between the two parties so that they can do business together.

The traditional view of the role of the manager is, as Milton Friedman (1970) put it 'to make as much money as possible while conforming to the basic rules of society'. This principal can be applied to project managers, as their role is to get the project completed on time and to budget, legally. This narrow definition is dysfunctional as it does not acknowledge the role other people play in fulfilling the objective of the project. A project cannot succeed without the help of senior management, the project team, suppliers, users and the customer. The above definition of project management implies a style of 'I win you lose', whereas projects are a non-zero sum game; both parties have to gain. Recognising this interdependence under the pressure of deadlines and budgets requires a developed skill or judgement of the manager, except under the most obvious circumstances, and the pursuit of the long term goal.

Projects are agencies of change, they upset the status quo, and as such they can expect to meet resistance. Not only do projects create change in the organization as their principal product, they create change by the process in which they go about it. They are unique and as no norms have been established for them, this may in itself create uncertainty within their own structure. Projects use a variety of resources to achieve their objectives which need to be integrated. They also produce change not only for the end users of the change (building, computer system, business process, office move etc) but also for those people involved in getting to this end state. During these times of change people may feel insecure, or threatened by the alteration of the status quo. These people will need to be able to trust the integrity and openness of the project in order to contribute to its success. If they feel that the project has some hidden threatening agenda, this will add one more reason to resist the change brought about by the project. This is not to say that the outcome of the project must be of benefit to all, but that it must be clear and sensitively handled. If the outcome of the project is to reduce staff numbers, then this must be clearly articulated and people kept informed at every stage of the process. In order to reduce the risk to a project, it must be seen as ethical and trustworthy. For the project manager, discrete moral leadership rather than a public relations exercise is the key to reaping the benefits of ethics for temporary projects, for individual project managers and for the organizations in the long term.

This constant change and instability is one of the factors that differentiates the management of projects from the management of operations. Projects do not have a stable background against which to build up norms of behaviour, value systems and procedures. Instead, these norms and procedures have to be built up in a very short space of time in a very dynamic environment. A side effect of this is that there is no time to adapt and evolve these procedures as by the time they have been tried the environment has moved on. As a consequence the project managers have a high degree of control over the health, welfare and well-being of all their team members and stakeholders. Another problem for project managers is that the members of their teams, customers and users will have their own different sense of morality, coming as they do from different backgrounds. This means project managers must clarify the values of the whole group to prevent any adverse clash of values in their relationships.

One of the duties of a project manager is to balance competing objectives of quality; cost; time and scope. Each project stakeholder, co-contractors, the project director, team members, the functional organization, subcontractors, users and society has expectations of how these objectives will be balanced according to their own perspectives. The relative weights applied to each stakeholder and the choices between the generic project goals will vary depending on the type and stage of the project (Mantel & Kloppenborg 1990). In most projects, cost is the most important goal once the specifications are set, and time becomes the most important as the project nears completion. It is this myopic concern with one or two variables in a project that may put the project manager under ethical pressure to disregard the holistic needs of the company and the other stakeholders. In this situation the project manager may find ways to manipulate the figures and make trade-offs that compromise certain aspects of the project in order to satisfy these small number of variables. The figures may be manipulated or have a different spin put on them in order for the project manager to look good in this period, in the hope that everything will be all right in the next. Many managers consider this practice to be not too unethical due to the intense pressure they are under to perform (Bruns and Merchant 1990).

Project managers are *leaders*; they have views and beliefs shaped by their background, education, and experiences. As *leaders* they must pervade all operations throughout the project. They therefore have a key responsibility to manage the values of the project to ensure they are effective in every action, and agendas of the many stakeholder groups are balanced and 'ethical'. The project manager must ensure the project is managed with a set of values congruent with those of society and the stakeholders. It is his or her responsibility to ensure a common set of values is communicated throughout the life of the project. It is not only the responsibility of the project manager to ensure that the values of the project match those of society, but also the project team members have a duty to themselves to ensure that their own work matches with these values. Unless the project manager is aware of all of these relationships and responsibilities he will not be providing the optimum base for his project.

There are many characteristics of the project manager's role that influence how ethically he or she performs the job, and how responsible he or she feels for the actions of the team. A major problem is the amount of information generated about progress, finance, decisions, views of stakeholders etc. If this information is all passed to the project manager there is a danger of 'information overload', causing a large amount of that information to be lost, degrading his or her performance. This can be avoided by ensuring the project manager delegates appropriately, and receives only relevant information. This relies on a hierarchy of team leaders deciding what is relevant and filtering the information. This filtering can introduce a bias at successive levels of management, removing information that shows them in a bad light, or is in their opinion not relevant. This bias, or blockage, may not allow the project manager to manage because he or she does not have all the relevant information. Secondly, and perhaps more importantly the blockage will allow the middle levels of management to cover up bad or unethical practice. This covering up may be due to the fact that they are trying to make themselves look good or feel they will be punished for bringing bad news. A more common problem is an emotional attachment they feel to a project. As people work on a project they become more committed to it and begin to feel any obstacle can be overcome (triumph of hope over experience) and this may prevent them from recognising real problems. It is the leader's role to ensure channels of communication are open to allow all team members access to the project manager to report any issues that give them cause for concern and not rely totally on the information filtering through the hierarchy.

The most serious problem in terms of the pressure put upon the project manager is perhaps its most basic function: the interface between management and the professional discipline. Normally a project manager is expected to have a high level of skill in the field in which the project is conducted; in most engineering projects this will involve the project manager being an engineer. An engineer deals with the facts of the profession, designs, calculations and the more abstract notion of engineering judgement. The engineers' role is to assemble data and perform calculations in order to determine the course of action. A manager co-ordinates resources, and takes decisions based on the recommendations of the team. However, the project manager is at the interface of these two roles, not only must he or she take decisions, but is also in a position to take them based on 'professional judgement'. In normal circumstances the distinction between the two roles can be maintained. However, when under pressure this distinction with its associated moral and ethical consequences can break down.

In this section it has been shown what pressures and complications are brought together in the role of project manager. The project manager has a great responsibility to the team, the public, the company and all other stakeholder groups. As a result of this the scope and nature of his job make this a demanding but very rewarding role.

ETHICS AS A DIFFERENTIATOR

Much has been written in the media about ethics and its detrimental effect on business. However, ethics can be used as a positive differentiator (for example the Co-op and the Ethical Investment Funds). By differentiating itself from the competition, a company may be able to gain advantage. Ethics and competition are not mutually exclusive; competition is an essential part of business. Once equality in cost of production is achieved in a market, or cost of execution of a project, then the only way to stay in business is either to become more efficient or differentiate. Many companies are already competing on these grounds, for example ethical investment funds, producers of green products, and firms that trade on their ethical image.

In any business or project a company can possess a number of competitive weapons; productivity, quality and new products. Ethics can be added as another weapon. To realize this edge, leadership, innovation and communication are needed. All of these are qualities of the good manager, and essential qualities of the project manager. In managing the ethics of a group, there are many parallels between ethics and quality. Both of these embody the long-term perspective, are customer led, doing things right, and doing the right things. Where organizations have adopted and internalised a strong ethical culture that they can sustain, they can exploit this as a competitive advantage. The organization's reputation with its customers, employees and even suppliers of some high value added products can build strong relationships and lasting confidence. This can act as a barrier to entry to new firms entering the market. This tactic must be used with care as stakeholders and observers will look for lapses from this policy which may be harmful to the project. These lapses may be exploited by competitors, or those who have some other agenda for the project, and do not wish to see it achieve some of its outcomes.

ETHICAL THEORY

In order to discuss the role that ethics play in project management it is necessary to present ethical points in terms of the underlying ethical theory. This section illustrates why it is important to understand this theory not only to use in this discussion, but for managers to think about and present their ethical arguments.

In order to argue the case of a moral viewpoint, managers need to be able to articulate these arguments in a form that is intellectually and theoretically valid. Some authors argue that in addition to the skills of ethical analysis and reasoning, ethical enquiry often requires an understanding of the nature of basic ethical principles, the status of knowledge in ethics and the relationships among ethics, law and religion (Benjamin and Curtis 1986). In many cases the moral values of managers, project managers and executives may often conflict with their role duties. What, according to Gandz and Hayes (1988), managers and executives are deficient in, are the skills of ethical analysis which allow them to reconcile their role as managers and that of socially integrated individuals. Not only must the managers be able to argue an ethical position in coherent terms, but they must be able to articulate this view to their peers and the various stakeholders in the company, or in the case of a project manager, the project.

> *No competent executive would think of taking the company to the bargaining table without a clear sense of objectives, limits and tactics. And yet some of the same executives lead their companies into the forum of public opinion with nothing but a grab bag of ethical platitudes (*Solomon 1989).

The traditional way of reducing the variety of values, whether ethical or not, is to seek general principles. The principles or theories try to avoid the arbitrary treatment of individuals and cases, and allows consistency in policy and judgements. To be able to reason, articulate and discuss ethical issues, it is important to understand some basic philosophical theories in the field of ethics. Figure 40.2 illustrates a framework for ethical theories.

The following paragraphs give an overview of the main ethical theories. There are two approaches to ethical theory, the first is the rule-based approach, and the

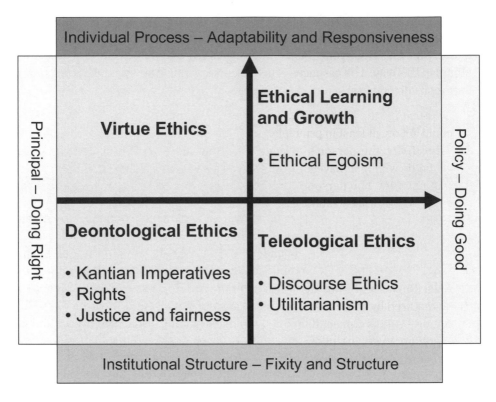

Figure 40.2   A framework for ethical theories (after Fisher and Lovell 2003)

second is the utilitarian approach. The first says there are a set of rules you must obey, the second suggests that you should do that which will produce most good.

RULE-BASED THEORIES

The central thesis of deontological ethics (rule-based) is that the consequences of actions are not the primary consideration in deciding what ought to be done (Bowie and Duska 1990); it is the consideration of fairness and justice that takes precedence over the consequences of actions. These rule-based theories can be broken down into two different types: absolute and conditional theories. The absolute theories, the main one of which is Kant's Categorical Imperative, say people must do certain things if they are to be morally right. The conditional theories, such as prima facie duties, also advocate a set of rules but suggest how and when it is appropriate to modify these duties.

The Categorical Imperative form of ethics was developed by Immanuel Kant (1724–1804). He attempted to show that there are certain moral rights and duties that all humans must follow, regardless of the benefits or otherwise that the exercising of these rights will accrue for the individual or for others (Velasquez 2003). This theory assumes that everyone should be treated as a free person equal to everyone else. Everyone has a right to such treatment and everyone must treat others in this way. The essence of the Categorical Imperative is based on 3 criteria for moral correctness:

1. *Universality:* the individual's reasons for acting must be reasons that everyone could act on, at least in principle.
2. *Transitivity:* the person's reasons for acting must be reasons that he or she would be willing to have all others use as a basis of how they treat him or her.
3. *Individuality:* The person 'should treat each human being as a person whose existence as a free rational person should be promoted' (Gandz and Hayes 1988).

The conditional rule-based ethics from the utilitarian aspect can be summarised in these principles (Velasquez 2003):

1. An action is right from an ethical point of view if, and only if, the action would be required by those moral rules that are 'correct'.
2. A moral rule is correct if, and only if, the sum total of the utilities produced if everyone were to follow that rule is greater than the sum total utilities produced if everyone were to follow some alternative rule.

In the rule-utilitarian approach, the fact that a certain action would maximize utility (goodness) does not make it moral. In this approach you must first find the correct rule and then apply the utility criterion. The most common form of conditional rule-based approaches from the adaptation of rule-based ethics is Prima-Facie Duties. A prima facie rule takes the form that other things being equal, one should tell the truth, obey the law and so on. The theory states that there are prima facie (at first sight) duties that are morally binding and that ethical decisions constitute deciding which is the more obligatory, if and when there is a conflict. The six prima facie duties are (Gandz and Hayes 1988):

- fidelity
- gratitude
- justice
- beneficence (the act of doing good)
- self improvement, and
- non-malfeasance

The main problem with this theory is determining which is the appropriate rule, causing the user to focus too narrowly on the means, rather than the ends. Another problem is when duties conflict, deciding what weight and merit should be applied to each. Some argue this form can degenerate into traditional utilitarianism, by allowing the rules that give beneficial expectations more utility than those that do not allow such expectations (Velasquez 2003).

UTILITARIAN THEORIES

There are a number of ethical theories that explicitly designate some intrinsic aspect of the human act as the criterion for moral goodness, or badness. Hedonism is an example of one of these forms of ethics. Its roots can be traced back to ancient Greece. The theory holds that as long as an act is capable of producing some pleasure (Hedone in Greek), it is good. This form of ethics has evolved throughout the years to emphasize more rational pleasures and the promotion of peace of mind. Utilitarian Ethics is a development of this theory. The theory is variously known as best result ethics, egoism or end point ethics. The main exponents of this theory were Jeremy Bentham (1748–1832), and John Stuart Mill (1806–1873). The essence of the theory can be stated as

> *An action is right from an ethical point of view if and only if the sum total of the utilities produced by the act is greater than the sum total of the utilities produced by any other act,* (Velasquez 1992).

This form of ethics it is argued will naturally lead to a division of labour that will produce the best outcome for society (Bowie and Duska 1990). Thus, if people take responsibility for their own roles, society (including the project) will flourish. However, there are many problems with this approach to ethics. Firstly, how does one estimate the plurality of values, happiness, pleasure, health, knowledge, friendship, comfort, pain, harm etc., to evaluate the consequences of a proposed course of action? Even if one can estimate the utility of an action, you cannot simply add and subtract the various positive and negative consequences of the alternative courses of action. Further problems arise with this theory, mainly due to the concept of justice.

RELATIVIST THEORIES

The relativist theory is perhaps the most contentious theory of all those discussed so far. It has become most fashionable since World War II. In its clearest form it is based on the existentialist philosophy of Jean Paul Sartre. The essence of this argument is that ethics is merely a matter of taste (Donaldson 1992), and if one culture or country prefers one set of rules there is little that can be said or done about it. Sartre argued that there is a basic human nature given to us by a great designer, God, and so nothing to bind us to a certain way of action (Varga 1984). In this form of ethics what people make of themselves is of their own free actions, they create their values depending on their own situations and circumstances. These sentiments can be summarised by the expression:

When in Rome its all right to do as the (good) Romans do

This perhaps gained in prominence when people worked in other cultures on their own and indulged in practices that would be condemned in their own cultures. This could take the form of working practices for employees, making payments to local 'middle men' to secure contracts. There are many arguments against this form of ethics. Bernard Williams in his book on Morality (1972) describes Relativism as:

> ... *the anthropologists heresy, possibly the most absurd view to have been advanced in moral philosophy*

Others have argued that if this theory were accepted without any restrictions, no order could be maintained in society and no State could function (Varga 1984). These objections forced even Sartre to modify the theory to a more acceptable form. However, as the evolution of what is 'good' continues (e.g. wearing seat belts, drink driving, and smoking in public) this theory still has its place.

ETHICS ABROAD

Many project companies now compete nationally and internationally. Many are global, with infrastructures or centres of expertise shared across national boundaries. When companies and their staff operate in this environment, problems can, and do, occur. They lose the backdrop of shared values, familiar laws, judicial procedures and standards of ethical conduct. Practices that worked in one country, may not work in another. They may have different ethical conduct or cultural norms. This is not to say that one set of standards is better than another, or that they must abide by the higher standard of the two moral codes. Some ethical theories, such as relativism, suggest there is no absolute measure of ethical standard, just statements of the fashion of society at the time. I have heard of examples of companies sending engineers to work on projects abroad where they have encountered problems. Some of these engineers and project staff have been recalled due to their inability to reconcile their own value systems, congruent with their home country, with those of the country in which they find themselves working. This causes problems not only for the individual, and their perception of their career, but for the company in how to manage and resource the project. A way of resolving this is to use cultural relativism.

Problems involved when projects are conducted in multi-cultural environments with no reference points are many, and not easy to resolve. However, the rest of this section provides some guidance on how practices that are just different may be distinguished from those that are wrong. Some cultures place different emphasis on equally valid ethical codes which may cause confusion. Americans place greater emphasis on liberty than loyalty, whilst the Japanese place the

849

emphasis on loyalty to their company and business networks. These issues may be addressed explicitly up front, before staff are exposed to these dilemmas. By giving staff a framework in which to think about these issues, they will be better equipped to deal with the issues for the benefit of themselves, the company and the project on which they are employed. When shaping the ethical behaviour of staff, or a company based in a foreign culture they must be guided by three principles (Donaldson 1996):

- respect for core human values, which determine the absolute threshold for all business activities
- respect for local traditions
- the belief that context matters when deciding what is right and what is wrong

In Japan the giving and receiving of gifts is an integral part of business life. Many western cultures may consider this as not just different, but wrong, as it could be seen as trying to unduly influence someone (bribery). Many companies have come to respect this tradition and have different limits for the giving and receiving of gifts in Japan than they do in the rest of the world. Respecting local traditions also means recognising the strengths and weaknesses of different ethical norms. In the Far East, stealing the credit from a subordinate is nearly an unpardonable sin. The phenomenon of globalisation in business leads to the conclusion that in order for this world to be ethical and just, there must be some global ethic. There are international regulatory frameworks, laws and their courts are emerging to deal with the technical issues in globalisation, but the global business ethic is not yet here to help the project manager; although there have been many events contributing towards the creation of a global ethic (Kung 1997). The basic principles of the global ethic which may be used in addition to the above are:

1. *Justice:* just fair conduct, fairness, exercise of authority in maintenance of right
2. *Mutual Respect:* love and respect for others
3. *Stewardship:* human beings are only the stewards of natural resources
4. *Honesty:* truthfulness and reliability in all human relationships (integrity)

The above principles are more abstract than those contained in a company's or professional institutions ethics statement, but they do provide a mental framework in which to address these issues at a macro level. In recent years the law has started to catch up with society's view of what is ethical. In 1998 the Organization for Economic Co-operation and Development (OECD) requested that its member states legislate for 'a criminal offence under its law for any person intentionally to offer, promise or give any undue pecuniary or other advantage, whether directly or through intermediaries, to a foreign public official, for that official or for a third party, in order that the official act or refrain from acting in relation to the performance of official duties, in order to obtain or retain business or other improper advantage in the conduct of international business.' By 2002 all of the member countries had enacted this legislation. The World Bank Estimates the cost of corruption or 'tainted procurement' at $1.5 trillion USD.

PRACTICAL HELP

Throughout this chapter, I have discussed the role of ethics in management and more specifically project management, the role of ethics in the long term view, the background to ethical theory, the specifics of managing ethics in a global business, or at least a project in a foreign country. However, there are times when the manager does not have the luxury to think about the philosophical dimensions of an ethical dilemma, and this is where a more prescriptive checklist or rule of thumb can be of use. The rules of thumb for ethical decision making (in the domestic setting) come in varying degrees of complexity, some of more use than others. A more comprehensive rule that provides a mental framework in which to draw out many of the issues in a decision is described below:

1. Which **goals or priorities** does this solution support or work against?
2. Does the solution reflect the **values** of the organization and the decision makers?
3. What are the **consequences** (in terms of benefit or harm) and ramifications (effect of time and outside influences) for each of the stakeholders in the following three areas: cost-to-benefit, rights-to-equity and duties-to-obligation? Are there any other consequences?
4. What qualms would the decision-maker have about the **disclosure** of a favourable decision to this solution to the CEO, board of directors, family and the public?
5. What is the positive or negative **symbolic potential** of this solution if understood – or misunderstood – by others? Will it contribute to building and maintaining an ethical environment? (Dreilinger 1994).

Whenever making a decision that has some ethical dimension, it is important to keep monitoring the outcomes of the decision at every stage. This is needed to ensure that the decision is still the best, and that any corrective action can be identified early.

Some companies have developed ethical training programme for their staff to ensure that there is a common ethical norm and that it is acceptable to do something about an issue.

CONCLUSIONS

I have discussed how ethics play an increasingly important role in business and project management. This is due to many factors, including heightened awareness of workers and the general public, and as a reaction against the recent high profile collapse of some companies. All managers, especially project managers, are under pressure to take short cuts, improve the figures and get immediate results; this also puts them under ethical pressure. The decisions that the project manager takes are much less restricted than those in line management. The result of this is that the project manager operates in a relatively unbounded, dynamic, and often international environment, giving them greater freedom and scope, and their decisions wider effects. A more serious characteristic of project management, putting them under more ethical pressure, is the weak distinction between professional and managerial roles. The international nature of many projects brings with it its own special set of ethical problems that must be handled for both the team members involved in the project, and the project manager executing the project. In order to help the project manager deal with these ethical pressures there needs to be a more structured framework in which to take decisions.

A point made in this chapter is that much of today's management and especially project management is conducted in a complex interrelated environment with a finite number of players. If project managers are to succeed in this environment, they must be aware of these interrelationships, and the impact they can have on the success of their company, their project, or their next project and their career.

Ethics in projects and business need not be a threat but an opportunity, a way of differentiating yourself from the competition and exploiting some form of competitive advantage. This differentiation is best handled subtly, not as a public relations exercise, and can bring lasting benefits which may not only attract new business, new and better motivated employees, but also ease the path to the completion of projects.

Several methods have been outlined that will assist project managers in their duties. These include; giving an understanding of the background of ethical theory, an understanding of the issues that may face project managers, the way in which ethics play a vital role in the success of a project, both from the ethical dilemmas, and from the relationship maintenance perspective. A rule of thumb has been provided to act as a first check to help project managers consider the issues involved. Where projects are conducted in an international environment a further framework has been included to help the manager also assess and resolve these issues.

REFERENCES AND FURTHER READING

Benjamin, M., and Curtis, J., 1986, *Ethics in Nursing,* Oxford: Oxford University Press.

Bowie, N.E., and Duska, R.F., 1990, *Business Ethics, 2nd edition,* Prentice Hall International.

Bruns, W.J. Jr., and Merchant, K.A., 1990, 'The dangerous morality of managing carnings', *Management Accounting,* August.

Donaldson, J., 1992, *Business Ethics: A European Case Book,* Academic Press.

Donaldson, T., 1996, 'Values in tension: ethics away from home', *Harvard Business Review,* September – October.

Dreilinger, C., 1994, 'Ethics, what about thou shalt?' *Journal of Business Strategy,* July-August.

Farrell O., Fraedrich J., Ferrell L., 2000, *Business Ethics: Ethical Decision Making and Cases,* 4th Edition. Hoghton Mifflin.

Fisher, C., and Lovell, A., 2003, *Business Ethics and Values,* Prentice Hall .

Friedman, M., 1970, 'The Social Responsibility of Business is to Increase Profits', *New York Times Magazine,* 13 September.

Gandz, J., and Hayes, N., 1988, 'Teaching business ethics', *Journal of Business Ethics,* 7.

Garvind, D.A., 1991, *Operations Strategy,* Englewood Cliffs, NJ: Prentice Hall.

Kung, H., 1997, 'A global ethic in an age of globalisation', *Business Ethics Quarterly,* 7(3).

Mantel, S.J., and Kloppenborg, T., 1990, 'Trade-offs on Projects: they may not be what you think', *Project Management Journal,* 21(1), March.

Soloman, R.C., and Hanson, K., 1989, *It's Good Business,* Anthenum, New York.

Velasquez, M.G.,2003, *Business Ethics: Concepts and Cases, 5th edition,* Prentice Hall International.

Varga, A.C., 1984, *The Main Issues in Bioethics,* New York: Paulst Press.

Williams, B., 1972, *Morality: An Introduction to Ethics,* Cambridge: Cambridge University Press.

Index